Per[illegible] Lorik Yadav

NANI PALKHIVALA

The

COURTROOM GENIUS

Dear Lorik,

I've known you for long enough and I know that you have it. You may become a lawyer or an IAS, you shall excel.

Best of Luck.

Love,

Gatik Bhaiya

First Edition 2012
Reprint 2012
Reprint 2012
Reprint 2012
Reprint 2012
Reprint 2012
Reprint 2012
Reprint 2015
Reprint 2016
Reprint 2016
Reprint 2016
Reprint 2017
Reprint 2018
Reprint 2018
Reprint 2018
Reprint 2018
Reprint 2018
Reprint 2019
Reprint 2019
Reprint 2019
Reprint 2019
Reprint 2019
Reprint 2020
Reprint 2020
Reprint 2020
Reprint 2020
Reprint 2021
Reprint 2021
Reprint 2021
Reprint 2021
Reprint 2022
Reprint 2022
Reprint 2023
Reprint 2023
Reprint 2023
Reprint 2023
Reprint 2024
[illegible]int 2024
2025
2025
2025
[illegible]025

NANI PALKHIVALA

The

COURTROOM GENIUS

Soli J Sorabjee
Former Attorney-General for India
Senior Advocate,
Supreme Court of India

Arvind P Datar
Senior Advocate,
Madras High Court

Foreword by
Behram A Palkhivala
Senior Advocate,
Bombay High Court

LexisNexis®

LexisNexis®

This book is a publication of LexisNexis
(A Division of RELX India Pvt Ltd)
14th floor, Building No 10, Tower-B, DLF Cyber City, Phase-II,
Gurgaon-122002, Haryana, India.
Tel : + 91 124 4774444 Fax: + 91 124 4774100
Website : www.lexisnexis.co.in / E-mail : help.in@lexisnexis.com

---

Nani Palkhivala: The Courtroom Genius, 2012

ISBN: 978-81-8038-754-8

Printed by: Saurabh Printers, Greater Noida, UP.

Printed and bound in India.

To the memory of

Nani Ardeshir Palkhivala

who lived and practised the essence of

Zoroastrianism

"Humata, Hukhta, Huvarshta"

Good Thoughts, Good Words, Good Deeds

His life will remain an example
of what we are all capable of.

To set a lofty example is the richest bequest
a man can leave behind him.
— Samuel Smiles (1812–1904)

That some achieve great success, is proof to all
that others can achieve it as well.
— Abraham Lincoln (1809–1865)

Every great example takes hold of us with
the authority of a miracle, and says to us,
'If ye had but faith, ye, also, could do the same things.'
— Jacobi (1804–1851)

Foreword

Justice H.R. Khanna said, 'If a count were to be made of the ten topmost lawyers of the world, I have no doubt that Mr. Palkhivala's name would find a prominent place therein. There have been occasions when his advocacy reached great heights, and long after we have heard him, we find his words echoing in our memory and leaving a trail of pleasant remembrance.' This book will have served a good purpose if it makes the readers feel that the statement must be true. How true, only those who had actually heard Nani argue cases that created India's destiny would know.

Nani was at his best in the *Kesavananda Bharati* case. But he excelled himself while opposing the government's attempt to get it overruled. Years later, while visiting Nani during his last illness, the same Judge recalled Nani's performance during the hearing of the review petition and told me, 'It was not Nani who spoke. It was Divinity speaking through him.' Justice Khanna was speaking for an astounded and grateful nation.

What made Nani truly special was not only his phenomenal mind, but also his deep sense of morality, his finely-tuned sense of justice, and an unshakeable belief in democracy, even through some of India's grimmest days. Which is why he was often considered the conscience of the nation. It was from this space that many of his most impassioned appeals in court emerged–they were made by a man who was ferociously guarding the rights and liberties of the common man and simultaneously trying to preserve the integrity of the nation.

Behram A Palkhivala

Preface

In 2004, the Nani A. Palkhivala Memorial Trust requested us to write a book on the important cases that had been argued by late N.A. Palkhivala. This was to be a book quite different from the biography written by M.V. Kamath.[1] Y. H. Malegam, the Chairman of the Trust, wanted us to highlight his legal journey and comment upon the important cases that he argued in various High Courts and the Supreme Court of India. The object was to record Palkhivala's contribution to the development of not only the law of income tax but other branches of law as well. We readily agreed and soon commenced the research necessary for this work, little realizing the enormous time that this was to consume. Starting with law reports from 1947, we found that literally hundreds of cases had been argued by him in various High Courts and the Supreme Court. One book notes that Palkhivala had appeared in the Supreme Court in not less than 150 prominent cases.[2] Equally staggering was the number of cases that he had argued before the Bombay High Court and other High Courts. If this was not enough, there were even more cases where he had appeared before the Income Tax Appellate Tribunal and the Industrial Tribunal. India was involved in three major international cases and he was engaged to defend our country in all three of them. And, to add all of this, he had a huge opinion practice!

We have chosen only those cases where new principles have been laid down or which had some interesting feature. It was a difficult task to select these cases and omit the remainder. It is quite possible that readers may feel that a particular case was wrongly left out. We can only apologise for such a lapse but this is inevitable in any selection.

Apart from the reading of judgments, interviews were conducted with judges who had heard his arguments and with lawyers and Chartered Accountants closely associated with him. These interviews were extremely helpful in the writing of this book and gave us invaluable insights into the nature of his advocacy, his method of preparing for his cases and his style of advocacy. As this book is confined to his contribution to the development of the law, we have not touched upon his work as a director in several leading companies, the numerous speeches that he delivered not only on the Union Budget each year but on various other subjects.

It was during the preparation of this book that one question kept cropping up. How could one man achieve all this in a lifetime? The

1. M.V. Kamath, *Nani Palkhivala : A life.*
2. Maj Gen Nilendra Kumar, *Nani Palkhivala — A Role Model,* Universal Law Publishing Co. (2006), pp. 376-408.

interviews indicated that there were certain special qualities that Palkhivala had cultivated and which, we believe, can be emulated with determination and practice. These, combined with his brilliance, led to a staggeringly successful career that is unlikely to be equaled in the near future. Finally, we hope this book will inspire younger members of the Bar to greater professional excellence. At the present time, there are very few role models, particularly at the Bar, and the life of Palkhivala as a lawyer is truly inspirational and will hopefully motivate younger lawyers to strive and attain professional excellence.

This book is confined to Palkhivala's career as a lawyer. Therefore, we have deliberately omitted references to his personal life, his stint as India's Ambassador to the United States and his role as a director of several companies.

Acknowledgements

From the start, Behram Palkhivala has been a pillar of support and this book would have been impossible without his continued and cheerful help. Apart from several meetings at his residence in Mumbai, he took the trouble of retrieving several old newspaper reports and articles. He has meticulously maintained all the opinions speeches and other material of his late brother. His methodical manner of working, the phenomenal attention to detail are qualities that we must emulate. Despite his age and frail health, he took the trouble of going through the entire typescript and made several corrections which were lessons in proof-reading. He was also kind enough to help us with several old photographs that have been printed in this book. His wife, Dhan Palkhivala, also gave us several interesting anecdotes.

Our grateful thanks must go to late Chief Justice Y.V. Chandrachud for a memorable interview. He knew Palkhivala from the time they were part-time lecturers at the Government Law College, Mumbai. Chandrachud noted how bitter and sad Palkhivala had become in the last years of his life. Justice S. Muralidhar of the Delhi High Court worked with Palkhivala in Seshan's *election* case and helped in writing that sub-chapter. Thanks are also due to former Chief Justice M.N. Venkatachaliah and former Supreme Court judges S.Ranganathan and Kuldip Singh. Justice R.V. Easwar, now a judge of the Delhi High Court and former President of the Income Tax Appellate Tribunal, helped us to shortlist the important tax cases.

From the Bar, D.M. Popat, Ravinder Narain and Harish N. Salve gave us several hours of their time that revealed several interesting facets of his personal and professional life. We also had the benefit of interviewing Senior Advocates, K. Parasaran, Fali S. Nariman, Anil Divan, Dinesh Vyas H.P. Ranina and Rohinton F. Nariman. Senior Advocate K.K. Venugopal gave us the written submissions made on behalf of the Union of India in the *Minerva Mills* case and his impressions of Palkhivala who argued for the petitioners. T.R. Andhyarujina gave us a wealth of information on the *Kesavananda Bharati* case. His latest book on the subject, *The Kesavananda Bharati Case – The Untold Story of Struggle for Supremacy by Supreme Court and Parliament;*[3] has also revealed new facts about that case and the subsequent review. Prashant Bhushan gave us several details about the *Kesavananda Bharati* review case and permitted us to reproduce certain portions from his excellent book *The Case that shook India.*[4] Thanks are also due to M.L. Bhakta, late N.C. Mehta, D.B. Engineer, N.H. Hingorani and Kapila Hingorani for their help.

Palkhivala was closely associated with several chartered accountants including Y.H. Malegam, Bansi Mehta, N.V. Iyer and Dileep Choksi. N.V. Iyer was a key member of the team that helped Palkhivala prepare his famous annual budget lectures. Y.H. Malegam carefully went through the final draft of this book and made several suggestions. Dileep Choksi gave up several months of his practice and helped Nani and Behram Palkhivala complete the eighth edition of his book. This book would have been incomplete without their help.

R.S. Gae, former Law Secretary, gave us several interesting insights into the *Bank Nationalisation* case. Our thanks to Chief Justice A.P. Shah for permitting us to access the 1951 *Copyright* case pleading and judgment and to Surendra Malik, Eastern Book Company, for allowing us to reproduce the written submission in the *Kesavananda Bharati* case.

This book would have been equally impossible without the help of our young colleagues at the Bar: Ananth Padmanabhan, Suchindran B.N., Vikram Ramakrishnan, Rishi Kumar Dugar, Karthik Sundaram, Sandeep Bagmar R. and V. Niranjan. They tirelessly helped in the research, assisted in preparing the drafts, cross-checking the citations and checking the proofs. Special thanks to Sandeep Bagmar R. for his assistance in final stages of the Book.

V.S. Jayakumar and M.V. Swaroop, Advocates, Madras High Court carefully tabulated all the important cases argued by Palkhivala on direct taxes before the Supreme Court and the High Courts as well as the ITAT. This saved considerable amount of time.

Capt. P.R. Datar meticulously corrected the proofs. Shri P.S. Seetharaman and R. Rajakumar patiently typed draft after draft over the last seven years. Thanks are also due to Shri R. Krishnamurthy, S. Sankar and Lazar for

---

3. Universal Law Publishing Co. (2011).
4. Vikas Publishing House Pvt. Ltd. (1978).

ensuring that the extensive research material was kept in an organized manner.

Ms. Shirin Bharucha, who was the Legal Advisor of the Tata Group for almost four decades with Palkhivala, was kind enough to permit us to reproduce a few of his opinions.

Ms. Thrity Dollykooka, his secretary for several years, was also very helpful and kind enough to show us numerous letters and spoke at length about his manner and style of working. Thanks are due to late M.R. Pa for giving us a lengthy interview despite his ill-health.

We are deeply grateful to the unfailing patience and kindness shown by Shri S. Divakara, Director-General of Forum of Free Enterprise, Mumbai over the last seven years. Without him, most of the interviews would not have been possible. Thanks are due to Himani Datar and the Wadhwa brothers for their constant encouragement and support.

Finally, we must thank Ms. Abha Thapalyal Gandhi, Publishing Director Ms. Supriti Narayanan, Publishing Manager and Mr. Arjun Bhargava Legal Research Editor of LexisNexis Butterworths Wadhwa Nagpur for the excellent manner in which the book has been brought out. They made several suggestions to improve the layout and presentation of the book And they were more than forgiving for the enormous time taken to write this book.

We started writing this book in 2004 and had the assistance of numerous individuals. We sincerely apologize to any person who has lent a helping hand on this seven year journey but has been missed out. For us, writing this book has been a remarkable experience. It is still difficult to believe that one man could have achieved so much in one life time. One of Palkhivala's favourite poems was Rudyard Kipling's "If" and we close our work with these immortal lines from the last para of that poem:

If you can talk with crowds and keep your virtue,
Or walk with Kings—nor lose the common touch,
If neither foes nor loving friends can hurt you,
If all men count with you, but none too much;
If you can fill the unforgiving minute
With sixty seconds' worth of distance run,
Yours is the Earth and everything that's in it,
And — which is more — you'll be a Man, my son!

New Delhi,
December 25, 2011

Soli J Sorabjee
Arvind P Datar

General Contents

Appendices

Table of Cases

D

E

J

K

L

M

T

Chapter 1

Secrets of Palkhivala's Success

Nanabhoy Ardeshir Palkhivala arguably had the most meteoric rise as an advocate in living memory. Without a privileged background, without a god-father in the legal profession, without a degree from Oxford or Cambridge or any foreign university, without being a barrister (as was fashionable at that time), handicapped by a severe stammer in his childhood, Palkhivala reached the very pinnacle of success in the legal profession in less than twenty years.

What was the secret of his stupendous success at the Bar? What makes one person reach unbelievable levels of achievement in his chosen field? Are there any lessons to be learnt from such success? Is there a formula that can be replicated by anyone – like ingredients of a recipe of a master chef that can be merely repeated? There is a theory that success leaves clues. If a person has succeeded by doing certain things, it is possible to do the same thing and achieve similar, if not the same, success.

As we came to the end of preparing the final chapters of this book, Malcolm Gladwell's *Outliers – The Story of Success* was published in late 2008.[1] Chapter II of this remarkable book dealt with three questions: Is achievement the result of innate talent? What roles do hard work and preparation play? Does the particular working environment play an important role? The answers Gladwell gives us are truly astonishing and explain, to a great extent, Palkhivala's success.

The 10,000 hour rule

Gladwell begins by referring to a study undertaken by an eminent psychologist, Prof. K. Anders Ericsson and his two colleagues, at Berlin's Elite Academy of Music in the early 1990s.

---

1. Gladwell is an international best selling author of three other remarkable books: '*The Tipping Point*', '*Blink*', and his latest offering '*What the Dog Saw: And Other Adventures*'.

The school's violinists were divided into three groups. The first group contained the very successful 'stars', those who had the potential to become world class violinists. In the second category were those who were merely 'good', and in the last category were students who were unlikely to ever play professionally and who intended to be music teachers in the public school system.

Prof. Ericsson found that all three groups had started playing at the same age – around five years old. All three groups played for about the same time – about two to three hours per week – till they were eight. But then the differences began to emerge – *the best students simply practised more than everyone else!* By age twelve, the first group was practising eight hours per week and reached thirty hours of practice per week by the time they were twenty – single-mindedly and purposefully playing their 'instruments with the intent to get better'. The study found that the top students had, by the age of twenty, totalled 10,000 hours of practice, the second group 8,000 hours and the last category 4,000 hours. (Amateur violinists practised even less – just 2000 hours).

Prof. Ericsson repeated his study with pianists and got the same results. Later, similar studies were made among music composers, basketball players, fiction writers, ice-skaters and chess players. Despite these diverse set of activities, in no area was world class expertise acquired in lesser time. Mozart, arguably the greatest musical prodigy of all time, did not hit his stride until he had put in 10,000 hours of practice. As Gladwell points out: '*Practice is not the thing you do once you are good. It is the thing you do that makes you good.*'

And music lovers will be delighted to know that the hugely popular rock band, Beatles, achieved excellence in their field by practising several hours a day, particularly in Hamburg where they played in night clubs between 1961 and 1964. The other rock bands performed for considerably less time. The gruelling practice put in by the Beatles made them 'sound like no one else'.

The 10,000-hour rule perhaps applies to Palkhivala as well. Without question, he worked harder and with greater speed than most of his contemporaries. 'You cannot imagine the speed with which he worked', said his brother, Behram. After working till 9.30 in the evening, Palkhivala (and sometimes his brother) would start working on the income tax commentary at 10 p.m. and continue till 2 a.m., day after day. 'In all his numerous visits to the Supreme Court, he never went to the canteen or the Bar Association even once,' remembers Ravinder Narain.[2] During the long years that they worked together in the High Court, Behram too had never seen Nani enter the Bar Association except to attend meetings convened on rare occasions for specific purposes.

Innate talent Palkhivala undoubtedly had, but extraordinary hard work was a greater factor that contributed to his success. In the words of Gladwell: 'Achievement is talent plus preparation. The problem with this view is that the closer the psychologists look at the careers of the gifted, *the smaller the role innate talent seems to play and the bigger the role preparation seems to play*'.

Stream of opportunities

The other factor that is responsible for extraordinary success, according to Gladwell, is the 'stream of opportunities' that comes one's way. Very often being in the right place at the right time helps and makes all the difference between modest and outstanding success.

The richest software billionaires – including Bill Gates and Steve Jobs – were all born in the mid 1950s and joined college at the starting point of the computer revolution. And fourteen of the seventy-five richest men in all human history were born between 1830 and 1840 and were young entrepreneurs in the 1860s and 1870s – the period of the greatest economic transformation in American history.

Palkhivala had his 'stream of opportunities' as well. *First,* he had the good fortune of joining the chambers of Sir Jamshedji Kanga, perhaps the busiest chamber at that time. Kanga had been the Advocate-General of the State of Bombay for several years and, at that time, the Commissioner of Income Tax was invariably represented by the Advocate-General in the Bombay High Court. After returning to private practice, Kanga was frequently briefed to appear for income tax assessees. Palkhivala, who joined his chambers in 1945, soon began to assist him in income tax cases where his accounting knowledge was particularly useful. Several of his other juniors became leading members of the Bar – R.J. Kolah, H.M. Seervai and F.S. Nariman, to name a few. Palkhivala was thus briefed frequently in income tax cases before the Bombay High Court as well as the Income Tax Appellate Tribunal. No

2. A Senior Advocate of the Delhi High Court and former partner of J.B. Dadachanji & Co. – the firm that briefed Palkhivala more than anybody else in New Delhi.

other chamber could have given him so much encouragement and support. A good senior can make all the difference to the career of a young lawyer.

Secondly, the Income Tax Appellate Tribunal (ITAT) had started functioning in 1941, and the number of tax appeals increased substantially. Palkhivala's knowledge of accountancy and quick grasp helped enormously in gaining the confidence of chartered accountants. As Kanga was busy in the High Court, Palkhivala was briefed frequently to appear before the ITAT.

Thirdly, most constitutional and tax cases were heard by Chief Justice Chagla, undoubtedly one of India's greatest judges. Chagla had the habit of delivering judgments immediately after arguments were concluded. Indeed, in his 18 year stint, he reserved judgments only twice. His judgments were extremely readable and seldom lengthy. Chagla was able to finish all tax references in 8 to 10 weeks, thus leaving Palkhivala ample time to appear before the Supreme Court, other High Courts and the Tribunals. The Bench of Chagla and Tendolkar perhaps delivered more important judgments on income tax than any other Bench of the High Court or Supreme Court.

Fourthly, the Industrial Tribunal also had an increasing workload with the rise in trade union activities and consequent confrontation with managements. Luckily, for Palkhivala, the Income Tax Appellate Tribunal worked only in the morning and the Industrial Tribunal only in the afternoon! After arguing the whole morning before the Tax Tribunal, he would be off to the Industrial Tribunal in the afternoon.

Fifthly, he had the advantage of setting up his practice in Bombay (now Mumbai) which was growing at a rapid pace and was soon to overtake Calcutta as the commercial capital of India. The early decades of independence saw a rapid growth in industrial and commercial activities in Bombay which inevitably led to tax and commercial litigation.

Sixthly, the Constitution came into force in 1950 – just four years after he commenced practice – leading to a boom in writ petitions. Palkhivala was briefed to appear in a large number of them – particularly in cases relating to requisition and evacuee property.

Lastly, there was also an increasing amount of work in the newly formed Supreme Court which had outstanding judges like Chief

Justice Kania, B.K. Mukherjea, Vivian Bose, M.C. Mahajan, Fazl Ali and T.L. Venkatarama Iyer.

Palkhivala thus had his 'stream of opportunities' and he took full advantage of all of them. He was given all the ingredients for remarkable success and, like a master chef, he turned himself into one of the finest advocates of all time. Behram remarked that Nani would not only utilize opportunities that came his way but *also make opportunities.* When, early in his career, he realized that there was no good book on income-tax, he set about writing one which helped propel him to the front ranks of his profession.

Finally, what about 'luck'? It has been said that luck is the *intersection* of hard work and opportunity. By this definition, Palkhivala was very 'lucky' indeed.

Apart from the 'stream of opportunities', Palkhivala had certain outstanding qualities, both innate and cultivated, that were vital ingredients of his phenomenal success. In several interviews, the qualities that were repeatedly highlighted were as follows:

(i) *Single minded determination to succeed*: Palkhivala was extremely driven and ambitious and even as a child, he would strive to come first in every debate or elocution competition. Behram Palkhivala recollects that he hated to come second. It was this drive that enabled him to come First-class First in the First LL.B. (1943), First-class First in the Second LL.B. (1944) and he passed the Advocate (OS) examination with the highest marks in every individual paper (1946).

(ii) *Capacity for hard work*: Dinesh Vyas[3] remarked that continuous hard work was Palkhivala's second nature. He just seemed to have limitless inner energy to keep going. His conferences with solicitors and advocates would often continue till midnight. Bansi Mehta, one of India's leading chartered accountants, recalls that a party from Delhi required an urgent opinion as certain amounts had to be paid to the Department the very next day which was the last date for payment. When he asked for an appointment, Palkhivala told him to come the next day. Bansi Mehta explained that the matter was very urgent and the client had to go back to Delhi the next day to pay the amount if Palkhivala felt that it was advisable to do so. Since the matter could

3. Palkhivala's junior and now a leading senior counsel specializing in tax matters. Dinesh Vyas prepared the ninth edition of Kanga and Palkhivala's 'Law and Practice of Income Tax'.

not be postponed to the next day, Palkhivala asked Bansi Mehta and his client to come to his residence at 12.30 a.m. in the night. After discussing the matter, he agreed to the proposal made by Bansi Mehta and suggested a few changes. The conference was over at 1.00 a.m. and the client left for Delhi the next day and paid the amount as per the opinion.

In the mid-1960s, Bakshi Ghulam Mohammed[4] had challenged his detention in a writ petition filed before the Jammu and Kashmir High Court. As the Government of that State was very keen to sustain the detention, Ravinder Narain suggested that the counter affidavit of the Government be settled by Palkhivala. There was only one day left for filing the counter. Accordingly, Jaswant Singh[5] and Ravinder Narain came to Bombay. Due to his hectic schedule, Palkhivala gave them an appointment at 10.30 p.m. and the three worked till 4.30 a.m and finalized the counter affidavit. Palkhivala drove his car and dropped them at the hotel. Without any sleep, they directly went to the airport and to Delhi. After having the counter affidavit cyclostyled, Ravinder Narain and Jaswant Singh flew to Jammu at 1.30 p.m and filed the counter at 4.00 p.m. – just half-an-hour before the deadline.

Thrity Dollykooka, Palkhivala's secretary for several years, recollects his giving an urgent appointment at 3.30 a.m. at his residence. This odd time was given because Palkhivala had to leave for the airport at 4.00 a.m!

(iii) *Time management*: A major factor that led to his success was his obsession with time management. Vyas has not seen any other man who valued the importance of time as much as Palkhivala did. Wasting time was a major crime. M.L. Bhakta,[6] who had briefed him in a number of cases, recollects that Palkhivala always came to court just five minutes before his case was expected to be called out or taken up. If the earlier case took more time than expected, he would get visibly annoyed and agitated, although he would not say anything. Bhakta found him very tense if he was kept waiting.

Ravinder Narain also reveals an interesting fact that showed his obsession in not wasting time. As soon as his case in the Supreme Court was over, he would rush back to his hotel for the next

---

4. He was the Deputy Prime Minister of Jammu & Kashmir and became the Prime Minister after the detention of Sheikh Abdullah in 1953.
5. An advocate, later became a judge of the Supreme Court of India.
6. A leading solicitor and partner of Kanga & Co.

meeting or to prepare for the next case or opinion. Behram also mentioned that he never spent time in the Bar library at the Bombay High Court or chatting with friends. He would never come back from court and relax over a cup of tea. As soon as he returned to his chamber in the Bombay High Court, he would immediately start working! Indeed, his inability to relax may have affected his health in later years. But the lesson to be learnt is that he took care not to waste even a few minutes.

(iv) *Concentration*: M.R. Pai noted that Palkhivala always gave complete attention to the task at hand. He would always focus on doing one thing at a time and avoided multitasking. Before he started a meeting, he would set aside all other papers and only concentrate on the particular topic for that meeting. His ability to concentrate and be completely focused on the task at hand was truly remarkable. This power, combined with a razor sharp intellect, enabled him to grasp and understand complex legal problems in a very short time. Consequently, his conferences would always be brief.

(v) *Speed reading*: Palkhivala had also mastered the art of speed reading. He would glance at a page from top to bottom in one sweep, grasping the contents therein. The essence of the case would then be retained in his photographic memory. Palkhivala told Pai that the powers of concentration, focusing and speed reading could be mastered by anyone.

(vi) *Continuous self-improvement*: Popat[7] noted that Palkhivala was very fond of reading Peter Drucker and was constantly finding ways to improve the methods of his working. He believed in the need for continuous self-improvement.

(vii) *Clear strategy and persuasive style of advocacy*: According to Vyas, he laid great emphasis on having a clear and consistent strategy in important cases. He would carefully analyze the facts, compartmentalize the legal issues and formulate his propositions. Once this was done, he never omitted any point or argument that was needed to be made. Harish Salve also recollects the great amount of preparation that went into the *Lohia Machines'* case.[8] The next attribute is Palkhivala's style of advocacy. He tried to summarise his arguments into brief points. He often argued by

7. D.M. Popat, Senior Partner of Mulla & Mulla & Craigie, Blunt & Caroe, Bombay (Mumbai).
8. *Lohia Machines Ltd. v. Union of India,* (1985) 152 ITR 308 : AIR 1985 SC 421 : (1985) 2 SCC 197 – interview with Harish N. Salve.

giving examples as to what would happen if his point of view was not accepted. Similarly, he tried to show that the stand taken by the other side would lead to unintended or absurd consequences. Palkhivala's style was persuasive and he almost never raised his temper or interrupted the other side. He advised his juniors to never lose their temper in court or offend the judge.

There have been other lawyers who were more learned in the law but, according to Iqbal Chagla,[9] Palkhivala was unsurpassable for sheer advocacy. His felicity of expression made dry legal arguments very interesting and often left the judges spellbound.

(viii) *No gossip*: M.R. Pai travelled with Palkhivala all over India for his Budget and other lectures. In an interview, Pai remarked that two of the most unusual things about Palkhivala was that he never indulged in gossip and he never criticised people behind their back.

Fali Nariman remarked that great batsmen were of two kinds: those belonging to the 'Hobbes class' and a very few belonging to the 'Bradman class'. By emulating Palkhivala's qualities and work habits, most lawyers can reach the Hobbes class if they are determined to do so. Perhaps, with exceptional hard work, and a bit of luck, one could even shatter the gravitational barrier and enter the stratospheric level of the 'Bradman class'.

❋

9. A leading senior counsel at the Bombay High Court and son of Chief Justice M.C. Chagla.

Chapter 2

Extraordinary Child and Lawyer by Accident

The early years

Nanabhoy Ardershir Palkhivala was born on January 16, 1920, the second of three children. His surname, like many Parsi surnames, was based on the business carried on by his ancestors.

The Palkhivalas manufactured *palkhis* or palanquins which were carried by four servants. Wealthy businessmen and lawyers travelled in *palkhis* in the days before the motor-car.[1] However, *palkhis* made by them were of outstanding quality and there was a waiting list for their products. With the popularity of horse-drawn carriages, the manufacture of *palkhis* became unnecessary.

His parents, Ardeshir and Sheroo, were a devoted couple. His father ran two laundries which were renowned for superb quality and customer service. The family was not affluent but there was no shortage of the basic necessities of life. His parents lavished affection on the three children and all were equally devoted to both of them. In interviews to various periodicals, Palkhivala often became emotional when he spoke of his parents. As Behram Palkhivala, his younger brother, said: 'From our parents, we learnt lessons which no school, no college, no university could impart. The children studied in school; they were educated at home'. A later edition of Palkhivala's classic commentary *The Law and Practice of Income Tax* was dedicated to the memory of his parents with these memorable words:

To the memory
of
my mother and father
'So now in the end, if this the least be good,
if any deed be done, if any fire
burn in the imperfect page, the praise be thine.

---

1. *M.V. Kamath, Nani Palkhivala: A life*, pp. 28-31.

Palkhivala was a studious child who loved reading more than anything else. He did extremely well in his school examinations and was a diligent, conscientious student. Apart from studies, he was good in music—playing the violin and the piano, palmistry, photography, sketching, painting and carpentry but he never pursued these hobbies after college. Behram Palkhivala recollects that he had a good sense of humour and sometimes played practical jokes. He was hopeless in sports but liked the game of cricket. With the enormous pressure on his time, he seldom witnessed a cricket match. Behram remembers that, even in his early years, Palkhivala was an extraordinary child and was conscious that he was 'born with a mission'. He was obsessed with time; always engaged in some work and always in a hurry.

A voracious reader from his childhood, Palkhivala invested all his savings in buying second hand books. Popular Publications had a book shop on Grant Road in Bombay and Shri Bhatkal, the proprietor, allowed him to use the bookshop late into the evening. Palkhivala would spend hours reading the latest arrivals in biography, history and literature. Little wonder that he developed an abiding love for literature and wanted to be a teacher in English.

Palkhivala's stammer has often been commented upon. A man who kept 100,000 people spell-bound at a cricket stadium, would, as a child, struggle to say even a few words. Behram recollects his elder brother's bad stammer – getting stuck with words and unable to complete a sentence. It was a terrible sight. His father made him run on the beach with an almond under his tongue. Perhaps, he took the cue from Demosthenes who placed pebbles in his mouth and practiced shouting at the waves to clear his stammer. (Incidentally, Palkhivala admired Winston Churchill who also had a stutter). Despite his stammer, Palkhivala took part in several debates and elocution contests. He was determined to get over this handicap and it is tempting to speculate that he may not have been such a great speaker if he did not have the stammer. Great achievements have often come from men driven to overcome insurmountable odds. His love and extensive reading of the classics, biographies and history proved useful in debates and elocutions which he frequently won. It was a happy childhood and he remained devoted to his brother and sister. They, in turn, lavished their affection on him.

Palkhivala studied at the Master's Tutorial High School—it still exists and was later taken over by a Sindhi trust. Apart from school subjects, Palkhivala attended accounting classes conducted by

Principal Banaji. This kind Principal was so impressed with Palkhivala's sincerity that he did not charge anything for these classes. This knowledge of accounting was invaluable in arguing income-tax cases. Palkhivala finished his matriculation examination in 1936, getting the highest marks in English. It is interesting to note that in 1937 he passed the first year arts exam with highest marks in Persian!

'My son – you are cut out for law'

Palkhivala's debating skills and clear thinking led his father to frequently advise him to become a lawyer. He said *'My son—you are cut out for law—become a lawyer'.* But Palkhivala wanted to be a lecturer in English and did not follow his father's suggestion. And how right his father was!

After completing his matriculation, Palkhivala joined the St. Xavier's College in 1940, and completed his B.A. with Honours in English literature. His future wife, Nargesh, had also joined the same college to pursue a degree in mathematics. R.S. Gae, the former Law Secretary of the Government of India, and now a sprightly nonagenarian, was a lecturer in mathematics and taught Nargesh. He recollects that the two students were friends. After his B.A., Palkhivala's ambition was to become a lecturer in a local college. But he was not selected. A lady candidate was selected because she had prior teaching experience. This was perhaps the first major twist of fate that was to have a decisive impact on his career. This episode has often been recounted; Palkhivala continued to be in touch with this lady lecturer and even invited her for lunch in later years.

He then went on to do his M.A. in English literature. Even at this time, he did not pursue a career in law although he could have taken up law immediately after the B.A. examination. Thus, two more years were spent in getting his M.A. degree.

Nargesh wanted Palkhivala to become a member of the Indian Civil Service (ICS). This was the ultimate dream for many young Indians at that time. The ICS entrance examination was held in New Delhi but a severe epidemic broke out that year resulting in several deaths. His parents were extremely worried and requested him not to go to Delhi. Palkhivala, as a devoted son, did not submit his application form and the last date was over. By another twist of fate, which must have seemed cruel at the time, the Government later declared that the examination would be held at

Bombay because of the epidemic. By this time, it was too late to submit the application form and Palkhivala never attempted the examination again.

Having failed in his attempt to become an English lecturer and to write the ICS exam, Palkhivala finally took up law and joined the Government Law College in 1942. At last, he paid heed to his father's advice. It is supremely ironical that the India's greatest lawyer became one by accident. If he had become an English lecturer, he may have retired as a Vice-Chancellor. As an ICS Officer, he would have eventually retired as a Secretary to the Government.

It was as if some unseen hand thwarted his attempts at other careers and gently steered him to the legal profession. His father's words were indeed prophetic. For a man obsessed with time, Palkhivala lost two precious years of practice. Looking back, Palkhivala seemed genetically coded to be an outstanding lawyer.

Palkhivala joined the Government Law College at Mumbai in 1942. He stood first in the First and Second LL.B. examinations in 1943 and 1944. At that time, lawyers who wanted to practice on the original side had to pass the difficult 'Advocate (OS)' examination. Palkhivala, true to form, not only stood first in this exam but secured the highest marks in *every* individual paper in this examination! It is unlikely that this feat will be equaled; in any event, it cannot be bettered.

❋

Chapter 3

Meteoric Rise to Legal Stardom

After a brilliant academic record at the law college, Palkhivala joined the chambers of Sir Jamshedji Kanga in 1944. Kanga was the leader of the Bombay Bar and had been the Advocate-General of Bombay from 1922 to 1935. He was also a judge of the Bombay High Court for one year between 1921-1922.[1] At that time, the person who held the post of Advocate-General was truly the leader of the Bar and, apart from judgeship, this was considered the zenith in any lawyer's career. Like so many constitutional offices, this office has also been devalued and appointments are often made on purely political considerations. Merit and ability have now become optional accessories.

No other lawyer in living memory had as rapid a rise in the legal profession as Palkhivala. The meteoric rise of Palkhivala is even more remarkable in the background of the galaxy of seniors who practised in the Bombay High Court in 1944. At that time, the leaders of the Bar were M.C. Setalvad, C.K. Daphtary, M.P. Amin and M.V. Desai to name a few. Sir Jamshedji Kanga was of course the tallest leader of the Bar but he had substantially reduced his practice by then.

Kanga's chamber had a formidable team of talented counsel. The seniormost lawyer working with Kanga was R.J. Kolah who was himself a leading practitioner at the tax Bar. Among other lawyers were Marzban Mistry (the senior of F.S. Nariman), Jal Vimadalal and K.H. Bhabha and the great H.M. Seervai. In 1946, these lawyers already had a large practice. For most lawyers, it takes a decade to get going. Nariman recollects that within a span of two years, Palkhivala had picked up an enormous amount of work and there was no important matter in the Bombay High Court in which he was not briefed.

---

1. Under Article 220 of the Constitution, any person who has been a permanent judge of a particular High Court cannot practice in that court. This prohibition did not exist earlier and Kanga could revert to the Bar after being a judge for a year.

His first brief was entrusted to him by Rustom Gagrat, founder of Gagrat and Company, a leading firm of solicitors. He expected Palkhivala to take about a week to finish the plaint as the case was quite complicated. To his surprise, Palkhivala drafted the plaint within two days. Gagrat was deeply impressed with the speed and quality of Palkhivala's work. This must have been the experience of other solicitors as well. His brilliant scholastic record must have also helped in gaining the confidence of solicitors.

Behram Palkhivala recollects one particular case that was a turning point in Palkhivala's life. One Abdul Ismail was the tenant on the first floor of the Paradise Building at Warden Road in Bombay. His landlord was Mr. N.B. Vakil. In January 1948, Ismail assigned his tenancy to Khushaldas Advani and his two relatives. All three assignees were refugees from Sindh and they took possession in February 1948. Three weeks later, P.V. Rao, Secretary to the Government of Bombay, Health and Local Government Department signed an order requisitioning this flat. The official order was issued in the name of the Governor of Bombay. This flat was allotted to another refugee from Sindh. At that time, the Constitution of India had not come into force and Advani filed a petition for a writ of *certiorari* under Section 45 of the Specific Relief Act, 1877.[2] The case was posted before Justice N.H. Bhagwati, the father of the former Chief Justice P.N. Bhagwati. R.J. Kolah, assisted by Palkhivala, appeared for Advani and M.P. Amin, as Advocate-General, appeared for the Government of Bombay.[3] R.J. Kolah and the Advocate-General concluded their arguments on a particular day and the judge posted the case on the next day for Kolah's rejoinder.

Unfortunately, Kolah was held up in another case the next day and he asked Palkhivala to complete the arguments in rejoinder. This was the moment of opportunity and Palkhivala made the most of it. One of the controversial questions in this case was whether a writ of *certiorari* would lie against the Provincial Government.

---

2. The relevant part of Section 45 reads as follows:
   'Any of the High Courts of Judicature at Fort William, Madras and Bombay may make an order requiring any specific act to be done or forborne, within the local limits of its ordinary original civil jurisdiction, by any person holding a public office, whether of a permanent or a temporary nature, or by any corporation or inferior Court of Judicature.'
3. The State of Maharashtra was later formed on May 1, 1960 under the States' Reorganisation Act, 1956.

Three judgments of the Madras High Court[4] and one of the Calcutta High Court[5] had taken the view that a writ of *certiorari* would not lie against the Provincial Government.

Palkhivala did not sleep that night as he had the formidable task of arguing that four decisions of the Madras High Court and Calcutta High Court did not represent the correct view. Palkhivala urged new points which are normally not permissible in a rejoinder. M.P. Amin was gracious enough not to object to Palkhivala's raising new points but he requested Justice Bhagwati that he should have the right of surrejoinder. Palkhivala began his arguments and continued for the day. Dhan Palkhivala (Behram Palkhivala's wife) was a student of the law college at that time. Word spread that young Palkhivala was arguing an important case before Justice Bhagwati. She and other students all rushed to the Bombay High Court to listen to him. It was a scintillating performance and Palkhivala ultimately persuaded the judge to take a contrary view. For a two-year old lawyer, this was a stupendous feat. M.P. Amin must also be complemented for allowing Palkhivala to raise new points in rejoinder.

The judgment was taken in appeal and heard by a Division Bench of Chief Justice Chagla and Justice Tendolkar.[6] The view of Justice Bhagwati that a writ of *certiorari* would lie against the Provincial Government was upheld although the order of Justice Bhagwati on certain other issues was reversed.

There is no doubt that even without this case, Palkhivala would have made good at the Bar. But *Rao v. Advani* was the equivalent of a booster rocket that quickly put him on a trajectory into the stratosphere.

Nariman recollects that Kanga's chamber was crowded with several juniors. Kanga had a large table and the other juniors (who included Kolah, Mistry and Seervai) had one table each. Soon Palkhivala also had a table with only one chair. He got so busy that he frequently had conferences in his car as there was simply no room in the chamber.

---

4. *Venkataratnam v. Secretary of State for India,* AIR 1930 Mad 896 : (1931) 53 ILR 979; *Thyagarajan v. Government of Madras,* AIR 1939 Mad 940 : (1940) ILR 204 : (1939) 2 MLJ 801; *Kandaswami v. Province of Madras,* AIR 1947 Mad 443 : (1948) ILR 283 : (1947) 2 MLJ 146.
5. *In Re Banwarilal Roy,* 48 CWN 766.
6. *P.V. Rao v. Khushaldas S. Advani,* AIR 1949 Bom 277 : (1949) 51 Bom LR 342.

Justice Y.V. Chandrachud, the former Chief Justice of India, also had a rapid rise at the Bar. Chandrachud was one year senior to Palkhivala and had also stood first in the first and second year LL.B. examinations. He remembers Palkhivala as a young lawyer who would not even waste a single minute and they would frequently meet in the library. One day there was an advertisement on the notice board inviting applications for the posts of part-time lecturers in the Government Law College. Chandrachud told Palkhivala that both of them should apply for this post. Palkhivala was skeptical but Chandrachud told him that they had nothing to lose.[7] At that time, to be appointed a part-time lecturer was a feather in the cap of any lawyer. The system of appointing practising lawyers as part-time lecturers was a wonderful idea and enabled several leading lawyers to teach students. Unfortunately, this was discontinued and the new rules now require lecturers to have at least a Masters' degree before they can be part of the faculty. The loss to students has been very heavy.

Chief Justice Chagla selected both of them and they started teaching in the law college. Both had a number of students who went on to become leaders of the Bar – Nariman, Sorabjee, Ashok Desai and Anil Divan,[8] to name a few. D.M. Popat, a leading solicitor, was also his student.[9] The lectures by Chandrachud and Palkhivala were very popular. Due to his court work, Palkhivala would be frequently late for class but the students would wait. Palkhivala continued as a lecturer from 1949 till 1952. According to Popat, Chandrachud was the better lecturer because his lectures could be followed even by the average student. Chandrachud also made his classes more interesting because he would explain legal concepts with interesting anecdotes and examples. Palkhivala was also offered the post of the Principal of the Government Law College which had an attractive salary of Rs. 1,500/- per month. This offer was made soon after he started practice, but he declined.

---

7. Interview with late Justice Y.V. Chandrachud.
8. F.S. Nariman was the Additional Solicitor-General of India during 1972-75. He resigned in 1975 in the wake of the Emergency. Soli Sorabjee and Ashok Desai both held the post of Attorney-General. Anil Divan is also a leading member of the Supreme Court Bar and had closely worked with Palkhivala in the *Kesavananda Bharati* case. Sorabjee assisted Palkhivala in a number of important cases, including *Kesavananda Bharati*. Nariman worked with Palkhivala in the *Golak Nath* case.
9. D.M. Popat is the Senior Partner of Mulla & Mulla & Craigie, Blunt & Caroe. He has also worked with Palkhivala in a number of cases.

From 1953, Palkhivala's name is regularly mentioned in the law reports. From the age of 33, Palkhivala regularly appeared in the Supreme Court on his own and without briefing any senior. This again was remarkable – particularly at a time when the Supreme Court had a galaxy of outstanding judges and the Bar at Delhi also comprised of great advocates like M.C. Setalvad (the first Attorney-General), C.K. Daphtary (the first Solicitor-General) G.S. Pathak, N.C. Chatterjee, and P.R. Das to name a few.

In 1957, at the age of 37, Palkhivala was also appointed a part-time member of the Law Commission at the behest of its Chairman, M.C. Setalvad.

Another important factor that helped in the meteoric rise of Palkhivala was the formation of the Income Tax Appellate Tribunal (ITAT), a few years earlier, in 1941. Even at that time tax laws were hideously complicated. It was the convention that the Advocate-General of the Province would appear in the High Court for the Commissioner of Income Tax (Revenue) and Kanga, as Advocate-General for 13 years, had appeared in numerous tax references. After he stepped down, he continued to be briefed in several income tax references for the assessees. (Incidentally, M.C. Setalvad, as Advocate-General of Bombay, also appeared in numerous cases for the Revenue). After 1946, the number of income tax cases before the Tribunal began to increase.

Palkhivala had started to appear as Kanga's junior in the High Court. As the great man could not appear often in the Tribunal, it was but natural that solicitors started briefing Palkhivala in several appeals before that forum. Several of his colleagues and juniors mention that Palkhivala appeared in countless cases before the Tribunal. In his career, he perhaps did more cases before the ITAT than in the High Courts and the Supreme Court combined!

When asked how Palkhivala could combine work in the High Court and the Tribunal, Behram points out that income-tax references were heard by a Bench headed by Chief Justice Chagla and Justice Tendolkar or the Chief Justice and another puisne judge. In those days, the Bench would quickly dispose of the tax cases within a few weeks and several months would be available to tax lawyers to appear before the Tribunal. This enabled Palkhivala to appear before the Tribunal more often.

Palkhivala, with his analytical ability, was able to handle the intricacies of tax laws. He was undoubtedly helped by his knowledge of accounting learnt from Principal Banaji. Finally, his dominant place on the tax side was assured by his treatise, *The Law and Practice of Income Tax* which Chief Justice Chagla famously called 'The Book'.

Within three years at the Bar, Palkhivala had an annual income of Rs. 60,000, the equivalent of more than Rs. 50 lakhs today. The Supreme Court has noted that rent of Rs. 12/- per month in 1940 would be equivalent to Rs. 800/- per month in 1996. Between 1940 and 1996, the wholesale price index had risen 66 times. Silver costing Rs. 52 per kg in 1940, was Rs. 7,000 per kg on December 31, 1996.[10] Today, it is almost Rs. 30,000 per kg. The staggering success Palkhivala had at the Bar can be reckoned from the fact that within seven years of joining the Bar, he purchased a large flat of about 5,000 sq.ft. at Commonwealth Building on the plush Marine Drive. He continued to live there till the end of his life and even refused the allotment of a flat by the Tatas several times.

Very, very few lawyers can boast of such rapid success which is unlikely to be repeated in the years ahead. Setalvad, the first Attorney-General and still the epitome of professional rectitude, joined the Bar in 1911 and till 1918 had very little work in court. In his superb autobiography, his *total earnings* in 1913 is shown as one gold *mohar* - which was equal to Rs. 15/-! After 1918, however, his practice picked up, and by 1930, he had a very large practice.

In fine, Palkhivala's practice had truly a meteoric rise. He successfully exploited every opportunity that came his way and reached the top in a very short time. With his increasing involvement with the Tata group of companies, his court apperances became less frequent after the 1970s but he continued to appear in landmark cases. In his later years, Palkhivala remarked that he was more interested in *causes* than in *cases.*

10. *Malpe Viswanath Acharya v. State of Maharashtra,* AIR 1998 SC 602, 613 : (1998) 2 SCC 1.

Chapter 4

Palkhivala as Defendant

The Sampath Iyengar Copyright Case

Palkhivala, as a law student, had no predilection for tax laws. He had never decided that he would be a tax lawyer. After joining the chambers of Sir Jamshedji Kanga, he found that Kanga was frequently briefed in tax references before the Bombay High Court and in tax appeals before the Income Tax Appellate Tribunal (ITAT). Palkhivala's knowledge of accounts was very useful and he seemed to have a natural inclination to these cases.

Just a year after passing his Advocate (OS) examination, in 1946, he thought of the idea of writing a commentary on the fast growing subject of income tax. At that time, a few other commentaries (by V.S. Sundaram, Sampath Iyengar,[1] Pal and A.N. Aiyar) were already in the market. Palkhivala discussed the idea with Kanga and commenced writing the book in March 1947. The task was to take him almost three years. Palkhivala would discuss the important parts of the book not only with Kanga but also with R.J. Kolah, who was also in Kanga's chambers and had a large tax practice of his own.

Palkhivala read each reported tax case in India and the United Kingdom and wrote the commentary on a 'section-wise' basis. Some commentaries are written topic-wise, like Seervai's *Constitutional Law of India* or Gower's *Principles of Modern Company Law*. The entire writing was done by Palkhivala and Kanga, whose task was mainly of a supervisory and advisory character, did not make any significant alteration. Palkhivala initially titled the book 'The Law and Practice of Income Tax' Kanga passed away shortly after the publication of the sixth edition. Thereafter, the title ran: *Kanga and Palkhivala's The Law and Practice of Income Tax*. The first edition ran into 744 pages of

---

1. The judgment of the Madras High Court refers to 'A.C. Sampath Ayyangar' but the name is spelt as 'Iyengar' in his published book.

commentary (Part-I) and 344 pages of statutory and other legal provisions and index (Part-II). The book, priced at Rs. 35, soon sold out.

Anyone who has written, or even attempted to write, a book on any stodgy and dreary legal subject will know how arduous the task is. Every reported case has to be read and a case-note prepared. One has to then decide the headings and sub-headings under each section and allocate the cases accordingly. Several cases have to be consigned to the foot-notes as they may not say anything new but one has to unfortunately read these cases to learn that they have nothing new to say! In a book on income tax, one is confronted with another occupational hazard: numerous amendments each year that necessitate rewriting several parts of the book.

And those were the days of manual typing, composing and printing by letter-press. Today, in the computer age, one takes for granted the enormous ease with which drafts can be revised and edited. Few people know that Behram Palkhivala typed almost the *entire manuscript* of the first edition. Both brothers continued to work as a team right till the eighth edition. From the fifth edition onwards, Behram would prepare the case-notes and commentary on various sections and Palkhivala, after discussions with him, would finalise the same. It was very heavy work for Behram, who had to give up his practice for several months each time. Indeed, for one edition, he gave up his practice for a whole year!

How did the two brothers work as a team to complete the book? Palkhivala would work in his High Court chamber till 9.30 p.m, completing his cases and opinion work. Behram, who finished his advocate's examination in 1949, would start working on the book after 10.30 p.m and often continue till 2.30 a.m. or later. This method continued till 1953 when Palkhivala shifted to his new apartment at 'Commonwealth'. Thereafer, till 1969, Behram would spend the entire day at Commonwealth preparing the new edition. After 1969, Behram completed the revisions at his home and sent the drafts to his brother for finalization.

The 'ill-advised' copyright suit

The first edition of the book received critical and popular acclaim and soon sold out. But trouble was brewing 1000 km southwards – in the city of Madras, now Chennai. A.C. Sampath

Iyengar[2] was an advocate practising in the Madras High Court. He gave up practice in 1948 and was an advisor to various Chambers of Commerce. In 1941, he had published his commentary on the Income Tax Act, 1922, after 2½ years of preparation. It was priced at Rs. 12/- per copy and 2000 copies were printed and sold. The second and third editions were published in 1945 and 1947, priced at Rs. 20/- and Rs. 25/-. All the editions were sold out and were popular with the tax bar. By 1951, he was already working on the fourth edition which was to be priced at around Rs. 40/- and have a print-run of 5000 copies.

Sampath Iyengar claimed to have seen a copy of Kanga & Palkhivala's 'Law and Practice of Income Tax' in a book-shop in Calcutta. On a reading of the book, Iyengar felt that several portions of his book had been pirated and asked his solicitors, M/s. Sanderson and Morgan, to issue a legal notice to Kanga and Palkhivala. The solicitors requested Iyengar to give them a list of specific passages that would demonstrate piracy before they could issue a legal notice to an eminent lawyer like Sir Jamshedji Kanga. Eventually, a legal notice was issued on August 1, 1951, claiming compensation for various acts of infringement of copyright like adopting similar treatment and analysis, copying passages, characteristic phraseology and coined expressions. As Kanga was then in England, a detailed reply was sent on September 12, 1951 denying the charges of infringement and refuting the claim for compensation.

On November 22, 1951, Sampath Iyengar filed a suit – in the Madras High Court under Sections 6 and 7 of the Copyright Act, 1911, paying a total court fee of Rs. 784, 11 annas (written as Rs. 784-11-00).[3] The five page plaint prayed for a decree for injunction, damages and for taking of accounts. The three defendants were Sir Jamshedji B. Kanga, N.A. Palkhivala and N.M. Tripathi Pvt. Ltd.[4] Justice Krishnaswami Nayudu initially granted an order of interim injunction on November 30, 1951 which was later vacated. Iyengar alleged that Kanga and Palkhivala had infringed his copyright by reproducing substantial portions of his book, particularly the 1947 edition. The two authors, he

2. The judgment of the Madras High Court refers to 'A.C. Sampath Ayyangar' but the name is spelt as 'Iyengar' in his published book.
3. C.S. No. 350 of 1951. The plaint, para 11, refers to Rs. 768-10-0. The court records show that he was called upon to pay additional stamp and transmission fees, totaling the amount to Rs. 784-11-0.
4. The publisher of the book. Tripathi was a well known publisher of several legal commentaries.

claimed, had cunningly changed words here and there, transferred passages from the footnotes to the body and *vice versa*, in a dishonest attempt to camouflage their acts of piracy.

A joint written statement was filed by Kanga and Palkhivala denying all allegations of infringement and piracy. They pointed out that the plaint was belated as their book was published in October 1950 and had sold out by February 1951. Their commentary was the result of careful and independent study of 'each and every case' cited in the book. Palkhivala, as second defendant, claimed that he had read not only the head-notes but also the judgments in each case that was mentioned in the book. Sir Jamshedji Kanga had a very large income tax practice from the beginning of the Income Tax Act, 1922 and had appeared in several important cases that had been dealt with in the book .

Palkhivala, the second defendant, also commanded a considerable practice in the field of income tax and other fields. On the charges of infringement, both Kanga and Palkhivala contended that the common phrases and sentences could be traced to well known decided cases which had been discussed in their book. These phrases and sentences had become the current-coin of income tax law and Iyengar could not claim any copyright to them. Their commentaries had followed the usual and well established plan of a legal commentary and their style and mode of expression was patently different. Even a cursory, comparative glance at the two commentaries would clearly indicate the originality of thought, substance, expression and presentation. They submitted that the plaintiff's charges of plagiarism and piracy were totally false, and Iyengar could not claim any copyright in the language and phraseology of classic judgments, well known legal expressions and propositions and dubbed Iyengar's claim as 'fantastic'. Finally, they submitted that their commentary was the result of an entirely different study and had nothing whatsoever to do with Iyengar's book. Kanga and Palkhivala also objected to the jurisdiction of the Madras High Court.

This suit, filed in 1951, came up for final hearing within just six months before an eminent ICS judge of the Madras High Court-Justice A.S. Panchapakesa Ayyar. M.C. Setalvad, the then Attorney-General, R.J. Kolah, an eminent tax lawyer, and H.M. Seervai, who later became India's leading commentator on constitutional law, appeared for Kanga and Palkhivala. The initial submissions were made by Setalvad who gave up the objection of jurisdiction. Kolah made legal submissions; and Seervai conducted the cross-examination, which went on for several days, and made the final submissions.

T.M. Krishnaswami Ayyar, a leading member of the Madras High Court, appeared for A.C. Sampath Iyengar. Justice Ayyar has elaborately discussed the legal position relating to copyright particularly in the context of legal commentaries. Surprisingly, this important judgment has not been reported in any law journal and is, therefore, produced in full in the appendix along with the plaint and the written statement.

Palkhivala stood his cross-examination very well and the answers he gave in the witness box virtually demolished the case of the plaintiff. On the other hand, Iyengar did not fare well and had emotional outbursts. The oral testimony of Palkhivala and Iyengar has been commented upon by Justice Ayyar as follows:

'The examination of P.W.1[5] and D.W.1[6] was elaborate and detailed, and D.W.1 fared better in cross-examination than P.W.1. He stood a detailed and skilful cross-examination exceedingly well, and was not materially shaken on any point, and struck me as a competent and alert lawyer, who was thoroughly conversant with the Income Tax Act and Law and was very well-informed with every part of his book, and could give a cogent account of any part of it, regarding the scheme, arrangement, analysis, conclusion, criticism etc. He struck me also as giving his evidence in a straight forward fashion. P.W.1 was not able to stand the cross-examination so well because of his emotion and often gave answers which cannot be said to be satisfactory. He was not able in some cases to refer to other portions of his book, or to the Act, or the Income-tax manual, or the decided cases, so quickly as D.W.1 possibly due to his greater age. Memory is notoriously stronger in a younger man.'

In his testimony, Palkhivala stated that he had conceived the idea of the book in March, 1947. As a lawyer, he had referred to the commentary of Iyengar and also the commentaries by Sundaram, Pal and A.N. Aiyar while arguing his cases. On oath, he swore that he had not kept these commentaries before him while writing his book. However, he remembered the opinions expressed by Iyengar on more than 20 points while writing the book and in fact, on one point, he had expressed a contrary opinion. Although Kanga had only a supervisory and advisory role, M.C. Setalvad

---

5. A.C. Sampath Iyengar.
6. N.A. Palkhivala.

informed the judge that Kanga took the fullest responsibility for every single sentence in their book.

In the witness-box, Palkhivala submitted that he had referred to various cases of Indian and English Courts, in addition to other leading reference books like *Halsbury's Laws of England*. He had discussed complicated problems with Kanga, Kolah and other colleagues in his chambers and with Mr. R.K. Dalal, who was an expert in insurance law.[7] Reference was also made to various select committee reports. Palkhivala wrote the book by systematically examining every relevant reported case and making extracts and notes. He had kept his notes and extracts of various rulings which he had relied on while conducting his own cases. He had also taken advantage of the vast experience of Kanga when writing the book.

Justice Ayyar remarked that both the commentaries were good but the book of Kanga & Palkhivala was 'more methodical, lucid and systematic'. The arguments at certain stages were very bitter. H.M. Seervai who argued for Palkhivala commented that Iyengar had made false claims of originality and his book 'resembled more a godown' whereas Palkhivala's book was like a 'well arranged store'. This argument was rejected by the judge.

T.M. Krishnaswami Ayyar, who appeared for Sampath Iyengar, argued that Palkhivala had admitted using his commentary from 1944 onwards. Even after the idea of writing the book occurred to Palkhivala in 1947, he continued to refer to Iyengar's book during the course of his practice right upto 1950. Therefore, it must be presumed that he had used Iyengar's commentary for writing the book. T.M. Krishnaswami Ayyar also pointed out the admission of Palkhivala that Iyengar's commentary was always in their chamber and Kolah and Palkhivala had continuous access to the book. It was therefore obvious that Palkhivala had used it for writing his commentary. The judge rejected this plea based on the possibility of access in the following words:

'Here the argument is obviously based on the analogy of presumption of adultery drawn in a divorce case, when a young man and a young woman are alone with each other in the same bed-room at night, and could have had access, should be presumed to have had access, or to the presumption in Mohammadan Law, in its theory of valid interval, when a man and his wife, of

---

7. In fact, Mr. Dalal, an eminent Chartered Accountant, had pointed out that the opinion of Palkhivala on a point of insurance law was contrary to the view taken by Sampath Iyengar.

co-habitable age, are alone, are presumed to be likely to have had sexual intercourse. I cannot agree that a man's being alone with a book belonging to a colleague in the same chambers, is in an exactly similar position to the young man and young woman being alone in a bed-room at night or a man and wife being alone under the Mohammadan Law. Each case must depend on the evidence in that case'.

The judge then pointed out that any infringement or violation of copyright would have to be established by demonstrating that there were too many similarities which could not be attributed to mere chance, tell-tale inadvertent slips and errors. If the defendant is unable to explain the similarities, the slips and errors, or is unable to point out the correct reference book from which he took the material, there would be no doubt that copying had taken place. The burden of proving this was heavily on Iyengar, and the judge eventually held that there was no proof of copying.

Much was made of certain common passages which were found in both the books. Palkhivala was able to demonstrate that the passages were not identical and there were important differences. Further, these passages had been taken directly from the judgments and Palkhivala had specifically referred to them in his book. It was the common practice for legal commentaries not to contain the entire extracts but a summary thereof. Out of three passages that were similar, none could lead to any finding of copying. The judge also pointed out that Iyengar must have got annoyed because one of the views expressed by him was referred to as 'absurd' in the book of Kanga & Palkhivala. According to the judge, this was one of the underlying causes in Iyengar filing 'his thin and unconvincing suit and for his irritability and emotion when giving answers in the witness-box.' The judge also rejected the plea of camouflaging. Showing some sympathy for Iyengar, Justice Ayyar held that he was not motivated by money while launching his 'ill-advised litigation'. Iyengar had sincerely believed that his observations in his book had been pirated. In the end, the suit was dismissed. Kanga & Palkhivala did not press for costs. Thus ended a famous litigation wherein Palkhivala withstood his cross-examination very effectively.

The book has now completed nine editions, and the commentary is now in two volumes. Sampath Iyengar's commentary is also good and very popular and is now in its tenth edition that has ten volumes. The suit filed was indeed unfortunate and Justice Ayyar rightly characterized it as 'ill-advised'.

Subsequent editions

The second edition was published in 1952 and the third in 1955. After the fifth edition, the intervals between each edition increased, perhaps because of Palkhivala's increasing involvement with various other activities. Contrary to normal practice, Palkhivala did not prepare the entire revised edition before sending it to the press. The commentary thus went to the press bit by bit. Thus, the three processes of Nani Palkhivala finalizing the new edition, the press preparing the proofs and sending them back, and Behram going through the proofs, went on simultaneously. The seventh edition was published in 1976, the eighth edition in 1990 and the ninth in 2004.[8]

Palkhivala was extremely particular about minor details in the book; meticulous cross-checking of references was insisted upon to be sure that there was no mistake in the book. Upto the sixth edition, Behram did the proof reading but this difficult task was allotted to about six persons for the seventh and eighth editions.

Dinesh Vyas, a well-known tax lawyer, suspended his large practice for many months to assist in the preparation of the seventh edition and Palkhivala gracefully acknowledged this in the preface. Dileep Choksi, an eminent Chartered Accountant, took time off from his extensive practice for several months to do substantive work for the eighth edition; and Palkhivala thanked him for his assistance in the 'acknowledgements'. Choksi recollects that Palkhivala would work very late into the night finalizing the new edition. He was proud of the fact that the book had been referred to by the House of Lords. A little before Palkhivala passed away, the copyright in the book was transferred to Butterworths, and they engaged Dinesh Vyas to prepare the ninth edition. Unfortunately, Palkhivala did not live to see its publication.

Introduction and preface – A unique style

The introduction and the preface to each edition of the book were very interesting. Palkhivala repeatedly protested against the chronic tinkering of the Act and lamented that it had been twisted completely out of shape. By the seventh edition in 1976, the Income-tax Act, 1961 had suffered more than 560 insertions, 600 substitutions and 190 omissions! The eighth edition came 14 years

---

8. The successive editions of the book were published as follows: 2nd (1952), 3rd (1955), 4th (1958), 5th (1963), 6th (1969), 7th (1976), 8th (1990) and 9th (2004). The 4th, 6th and 7th editions were also reprinted due to heavy demand.

later in 1990 by which time the Income Tax Act was almost 30 years old and had been mutilated by more than 3,300 amendments. Sections 11 to 13 that deal with charitable trusts had suffered no less than 50 amendments. Palkhivala lamented that 'we legislate first, and think afterwards; complexity is heaped upon complexity and the confusion becomes worse confounded.' The avalanche of amendments only resulted in more litigation. In his last preface, written for the eighth edition, Palkhivala observed:

'In the United Kingdom there are 29 million income-tax payers but the number of references filed in the High Court is only around thirty in a year. In India there are only seven million income-tax payers but the number of references filed in our High Courts is over 6,000 a year, in addition to more than 1,000 writ petitions. These figures reflect the tremendous public dissatisfaction with the quality of the law and of fiscal administration. Our Law Reports bear witness to the fact that generally a case reaches hearing in the High Court twenty years, and in the Supreme Court thirty years, after the relevant assessment year. The situation is continuously aggravated by the deluge of new amendments – the indigestible verbiage; and the flood of litigation is heavier today than ever before.'

In 2011, the Income Tax Act, 1961 completed 50 years and this Act is expected to be replaced by the Direct Taxes Code. The new legislation is only going to make the law more complex, leaving the assessees confused and confounded. In the name of simplification, the new Code contains a definition section that has 318 definitions. Incredibly, no Indian will be able to 'leave the territory of India unless he furnishes to the prescribed authority an undertaking to the effect that he has made satisfactory arrangement for discharging his tax liability.' On this undertaking, the prescribed authority has to give a 'no objection certificate' to leave India. If an airline commits the mortal sin of carrying a passenger who has not obtained the 'no objection certificate', the airline will be treated as an assessee in default and be liable to pay the tax of the passenger![9] There are several other absurd provisions in the Direct Taxes Code and nothing can better describe it than the following passage of Palkhivala in the preface to the eighth edition:

'G.K. Chesterton, in his brilliant essay "The Mad Official", analyses how a society goes mad. The rot begins, he says, when wild actions are received calmly by society. "These are people that have

9. See clause 222 of the Direct Taxes Code Bill, 2009.

lost the power of astonishment at their own actions. When they give birth to a fantastic passion or foolish law, they do not start or stare at the monster they have brought forth...These nations are really in danger of going off their heads *en masse,* of becoming one vast vision of imbecility." India is one such country in respect of budgeting and fiscal laws. Today the monster of our direct tax structure has become more monstrous than ever before.'

It is indeed unfortunate that the complexity and chronic tinkering is equally rampant in the field of indirect taxes as well. There is complete absence of any fair-play in the administration of tax laws. If a decision of the court or the tribunal is in favour of the assessee, the relevant statutory provision is promptly amended retrospectively with very little regard for the enormous hardship that it causes to the assessees. One can only conclude with the last passage of the last preface written by Palkhivala:

'Every Government has a right to levy taxes. But no Government has the right, in the process of extracting tax, to cause misery and harassment to the taxpayer and the gnawing feeling that he is made the victim of palpable injustice'.

Chapter 5

Constitutional Law Cases

An Amazing Journey

Palkhivala is mainly remembered for his arguments in the *Bank Nationalisation, Privy Purses* and *Kesavananda Bharati* cases. But Palkhivala's constitutional journey began as soon as the Constitution came into force and the Supreme Court was established. Behram Palkhivala remembers that his brother had argued a number of constitutional cases in the Bombay High Court from 1950 onwards. A little after his 31st birthday, Palkhivala argued an important case in that court that dealt with the construction of legislative entries in the Seventh Schedule to the Constitution, how far legislation could be *ultra vires* the Constitution and, equally important, whether the complete exclusion of the jurisdiction of the civil courts was permissible. A writ of *certiorari* was filed against an order passed by the Custodian of Evacuee Property and Palkhivala likened the position of an evacuee to that of a Roman slave. Chief Justice Chagla rejected his arguments on the Constitution but allowed the appeal on a narrow ground. His judgment is superb and all the more remarkable because it was dictated in open court and immediately after the arguments concluded.[1] In the early 1950s, Palkhivala appeared in a number of cases relating to evacuee property – a legal legacy of the partition.

Another important case argued brilliantly by Palkhivala was *State of Bombay v. Heman Santlal Alreja*[2] which related to an order of requisition under the Bombay Land Requisition Act, 1948. Justice Tendolkar had struck down certain provisions of this Act and had issued a writ of *mandamus* against the State of Bombay restraining it from enforcing or taking any proceedings in the enforcement of

---

1. *Abdul Majid Haji Mahomed v. P. R. Nayak,* (1951) 53 Bom LR 621 : (1952) ILR Bom 378. Chief Justice Chagla had the remarkable ability to dictate judgments in open court in even the most complicated cases after the arguments were over. In his autobiography, *Roses in December,* he has mentioned that he reserved judgments only twice in his 18-year stint as a judge!
2. AIR 1952 Bom 16 : (1951) 53 Bom LR 837.

that order. The State of Bombay appealed and the appeal was heard by Chief Justice Chagla and Justice Gajendragadkar.

The Chief Justice remarked that Palkhivala had advanced a 'very interesting and able argument' that the Constitution made a distinction between 'existing law' and 'law in force'. While 'existing law' meant actual law in operation, 'law in force' included not only law actually in force but also law potentially in force in the sense of the law being capable of being extended by means of a notification or by other methods. The Constituent Assembly drew a deadline at laws actually in operation and refused to save laws beyond that line if they contravened any of the fundamental rights. Further, while Section 299(4) of the Government of India Act, 1935, provided that 'nothing in this section shall affect the provisions of any law in force at the date of the passing of this Act', Article 31(5)(a) uses the expression 'existing law' and not 'law in force'. Chief Justice Chagla rejected this argument in an equally remarkable manner and, after reference to earlier cases and the Government of India Act, 1935, held that there was no difference or distinction between 'laws in force' and 'existing laws'.

The first case in the Supreme Court where his name finds a mention is *State of Bombay v. F.N. Balsara.*[3] R.J. Kolah, a doyen of the tax bar, and Palkhivala assisted Sir N.P. Engineer, a former Advocate-General of India although the law report does not refer to the arguments of Engineer. The case was to challenge certain provisions of the Bombay Prohibition Act, 1949, and went up to the Supreme Court from a Full Bench decision of the Bombay High Court which had held several sections of this Act to be unconstitutional. The decision was substantially reversed by the Supreme Court and only a few provisions dealing with medicinal and toilet preparations that contained alcohol were struck down. Palkhivala was just 31 years when he assisted Sir N.P. Engineer before the newly formed Supreme Court. For a lawyer who was just five years at the Bar, this was a remarkable achievement.

It was not long before Palkhivala started appearing himself in the Supreme Court. In 1954, at age 34, he appeared in an important case which dealt with the power of the State to direct education to be conducted only in the local language.[4] The facts showed that out of 1,403 secondary schools in the State of Bombay

3. AIR 1951 SC 318 : [1951] SCR 682.
4. *State of Bombay v. Bombay Education Society,* AIR 1954 SC 561 : [1955] SCR 568.

(since bifurcated into Maharashtra and Gujarat), 1,285 schools imparted education through some language other than English and only 118 schools had English as the medium of instruction. Of these, 30 schools were Anglo-Indian schools. The Education Department issued a circular prohibiting primary and secondary schools from using English as a medium of instruction except to those citizens who were Anglo-Indians and of 'non-Asiatic descent'. The Supreme Court struck down this circular as violative of Article 29(2) which prohibits any citizen being denied admission in any educational institution which is either maintained by the State or receives aid from the State on grounds of religion, race, caste, language or any of them.[5]

This appeal also showed the quick and unconventional method by which Chief Justice Mahajan disposed of his cases. Palkhivala was opposed by Motilal Setalvad, the then Attorney-General, who appeared for the then State of Bombay. The law which was challenged stipulated that only those children whose mother-tongue was English could go to an English medium school. Palkhivala called this an 'oppressive tyrannical law'. When the matter came before Chief Justice Mahajan, Setalvad had to open the argument as Palkhivala had succeeded before the High Court. Within two minutes, he asked Mr. Setalvad *'Well, Mr. Attorney General, I do not want to interrupt you. I only want to ask you one question: where is your own son being educated?'* Setalvad's son was studying in England and to avoid embarrassment, he told the court that his personal viewpoint was not relevant and he was only representing the State of Bombay. Chief Justice Mahajan said: *'Very well, Mr. Attorney General, we understand you now, but cut the matter short because we do not want time to be wasted. I can tell you here straightaway which way the decision is going to be.'* The entire appeal then fizzled out in ten minutes.[6]

In this case, the Supreme Court also decided another important point: even if the object or motive of teaching a child through the mother tongue was laudable, its validity had to be judged by the

---

5. Article 29 reads as follows:–'29. Protection of interests of minorities.–(1) Any section of the citizens residing in the territory of India or any part thereof having a distinct language, script or culture of its own shall have the right to conserve the same.

   (2) No citizen shall be denied admission into any educational institution maintained by the State or receiving aid out of State funds on grounds only of religion, race, caste, language or any of them.'
6. Extracts from a speech by Palkhivala at a function organized by the ITAT Bar Association.

method of its operation and its effect on the fundamental right guaranteed under Article 29(2). All citizens under Article 29(2) had a right to get admission in educational institutions maintained or aided by the State. It would not be open to the Government to limit this right only to citizens belonging to a minority group. The curse of linguistic chauvinism coupled with an anti-English bias was prevalent from the beginning of free India and our short-sighted politicians have never fully recovered from this obsession.

The next important case that Palkhivala appeared in before the Supreme Court was the *State of Bombay v. Bhanji Munji.*[7] The city of Bombay seems to have always been in the grip of a housing shortage. After independence, the situation became particularly grim due to the influx of a large number of refugees from Pakistan. Justice Bose, in the Supreme Court, described the situation thus:

> *A race of proprietors in the shape of rapacious landlords who thrived on the misery of those who could find no decent roof over their heads sprang into being. Even the efficiency of the administration was threatened because Government servants could not find proper accommodation. Milder efforts to cope with the evil proved ineffective.*[7]

The Bombay Land Requisition Ordinance enabled the Government to acquire vacant houses and allot them to Government servants who did not have accommodation, and a special allotment was also made to persons who informed the Government about undisclosed vacancies. This was a kind of reward to these informers and they were to be given housing for informing the Government about a vacant house which had not been done by the landlord. Palkhivala had succeeded before the Bombay High Court which held that the allotment of housing to spies and informers as a reward for their service was outside the scope of the Ordinance and that the burden was on the State Government to establish that a particular property was vacant and available for allotment. In the Supreme Court, Palkhivala's arguments were not accepted. The decision to allot homes to spies and informers was part of a policy of the Government and if it felt that this was a good incentive, the courts would not interfere. The court also observed that the burden of proof could not be placed on the Government. Although Palkhivala was not successful before the Supreme Court in this case, the earlier decision in the education

7. AIR 1955 SC 41 : [1955] 1 SCR 777.

case where he had succeeded firmly established his reputation in the Supreme Court. By 1954, it was clear that his trips to Delhi would increase significantly in the years ahead.

In 1957, Palkhivala argued an interesting case before the Supreme Court in *State of Bombay v. R.M.D Chamarbaugwala.*[8] Chamarbaugwala printed and published a weekly newspaper called 'Sporting Star'. It had a licence to run a prize competition called 'Littlewood's Football Pool Competition'. After its licence was not renewed by the Bombay Government, it shifted its activities to the then State of Mysore. There was a purpose of shifting the business to Mysore because, until 1952, the tax on prize competitions levied by the State of Bombay was confined to lotteries and prize competitions conducted within that State. A new Section 12A was inserted which levied tax on lotteries and prize competitions conducted through newspaper publications printed outside the State of Bombay but circulated within that State. Tax was now imposed on entry fees paid by participants who submitted entries from outside the State of Bombay.

Palkhivala raised several interesting arguments but these were partly accepted and partly rejected by the Bombay High Court. The Bombay High Court had agreed with his submission that tax on prize competitions was not a 'tax on betting and gambling' falling under Entry 62[9] but a tax on trade and commerce under Entry 60[10] which had a ceiling limit of Rs. 250 per annum at that time (and subsequently raised to Rs. 2,500). The Bombay High Court also accepted Palkhivala's arguments that a tax on prize competitions was violative of Article 304(b).[11] Under this provision, any restriction on trade was permissible only if the relevant Bill was introduced with the previous sanction of the President. Most importantly, the Bombay High Court held that prize competitions were not activities against public interest. Finally, he argued that the Bombay Legislature did not have legislative competence to tax prize competitions conducted outside that State and the law could not have extra-territorial operation, but this plea was rejected. The weekly was printed and published from Bangalore and sold throughout India. In the State of Bombay,

8. AIR 1957 SC 699 : [1957] 1 SCR 874.
9. Entry 62 of List II of Schedule VII: 'Taxes on luxuries, including taxes on entertainments, amusements, betting and gambling'.
10. Entry 60 of List II of Schedule VII: 'Taxes on professions, trades, callings and employments'.
11. The text has been reproduced in footnote 13, *infra.*

Chamarbaugwala appointed agents to collect entry forms which were then forwarded to Bangalore.

Chamarbaugwala submitted that the tax made it impossible to carry on business except at a loss and the restrictions in Bombay were different and in addition to the restrictions imposed by the State of Mysore. The Bombay High Court struck down the tax as violating Article 276(2)[12] and the rules imposing the restrictions as violating Article 304(b).[13] The State of Bombay appealed and engaged H.M. Seervai to appear in the case.[14] The Supreme Court, however, held that the freedom to carry on trade, business and commerce throughout India did not apply to gambling activities. Finally, it held that the tax was on betting and gambling and could be levied without any ceiling limit.

In a lengthy judgment by Chief Justice S.R. Das,[15] the Supreme Court held that unless success in a competition required a substantial degree of skill, such competitions would be gambling in nature. Such activities were anti-social and deserved to be condemned. The fundamental right to carry on business under Article 19(1)(g) would not include the right to carry on gambling activities that deserved to be characterized as '*res extra commercium*'.[16] It also rejected the objection that the Bombay law was extra-territorial in operation. Once the weekly was sold in Bombay and the company had established depots in Bombay, the State of Bombay had jurisdiction to pass laws either banning or taxing such activities. It also rejected the objection that such laws would affect inter-State trade and commerce.

---

12. Article 276(2) at the relevant time read as follows: '(2) The total amount payable in respect of any one person to the State or to any one municipality, district board, local board or other local authority in the State by way of taxes on professions, trades, callings and employments shall not exceed two hundred and fifty rupees per annum.'
13. Article 304(b) reads: '304. Restrictions on trade, commerce and intercourse among States.–Notwithstanding anything in Article 301 or Article 303, the Legislature of a State may by law – (a) ....; and (b) impose such reasonable restrictions on the freedom of trade, commerce or intercourse with or within that State as may be required in the public interest: Provided that no Bill or amendment for the purposes of clause (b) shall be introduced or moved in the Legislature of a State without the previous sanction of the President.'
14. Seervai was later appointed the Advocate-General of Bombay (later Maharashtra) in 1957 and continued till his resignation in 1974.
15. *State of Bombay v. R.M.D. Chamarbaugwala*, AIR 1957 SC 699 : [1957] 1 SCR 874.
16. The Supreme Court wrongly used the phrase '*res extra commercium*' in this case and in several later decisions. For the scope of this expression, see author's article in National Law School of India University Law Review, 21(1) NLSI. Rev. 133 (209).

Chamarbaugwala filed another petition[17] directly before the Supreme Court under Article 32 questioning the validity of certain provisions of the Prize Competition Act, 1955.[18] Palkhivala argued that the definition of 'prize competition' included not only competitions which depended on mere luck or chance but also those which depended on a substantial degree of skill. As the definition was not severable, it had to be struck down in its entirety. Seervai, appearing for the Union of India, fairly conceded that the definition of 'prize competition' would only apply to competitions where success did not depend on skill and were essentially gambling in nature.

Palkhivala argued that the other provisions of the Act and the rules made thereunder were wholly unworkable and would render it impossible to run the competitions and such unreasonable restrictions seriously encroached the petitioner's fundamental right to carry on business.

In an outstanding judgment, Justice T.L. Venkatarama Ayyar beautifully summed up the doctrine of severability. In simple terms, if a law has valid and invalid parts which are separable, the court can strike down the invalid part and uphold the valid portion. However, if the valid and invalid parts are so inextricably mixed up that they cannot be separated from one another, then the invalid portion would result in the invalidity of the Act in its entirety. He set out seven principles of severability which remain the classic exposition on the subject.[19] Finally, Justice Ayyar concluded that the definition of 'prize competition' was severable and would only apply to those competitions in which success did not depend to any substantial extent on skill. The net result was that the appeal argued by Seervai was allowed and the writ petition argued by Palkhivala was dismissed. Effectively, Palkhivala lost both cases and Seervai succeeded.

---

17. *R.M.D. Chamarbaughwala v. Union of India*, AIR 1957 SC 628 : [1957] 1 SCR 930.
18. Readers would have noticed that the laws which were initially passed by the State of Bombay and certain other States were replaced by an Act of Parliament - the Prize Competition Act, 1955. This was because the Bombay High Court had held that a tax on prize competitions conducted from Mysore, would be a restriction on inter-State trade and commerce. In view of the serious consequences of the Bombay High Court judgment, various States including Andhra Pradesh, Bombay Madras, Orissa and U.P. passed resolutions under Article 252(1) giving Parliament the power to enact the requisite legislation. Thus, lotteries and prize competitions, which were within the domain of the State Governments, were now regulated by a Parliamentary or Central law.
19. Interested readers may see para 22 of the judgment at pages 636–637 of the decision reported in AIR 1957 SC 628 : [1957] 1 SCR 930.

Another important case argued by Palkhivala was *Tata Engg. & Locomotive Co. Ltd. v. State of Bihar.*[20] The sales tax authorities sought to levy sales tax on certain transactions which were claimed to be inter-State transactions and therefore beyond the jurisdiction of the State authorities. Writ petitions were filed directly before the Supreme Court under Article 32 of the Constitution of India pleading violation of a citizen's fundamental right to carry on trade or business under Article 19(1)(g). The great M.C. Setalvad, the first Attorney-General of India, raised a preliminary objection on the maintainability of the writ petition. He argued that a company is not a 'citizen' and could not file a writ petition for the enforcement of the fundamental right to carry on trade or business. Setalvad argued that if sales tax had been wrongly levied on certain transactions, these companies should prefer an appeal to the appellate authority and then to the Tribunal constituted under the relevant sales tax laws.

The judgment of the Supreme Court contains Palkhivala's arguments in detail and indicates the passion with which he had argued the case. Palkhivala tried to adopt the clever move of adding two shareholders as the petitioners along with the company. He pleaded that the court should not adopt a doctrinaire or technical approach. A company, after all, was nothing but a combination of several shareholders. If the rights of the shareholders were being affected, then the writ petitions were maintainable. Justice Gajendragadkar rejected all the points raised by Palkhivala 'as somewhat ingenious'. He held that Article 19 gave rights only to citizens while other rights like equality under Article 14 applied to all persons. It was for Parliament to amend the Citizenship Act, 1955, and extend the fundamental right to carry on business to companies. He also rejected the plea of a company being an amalgam of several shareholders. Once the shareholders got together and formed a company, they exercised their right to form an association under Article 19(1)(c) thereof. A company is a separate legal entity and the business of the company is not the business of its shareholders. Thus, the writ petition was dismissed on the basis of a preliminary objection.

Eight years later, in *Bennett Coleman & Co. Ltd. v. Union of India,*[21] the Supreme Court upheld the right of a company to file a writ petition if the rights of the shareholders were also affected.

---

20. AIR 1965 SC 40 : [1964] 6 SCR 885.
21. AIR 1973 SC 106 : (1972) 2 SCC 788.

This was a decision of five judges but in all fairness, it must be admitted that if a literal interpretation is adopted, the arguments of Palkhivala are wrong and the judgment of Justice Gajendragadkar is the correct view. It is ironical that a large company carrying on business to the tune of thousands of crores has no fundamental right to carry on business but a small shop-keeper has the right to do so. The law, particularly the Citizens Act, 1955, should be amended to remove this lacuna.

Palkhivala was engaged to appear for the Chief Justice of the Bombay High Court in a historic case before the Supreme Court that related to privileges of Parliament and the State Legislature.[22] At the age of 44, he was in the position of one of the leaders of the Bar. It is significant that the Chief Justice thought him to be the appropriate person to represent the Bombay High Court. Although there is no reference to his arguments, the case was of great importance and was argued primarily by H.M. Seervai, the great constitutional scholar, who appeared for the U.P. Vidhan Sabha. M.C. Setalvad appeared for the Allahabad High Court. While Seervai argued for several days, Setalvad took just one-tenth of the time and Chief Justice Gajendragadkar complimented him for his brevity: 'Mr. Setalvad who appeared for the Allahabad High Court addressed to us a very able argument with characteristic brevity and lucidity'. M.C. Setalvad was the Attorney-General from 1950 to 1963, and till date remains the epitome of professional integrity and rectitude. A man of few words, he was known for his brief arguments. He would state his points clearly and logically without any flourish and sit down. This came to be called the 'Setalvad style of advocacy'. Fali S. Nariman pays a brilliant tribute to Setalvad in these words:

> *Motilal was both a great lawyer and a great advocate. He ennobled the consummate art of the advocate. A brief, cogent and logical argument came to be described in his own lifetime as being in the Motilal Setalvad style – the greatest tribute to an advocate. Brevity to him was not just a piece of advice for the practising lawyer – it was a word to live by. There were no cobwebs in his well-stocked and well-ordered mind. He was precise – at times so precise that after having expressed himself in a few short sentences he felt there was really nothing more to be said in the case.*

---

22. In Re *Powers, Privileges and Immunities of State Legislatures,* [1965] 1 SCR 413 : AIR 1965 SC 745.

> *Those who saw and heard Motilal know that his greatest contribution as an advocate was the example he set – putting across the best points in the briefest possible space of time.*[23]

The facts of this case are most interesting. In March 1964, the Speaker of the U.P. Legislative Assembly punished one Keshav Singh for contempt of the U.P. Assembly and directed that he should be imprisoned for seven days in the District Jail, Lucknow. His crime was that he published a pamphlet derogatory of the U.P. Assembly. Two judges of the Allahabad High Court granted bail to Keshav Singh. Furious at this order, the U.P. Assembly passed a resolution stating that the two High Court judges who passed the order of bail and the counsel for Keshav Singh, D. Solomon, had committed contempt of the House. They further directed that whilst Keshav Singh should be taken into custody and kept in the District Jail, Lucknow, the two judges and the advocate were to be brought in custody before the House. The two judges learnt about this order on the radio and the next morning in the newspapers. The two judges filed a writ petition in the High Court against the order of the Assembly. A Full Bench consisting of 28 judges of the Allahabad High Court took up this petition filed by the two judges. The House withdrew the arrest warrant issued to the two Judges and the lawyer but all three were placed under an obligation to appear before the House and explain why they should not be proceeded against for contempt. This was a shocking turn of events, but the embarrassing crisis was defused by the President making an order of reference under Article 143(1).[24] A five judge Bench headed by Justice Gajendragadkar finally held that no contempt had been committed. Thus ended the sensational case which could have led to the possible arrest of two High Court judges by the Speaker of the Legislative Assembly. In the end, neither the High Court judges nor the lawyers had to appear before the Assembly.

Another important matter which Palkhivala argued for Tata Engg. & Locomotive Co. Ltd. as an intervener was the famous

---

23. This tribute is contained in the foreword to Setalvad's autobiography, *My Life, Law and Other Things,* Universal Law Publishing Co. Pvt. Ltd.
24. '143. Power of President to consult Supreme Court.—(1) If at any time it appears to the President that a question of law or fact has arisen, or is likely to arise, which is of such a nature and of such public importance that it is expedient to obtain the opinion of the Supreme Court upon it, he may refer the question to that Court for consideration and the Court may, after such hearing as it thinks fit, report to the President its opinion thereon'

Ujjam Bai case.[25] The Supreme Court had to consider the circumstances under which a person could directly approach the Supreme Court under Article 32. Palkhivala's argument was rejected and the court held that if an assessment order was passed under a valid taxing statute, it could not be questioned in a petition under Article 32 on the ground of violation of fundamental rights. Consequently, an assessment order was passed by the Income Tax Officer under the Income Tax Act, 1961 – a valid Act – even if it is erroneous, cannot be challenged directly before the Supreme Court under Article 32 of the Constitution. The decision is important as different judges constituting a seven-judge Bench have given different interpretations to the scope of Article 32.

Palkhivala was not confined to arguing constitutional cases on tax matters alone. For example, an important case which he argued related to the power of the State Government to make Gujarati compulsory as a medium of instruction.[26] Referring to various constitutional provisions, the court held that the State of Gujarat did not have the competence to impose a regional language or Hindi as the exclusive medium of instruction. The Court rightly pointed out the difficulty of imposing a regional language as the medium of instruction particularly in imparting scientific or technical instructions or in training students for professional courses like law, engineering and medicine. The absence of adequate text-books, proper journals and other literature, availability of competent instructors and the capacity of students to understand the instructions in a regional language or in Hindi were all matters that had an important bearing on the issue. This would result in the lowering of standards. Surprisingly, Justice Subba Rao took a dissenting view and accepted the plea of the State Government. If the judgment had gone the other way, all other States would have followed suit with each making its regional language as the exclusive medium of instruction.

We often forget the significance of these decisions that have had a vital but quiet role to play in preserving the unity of the nation. It is unfortunate that, even today, few politicians have paused to consider the devastating long-term effect of short-term populist measures.

---

25. *Ujjam Bai v. State of U.P.*, AIR 1962 SC 1621 : [1963] 1 SCR 778.
26. *Gujarat University v. Krishna Ranganath Mudholkar,* AIR 1963 SC 703 : [1963] Supp (1) SCR 112 : 1963 GLR 450.

By the early 1960s, Palkhivala had established a reputation amongst the legal fraternity as not only a tax lawyer but as a Constitutional lawyer as well. At that time, even he would not have expected that in the next decade, he would have to play a leading role in almost all major constitutional cases.

❄

(i)

The Case Palkhivala Missed

Sajjan Singh v. State of Rajasthan

The controversial Ninth Schedule was first inserted by the Constitution (First Amendment) Act, 1951, after several statutes to implement land reforms were struck down by various High Courts. Alarmed at the turn of events so soon after the Constitution came into force, Pandit Nehru realised that the entire programme of agrarian reforms would be in jeopardy. Right from the beginning, it was the Government's attempt to pay absurdly low amounts of compensation that triggered these writ petitions. If the compensation paid had been fair, there would have been no reason to challenge the statutes. The Land Acquisition Act was first enacted in 1896 and as long as landowners were paid reasonable compensation, there was no cause for any complaint.

The first Parliament consisted of virtually the same people who had formed the Constituent Assembly and included Dr. Ambedkar. This Parliament passed the Constitution (First Amendment) Act, 1951 and created the Ninth Schedule. This was to be a one-time measure to protect land reform legislation. As events turned out, it was grossly abused and, by 1974, various enactments that had nothing to do with land reform, including the Monopolies and Restrictive Trade Practices Act, 1969 and the Foreign Exchange Regulation Act, 1973, were added to the Ninth Schedule to make them immune from judicial review. The Government could thus pass any law and once it was placed in the Ninth Schedule, it could never be challenged as being violative of Articles 14, 19 and 31.[1]

1. In 2007, the Supreme Court held that a constitutional amendment made to add a new enactment in the Ninth Schedule could be challenged if it violated the basic structure of the Constitution. *I.R. Coelho v. State of Tamil Nadu,* (2007) 2 SCC 1 : AIR 2007 SC 861.

Origins of the Ninth Schedule

The Ninth Schedule has a very interesting origin. It was suggested by the former Advocate-General of Tamil Nadu, V.K.T. Chari, whose knowledge of law was profound. Although not very articulate, Chari had a brilliant mind and was capable of the most original and incisive arguments. He wrote to the then Law Secretary suggesting that a new schedule could be created which could contain all the laws relating to land reform legislation. These laws could be made valid retrospectively and, for the future, these laws could be made immune from being challenged as violative of Articles 14, 19 and 31. The Ninth Schedule is, therefore, a unique feature of our Constitution. Gajendragadkar J. remarked that only India had a Constitution that contained a provision for protection against itself! Thus, a letter written by the Advocate-General from the city of Madras (now Chennai) became the foundation for the Ninth Schedule.[2]

Is the amending power unlimited?

In October 1951, the Supreme Court upheld the validity of the First Amendment.[3] In this case, the Supreme Court held that the power of Parliament to amend the Constitution was *without any limitation*. Interestingly, Article 13(2) specified that any law which abridged or took away any of the fundamental rights would be void. If this Article was given a literal interpretation, fundamental rights would be unamendable. The Supreme Court got over this difficulty by holding that the word 'law' in Article 13(2) would only mean Parliamentary legislation or 'ordinary law' and not constitutional amendments. Thus, any or all fundamental rights could be taken away by a constitutional amendment made in exercise of the 'constituent power' and Article 13(2) would not apply.[4] From 1951 to 1965, the power of Parliament to amend any part of the Constitution was unlimited.

---

2. *Granville Austin, Working A Democratic Constitution, The Indian Experience,* Oxford University Press (1999), p. 85. Austin, by meticulous research, has traced Chari's letter dated March 14, 1951 to the then Law Secretary. This letter has been sourced from the Law Ministry files in the National Archives of India.
3. *Shankari Prasad Singh Deo v. Union of India,* AIR 1951 SC 458 : [1952] SCR 89.
4. Article 368 enabled the Parliament to amend the Constitution. Certain provisions require not only two-thirds majority but also ratification by at least half of the State Legislatures throughout the country. Shockingly, an amendment to fundamental rights can be passed by a 2/3rd majority and does not require ratification by the State Legislatures.

When the *Sajjan Singh*[5] case was to be argued in 1965, D.M. Popat had a detailed conference with Palkhivala. The question they discussed was if Parliament had the unlimited power to take away fundamental rights or amend any part of the Constitution, could they take away all the fundamental rights? Was the amending power of Parliament unlimited or was it subject to certain inherent limitations? In other words, was there some portion of the Constitution which could not be altered? Was there a 'core' that could not be touched even if the ruling party had an overwhelming majority to pass the Constitutional amendment?

Palkhivala's inability to attend

Palkhivala hated to wait in court and told Popat that he would come on the last day and appear in the matter.[6] Popat warned that Chief Justice Gajendragadkar would abruptly complete the hearing and advised Palkhivala not to take a chance and come to the Supreme Court. Palkhivala felt that the case was of great importance and would take several days of hearing. He thought that he could go to the Supreme Court at a later date. Popat's apprehension that the Chief Justice would end the hearing within a few days came true and the arguments were treated as concluded. The judgment was reserved and Palkhivala lost the chance of making his submissions on the 'implied limitations' on the amending powers of Parliament.

Parliament's power unlimited

By 3 : 2, the majority held that Parliament could amend fundamental rights and did not go into the question of any limitation on the amending power. Chief Justice Gajendragadkar, in a terse and conservative judgment, adopted the principle of strict construction and observed that there was no need to reconsider *Shankari Prasad's* case. He observed that the word 'law' in Article 13 would exclude amendments made in exercise of 'constituent power'. Strangely, he observed that the correctness of the conclusion in *Shankari Prasad's* case 'had not been questioned' before the Supreme Court in the course of arguments and there was no need to refer the matter to a larger Bench for further examination of the problem. The judgment of the Chief Justice does not set out the arguments of M.C. Setalvad and G.S. Pathak

---

5. *Sajjan Singh v. State of Rajasthan,* AIR 1965 SC 845 : [1965] 1 SCR 933.
6. Palkhivala was to appear for Maharashtra Pragati Shetkari Sangh as intervener and J.B. Dadachanji & Co. were the solicitors.

who appeared for the petitioners or those of C.K. Daftary who was the then Attorney-General of India. On such an important issue, one would have thought that the judgment would set out the submissions made by eminent counsel who appeared in the matter. Instead, he summarises the submissions by stating that, 'in substance, the points urged before us in the present proceedings are really concluded by the decision in the *Shankari Prasad* case'. He declined to consider the possibility of reconsidering *Shankari Prasad* because it would result in rendering earlier amendments invalid and would also have a serious impact on the validity of Acts included in the Ninth Schedule. The applicability of the doctrine of prospective overruling was never urged before the court. Without much ado, the majority upheld the Seventeenth Amendment to the Constitution.

The net result was that a constitutional amendment, even if it substantially eroded or even abolished fundamental rights, could not be questioned if the amendment had been passed with the requisite majority. This was possible by treating the word 'law' in Article 13(2) as applicable only to an ordinary parliamentary legislation and not a constitutional amendment. By this judgment, any ruling party which had two-thirds majority in Parliament and had control over half of the States could amend the Constitution to any extent and the judiciary could not interfere. In 1965, the Supreme Court could not comprehend the possibility of Parliament doing anything that would damage the Constitution; little did it know that the worst was yet to come in the ensuing decade.

Two path-breaking judgments

The danger of giving Parliament unfettered power to amend the Constitution was considered by Justice Hidayatullah and Justice Mudholkar – who were the two-member minority. Justice Hidayatullah, while upholding the Seventeenth Amendment, expressed reservation as to whether fundamental rights could be taken away by a simple majority in Parliament. Although Article 368 gave the power to amend any provision of the Constitution, Justice Hidayatullah observed that he was not inclined to play the role of a 'grammarian'. The power to make amendments ought not to be used ordinarily to escape from absolute constitutional restrictions. Unfortunately, Justice Hidayatullah did not spell out what he meant by 'absolute constitutional restrictions'. He reserved his opinion on how wide the word 'law' in Article 13 in the Constitution was. Although not clearly articulated in his judgment, Justice Hidayatullah's fear was the possibility of Parliament resorting to Article 368 and making drastic amendments that would take away fundamental rights. He remarked:

> *The Constitution gives so many assurances in Part III that it would be difficult to think that they were the play things of a special majority. To hold this would mean prima facie that the most solemn parts of our Constitution stand on the same footing as any other provision and even on a less firm ground than that on which the articles mentioned in the proviso stand.*

Justice Mudholkar's judgment is extremely elegant and deserves to be carefully read. He expressed doubt on whether the word 'law' occurring in Article 13(2) would exclude a constitutional amendment. When Parliament amends the Constitution, it does not act in a different capacity. An amendment of the Constitution is equally a law just as any other legislation. Further, unlike the British Parliament, the Indian Parliament and several other organs of the State could function only within the limits of the power which the Constitution has conferred upon them. This would also be so when, in the exercise of legislative power, it made an amendment to the Constitution or to any of its provisions. It was necessary to consider whether certain fundamental rights are the minimum rights reserved by people to themselves and are, therefore, unalterable. The view that legislative reforms would be hampered if fundamental rights were treated as unalterable was also not correct. Justice Mudholkar pointed out that the Directive Principles are equally fundamental in the governance of the country and the provisions of Part III (Fundamental rights) had to be interpreted harmoniously with Part IV (Directive Principles).

Origins of the basic structure theory

Most interestingly, Justice Mudholkar introduced the concept of 'basic feature'. He pointed out that the Constitution contained a 'solemn and dignified preamble' which appeared to be the epitome of the 'basic features' of the Constitution. Can it not be said, he asked, that these are indicia of the intention of the Constituent Assembly to give a permanency to the basic features of the Constitution? He observed:

> *It is also a matter for reconsideration whether making a change in a basic feature of the Constitution can be regarded merely as an amendment or would it be, in effect*

> *rewriting a part of the Constitution; and if the latter, would it be within the purview of Article 368?*

What is remarkable is that Justice Mudholkar referred to a decision of the Supreme Court of Pakistan,[7] where Chief Justice Cornelius[8] held that the power of the President to remove defects will not extend to making an alteration in the fundamental features of the Constitution. Justice Mudholkar, however, used the expression 'basic features' which expression was later adopted extensively in the *Kesavananda Bharati* case.

Equally important was his conclusion:

> *Before I part with this case, I wish to make it clear that what I have said in this judgment is not an expression of my final opinion but only an expression of certain doubts which have assailed me regarding a question of paramount importance to the citizens of our country; to know whether the basic features of the Constitution under which we live and to which we owe allegiance are to endure for all time – or at least for the foreseeable future – or whether they are no more enduring than the implemental and subordinate provisions of the Constitution.*

Only eight years later, the basic structure theory became part of the Constitution. It is interesting to speculate whether Palkhivala's appearance would have tilted the balance in 1965. Two judges held that it was necessary to further examine whether Parliament had unlimited power to amend the Constitution. It is quite probable that he may have persuaded one more judge to accept that the matter required reconsideration and perhaps a larger Bench would have been constituted in 1965 itself. If the basic structure theory had been laid down in 1965, the entire tussle between the judiciary and the Legislature could have been avoided. Fortunately, we had then the remarkable Lal Bahadur Sastri at the helm of affairs. The limits of Parliament's power could have been laid down at that time and much of the unnecessary tension between the two branches may not have arisen. Consequently, the ugly theory of a 'committed judiciary' and the supersession of judges could also have been avoided.

❋

---

7. *Fazlul Quader Chowdhry v. Mohd. Abdul Haque,* 1963 PLD 486 (SC).
8. Former Chief Justice of Pakistan.

(ii)

The Case that Changed the Constitutional Landscape

IC Golak Nath v. State of Punjab

The conservative and traditional view adopted in *Shankari Prasad's* case,[1] was followed, albeit by a very slender majority of 3:2, in *Sajjan Singh's* case.[2] Seventeen years after the Constitution came into force, the misuse of the Ninth Schedule gradually came to light. At least two of the five judges had felt that it was necessary to consider whether Parliament could be trusted with the power to amend the Constitution in any manner it chose. There was a clear danger of erosion of Fundamental Rights and the Supreme Court now had to consider this issue in a case that would permanently alter the constitutional landscape of the country. For the first time, the court had to constitute a Bench of eleven judges to hear a case.

Golak Nath and Bhatte – The two petitioners

Henry Golak Nath was a Christian missionary of Bengali origin. Henry's father, Golak Nath Chatterjee had to leave Bengal and come to Punjab after converting to Christianity in the mid-nineteenth century. He had walked across the country to Punjab and married a Kashmiri. Henry, over the years, had acquired a large amount of land. He died in 1953 leaving behind his son, daughter and grand-daughters. In January 1962, 418 acres of land were declared surplus under the Punjab Security of Land Tenures Act, 1953.[3] At the same time, at the other end of India, the Mysore Land Reforms Act, 1961, imposed a ceiling limit on land holdings and tenants were conferred the ownership of lands which were 'surplus' or in excess of the ceiling limit. Writ petitions were filed under Article 32 directly to the Supreme Court challenging both the Punjab Security of Land Tenures Act, 1953, and the

---

1. *Shankari Prasad v. Union of India,* AIR 1951 SC 458 : [1952] 1 SCR 89.
2. *Sajjan Singh v. State of Rajasthan,* AIR 1965 SC 845 : [1965] 1 SCR 933.
3. The details of Henry Golak Nath are set out in Granville Austin, *Working a Democratic Constitution, The Indian Experience,* pp. 196-208.

Mysore Land Reforms Act, 1961.[4] These enactments were included in the Ninth Schedule to the Constitution by the Constitution (Seventeenth Amendment) Act, 1964. The Ninth Schedule made these laws immune from attack on the ground of violating Article 14, 19 or 31.

As we have just seen, the Seventeenth Amendment had been upheld by the Supreme Court just two years earlier in *Sajjan Singh's* case.[5] *Sajjan Singh*, in turn, had followed the earlier decision of the Supreme Court in the *Shankari Prasad*[6] case rendered in 1952. The petitioners, therefore, challenged the validity of the Constitution (First Amendment) Act, 1951, the Constitution (Fourth Amendment) Act, 1955 and the Constitution (Seventeenth Amendment) Act, 1964.[7] Unless the earlier decisions of *Sajjan Singh* and *Shankari Prasad* were overruled, the petitioners could not succeed.

Bench of eleven judges

As the issue was extremely important, a Bench of eleven judges was constituted to hear this case.[8] Chief Justice Subba Rao gave another reason for constituting a Bench of eleven judges. He pointed out that the correctness of the decision in the *Shankari Prasad* case had not been questioned in the *Sajjan Singh* case. Indeed, Chief Justice Gajendragadkar had held that there was no reason to reconsider the earlier decision rendered in 1951. At the same time, there was a conflict between the views taken by the majority and the minority in the *Sajjan Singh* case which had to be resolved.[9] In *Sajjan Singh's* case, as we have just seen, two of the judges (Hidayatullah and Mudholkar JJ) expressed grave doubts as to whether Parliament could be treated as having unlimited power to amend the Constitution.

Thus, the reason for setting up an eleven-judge Bench was really to define the limits of the powers of Parliament to amend the

---

4. The petitioner from Mysore was N. Krishna Bhatte. If he had filed his writ earlier, his name would have been immortal and no one would have heard of Golak Nath.
5. *Sajjan Singh v. State of Rajasthan*, AIR 1965 SC 845 : [1965] 1 SCR 933.
6. *Shankari Prasad Singh Deo v. Union of India*, AIR 1951 SC 458 : [1952] 1 SCR 89.
7. *I.C. Golak Nath v. State of Punjab*, AIR 1967 SC 1643 : [1967] 2 SCR 762.
8. Of the eleven judges, only Hidayathullah was on the Bench of five judges that had heard the *Sajjan Singh* case in 1965.
9. There is no logic in this statement. There will always be conflict between the majority and the minority. A larger Bench is constituted only when there is a conflict between two Benches having the same strength of judges.

Constitution and, in particular, Fundamental Rights. If Parliament were to have unlimited power to amend the Constitution, could it, for instance, abolish the post of President? Could it obliterate the concept of federalism? Could Fundamental Rights be abrogated and a democratic republic be converted into a totalitarian system of Government–which, effectively, did happen during the Emergency from 1975-77?

As the case was extremely important, the Supreme Court issued notices to the Advocates-General of various States and a galaxy of lawyers appeared in the matter. Golak Nath was represented by R.V.S. Mani and for the interveners, some of the eminent counsel were M.C. Setalvad, M.K. Nambiar, A.K. Sen, R.K. Garg and K. Parasaran. The State of Punjab was represented by Niren De who was then the Solicitor-General of India and later became the Attorney-General of India. Lal Narain Sinha was the Advocate-General of the State of Bihar[10] and Mohan Kumaramangalam was the Advocate-General of the State of Madras (now Tamil Nadu). Mohan Kumaramangalam, a Communist, later joined the Indira Gandhi's cabinet as a Minister. He propounded the obnoxious theory of a 'committed judiciary' and was mainly responsible for the supersession of judges. The damage to the judiciary was immense and long-lasting. He died in a tragic air crash in May 1973.

Palkhivala's one day appearance

D.M. Popat strongly believes that if Palkhivala had listened to him and appeared in the *Sajjan Singh* case, the result may have been different. The Supreme Court could have been persuaded to reconsider the scope of the powers of Parliament. A golden opportunity to reconsider the earlier decision in *Shankari Prasad's* case had been lost. Chief Justice Subba Rao had issued directions to constitute an eleven Judge Bench and Palkhivala was then in Delhi for some other case. He spoke to Popat and informed him about the good news of a larger Bench being constituted and said, 'Popat, this is a God sent opportunity and we should not miss it'.

Unfortunately, when the *Golak Nath* case was taken up, Palkhivala was held up at Geneva where he was arguing, ironically, for the Union of India in an international dispute. When Popat asked Palkhivala to appear, he initially expressed his reluctance. Noticing that Popat was unhappy with his decision, Palkhivala agreed to come to Supreme Court for just one day! Palkhivala

---

10. He later became Attorney-General and argued the *Minerva Mills* case.

reached Delhi on Sunday night and was to argue on Monday. He had to return to Geneva on Monday night. F.S. Nariman and Popat went to Palam Airport (as Delhi Airport was then called) to receive Palkhivala and Nariman briefed him about what had been argued in court and what questions were raised by the judges. Nariman mentioned that Chief Justice Subba Rao had spoken about prospective overruling. While alighting from the car, Palkhivala briefly explained the genesis and ambit of 'prospective overruling' and referred to a Supreme Court decision on this point. He casually mentioned about the book by Julius Stone titled 'Dimensions of Social Justice' which would be relevant for the case. Popat remembered that he was speechless at Palkhivala's knowledge of prospective overruling which he explained in less than three minutes. Among few other lawyers who had an equally profound knowledge of the law was perhaps A.V. Viswanatha Sastri.

Palkhivala asked Popat to make sure that he got his turn on Monday. Popat had earlier told M.K. Nambiar, who was then arguing the case, that Palkhivala had only one day to spare and had to rush back to Geneva. Nambiar gracefully agreed to allow Palkhivala to make his submissions. At the same time, he (Nambiar) could not abruptly end his argument and allow Palkhivala to argue and then resume his arguments again. How was Palkhivala to be allowed to argue for a short while before Nambiar could continue?

On that fateful Monday, Nambiar continued his arguments from 10.30 a.m. till 11.30 a.m. There was no sign of his stopping and giving Palkhivala a chance to argue. Palkhivala was getting increasingly restless. At 11.30 a.m., the judges started questioning him on several legal issues. Deftly, he replied that the questions raised by the judges were 'extremely important' and he would require some time to reflect upon them and come back with an answer! He then told the Supreme Court that Palkhivala would like to make his submissions and after he concluded, he (M.K. Nambiar) would respond to the questions raised by the Bench. This gave Palkhivala the necessary time to make his submissions!

Earlier that morning, Palkhivala decided to confine his arguments only to the question of implied limitations on the power of Parliament to amend the Constitution. Popat also told Palkhivala that the judges had repeatedly raised questions on prospective overruling. Palkhivala made an impassioned plea for a reconsideration of the earlier view that Parliament had the unfettered power to amend the Constitution. He pointed out the dangerous consequences of not placing any limitation on the amending power of Parliament under Article 368. Could Parliament delete all Fundamental Rights? Could it alter the federal structure of India? Or, was there a core area of the Constitution that could not be touched? Unfortunately, none of the judgments have set out the arguments of Palkhivala or the other eminent counsel. Indeed, M.K. Nambiar had cited an article by a German jurist, Dieter Conrad, titled 'The Implied Limitations of the Amending Power'[11] but this was also not referred to. Justice Wanchoo characterized these submissions as 'arguments of fear'; the so-called fear of frightful consequences, he held, was not a ground to impose implied limitations on the amending power for 'we have no reason to suppose that Parliament on whom such power is conferred will abuse it.' Justice Wanchoo's faith in our Parliamentarians was quite misplaced – he could not have foreseen the rapid deterioration that was to take place in the next two decades.

The case was argued for several days and the stage was set for the Supreme Court to decide issues of grave and fundamental importance. As it turned out, the *Golak Nath* case altered the course of constitutional law of India.

The majority view

Chief Justice Subba Rao gave the judgment for himself and four other judges.[12] He began by discussing the earlier two decisions in the *Shankari Prasad* and *Sajjan Singh* cases. In both these decisions, it was accepted that Parliament had unlimited power to amend the Constitution. It was held that the word 'law' in Article 13(2) did not include a constitutional amendment but referred to an ordinary statute. Tracing the history of fundamental rights, Chief Justice Subba Rao referred to the resolution passed at the Madras Congress in May 1928. Motilal Nehru had presided over this meeting and observed that Fundamental Rights should be guaranteed in such a manner that they could not be withdrawn under any circumstances. He referred to the unfortunate existence of communal differences in the country and pointed out that there was a need to create a sense of security amongst people, particularly to secure full enjoyment of religious and cultural rights. On April 30, 1947,

11. Palkhivala relied on the same article in the *Kesavananda Bharati* case, see (1973) 4 SCC 225, at page 562.
12. The majority consisted of Subba Rao C.J., Sikri, Shah, Shelat, Vaidialingam and Hidayatullah JJ. The minority view was by Wanchoo, Bhargava, Mitter, Bachawat and Ramaswami. JJ.

Pandit Nehru proposed the adoption of the interim report on Fundamental Rights before the Constituent Assembly and remarked that Fundamental Rights were something that had to be permanent in the Constitution. Reference was also made to certain speeches of Dr. Ambedkar who observed:[13]

> *Now, what is it we do? We divide the articles of the Constitution under three categories. The first category is the one which consists of articles which can be amended by Parliament by a bare majority. The second set of articles are articles which require two-thirds majority. If the future Parliament wishes to amend any particular article which is not mentioned in Part III or Article 304, all that is necessary for them is to have a two-thirds majority. Then they can amend it.*

Thus, Dr. Ambedkar, according to Chief Justice Subba Rao, was of the view that Fundamental Rights were so important that they could not be amended. Even the Supreme Court had observed that Fundamental Rights were sacrosanct[14] and were 'unalienable and unviolable'.[15] Referring to the views of Pandit Nehru and Dr. Ambedkar, Justice Subba Rao referred to the 'transcendental character' given to Fundamental Rights by two of the important architects of the Constitution. The paradox of accepting the view that Fundamental Rights could be amended or abrogated by Parliament was demonstrated by referring to Article 13(2). This clause states that any 'law' which takes away or abridges Fundamental Rights would be void to that extent. Therefore, even if a unanimous Parliament were to pass an ordinary law, seriously interfering with the religious rights of a minority community, it would be unconstitutional as violating the fundamental right to practise one's religion. At the same time, Parliament could theoretically delete this fundamental right completely and no one would have the right to practise their own religion. Alternatively, Parliament could amend the Constitution and make a particular religion as the State religion and still it would be unquestionable. Thus, an ordinary law which was contrary to even *one* fundamental

---

13. Speech on September 18, 1949—Speaking on an amendment to draft Article 304 (the present Article 368) proposed by H.V. Kamath. Although Ambedkar refers to 'three categories', only two are mentioned.
14. *M.S.M. Sharma v. Sri Krishna Sinha,* AIR 1959 SC 395 : [1959] Supp (1) SCR 806.
15. *Ujjam Bai v. State of U.P.,* AIR 1962 SC 1621 : [1963] 1 SCR 778.

right would be unconstitutional but an amendment that deleted all Fundamental Rights would be permissible!

The majority also rejected the argument that amending the Constitution was a political question which was outside the scope of judicial review. The majority held that the amending power would not enable Parliament to override all express or implied limitations on that power and that Parliament could not amend Part III (Fundamental Rights) of the Constitution. Thus, the pendulum swung to the opposite extreme: while *Shankari Prasad* and *Sajjan Singh* cases had held that Parliament had unlimited power to amend the Constitution, the majority in *Golak Nath* held that Parliament could not amend any part of the Constitution in Part III that dealt with Fundamental Rights.

The majority judgment delivered by Chief Justice Subba Rao reflected his serious concern at the erosion of Fundamental Rights. This was justified because of the misuse of the Ninth Schedule and the frequent constitutional amendments. What was intended to be a one time measure was frequently resorted to and several laws that had nothing to do with agrarian reforms were included in the Ninth Schedule and could not be challenged even if they violated Articles 14, 19 and 31 – the main grounds on which a legislation is normally struck down. Perhaps Chief Justice Subba Rao went too far, but the manner in which Articles 13 and 368 were worded left him with little choice.

Doctrine of prospective overruling

At the end of his judgment, Chief Justice Subba Rao referred to a request made to the Supreme Court for not taking a different view from *Shankari Prasad* case observing that ordinarily the Supreme Court is reluctant to reverse its previous decision. He held, on the other hand, that it is the court's duty to correct its erroneous decision as early as possible. As the Supreme Court was convinced that the *Shankari Prasad* case was wrong, it was necessary to overrule it because the longer it held the field, the greater would be the scope for erosion of Fundamental Rights. Significantly, he observed that the *Shankari Prasad* case contained seeds of destruction of the cherished rights of the people, and the sooner it was overruled, the better for the country.

Now, this conclusion would have led to a serious problem. Any judgment of the Supreme Court applies retrospectively. In other words, a judgment delivered in 2008 on an income tax case which started in 1998 would apply from 1998 itself. On the other hand, laws made by Parliament or by a State Legislature usually have prospective effect. If *Golak Nath* overruled the views in *Shankari Prasad* (1952) and *Sajjan Singh* (1965), Parliament would have had no power to amend any fundamental right from 1950 onwards. This would render the First, Fourth and Seventeenth Amendments unconstitutional and all the land reform legislations made from 1950 to 1967 would be invalid. It would have led to complete chaos as a number of zamindari estates had been abolished and thousands of acres of land had been acquired and distributed to cultivating peasants for 17 years. It would be impossible to set the clock back. Therefore, the court invoked the American constitutional doctrine of 'prospective overruling'.[16]

Justice Hidayatullah's concurring view

Equally important is the concurring view[17] of Justice Hidayatullah who had taken a dissenting view in the *Sajjan Singh* case and was the only common judge who had heard both cases. His judgment is remarkable for the scholarship and analysis of the dangers of giving Parliament absolute power to amend Fundamental Rights. He cautioned against the dangers of eroding Fundamental rights for the ostensible object of promoting Directive Principles. He also seriously questioned the patent abuse of the Ninth Schedule. This was intended to protect agrarian reforms but Parliament subsequently included laws that had no connection whatsoever with the abolition of the zamindari estates or other reformative legislation. For example, the Railway Companies (Emergency Provisions) Act, 1951, amongst various statutes, had nothing to do with the agrarian reforms or the basic purpose for which the Ninth Schedule was inserted. Hidayatullah referred to the fear of Madison: 'the danger of an elected Government who could, for reasons of prejudice, sinister design, intrigue, corruption or other means, first get elected and then betray the interest of the people'.[18] Madison's fear has proved true time and time again in India. Virtually, every ruling party in the Centre and the States had betrayed the interest of the people. Hidayatullah's conclusions were far reaching. He held that Fundamental Rights could be abridged or taken away only if

---

16. For a detailed analysis of this doctrine, see Arvind P. Datar, 'Prospective Overruling: Correct Doctrine, Incorrect Application', (2008) 7 SCC (Jour.) J-41.
17. The text of his judgment is on pp. 1692-1718 of AIR 1967 SC 1643.
18. Federalist No.10.

another Constituent Assembly was formed; Parliament could not take them away by amending the Constitution under Article 368.

The minority view

The minority judgments adopted a conservative approach. Justice Wanchoo reiterated the earlier views taken in *Shankari Prasad* (1952) and *Sajjan Singh* (1965) and held that there was no limitation on the power of Parliament to amend the Constitution.

Similarly, Justice Bachawat observed that a static system of laws was the worst and an unamendable Constitution meant that agrarian reform and progress would be at a standstill; even the unique feat of 500 million citizens at a special convocation would not be able to amend the Fundamental Rights contained in Part III. The only way for the deadlock to be resolved was by a revolution and such a situation was not intended by the framers of the Constitution.[19]

The consequences of the *Golak Nath* verdict

Unfortunately, the consequence of the majority judgment was that Parliament became completely powerless to amend or alter any of the Fundamental Rights contained in Articles 14 to 32 of the Constitution; it was a shift from total freedom to a total embargo and this was difficult for Parliament to accept. The majority verdict in *Golaknath* was widely criticized and almost all constitutional scholars took the view that the decision was wrong. Six years later, it was overruled unanimously by all the thirteen judges in the historic *Kesavananda Bharati* case. Nevertheless, it was a major step towards limiting the uncontrolled power of Parliament to amend/ alter the Constitution.

This verdict set the Supreme Court on a direct collision course with Parliament and the ruling Congress party led by Mrs. Indira Gandhi. The battle continued for almost 15 years and culminated in the *Judges' Transfer* case.[20] In its wake, the Supreme Court delivered landmark judgments in the *Bank Nationalisation* case,[21] the *Privy Purses* case,[22] the *Bennett Coleman* case,[23] the

19. The minority judgment of Justice Bachawat is on pp. 1718-1730 and that of Justice Ramaswami is on pp. 1730-1742 of AIR.
20. *S.P. Gupta v. Union of India*, AIR 1982 SC 149 : 1981 Supp (1) SCC 87.
21. *R.C. Cooper v. Union of India*, AIR 1970 SC 564 : (1970) 1 SCC 248.
22. *Madhav Rao Scindia v. Union of India*, AIR 1971 SC 530 : (1971) 1 SCC 85.
23. *Bennett Coleman & Co. v. Union of India*, AIR 1973 SC 106 :(1972) 2 SCC 788.

Kesavananda Bharati case,[24] the *ADM Jabalpur* case[25] and the *Minerva Mills* case.[26] Except *ADM Jabalpur*, Palkhivala had appeared and substantially succeeded in all of these cases.

As a postscript, it must be mentioned that Chief Justice Subba Rao resigned as Chief Justice and then contested for the office of President, a step that was widely, and rightly, criticized. An outstanding judge, he had the courage to take bold decisions and his judgments had the imprint of legal scholarship[27] but his entering the political arena dented his stature.[28]

For Golak Nath and Bhatte, this marathon judgment was only of academic interest as they got no relief. The laws they challenged were upheld and so were the First, Fourth and Seventeenth Amendments. The doctrine of prospective overruling, as applied, meant that laws taking away Fundamental Rights could not be made in future. Golak Nath and Bhatte could only have the consolation of contributing significantly to the development of constitutional law. Golak Nath had the additional bonus of having his name become immortal.

❋

24. *Kesavananda Bharati v. State of Kerala,* AIR 1973 SC 1461 : (1973) 4 SCC 225.
25. *ADM Jabalpur v. Shivakant Shukla,* AIR 1976 SC 1207 : (1976) 2 SCC 521.
26. *Minerva Mills v. Union of India,* AIR 1980 SC 1789 : (1980) 2 SCC 591.
27. Justice Jeevan Reddy, a former Supreme Court Judge, paid rich tributes to Chief Justice Subba Rao at the latter's centenary celebrations. Reddy J. refers to Subba Rao's self-discipline, high learning and total integrity. See (2003) 8 SCC (Jour) 41.
28. It is a matter of deep regret that quite a few judges, including a former Chief Justice, have contested elections to the Lok Sabha and Rajya Sabha. This seriously erodes the confidence of the people in the judiciary. In pursuit of personal ambition, these judges forget the serious damage they cause to the image and reputation of the judiciary.

(iii)

The Bank Nationalisation case

A Turning Point in the Interpretation of Fundamental Rights

After *Golaknath,* the next major case argued by Palkhivala was *R.C. Cooper v. Union of India,*[1] popularly called the *Bank Nationalisation* case. The much maligned and misunderstood verdict in this case was portrayed as 'undemocratic' and a serious setback to the Government's avowed objective of socialism. As often happens, several politicians and even lawyers have condemned this decision without reading it or understanding the basis on which the decision was rendered by the Supreme Court. It is often forgotten that the power of the Central Government to nationalize banks was upheld. This, according to the court, was a matter of policy and the court would not interfere in the decision of the Government to exercise State control over any particular industry. But the court rightly struck down the provisions relating to compensation. The case also marked a turning point in the interpretation of fundamental rights and was the foundation of several subsequent important Supreme Court judgments that expanded the scope of judicial review.

Pandit Nehru firmly believed that socialism was the economic model most suited to India. In fact, Fabian socialism was popular in several developing countries. State control of important industries was seen as the means to achieve the objective of the greatest good of the greatest number. The commanding heights of the Indian economy were to be controlled by Government-owned corporations. After independence, several States nationalized transport undertakings; electricity was made a State monopoly and the insurance sector was nationalized. In the late 1960s, several refineries and oil companies were nationalized. It was only a matter of time before major banks would be taken over by the State. Indeed, the proposal to nationalize banks was mooted by the

---

1. AIR 1970 SC 564 : (1970) 1 SCC 248.

All-India Congress Committee in 1948. R.K. Shanmugham Chetty, the first Finance Minister, wanted to nationalize the Imperial Bank but the suggestion was dropped at the behest of Sardar Patel.[2]

In 1955, the Imperial Bank of India was taken over under the State Bank of India Act, and four years later, seven of its subsidiaries were also taken over. With this partial nationalisation, one-third of commercial banking in the country came under State control. The Reserve Bank of India took a pro-active role in regulating the banking sector and reduced the number of commercial banking institutions from 566 in 1951 to 89 in 1969. Given below is a tabular analysis of the commercial banking sector in India in June, 1969:

	No. of banks	**No. of officers**	**Deposits (in crores)**	**Credit (in crores)**
State Bank of India	1	1,566	948	967
Subsidiaries of State Bank of India	7	888	291	219
Indian Scheduled Commercial Banks (each with deposit exceeding Rs. 50 crores)	14	4,130	2,632	1,829
Banks incorporated in Foreign Countries– Only 13 were operating.[3]	15	130	478	385
Other Indian Scheduled Banks	36	1,324	296	197
Non-scheduled Commercial Banks	16	216	28	16

Some leaders opposed nationalisation on the ground that the compensation (initially estimated at Rs. 85 crores) could be used to stimulate the economy. There was an increasing tussle between Indira Gandhi and her close advisors and the old guard of the Congress. Morarji Desai, who was then the Deputy Prime Minister and also the Finance Minister, was of the view that instead of paying Rs. 85 crores, they could control the banks and channel the credit to the social sectors by amending the banking laws.

---

2. In retrospect, nothing was more damaging in the early years of India's independence than the demise of Sardar Patel very soon after independence.
3. The figures are from the reported judgment in *R.C. Cooper v. Union of India,* AIR 1970 SC 564, 581 : (1970) 1 SCC 248.

On July 17, 1969, Morarji Desai was dropped as Finance Minister. The next day, on July 18, 1969, Morarji Desai resigned as Deputy Prime Minister.

July 19, 1969 was a Saturday and the acting President promulgated the Banking Companies (Acquisition and Transfer of Undertaking) Ordinance, 1969, nationalizing 14 banks having deposits exceeding Rs. 50 crores.[4] Mrs. Indira Gandhi announced the nationalisation in a late-afternoon radio broadcast to the nation. At that time, C. Rajagopalachari[5] criticized the proposal and particularly denounced the promulgation of an ordinance on a Saturday when Parliament was about to start the monsoon session just two days later.[6] The obvious intention was to present Parliament with a *fait accompli*.

The Ordinance was a closely guarded secret and, at one stroke, more than 75% of the banking sector came under State control. The entire paid-up capital, all assets and liabilities, contracts, and agreements were to vest with the Central Government. All directors of the fourteen nationalized banks would vacate their respective offices but services of other employees were to continue with the nationalized banks. The most shocking part of the Ordinance was the Second Schedule which spelt out the compensation that was to be paid. To determine the quantum of compensation, two methods were specified:

(a) Where the amount of compensation could be fixed by an agreement, it would be determined in accordance with such agreement;

---

4. *The fourteen banks were:* (1) The Central Bank of India Ltd.; (2) The Bank of India Ltd. (3) The Punjab National Bank Ltd. (4) The Bank of Baroda Ltd.; (5) The United Commercial Bank Ltd.; (6) Canara Bank Ltd. (7) United Bank of India Ltd.; (8) Dena Bank Ltd.; (9) Syndicate Bank Ltd.; (10) The Union Bank of India Ltd.; (11) Allahabad Bank Ltd.; (12) The Indian Bank Ltd.; (13) The Bank of Maharashtra Ltd.; and (14) The Indian Overseas Bank Ltd.
5. Affectionately called Rajaji, he was the first Governor-General of India. He was the Chief Minister of the Madras Presidency in 1937 and was the first to introduce prohibition and also sales tax. A pragmatic and brilliant Statesman, he saw the evils of a controlled, socialist economy and called it the 'licence-permit raj'. He was the founder of the Swatantra Party. Palkhivala had immense admiration for him. In a speech at Madras (Chennai), Palkhivala remarked that the destiny of India would have been different if Rajaji had been at the helm of affairs. Rajaji passed away on December 25, 1972, just a few days after his 94th birthday. Gandhiji called him as the 'keeper of my conscience'.
6. For a detailed and excellent account of the political events that led to bank nationalisation in 1969, see Granville Austin, *Working a Democratic Constitution, The Indian Experience*, Oxford University Press (1999), pp. 210-215.

(b) Where no such agreement could be reached, the Central Government had to refer the matter to a Tribunal within a period of three months from the date on which the Central Government and the existing bank failed to reach an agreement regarding the amount of compensation.

The compensation so determined was to be given not in cash but in marketable Central Government securities payable *after ten years*. This was most unfair and virtually amounted to State plunder. The shareholders of these fourteen banks would consequently get nothing; indeed, a senior citizen may not even be alive to get his security encashed after ten years. In retrospect, the entire litigation could have been avoided if the Central Government had paid about Rs. 75 crores as compensation either in one lump sum or in three instalments. Any Government that acts unfairly towards a section of its citizens will only generate contempt for the law; if the Government cannot act in a fair manner, it can hardly expect its citizens to reciprocate. If leadership is an example, then the manner in which the banks were nationalized with a ten-year deferred compensation was a terrible example. Slowly but surely, all constitutional and democratic values were systematically eroded from the late 1960s. If the Government of India owned shares in any foreign enterprise and its assets had been expropriated and compensation was made payable after ten years, would it be acceptable? Do unto others as you would have others do unto you applies equally to State action. In a nutshell, the provisions of the Ordinance were draconian and the Government was quite naïve to expect it to remain unchallenged.

Less than 48 hours after the ordinance was promulgated, Palkhivala moved a petition before the Supreme Court. Ravinder Narain[7] recollects that Palkhivala flew down to Delhi that Sunday (just a day after the ordinance) and the petition was drafted and finalised in two hours! R.C. Cooper was the petitioner and was then a director of the Central Bank of India Ltd.. Cooper held shares in this bank, Bank of India Ltd. and Bank of Baroda Ltd. He had also deposits and current accounts with these banks. At that time, shares in the banks were considered a safe and attractive investment. To challenge such a major Ordinance in so short a time was truly a remarkable feat. A writ petition was filed on

---

7. Former partner of Dadachanji & Co. and now a Senior Advocate of the Supreme Court of India.

July 21, 1969 (Monday) and the interim application was heard on July 22, 1969; an interim order restraining the removal of the Chairmen of the banks was granted.

Legal issues

This case raised several important legal issues which can be summarised as follows:

(i) Whether a shareholder could file a petition for violation of his fundamental rights when the company in which the shares are held had been taken over ?

(ii) Whether the Ordinance was validly promulgated ?

(iii) Whether the Banking Companies (Acquisition and Transfer of Undertaking) Act, 1969, which replaced the Ordinance was within the legislative competence of Parliament ?

(iv) Whether the said Act was violative of Articles 19(1)(f) and 31(2) – provisions pertaining to the fundamental right to acquire, hold and dispose of property ?

(v) Whether the quantum or method adopted for payment of compensation was valid ?

Maintainability of the petition

Those who are not lawyers may wonder why R.C. Cooper chose to challenge the Ordinance nationalizing the banks, particularly when no bank had chosen to do so. How did it matter to a shareholder of a bank if it was nationalized? Was it not necessary for the banks to challenge the take-over of their assets? Surprisingly, none of them did. R.C. Cooper contended that he lost his right to receive dividend, the value of his investments had been substantially eroded and that he was deprived of his right as a shareholder to carry on business, albeit through the agency of the banking company. Effectively, he was converted to a mere deposit-holder of a nationalized bank without his consent. On the other hand, the Attorney-General argued that a shareholder, depositor or director was not entitled to move a petition for infringement of the rights of a company. The fundamental right to carry on business was available only to citizens and not to limited companies.

Rejecting the objection, the Supreme Court ruled that both these cases would not apply. It held that R.C. Cooper had challenged the infringement of his own rights and not of the bank of which he was the shareholder and director and where he had current and fixed deposit accounts. Cooper claimed that as a result of nationalisation, he suffered great financial loss and was deprived of the rights of a shareholder to carry on business through the agency of the company. The Supreme Court observed that an executive or legislative measure may impair the rights not only of the company but also of its shareholders. The court could grant relief if the State action impaired the right of the shareholders as well as the company. The court would not deny itself the jurisdiction to grant relief in such cases by concentrating upon technicalities.

The correct view was that subsequently expressed in the *Bennett Coleman*[8] case: a shareholder could challenge State action if it affected his rights as a shareholder. In this case, Chief Justice Ray pointed out that the newsprint policy affected not only the newspaper company but also the rights of its shareholders. If the action is likely to affect the fundamental rights of the shareholders as well, it is open to the company to file a writ petition along with the aggrieved shareholders. The rights of shareholders were 'projected and manifested by the newspapers owned and controlled by the shareholders through the medium of the corporation.' The fact that the company is one of the petitioners will not prevent the court from giving relief to the shareholders.[9]

In the end, the petition filed by R.C. Cooper was held to be maintainable. The first hurdle was crossed.

Validity of the Ordinance:

Having rejected the preliminary objection, the Supreme Court dealt with the constitutional validity of the Ordinance. Palkhivala, using the language of Article 123 of the Constitution,[10] contended

---

8. *Bennett Coleman & Co. Ltd. v. Union of India,* AIR 1973 SC 106, 114 : (1972) 2 SCC 788. In this case, each petition had clearly included not only the company but also some shareholders, the editor and the publishers.
9. The interested reader may also see the decision of the Supreme Court in *Delhi Cloth & General Mills Ltd. v. Union of India,* AIR 1983 SC 937 : (1983) 4 SCC 166. Earlier, the Supreme Court had held that a limited company, not being a citizen, could not claim the fundamental right to carry on business under Article 19(1)(g). See *State Trading Corporation Ltd. v. CTO,* AIR 1963 SC 1811 : [1964] 4 SCR 99 and *Tata Engineering and Locomotive Co. Ltd. v. State of Bihar,* AIR 1965 SC 40: [1964] 6 SCR 885.
10. Article 123 conferred power on the President to promulgate an ordinance during recess of Parliament. A similar power is conferred on the Governor of each State under Article 213.

that the President was not the final arbiter on whether the conditions necessitating an ordinance existed. He submitted that in so far as the power of judicial review went, there was absolutely no difference between the power to promulgate an ordinance, and statutory powers exercised by an authority based on his subjective satisfaction that certain pre-conditions prescribed for the exercise of such power existed. Therefore, the Supreme Court had the power to annul the Ordinance if it found that there were no circumstances rendering it necessary for the President to take immediate action. The Attorney-General argued that the Presidential satisfaction under Article 123 was purely subjective, and could not be questioned in a court of law. The language of Article 123, he submitted, acted as a mere guidance and not as a pre-condition for the exercise of this power. The majority did not deal with this interesting question as the Ordinance had by then been replaced by an Act of Parliament which was eventually held to be unconstitutional.

The challenge to the Ordinance was not a strong point in Palkhivala's favour although, by convention, it was wrong to have promulgated an ordinance when Parliament was to begin its session just two days later. It displayed utter disregard for constitutional conventions and norms that soon became a hallmark of the 1970s.

Legislative competence of the acquisition process

The focus of the judicial enquiry thus shifted towards the *vires* of the Banking Companies (Acquisition and Transfer of Undertaking) Act, 1969 ('Acquisition Act'). Palkhivala challenged the legislative competence of Parliament to enact the Acquisition Act. While conceding that Parliament could validly legislate in respect of acquisition of that part of the undertaking which related to the business of banking as defined in Section 5(b) of the Banking Regulation Act, 1949,[11] he contended that the competence in respect of any other business carried on by these banks prior to the date of acquisition fell within Entry 26 of List II.[12] As a corollary,

11. Under Section 5(b) of this Act, 'banking' meant 'the accepting, for the purpose of lending or investment, of deposits of money from the public repayable on demand or otherwise, and withdrawable by cheque, draft or otherwise.' This definition did not include other commercial activities engaged in by a banking institution.
12. The Seventh Schedule of the Constitution of India contains three Lists which demarcate the fields of legislation given to Parliament (List I), to the State Legislatures (List II), and concurrently to both Parliament and State Legislatures (Footnote No. 12 Contd.)

the power to legislate in respect of acquisition under Entry 42 of List III[13] could be exercised by Parliament only for effectuating legislation under any Entry falling in List I or List III of the Schedule VII. The Attorney-General, on the other hand, pushed for an expansive construction to the term 'banking' as used in Entry 45 of List I,[14] to cover all commercial activities carried on by banks. Briefly, Palkhivala argued that Parliament had the power to acquire only the banking business; other trading activities could be acquired only by the respective State Legislatures. The power of acquisition under Entry 42 of List III could not be exercised unless basic legislation was enacted either under Entry 45 of List I or Entry 26 of List II.

The majority rejected this plea by the Attorney-General, and held that if all commercial activities carried on by a bank at any given time were to be used for determining the ambit of the term 'banking', it would create substantial ambiguity. However, they also expressly rejected the limitation suggested by Palkhivala to the legislative competence of Parliament under Entry 42 of List III, and held that the power to legislate for acquisition of property was exercisable only under this Entry, and not as an incident of the power to legislate in respect of a specific head of legislation in any of the three Lists. According to the majority, the term 'property' as used in this Entry was wide enough to include not only the assets, but also the organization, liabilities and obligations of any going concern. Based on this reasoning, they concluded that a law could be validly enacted under this Entry for the compulsory acquisition of an 'undertaking' as defined in Section 5 of the Acquisition Act. This was an important principle laid down by the Supreme Court. The power to acquire property was held to be an independent power and there was no need to have any basic or separate legislation under one of the entries under List I or List II. Thus, if Parliament wanted to acquire or nationalize the airline business, it could do so directly by passing a law under Entry 42 of List III and it need not make any law under Entry 29 of List I that deals with airways and aircrafts.

(Footnote No. 12 Contd.)
(List III). The exclusive legislative competence with respect to 'trade and commerce within the State, subject to the provisions of entry 33 of List III' was vested in the State Legislatures.

13. Under this Entry, the legislative competence for 'acquisition and requisitioning of property' was vested in both the Parliament as well as the State Legislatures.
14. The exclusive legislative competence with respect to 'banking' was vested in Parliament under this Entry.

The overruling of the 'mutual exclusivity' theory

The most important legal contribution of the *Bank Nationalisation* case was the overruling of the 'mutual exclusivity theory'. After rejecting the challenge to Parliament's competence to nationalize banks, the majority went on to examine the Acquisition Act on the touchstone of fundamental rights. At the outset, the stand taken by the Union was that the Acquisition Act could not be tested for violation of all fundamental rights, but only for the violation of Article 31, which specifically dealt with acquisition. This contention was based on the theory of 'mutual exclusivity' of rights, propounded by the Supreme Court in *A.K. Gopalan v. State of Madras*.[15] This was perhaps the first landmark decision rendered by the Supreme Court, oddly by a Bench of an even number of judges.[16] The Constitution initially provided for a strength of nine judges of the Supreme Court and in 1950 only six judges had been appointed. All of them sat in this matter. It was truly a hearing by the full court.

A.K. Gopalan, a communist, was detained in the Madras Jail from December 1947. In the criminal cases filed against him, the convictions had been set aside. But he continued to be incarcerated under the Preventive Detention Act, 1950. After the Constitution came into force, he directly filed a writ petition before the Supreme Court under Article 32 stating that the law of preventive detention violated Articles 13, 19, 21 and 22.[17] He argued that under Article 19, he had several fundamental rights, in particular, the right to move freely throughout the territory of India. But this right was infringed because he was preventively detained. He also argued that his right to liberty under Article 21 had also been infringed. The Indian Constitution permitted preventive detention under Article 22. This is a peculiar provision whereby a person can be detained without trial and this power, ironically, is contained in the chapter on fundamental rights.[18]

---

15. [1950] SCR 88 : AIR 1950 SC 27.
16. The six judges were: Kania C.J., Fazl Ali, Patanjali Sastri, Mahajan, B.K. Mukherjea and S.R. Das JJ.
17. For the text of these articles, see Appendix I.
18. In the words of Patanjali Sastri J., 'This sinister-looking feature, so strangely out of place in a democratic Constitution which invests personal liberty with the sacrosanctity of a fundamental right, and so incompatible with the promises of its preamble, is doubtless designed to prevent an abuse of freedom by anti-social and subversive elements which might imperil the national welfare of the infant Republic.'

The majority of the Supreme Court held that the various fundamental rights operated in separate compartments and were mutually exclusive – each article enacting a code relating to protection of distinct rights. If Gopalan was detained by a valid order of detention under Article 22, he could not complain of violation of Article 21. He would have the right to move freely throughout India only if he was not in jail. Patanjali Sastri J. held that Article 19 would apply only if a citizen was free; if he was under preventive detention, he would not be able to enjoy the freedom under Article 19. Fazl Ali J. struck a different note and observed that the fundamental rights are not to be treated as independent of each other. The fact that different aspects of the same rights have been dealt with in three different articles will not make them mutually exclusive. Article 22 does not exclude the operation of Articles 19 and 21; conversely, Articles 19 and 21 must be read subject to Article 22. But Justice Fazl Ali was in the minority and twenty years ahead of his time.

Gopalan laid down the mutual exclusivity theory which was followed for 20 years in various judgments till it was overruled by the *Bank Nationalisation* case.

How would this mutual exclusivity theory apply to property rights under the *Bank Nationalisation* case? Article 31 permitted the acquisition of property for a public purpose. At the same time, Article 19(1)(f), deleted in 1978,[19] conferred the fundamental right to acquire, hold and dispose of property. Article 19(5) enabled the State to impose restrictions on this right. The Union of India took the plea, on the basis of *Gopalan's* case, that when property was acquired, the restrictions imposed under Article 19(5) would have no application. If the property had been acquired, the court could only examine whether the provisions of Article 31 had been complied with. The question of the fundamental right to hold property under Article 19(1)(f) would automatically cease as soon as the property had been acquired. In other words, acquisition of property would be governed only by Article 31 and Article 19 had no application at all.

The mutual exclusivity theory was closely examined in the *Bank Nationalisation* case in the context of a few earlier cases. In 1960, Subba Rao J.[20] observed that Article 31 contemplated acquisition of

19. Articles 19(1)(f) and 31, that dealt with the right to property, were omitted by the Constitution (Forty-fourth Amendment) Act, 1978.
20. *K.K. Kochuni v. State of Madras*, AIR 1960 SC 1080 : [1960] 3 SCR 887.

property by 'authority of law' which meant authority of a *valid* law. Such a law could not violate other fundamental rights. Now, there were two divergent lines of authority. One view was that a law of acquisition could be tested on the ground that it violated other fundamental rights including the right to property under Article 19(1)(f). The other view was that the law of acquisition could not be questioned on the ground that it violated Article 19(1)(f).

The majority in *Bank Nationalisation* case rightly held that the theory of 'mutual exclusivity' was based on an improper understanding of the protection guaranteed by fundamental rights. According to them, such protection was determined by the nature of the right, the interest of the aggrieved party and the degree of harm resulting from State action. This view taken by the majority was a definitive and important break from the earlier pronouncements, where the Supreme Court had held that the extent of this protection was circumscribed by the object behind the State action. If a law of acquisition permitted the deprivation of property without granting any hearing to the person whose property was compulsorily acquired, the law would be struck down as violating Article 19(1)(f). It may be added that if the law of acquisition seeks to acquire only a few properties in a particular area and deliberately omits other properties which are similarly placed, the law of acquisition can be challenged as violating Article 14. Therefore, the mutual exclusivity theory was flawed and ignored the inter-dependence of fundamental rights.

The Supreme Court thus overruled the 20 year old rule of mutual exclusivity laid down in *Gopalan's* case. The theory of mutual exclusivity was rightly rejected and this paved the way for all the fundamental rights being considered together. Eight years later, in *Maneka Gandhi's* case,[21] the Supreme Court held that Articles 14, 19 and 21 formed an inter-linked and composite code, thereby protecting the citizens from any sort of unfair, unreasonable or arbitrary action by the State. The *Maneka Gandhi* judgment extensively relied on the *Bank Nationalisation* case and expanded the frontiers of judicial review. The heavily criticized *Bank Nationalisation* case thus became the basis for a completely new approach to fundamental rights. This new approach has also vastly expanded the power of the High Courts under Article 226.

---

21. *Maneka Gandhi v. Union of India,* AIR 1978 SC 597 : (1978) 1 SCC 248.

Compensation – The Achilles' heel of the Government's case

The payment of compensation was the major source of friction between the Central and State Legislatures on the one hand and the Supreme Court and the High Courts on the other. Ever since independence, several legislative initiatives for acquisition of property were struck down by the Supreme Court and the High Courts on the ground of inadequate compensation. Article 31(2) placed two major restrictions on the power of the State to acquire private property: first, such acquisition had to be for a public purpose and, secondly, compensation had to be paid for the same. The *Bank Nationalisation* case was fought and won by making full use of the second limitation. In retrospect, a large amount of judicial time would have been saved if adequate compensation had been paid. The fact that land is being acquired for a public purpose does not justify the payment of a paltry or illusory sum as compensation. If land is acquired at a fraction of its cost, it is not acquisition but State plunder.

As already stated, this was not the first case where the issue of compensation was fatal to the case of the State Government. In *State of West Bengal v. Bela Banerjee,*[22] the Supreme Court interpreted the expression 'compensation' as used in Article 31(2) to mean 'full indemnification'. The Parliament responded to this judgment with the Constitution (Fourth Amendment) Act, 1955, thereby clarifying that inadequacy of compensation could not be used to challenge laws providing for acquisition of private property. Despite this, the Supreme Court, in *P. Vajravelu Mudaliar v. Special Deputy Collector, Madras,*[23] as well as some other decisions,[24] held that the expression 'compensation' in Article 31(2) continued to mean 'just equivalent' even after this amendment. Further confusion was caused when the Court, in *State of Gujarat v. Shantilal Mangaldas,*[25] held that the compensation, which was fixed or determined using the principles specified by the Legislature, was not open to challenge on the somewhat indefinite plea that it failed to meet the standard of a just or fair equivalent. Going by this

---

22. [1954] SCR 538 : AIR 1954 SC 170.
23. [1965] 1 SCR 614 : AIR 1965 SC 1017. Hereinafter referred to as Vajravelu Mudaliar.
24. See *Union of India v. The Metal Corporation of India Ltd.,* AIR 1967 SC 637 : [1967] 1 SCR 255; *Lachhman Dass v. Municipal Committee, Jalalabad,* AIR 1969 SC 1126 : [1969] 3 SCR 645.
25. (1969) 1 SCC 509 : [1969] 3 SCR 341. Hereinafter referred to as *Shantilal Mangaldas.*

judgment, only the principles for determination of compensation could be challenged as being irrelevant.

Thus, the Court, in the *Bank Nationalisation* case, had to choose between expansive judicial review, as brought in by the 'just equivalent' test, and a narrower review, as propounded in *Shantilal Mangaldas*. Without making this choice, the majority held that the Acquisition Act was liable to be struck down as it failed to provide compensation based on relevant principles. This test, according to the majority, was accepted by both *Vajravelu Mudaliar* as well as *Shantilal Mangaldas*. However, the majority also felt that the broad object underlying the principle of valuation was to give the owner an equivalent of his property, with its existing advantages and potentialities. From this observation, as well as the factual grounds adduced by the majority for its conclusion, it is quite evident that they preferred the principle laid down in *Vajravelu Mudaliar*. It was squarely due to this approach taken by the Supreme Court, whereby they rendered the Constitution (Fourth Amendment) Act, 1955 ineffective for all practical purposes, that this case came to symbolise the growing rift between the judiciary and the legislature.

There was really no need to try and reconcile these two decisions. Although the quantum of compensation could not be challenged, *Shantilal Mangaldas* clearly laid down that 'principles' could be challenged on the ground that they were irrelevant to the determination of compensation. The principles which were laid down in the Acquisition Act satisfied these tests as they were truly irrelevant and absurd. As pointed out below, the majority clearly and rightly found several principles for determining the compensation as being irrelevant and thus unconstitutional. The *Bank Nationalisation* case could have struck down the Acquisition Act even on the basis of the tests laid down by *Shantilal Mangaldas*.

The majority observed that the Acquisition Act, instead of valuing the entire undertaking as a unit, provided for determination of the value of only some of the components that constituted the undertaking. It also prescribed different methods for valuing each such component. This method, in the opinion of the majority, was *prima facie* not relevant to the determination of compensation for the whole undertaking. In their view, it was an important principle of valuation that the acquired property be valued as a unit, and not as an aggregate of the value of different components constituting this unit. They felt that the Acquisition Act was liable to be struck down purely on this ground.

A summary of the absurd and wholly unjustified principles laid down for payment of compensation in the Ordinance and the subsequent Acquisition Act is as follows:

(i) There was no provision for valuing the entire undertaking as a unit but only a provision for valuing some of the components that constituted an undertaking.

(ii) Goodwill of the banks was not even included as an asset for the purpose of valuation.

(iii) There was no compensation for the rent paid for the unexpired period for long term lease entered into by the banks.

(iv) Value of land and buildings was deemed to be twelve times of the annual rent or reasonably expected rent. Due to several States having rent control legislation, there was an absurdly low ceiling limit on the rent chargeable for buildings. Thus, payment of twelve times of the annual rental value had no connection whatsoever with the value of the acquired property.

(v) Interest payable on certain mortgages and capital charges were to be deducted twice for determining the quantum of compensation – first, while fixing the value of assets and secondly, under the head 'liabilities'. This obviously resulted in unfair deduction of compensation payable to the banks.

(vi) Palkhivala was able to demonstrate that if a building had been mortgaged and partly let-out, the formula prescribed for payment of compensation would actually result in a *negative value.*

(vii) The total compensation that was determined after applying these irrational principles was then *payable after ten years.*

All these factors, the majority observed, contributed to the determination of compensation based on irrelevant principles, replying in this manner to the submission by the Attorney-General that these factors merely rendered the compensation inadequate. They also concluded that Sections 4, 5 and 6 of the Acquisition Act, read with Schedule II, which provided for the statutory transfer and vesting of the undertaking of these banks in newly created banks, and the method for determining compensation, were void as they impaired the fundamental guarantee of 'compensation' under Article 31(2). Since these provisions were not severable from the rest of the Act, the entire Act was thereby declared void.

Violation of rights to equality and to carry on business

The Acquisition Act prohibited the nationalised banks from carrying on banking business. This could not be challenged as violating their right to carry on business in banking; under the Constitution, the State could always create a partial or complete monopoly. Until recently, the petroleum industry was completely nationalized whilst the power sector had a partial monopoly – with a few private sector units which were permitted to generate power. But the ban on banking business violated the right to equality under Article 14. The Supreme Court observed that while the fourteen banks were prohibited from doing banking business, other banks, including foreign banks, could continue to carry on banking business in India and abroad. There was also no bar on new banks being formed. The Union of India, in its affidavit, had made no serious attempt to explain why the fourteen named banks should be subject to this disability. The court accepted Palkhivala's argument that this was a 'flagrantly hostile discrimination' that 'impaired' the guarantee of equality.

The fourteen banks were magnanimously permitted to carry on 'non-banking business'. As companies, the fourteen banks were prohibited from using the words 'bank' or 'banking' in their corporate name. The nationalised banks found themselves in a pathetic situation. They were deprived of their entire assets, including their premises, their corporate names, their managerial and other staff and the pitiful compensation that was payable was to be received after *ten years.* The court had no hesitation in holding that the 'theoretical right' to carry on business was an 'empty formality' and was liable to be struck down as being unreasonable.

The court also agreed with Palkhivala's submission that the Acquisition Act violated the right to equality under Article 14 as it prohibited these 14 banks from carrying on the business of banking, when other existent banks as well as newly created banks could very well carry on this business. According to the majority, this was a clear disability cast upon these banks. They felt that a rational explanation for this was imperative, especially since the Union had conceded that these banks had, by their superior management, established an extensive business organization with each bank having more than Rs. 50 crores of deposits. On failing to see any such explanation in the affidavits of the Union, they struck down Section 15(2)(e) of the Acquisition Act as unconstitutional and held that flagrantly hostile discrimination was being practised when, after acquiring the assets, undertaking, organization, goodwill and the names of these 14 banks, they were prohibited from carrying on banking business whereas other banks, Indian as well as foreign, were permitted to do so. This was an excellent example of the 'effect' test in operation, as the majority used Article 19(1)(g) against the restrictions on non-banking business activities, and Article 14 to strike down the legal prohibition on banking business.

Object and effect test

Another important point that was decided in the *Bank Nationalisation* case was the 'effect test'. The assumption in *A.K. Gopalan's case* was that the *object* of State action alone had to be considered while examining the infringement of guaranteed fundamental rights. This was held to be incorrect and the effect of laws on fundamental rights could not be ignored. The *object and effect* test also demonstrated the inter-dependence of fundamental rights. The object of a law may be to achieve a particular fundamental right but in doing so, the *effect* may be the contravention of another fundamental right. The court then has to examine the inter-dependence of these rights and decide the validity of State action. Thus, if a person has been detained in accordance with the prescribed procedure and his detention is lawful, he cannot complain of losing his right to move freely throughout the territory of India. The same is the position of a person who is jailed for committing a crime. Similarly, if the relevant law for acquiring property for a public purpose is valid in terms of Article 31 and gives full opportunity to the owner of property before deciding the quantum of compensation, the person whose property is acquired cannot complain of losing his (erstwhile) right to property. The majority in the *Bank Nationalisation* case thus accepted Palkhivala's contention that emphasis had to be placed on the 'effect' of State action. This 'effect' test, as propounded by the majority, has thereafter been used in several decisions for testing the validity of State action. It is precisely due to this 'object and effect test' that the *Bank*

Nationalisation case has attained a status of permanence in Indian constitutional jurisprudence.[26]

Nationalisation upheld

Contrary to popular belief, the Supreme Court upheld the right of the Union and State Governments to nationalize banks, or, for that matter any industry. Palkhivala tried to demonstrate that commercial banks had achieved much better results than the Government-owned State Bank of India and its subsidiaries. A comparison was sought to be made with the banking structure in countries like Canada, Japan, France, U.S and U.K. The Attorney-General of India had submitted that nationalisation was necessary to ensure that the banking sector played a greater role, particularly in the rural areas. It was submitted that major banks catered only to large scale industries. The court refused to consider the relative merits of different political theories or economic policies. The majority rejected the plea that nationalisation was not in the larger interest of the nation. It held that there was no satisfactory proof that nationalisation would serve political ends.

Palkhivala had argued that the selection of these fourteen banks from the very many banking institutions in the country, for the purpose of compulsory acquisition, was liable to be struck down as hostile discrimination since there was no reasonable nexus between this classification and the object of the Act. He presented voluminous data before the Court to show how even the acquisition of all private banks in India would not suffice to substantially serve the needs of development of the national economy. The Attorney-General countered this by resorting to the Directive Principles of State Policy, and submitted that the policy of the Union was to control the concentration of private economic resources. These fourteen banks were selected as they had larger business and wider coverage, larger organization, better managerial resources, and better trained and equipped employees, when compared to the other banks. The majority refused to express an

26. In this process, the majority overruled the judgment in *Gopalan's* case, and held as follows:

'In our judgment, the assumption in *A K. Gopalan's case that certain articles in the Constitution exclusively deal with specific matters and in determining whether there is infringement of the individual's guaranteed rights, the object and the form of the State action alone need be considered and effect of the laws on fundamental rights of the individuals in general will be ignored, cannot be accepted as correct.*' See *R.C. Cooper v. Union of India,* AIR 1970 SC 564, 597.

opinion on this contention raised by Palkhivala because of the insufficiency of reliable data for arriving at a decision on this point.

Palkhivala raised another interesting argument and claimed that the nationalisation was wholly irrational as it penalized efficiency and good management. Section 36AE of the Banking Regulation Act, 1949 conferred power on the Central Government to acquire the undertakings of banking companies that were badly managed but the fourteen nationalized banks had complied with all the directives of the Reserve Bank of India. The banks that were nationalized were just the opposite of those that were contemplated under the law to be acquired. The Supreme Court merely said: 'We need express no opinion on this part of the argument'.

A misunderstood decision

The decision in the *Bank Nationalisation* case is much misunderstood. Socialists and communists viewed this judgment only in the context of the 'class struggle'. At that time, it was thought that nationalisation was a panacea for most social evils and the judiciary was a hindrance in the way of social reforms. It had also become fashionable to criticize the judges. The Marxist Chief Minister of Kerala, E.M.S. Namboodiripad remarked that judges 'were guided and dominated by class hatred, class interests and class prejudices; where the evidence is balanced between a well-dressed pot-bellied rich man and the poor ill-dressed and illiterate person, the judges would instinctively favour the former. The judiciary was weighed against workers, peasants and other section of the working classes and it essentially served the exploiting classes. Even though the judiciary was separated from the executive, it was still subject to the influence and pressure of the executive.'[27]

Socialism, in retrospect, has been disastrous to our country's economy and almost led India to bankruptcy. Indeed, socialism

27. *E.M.S. Namboodripad v. T.N. Nambiar,* AIR 1970 SC 2015 : (1970) 2 SCC 325. It was supremely ironical for a Marxist Chief Minister to speak about the judiciary being influenced by the executive. In no communist regime in the world has there been an independent judiciary. Every Communist State has been totalitarian with complete absence of the rule of law. These remarks of the former Chief Minister led to a contempt petition. The Chief Minister was found guilty of contempt by the Kerala High Court but the fine was substantially reduced to Rs. 50/- by the Supreme Court because Justice Hidayatullah observed that the ends of justice were substantially met by exposing Namboodripad's misunderstanding of the true teaching of Marx and Engles. Hidayatullah extensively refer to several sources to prove that Namboodripad had not properly understood Marxism! This was a tangential argument not relevant to the question of whether the Chief Minister had committed contempt.

and State control of industry has dismally failed throughout the world. The entire economic miracle of China has been possible only by encouragement of the private sector. However, socialism was a popular philosophy at that time and it was the right of the elected Government to choose a socialistic path. But socialism does not justify payment of compensation based on absurd principles. Valuing property at twelve times the annual rent in Bombay (Mumbai) would not even make up one-hundreth of its market value. And even this paltry compensation was to be paid in bonds that matured after ten years! The Supreme Court, therefore, rightly struck down the Act on the manner in which the compensation was to be paid but upheld the right of the State to nationalize banks.

After this decision, Mrs. Gandhi called for elections and led the Congress party to a stunning victory. This was taken as the mandate of the people to further pursue the socialistic agenda. Article 31(2) was further amended and the word '*compensation*' was replaced by the word '*amount*'. Compensation meant a just equivalent but 'amount' would mean 'a sum of money' – which could be anything. Flush with victory, several more amendments were made including the highly controversial Article 31C which sought to prohibit judicial scrutiny of any law if it merely contained a declaration that the law was intended to give effect to the directive principles of State policy. This has been dealt with in great detail in the *Kesavananda Bharathi* case.

Re-enactment of the Bank Nationalisation Act

After this decision, the Parliament re-enacted the Bank Nationalisation Act and an additional sum of Rs. 58 crores was paid to the fourteen banks. In his book, '*Legend of Palkhivala*', M.R. Pai wrote that not even one bank wrote a 'thank you' letter to Palkhivala for all the effort that he had put in. The entire controversy could have been avoided in the first place even if an extra Rs. 50 crores had been paid to the banks or if more reasonable yardsticks to determine compensation had been adopted. More importantly, the confrontation with the judiciary could have been avoided.

The details of the compensation eventually paid are set out in the autobiography of Justice P. Jaganmohan Reddy who was in the majority that struck down certain provisions relating to compensation. The details of the compensation paid, as given in his autobiography, are as follows:

Second Schedule to the Banking Companies (Acquisition and Transfer of Undertakings) Act, 1970

Name of the Existing Bank	Amount of Compensation (Rs. in lakhs)
The Central Bank of India Ltd.	1750
The Bank of India Ltd.	1470
The Punjab National Bank Ltd.	1020
The Bank of Baroda Ltd.	840
The United Commercial Bank Ltd.	830
Canara Bank Ltd.	360
United Bank of India Ltd.	420
Dena Bank Ltd.	360
Syndicate Bank Ltd.	360
Union Bank of India Ltd.	310
Allahabad Bank Ltd.	310
The Indian Bank Ltd.	230
The Bank of Maharashtra Ltd.	230
The Indian Overseas Bank Ltd.	250
	87.40 crores

In Chapter 16 of his book,[28] Justice Reddy deals with the *Bank Nationalisation* case and points out the factors that led to the majority holding certain provisions relating to compensation as unconstitutional. Justice Reddy points out that Justice J.C. Shah had prepared the draft decision of the majority and this was circulated to all judges. They had several conferences at Justice Shah's house and the draft was gone into in great detail. All the judges debated the draft for hours and extensively edited it. Justice Ray who delivered dissenting judgment, had also participated in these deliberations.

Justice Reddy also refers to an interesting controversy. The 11 Judge Bench was presided over by Justice J.C. Shah. This was because Chief Justice Hidayatullah, as acting President, had signed

28. P. Jaganmohan Reddy, *The Judiciary I Served*, Orient Longman, (1999) pp. 171-182.

the Ordinance and, therefore, did not hear the case. At the commencement of the arguments, Justice Sikri informed the Attorney-General Niren De, that he had a few shares in one of the nationalized banks and asked whether there was any objection to his being part of the Bench. The Attorney-General replied that there was no objection but later when the judgment went against the Govenment, this issue was raked up before Parliament! Chief Justice Hidayatullah and the Speaker of the Lok Sabha, G.S. Dhillon amicably resolved the dispute.

In retrospect, it is indeed deeply unfortunate that so much of bitterness should have been generated between the judiciary and the legislature over the payment of just Rs. 87.4 crores to all banks.

The shareholders gained little but the hostility of the then ruling Government towards the judiciary that began with *Golak Nath* further increased with the *Bank Nationalisation* case. After *Golak Nath* and *Bank Nationalisation*, the relationship between the judiciary and Mrs. Gandhi became even more strained. The *Privy Purses* case made matters even worse and we shall shortly turn to this case. The strained relations continued for several years culminating in supersession and arbitrary transfers of judges.

❋

(iv)

The Privy Purses Case

A Constitutional Betrayal

The historic verdict in the *Bank Nationalization* case was pronounced on February 10, 1970. Less than a year later, the Supreme Court delivered another major ruling on constitutional law – it declared the Presidential Order de-recognising the Princes as unconstitutional. The abolition of privy purses was perhaps one of the most shameful episodes in our constitutional history. No one can forgive a Government that reneges on solemn assurances made in its Constitution.

The pre-independence background

The policy of annexation initiated by Lord Dalhousie resulted in large parts of undivided India becoming part of the territories of the East India Company. The company installed a Resident in each of the conquered States that accepted a 'subsidiary alliance'. Lord Dalhousie also applied the 'Doctrine of lapse' to annexe the States of Satara, Nagpur, Jhansi, Sambalpur, Bhagat and other States. The policy of annexation brought in its wake large scale corruption. During the Mutiny of 1857, most of the Indian rulers did not support the uprising but several rulers actively assisted the British. V.P. Menon, in his excellent book,[1] refers to Lord Canning's acknowledgement of the role of the States as 'breakwaters in the storm which would have swept over us in one great wave'. The policy of annexation was replaced by assuring the rulers that their rights, dignity and honour would be preserved. The Princes were given the power to adopt heirs according to their own customs, although this was subject to approval by the British Government. The policy of annexation was formally buried as was made clear in the proclamation of 1858:

---

1. V.P. Menon, *Integration of the Indian States*, Orient Longman Ltd., (1956), p. 10.

> *We desire no extension of our present territorial possessions; and while we will permit no aggression upon our dominions or our rights to be attempted with impunity, we shall sanction no encroachment on those of others. We shall respect the rights, dignity, and honour of Native Princes as our own; and we desire that they as well as our own subjects should enjoy that prosperity and that social advancement which can only be secured by internal peace and good government.*

The princely States thus became an integral part of the British Empire and were treated as territories under the direct domination of the Crown. Lord Canning wrote:

> *The territories under the sovereignty of the Crown became at once as important and as integral a part of India as territories under its direct domination. Together they form one direct care and the political system which the Moghuls had not completed and the Mahrattas never contemplated is now an established fact and history.*[2]

Legally, the princely States were not a part of British India and inhabitants of these States were not treated as British subjects. In theory, the Princes were sovereign rulers of their own States. In practice, they were completely subordinate to the British Government. Menon cites several examples of encroachment into the so-called internal sovereignty of the rulers. He writes:

> *The ruler thus did not inherit his gaddi as of right, but as a gift from the paramount power. This, coupled with the right of the Crown to regulate the status and salutes of the rulers and to confer titles and decorations, had the effect of binding the rulers more closely to the Crown.*[3]

By 1947, the princely States covered 48% of the area of the Indian Dominion and formed 28% of its total population. The Indian Independence Act, 1947 provided for the lapse of paramountcy of the British crown in India over the Indian States and each Ruler had the option of either acceding to the dominion of India or Pakistan or to continue as an independent sovereign State. If the rulers had not joined the Union of India, the country would have consisted of the major Presidencies of Madras, Bombay and Calcutta and the Chief Commissioners Provinces as

---

2. V.P. Menon, *Integration of the Indian States*, Orient Longman Ltd., (1956), p.11.
3. *Ibid* at p. 13.

independent India on the one hand, and the princely States on the other. Free India would have had no control over these princely States as independent mini-states. Sardar Patel understood that in the absence of a peaceful and friendly settlement with the Princes, there would be confusion and turmoil. After the horror of partition, stability was the most important need and the only option was to negotiate an amicable settlement with the rulers.

Efforts of Sardar Patel and V.P. Menon

V.P. Menon was the Constitutional Advisor to Lord Mountbatten. At a meeting of Lord Mountbatten with the leaders of the Congress and the Muslim League, a new 'States Department' was set up which had one minister from the Congress and the other from the Muslim League. Pandit Nehru suggested the name of Sardar Patel and Jinnah suggested Abdur Rab Nishtar. Looking back, Panditji could not have appointed a better person. Menon recounts the Herculean efforts made by Sardar Patel to persuade the rulers to join the Indian Union. This long-drawn process of negotiations between the Union and these rulers finally culminated in the creation of a geographically unified India. The rulers signed Instruments of Merger, Instruments of Accession, or formed themselves into Unions or 'United States' by signing common covenants, with the Unions in turn signing the Instruments of Accession. In the end, 552 of the 555 erstwhile States formed part of the Indian Union through one of these means.[4] C. Rajagopalachari signed the Instruments of Accession as the Governor-General of India.

The details of this integration of the princely States into the Dominion of India are set out in Menon's book. Fifty two years after it was written, it still remains spellbinding.

From the beginning, the Princes were worried about their rights and privileges. In February, 1947, Pandit Nehru assured these rulers that the monarchical form of Government or the integrity of the States would not be touched. Sardar Patel reiterated this guarantee on July 5, 1947 and promised to scrupulously respect their autonomous existence. In a speech to the Chamber of Princes on July 25, 1947, Lord Mountbatten promised that the Central Government would not encroach on the internal autonomy or sovereignty of the States. These assurances eventually persuaded the

---

4. The three notable exceptions were the States of Mysore, Hyderabad, and Jammu and Kashmir.

rulers to agree on integration which would require the surrender of most of their assets and dissolution of the princely States. Menon states that the grant of privy purses was a sort of *quid pro quo* to the rulers in return for handing over to the dominion of India their States unconditionally and for ever.

Privy purses – What the Princes got and what they gave up

The privy purses were fixed on the basis of a formula whereby a ruler whose State had an annual revenue of Rs. 15 lakhs would get an annual privy purse of Rs. 1,30,000/-, about 8.5% of the annual revenue. Out of 554 States, over 450 had annual revenues of less than Rs. 15 lakhs. For larger States, privy purses were fixed on an *ad hoc* basis. They were:

Gwalior (Rs. 25 lakh), Indore (Rs. 15 lakh), Patiala (Rs. 17 lakh), Baroda (Rs. 26.5 lakh), Jaipur (Rs. 18 lakh), Jodhpur (Rs. 17.5 lakh), Bikaner (Rs. 17 lakh), Travancore (Rs. 18 lakh), Bhopal (Rs. 11 lakh), Mysore (Rs. 26 lakh) and Hyderabad (Rs. 50 lakh in Hyderabad currency equal to Rs. 43 lakhs in Indian currency).[5]

In contrast, 396 rulers drew below Rs. 50,000/- per annum. 22 small States in Vindhya Pradesh drew less than Rs. 700/- per month. The least was the ruler of Katodia in Saurashtra who drew Rs. 192/- per annum – Rs. 16 per month! The privy purses were to cover all the expenses of the ruler and his family. The ruler had to maintain his family and other staff within this amount. Moreover, the successors to the individual *gaddi* (throne) would only get such amount as would be decided by the Government of India. The total cost to the Indian exchequer was less than Rs. 6 crores in 1947 and this was reduced to Rs. 4 crores by 1970 when the purses were sought to be abolished. Menon remarked that the privy purses were fixed for 554 States on 'an equitable basis within a remarkably short period and without recourse even of a single case to arbitration. This was due in large measure to the accommodating spirit shown by the rulers and the local ministry concerned'.[6]

In return, the rulers had surrendered several villages, thousands of acres of scattered areas of *jagir* land, palaces, museums, buildings, aeroplanes and cash balances and investments amounting to Rs. 77 crores. In addition, was the railway system of about 12,000 miles which the States had surrendered to the Centre

5. V.P. Menon, *Integration of the Indian States*, Orient Longman Ltd., 1956, p.550.
6. *Ibid* at p. 555.

without any compensation. On 12th October, 1949, Sardar Patel informed the Constituent Assembly that the cash assets given by the rulers of Madhya Bharat alone were sufficient, if invested, to cover the payment of privy purses to all Princes. *The payments made to the Princes were one-fourth of what they had earlier enjoyed.*[7] (emphasis supplied)

Objections by Congressmen

From the beginning, members of the Congress party were reluctant to give anything to the former rulers. Most of the rulers had done little to support the freedom struggle and they were looked upon, perhaps rightly, as lackeys and stooges of the British Empire. In the Constituent Assembly, several Congressmen had objected to the payment of privy purses to the rulers who had clearly supported the British Government and not sympathised with the freedom struggle.[8] To many freedom fighters, the rulers had betrayed their cause and there was no reason to give any amount to them. As explained above, it was Sardar Patel who took the initiative of persuading the Constituent Assembly to permit the payment of privy purses and guarantee the same in the Constitution. While commending the adoption of Article 291 to the Constituent Assembly, he remarked:

> *The privy purse settlements are therefore in the nature of consideration for the surrender by the rulers of all their ruling powers and also for the dissolution of the States as separate units... Need we cavil then at the small – I purposely use the word small – price we have paid for the bloodless revolution which has affected the destinies of millions of our people? ...*
>
> *The capacity for mischief and trouble on the part of the rulers if the settlement with them would not have been reached on a negotiated basis was far greater than could be imagined at this stage. Let us do justice to them; let us place ourselves in their position and then assess the value of their sacrifice. The rulers have now discharged their part of the obligations by transferring all ruling powers by agreeing to*

7. Speech made in the Constituent Assembly by Sardar Patel dated 12.10.1949. See *Constituent Assembly Debates,* Vol. X .
8. A number of Congress members of the Constituent Assembly tried to have them annulled. For details on this divide, *see* Granville Austin, *Working a Democratic Constitution, The Indian Experience,* Oxford University Press (1999), pp. 220- 222.

the integration of their States. The main part of our obligation under these agreements is to ensure that the guarantee given by us in respect of privy purses are fully implemented. Our failure to do so would be a breach of faith and seriously prejudice the stabilisation of the new order.[9]

Constitutional safeguards

The rulers had signed Instruments of Merger and Instruments of Accession before 1950. The assurances given by the Government of the Dominion of India were set out in Articles 291[10] and 362.[11] The privy purses were thus constitutionally guaranteed and charged on the Consolidated Fund of India. Under Article 114(2), parliament cannot vary or alter any amount that is charged on the Consolidated Fund. The privy purses were also exempted from all taxes. In 1949, Pandit Nehru wrote to Sardar Patel stating that he was 'a little surprised and taken aback' that the privy purses were tax free and payable in perpetuity.

Post-independence – Objections once again

After independence, Congressmen once again questioned the need for payment of privy purses. In the 1950s, Pandit Nehru wrote to the rulers asking them to 'voluntarily' reduce the privy purse. This itself was highly objectionable; once a promise had been

---

9. Speech made in the Constituent Assembly by Sardar Patel dated 12.10.1949. See *Constituent Assembly Debates,* Vol. X.
10. Article 291 of the Constitution provided: 291. Privy Purse sums of rulers.–(1) Where under any covenant or agreement entered into by the Ruler of any Indian State before the commencement of this Constitution, the payment of any sums, free of tax, has been guaranteed or assured by the Government of the Dominion of India to any Ruler of such State as privy purse.
    (a) such sums shall be charged on, and paid out of, the Consolidated Fund of India; and
    (b) the sums so paid to any Ruler shall be exempt from all taxes on income.
    (2) Where the territories of any such Indian State as aforesaid are comprised within a State specified in Part A or Part B of the First Schedule, there shall be charged on, and paid out of, the Consolidated Fund of that State such contribution, if any, in respect of the payments made by the Government of India under clause (1) and for such period as may, subject to any agreement entered into in that behalf under clause (1) of Article 278, be determined by Order of the President.'
11. Article 362 provided: '362. Rights and privileges of Rulers of Indian States.—In the exercise of the power of Parliament or of the Legislature of a State to make laws, or in the exercise of the executive power of the Union or of a State, due regard shall be had to the guarantee or assurance given under any such covenant or agreement as is referred to in clause (1) of Article 291 with respect to the personal rights, privileges and dignities of the Ruler of an Indian State.'

made and given effect to by specific provisions in the Constitution, it was wholly inappropriate to request any kind of reduction in the quantum of privy purse.

In the early 1960s, several leaders of the Congress yet again proposed abolition of the privy purses and privileges given to the rulers. To the credit of Pandit Nehru, he rejected this proposal on the ground that the Government should not break its promise. He also pointed out that the expenditure on privy purses was diminishing. Thus, a formal resolution moved at the Bhubhaneswar convention of the Congress party was rejected. This shows that Pandit Nehru preserved the sanctity of the Constitution and did not countenance any proposal for abolishing the privy purses. After Pandit Nehru and Lal Bahadur Shastri, respect for constitutional conventions died. Before 1967, the policy of the Government was kept within the framework of the Constitution. After 1967, the framework of the Constitution was sought to be brought within the framework or the policy of the ruling party.

V.P. Menon rightly criticised the repeated attempts to go back on the solemn assurances made to the former rulers. He observed:

> *The merger agreements and covenants are bilateral documents. As Sardar very rightly remarked, the rulers discharged their part of the contract by surrendering their States and powers. They are now bereft of any bargaining power. Because a creditor is too weak or poor to enforce his rights, a debtor should not, in honour, refuse to discharge his debt. As an honourable party to an agreement, we cannot take the stand that we shall accept only that part of the settlement which confers rights on us, and repudiate or whittle down that part which defines our obligations. As a nation aspiring to give a moral lead to the world, let it not be said of us that we know the 'price of everything, and the value of nothing'.*
>
> *After integration, the rulers settled down and adjusted themselves to the new order of things. By reopening the question of the privy purse we are again unsettling them.*

The final step to abolish the privy purses was perhaps prompted by the fact that most of the Princes had joined the Swatantra Party headed by Rajagopalachari. In the 1967 elections, many of them stood against Congress candidates and defeated them.[12]

12. In Jaipur, Maharani Gayatri Devi defeated her Congress rival by over 4 lakh votes. This was a Guinness Book record.

Indira Gandhi, the new Prime Minister was therefore determined to abolish the privy purses. On 25th June, 1967, the All India Congress Committee passed a resolution to abolish the privy purses. The Government of India was prepared for a 'negotiated settlement' on the basis of which the abolition should take place. The Concord of Princes were not prepared to enter into any negotiations and were rightly worried that any such fresh settlement would be broken just as simply as past solemn assurances.

Fiasco in Parliament

Mrs. Indira Gandhi was in no mood to relent and her Government introduced the Constitution (Twenty-fourth Amendment) Bill, 1970 on 2nd September, 1970. As Parliament could not vary or alter the privy purses, the only step was to delete Articles 291 and 362. The ostensible objective of this Bill was to build an 'egalitarian social order'. If this Bill was passed, the two Articles 291 and 362 would stand deleted and, at one stroke, the payment of privy purses would be immediately stopped. The Lok Sabha passed the Bill with a good majority – 332:154 votes. Unfortunately for Mrs. Gandhi, the Bill failed to muster the requisite 2/3rd majority and on September 5, 1970, it was defeated in the Rajya Sabha – 149:75. This was a serious embarrassment to the ruling party. But having abandoned all sense of constitutional propriety, the Cabinet met that evening and it was decided to advise the President to withdraw the recognition granted to the rulers. Rumour has it that the Presidential Order was sent by a special aircraft to Hyderabad where President Giri was on a visit. At midnight, the President signed separate but identical orders, withdrawing the recognition of all rulers. As a sample, the order issued to the Maharaja of Gwalior is reproduced:

> *In exercise of the powers vested in him under Article 366(22) of the Constitution, the President hereby directs that with effect from the date of this Order His Highness Maharajadhiraja Madhav Rao Jiwaji Rao Scindia Bahadur do cease to be recognised as the Ruler of Gwalior.*
>
> *By order and in the name of*
> *the President*
> *Sd. L.P. SINGH*
> *(L.P.SINGH)*
> *Secretary to the Government of India'*

Separate orders were issued to all rulers on September 6, 1970 and an appropriate notification was issued in the Official Gazette on September 19, 1970. Although the constitutional guarantee could not be abrogated, the payment of privy purses was discontinued by resort to Article 366(22). This provision was never intended to be indirectly used to abolish the privy purses. The power was reserved to the President to recognise or not to recognise a ruler in exceptional circumstances. Therefore, a Prince was the person recognised by the Government of India as a Ruler of a particular State. This was similar to the power which had been exercised by the Viceroy. What could not be done directly by a constitutional amendment was sought to be done indirectly by an executive order passed by a rubber stamp President. The signing of the Presidential Order on September 6, 1970 marks the most shameful date in the constitutional history of India.

The decision of the Supreme Court in *Madhav Rao Scindia v. Union of India,*[13] more popularly known as the *Privy Purses* judgment, was in large measure a product of the effort and perseverance of Nani Palkhivala, who ever so passionately defended the sanctity of the promise given to the erstwhile rulers of this land. The forensic arguments as well as the clear reasoning adopted by both the counsel and the judges of the Supreme Court make it one of the best constitutional law cases ever decided by the Indian Supreme Court. Shri C. Rajagopalachari's observations on this judgment rightly sum up its significance and are worth quoting here: 'The Supreme Court has, if I may say so respectfully, justified its existence. It has saved India's honour. The Court has justified the people's confidence in it as an impregnable bulwark for safeguarding justice and democracy against authoritarianism.'

It was with the Constitution coming into force that the rights of the rulers gained an elevated status in the form of specific constitutional provisions such as Articles 291 and 362. Though these provisions did not spell out in detail the privileges and payment particulars, the rulers finally had an assurance more concrete in nature when compared to the covenants and instruments signed by them. This in turn led to the above-mentioned writ petitions filed by Madhav Rao Scindia and the other Princes before the Supreme Court.

---

13. (1971) 1 SCC 85 : AIR 1971 SC 530.

De-recognition of Princes challenged in the Supreme Court

The de-recognition of the Princes was challenged by Madhav Rao Scindia,[14] the Maharaja of Gwalior and seven other rulers. All these writ petitions were filed directly before the Supreme Court under Article 32 of the Constitution of India. Surprisingly, Palkhivala had considerable difficulty in getting the writ admitted before the Supreme Court.[15]

In supporting these petitions, Palkhivala contended that rulership itself amounted to property. He also pointed out that the act of de-recognition had led to considerable deprivation of property and personal liberty. The other major contention raised by him, being the one on which the majority of the eleven Supreme Court judges hearing this matter decided in favour of the petitioners, was that the Presidential Order was invalid, and violative of important constitutional provisions. He submitted that Articles 291, 362 and 366(22) of the Constitution formed a single scheme which could not be dislocated by a Presidential Order. Moreover, the Supreme Court, he submitted, had the jurisdiction to decide on this as Article 363[16] was a provision with limited effect, and not a complete bar on any dispute relating to the rulers' privileges as was contended by Niren De, the Attorney–General for India. These arguments need to be examined closely in order to appreciate their clarity and incisiveness.

---

14. Ironically, Madhav Rao Scindia joined the Congress later and became the Minister for Railways. He remained a Congressman till his tragic and early demise in an air crash.
15. Interview with Ravinder Narain, Senior Advocate.
16. Article 363 provides: '363. Bar to interference by courts in disputes arising out of certain treaties, agreements, etc.—(1) Notwithstanding anything in this Constitution but subject to the provisions of Article 143, neither the Supreme Court nor any other court shall have jurisdiction in any dispute arising out of any provision of a treaty, agreement, covenant, engagement, *sanad* or other similar instrument which was entered into or executed before the commencement of this Constitution by any Ruler of an Indian State and to which the Government of the Dominion of India or any of its predecessor Governments was a party and which has or has been continued in operation after such commencement, or in any dispute in respect of any right accruing under or any liability or obligation arising out of any of the provisions of this Constitution relating to any such treaty, agreement, covenant, engagement, *sanad* or other similar instrument.
    (2) In this article:
    (a) 'Indian State' means any territory recognised before the commencement of this Constitution by His Majesty or the Government of the Dominion of India as being such a State; and
    (b) 'Ruler' includes the Prince, Chief or other person recognised before such commencement by His Majesty or the Government of the Dominion of India as the Ruler of any Indian State.'

Palkhivala made full use of the failed attempt by the Government to push through the Constitution (Twenty-fourth Amendment) Bill. It was contended that the presence of Articles 291 and 362 in the Constitution hindered the President from passing any Order such as the one under challenge, and that the legal effect of this Order could be realized only by way of a constitutional amendment. According to him, Articles 291 and 362 in particular, and even the other articles in the Constitution pertaining to the rights of these rulers, continued the obligation of the Government to pay the privy purses and also to recognise the privileges. He explained that it was precisely for this reason that the privy purses stood charged on and were to be paid out of the Consolidated Fund of India, thus barring even parliament from voting upon them. Since these assurances and guarantees were constitutionally provided for, the Executive could not, by an indirect device such as this Order, withdraw the recognition of these rulers and thereby avoid these constitutionally guaranteed obligations. Though the fixation of privy purses and recognition of privileges may have been a historical fact, they were still guaranteed by the Constitution and had to be carried out according to the constitutional provisions. Thus, Palkhivala instead of basing the claims on the agreements or covenants between the Rulers and the Sovereign entered into at or about the time of Independence, founded them upon the constitutional provisions themselves, and argued that the historical reasons for these privileges could not in any way take away the sanctity of the constitutional mandate imprinted upon their continuance. The Presidential Order was therefore contended to be a violation of the spirit and meaning of Articles 366(22), 291 and 362, an affront to Parliament which had rejected the earlier amendment, and a device to indirectly amend the Constitution.

Specifically countering the reliance placed by the Attorney–General on Article 366(22) for deriving the power of de-recognition of rulers, Palkhivala pointed out that the President's power under Article 366(22) was meant to be exercised only for recognising a Ruler at a time and for the time being, or to withdraw recognition from a Ruler for cogent and valid reasons, naming in his place a successor, and not for withdrawing the recognition for all rulers *en masse* for no reason except that the concept of rulership was considered outmoded or that some persons were against its continuance. The mastery over various laws of the land, which Palkhivala had cultivated through years of practice and learning, was displayed when he took these submissions to their logical end by showing how the Presidential Order in fact had the effect of amending and affecting various legislations such as the Wealth Tax Act of 1957, the Gift Tax Act of 1958, the Hindu Succession Act, 1956, the Income Tax Acts of 1922 and 1961, the Estate Duty Act of 1953, the Sea Customs Act of 1878, the Code of Criminal Procedure of 1898, and the Code of Civil Procedure of 1908, all of which conferred certain benefits, exemptions and privileges to the rulers. The fact that these provisions, validly passed by a competent law-making body, were rendered nugatory by a Presidential Order, merely executive in nature, spoke volumes about the legality of this measure.

The Union relied more on political theories than on legal principles to counter these weighty submissions well-rooted in constitutional law. The Attorney-General contended that the Presidential Order was a political act falling outside the purview of judicial scrutiny. He relied on the doctrines of paramountcy of the Indian Union, and 'Act of State', to further this contention. According to him, the bar on jurisdiction of courts contained in Article 363 of the Constitution was the direct fallout of these doctrines. He also raised the plea of state policy in order to defend the Presidential Order. Explaining the effect of Article 291, he submitted that only 'imperfect obligations' were created through this provision. Such obligations according to him were unenforceable by the rulers, and more in the nature of a 'gift' given by the Union of India. If these arguments were correct, it would mean that the President while exercising his executive power on the aid and advice of the Council of Ministers, could in some situations exercise unbridled power with no, or very limited, judicial scrutiny over his action. Precisely due to these arguments, the *Privy Purses* case became an important landmark in Indian constitutional law.

Palkhivala forcefully countered these arguments and submitted that the stand of the Government was totally misconceived and betrayed ignorance both of history and of law. With the coming into force of the Indian Independence Act, 1947, British paramountcy lapsed and both erstwhile British India and the erstwhile Indian States became completely sovereign and independent. The Indian States voluntarily acceded to the Dominion of India and became part of the Republic of India. Thus the Republic of India was an immediate successor to the Dominion of India and the Indian States. At no stage did paramountcy get transferred to the Dominion of India. Besides, paramountcy can only be exercised over other States and not over the so-called rulers who were mere citizens without any state. After 26th January, 1950, the only paramountcy is that of the Constitution. Next, there can be no 'Act of State' against the citizens of a country; it can be exercised only against a foreign state or an alien. Finally, recognition or derecognising of a Ruler was purely a constitutional power and had nothing to do with politics; there was no such thing as a 'political act' outside the Constitution; whatever the Government did had to be within the boundary line drawn by the Constitution. The Constitution did not recognize any 'political power' of the Government to override the Constitution. Palkhivala submitted that the Government could not, in any situation, breach constitutionally binding obligations. Article 291, he argued, was mandatory in nature. This provision created new and independent rights and obligations that were beyond the reach of the legislature and the executive, due to their inclusion in the Constitution. He brought out a clear distinction between the covenants entered into by the rulers, and the guarantee contained in Article 291 to effectively counter the argument raised by the Attorney-General that Article 291 created 'imperfect obligations' which could not be enforced by the rulers. Moreover, the broad exemption from all taxes guaranteed in the various covenants was restricted to an exemption from all taxes on income in Article 291. Thus, the covenants promised several privileges, immunities, benefits, and exemptions to the rulers, while the object of Article 291 was to constitutionally protect and guarantee a certain minimum of these promises.

These distinctions brought out between the covenants on one hand, and Article 291 on the other, were pivotal in overcoming the jurisdictional barrier imposed by Article 363. Article 363 excluded the jurisdiction of the court only in two situations, namely:

(a) in disputes arising out of provisions of any covenant entered into before the commencement of the Constitution by any Ruler, to which the Government of the dominion of India was a party and which had been continuing in operation after the commencement; and

(b) in disputes in respect of any right accruing under, or any liability or obligation arising out of, any of the provisions in the Constitution relating to any such covenant or other similar instrument. The decision hinged on the interpretation of Article 363 because this formidable defence from the Attorney–General, if accepted, would bar the Rulers from seeking any remedy before any court of law.

Palkhivala had convincingly shown that Article 291 was not in the same league as the covenants entered into by the Rulers, and that this dispute was not one arising out of the provisions of any covenant but one pertaining to an independent right which was constitutionally guaranteed. However, for the erstwhile Rulers to succeed, it was still required to show that Article 291 itself was not a constitutional provision 'relating to' any such covenant, and therefore that the second category of jurisdictional bar envisaged in Article 363 was not attracted to the dispute in this case. Though Article 291 did make a reference to the covenants, Palkhivala persuasively explained this seemingly adverse fact by pointing out that this was only for the limited purpose of identifying the privy purses, which in turn were the subject matter of Article 291. In other words, Article 291 could not be branded as 'relating to such covenants' merely because it referred to them for the limited purpose of identifying the privy purses. Moreover, Article 363 being a provision that excludes the jurisdiction of the Supreme Court, Palkhivala argued that it had to be construed strictly. In his submission, any remote connection or reference to the covenants in the relevant constitutional provision would not exclude the jurisdiction of the Supreme Court to grant relief in disputes involving that provision, as the constitutional provision had to be one whose dominant purpose was directly connected with the covenants, for the bar to operate. As an incidental point, a novel submission was raised that Article 363 could anyway be used only for *bonafide* disputes and not for disputes that made a mockery of the Constitution. Therefore, Article 363 had to be construed harmoniously without violating the effect and mandate of Articles 112, 113, 114,[17] 291 and 366(22). Driving the proverbial last nail into the coffin, he submitted that jurisdictional power could not be interpreted in a manner whereby an *ultra vires* act went unchallenged before a court of law. An *ultra vires* action was a nullity in law, and the bar under Article 363 could not be pleaded to protect a nullity. To buttress this final point, he relied on precedents such as *Pratap Singh v. State of Punjab*,[18] *Makhan Singh*

17. On a joint reading of these provisions, the expenses charged on the Consolidated Fund of India, including the privy purses payable under Article 291, shall not be submitted to the vote of Parliament though they are open to discussion in the Parliament.
18. [1964] 4 SCR 773 : AIR 1964 SC 72.

v. State of Punjab,[19] *Ram Manohar Lohia v. State of Bihar,*[20] *Dhulabhai v. State of Madhya Pradesh,*[21] and *Anisminic Ltd. v. Foreign Compensation Commission.*[22]

Majority (7:2) holds derecognition unconstitutional

The Supreme Court, by a majority of nine judges, with two judges (A.N. Ray J. and Mitter J.) dissenting, struck down the Presidential Order as unconstitutional. Shah, J. speaking for himself and six other learned judges of the Supreme Court, clearly held that the power conferred by Article 366(22) was exercisable only for *bona fide* purposes. Articles 366(22), 291 and 362 made the privileges of rulers an integral part of the constitutional scheme. This class of citizens were accorded special privileges due to historical reasons, and they could not be deprived of those privileges arbitrarily. The learned judge rejected all arguments of 'State policy' and conclusively held that the foundation of our Constitution being firmly laid in the rule of law, no instrumentality of the Union including the President could be invested with any arbitrary authority. The Union's reliance on 'political power', paramountcy, and 'Act of State', also met the same fate.

The majority accepted Palkhivala's submission that Article 366(22) did not invest the President with the arbitrary authority to recognise or not to recognise a Ruler. Moreover, they reasoned that Article 291 read with Articles 112, 113 and 114 formed part of a single scheme. As per this scheme, the privy purse had to be included in the financial statement as charged upon the Consolidated Fund; it was beyond the voting power of parliament; its destination was not to be altered; it was to be paid to the Ruler after the Appropriation Bill was passed; and when paid it was to be free from the liability to pay taxes on income. This was an integrated process, which could not be interrupted without dislocating the constitutional mechanism.

The jurisdictional bar in Article 363 was considered inapplicable by the majority because, as submitted by Palkhivala, Article 291 created an independent obligation and the reference in this provision to the covenants was only for the limited purpose of identifying the privy purses and for no other reason. This reference

19. AIR 1964 SC 381 : [1964] 4 SCR 797.
20. AIR 1966 SC 740 : [1966] 1 SCR 709.
21. AIR 1969 SC 78 : [1968] 3 SCR 662.
22. (1969) 1 All ER 208 : (1969) 2 AC 147.

did not make Article 291 a provision relating to the covenant. They accepted the strict construction placed by him upon the words of Article 363. According to the majority, any provision excluding the jurisdiction of the Court had to be strictly construed, and there would be no barrier operating 'at the very threshold' as was submitted by the Attorney–General. Constitutional provisions, in order to fit within the second limb of Article 363, had to have a dominant and immediate connection with the covenants signed by the rulers or their predecessors, as submitted by Palkhivala. After subjecting Article 366(22) to this test, the majority expressed the view that the direct and only purpose of this provision was to recognise rulership, and it was not a provision relating to the covenants. So, the majority concluded that the Constitution, and not the covenants, vested in the Rulers this right to receive privy purses. Consequently, this right could probably be abolished through a constitutional amendment but not through a Presidential Order de-recognising the Rulers.

Hidayatullah, J. in his concurring opinion upheld Palkhivala's arguments, and held that however wide the power under Article 366(22) may be, it did not extend to withdrawing recognition of all the Rulers by a 'midnight order'. This question, in his view, was in fact independent of Article 363 and had no bearing upon any covenant. On Article 363 itself, the learned judge was of the view that a right under Article 291 was not rendered unenforceable merely due to the presence of this provision, as Article 291 was not a provision 'relating to' the covenants. The learned judge went into the concept of property in great detail and concluded that the privy purses payable to the Rulers neatly fitted within the modern notion of property, this being an aspect of the case to which the majority opinion had not given much attention.

Hegde J. also gave a concurring opinion in which he clearly stated that the policy of the Constitution had to prevail over any 'State policy'. Questions of public opinion, the learned judge observed, were not for the Court to take into account or consider when pronouncing on the constitutional validity of a particular State action. The power under Article 366(22) was, in his opinion, limited in nature and to be exercised quasi-judicially as this power was in fact coupled with a duty. The learned judge substantiated this view by referring to several other provisions of the Constitution which at first glance appeared to be conferring unbridled discretion on the President, but actually cast a duty upon the President to exercise his power without eroding the delicate constitutional scheme.[23] He agreed with the view taken by the majority on the scope and ambit of Article 291 as well. The learned judge sagaciously observed that breach of any of the constitutional provisions even if made to further a popular cause was bound to be a dangerous precedent. Using the Weimar Constitution as an example, he cautioned that disrespect to the Constitution was bound to be broadened from precedent to precedent and before long the entire Constitution may be treated with contempt and held up to ridicule. This observation turned out to be prophetic, looking at the subsequent turn of events. He correctly pointed out that the basic issue arising for decision in this case was whether the executive could flout the constitutional mandate and set at naught legislative enactments at its discretion. The learned judge felt that if this could be done, the assumption that citizens of India were ruled by law and not by men would have to be given up as erroneous.

An interesting point to be noted here is that Palkhivala's arguments on the violation of right to property were not considered in detail by the majority, except for the fact that the learned judges recognised the proprietary interest of the Rulers to be adversely affected. This exercise was only meant to decide on the admissibility of the petitions under Article 32 of the Constitution, as per which some fundamental right had to be violated if the petitions were to be entertained.

Apart from the Attorney–General, Mr. Niren De, Shri Mohan Kumaramangalam also supported the abolition of the privy purses. The main plea taken by the Attorney–General and Mohan Kumaramangalam was that the order of the President was not questionable in any court of law under Article 363. This Article barred the Supreme Court or any other court from dealing with any dispute arising out of a treaty, agreement, covenant, engagement, *sanad*, or other similar instruments entered into between the Ruler and the Government of the Dominion of India. Barring this technical objection, the abolition of the privy purses could not be sustained on any legal ground. In effect, what was argued was that the courts were powerless to interfere in this matter, regardless of the illegality and, indeed, immorality of what had been done. The Union had no regard for the sanctity of the

23. Some provisions of this nature pointed out by the learned judge were Articles 341(1) and 342 (1) of the Constitution, which vested the President with the power to specify Scheduled Castes and Scheduled Tribes, and Article 324 under which the President was vested with the power to appoint the Chief and other Election Commissioners.

promises made to the Princes. Even worse, they had no regard for the Herculean efforts made by Sardar Patel and V.P. Menon less than 25 years earlier.

Interestingly, Justice Mitter observed that the petitions were not maintainable but at the same time, he held that the action of the President 'appeared to be unjustified' – a mild rebuke which, of course, made no difference.

It is through the *Bank Nationalization case* that Palkhivala contributed extensively to the constitutional protection of property rights in India. However, the *Privy Purses* judgment put the judiciary in open confrontation with the Congress party. This issue joined with bank nationalization to fuel the demands for unlimited parliamentary power of constitutional amendment, and the consequent clash with the judiciary.[24]

Constitutional amendment nullifies judgment

The move by Indira Gandhi, nine days after this decision, to call upon the President and advice fresh elections, was probably an indication of the approaching storm. Mrs. Gandhi's vision of a 'just social order', effectively marketed through her election campaign, was well received by the people, who saw the judiciary as an impediment in the process of social reform. In the 1971 elections, the Congress party managed a clear and convincing mandate from the people: 350 seats in Parliament to be precise. Thus began the process of constitutional amendments to override the existing barriers to an 'egalitarian society'. The large majority gained by Mrs. Gandhi enabled her to ultimately achieve her ambition of abolishing privy purses. The Constitution (Twenty-sixth Amendment) Act, 1971 was introduced to delete Articles 291 and 362; and Article 363A was inserted to declare that privy purses stand abolished and all rights, liabilities and obligations in respect of privy purses are extinguished. Accordingly, the Article stated that no Ruler shall be paid any sum towards privy purses. The Statement of Objects and Reasons was signed not by the Law Minister but by Mrs. Gandhi herself. The Objects and Reasons to the Twenty-sixth Amendment reads:

---

24. Granville Austin, *Working a Democratic Constitution, The Indian Experience*, Oxford University Press (1999), p. 220.

> *The concept of rulership, with privy purses and special privileges unrelated to any current functions and social purpose, is incompatible with an egalitarian social order. Government have, therefore, decided to terminate the privy purses and privileges of the Rulers of former Indian States. It is necessary for this purpose, apart from amending the relevant provisions of the Constitution, to insert a new Article therein so as to terminate expressly the recognition already granted to such Rulers and to abolish privy purses and extinguish all rights, liabilities and obligations in respect of privy purses. Hence this Bill.*
>
> New Delhi — Indira Gandhi
>
> The 31st July, 1971.

Outrage and sadness

Of all the cases argued by Palkhivala, the *Privy Purses* and the *Minerva Mills* cases give a feeling of outrage and sadness at the enormous damage that what was done to the Constitution and constitutional principles. Even if the former Rulers, as a class, were reprehensible, it could not be forgotten that the privy purse was a solemn constitutional guarantee on the basis of which they agreed to give up all they had. Except by use of force, India could never have achieved unification. A paltry sum of Rs. 4 crores per annum was the price for a unified India and this unification would have been simply impossible but for the efforts of Sardar Patel and V.P. Menon. The *Bank Nationalization* case or the other *Zamindari* abolition cases were matters of socialist policy which the elected Government of the day had the right to pursue. But no Government in any civilised society could breach its constitutional guarantee. India must permanently hang its head in shame for what it did to the privy purses. Worse, all this was wholly unnecessary as the amount payable as privy purses would have gradually dwindled. As rightly observed by Granville Austin, the privy purses would have become a 'footnote to history had abolishing them not been adopted as a cause by Mrs. Gandhi and the social-economic activists.'[25]

❋

---

25. Granville Austin, *Working a Democratic Constitution, The Indian Experience,* Oxford University Press, (1999), p. 220.

(v)

Newsprint Control or Newspaper Control?

Bennett Coleman v. Union of India

A very important case argued by Palkhivala, but now almost forgotten, is *Bennett Coleman v. Union of India.*[1] It is today difficult to imagine the extent to which the supply of essential commodities was controlled until the 1980s. In theory, the policy of equitable distribution of scarce resources through 'Control Orders' sounds very attractive. In practice, it only led to a thriving parallel economy where controlled commodities were sold in the black market at inflated prices. The policy of State control led to large generation of black money, the evil consequences of which are felt to this day. One of the items controlled was newsprint. The Newsprint Control Order, 1962 was made under the Essential Commodities Act, 1955 and its import was regulated by the Import Control Order, 1955. Shorn of details, quotas were allotted to different newspapers on the basis of their circulation in 1961-62. A limited annual increase was permitted. The Newsprint Policy of 1972-73 introduced four restrictions which were challenged before the Supreme Court:

(i) No newspaper or new edition could be started even if a particular company or newspaper did not apply for increased quota. In other words, even within the authorised quota, a new edition or a new newspaper could not be started;

(ii) The maximum number of pages was limited to ten. No adjustment was permitted between circulation and pages; a newspaper could not reduce circulation and increase the number of pages or vice versa.

(iii) No interchangeability was permitted between different newspapers published by a group or between different editions of the same paper;

---

1. AIR 1973 SC 106 : (1972) 2 SCC 788.

(iv) Newspapers, having less than ten pages, were permitted an increase of 20% in page level up to a maximum of ten pages;

Writ petitions were filed by leading newspapers – *The Times of India*, *Hindustan Times* and *Indian Express*. Palkhivala appeared for Bennett Coleman & Co. Ltd. – the publishers of *The Times of India*. C. K. Dapthary, M. K. Nambiar and Soli Sorabjee were the other leading lawyers who appeared in this case which was heard by a Bench of five judges.[2] Palkhivala argued that the newsprint control policy was really a policy of 'newspaper control'; it was a subtle and sophisticated device to control newspapers. Newsprint control could validly be done through rationing of newsprint but what had been imposed were objectionable post-quota restrictions. The policy imposed draconian conditions which completely banned new editions or the interchangeability or re-allocation of newsprint amongst various newspapers published by a group.

Justice Ray, speaking for the majority, struck down the newsprint control policy as violative of Articles 14 and 19(1)(a).[3] He observed that the imposition of the ten-page limit violated the right to freedom of speech and expression. The judgment contains an elaborate discussion on how a free press is vital to a democracy. He further held that if there was shortage of newsprint, the Government could have allotted newsprint to various newspapers by a margin of fair and equitable basis. But the policy went way beyond that by imposing various other restrictions. Newspapers were able to factually demonstrate that the new policy could result in reduction in pages of various newspapers by a margin of 23.8 - 43.8%. He rejected the Government's stand that the policy would enable smaller newspapers to attain equality of position with those operating above the ten-page level. According to Justice Ray, the object of helping smaller newspapers could not be allowed to 'strangulate the freedom of speech and expression of the big dailies'. The policy resulted in drastic reduction in advertisement revenue which, in turn, made the newspapers unviable economically. The policy was also very rigid; it did not permit newspapers belonging to a particular group from reallocating newsprint amongst various newspapers within the overall quota allotted to that group. The policy also permitted newspapers having circulation of less than one

---

2. Chief Justice S.M. Sikri, and Justices A.N. Ray, P. Jaganmohan Reddy, K.K. Mathew, M.H. Beg . Justice K.K. Mathew dissented from the majority.
3. Article 14 is the fundamental right to equality. Article 19(1)(a) is the fundamental right to freedom of speech and expression.

lakh to have a 10% increase whereas newspapers having more than one lakh circulation were permitted only a 3% increase in circulation. Extensive data was furnished to the court that clearly showed that the newspaper policy would have drastically affected advertising revenue and threatened the viability of several big dailies.

Surprisingly, Justice Mathew dissented and upheld the newsprint policy. His judgment was primarily based on the fact that newspapers were effectively controlled by private business groups but his reasoning is rather strange. The right to freedom of speech, he held, did not mean the right to use unlimited quantity of newsprint. This right was not a guardian of 'unlimited talkativeness'. Strangely, he held that the newsprint policy would enrich and enlarge the freedom of speech but did not explain how!

If newsprint was in short supply, then there could be no objection to ration it equitably but to further dictate the number of pages that could be published, and ban any new edition was clearly aimed at controlling the newspapers. As Justice Ray in the majority rightly observed, the ostensible object of control of newsprint had been subverted to newspaper control.

This judgment was instrumental in preserving and protecting the right of newspapers to start new editions and to print more pages if they so chose. In later years, these controls were abolished but the argument of Palkhivala and other learned counsel played an important role in protecting free speech. If this newsprint policy had been upheld, it would have been a matter of time before the Government took further steps to, at least indirectly, strangulate the free press.

❋

(vi)

Kesavananda Bharati and Fundamental Rights

The Saving of India's Constitution

On April 24, 1973, Chief Justice Sikri and 12 other judges assembled in the Chief Justice's court. This was the largest Bench that had heard the lengthiest arguments and covered the widest area of case law and legal literature in the history of the Supreme Court. The judgment profoundly altered the future of the Indian Republic. The verdict was a virtual judicial photo-finish with six judges upholding Parliament's claim of having unlimited power to alter the Constitution in any manner it chose, while six other judges held that Parliament's amending power was limited and it could not alter the basic structure or the essential features of the Constitution. By a strange twist of fate that made this case even stranger than fiction, Justice Khanna traveled for a long distance on the road that upheld Parliament's claim but, at the last moment, held that the power of Parliament to amend the Constitution would not include the power to alter its basic structure or essential features. This portion of Justice Khanna's judgment, as future events would show, saved democracy and prevented India from degenerating into a totalitarian regime or a one-party Government.

If there is one case that Palkhivala will always be remembered for, it is *Kesavananda Bharati v. State of Kerala,*[1] more popularly known as the *Fundamental Rights* case. At the core of this case was a single question: did Parliament have unlimited power to amend the Constitution or was there any implied or inherent limitation on such amending power? By a wafer-thin majority of 7:6, the Supreme Court held that the power of Parliament is not unlimited and that the amending power cannot be used to alter the basic structure or the essential features of the Constitution. In fact, the

1. AIR 1973 SC 1461 : (1973) 4 SCC 225.

majority is not really 7:6. If the decision of Justice Khanna is vivisected carefully, one would find that the verdict is really 6.6:6.4 !

One of the staunchest supporters of the unlimited power of Parliament to amend the Constitution was H.M. Seervai. With his characteristic honesty, he later admitted that if the basic structure doctrine had not been laid down, the consequences would have been very grave and India would have been in danger of being converted into a police State 'as the experience of the emergency clearly showed'. Indeed, the subsequent amendments, which are referred to later, show that Parliament would have most certainly 'defaced and defiled'[2] our Constitution.

Every major constitutional decision has a political or social background and the historic verdict in *Kesavananda Bharati* can be best understood in the context of various political events and important judgments that preceded it. Stung by the adverse verdict in the *Privy Purses*[3] case, Mrs. Indira Gandhi requested the President to dissolve Parliament and call for fresh elections. The election manifesto of the Congress Party called for major constitutional amendments, including the abolition of Privy Purses which were dubbed as 'anachronistic'. Socialist rhetoric was at its zenith and it was extremely fashionable to repeatedly condemn the privileges of the few and the abject poverty and misery of the many. The right to property was portrayed as the villain in the path of socialistic reform. Anybody opposing socialism was branded as a monopolist and a fascist. Astonishingly, a vast number of people believed that the abolition of the right to property would cure the problems of abject poverty. History tells us that abolishing the right to property does not in any manner alleviate poverty and it is ironical that a vast majority of current day politicians, who continue to swear by socialism, have declared assets that run into crores of rupees.

Mrs. Gandhi fought the 1971 election on a catchy slogan – '*garibi hatao*'.[4] Undoubtedly, her charisma and this slogan helped and she led her party to a stunning victory, gathering almost 350 seats out of the total strength of 540.

---

2. Palkhivala wrote a book titled *Our Constitution Defaced and Defiled,* Macmillan, 1974. The book criticized the 'hasty and ill-considered' amendments that almost destroyed the integrity of our Constitution.
3. *Madhav Rao Scindia v. Union of India,* (1971) 1 SCC 85 : AIR 1971 SC 530.
4. Translated, it means 'abolish or remove poverty'.

Mohan Kumaramangalam, Siddharth Shankar Ray and H.R. Gokhale, who were Mrs. Gandhi's close advisers, soon got down to the task of making major changes to the Constitution. Top priority was obviously given to overruling the three important judgments which had gone against Mrs. Gandhi – *Golak Nath, Bank Nationalization* and *Privy Purses*. These amendments had a clear agenda of reducing the power of courts and curtailing judicial review. Mohan Kumaramangalam publicly stated that courts could not be permitted to sit in judgment on issues which were really political and that Parliament, and not the courts, had to decide whether laws, in reality, would implement the Directive Principles. He also made other disparaging remarks about the judiciary, accusing judges 'of obstructing social and economic justice'. Granville Austin[5] reproduces this statement made by Mrs. Indira Gandhi: 'It is unacceptable to us that a few should skim the cream of social investments, defrauding society as a whole. The whole idea of private profit at the cost of the common man is repugnant to me, to my party, and, I think, to the nation.' Looking back, one wonders whether she was referring to the new class of sycophantic politicians that emerged in the 1970s! It was also made clear that Directive Principles would be given precedence over fundamental rights. In essence, the Congress party promised radical constitutional changes that would be the basis for economic and social reform. Flushed with victory, no time was lost in introducing several constitutional amendments of far reaching consequence.

Constitutional Amendments

On July 22, 1971, the Twenty-fourth and Twenty-fifth Amendment Bills were introduced in Parliament. The former bill had the clear objective of getting over the decision in the *Golak Nath* case which had held that Parliament had no power to take away or curtail any of the fundamental rights guaranteed by Part III of the Constitution. The Twenty-fourth Amendment Bill made just two amendments to the Constitution–to Article 13 and Article 368 – but both had a deadly impact. Article 13 stipulated that no law could take away or abridge fundamental rights and any law that did so was void. *Golak Nath* had held that the word 'law' would also include a constitutional amendment – reversing the view held from 1950 to 1967 that the word 'law' did not do so. The earlier view had made a distinction between an 'ordinary law' made under

5. Granville Austin, *Working A Democratic Constitution*, page 251.

Parliament's 'legislative power' and constitutional amendments made under its 'constituent power'. The amendment to Article 13 restored the earlier view, and therefore constitutional amendments would not be void merely because they infringed fundamental rights. Similarly, Article 368 – which dealt with amendments to the Constitution – was also changed to enable Parliament to add, vary or repeal any provision of the Constitution. Thus, even fundamental rights were not saved and Parliament had the power to repeal even the right to freedom of speech or the right to practise one's own religion. Earlier, any Bill presented to the President could be sent back by him for reconsideration. The amendment to Article 368 made it mandatory for the President to give his assent and reduced him to a constitutional rubber stamp.

The Twenty-fifth Amendment Bill contained two vicious provisions. First, the word 'compensation' in Article 31 was substituted by the word 'amount' and it was made clear that even such 'amount' could be paid 'otherwise than in cash'. In the *Bank Nationalization* case, the Supreme Court had made it clear that illusionary amounts paid as compensation for acquiring property would be impermissible. In other words, the compensation paid would be subject to judicial review. The stated object of this amendment was to ensure that any 'amount' paid for acquiring property, however ridiculous, would not be subject to any kind of challenge. No court could entertain a petition that questioned the amount paid for acquiring property. Thus, even the pittance that was paid in the *Bank Nationalization* case – and that too payable after ten years – could not be questioned in any court of law. Secondly, Parliament inserted a new Article 31C which had far reaching consequences. Article 31C had the ostensible object of protecting laws for implementing the Directive Principles specified in Article 39(b) and (c).[6] This was presumably to protect legislation that nationalized various industries and implemented other socialistic measures. What was deadly was the latter part of Article 31C which prohibited any court from entertaining any petition which sought to establish that a particular law would not secure the

---

6. Article 39(b) and (c) reads as under:

    39. Certain principles of policy to be followed by the State: The State shall, in particular, direct its policy towards securing—

    ...

    (b) that the ownership and control of the material resources of the community are so distributed as best to subserve the common good.

    (c) that the operation of the economic system does not result in the concentration of wealth and means of production to the common detriment;

principles laid down in Article 39(b) and (c). Such a law got immunity if it merely contained a declaration in the preamble that it was to give effect to the Directive Principles contained in Article 39(b) or (c). Article 31C actually prohibited even the filing of such a petition. Thus, a petitioner would not be allowed to logically demonstrate that a particular legislation whose ostensible object was to secure the principles specified in Article 39(b) or (c) was actually meant for some other purpose!

The Constitution (Twenty-ninth Amendment) Act, 1972 inserted the two land reform amendments made in 1969 and 1971 to the Kerala Land Reforms Act, 1963, in the Ninth Schedule to the Constitution, thus protecting them from any challenge of their violating fundamental rights. This constitutional amendment was also eventually challenged.

The Constitution (Twenty-sixth Amendment) Act, 1971, was passed by Parliament abolishing privy purses by making suitable changes in the Constitution itself. Although the validity of this amendment came up for consideration before the Supreme Court in the *Kesavanada Bharati case*, the court did not consider it; this issue was relegated to another Constitution Bench of five judges.

Palkhivala's initial reluctance

Initially, Palkhivala was reluctant to appear as it was obvious that this case would take a very long time to complete.[6a] The sugar mills then tried to brief M.C. Chagla but they found that he was not keeping very good health and would be unable to stand the strain of arguing for several days. C.K. Dapthary also expressed his reluctance to be the lead counsel. In a lighter vein, he quoted a Gujarati saying to Popat which meant that he did not want to put in all the hard work and let several others reap the benefit. Finally, Palkhivala was persuaded to lead the arguments and the rest, as they say, is history. The case eventually took much more time than anyone expected. Apart from Palkhivala, C.K. Daphtary and M.C. Chagla also appeared on behalf of the petitioners. Palkhivala was assisted by a highly competent team of lawyers including Soli Sorabjee, Anil Divan, D.M. Popat, M.L. Bhakta, Ravinder Narain and the late J.B. Dadachanji.

6a. Interview with D.M. Popat, Senior Partner, Mulla & Mulla & Craigie, Blunt & Caroe.

A marathon 68–day hearing

As is well-known, the case was heard by the largest Bench in the history of the Supreme Court – 13 judges – and for the longest number of days. Palkhivala and other counsel for the petitioners argued for 31 days, the case being heard on Tuesday, Wednesday and Thursday of each week. In rejoinder, the arguments of Palkhivala took two days. He had to cut short his submissions because of Justice Beg's illness and this is discussed later in this chapter.

H.M. Seervai appeared for the State of Kerala and was assisted by T.R. Andhyarujina.[7] At that time, he was the Advocate-General of Maharashtra and his commentary on the Constitution of India had been published to great acclaim in 1967. Seervai argued for 21 days. The Union of India was represented by the Attorney-General Niren De and the Solicitor-General Lal Narain Sinha, both of whom together took 12 days to complete their submissions and an additional day for reply. Apart from these two, Byra Reddy, Advocate-General of Mysore and Dr. L.M. Singhvi, Advocate-General of Rajasthan also made submissions on behalf of those two States. The case totally took 68 working days[8] commencing on October 31, 1972, and concluding on March 23, 1973. The written arguments were submitted by March 27, 1973.

Some of the exchanges between the judges and Palkhivala are interesting. Palkhivala had repeatedly referred to Hitler's subversion of the Weimar Constitution and converting Germany into a dictatorship. Hitler had been allowed to amend the Constitution and the world knows what followed. These repeated references irked Justice Grover.

Justice Grover: What is the point in taking us to these facts? If the Parliament has the power to amend fundamental rights, it

---

7. Andhyarujina also became Advocate-General of Maharashtra and Solicitor-General of India. He now practises in the Supreme Court. Andhyarujina maintained a diary and noted the proceedings on a day-to-day basis; on the basis of which he has now written *The Kesavananda Bharati Case – The Untold Story of Struggle for Supremacy by Supreme Court and Parliament*, Universal Law Publishing Co. (2011).
8. There is a slight variation in the number of days. V. G. Ramachandran in (1973) 4 SCC (Jour) 35, 50 mentions that the case took 65 days, while Prof. P. K. Tripathi mentions 68 days in (1974) 1 SCC (Jour) 3. Andhyarujina informed us that although the hearing was for 68 days, two days were lost at the final stage due to Justice Beg's illness and Palkhivala could not complete his arguments in rejoinder; the hearings were, therefore, for 66 days.

would remain unaffected irrespective of what happened in Germany or is likely to happen anywhere.

A few days later, Justice Grover told Palkhivala not to go into politics.

Justice Grover: We need not go into politics.

Palkhivala: I accept.

Justice Grover: Sometimes you go into politics and we are provoked to go into it.

Palkhivala: I want to know whether this case can be decided without going into the ambit of politics. But when I talk of totalitarian regimes and democracy, they form part of the constitutional argument.

When Justice Grover objected to the use of the word 'totalitarian', Palkhivala replied that he would use the word 'undemocratic'.

But the best exchange that was reported in the *Times of India,*[9] was with Justice Dwivedi:

Justice Dwivedi: Has any court decreed that there is an implied limitation on the power to wage war?

As though taken aback by the sudden question, Mr Palkhivala paused, took off his spectacles and wiped them, and then softly answered: 'With the utmost respect, your lordship, may I say that no express power to make war is provided in the Constitution. May I ask the indulgence of this court to be excused from dealing with this topic, since it is not germane to the present case'.

Excellent team work

Andhyarujina felt that the petitioners had excellent team work which was lacking on the side of the Union of India. Seervai and Niren De did not work as a team. There was an initial tussle between them as to who would open the submissions on behalf of the respondents – the Union of India, the State of Kerala and other States. Justice Jaganmohan Reddy, in his autobiography, has this to say: 'The Attorney-General had precedence and he should begin and pointed out that the Chief Justice, Shelat and Hegde in the *Bank Nationalization* case had said that this reversal of order could

9. November 30, 1972.

not be allowed. In any case, Chief Justice Sikri later said it is for both Seervai and Niren De to settle the issue and if De permitted, Seervai could start first. This, of course, was right but evidently by then at the instance of Gokhale, De was asked to give way to Seervai. I understand on authentic information that De had gone to the Prime Minister and complained. She asked him to come and see her again and when he did she told him, there was nothing she could do because she was dependent on the advice of the legal members of her Cabinet. De quietly lumped this insult and later tried to make a virtue of it. Talking to me, Niren De said he did not want to create trouble in Court and even suggested why the Court was not stopping Seervai's meandering arguments.'[10]

Thus, Seervai initially argued for 21 days and was followed by Niren De and a few other lawyers.

As mentioned earlier, the petitioner's team included Soli Sorabjee, Anil Divan, D.M. Popat, Ravinder Narain and several other lawyers. D.M. Popat would meticulously make a list of things to be done, noting against each item the name of the team member to whom the assignment was given. The research material and the judgments to be cited would be scrutinized by Sorabjee and Divan and then given to Palkhivala at night. Sorabjee and Divan also had a conference with Palkhivala each morning before the case. Before the morning conference, Palkhivala would have read the research material and the case law.

A number of interesting incidents took place during the hearing of this case. Each morning, Palkhivala would indicate the outline of submissions that he proposed to make during that day and his team had to ensure that all the books and papers were kept ready. As and when he was completing a point, the set of books and papers required for the next point would be kept ready. One day, while he was starting a new point, he asked Sorabjee to keep the papers for the next point ready. Sorabjee asked Popat for the papers who, to his horror, found that the next set of papers had been left behind at the hotel. Palkhivala was arguing his case with great passion and the papers he wanted were vital to the case. He was expected to come to the next point within the next half hour and Popat had no option but to get the papers from the hotel. When Popat came out of the Supreme Court, he found that their car and driver had gone away. There was no other vehicle available except one taxi which

10. Justice P. Jaganmohan Reddy, *The Judiciary I Served,* Orient Longman (1999), pp. 230-231.

was open with its key in the ignition. The driver of the taxi was nowhere in sight. As the matter could brook no delay, Popat got into the taxi and drove it himself to the hotel! He got the important documents and drove back to the Supreme Court and left the taxi exactly where it was. He then rushed back to the court and Palkhivala had the necessary papers just in time.

Justice Beg's illness

Few people know that the entire case came close to being re-heard because of the illness of Justice Beg.[11] He fell ill in February and March, 1973 and was hospitalized thrice. Andhyarujina records that Justice Beg was first hospitalized on February 6, 1973 for three days and one week was lost. He resumed work on February 12, 1973 but fell ill on March 5, 1973 and was hospitalized for a week. The hearing once again resumed on March 12 and continued for a short while thereafter. Palkhivala began his arguments in reply on March 14 and continued till the March 16. There was a special session during the Holi vacation to enable him to complete his rejoinder and the case was fixed for hearing on March 22 and 23, 1973. Justice Beg was once again hospitalized the previous evening and was advised complete rest for three weeks.[12] At that time, Chief Justice Sikri had to go on a two-week trip to Europe in the last week of March and was to retire on April 24, 1973. If Beg did not sit again or if Chief Justice Sikri retired, the hearings, which had already taken five months, would have to commence once again.

Popat remembers that the Chief Justice summoned to his chamber all the advocates who were arguing the case and suggested that the hearing could continue without Justice Beg. This suggestion was promptly, and perhaps rightly, rejected by Seervai and Niren De and the latter even threatened to boycott the court hearings if the matter was continued without Justice Beg. There was an unpleasant exchange of words between Palkhivala and De. Palkhivala, who had been given four days for his rejoinder, had completed only two days of arguments. The illness of Justice Beg left him with no choice but to give up his arguments for the last two days. Palkhivala was allowed

---

11. V.G. Ramachandran records that Justice Beg's illness had earlier interrupted the hearings for four days in February and then for six days in March. See (1973) 4 SCC (Jour) 35, 50.
12. T.R. Andhyarujina, *The Kesavananda Bharati Case – The Untold Story of Struggle for Supremacy by Supreme Court and Parliament*, Universal Law Publishing Co. (2011).

to file written submissions. In the end, the hearing concluded on March 23, 1973 and the judgment came exactly a month later.

Who was Kesavananda Bharati?

Kesavananda Bharati's name has perhaps been repeated more often than any other in the Supreme Court and the High Courts. He was a religious leader whose full name was 'His Holiness Kesavananda Bharati Sripadagalvaru' and was the head of a *math*[13] in Kerala. On March 21, 1970, he directly filed a writ petition under Article 32 before the Supreme Court to challenge certain provisions of the Kerala Land Reforms Act, 1963, and the Kerala Land Reforms (Amendment) Act, 1969.

The Full Bench of the Kerala High Court had struck down certain provisions of the Kerala Land Reforms Act, 1963, as amended in 1969 and 1971. The Supreme Court partly allowed the appeal, thereby invalidating certain crucial provisions. It was felt that this decision would adversely affect the interests of tenants in the land reform programme. There were certain other appeals pending in the Supreme Court and to put an end to any uncertainty, the Constitution (Twenty-ninth Amendment) Act, 1972 was passed on June 9, 1972. It contained just one provision: the two Land Reform Amendment Acts passed by the Kerala Legislature in 1969 and 1971 were inserted in the Ninth Schedule to the Constitution and, therefore, immunised from challenge as being violative of fundamental rights. Accordingly, Kesavananda Bharati filed an application to amend his petition to challenge the Kerala Land Reforms (Amendment) Act, 1971, and the Constitution (Twenty-ninth Amendment) Act, 1972.

Ironically, Kesavananda Bharati, neither met Palkhivala nor even spoke to him. T.R. Andhyarujina was having his lunch in the canteen when an advocate from Kerala told him that Kesavananda Bharati was quite surprised to see his name appearing in the papers every day and wondered why the case was taking so much time. His Holiness would never have imagined that his name would soon become immortal.

Kesavananda Bharati was not the only petitioner in this historic case. Two erstwhile Rulers and some mining, sugar and coal companies filed in all six writ petitions and there were 20 interveners.

---

13. Pronounced '*mutt*' and also spelt as such in North India. A 'math' or 'mutt' is a Hindu religious institution with properties attached thereto and presided over by a person who exercises spiritual leadership over a body of disciples.

As the questions involved in this case had far reaching effect, notices were issued to the Advocates-General of various States.

Funding of the litigation

D.M. Popat confirms that the entire litigation of Kesavananda Bharati was mainly funded by the coal, mining and sugar companies unlike the *Bank Nationalization* case or the *Mandal* case where Palkhivala had appeared without any fees. Further, a large team of eminent lawyers, including Soli Sorabjee and Anil Divan, were also present throughout the hearing and all of them stayed at the Oberoi Hotel during the hearing.

Palkhivala's submissions

In the *Golak Nath* case, it was held that the word 'law' in Article 13(2) would include amendments to the Constitution as well. Now, Article 13(2) states that 'The State shall not make any law which takes away or abridges the rights conferred by this Part and any law made in contravention of this clause shall, to the extent of the contravention, be void'. The implications of this judgment were indeed drastic. If the word 'law' included a 'constitutional amendment', any infringement of fundamental rights would be void and Parliament would not be able to abridge or take away all or any of the fundamental rights. This judgment overruled the earlier view that an amendment to the Constitution was in exercise of 'constituent power' and the word 'law' in Article 13(2) would not include a constitutional amendment. The decision in the *Golak Nath* case applied prospectively, and until 1971, Parliament had no power to amend, take away or abridge fundamental rights.

The Twenty fourth Amendment, as mentioned earlier, was intended to supersede the *Golak Nath* case. Of the two issues, the more important was the limit on the power of Parliament to amend the Constitution. In the first para of his written submissions,[14] Palkhivala succinctly stated:

> *The whole ratio of the majority judgments as well as the minority judgments in Golak Nath's case, turns entirely on the meaning to be attached to two words – the word law in Article 13(2) and the word amendment in Article 368. Therefore, the crucial question is – what is the precise meaning to be attached to these two words. To start with*

14. The text of these submissions are set out in (1973) 4 SCC (Jour) 1-34.

any assumption that the word "amendment" should be construed in its widest sense is to start with the answer instead of starting with the question.

On the very first day of the hearing, Palkhivala was told by Chief Justice Sikri that he should primarily concentrate on the implied limitations on Parliament's amending power. The judges made it clear that the judgment in the *Golak Nath* case was very difficult to sustain. Right at the start, it was clear that the thirteen-judge Bench would overrule the *Golak Nath* view that Parliament could not take away or abridge any of the fundamental rights on a proper construction of the word 'law' in Article 13(2). Popat recalls that this was also a hint or suggestion to Palkhivala to focus his arguments on the implied limitations to the amending power rather than justify the *Golak Nath* view.

Palkhivala first made his submissions on Articles 13 and 368 as they stood before the Twenty-fourth and Twenty-fifth Amendments to the Constitution, and then challenged the validity of these Amendments which mutilated or nullified those Articles. His main submissions, supported by detailed arguments over a month, may be summarized as under:

I. Parliament's power of amendment – Article 368:

1. Article 368 referred to the topic of constitutional amendment. It was silent as to:
   (a) the subject matter in respect of which the amending power could be exercised; and
   (b) the extent or width of the amending power.
2. The word 'amendment' is of the most elastic ambit and has a gradation of meanings. In Article 368 it must be understood having regard to the genesis and general scheme of the Constitution, the basic constitutional structure behind the text of the constitutional document, and all other relevant circumstances.
3. In Article 368, the word 'amendment' had a restricted meaning and precluded the power to destroy or alter the essential features, the basic elements or the fundamental principles of the Constitution. This view was supported not only by the language of Article 368 itself and inherent evidence within it, but also by comparing its language with that in other relevant

Articles. First, Article 368 did not start with the non obstante clause 'notwithstanding anything in this Constitution'; and, secondly, it used the word 'amendment' simpliciter, whereas other less significant Articles specifically use the words 'add', 'alter', 'repeal' or 'vary' in addition to the word 'amend'.

4. The Preamble cannot be amended by Parliament. Article 368 deals only with the amendment of 'this Constitution'. First, the Preamble is not a part or provision of the Constitution. Secondly, its very nature and contents make it incapable of being amended. It refers to the most momentous event in Indian history, and sets out what the people of India resolved to do for their unfolding future. No Parliament can amend or alter past history. If the Preamble is unalterable, it necessarily follows that those features of the Constitution which are necessary or intended to give effect to the Preamble are unalterable, and the fundamental rights are amongst them.

5. In a Constitution, what is left unsaid is as important as what is said, what is implied is as much a part of the instrument as what is expressed. There are inherent and implied limitations on the amending power of Parliament. They debar Parliament from destroying or altering the basic or essential features of the Constitution. This principle of inherent or implied limitations stems from the fact that Parliament is only a creature of the Constitution, while the power to impair the essential features of the Constitution is an attribute of ultimate legal sovereignty, which resides only in the people. But people are not associated with the amending process at all. Parliament cannot be equated with the people, and Parliament's will is not the people's will.

6. The test to be applied in determining the scope and width of the power is to see what can possibly be done in exercise of that power. If Article 368 were to be construed as giving Parliament unlimited power of amendment, then Parliament can destroy the sovereign status or the democratic character of the country, abolish the judiciary, abrogate all basic human freedoms, and, indeed, thereafter repeal Article 368

itself and provide that henceforth the Constitution would be unamendable.

7. Article 368 should not be read as expressing the death-wish of the Constitution or as a provision for its legal suicide. Parliament cannot arrogate to itself under this Article the role of the Official Liquidator of the Constitution.

Palkhivala mentioned the following as some of the essential features of the Constitution:

1. The supremacy of the Constitution.
2. The sovereignty of India.
3. The integrity of the country and the unity of the nation.
4. The democratic way of life, as distinct from mere adult franchise.
5. The republican form of government, as distinct from monarchy.
6. The guarantee of basic human rights, elaborated in Part III of the Constitution.
7. A secular state in which all religions are equal and none is favoured.
8. A free and independent judiciary, without which all rights would be writ in water.
9. The dual structure of the Union and the States, which permits centralisation and decentralisation to coexist.
10. The balance between the legislature, the executive and the judiciary.
11. The parliamentary form of government, as distinct from an authoritarian type of presidential form of government.
12. The amendability of the Constitution according to the basic scheme of Article 368: the Constitution must continue to be amendable without being alterable in its essentials. Article 368 itself can be amended but not so as to destroy its basic scheme: it cannot be so amended as to empower Parliament to alter or destroy any of the essential features of the Constitution.

II. Fundamental Rights – Article 13:

1. The word 'law' in Article 13(1) and (2) would include constitutional law, and therefore, a constitutional amendment. There were several indications to support this view. Therefore, Parliament, in exercise of its amending power, could not abrogate or abridge the fundamental rights.
2. If the word 'law' did not include a constitutional amendment, the consequences would be quite startling. Parliament could not even unanimously pass an ordinary law which took away a single fundamental right; but it could by a requisite majority repeal the entire chapter on fundamental rights merely by calling the law a constitutional amendment.
3. Such a narrow interpretation would threaten the integrity of the country and 'the unity of the nation' referred to the Preamble: the fundamental rights could be made applicable to certain communities or certain parts of India and not to others, and overtly favourable treatment could be given to members of a political party and not to the rest of the citizenry.
4. The fundamental rights are the basic human freedoms which people of India had reserved for themselves while giving to themselves the Constitution, and therefore, they could not be destroyed or curtailed by Parliament.
5. The proceedings before the Constituent Assembly indicate that the fundamental rights, most of which are inalienable natural rights, were intended to be permanent.

III. The Constitution (Twenty-fourth Amendment) Act, 1971:

1. Parliament, being a creature of the Constitution, had only such constituent power as was originally conferred by the Constitution. In exercise of its amending power Parliament could not enlarge its own constituent power or assume power not originally conferred by the Constitution.
2. By the Twenty-fourth Amendment, Parliament effected a silent revolution. It ceased to be a creature of the Constitution, and became its master.

3. By amending Articles 13 and 368 Parliament did indirectly what it could not do directly: it first repealed the limitations on its own constituent power and then purported to do what was forbidden by those limitations. It enlarged its own constituent power; it empowered itself to destroy or alter the essential features of the Constitution; and it usurped from the people their ultimate legal sovereignty. This Parliament was not entitled to do.

IV. The Constitution (Twenty-fifth Amendment) Act, 1971:

The Twenty-fifth Amendment amended Article 31 and inserted Article 31C.

A. Article 31:

1. In Article 31(2) the word 'amount' was substituted for the concept of 'compensation' for the property acquired. The amount might be illusory, and acquisition might virtually be confiscation.
2. The right to property was a fundamental right and had to be protected. This right was essential for the meaningful exercise of several other fundamental rights. The rights to have a free press, to form trade unions, to carry on business, to reside in any part of India, to practise religion, would all be meaningless if the printing plant of the publisher, the assets of the trade union or the businessman, the house or household effects of the individual, and the institutions maintained by a community for its religious purposes were acquired without payment of compensation.
3. The injustice was compounded by making the amount payable 'otherwise than in cash'. In view of the State's tendency to repudiate even solemn constitutional guarantees, a government's promise to pay at a future date might be almost worthless.
4. In any event it should be held that the 'amount' could not be illusory or arbitrary. The amount fixed or the principles specified for fixing it must have a reasonable relation to the property and its value, though the amount may not be equivalent to 'compensation' in the legal sense.

B. Article 31C:

Article 31C destroyed or damaged the core or essence of several essential features of the Constitution:

1. It destroyed the supremacy of the Constitution, and gave a blank charter to Parliament and all the State Legislatures to defy and ignore the Constitution.
2. It not only subordinated the fundamental rights to the Directive Principles of State Policy, but virtually abrogated them in respect of laws which the legislature declared to be for giving effect to the Directive Principles.
3. Such legislative declaration would make even the fundamental right to move the Supreme Court under Article 32 unexercisable.
4. It effectively enabled the State Legislatures to make fundamental rights unenforceable.

Article 31C was a monstrous outrage on the Constitution. It had a built-in mechanism for the dissolution of the true democracy that India had so far been, cessation of the rule of law, disintegration of the nation, and the birth of a totalitarian regime.

Arguments for the Union and the States

H.M. Seervai, the then Advocate-General of Maharashtra, appeared for the State of Kerala and argued for 21 days. His submissions can be briefly summarized as follows:

(1) The extent of amending power should not be viewed in the context of possible abuse of that power. It was wrong to assume that elected representatives of the people would abuse their unlimited legislative power.

(2) It was essential that the three wings of the Government– legislature, judiciary and executive – harmoniously run the machinery of Government.

(3) The Twenty-fourth Amendment was to remove some of the doubts on the scope of limits on the amending power. In *Golak Nath*, the minority rejected the theory of implied or inherent limitations on the amending power but the majority did not decide this issue.

(4) The Preamble was very much a part of the Constitution and could be amended. The fundamental rights are not human rights or natural rights. They are only social rights which can be changed from time to time.

(5) The basic features of the Constitution like parliamentary democracy, judicial review, religious rights were not meant to be permanent by the founding fathers of the Constitution.

(6) The court should be guided by the language used in the relevant articles and should not be guided by the so-called underlying or unfettered spirit thereof.

(7) The judiciary and the legislature have co-extensive powers. If the former invalidates an amendment as *ultra vires*, the latter has the necessary power to pass a law to meet the situation created by the judicial verdict.

(8) The power to amend the Constitution in Article 368 includes the power to amend any provision of the Constitution including fundamental rights in Part III.

(9) There was a distinction between legislative power and constituent power. The word 'law' in Article 13(2) would not include constituent power which was distinct and superior to ordinary law making power under Article 245.

(10) The argument which sought to portray adverse consequences were 'political arguments' which should not be countenanced.

(11) Similarly, there was no justification in the theory of implied limitation on amending power. There was no case to treat certain provisions as 'core and essence of the Constitution' and to invoke vague standards to discover implied limitations on the amending power.

(12) Article 368 had enjoyed a large and liberal interpretation till the *Golak Nath* decision in 1967. The Supreme Court had upheld the First, Fourth and Seventeenth Amendments and the Twenty-fourth Amendment was only to restore to Parliament the power it already possessed.

(13) Judicial review was not an essential feature of the Constitution. Reference was made to various

Constitutions of other countries to reject this theory. Further, the thumping majority secured by the Congress party in 1971 showed that people's approval had been obtained to the policy of constitutional amendment. The democratic will of the people must prevail. If there is a doctrine of implied limitation, the judiciary gets the last word on the Constitution, thereby usurping a superior status not warranted under the Constitution.

(14) 'A Government by judges' must be avoided in a federal democracy. The very fact that the first Parliament, which consisted only of members of the Constituent Assembly, amended Part III showed that the amending power included the power to amend all the fundamental rights in Part III.

(15) On the issue of Twenty-fifth Amendment which replaced the word 'compensation' with the word 'amount', it was only to do away with the confusion and uncertainty in the law created by earlier conflicting decisions. Any limited judicial review that would be permissible was only to determine whether the amount was illusory.

Seervai's scholarship was truly outstanding and he strongly felt, at that time, that there should be no limitations on the amending power of Parliament. Justice Reddy remarks, 'Seervai was most courteous and his court manners were unexceptionable except when it came to views held by the Court being contrary to the views expressed by him in his book on the Constitution.'[15]

Niren De, the learned Attorney-General, then made his submissions reiterating most of the points argued by Seervai. Both Justice Chandrachud and Justice Jaganmohan Reddy have mentioned that his arguments were often abrasive and even threatening. Justice Reddy wrote, 'Once or twice the Attorney-General, who was most arrogant and rude, suggested though not in so many words that the Court's future would be at stake. He said at one stage that the consequences have to be borne in mind if the decision went against the government. This, I felt, was an attempt to browbeat us. The impression one gathered during the arguments can never really be conveyed by the words used because of the

---

15. Justice P. Jaganmohan Reddy, *The Judiciary I Served*, Orient Longman (1999), p. 203.

manner of saying it, the tone adopted, the emphasis placed and the menacing nature of the insinuations hurled at the Bench. Some of the senior judges reacted by conveying their displeasure. The attacks on the Court were often vicious and showed the venom and pique which these persons had against it. Even the Attorney-General was no exception.'[16]

Justice Chandrachud remarked, 'He ticked off the judges as if they were errant school boys. His style of argument did not go well with several judges on the Bench.'[17]

At the same time, he was reputed to be a very intelligent and competent counsel. It was just bad luck that he had the misfortune to support so many constitutional amendments that were often shocking in nature. Mr. Niren De submitted that several constitutions had expressly set out limitations on the amending power. Article 368, on the other hand, did not contain any limitation and the word 'amendment' would mean addition, repeal, variation and even substitution. But he fairly conceded that repeal *in toto* was not included. He also submitted that the argument of fear that there would be several abuses of the amending power was meaningless. The 'political realities would prevent such a situation'. On the issue of compensation, he pointed out that by using the word 'amount', the legislature was the sole authority to fix what had to be paid for acquiring land or property and no court could go into the question at all. He remarked, tongue-in-cheek, that Justice Hegde, as a member of Parliament, had expressed the view that the legislature was the sole judge for fixing compensation. He submitted that fundamental rights were subservient to the Directive Principles to the extent it was necessary to achieve the socio-economic progress of the people.

N.H. Hingorani[18] had worked with Niren De in the *Bank Nationalization* and *Privy Purses* cases. In the *Kesavananda Bharati* case, Hingorani was also present at the hearing on a number of days. He recollects that Niren De was, unfortunately, much maligned. It was Niren De who asked Indira Gandhi to stop the transfer of judges during the Emergency. The transfers started when he was in England and, on his return, he told Indira Gandhi

---

16. Justice P. Jaganmohan Reddy, *The Judiciary I Served,* Orient Longman (1999), p. 230.
17. Interview with late Justice Y.V. Chandrachud.
18. A senior advocate of the Supreme Court. This is based on an interview with him and his wife Mrs. Kapila Hingorani who also practises in the Supreme Court and has spearheaded important public interest cases.

that the wholesale transfer of judges had to be stopped. Fortunately, she listened to his advice. Niren De, according to Hingorani, was also an important balancing factor. Mohan Kumaramangalam and S.S. Ray wanted to make radical changes that would have effectively implemented the concept of committed judiciary. It was Niren De who cautioned Indira Gandhi against taking such extreme steps.

Palkhivala's rejoinder

Palkhivala rejoined for two days and argued that Directive Principles were the ends of Government and fundamental rights were the permissible means to achieve those ends. In any democracy, there had to be a limitation on the exercise of legislative power because elected representatives seldom paused to consider the legitimacy of the means. In particular, he attacked the new Article 31C which, according to him, was the forerunner of a totalitarian State.

Responding to the criticism that the portrayal of adverse consequences was an argument of fear, Palkhivala argued: 'The question of abuse or misuse of power is entirely irrelevant. To say that taking into account consequences involves consideration of abuse of power is to confuse the extent of power with its exercise, and its scope with the manner of its use. When the question is as to the width of the power, the hope and expectation that it will never be used is as wholly irrelevant as an imminent danger of its use. The test of the true width of a power is not how probable it is that it may be exercised, but what can possibly be done under it.'

As mentioned earlier, due to the illness of Justice Beg, Palkhivala who had been given two more days for his rejoinder, agreed to stop and file written submissions.

The longest judgment

The marathon hearing finally ended on March 22 and all the written submissions were given by March 28, 1973. The mammoth judgment, covering 703 pages, was delivered on April 24, 1973.[19] As expected, the Bench was clearly divided. Six of the judges held that Parliament's power to amend the Constitution was indeed limited and it could not alter the basic or essential features of the

---

19. The reported judgment starts at p. 225 in (1973) 4 SCC, and the headnotes alone take up 80 pages.

Constitution. The other six took the diametrically opposite view and held that there was no such limitation on the amending power. As pointed out later, it was the last part of Justice Khanna's decision that tilted the balance in favour of democracy and the rule of law.

Based on the arguments advanced, the main issues that arose for consideration were the following:-

(i) Was *Golak Nath* correctly decided or was it liable to be overruled ?

(ii) Was the Twenty-fourth Amendment, which gave unlimited powers to Parliament to add, vary or repeal any provision of the Constitution valid ?

(iii) Was Section 2 of the Twenty-fifth Amendment that substituted the word 'amount' for the word 'compensation' valid ?

(iv) Was Section 3 of the Twenty-fifth Amendment which inserted Article 31C valid ?

(v) Was the Twenty-Ninth Amendment, which inserted two Kerala Land Reform Amendments in the Ninth Schedule valid ?

The validity of the 26th Amendment was also challenged but this issue was not decided. The controversial 'summary' signed by nine judges stated that another Constitution Bench would determine its validity.

The wafer thin majority demonstrated that any change in the composition of the Bench may have resulted in a different verdict. Two of the judges who were part of the majority in the *Golaknath* case–Justices Sikri and Shelat were also part of the 13 member Bench. Seervai, in an article written after the judgment, criticized the presence of these two judges. If two other judges would have been appointed, the verdict may have been different![20]

Golak Nath overruled

Nine of the thirteen judges expressly overruled *Golak Nath* and made a clear distinction between an ordinary law and the Constitution. The distinction between the two was based on the 'criterion of validity'. This was based on the premise that while an ordinary law depended on a higher law for establishing its own

20. H.M. Seervai, *Fundamental Right case, At the Cross Roads,* (1973) 75 Bom LR 47 (48).

validity, a provision of the Constitution did not depend on another law and, instead, generated its own validity.[21]

Limitations on amending power

On the Twenty-fourth Amendment, six judges, namely Chief Justice Sikri and Justices Shelat, Grover, Hegde, Reddy and Mukherjea, held that fundamental rights, being part of the essential elements or basic features of the Constitution, could not be abrogated or emasculated by the exercise of the power of amendment under Article 368. However, reasonable abridgement of fundamental rights, as distinct from their abrogation or emasculation, was permissible.

The other six judges, namely Justices Ray, Palekar, Mathew, Beg, Dwivedi and Chandrachud, held that the power of amendment did not have any limitation or restriction. Astonishingly, Justice Khanna accepted this view in the first part of his judgment but in the latter part, while dealing with Article 31C, held that the basic structure or framework of the Constitution could not be abrogated by the exercise of the power of amendment.

All the six judges who upheld the unlimited power of amendment, plus Justice Khanna, placed extraordinary faith in our elected representatives. Repeatedly rejecting the possibility of abuse as an argument of fear, these judges placed trust in Parliament and the State Legislatures who were supposed to have the welfare and good Government of the country at heart. There was no reason to believe that the elected representatives would do anything drastic and it was wrong to uphold implied limitations on the amending power by giving examples of drastic consequences that could arise. Justice Ray dubbed such a test as absurd and quoted the words of Chief Justice Taft of the US Supreme Court: 'If those who were in separate control of each of the three branches of Government were bent upon defeating the actions of each other, normal operation of Government would come to a halt and could be paralyzed.' These judges placed faith in the 'collective wisdom' and 'innate good sense' of Parliamentarians and legislators.

Palkhivala had given several examples of different countries where the amending power in a democratic Constitution was

---

21. For an excellent discussion on 'criterion of validity', see P.K. Tripathi : *Some Insights into Fundamental Rights,* University of Bombay, (1972), Ch. I,. Golak Nath: A Critique, p. 17; see also the article 'Kesavananda Bharati v. State of Kerala – Who Wins?' by Prof. P.K. Tripathi (1974) 1 SCC (Jour) 35, 50.

utilised to establish one party rule or rule by a small oligarchy. He had frequently referred to the manner in which the Weimar Constitution was subverted by Hitler who converted the German State into the most repressive and brutal dictatorship. By amending the German Constitution, Hitler systematically arrogated to himself virtually unlimited powers, and any kind of dissent was ruthlessly muzzled. But these examples were rejected by the judges as not being relevant in considering the scope of the amending power. Palkhivala had argued that if the amending power is unlimited, one generation can exercise such power and then pass a law taking away the power of amendment from future generations and foreclose them from ever exercising it. Justice Mathew rejected this argument with the observation:

> *I think the argument is too speculative to be countenanced. It is just like the argument that if men and women are given the freedom to choose their vocations in life, they would all jump into a monastery or nunnery, as the case may be, and prevent the birth of a new generation, or the argument of some political thinkers that if freedom of speech is allowed to those who do not believe in it, they would themselves deny it to others when they get power and, therefore, they should be denied that freedom today, in order that they might not deny it to others tomorrow.*

In retrospect, the courts must take into account the possibility of abuse as no one, including the judiciary, can be trusted with unlimited power. Indeed, an essential feature of any responsible Constitution is the existence of both implied and express limitations.

'Compensation' and 'amount'

Section 2 of the Twenty-fifth Amendment primarily sought to nullify the *Bank Nationalization* judgment by substituting Article 31(2). In its new *avatar*, it read:

> *(2) No property shall be compulsorily acquired or requisitioned save for a public purpose and save by authority of a law which provides for acquisition or requisitioning of the property for an amount which may be fixed by such law or which may be determined in accordance with such principles and given in such manner as may be specified in such law; and no such law shall be called in question in any court on the ground that the*

> *amount so fixed or determined is not adequate or that the whole or any part of such amount is to be given otherwise than in cash.*

While all the judges upheld the substitution of the word 'amount' for the word 'compensation', six judges[22] held that the amount and the principles on which such amount was arrived at would still be subject to judicial scrutiny. The court could intervene if the amount was illusory or arbitrary or had no relationship to the market value of the property. Six judges[23] held that the amount actually paid was completely excluded from any kind of judicial scrutiny. Justice Khanna also agreed and held that the legislature could, if it so chose, pay an amount which was plainly inadequate. Justice Chandrachud held that the court could interfere with the amount paid if it was illusory or the law specifying the amount was in the nature of a fraud on the Constitution. Thus, in the context of Article 31(2), it was Justice Chandrachud, who tilted the balance in favour of judicial review.

The notorious Article 31C

The next part of the Twenty-fifth Amendment was Article 31C which was a startling section that made the fundamental rights subservient to the directive principles. The section read as follows:

> ***31C. Saving of laws giving effect to certain directive principles:*** *Notwithstanding anything contained in Article 13, no law giving effect to the policy of the State towards securing the principles specified in clause (b) or clause (c) of Article 39 shall be deemed to be void on the ground that it is inconsistent with, or takes away or abridges any of the rights conferred by Article 14, Article 19 or Article 31; and no law containing a declaration that it is for giving effect to such policy shall be called in question in any court on the ground that it does not give effect to such policy:*
>
> *Provided that where such law is made by the Legislature of a State, the provisions of this article shall not apply thereto unless such law, having been reserved for the consideration of the President, has received his assent.*

---

22. Chief Justice Sikri and Justices, Shelat, Hegde, Grover, Reddy and Mukherjea.
23. Justices Ray, Palekar, Mathew, Beg, Dwivedi and Khanna.

Once again the Chief Justice and four other judges[24] declared the entire Article 31C as unconstitutional. Justice Reddy upheld the first part but declared the second part as unconstitutional. Justice Khanna held that the second part was unconstitutional as it would destroy the basic structure of the Constitution. The remaining six judges[25] held that Article 31C was completely valid. Thus, seven out of thirteen judges held that the latter part of Article 31C was invalid.

Justices Hegde and Mukherjea pointed out that valuable constitutional guarantees are generally encroached upon imperceptibly and with the best of intentions. Once an attempt is successful, further encroachments follow as a matter of course, not perhaps made with any evil motive but out of strong convictions about the righteousness of the course adopted and the objects intended to be achieved, but they may all the same be wholly unconstitutional. They quoted this classic passage of Lord Atkin which deserves to be reproduced:[26]

> *Both the Act and the sections have a legislative history which is relevant to the discussion. Their Lordships entertain no doubt that time alone will not validate an Act which when challenged is found to be ultra vires; nor will a history of a gradual series of advances till this boundary is finally crossed avail to protect the ultimate encroachment.*

Article 31C, inserted by the Twenty-fifth Amendment, they held, had finally crossed this boundary.

Justice Ray pointed out that the two basic postulates in democracy are faith in human reason and faith in human nature and there is no higher faith than faith in the democratic process. The learned judge apparently forgot that when the democratic process is sought to be subverted and human nature and human reason do not act for the benefit of the nation but for narrow, short-term political considerations, such faith is wholly misplaced and the court has to interfere.

Justice Khanna was particularly harsh in his remarks on the second part of Article 31C. He pointed out that Parliament or a State Legislature could pass a law, with just the minimum number of members present as a quorum which would reduce Articles 14,

---

24. Justices Shelat, Hegde, Grover and Mukherjea.
25. Justices Ray, Palekar, Matthew, Beg, Dwivedi and Chandrachud.
26. *Proprietary Articles Traders Association v. Attorney-General of Canada*, 1931 AC 311, at 317.

19 and 31 to a 'dead letter' and make them 'ineffective purposeless showpieces'. All that was required was just a mere declaration that the particular law was intended to give effect to the objects mentioned in Article 39(b) and (c). He also pointed out the danger of State Legislatures resorting to declarations made for various legislations and, in effect, enabling State laws to effectively abrogate Articles 14, 19 and 31. Thus, the same judge who rejected the 'argument of fear' in the context of the amendment to Article 368 and upheld the Twenty-fourth Amendment, was not willing to place the same trust in the 'collective wisdom' and 'innate good sense' of the elected representatives when it came to the drastic provisions in the latter part of Article 31C as inserted by the Twenty-fifth Amendment.

As Upendra Baxi rightly pointed out,[27] judges who had no hesitation in giving unlimited amending power to Parliament on the ground that there was no justification in assuming that the power would be abused, made strong remarks about the need to preserve judicial review in the context of Article 31C. In his words:

> *To concede power on the assumption, hope or faith that Legislatures will always act wisely and fairly is (with respect) no better than to deny this power on the ground that it may possibly be abused. The latter, it has been reiterated ad nauseum, is no ground for denying power. When indeed will it be realized that, by the same token, the possibility of the benign use of the power is likewise no ground for conferring it ?*

On the other hand, Justice Mathew echoed the sentiments of the other six judges who had no hesitation in upholding Article 31C despite the enormous potential for abuse. His words are instructive:

> *The supposed bad odour about the article should not upset our judgment in adjudging its constitutionality. We have no power under the Constitution to adjudge a constitutional amendment as unconstitutional on the ground that the amendment would in effect vest large powers in Parliament and State Legislatures to pass laws which might violate Articles 14, 19 and 31.*

---

27. 'The Constitutional Quicksands of Kesavananda Bharati and the Twenty-fifth Amendment' (1974) 1 SCC (Jour) 45, 61.

The Twenty-Ninth Amendment

Finally, with regard to the Twenty-ninth Amendment, the majority upheld the amendment as being within the amending power but left it to the Constitution Bench to decide whether the insertion in the Ninth Schedule was violative of the basic structure.

A controversial summary

Another unique feature of this thirteen-judge case was this summary that was signed only by nine judges.

Summary

'The view by the majority in these writ petitions is as follows:

1. *Golak Nath's* case is overruled.
2. Article 368 does not enable Parliament to alter the basic structure or framework of the Constitution.
3. The Constitution (Twenty-fourth Amendment) Act, 1971 is valid.
4. Section 2(a) and (b) of the Constitution (Twenty-fifth Amendment) Act, 1971, is valid.
5. The first part of Section 3 of the Constitution (Twenty-fifth Amendment) Act, 1971, is valid. The second part, namely, "and no law containing a declaration that it is for giving effect to such policy shall be called in question in any Court on the ground that it does not give effect to such policy" is invalid.
6. The Constitution (Twenty-ninth Amendment) Act, 1971 is valid.

The Constitution Bench will determine the validity of the Constitution (Twenty-sixth Amendment) Act, 1971,[28] in accordance with law.

The cases are remitted to the Constitution Bench for disposal in accordance with law. There will be no order as to costs incurred upto this stage.'

The nine signatories were Chief Justice Sikri and Justices Shelat, Hegde, Grover, Jaganmohan Reddy, Palekar, Khanna, Mukherjea and Chandrachud. The other four (Justices Ray, Mathew, Beg and

---

28. This amendment abolished privy purses by amending the Constitution.

Dwivedi) refused to sign it and Seervai has severely criticized this summary. Actually, the summary has served a very useful purpose of informing the public at large of what the 703-page decision contained. It served as a useful guide to the High Courts as well. It also prevented the need for reading the eleven lengthy judgments that were sometimes at variance with one another.

In *Minerva Mills,*[29] Justice Chandrachud, who had become Chief Justice by then, had a dig at critics of the summary and stated:

> *Whether or not the summary is a legitimate part of the judgment, or is per incuriam for the scholarly reasons cited by authors, it is undeniable that it correctly reflects the majority view.*

Breathtaking scholarship

A reading of the eleven opinions leaves one awestruck by the enormous amount of hard work that had gone into the preparation of the case. The Attorney-General had submitted a comparative chart analyzing the provisions of no fewer than 71 Constitutions. Apart from earlier Supreme Court decisions, Palkhivala, Seervai and Niren De had referred to decisions from the United States, England, Australia, Canada, Ireland and Ceylon. Numerous references were made to various text books not only on constitutional law and other legal subjects but also on political science, economics and history. The table of cases cited alone extends to about 18 pages and the list of treatises, reference books and articles that were cited runs into seven pages.[30] Not only were different Constitutions referred to, references were also made to bills passed by the New South Wales Legislature in 1930. It must have been a Herculean task for the counsel concerned and an equally mammoth task for the judges to sift through the mass of materials produced.

Basic structure theory

The most important contribution of this judgment is the basic structure theory. This theory or doctrine effectively arrived at a workable compromise between two diametrically opposite views represented by the pre and post *Golak Nath* phases. Either view

---

29. *Minerva Mills Ltd. v. Union of India,* (1980) 3 SCC 625 : AIR 1980 SC 1789.
30. The books and treatises have been set out in the beginning of (1973) 4 SCC (Journal) 1-64 along with the written submissions of Palkhivala.

would not have worked given the changed political scenario and dwindling adherence to constitutional conventions. The basic structure theory restores the power of Parliament to amend any part of the Constitution. At the same time, Parliament's power is not unlimited and no amendment can violate the fundamental or essential features or, as they are now popularly called, the basic structure of the Constitution. There is no such phrase in the Constitution and no part of the Constitution can be said to constitute the basic structure. Indeed, different judges in the *Kesavananda Bharati* case have given different definitions of the basic structure. Its lack of rigidity is itself its most important virtue. As long as Parliament does not drastically amend the Constitution, it can virtually make any change to the constitutional structure. At the same time, the core or the essence must be retained.

As explained earlier, the first reference to the fundamental features was made by Justice Mudholkar in the *Sajjan Singh's* case and later elaborated in *Golak Nath*. This was taken a step further in *Kesavananda Bharati* as it was the primary issue to be determined in the context of the Twenty-fourth Amendment. The essential features of the Constitution enumerated by Palkhivala have been set out earlier and have also been reproduced in the judgment of Justice A.N. Ray.

But his submissions were not accepted *in toto*. Indeed, different examples of what constitutes basic structure were given by different judges and these have been enumerated below:

I. View of Sikri CJ:

(i) Supremacy of the Constitution;

(ii) Republican and Democratic forms of Government;

(iii) Secular character of the Constitution;

(iv) Separation of powers between the legislature, the executive and the judiciary;

(v) Federal character of the Constitution.

II. View taken by Shelat and Grover JJ:

(i) The supremacy of the Constitution;

(ii) The Republican and Democratic forms of Government and sovereignty of the country;

(iii) Secular and federal character of the Constitution;

(iv) Demarcation of power between the legislature, the executive and the judiciary;

(v) The dignity of the individual secured by the various freedoms and basic rights in Part III and the mandate to build a welfare State contained in Part IV;

(vi) The unity and the integrity of the nation.

III. View taken by Hegde & Mukherjea JJ.:

(i) Sovereignty of India;

(ii) The democratic character of our policy;

(iii) The unity of the country;

(iv) The essential features of the individual freedoms secured to the citizens;

(v) Welfare State and egalitarian society.

IV. View taken by Jaganmohan Reddy J.:

(i) Sovereign Democratic Republic;

(ii) Justice, social, economic and political;

(iii) Liberty of thought, expression, belief, faith and worship;

(iv) Equality of status and of opportunity.

Thus, there was no unanimity on what constituted the basic structure of the Constitution. However, this uncertainty has not come in the way of the Supreme Court applying the doctrine of basic structure in several cases. Important principles like 'due process' are also undefined and have been invoked from generation to generation in the United States to solve complex constitutional issues. The Supreme Court has applied the doctrine to strike down certain provisions of the Constitution (Thirty-ninth Amendment) Act, 1975 (which sought to nullify the Allahabad High Court's judgment against Indira Gandhi and make elections of the President, Vice-President, Prime Minister and Speaker not questionable in any court of law) and also certain sections of the Constitution (Forty-second Amendment) Act, 1976 in the *Minerva Mills* case. The basic structure doctrine has been applied to preserve the writ jurisdiction of the High Courts.[31] For the last

31. *L. Chandrakumar v. Union of India,* (1997) 3 SCC 261 : AIR 1997 SC 1125. See also *Kihoto Hollohan v. Zachillhu,* 1992 Supp (2) SCC 651, 715, para 120, where excluding the judicial review of the Speaker's decision on the question of disqualification of MPs and MLAs was held to be violative of the basic structure.

thirty-seven years, this doctrine has proved remarkably useful in preserving democracy and the rule of law.

Justice Mathew, though in the minority, rejected the criticism that it was not possible to ascertain what the essential features were:

> *I am not dismayed by the suggestion that no yardstick is furnished to the Court except the trained judicial perception for finding the core or essence of a right, or the essential features of the Constitution... Few constitutional issues can be presented in black and white terms. What are the essential features and non-essential features of the Constitution? These are not matters of icy certainty; but, for that reason, I am not persuaded to hold that they do not exist, or that they are too elusive for judicial perception. Most of the things in life that are worth talking about are matters of degree and the great judges are those who are most capable of discerning which of the gradations make a genuine difference.*
>
> *Nor do I think that all the provisions in the Constitution are equally essential. And our Constitution could very well have dropped many of its provisions. Merely because all the provisions of the Constitution have equal importance in one respect, namely, they are all embodied in one document, and can be amended only by the procedure prescribed in Article 368, it does not follow that all of them are essential features of the document in all other respects.*
>
> *But the question will still remain, even when the core or the essence of a fundamental right is found, whether the amending body has the power to amend it in such a way as to destroy or damage that core.*[32]

Criticism of *Kesavananda Bharati*

It has been repeatedly commented that the case was essentially one with a political background. In his autobiography, Justice Jaganmohan Reddy recollects: 'I got the impression [from the first day] that minds were closed and views were determined.'[33]

Andhyarujina also recollects that the Bench was clearly divided and some judges were clearly in favour of the petitioners, while

---

32. *Kesavananda Bharati v. State of Kerala,* (1973) 4 SCC 225, 826-827 : AIR 1973 SC 1461.
33. Justice P. Jaganmohan Reddy, *The Judiciary I Served,* Orient Longman, (1999), p. 227.

others were on the opposite side. From the beginning, there was no doubt as to which side some judges were inclined. According to him, the final verdict was a political one and although the verdict eventually proved useful, the manner in which the case was conducted and judgments delivered left much to be desired.

> *In so far as the hearing of the case was concerned, from the day the case began on 31st October 1972 and before it had even progressed a week, it became clear that there was a sharp cleavage between the two points of view: one, that the word "amendment" had a limited scope, that there were implied limitations, that the essential features and the basic structure could not be altered, and the other that it was wide in interpretation, and the sky was the limit. While the Chief Justice (Sikri), Hegde and Grover were constantly asking questions, and letting fall suggestions in support of the first view, and gave extreme examples, Ray, Palekar, Mathew and Dwivedi were countering these suggestions and asking Palkhivala where he had got implied limitations, essential features and basic structure from. This process continued for 32 days, and we were presented with Conrad and his views, the Irish case, the Ceylonese cases, debate showed a sharp division which appeared irreconcilable. I got the impression throughout that minds were closed and views were predetermined.*[34]

Another judge spoke about 'unusual happenings', and Andhyarujina wrote: 'If the several "unusual happenings" in the case are related in detail, they will make one doubt if the decision in the case was truly a judicial one – expected from judges with detachment from the results of the controversy before them.'[35] Reddy also refers to an unusual suggestion by Justice Dwivedi:

> *There was one occasion when Dwivedi made a startling proposal to Palkhivala. He said if he (Palkhivala) agreed to property rights being taken away, he (Dwivedi) would get Parliament to declare that other fundamental rights would not be taken away. Palkhivala replied: "Have I referred so far at any time to property rights? I was dealing with the implied limitations and natural rights, etc." How a judge*

34. *The Hindu,* May 21, 2007.
35. *Ibid.*

> *could give such an assurance as Dwivedi offered and what authority he had to do so passed everyone's comprehension.*[36]

A shocking revelation by Andhyarujina is that the Government was in possession of some of the draft judgments even before they were delivered on April 24, 1973 and had consequently decided to appoint Justice Ray as the Chief Justice by superseding three senior judges. In Andhyarujina's words:

> *Towards the end of the hearing in the Kesavananda case Government came to know of the opinions of the Chief Justice and three senior-most judges who were against conceding unlimited power of amendment to Parliament and was in possession of some of the draft judgments prior to their delivery on 24 April, 1973. With the knowledge that C.J. Sikri and three senior-most judges were deciding against it, Government decided to supersede them even before the official delivery of the judgments on 24 April, 1973 on the retirement of C.J. Sikri the next day on 25 April, 1973 and appointed Justice A.N. Ray as the next Chief Justice who it was known to the Government would be deciding in its favour.*[37]

Another area of criticism has been the lack of consultation amongst the judges before the judgments were delivered. Justice Chandrachud opened his judgment with the following remarks:

> *I wanted to avoid writing a separate judgment of my own but such a choice seems no longer open. We sat in full strength of 13 to hear the case and I hoped that after a free and frank exchange of thoughts, I will be able to share the views of someone or the other of my esteemed Brothers. But we were overtaken by adventitious circumstances. Counsel all round consumed so much time to explain their respective points of view that very little time was left for us to elucidate ours. And the time factor threatened at one stage to assume proportion as grave as the issues arising in the case. The Court very soon will be poorer by the retirement of the learned Chief Justice and that has set a date-line for the*

---

36. Justice P. Jaganmohan Reddy, *The Judiciary I Served,* Orient Longman, (1999), p. 227. Justice Reddy also records that Justice Dwivedi had made a favourable speech at the Allahabad High Court and openly remarked that he was going to the Supreme Court to see that the *Golaknath* case was overruled.
37. T.R. Andhyarujina, *The Kesavananda Bharati Case – The Untold Story of Struggle for Supremacy by Supreme Court and Parliament*, Universal Law Publishing Co. (2011).

> *judgment. There has not been enough time after the conclusion of the arguments, for an exchange of draft judgments amongst us all and I have had the benefit of knowing fully the views of only four of us. I deeply regret my inability to share the views of the learned Chief Justice and of Hegde J., on some of the crucial points involved in the case.*[38]

Normally, in important cases, there are extensive consultations after arguments are over. Jaganmohan Reddy's autobiography refers to the discussions that took place after the arguments were concluded in the *Bank Nationalization* case.[39] However, in *Kesavananda Bharati*, Chief Justice Sikri had consultations only with seven other judges. In Justice Reddy's words:

> *During the hearing of the case and when it was coming to a close, I, one day, sent some grapes which I received from Hyderabad to Sikri and other brother judges. Sikri rang me up and while thanking me he asked me what was I doing the next day Sunday. I said, nothing. He asked me if I would like to come to a conference of judges at his house to discuss the case. I said, of course, it was my duty to do so. Next day in my walk with Ray I asked him whether he was coming to the judges' meeting. I was surprised when he said he had not been asked. I told him perhaps Sikri was planning to invite him. When we met in Sikri's house that day at about 10.30 a.m. I found we were only eight of us there. Sikri, Shelat, Hegde, Grover, myself, Khanna, Mukherjee and Chandrachud. I asked Sikri why the others were not called. He said he knew their views but not ours; that was why he had called us. I made it clear that I felt that was not proper. Sikri's explanation was that whenever he called all of us together it was a cacophony of noise and sterile talk. I did not remember being invited to such a meeting. In any case he said during the hearing of the case he came to know the views of individual judges who were frequently expressing their comments from the Bench.*[40]

---

38. Justice Chandrachud confessed that he had the chance hurriedly to read draft judgments only of some of his colleagues.
39. Justice P. Jaganmohan Reddy, *The Judiciary I Served*, Orient Longman, (1999), at p. 177.
40. *Ibid*, p. 231.

The lack of consultation has been severely criticized by Andhyarujina: 'The Chief Justice's action has been described by some as an act of statesmanship. Others believe it was a manoeuvre to create a majority that did not exist.'[41] And in the same article, he criticizes the manner in which the basic structure came to be formulated:

> *However, in the glorification of the basic structure theory, it is important to bear in mind its infirm roots and how predilections and prejudices of judges, chance, and accidental circumstances have played a greater part rather than any logic or conscious formulation of it.*[42]

The judgment evoked mixed response and two articles[43] criticized the view and opined that the entire Constitution was amendable and there were no limits on the power of Parliament to take away any or all of the fundamental rights. Indeed, Prof. Tripathi criticised the concession made by H. M. Seervai and Niren De that the power of amendment under Article 368 did not extend to the repeal or abrogation of the whole Constitution. This, according to him, was counter-productive as no Parliament could be capable of taking such an extremely unwise step. As subsequent events showed, Tripathi's criticism proved unfounded. A Parliament may not abrogate or repeal the whole Constitution but it could make changes in just a few clauses and render the whole Constitution a meaningless document. One cannot forget that even the People's Republic of China has a Constitution that confers rights on its people in theory, but everyone knows that these are non-existent in practice.

Seervai's critical article analyses the decision carefully. As mentioned earlier, Seervai himself later changed his views and felt that the doctrine of basic structure was essential to prevent India from degenerating into a police state. Indeed, despite the basic structure theory, most political parties have become dynastic with virtually no inner-party democracy. Coalition politics has also taken its toll on democratic values. Recent political developments have threatened the unity of India and may lead to further fragmentation of the Indian Republic. It is only the theory of basic structure that keeps India together and ensures that the Constitution will survive in the present democratic set-up.

---

41. *The Hindu,* May 21, 2007.
42. *Ibid.*
43. Tripathi, (1974) 1 SCC (Jour) 3, *supra*, and Seervai LXXV Bom LR 47.

Upendra Baxi, in his article on *Kesavananda Bharati* referred to earlier, rightly remarked that this lengthy judgment was likely to create 'an illiterate Bar' in the country as the decision which ran into more than 700 closely printed pages was unlikely to be read by the majority of the Bar. This is very true and, without the controversial summary, it would have been very difficult to discern the main points that were decided. The other advantage is that all eleven opinions have summarized their conclusions.

Kesavananda Bharati, in a sense, was a judicial compromise as the power of Parliament to amend the Constitution to a very large extent was restored. The only limitation was that it could not alter the basic structure or essential features. While conceding this power to Parliament, the Supreme Court reserved to itself the power of judicial review and thus ensured a system of checks and balances amongst the three wings of Government.

Role of Palkhivala

By all accounts, Palkhivala single handedly argued this case to its wafer thin victory. He had the benefit of a superb team of lawyers to assist him, but arguing a case for 31 days, spread over a few months, was a feat that is unlikely to be equaled or surpassed. Several lawyers who were present during the hearing remember the spell-binding advocacy of Palkhivala. One young lawyer, who later became an eminent High Court judge, described Palkhivala's advocacy as 'scintillating'. He remembers that Palkhivala seldom raised his voice but was able to make his submissions with excellent examples and illustrations. But Palkhivala was not without his critics. Justice Jaganmohan Reddy, in his autobiography, remarked that Palkhivala's arguments were unnecessarily lengthy and sometimes political in nature:

> *One of the tendencies which I noticed in Palkhivala was that he was in the habit of answering with enthusiasm anything which fell from Chief Justice, Hegde and Grover and with some difference to the questions of Ray, Mathew, Palekar and Khanna. Palkhivala however often ignored questions from Dwivedi and Beg who he assumed had already formed their opinions, because more often theirs were not questions but dissertations. Mukherjee hardly ever said anything but when he did during Seervai's arguments, the implications of the questions posed by him were very significant and it took Seervai quite some time to formulate*

his answer, which when he did hardly touched the fringe of it. Chandrachud and I were frugal in our questions.[44]

No ambiguity

It is submitted that the general criticism that the *Kesavananda Bharati* judgment did not indicate any majority or minority view is not correct. A reading of the decision makes it clear that:

(i) The Twenty-fourth Amendment, which overruled *Golak Nath* view, was upheld. Therefore, Parliament was given the power to amend any part of the Constitution (subject to basic structure);

(ii) The Twenty-fifth Amendment replacing the word 'compensation' with 'amount' in Article 31 was also upheld.

(iii) The Twenty-fifth Amendment, which inserted Article 31C, was also upheld except the latter part of Article 31C.

(iv) The Twenty-ninth Amendment was upheld – this amendment had included two Kerala land reform laws in the Ninth Schedule.

(v) Parliament cannot alter the basic structure or framework of the Constitution.

These five principles summarise the essence of the *Kesavananda Bharati* case.

Narrow victory for democracy

The decision shows that but for the latter part of Justice Khanna's judgment, the entire case would have gone against the petitioners. One can only shudder to think as to what would have happened if the decision had gone the other way. To start with, the Thirty-ninth Amendment passed by Parliament, when all the opposition members were in jail, would have become the law. This granted immunity to Indira Gandhi and nullified the decision of the Allahabad High Court. The Forty-first Amendment Bill, which lapsed eventually, granted complete immunity from all civil and criminal proceedings to the President, Vice-President, Prime Minister and Governors. Thus, even a person accused of murder or

---

44. Justice P. Jaganmohan Reddy, *The Judiciary I Served,* Orient Longman (1999), p. 229.

rape could not be prosecuted if he had functioned as Governor for just one day. The Forty-second Amendment was equally devastating to the Constitution. All these amendments could never have been challenged. With increasing degradation in standards of public life, it would have been a matter of time before the country descended into a dictatorship or one-party rule.

Postscript – Shameful supersession of judges

The judgment in *Kesavananda Bharati* was delivered on the last working day of Chief Justice Sikri. He retired on April 25, 1973. The tradition of appointing the senior most judge as the Chief Justice was abandoned and Justice Ray, who was the fourth in the line of seniority, superseded Justices Shelat, Hegde and Grover. Shamefully, this announcement was first made known through a radio broadcast over the All India Radio. The three superseded judges resigned, leading to widespread protest throughout the country. In several High Courts, there was a boycott of one day. Chief Justice Ray never commanded the respect that was due to a Chief Justice. Over the years, his judgments were mainly in favour of the Union of India. To be fair, he had struck down the Thirty-ninth Amendment which sought to nullify the Allahabad High Court judgment and make the election of the Prime Minister unquestionable in any court of India. This was done despite the Emergency. Similarly, he also struck down the Newsprint Control Order in the *Bennett Coleman* case[45] in late 1972. But the Bar never forgave him for being a party to the supersession of senior judges. It is reported that when there were earlier attempts to supersede the senior most judge, all the remaining judges threatened to resign. If Ray had set a similar example, he would have greatly contributed to the independence and prestige of the judiciary. The supersession of judges was just the beginning of a continued onslaught on the judiciary which extended till 1977 and was resumed once again after Mrs. Gandhi came back to power.

Basic structure doctrine – Saviour of the rule of law

Subsequent events have shown the necessity of the basic structure doctrine and it has been the bulwark against repeated attempts of politicians to subvert the Constitution. It is now accepted by everyone in India that Parliament should not be given unlimited power to amend the Constitution.

---

45. *Bennett Coleman & Co. v. Union of India,* AIR 1973 SC 106 : (1972) 2 SCC 788.

Whatever its defects and the manner in which the case was heard and judgment delivered, the formulation of the basic structure theory saved democracy and preserved the rule of law. Our political leaders, with nothing else in mind but political vote banks and the next election, will never be able to destroy the basic features of our Constitution.

And, finally, the marathon hearing yielded no relief to His Holiness Kesavananda Bharati or any of the other petitioners. But they have the consolation of being responsible for the basic structure doctrine and saving Indian democracy.

(vii)

The Clumsy Attempt to Review Kesavananda Bharati

The historic verdict in *Kesavananda Bharati* came on April 24, 1973. It continues to be remembered for formulating the basic structure theory and imposing a limitation on the power of Parliament to amend the Constitution. This was perhaps its biggest contribution. At the same time, it is often forgotten that Union of India succeeded on virtually all other points. The 24th and 29th Amendments were upheld in full and the 25th Amendment, which sought to introduce Article 31C was partly struck down by a wafer thin majority of 7:6. Indeed, the decision in the *Kesavananda Bharati* case was more than adequate to enable the Government to carry out its socialistic reforms, especially after the categorical verdict that the right to property was not a fundamental right. With this, the basic complaint of the Central Government was over. Even the six judges who had held that the Parliament could not alter the basic structure or essential features of the Constitution accepted Parliament's power to amend any fundamental right. The *Golak Nath* view had been decisively overruled and the 24th Amendment had been upheld subject to the basic structure doctrine.

Similarly, the deletion of the word 'compensation' had been upheld and it was made clear that the amount paid need not be the market price. Indeed, it could be much less than that. All that the Supreme Court required was the amount to be paid should not be illusory. This was a perfectly valid view as it would be immoral for any Government that respected the rule of law to take away property and pay something that was ridiculously low. No court of any democracy could be expected to uphold payment of an amount that was totally absurd.

If the *Kesavananda Bharati* judgment is read dispassionately, the only part that was really against the Government was striking down the latter part of Article 31C which again was utterly incapable of being defended. Thus, the Union of India should have been perfectly content with this judgment as there could be no legal hurdle in implementing any socialistic reform programme.

In the latter half of 1973, things became politically more difficult for Mrs. Indira Gandhi with an increasingly strident opposition. The railway strike of May 1974 had a crippling effect on the economy; strikes, lockouts and *bandhs* became more widespread. Meanwhile, the nationalization programmes continued with coal companies being nationalized. Similarly, several other companies were taken over. The Monopolies and Restrictive Trade Practices Act, 1969, was also being implemented vigorously. The economy of India was on a clear socialist path.

Appeal against the Allahabad High Court decision

In June 1975, the historic Allahabad judgment found Indira Gandhi guilty of two corrupt election practices under Section 123(7) of the Representation of the People Act, 1951, and she was disqualified for six years. Indira Gandhi appealed to the Supreme Court and Palkhivala initially appeared for her but later withdrew from the case after the imposition of the Emergency. Mrs. Indira Gandhi eventually succeeded in her appeal but the Supreme Court struck down a part of the 39th Amendment that prevented the election of a Prime Minister from being questioned in a court of law.

On September 1, 1975, an oral application was made by Govind Swaminathan, the then Advocate-General of Tamil Nadu along with the Attorney-General, Niren De, for fixing an early date to hear certain land ceiling cases where the question of violation of the basic structure was involved. This request was made when the appeal of Mrs. Indira Gandhi was being heard by a Constitution Bench of five judges. Niren De had been highly critical of the basic structure theory while arguing in support of the 39th Amendment in the appeal of Mrs. Indira Gandhi.

The arguments in her appeal were concluded on October 9, 1975 and judgment was reserved. On October 20, 1975, Chief Justice Ray passed a written order constituting a Bench of 13 judges who were to hear arguments on two questions:-

(i) Whether or not the basic structure doctrine restricted Parliament's power to amend the Constitution ?

(ii) Whether or not the *Bank Nationalization* case had been correctly decided ?

This order was indeed surprising because no review petition had been filed by any of the parties to the *Kesavananda Bharati* case. It must also be noted that the first question was also inappropriate because the Supreme Court had effectively held that the Parliament's power to amend the Constitution would not include the power to alter its basic structure. If at all this view was to be overruled, then it would be necessary to constitute a Bench of 15 judges just as a Bench of 13 judges had to be constituted to reconsider the decision of 11 judges in the *Golak Nath* case.

It is also mysterious as to why the correctness of the *Bank Nationalisation* case had to be re-examined. The Government had already paid the higher compensation and passed the Bank Nationalisation Act. Fourteen banks had been nationalized and there was no controversy left.

As scheduled, the Bench of 13 judges assembled on November 10, 1975 to hear what effectively was a review of the *Kesavananda Bharati* judgment. Of the 13 judges who had heard that case, only five judges had continued in office: Chief Justice A.N. Ray, Justice H.R. Khanna, Justice K.K. Mathew, Justice M.H. Beg and Justice Y.V. Chandrachud. The eight new judges on the Bench were: P.N. Bhagwati, V.R. Krishna Iyer, P.K. Goswami, R.S. Sarkaria, A.C. Gupta, N.L. Untwalia, M. Fazl Ali and P.M. Singhal.

An 'improper' letter

Palkhivala who had been engaged to appear in the review petition, wrote a personal letter to Mrs. Indira Gandhi just a day before the hearing.[1] In a recent article,[2] T.R. Andhyarujina remarked that this the letter was of 'doubtful propriety'. Palkhivala congratulated Indira Gandhi on the success of her appeal but went on to request her to withdraw the Government's attempt to get the *Kesavananda* judgment reconsidered. Palkhivala also praised Indira Gandhi by pointing out that India was the only country that continued to have political stability while Pakistan, Burma and Ceylon, which had become independent at the same time, were facing political instability and wrote: 'The greatest credit for this achievement is due, apart from the outstanding personality of your father and yourself, to the basic structure of our Constitution'.

---

1. *M.V. Kamath, Nani Palkhivala : A life*, pp. 190-194.
2. 'The Untold Story of How Kesavananda Bharati and the basic Structure Doctrine Survived an Attempt to Reverse them by the Supreme Court', (2009) 9 SCC J-33.

At the end of the letter, Palkhivala 'beseeched' Indira Gandhi to reconsider the review plea as this would save several months of hearing and prevent wastage of judicial time. Apparently, Indira Gandhi simply ignored this letter and the hearing commenced on November 10, 1975. Perhaps, she had not forgiven him for refusing to appear in her case after she declared the emergency in June 1975.

Palkhivala's finest hour

As has been repeatedly pointed out, the two days of arguments on November 10 and 11, 1975 represented the finest hour of Palkhivala's legal career. Justice Khanna and other judges were of the view that the heights of eloquence and advocacy reached on these two days were really unparalleled and that Palkhivala's feat would perhaps never be equalled in the Supreme Court. Talat Ansari,[3] who was also instructing him, recollects that Palkhivala came to Delhi the previous night and they had only one discussion in the morning. Palkhivala asked the instructing lawyers to keep their judgments ready. He had already formulated his objections to the review.

The necessity of the basic structure doctrine was amply demonstrated by two constitutional amendments. The 39th amendment prohibited any challenge to the election of the President, Vice-President, Prime Minister and Speaker. Shockingly, the amendments stipulated that even pending cases or appeals would stand dismissed. There was no doubt that the amendment was only to protect Indira Gandhi and nullify the Allahabad High Court's judgment that had set aside her election. This amendment was most unfortunate because her appeal was pending in the Supreme Court.

Even more shocking was the 41st Amendment Bill which later lapsed. This bill prohibited any civil or criminal proceedings against the President, Vice-President, Prime Minister and Governors. Palkhivala pointed out that if this Bill had become law, any criminal would not be punished if he became the Governor for just one day. This would give him a complete immunity for the rest of his life however heinous his crime may have been. It is amazing how any one could have thought of such an amendment in a democratic republic. Palkhivala used these amendments to devastating advantage

---

3. Now a partner with Kelley Drye & Warren LLP, a firm of attorneys in the United States.

and pointed out that without the basic structure theory, these amendments would be valid. He then asked the thirteen judges to imagine what could happen if they reviewed and overruled the basic structure doctrine in *Kesavananda* case. Thus, these two outrageous amendments did more than anything else to justify the need for the basic structure theory. Parliament could no longer be trusted to protect and preserve the Constitution.

An excellent account of what transpired is contained in a recent article written by T. R. Andhyarujina[4] and in a book by Prashant Bhushan.[5] Bhushan was present at the hearing and had noted the interesting exchanges that took place before the Supreme Court. Some of the questions put to Palkhivala and his replies were noted in great detail by Prashant Bhushan and deserve to be reproduced.

Palkhivala began by pointing out that no review petition had been filed. Was the intended review based on any oral request for review by the Union of India? he asked.

Chief Justice Ray: No, the request had also come from the petitioners. Ever since the *Kesavananda Bharati* case, we have been flooded with requests for review from these petitioners.

Palkhivala: I beg your pardon, my Lord. It is impossible that the petitioners had requested a review. Why should they ask for a review which could only damage their case? If the basic feature theory disappears, then no Constitutional amendment can be struck down.

Chief Justice: Even the Tamil Nadu Government had asked for a review.

Tamil Nadu Advocate-General: I beg your pardon, my Lord. We never even once asked for a review.[6]

Chief Justice: Well, you were all asking for some constitutional amendment to be struck down on the doctrine of basic features. The Government said that it could not understand the theory, so the question arose.

---

4. 'The Untold Story of How Kesavananda Bharati and the basic Structure Doctrine Survived an Attempt to Reverse them by the Supreme Court', (2009) 9 SCC J-33.
5. *The Case that Shook India,* Vikas Publishing, Appendix 3, pp. 256-268. This book was published in 1978 and contains an excellent account of Indira Gandhi's election case in the Allahabad High Court, her subsequent appeal to the Supreme Court and the review petition.
6. The Advocate-General was S. Govind Swaminathan, a fearless advocate.

Palkhivala: The question would, of course, arise whenever a constitutional amendment is to be struck down on that theory, but that does not mean that it should be reviewed. If a principle has to be reviewed every time that it arises, then every case of the Supreme Court would have to be reviewed within a few days.

Palkhivala was particularly blunt in his response to queries raised by Justices Beg and Murtaza Fazl Ali.

Justice Beg: Mr. Palkhivala, how can you assume that we will overrule that case?

Palkhivala: Then are we going to waste five months of the Supreme Court's time merely to reaffirm an old judgment? We are not a debating society that we argue in order to reaffirm a judgment. Therefore, we have to consider the possibility of its being overruled.

Justice Beg: You see, I don't know what these basic features are.

Palkhivala: With the greatest respect, my Lord, it is inconceivable that the Supreme Court cannot understand its own judgment. If the Supreme Court cannot understand its own judgment, then who will? I have absolutely no doubt in my mind as to what the basic features are, and anybody who reads the judgment carefully cannot have any doubt.

Justice Beg: But I think every article in the Constitution is basic.

Palkhivala: If you take that view, my Lord, I will be the happiest man, because then the Constitution will remain substantially unchanged throughout.

Justice Beg: No, I mean I cannot tell the difference between basic and non-basic features.

Palkhivala: Suppose Article 368 of the Constitution itself said that the basic structure of the Constitution cannot be damaged or destroyed. The judiciary as the interpreter of the Constitution would have had to interpret it. Could it have said that it did not understand the Constitution?

Justice Murtaza Fazl Ali tried to justify the review on the ground that the *Kesavananda Bharati* decision was not clear.

Justice Murtaza Fazl Ali: Mr. Palkhivala, it seems that the judgment in *Kesavananda Bharati* is ambiguous, and by reconsidering it we might only clarify the issues.

Palkhivala: I do not think it is ambiguous, but assuming that it is, we have judges of enough competence to interpret even ambiguous judgments. Ambiguous judgments involving general principles are interpreted every day by this Honourable Court. What about the dictum that 'the essential powers of legislation' cannot be delegated? What are the essential powers of legislation? Or take the due process clause of America. For 200 years, the US Supreme Court has been interpreting and evolving that principle. Does it have any precise meaning? We can't have cut and dried definitions of general principles. They are not things which can be applied like mathematical formulae.

Justice Murtaza Fazl Ali: But we might only clarify and lay down as to what the basic feature is.

Palkhivala: We don't need the Full Court of 13 judges to lay down what the basic structure is. Each Constitution Bench can come to its own conclusion on that. Moreover, that is not the question referred to this Bench. The question referred to this Bench is whether the Parliament's powers are limited by the basic feature theory. And even if this Court does try to clarify, how can we assume that the judgment will be any less ambiguous than in the *Kesavananda Bharati* case?

Justice Murtaza Fazl Ali: Suppose the *Kesavananda Bharati* decision had gone against you. Would you not have been entitled to come and ask for a review now. So why should you object to the Government asking for a review?

Palkhivala: Let me answer this without any flippancy, my Lord. If the *Kesavananda Bharati* decision had gone against us, then there would be no Supreme Court today before which I could come for a review. But supposing that by some stroke of good fortune some part of the Court survived, I would have perhaps been entitled to ask for a review because of its baneful effect on public interest. But here the case is just the opposite. If the decision is reversed, then it will have a baneful effect on public interest.

In a similar vein, Justice Untwalia tried to suggest that errors, if any, in the *Kesavananda Bharati* decision could be corrected by the review petition.

Justice Untwalia: Suppose there is a manifest error, but we are not sure of the baneful effect on public interest. In that case, can we review a judgment?

Palkhivala: My Lord, if a case goes on for five months, is heard by 13 judges and literally thousands of authorities are quoted in the judgment, can anyone say that there is a manifest error in the judgment?

Palkhivala reminded the court that judicial discipline demanded that cases should not be reviewed because the constitution of the court changes and asked: What respect would the people have if the court behaved in a capricious way?

Justice Mathew: You can't say that we didn't observe judicial discipline. We struck down the 39th Amendment by respecting the majority decision.

Palkhivala: I never said that you didn't observe judicial discipline. In fact, until now the Supreme Court has had the most glorious tradition of observing judicial discipline and it would be very sad if this tradition is broken now.

And there were some lighter moments when Palkhivala complained about press censorship and the ban on public debate on many important public issues. Palkhivala remarked that even proceedings in court were not allowed to be published.

Justice Krishna Iyer: Are there any written orders about censorship of court proceedings?

Palkhivala: Yes, there are, and we have enough documentary evidence to prove it to the hilt. The Delhi High Court's judgment on the *habeas corpus* petition of Mr. Kuldip Nayar was not allowed to be published. The only way one heard of it was by tuning in to the BBC which reported parts of it. What I am saying now also will not be reported in tomorrow's newspapers due to censorship. If I say anything about the recent amendments in public, I shall probably be arrested. In fact, the only place where there is any freedom of speech in this country is the few hundred square feet of various courtrooms. In fact, I am very grateful to the Government for giving me the opportunity of expressing my views in this court.

Justice Krishna Iyer (amidst laughter): You should thank the Court for this.

Palkhivala: My Lords, I do thank the Court.

Niren De, arguing for the Union of India, called Palkhivala's argument a 'political lecture'. He submitted that the 'incoherent decision' in *Kesavananda Bharati* case had created chaos and everyone was giving different interpretations to the decision. Nowhere in the world was there a limitation on the amending power on the basis of a basic structure theory. The Government was finding it difficult to follow this doctrine and it was necessary that the judgment should be reconsidered so that not only the Government but also the citizens should know the correct position in law. He also criticised Palkhivala for not earlier objecting to the decision of the court to constitute a Bench to review the *Kesavananda Bharati* judgment. Palkhivala had 'sprung a surprise' by objecting to the review and a furious De remarked that he had not come across such submissions ever being made by a lawyer. Therefore, it was necessary for the court to clear up the issues.

Several judges asked De what exactly were the problems created by *Kesavananda Bharati.* Was there even one concrete instance where the basic structure theory had come in the way of passing socio-economic legislation?

Justice Khanna: Has the theory of basic features impeded any legislation about socio-economic measures?

De: Socio-economic measures are not the only thing, important as they are. The very structure of Government is the fundamental object of the amending process. You don't need the amending power for non-essential features of the Constitution.

Justice Untwalia: Is there any example where the Government wanted to amend the Constitution in public interest and has been prevented by the basic feature theory?

De: Take the case of the 39th Amendment.

Justice Untwalia: I am talking of amendments in public interest.

Justice Krishna Iyer: Are you asking for a clarification of the basic structure, or do you want us to annihilate the theory?

De: Mr. Palkhivala has raised preliminary objection that we can't go into that case. At least the court can go into it to clarify it.

On November 12, 1975, the case was posted for the third day of hearing and the Attorney-General was to continue his arguments. As soon as the Bench assembled, the Chief Justice announced 'This Bench is dissolved'. Before rising, he directed that the Constitution Bench would hear the petition from Andhra Pradesh which had challenged the Administrative Tribunal in Andhra Pradesh created by the Constitution (Thirty-second Amendment) Act, 1973, and that Bench could refer the case to the Full Court if it found any difficulty in applying the *Kesavananda* case.

The constitution of the 13-judge Bench was a pathetic attempt to overrule *Kesavananda Bharati*. The hearing was scheduled without any request from any party and there was nothing to indicate that the basic structure doctrine had created serious complications in the functioning of Parliament. A large part of the credit should also go to Govind Swaminathan, a fearless advocate, who was then the Advocate-General of Tamil Nadu. He, without any hesitation, dramatically got up and called the Chief Justice's bluff. Similarly, J.M. Thakore, the then Advocate-General of Gujarat, also informed the court that they too had not asked for any review. This was obviously very embarrassing to the Chief Justice.

The sudden dissolution of the Bench was a total surprise and an anti-climax. Andhyarujina believes that even the remaining 12 judges or at least some of them had no knowledge that the Bench would be dissolved. This tragic attempt on the part of Chief Justice Ray was a further set-back to his reputation. He continued as Chief Justice till he retired on January 28, 1977. Ray returned to Calcutta and recently passed away at the age of 99. History is the cruelest judge and Justice Ray will be remembered as having presided over the Supreme Court during its darkest period.

Till this day, it remains a mystery as to why a review Bench was constituted. Perhaps the Chief Justice thought that barring Justice Khanna, the other judges who heard *Kesavananda Bharati* and continued on the Bench had held against the basic structure doctrine. Even if three of the new judges decided against the doctrine, they could easily set it aside. What was missed by a hair's breadth in *Kesavananda Bharati* was attempted to be achieved through the review petition, a clumsy attempt that miserably failed.

❋

(viii)

St. Xavier's Case

Protecting Minority Rights

Consolidating minority rights

Articles 29 and 30 deal with cultural and educational rights and are intended to protect the interests of minorities. The draft articles were debated extensively in the Constituent Assembly as it was clear that an independent India could not be held together unless there was unity amongst the diverse linguistic and religious minorities. A special advisory committee was constituted which made important recommendations that formed the foundation for Articles 29 and 30. Article 29(1) confers on 'any section of the citizens'[1] the fundamental right to preserve their language, script or culture. Under Article 29(2), no citizen can be denied admission into any school or college which receives State aid on the basis of his religion, race, caste or language. Article 30(1) goes a step further and gives all minorities, whether linguistic or religious, the right to establish and administer educational institutions of their choice. Article 30(2) prohibits the Central and State Governments from discriminating against minority institutions while granting financial aid.[2]

---

1. This phrase was substituted for 'minorities'. Article 30, however, uses the word 'minorities'.
2. The text of Articles 29 and 30 is:

   '29. Protection of interests of minorities.—(1) Any section of the citizens residing in the territory of India or any part thereof having a distinct language, script or culture of its own shall have the right to conserve the same. (2) No citizen shall be denied admission into any educational institution maintained by the State or receiving aid out of State funds on grounds only of religion, race, caste, language or any of them.

   30. Right of minorities to establish and administer educational institutions.—(1) All minorities, whether based on religion or language, shall have the right to establish and administer educational institutions of their choice. (2) The State shall not, in granting aid to educational institutions, discriminate against any educational institution on the ground that it is under the management of a minority, whether based on religion or language.'

Thus, minorities have the fundamental right to establish their own schools and colleges. But the controversy that arose from time to time was the extent of autonomy that these institutions could enjoy. Could they have total freedom in recruiting staff, having their own curriculum and admitting students of their choice? From time to time, several State Governments tried to impose stringent regulations that interfered with the rights of management or administration of these minority institutions. It was only a matter of time before the Supreme Court would be called upon to demarcate the legal boundary that limited the right of the State Government to interfere with these educational institutions.

The unsuccessful experiment in Kerala

Article 30(1) has caused considerable controversy since 1957, when the then Communist Government in Kerala attempted sweeping educational reforms which led to widespread protests within the State that ultimately provoked the imposition of emergency under Article 356 of the Constitution. The President referred certain questions to the Supreme Court, seeking its opinion on the constitutional validity of the controversial provisions of the Kerala Education Bill.[3] The Kerala Education Bill, 1957, contained provisions for taking over the management of aided educational institutions as well as prescribing the mode and manner of appointment of the manager, teachers and non-teaching staff to these institutions. The aided institutions could not charge any fee other than the special fee that they were authorized to charge under this Act. In the case of primary education, neither aided nor unaided institutions were permitted to charge any fee at all. Stringent conditions for disclosure of assets and restrictions on alienation of the properties owned by aided institutions were also prescribed. There was also a prohibition on the manager of the concerned educational institution from shutting down the school without giving prior notice of one year. Amounts due to be paid by the manager could be recovered as an arrear of land revenue. Viewed as a whole, this Bill raised serious doubts in the mind of the

3. Article 143 enables the President to consult the Supreme Court on questions of law that are of major public importance. Article 143(1) is relevant and reads as follows:

'(1) If at any time it appears to the President that a question of law or fact has arisen, or is likely to arise, which is of such a nature and of such public importance that it is expedient to obtain the opinion of the Supreme Court upon it, he may refer the question to that Court for consideration and the Court may, after such hearing as it thinks fit, report to the President its opinion thereon.'

then President[4] as to its constitutional validity *vis-à-vis* Article 30(1). Therefore, acting under Article 143(1), the President referred certain questions to the Supreme Court, seeking its opinion on the constitutional validity of the controversial provisions of the Kerala Education Bill.

The Presidential reference in *In Re: The Kerala Education Bill, 1957*,[5] was decided by a Bench of seven judges. While six of the judges formed the majority and S.R. Das C.J. delivered the judgment on their behalf, Venkatarama Aiyar J. was the lone dissenter. The majority was of the view that many of the provisions contained in this Bill would qualify as reasonable, or at least constitutionally permissible, regulations. However, with regard to aided institutions, the majority felt that the power vested in the State, under Clause 14 of this Bill, to take over the management of these institutions in case of negligence on the part of the manager, or on the ground of larger public interest, would be violative of Article 30(1). The majority also held that Clause 15 of this Bill, which vested the Government with power to acquire any category of schools for standardising general education in the State or for improving the level of literacy in any area or for more effectively managing the aided educational institutions in any area or for bringing education of any category under their direct control, would infringe the rights of the aided institutions guaranteed by Article 30(1).

In the case of unaided institutions that merely sought recognition, the majority felt that they could not be compelled to provide primary education for free. While this condition could be validly imposed on aided institutions since the Government was obliged to pay the teachers and the non-teaching staff, there was no justification for imposing it on the unaided institutions as well.

Thus, the majority in *In Re: The Kerala Education Bill, 1957*, gave some guidance on the scope of Article 30(1). The clauses that were ultimately considered unconstitutional were those that directly infringed the rights of the minority institutions, by permitting the Government to take over or acquire the management of these institutions and thus destroy their minority character, or by mandating them to provide free education thereby hampering their commercial viability. The legality of other restrictions, of a more indirect nature, was not examined in detail by the Supreme Court.

4. President Rajendra Prasad, who was a very successful and astute lawyer.
5. AIR 1958 SC 956 : [1959] SCR 995.

The continuing conflict

The conflict between the States, which continued to assert their authority and control through indirect methods, and the minority educational institutions, which desired to retain their autonomy, continued to fester.

In some of the subsequent decisions, provisions analogous to the ones that were considered constitutionally permissible by the majority in *In re: The Kerala Education Bill* were struck down as being violative of Article 30(1).[6] All this while, there were continued attempts by various State Governments to increase the extent of their control over educational institutions. It was only a matter of time when the Supreme Court would have to reconsider the law on the effect of Articles 29 and 30 and the extent to which minority institutions could retain their autonomy. The Supreme Court did not have to wait long and, in 1974, Chief Justice A. N. Ray constituted a nine-judge Bench to consider this constitutional controversy in a writ petition filed by the Ahmedabad St. Xavier's College Society.[7]

St. Xavier's case – Challenging drastic interference in management

The seeds of the controversy in this case[8] dated to a period even prior to the Kerala Education Bill. The Gujarat University Act was enacted in 1949. Section 40 of this Act provided that the Senate of the Gujarat University could, within a period of seven years from the date on which this University was incorporated, determine that in the City of Ahmedabad, all instructions, teaching and training beyond the stage of Intermediate Examinations would be conducted by this University and imparted by its teachers. Upon such determination, Section 41 of this Act would apply and all educational institutions within Ahmedabad would become constituent institutions of the Gujarat University. Section 41 also prohibited these educational institutions from associating with, or seeking admission to, the privileges of any other University without

---

6. *State of Kerala v. Very Rev. Mother Provincial,* AIR 1970 SC 2079 : (1970) 2 SCC 417 : 1970 KLT 630; *D.A.V. College, Bhatinda v. State of Punjab,* AIR 1971 SC 1731 : (1971) 2 SCC 261. The entire sequence of decisions before *St. Xavier's* case, the nature of the provisions/ governmental action called into question in each of these decisions, and the view taken by the Supreme Court, have been discussed in Ray C.J.'s opinion as well as by Khanna J.
7. The nine judges were: Ray C.J., and P. Jaganmohan Reddy, Palekar, Khanna, Mathew, Beg, Dwivedi, Chandrahud and Alagiriswami JJ.
8. *Ahmedabad St. Xavier's College Society v. State of Gujarat,* AIR 1974 SC 1389 : (1974) 1 SCC 717.

the prior consent of the Gujarat University and the sanction of the State Government. The determination under Section 40 was not made within the prescribed seven year period thereby keeping dormant the wide powers vested in the University.

Meanwhile, St. Xavier's College of Arts and Commerce was established in Ahmedabad in June 1955 by the Society of Jesus, which was a religious order of Catholic priests and brothers. The college sought to provide higher education to Christian students, but admitted children of all religions to the college if they fulfilled the qualifying academic standards. St. Xavier's College was also accorded affiliation under Section 33 of the Gujarat University Act, 1949, in or about June 1955.

Imposing various controls

In 1971, the Senate's attempt to exercise the powers conferred on it under this Act was challenged on the ground that the seven year period had lapsed. This, in turn, led to the enactment of the Gujarat University (Amendment) Act, 1972. Section 41 of the amended Act converted all affiliated colleges of the University into its 'constituent' colleges, thereby integrating them. Section 41(4) conferred on the University vast powers: (i) to approve the appointment of teachers to these colleges, (ii) to require these colleges to contribute teachers for teaching on behalf of the University, (iii) to co-ordinate and regulate the facilities provided and expenditure incurred by these colleges and institutions on libraries, laboratories and other equipments for teaching and research, (iv) to require these colleges and institutions to confine the enrolment of students in certain subjects, and (v) to levy contributions from these colleges and institutions and to make grants to them.

Section 33A(1)(a) of the amended Act made further inroads into the management of these colleges by providing for a governing body consisting of a representative of the University nominated by the Vice-Chancellor, and representatives of teachers, non-teaching staff and students of these respective colleges. Section 51A interfered with the autonomy of these colleges to deal with cases of disciplinary misconduct by requiring the prior approval of the Vice-Chancellor or any other authorised officer of the University before any member of the teaching or non-teaching staff of any of these colleges could be dismissed, removed or reduced in rank. Section 52A created a new Tribunal of Arbitration to adjudicate any disputes between the governing body and any member of the teaching or non-teaching staff of an affiliated college that related to the conditions of service. This Tribunal was to consist of one member nominated by the governing body of the college, one member nominated by the member concerned, and an umpire appointed by the Vice-Chancellor. Thus, the control of the University was all pervasive and minority institutions were left with very little autonomy.

Serious erosion of minority rights

Nani Palkhivala appeared for St. Xavier's College Society, which had directly filed a writ petition before the Supreme Court under Article 32 of the Constitution. According to Palkhivala, the rights conferred by Article 30(1) could neither be taken away nor abridged by the State on account of the injunction in Article 13(2).[9] He submitted that the 'right to administer' guaranteed autonomy in administration. The management had the right to mould the minority institution as it considered fit. The regulatory measures adopted by the State could not restrict this right and could only facilitate the same through the instrumentality of the management of the minority institution. If the management of the minority institution were to be displaced, that would amount to a violation of the right to administer.

As in the other important cases argued by him, Palkhivala once again created a prism from which the judges could view the different facets and components of the impugned Act. This prism was built on the theme of autonomy of religious minorities. Using this theme, he attacked various provisions of this Act. He contended that any requirement of prior approval by the Vice-Chancellor or any other officer of the University authorised by him before awarding punishment in cases of disciplinary misconduct, and that too without any guidelines for the grant or refusal of such approval, would virtually deprive the management of any control whatsoever over its staff. Similar criticism was raised against the power of the University to appoint its own representative to the Governing Council. The State's power to interfere with the curriculum and syllabus for religious, cultural or linguistic instruction being imparted in unaided and unrecognised educational institutions run by a religious or linguistic minority,

---

9. Article 13(2) reads: 'The State shall not make any law which takes away or abridges the rights conferred by this Part and any law made in contravention of this clause shall, to the extent of the contravention, be void.'

was also challenged. Similarly, Section 52A was challenged on the ground that the reference of disputes to the Tribunal envisaged by this provision amounted to an external interference with the management of the college's affairs.

The arguments raised by Palkhivala were incisive as subsequently seen from the outcome. Earlier attempts were made in vain to control such educational institutions and there were earlier judgments in his favour. Palkhivala was able to take these cases as a foundation and get the legal position clarified by the Constitution Bench. In that sense, there were lesser hurdles for him to overcome as compared to the *Bank Nationalization* case or the *Fundamental Rights* case.[10]

The broad issue in this case was whether, and if yes to what extent, the religious and linguistic minorities had the right to establish and administer educational institutions for imparting general secular education within the meaning of Article 30 of the Constitution. Relying on the decisions in *In Re: The Kerala Education Bill,*[11] *Rev. Sidhajbhai Sabbai v. State of Gujarat,*[12] *Rev. Father Proost v. State of Bihar,*[13] *Rt. Rev. Bishop S. K. Patro v. State of Bihar,*[14] *State of Kerala v. Very Rev. Mother Provincial,*[15] and *D.A.V. College, Bhatinda v. State of Punjab,*[16] Palkhivala submitted that the State could not impose onerous pre-conditions for granting affiliation to minority educational institutions that would have the effect of infringing on their autonomy. According to him, the right of these minority institutions to administer consisted of four principal matters, namely (i) the right to choose their managing or governing body, (ii) the right to choose their teachers, (iii) the right to choose their students, which includes the right not to be compelled to refuse admission to students of their choice, and (iv) the right to use their properties and assets for the benefit of the institution. The amendments to the Gujarat University Act had unreasonably infringed these facets of the right to administer.

---

10. As rightly observed by Justice Jaganmohan Reddy, 'The attempt on behalf of the State of Gujarat has been to once again raise the same crucial issues which go to the root of the rights conferred on the minorities to establish educational institutions of their choice and whether the State could treat the majority and minority educational institutions equally, an issue upon which this Court has pronounced in no uncertain terms on earlier occasions.'
11. AIR 1958 SC 956 : [1959] SCR 995.
12. AIR 1963 SC 540 : [1963] 3 SCR 837.
13. AIR 1969 SC 465 : (1969) 2 SCC 73.
14. AIR 1970 SC 259 : (1969) 1 SCC 863.
15. AIR 1970 SC 2079 : (1970) 2 SCC 417.
16. AIR 1971 SC 1737 : (1971) 2 SCC 269.

The State's jurisdiction

The State countered these submissions raised by Palkhivala and contended that no educational institution, minority or non-minority in character, could claim a fundamental right to affiliation. It was open to the State to bring in permissive regulatory measures for ensuring efficient and transparent administration of any affiliated college. Relying on the principle that the right to administer did not include the right to 'maladminister', the counsel for the State submitted that the impugned provisions in the amended Act were only meant to introduce certain checks and balances on the administration of these educational institutions. Once an institution sought affiliation from the University, it was estopped from challenging these checks and balances.

A pro-minority rights verdict

Seven judges were of the view that the conditions for affiliation, while they could validly be prescribed, had to remain within constitutional limits and not infringe on the rights of minorities under Article 30(1). On this common ground, seven judges delivered four opinions[17] striking down as unconstitutional the impugned provisions of the Gujarat University Act as amended. Beg and Dwivedi JJ. wrote dissenting opinions.

In the words of Ray C.J. : '[T]he real reason embodied in Article 30(1) of the Constitution is the conscience of the nation that the minorities, religious as well as linguistic, are not prohibited from establishing and administering educational institutions of their choice for the purpose of giving their children the best general education to make them complete men and women of the country.' According to him, affiliation served the primary purpose of ensuring that students from affiliated educational institutions finished their education with degrees necessary for a useful career. Viewed from this angle, the establishment of a minority institution would not only be ineffective but also unreal unless such institution was affiliated to a University for the purpose of conferment of degrees on students. He felt that the rationale behind Article 30 would be defeated if affiliation was on terms that would make minority educational institutions surrender and lose their rights under Article 30.

---

17. Ray C.J. delivered judgment on behalf of himself and Palekar J.; Jaganmohan Reddy J. on behalf of himself and Alagiriswami J.; Mathew J. on behalf of himself and Chandrachud J. and Khanna J. wrote a separate judgment. Beg J. and Dwivedi J. wrote separate dissenting opinions.

Ray C.J. split the conditions of affiliation into two categories: one consisting of prescription of syllabi, curricula, courses of instruction, the qualifications of teachers, libraries, laboratories and conditions regarding health and hygiene of students, and the other consisting of terms and conditions regarding management and administration of such institutions. He felt that when it came to the first category, it was implicit that when a minority educational institution approached the University for affiliation, it was willing to adhere to the University's prescribed standards. However, the second category of conditions that pertained to management and administration of these colleges did not throw up such an easy solution because the University had less of a legitimate interest in the day to day running of these colleges than in the prescription of general standards.

Ray C.J. held that regulations were permissible only to ensure that there was no maladministration. Applying this yardstick, he felt that Section 40 of the amended Act, which made all affiliated colleges as 'constituent' colleges where the teaching would be conducted by teachers of the University, was destructive of the minority character of the petitioner and other such institutions and hence violated Article 30(1). He also held that Section 41 would be inapplicable to these institutions once it was concluded that Section 40 could not be made compulsorily applicable to them.

Accepting Palkhivala's contention that the right of administration could not be usurped, and the State could only facilitate better administration, Ray C.J. also held Section 33A(1)(a) and (b) to be inapplicable to minority educational institutions. He reasoned that immediate and effective action in cases of disciplinary misconduct was again an integral part of this right of administration, and provisions such as Sections 51A and 52A would hamper the speed and efficacy of decision making by the management. On this ground, he considered these provisions also to be inapplicable to minority educational institutions.

Jaganmohan Reddy J. agreed with the conclusions of Ray C.J. but wrote a separate opinion where he chastised the State of Gujarat for coming up with these provisions despite 'the consistent and categorical decisions which have held invalid certain provisions of the University Acts of some of the States as interfering with the fundamental rights of management of minorities in situations inherent in the right to establish educational institutions of their choice under Article 30(1)'. He felt that '[A] kind of instability in the body politic will be created by action of a State which will be construed as a deliberate attempt to transgress the rights of the minorities where similar earlier attempts were successfully challenged and the offending provisions held invalid.'

H.R. Khanna J. discussed in detail the extent of the right of minorities to establish and administer educational institutions placing great reliance on the earlier decisions of the Supreme Court. The learned judge explained the purpose of the rights conferred under Article 30(1) in language that merits reproduction:

> *A liberal, generous and sympathetic approach is reflected in the Constitution in the matter of the preservation of the right of minorities so far as their educational institutions are concerned... The principle which can be discerned in the various decisions of this Court is that the catholic approach which led to the drafting of the provisions relating to minority rights should not be set at naught by narrow judicial interpretation.*
>
> *The right conferred by Article 30(1) is intended to be real and effective and not a mere pious and abstract sentiment; it is a promise of reality and not a teasing illusion. Such a right cannot be allowed to be whittled down by any measure masquerading as a regulation. Balance has, therefore, to be kept between the two objectives, that of ensuring the standard of excellence of the institution and that of preserving the right of the minorities to establish and administer their educational institutions. Regulations which embrace and reconcile the two objectives can be considered to be reasonable.*

Based on this reasoning, the learned Judge held that Sections 33A, 40, 41, 51A(1)(b) and (2)(b) and 52A were unconstitutional.

Mathew J. (on behalf of himself and Chandrachud J.) wrote a concurring judgment that examined the comparative jurisprudence on the issue of minority rights and concluded that the provisions of Sections 33A, 40, 51A(1)(b) and (2)(b) and 52A were violative of Article 30(1) of the Constitution. Therefore, they could have no application to educational institutions established and administered by religious or linguistic minorities.

Two dissenting judgments

Justices Beg and Dwivedi dissented and upheld the provisions of the Gujarat University Act as constitutionally valid. According to

Justice Beg J., the principles of estoppel and acquiescence would permit the State to impose the impugned regulations once the minority institution had consented to the affiliation. In his words:

> *[T]he essence of the right guaranteed by Article 30(1) of the Constitution is a free exercise of their choice by minority institutions of the pattern of education as well as of the administration of their educational institutions. Both these, taken together, determine the kind or character of an educational institution which a minority has the right to choose... In a case in which the pattern is accepted voluntarily by a minority institution, with a view to taking advantage of the benefits conferred by a statute, it seems to me that it cannot insist upon an absolutely free exercise of the right of administration. Here, the incidental fetters on the right to manage the institution, which is only a part of the fundamental right, would be consequences of an exercise of the substance or essence of the right which, as I see it, is freedom of choice. No doubt, the rights protected by Article 30(1) are laid down in "absolute" terms without the kind of express restrictions found in Articles 19, 25 and 26 of the Constitution. But, if a minority institution has the option open to it of avoiding the statutory restrictions altogether, if it abandons, with it, the benefits of a statutory right, I fail to see how the absoluteness of the right under Article 30(1) of the Constitution is taken away or abridged. All that happens is that the statute exacts a price in general interest for conferring its benefits......This article, meant to serve as a shield of minority educational institutions against the invasion of certain rights protected by it and declared fundamental so that they are not discriminated against, cannot be converted by them into a weapon to exact unjustifiable preferential or discriminatory treatment for minority institutions so as to obtain the benefits but to reject the obligations of statutory rights.*

This dissenting opinion bears striking similarity with the dissent of Justice T.L. Venkatarama Ayyar in *In Re: The Kerala Education Bill.*[18] Dwivedi J. also employed similar reasoning to strike a dissenting note.

---

18. AIR 1958 SC 956 : [1959] SCR 995.

Controversy set at rest

In effect, Palkhivala's submissions in this case were accepted by the majority and went on to become the law of the land. With the passage of time, this would also become the law for unaided private educational institutions of a non-minority character as the scope of Article 19(1)(g) was extended to confer the highest degree of autonomy on such institutions.[19] *St. Xavier's* case clearly laid down the constitutional boundary that the State Governments could not cross.

❄

19. See *P.A. Inamdar v. State of Maharashtra,* (2004) 8 SCC 139 : (2004) 6 SCALE 245.

(ix)

The Habeas Corpus Case

Palkhivala's Critical Absence

The darkest period in the history of the Supreme Court was its judgment in *A.D.M., Jabalpur v. Shivakant Shukla,*[1] also known as the *Habeas Corpus* case. Several detenues had successfully challenged their detention before various High Courts and appeals were filed before the Supreme Court by the State authorities. Allowing the appeals, the Supreme Court dealt a fatal blow to liberty and during the Emergency enabled the imprisonment or detention of any person without trial. In all, 1,10,806 persons were arrested, tortured and detained without trial during the Emergency (1975-77).[2] The helpless citizen, according to the Supreme Court, would have absolutely no remedy so long as the Emergency continued. It is necessary to set out a brief factual background that led to this bitterly criticized decision.

Sensational Allahabad High Court verdict:

On June 12, 1975, Justice J.M.L. Sinha of the Allahabad High Court found Prime Minister Indira Gandhi guilty of certain electoral malpractices. An appeal was immediately filed before the Supreme Court and on June 23, 1975, Justice Krishna Iyer – then the vacation judge – heard a petition seeking stay of this judgment. Surprisingly, Palkhivala was engaged to appear for Indira Gandhi even though he had been a bitter critic of her policies. On June 24, 1975, Justice Krishna Iyer granted a partial stay of the judgment and allowed her to continue as Prime Minister but without any voting rights in Parliament.

On June 25, 1975, the President declared an Emergency under Article 352(1) on the ground that the 'security of India was

---

1. AIR 1976 SC 1207 : (1976) 2 SCC 521. The initials *A.D.M.* refer to Additional District Magistrate.
2. 'Shah Commission Report – Lost and Regained', p. 8 – compiled and edited by Era Sezhiyan (former Member of Parliament), Azahi Publisher.

threatened by internal disturbances'. Soon after midnight, that is on June 26, most leaders of the opposition were arrested in different parts of the country. On June 27, 1975, the President made a declaration under Article 359(1) whereby no person could move the courts for the enforcement of Articles 14, 21 and 22.[3]

Palkhivala resigned that very day, that is June 26, and informed the Law Minister that he could not appear for the Prime Minister anymore. In a press statement that was not published in full because of pre-censorship during the Emergency, he informed the nation that 'the measures taken by the government this morning are such that, consistent with my lifelong convictions and the values I cherish, I have requested the Law Minister to convey to the Prime Minister my decision to withdraw as counsel from the appeal.'

Several of the arrested leaders had filed writs of *habeas corpus* to challenge their detention. The High Courts of Allahabad, Bombay (Nagpur Bench), Delhi, Karnataka, Madhya Pradesh, Punjab and Rajasthan had held that even though Article 359 suspended enforcement of Articles 14, 21 and 22, the High Courts were entitled to examine the orders of detention and see whether they complied with the mandatory provisions of the Maintenance of Internal Security Act, 1971 (MISA), or whether the orders were *mala fide* or based on irrelevant material. Therefore, even if the High Courts could not question the order of detention as being violative of Articles 14, 21 and 22, judicial scrutiny could not be shut out. These were courageous decisions made by several High Courts which were taken up in appeal before the Supreme Court. The High Courts were clearly right: Article 359 may suspend Articles 14, 21 and 22 but the detention orders could be set aside if they were contrary to the provisions of MISA. To illustrate, an income-tax assessment order may not violate Article 14, but it can be set aside, if it is contrary to the Income Tax Act, 1961. When one reads the galaxy of advocates who appeared before the Supreme Court, Palkhivala's name is conspicuous by its absence. In 1975, his position as the pre-eminent counsel in constitutional law and a popular defender of liberty was well established. He had also appeared successfully for Ram Jethmalani before the Bombay High Court during the Emergency. Why then was he absent during the hearing of these appeals?

---

3. For the text of Articles 14, 21 and 22 see the Appendix.

Sorabjee and other advocates had requested Palkhivala to come to Delhi to appear in the Supreme Court. Palkhivala's response was that there was no way that the Supreme Court would allow the appeals of the Government especially after seven High Courts had delivered well-reasoned decisions in favour of the citizen. His view was that it was an open and shut case and nothing would be gained by his appearing before the Supreme Court. Palkhivala felt that Chief Justice Ray and Justice Beg would possibly hold in favour of the Government. He was completely confident about Justice Chandrachud and Justice Bhagwati holding in favour of the citizen. Indeed, ironically, he felt that it was Justice Khanna who could be 'the dark horse' but could be persuaded to dismiss the appeal and uphold the right to liberty.

In perhaps its worst decision, by a majority of 4:1, the Supreme Court held:

(i) Article 359 not only prohibited enforcement of Articles 14, 21 and 22, it also barred a person detained from approaching the High Court to question his detention on *any ground whatsoever.*

(ii) Liberty is the gift of law and can be forfeited by law.

(iii) Once a presidential order is passed under Article 359, there is a complete bar on any person moving the court for violation of Articles 14, 19 and 21.

(iv) During the Emergency, no person can question his detention for any reason whatsoever or on the ground that it is illegal or *mala fide*. (Shockingly, the majority held that the Supreme Court was not competent to examine the question of *mala fides* or the character of the order of detention).

In brief, the Supreme Court held that any citizen or foreigner could be detained in an Indian jail under the MISA or any other preventive detention law for the prescribed period and the person arrested had no remedy whatsoever. (This was the Indian equivalent of being sent to Siberia).

In fact, during the hearing, Attorney-General Niren De was asked whether a person could be shot without any remedy. De replied that so long as the Emergency continued the court could do nothing if such an event occurred! Indeed, the nail in the coffin of judicial independence and freedom was the following oft-quoted remark of Justice Beg J.:

> *We understand that the care and concern bestowed by the State authorities upon the welfare of detenus who are well-housed, well-fed, and well-treated, is almost maternal. Even parents have to take appropriate preventive action against those children who may threaten to burn down the house they live in.*

In a bold dissenting judgment that cost him the office of Chief Justice, Justice H.R. Khanna held that even during the Emergency, the right of a person to approach the courts for redressal could not be taken away.[4] This was an 'essential postulate and basic assumption of the rule of law in every civilized society'. If the detention order did not comply with the prescribed procedure, it could be questioned under Article 226 in a writ of *habeas corpus.* Even during the Emergency, no authority could suspend the power of the High Court to issue such writs. The presidential order under Article 359(1) only suspended the right to enforce fundamental rights. The procedural safeguards under MISA were rights created by an ordinary law and were not fundamental rights.

When the judgment came on April 28, 1976, Justice Khanna was indeed the dark horse but not in the manner Palkhivala and the others imagined! The ruling was 4-1 in favour of the Government. The majority held that no citizen who had been arrested and detained, had the right to move a writ of *habeas corpus* before a High Court under Article 226, after the order under Article 359[5] was passed on of June 27, 1975. Section 16A(9) of the Maintenance of Internal Security Act, 1971, which enabled the State not to inform the grounds of arrest to the detenue was also unfortunately upheld by the majority. India, thanks to this

---

4. Justice H. R. Khanna was superseded, not surprisingly, by Justice M.H. Beg.
5. Article 359(1) reads as under: 'Suspension of the enforcement of the rights conferred by Part III during emergencies.–(1) Where a Proclamation of Emergency is in operation, the President may by order declare that the right to move any court for the enforcement of such of the rights conferred by Part III as may be mentioned in the order and all proceedings pending in any court for the enforcement of the rights so mentioned shall remain suspended for the period during which the Proclamation is in force or for such shorter period as may be specified in the order.

   It had the effect of preventing any person from filing a writ petition challenging the detention order as violating any fundamental right during the period for which Emergency was proclaimed. This Article was amended in 1978 and thereafter enables any detenue to challenge a detention order if it violates Article 20 or 21. The 44th Amendment substituted the words "the rights conferred by Part III" with the words "the rights conferred by Part III (except Articles 20 and 21)."'

Supreme Court decision, virtually became a police state till the Emergency was lifted in 1977.

When the judgment was delivered, Palkhivala was in the midst of a meeting at Bombay. The news received via telex was that the verdict was 4:1. The first reaction of everybody present was jubilant as all of them thought that the citizens had succeeded and one judge alone had dissented. When the actual result was learnt, a few minutes later, Palkhivala sat in stunned silence for a whole minute. Then he seemed to want to distract himself by returning to the work at hand and continued with the meeting.

It would be presumptuous to imagine that Palkhivala's presence would have made a decisive difference had he been present. The decision was clearly influenced by much that happened outside the courtroom and subsequent research seems to suggest that there were many extraneous considerations that played a role in the rendering of that decision. However, the record might have reflected another brilliant defence of liberty from one of its most glorious champions. And for that reason alone, Palkhivala's appearance would have served a purpose. Given the fact that several persons had been detained without trial, Palkhivala ought to have appeared in the case.

In the end, Justice Khanna lost the office of Chief Justice but gained the admiration and respect of millions of citizens. Long after the names of the four judges constituting the majority are forgotten, the name of Justice Khanna will still be remembered for his courage in adhering to constitutional values. In a tribute entitled 'Salute to Justice Khanna' published in the *Indian Express* soon after, Palkhivala described him in the following words:

> *In deciding the habeas corpus matter as he did, H.R. Khanna played a memorable role at the most critical juncture in our history. Generations unborn will admire his historic judgment as a shining example of judicial integrity and courage and cherish it for the abiding values it embodies.*
>
> *H.R. Khanna has the priceless inner satisfaction of feeling that he has lived above the fog in public duty and in private thinking. When he pronounced his glorious dissent in the habeas corpus case, the New York Times remarked that surely a statue would be erected to him some day in an Indian city. His real monuments are his rulings upholding the basic structure of the Constitution and the citizen's*

> *right to his life and personal liberty. To the stature of such a judge, the Chief Justiceship of India could have added nothing.*

The disgraceful policy of superseding independent judges continued and Justice Beg was appointed as the Chief Justice superseding Justice H.R. Khanna who retired on March 12, 1977. The least that Indira Gandhi could have done was to have gracefully appointed Justice Khanna as the Chief Justice of India for the remaining six weeks of his tenure.

❋

(x)

The Minerva Mills Case

Challenging a Constitutional Outrage

Having failed in a clumsy judicial attempt to destroy the basic structure theory, the then ruling party introduced what H.M. Seervai called a 'constitutional outrage' – the Forty-second Amendment to the Constitution. This was really the second outrage on the Constitution; the dubious distinction of winning the first prize must go to the Thirty-ninth Amendment.

The Thirty-ninth Amendment

The Thirty-ninth Amendment to the Constitution introduced during the Emergency of 1975-77, was a shocking attempt to specifically nullify the Allahabad High Court's judgment which set aside the election of Mrs. Indira Gandhi. It was the first manifestation of what damage a Government, that had little regard for constitutional propriety, could do to the Constitution. Section 4 of this amendment specifically stated that the elections of the President, Vice-President, Prime Minister and Speaker could not be called in question before any court of law. Not content with this monstrous provision, it went on to provide that the elections of these four functionaries could not be questioned even in election petitions filed before 1975! It added that any order made by any court setting aside an election of any of these four functionaries would be deemed to be void and have no effect and that elections of all these four functionaries shall *always be deemed to have been valid in all respects.* If there was any appeal pending regarding President, Vice-President, Prime Minister or Speaker, the Supreme Court had to order that the election was valid and any judgment of any lower court had to be set aside.[1] Even a student with an elementary knowledge of constitutional

1. The amendment was only to protect Mrs. Gandhi; the addition of the President, Vice-President and Speaker was an immature attempt not to make it too blatant. The Thirty-ninth Amendment made other amendments to the Constitution including adding the Sick Textile Undertaking (Nationalization) Act, 1974 in the Ninth Schedule. Minerva Mills had been nationalized under this Act.

law would not have drafted such an amendment. Mercifully, Section 4 of this Amendment Act, introduced on August 10, 1975, was struck down on November 7, 1975.[2]

While it is not surprising that Section 4 of this amendment was struck down; what is shocking is that Justice Beg upheld it in a remarkably lengthy, incomprehensible and convoluted judgment.[3]

Not many people are aware of another deplorable amendment that eventually lapsed. Two days after the infamous Thirty-ninth Amendment, Gokhale[4] introduced the Forty-first Amendment Bill that sought to amend Article 361 and prohibit any civil and criminal proceedings against the President, Vice-President, Prime Minister and Governors. The Rajya Sabha passed the bill but the Lok Sabha was dissolved in 1977 and this bill, which was pending, lapsed. While arguing against the infamous review petition of *Kesavananda Bharati,* Palkhivala pointed out that if this bill had become law, then any person could commit the most heinous crime and could go scot-free if he had sufficient political influence to become the Governor of any State just for one day. He remarked that if these amendments could be passed when *Kesavananda Bharati* was still good law, one could only imagine what would follow if *Kesavananda Bharati* was reviewed and overruled.

The Forty-second Amendment

The Forty-second Amendment was introduced a year later – on August 28, 1976, by the then Law Minister, H.R. Gokhale, who was part of the coterie of advisors to Mrs. Indira Gandhi. The statement of objects and reasons to this shameful amendment deserves to be reproduced. It shows the devious manner in which the country was sought to be misled:

> *1. A Constitution to be living must be growing. If the impediments to the growth of the Constitution are not removed, the Constitution will suffer a virtual atrophy. The question of amending the Constitution for removing the difficulties which have arisen in achieving the objective of socio-economic revolution, which would end poverty and ignorance and disease and inequality of opportunity, has been engaging the active attention of Government and the public for some years now.*

---

2. *Indira Nehru Gandhi v. Raj Narain,* AIR 1975 SC 2299 : (1975) Supp 1 SCC 1.
3. See paras 562-637, particularly para 636 in the AIR Report.
4. The then Law Minister .

2. The democratic institutions provided in the Constitution are basically sound and the path for progress does not lie in denigrating any of these institutions. However, there could be no denial that these institutions have been subjected to considerable stress and strains and that vested interests have been trying to promote their selfish ends to the great detriment of public good.

3. It is, therefore, proposed to amend the Constitution to spell out expressly the high ideals of socialism, secularism and the integrity of the nation, to make the Directive Principles more comprehensive and give them precedence over those fundamental rights which have been allowed to be relied upon to frustrate socio-economic reforms for implementing the Directive Principles. It is also proposed to specify the fundamental duties of the citizens and make special provisions for dealing with anti-national activities, whether by individuals or associations.

4. ...

..

8.[5] ...

New Delhi *H.R. Gokhale*

28th August, 1976

It does not require much intelligence to understand the absurdity of these objects. How does a Constitution grow? It can only be amended by Parliament or interpreted by the courts. The amendment was ostensibly made with the object of ending poverty, ignorance, disease and inequality of opportunity. In reality, these problems only increased till the early 1990s when the Government was forced to abandon the economic policy of socialism. In the second paragraph, there is a pathetic reference to the need for not denigrating any of the democratic institutions in the Constitution. Ironically, the Forty-second Amendment had its clear object of precisely denigrating the Supreme Court and the High Courts. And what were the vested interests that were trying to promote their selfish ends? Was it not a group of persons of the then ruling party who wanted to perpetuate their power to the detriment of the public good?

---

5. Paras 4-8 are not relevant and have not been reproduced.

This amendment had really two main objectives: first, to emasculate the judiciary and, secondly, to establish the foundations of authoritarian rule. The Government wanted no interference, and irritants like fundamental rights and other checks on political power were sought to be eliminated. In retrospect, it is sad that a democratically elected Government would have thought of so badly mutilating a glorious Constitution put together after a three-year effort (from 1946 to 1949). The 'constitutional outrage' inflicted by the Forty second Amendment can be illustrated by a few examples:

(a) Parliament could make a law to prohibit 'anti-national activities' or 'anti-national associations'. These were wide expressions and could give virtual dictatorial power to the ruling party. Moreover, such a law could not be questioned on the ground that it violated Article 14, 19 or 31.

(b) A new article, Article 32A, prohibited the Supreme Court from deciding the constitutional validity of any State law unless the constitutional validity of any Central law was also an issue in such proceedings.

(c) By amending Article 31C, fundamental rights were made subservient to Directive Principles. (This is discussed in detail later in this chapter).

(d) All constitutional amendments from the beginning, i.e. 1950, were saved by a simple amendment to Article 368.

(e) Article 77 enabled the President to frame rules for the convenient transactions of the business of the Government of India. Typically, this enables allocation of business amongst various ministries. The Forty second Amendment prohibited any court from summoning any rule to be produced in court.

(f) The Supreme Court could not decide the constitutional validity of any law unless the case was heard by a Bench of seven judges and the verdict was by a two-thirds majority. In other words, unless five judges held that a provision was unconstitutional, the law could not be struck down.[6]

---

6. The U.S. Supreme Court has rendered several landmark verdicts by a 5:4 majority.

(g) The High Courts could not decide the validity of any Central law. The High Court's power of supervision over tribunals, under Article 227 was removed.

(h) The writ jurisdiction of High Courts was also substantially curbed.

(i) Article 323A and 323B enabled the creation of Tribunals and could, and did, take away the jurisdiction of the High Court in various areas.

Calling such an amendment a 'constitutional outrage', as Seervai did, is really an understatement. It marked one of the saddest parts of our constitutional history.

Two lethal amendments

Sections 4 and 55 of the Constitution (Forty-second) Amendment Act, 1976, made two seemingly innocuous but actually lethal amendments to Article 31C and Article 368. Article 31C, before and after the amendment,[7] read as follows:—

> *Before amendment: '31C. Notwithstanding anything contained in Article 13, no law giving effect to the policy of the State towards securing [the principles specified in clause (b) or clause (c) of Article 39] shall be deemed to be void on the ground that it is inconsistent with, or takes away or abridges any of the rights conferred by Article 14, Article 19 or Article 31; and no law containing a declaration that it is for giving effect to such policy shall be called in question in any court on the ground that it does not give effect to such policy:*
>
> *Provided that where such law is made by the Legislature of a State, the provisions of this article shall not apply thereto unless such law, having been reserved for the consideration of the President, has received his assent.'*[8]
>
> *After amendment: '31C. Notwithstanding anything contained in Article 13, no law giving effect to the policy of the State towards securing [all or any of the principles laid down in Part IV] shall be deemed to be void on the ground that it is inconsistent with, or takes away or abridges any of*

7. The portion in square bracket was substituted by the 42nd Amendment to expand the scope of Article 31C.
8. The unamended Article came up for consideration before the Supreme Court in the *Kesavananda Bharati* case and has been discussed in that sub-chapter, *supra.*

the rights conferred by Article 14, Article 19 or Article 31; and no law containing a declaration that it is for giving effect to such policy shall be called in question in any court on the ground that it does not give effect to such policy:

Provided that where such law is made by the Legislature of a State the provisions of this article shall not apply thereto unless such law, having been reserved for the consideration of the President, has received his assent.'

The result of this amendment was that the earlier protection that was limited to laws made to implement only Article 39(b) and (c)[9] was now extended to any law that purported to give effect to all or any of the Directive Principles. Thus, the Central or any State Government could pass any law on any subject and could merely declare that the law was to give effect to securing any of the Directive Principles in Part IV. Such a simple declaration rendered it impossible for the Supreme Court or the High Courts to strike it down. Thus, even if the law was patently discriminatory or even took away the fundamental right to freedom of speech, the courts could do nothing to protect the citizens of India. At that time, it was part of official propaganda to state that the laudatory objectives of the Directive Principles of State Policy, contained in Part IV of the Constitution, were being frustrated by fundamental rights. If the stumbling block or nuisance of fundamental rights was removed, it was argued, then there would be no impediment in achieving these Directive Principles and India would become a socialistic paradise. Strangely, no one could point out a single economic plan of the Government that had floundered because of fundamental rights. The only collision between the judiciary and the Parliament was on the issue of payment of compensation for acquiring property and the courts, rightly, had set at naught every attempt to pay an illusory amount as compensation. In over 95% of the cases, laws enacted by the Central and State Legislatures were upheld by the Supreme Court, sometimes even by straining the language to save a badly drafted law. But the amended Article 31C now enabled any Central or State law to simply add a label or sticker at the beginning of the Act that stated that it was to further Directive Principles.

---

9. Article 39(b) and (c) read as follows:—**39(b)**: that the ownership and control of material resources of the community are so distributed as best to subserve the common good; **39(c)**: that the operation of the economic system does not result in the concentration of wealth and means of production to the common detriment.

But was it open to a citizen to demonstrate that a particular law had no nexus to any Directive Principle or that such a law would actually defeat a Directive Principle? The latter part of the amended Article 31C took care of this eventuality and made it clear that nobody could raise such a question in any court of law! Thus, a mere declaration that a law was to secure all or any of the Directive Principles created an impenetrable wall and rendered Articles 14, 19 and 31 impotent.

Section 55 was equally shocking. Article 368 confers power on Parliament to amend the Constitution. For certain matters, the amendment requires the basic two-thirds' majority and the additional concurrence of at least half of the State Legislatures.[10] In *Kesavananda Bharati*, it was held that the power to amend the Constitution would not include the power to destroy the basic structure or basic features of the Constitution. Chandrachud C.J. observed that the 'theme song' of the majority decision in *Kesavananda Bharati* was:

> *Amend as you may even the solemn document which the founding fathers have committed to your care, for you know best the needs of your generation. But, the Constitution is a precious heritage; therefore, you cannot destroy its identity.*

Parliament, therefore, did not have unlimited power to amend the Constitution. Now, see how Section 55 of the Forty-second Amendment amends Article 368 by inserting two new sub-sections:

> *55. Amendment of Article 368.—In Article 368 of the Constitution, after clause (3), the following clauses shall be inserted, namely:—*
>
> *(4) No amendment of this Constitution (including the provisions of Part III) made or purporting to have been made under this article [whether before or after the commencement of Section 55 of the Constitution (Forty-second Amendment) Act, 1976] shall be called in question in any court on any ground.*
>
> *(5) For the removal of doubts, it is hereby declared that there shall be no limitation whatsoever on the constituent*

10. Ironically, the amendment to fundamental rights does not require ratification by not less than one-half of the States. A ruling party having the necessary majority in Parliament could have amended or deleted any of the fundamental rights but for the basic structure doctrine.

> *power of Parliament to amend by way of addition, variation or repeal the provisions of this Constitution under this Article.*

The lethal effect of this amendment is apparent even to persons who are not acquainted with constitutional law. Sub-section (4) permanently closed the door on *any* challenge to *any* amendment on *any* ground. It applied to all past amendments from 1950 and granted immunity to all future amendments. Sub-section (5) loudly declares that Parliament's power to amend the Constitution is unlimited and unquestionable. Village panchayats are covered by Article 40, and no amendment to this Article could be challenged even if it seriously discriminated between panchayats within a particular State; Article 14 would simply not apply. Further, if the amendment contained a clause that prohibited any report about corruption in any panchayat or any Government department, it could not be challenged as violating the right to a free press or the right to freedom of speech and expression.

Thus, even if the Constitution was amended to make Mrs. Indira Gandhi or any other person as Prime Minister for life, such an amendment could not be questioned in any court. And even if an amendment provided for dynastic rule and converted India into a monarchy, the courts would be totally helpless. This was not an imaginary scenario: the Thirty-ninth Amendment to the Constitution actually provided that the election of any Prime Minister could never be questioned in any court of law.[11] Most important of all, the amendment to Article 368 threw the basic structure principle out of the window and effectively nullified the decision in *Kesavananda Bharati.*

The historic verdict of 1977

Throughout the Emergency, the Forty-second Amendment itself could not be questioned because of Article 368(5). The Forty-second Amendment was passed without any debate or discussion. At that time, most Parliament members from the opposition were in jail and what remained was a rubber stamp Parliament that would grant approval to virtually anything. The Emergency ended

---

11. This was to overcome the adverse judgment of the Allahabad High Court which had set aside Mrs. Gandhi's election. Although the case was pending in the Supreme Court, the Government wanted to take no chances and effectively make Mrs. Indira Gandhi's election unquestionable in any court. One more shameful attempt to amend the Constitution was fortunately struck down. Even Chief Justice Ray held this provision to be unconstitutional.

in 1977 and, in a historic election, the Janata Party came to power defeating Mrs. Indira Gandhi. For the first time in Indian history, a non-Congress Government ruled at the Centre. The new Government promised to repeal the entire Forty-second Amendment as part of its election manifesto. It first introduced the Forty-third Amendment in 1978 and omitted several provisions inserted by the Forty-second Amendment. Another major amendment, the Forty-fourth Amendment, was brought into force a year later. It is rather strange that the Janata Party did not delete the amended provisions of Article 31C or Article 368. In fact, the Constitution (Forty-fourth Amendment) Act, 1978, deleted several sections of the Forty-second Amendment but, strangely and inexplicably, did not touch Section 4 or Section 55 even though these constituted a grave onslaught on the Constitution. The failure of the Janata Party to delete these provisions is inexplicable.[12]

The *Minerva Mills* case

Minerva Mills Ltd. was a company that had its textile undertaking – also called Minerva Mills – at Bangalore. On allegations of mismanagement, this undertaking was nationalized under the Sick Textile Undertakings (Nationalisation) Act, 1974. The company challenged the constitutional validity of this Act and the validity of Sections 4 and 55 of the Constitution (Forty-second) Amendment Act, 1976.

The stage was thus set for the Supreme Court to decide whether Parliament could amend or even repeal the provisions of the Constitution. What was particularly dangerous was Article 368(4) which provided that any constitutional amendment, either made before or after 1976, could not be called in question '*in any court on any ground*'. The Forty-second Amendment was a direct attempt to nullify the basic structure theory laid down in *Kesavananda Bharathi.*

Palkhivala had returned to practice after a brief stint as India's Ambassador to the United States. The *Minerva Mills*[13] case was heard by a Bench of five judges. The hearings commenced on October 22, 1979 and the Supreme Court reserved judgment on November 16, 1979. The *Minerva Mills* case was very important

12. According to Seervai, the Janata Party did not have the requisite majority in the Rajya Sabha. But this is not convincing. If they could amend some portions of the 42nd Amendment, they could have certainly deleted the draconian amendments made to Article 31C and Article 368.
13. *Minerva Mills Ltd. v. Union of India,* AIR 1980 SC 1789 : (1980) 3 SCC 625.

and the future of Indian democracy would be once again decided by five learned judges.

Palkhivala's submissions have been neatly summarized by Chief Justice Chandrachud who delivered the judgment for the majority. The five essential points pleaded by Palkhivala to challenge the validity of the amended Article 31C were:

(i) Article 31C destroys the harmony between Parts III and IV of the Constitution by making fundamental rights (Part III) subservient to Directive Principles of the State Policy (Part IV).

(ii) The basic structure of the Constitution rests on the foundation that while Directive Principles are the *mandatory ends* of Government, they can be achieved only through *permissible means* set out in Part III of the Constitution.

(iii) In other words, Article 31C as amended, conferred unrestricted licence on the legislature and the executive to both destroy democracy and establish an authoritarian regime.

(iv) The destruction of fundamental freedoms guaranteed by Part III was not necessary to achieve the objectives of Directive Principles like organising village panchayats, fixing minimum wages, compulsory education and protection of environment and wildlife.

(v) The Constitution permits fundamental rights to be suspended only during an emergency but the amended Article 31C virtually abrogates them even in normal times.

Palkhivala was assisted by Rohinton F. Nariman and Shylendra Swaroop. Nariman recollects that Palkhivala would ask them to research on certain legal issues that arose for consideration. As a young lawyer, what impressed him was Palkhivala's ability to put his propositions in the simplest possible language; he consciously avoided using bombastic words and phrases. The other remarkable feature was his ability to convince the court by pointing out the adverse consequences of the contrary view. Only once did Palkhivala lose his cool. Justice Untwalia repeatedly interrupted him by extolling the virtues of socialism. Exasperated, Palkhivala replied: '*Not even a lunatic would jump the wall from West Berlin to East Berlin.*' – loudly emphasizing the word 'lunatic'.[14]

Harish Salve, who was also present, remembers the passion with which the case was argued. The argument of fundamental rights being the 'end' while Directive Principles being the 'means to that end' was superbly articulated before the Supreme Court. The Union of India was ably represented by the Attorney-General, Lal Narain Sinha and the Additional Solicitor-General, K.K. Venugopal. Palkhivala had repeatedly referred to a letter of the then Law Minister[15] who stated in Parliament that the Government had introduced the Forty-second Amendment as it wanted to remove the 'let and hindrance of fundamental rights'. Lal Narain Sinha effectively demolished the initial impact created by Palkhivala's repeated reference to the letter of the Law Minister. It is necessary to give a brief background to understand the excellent impact of Sinha's argument.

During the Emergency, the Supreme Court had delivered a widely criticised decision.[16] The Supreme Court had held that Article 21 was completely suspended and that any person detained during the emergency could not question his detention on any ground whatsoever. No other judgment has been as bitterly criticised as this decision and it severely dented the reputation of the Supreme Court. It was felt that the Supreme Court had badly let down the people and failed to be a bulwark against authoritarian rule. On the other hand, several High Court judges who displayed remarkable courage by striking down detention orders as illegal were transferred during the Emergency.

Justice H.R. Khanna gave a dissenting verdict that cost him the office of Chief Justice. Justice M.H. Beg, who gave a favourable verdict, superseded Justice Khanna and became Chief Justice. The message was clear: 'toe the line of the Government and be rewarded'. H.R. Khanna lost the Chief Justiceship of India but earned the affection and goodwill not only of the entire Bar but millions of Indians as well.

Thus, when the *Minerva Mills* case was being argued, Lal Narain Sinha effectively countered the arguments of Palkhivala by

---

14. This was ten years before the Berlin Wall was torn down.
15. Late H.R. Gokhale.
16. *ADM, Jabalpur v. Shiv Kant Shukla,* AIR 1976 SC 1207 : (1976) 2 SCC 521. This decision is commonly referred to as the '*Habeas Corpus* case' and has been discussed in chapter 6(j).

remarking that just as one wrong judgment could not be a ground to condemn the Supreme Court, one letter of the Law Minister could not be the basis to condemn the functioning of the Government!

The arguments of the Attorney-General and the Addl. Solicitor-General of India have also been set out in the judgment.[17] The main stand of the Union of India can also be summarized into a few propositions:

(1) The law made to secure the objective of Directive Principles would necessarily be in public interest and would not violate fundamental rights.

(2) The elimination of obstructive legal procedures could not destroy the basic features of the Constitution.

(3) The earlier amendments of Articles 31A, 31B and the unamended Article 31C had been upheld.

(4) The amended Article 31C would equally fall within the amending power given to Parliament.

(5) Great stress was placed on Article 38 which enjoins the State to promote the welfare of the people by securing a social order in which justice, social economic and political, shall inform all institutions of national life.

(6) Even if Article 31C excluded the challenge of Articles 14 and 19, there could be cases where a particular law was not relatable to any of the Directive Principles. Such laws could always be challenged.

(7) The Supreme Court, as an alternative, was requested to 'read down' Article 31C so that only laws which did not damage or destroy the basic structure would be saved.

In an unusual move, Chief Justice Chandrachud passed an order on behalf of four judges setting out their conclusions. This was done on the last working day – May 9, 1980 – and he stated that the reasons would follow later. Justice Bhagwati refused to concur, stating that the questions involved had 'grave and momentous consequences' and it would be appropriate to pass a reasoned judgment on the reopening of the court after the summer vacation. Later, he criticized the delivery of this skeletal order.

---

17. K.K. Venugopal was then the Additional Solicitor-General and sent us the written submissions he made on behalf of the Union. Palkhivala, according to him, was at his peak and did brilliantly in the *Minerva Mills* case.

The majority judgment[18] was delivered by Chandrachud C.J., on July 31, 1980, which accepted the main submissions of Palkhivala and held that the amendment to Article 31C was void as it damaged the basic or essential features of the Constitution. The total prohibition from challenging any law on the ground that it was inconsistent with or abridged any of the rights conferred under Articles 14 and 19 was impermissible. The court observed that the Indian Constitution was founded on the bedrock of the balance between Parts III and IV – i.e. between fundamental rights and Directive Principles. Any attempt to give primacy to the Directive Principles would disturb the harmony of the Constitution. This harmony and balance between fundamental rights and Directive Principles was an essential feature of the basic structure of the Constitution. Goals or objectives set out in Part IV had to be achieved without abrogation of the means provided in Part III.

The Supreme Court noticed the devastation that could have been caused by Article 31C. No law was open to challenge as long as the object was to ostensibly secure the Directive Principles of State Policy. Most laws would have some bearing directly or indirectly, on Directive Principles. The court stressed the importance of the right to equality under Article 14 and the importance of basic freedoms like free speech, religion, business and the right to reside anywhere in India that were conferred by Article 19. Indeed, as long as the law declared that it was to attain the objective of Directive Principles, the law became fully protected. Even if the law did not achieve its purpose, it could not be questioned. Interestingly, the court also rejected the plea of 'reading down' Article 31C which was clearly intended to shut out all judicial review. The principle of reading down applied only when words of width were used inadvertently. Finally, the Supreme Court rejected the argument that Article 31C was similar to Articles 31A and 31B and since the latter two had been upheld, the amended Article 31C should also be upheld. The court held that Article 31A was to preserve specific laws including those relating to agrarian reforms whereas Article 31C sought to give protection to an 'uncatalogued variety of laws'. If Article 31C was not suspended, fundamental freedoms would become a 'parchment in a glass case' to be viewed as a matter of historical curiosity.

---

18. The judges in the majority were; Chandrachud C.J., A.C. Gupta, N.L. Untwalia and P.S. Kailasam JJ. Bhagwati J. partly dissenting.

The Supreme Court thus foiled the attempt of the Forty-second Amendment to subvert democracy. If the verdict had gone the other way, our democracy would not have survived for long.

Justice Bhagwati's dissent

In January 1980, Bhagwati J. wrote a sensational letter to Indira Gandhi, congratulating her on her victory in the general election when the *Minerva Mills* case was still being deliberated by the judges. Amongst other adulatory remarks, he praised her 'iron will', 'uncanny insight' and 'dynamic vision'. He wrote that her 'heart... identified with the misery of the poor and the weak'. He further commented that the 'judicial system in the country is in a state of utter collapse' and that there was a need to have a 'fresh and uninhibited look' at it. This letter somehow leaked to the press and was published in the *Hindustan Times*, amongst other newspapers. This letter, especially since the judgment in the *Minerva Mills* case was not delivered, came in for grave criticism from all quarters. Senior journalists and political commentators had serious reservations about the timing and nature of these remarks, and that too in a congratulatory letter to the Prime Minister. The Supreme Court Bar Association discussed the propriety of the letter and issued a statement from a section of its members taking 'strong exception' to it. Indeed, this letter was extremely inappropriate and should never have been written.

Justice P.N. Bhagwati, who partly dissented, started his judgment with a note of anguish. He expressed his displeasure at the lack of consultation amongst the judges who constituted this important Bench. The case was heard at great length lasting over three weeks and the judgment was reserved on November 16, 1979. There was no reason, Bhagwati J. said, for suddenly delivering the skeletal judgment on May 9, 1980 which was the last working day before the summer vacation.[19] Bhagwati J. pointed out that there was no reason for not having a full consultation and delivering the judgment after the court re-opened in July, 1980. Bhagwati J. rightly pointed out the need for consultation so that there was a full and frank discussion on a draft judgment.

19. An order dated May 9, 1980 was passed by Chandrachud C.J. and Gupta, Untwalia and Kailasam JJ. It briefly held that Sections 4 and 55 of the Forty-second Amendment Act were beyond the amending powers, since they damaged the basic or essential features of the Constitution. The order also stated that 'fuller reasons' would follow later. Bhagwati J. 'preferred' to pass a final order when he delivered his reasoned judgment after the summer vacation. Detailed judgments were passed on July 31, 1980.

Obviously very annoyed at the lack of consultation, he pointed out that if there is no proper collective decision making, it would introduce a 'chaotic' situation in the judicial process and would set an unhealthy precedent. The Supreme Court, being the highest court in the land, was expected to set the tone for the entire judiciary in the country. Having waited for five and a half months after conclusion of arguments, a delay of another two and a half months in making the order would not injure the interests of any party. It was in this background that he had refused to pass an unreasoned order in May, 1980. It appears that Bhagwati's refusal to pass any order had led to considerable misunderstanding and that is why he had to explain why he acted in the manner he did.

Bhagwati J. also pointed out that the question of deciding the validity of Article 31C was an 'academic issue'. He pointed out that the challenge in the *Minerva Mills* case was primarily directed against the order dated October 19, 1971, which had been passed under Section 18A of the Industries (Development and Regulation) Act, 1951. By this order, the management of the mills had been taken over. Later, the mills were nationalized under the Sick Textile Undertakings (Nationalization) Act, 1974. (In legalese, the right, title and interest in the entire industrial undertaking stood transferred to and vested in the Central Government!) This Act had been included in the Ninth Schedule by the Constitution (Thirty-ninth Amendment) Act, 1975. Unless the Thirty-ninth Amendment was struck down, according to Justice Bhagwati, they could not question the Nationalization Act. Now, Section 55 of the Constitution (Forty-second Amendment) Act, 1974, sought to amend Article 368 and completely bar any judicial scrutiny of the validity of any constitutional amendment. Bhagwati J. observed that if Section 55 was declared to be invalid, it would be sufficient for Minerva Mills and other petitioners to question the constitutional validity of the Nationalization Act but the petitioners had proceeded further and challenged the amendments made to Article 31C as well. Palkhivala had conceded before the Bench that he accepted the validity of Articles 31A, 31B and the unamended Article 31C. It was the amendment to Articles 31C and 368 which, according to Palkhivala, destroyed the basic structure of the Constitution and was beyond the amending power of Parliament. The Attorney-General pointed out that the Nationalization Act contained a declaration that it was to give effect to the Directive Principles set out in Article 39(b); if so, it would be protected by the unamended Article 31C and it would be unnecessary to go into the question whether the amendment to Article 31C was at all valid.

In other words, it was not necessary to put the amendment to Article 31C out of the way as that did not block the challenge of validity of the Nationalization Act. Therefore, he was of the view that the entire argument raised on the constitutional validity of Article 31C was academic and the court could have declined to go into that question. However, as the court had embarked upon an 'academic exercise at the invitation of Palkhivala'[20] and had spent considerable time over it and because the issues raised were of the gravest significance for the future of the nation, Justice Bhagwati then proceeded to examine this question on merits.

Justice Bhagwati had no difficulty in accepting the argument that giving Parliament uncontrolled power to amend the Constitution was impermissible. Characterising the amendment as a case of zeal overriding discretion, he observed:

> *Now, if by constitutional amendment, Parliament were granted unlimited power of amendment, it would cease to be an authority under the Constitution, but would become supreme over it, because it would have power to alter the entire Constitution including its basic structure and even to put an end to it by totally changing its identity. It will therefore be seen that the limited amending power of Parliament is itself an essential feature of the Constitution, a part of its basic structure, for if the limited power of amendment were enlarged into an unlimited power, the entire character of the Constitution would be changed. It must follow as a necessary corollary that any amendment of the Constitution which seeks, directly or indirectly, to enlarge the amending power of Parliament by freeing it from the limitation of unamendability of the basic structure would be violative of the basic structure and hence outside the amendatory power of Parliament.*

On the other important issue of the amendment to Article 31C, Justice Bhagwati took a dissenting view. He observed that Palkhivala had made a 'passionate plea with deep emotion and feeling' that the amended Article 31C was an open licence to the legislature and executive to destroy democracy and establish an authoritarian or totalitarian regime. He observed that although

20. This was an unnecessary, sarcastic remark by Justice Bhagwati.

Palkhivala had put forth his arguments against the pernicious consequences of the amended Article 31C with great force and persuasiveness, it did not appeal to him. Bhagwati J. then goes into a lengthy discussion on the importance of the Directive Principles and how critical they were to attain India's socialistic objectives. Directive Principles were intended to bring about a socio-economic revolution and create a new socio-economic order where there would be social and economic justice not for a 'fortunate few' but for the 'teeming millions of Indians, for the have-nots and the handicapped, the lowliest and the lost'. The emptiness of this lofty rhetoric is amply demonstrated by the disastrous economic consequences that socialism had on India's economy and drove it to near bankruptcy by 1991. It is very easy to talk about a socio-economic revolution and a new economic order. But nobody has been able to turn these lovely English phrases into economic reality.

Bhagwati J. pointed out that Article 31C did not completely exclude judicial review. It was open to the court to still examine whether there was a real and substantial connection between a particular enactment and the Directive Principles. The court could examine the objective and scope of the enactment, its pith and substance, its true nature and character. If on such examination, the court found that the Act was really to accomplish a purpose not covered by a Directive Principle then it would not get the protection of the amended Article 31C. He characterized Palkhivala's fear that every law could get the protection of Article 31C as an argument of despair – an extreme argument which was not justified. If the court found that a particular provision was subsidiary or incidental or not essentially and integrally connected with the implementation of the Directive Principle or the dominant object of such a provision was to achieve an unauthorized purpose, it would be outside the amended Article 31C and would have to meet the challenge of Article 14 and 19.

It is strange that Bhagwati J. lost sight of the latter part of Article 31C which expressly stated that no such law shall be called in question on the ground that it does not give effect to 'such policy' (of securing the Directive Principles). Was it then open to any petitioner to raise questions of 'pith and substance' and 'dominant object'?

If Justice Bhagwati's view was accepted, it would have virtually destroyed Indian democracy. It would have been very difficult to demonstrate that a particular law was not intended to achieve a purpose set out in the Directive Principles which are so vast that they cover almost everything under the sun. It is very easy to establish a theoretical nexus between any law and a Directive Principle. The fact that the law would never achieve the Directive Principle could never be examined by the courts.

Thus ended another major battle that Palkhivala fought to protect the Constitution. It was a case which ended the controversy between fundamental rights and Directive Principles. The majority judgment brings about a nice balance between the two.

It was extremely unfortunate that repeated attempts were made to destroy or damage the Constitution. No single individual stood up against this parliamentary onslaught as Palkhivala did. Indeed, it will be no exaggeration to call him a 'one man army' against the repeated attempts of the then ruling party to subvert democracy and destroy the judiciary. It is easier to underestimate than exaggerate the contribution of this one man in preserving democracy and the rule of law.

❋

The Mandal Case

Legitimising Caste-Based Reservations

If the decision in *Kesavananda Bharati* helped to preserve the unity and integrity of India, the decision of the Supreme Court in *Indra Sawhney v. Union of India*[1] popularly called the *Mandal* case – polarized Indian society by upholding reservations that are almost exclusively based on caste.

Historical overview of the reservation policy

Articles 15 and 16 provide the basic framework for reservation in matters of education and Government jobs respectively. The scope and ambit of these provisions has been the topic of much controversy since the coming into effect of our Constitution. Article 16 of the Constitution finds its genesis in draft Article 10(3) which was the precursor to Article 16(4). This provision had evoked passionate debate among the distinguished members of the Constituent Assembly. The expression 'any backward classes', as used in this draft article, was highly nebulous. Despite this ambiguity, a convincing speech by Dr. B.R Ambedkar was successful in bringing a temporary hiatus to the discussion and casting the dice in favour of using the expression 'any backward class' in Article 16.

Reservations – Earlier cases

Soon thereafter, in *State of Madras v. Champakam Dorairajan*,[2] a Government Order issued by the State of Madras which apportioned seats in medical and engineering colleges on the basis of one's caste, was challenged before the Supreme Court. In a powerful decision, S.R. Das J. held that the ineligibility created by this 'communal G.O.' whereby a Brahmin, who was otherwise

1. AIR 1993 SC 477 : 1992 Supp (3) SCC 217.
2. AIR 1951 SC 226 : [1951] SCR 525.

eligible, was rendered ineligible by virtue of his caste, was repugnant to Articles 15 and 16. This judicial view led to the insertion of Article 15(4) by way of the Constitution (First Amendment) Act, 1951, which authorized the State to make special provisions for the advancement of 'socially and educationally backward classes of citizens'. In *M.R. Balaji v. State of Mysore*,[3] the Supreme Court held that Article 15(4) was only an exception to Article 15(1) and that caste could not be the sole and dominant test for the purpose of identifying socially and educationally backward classes. While the exact percentage may vary, it could not cross the 50% limit. Indeed, in the *Balaji* case, it was held that classification of socially backward classes based only on caste and without reference to other factors, which were undoubtedly relevant, would be unconstitutional.

In India, the opportunity for education and for public employment has always been limited. In large parts of India, a Government job is still the most desired form of employment and the reservation quota for education and public employment has always been a politically sensitive issue. With political parties having very little to show by way of good governance, the easiest way to garner votes is to promise more reservations and more freebies.

Kaka Kalelkar Commission

Although Article 16(4) uses the expression 'any backward class', the meaning of this expression never came up for consideration before the Supreme Court till the decision in *Indra Sawhney*. This was because the benefits of reservation in public employment were confined to Scheduled Castes and Scheduled Tribes. The first Backward Classes Commission headed by Kaka Kalelkar submitted its report on March 30, 1955, recommending that factors such as traditional occupation and profession, percentage of literacy and general educational advancement, estimated population, and distribution throughout the State, have to be taken into account for classifying a community as a 'backward class'. The Commission also opined that the social position occupied by a community in the caste hierarchy would have to be taken into account when identifying backward classes for the purpose of job reservation. Interestingly, Kaka Kalelkar, who was the Chairman of this

3. AIR 1963 SC 649 : [1963] Supp (1) SCR 439 (A reservation of 68% in professional and technical colleges was struck down).

Commission, had second thoughts after signing the report and, in his covering letter addressed to the President of India, he virtually pleaded for the rejection of this report on the ground that the recommendation for caste-based reservations would be detrimental to national interest and unity!

This report was never implemented and in 1961, the Central Government wrote to all the State Governments expressing its view that it would be better to apply economic tests rather than caste for the purpose of reservations. Even at this time, the recommendation was confined to matters of education since there was no reservation for 'other backward classes' (OBCs) in Government jobs. Pandit Jawaharlal Nehru pointed out the dangers of reservation based exclusively on the basis of caste and without reference to economic consideration. In a famous letter to all the Chief Ministers sent on June 27, 1961, he observed:

> *...help should be given on economic considerations and not on caste...I dislike any kind of reservation, more particularly in service. I react strongly against anything which leads to inefficiency and second-rate standards... The only real way to help a backward group is to give opportunities of good education...But if we go in for reservations on communal and caste basis, we swamp the bright and able people and remain second-rate or third-rate. I am grieved to learn of how far this business of reservation has gone based on communal consideration. It has amazed me to learn that even promotions are based sometimes on communal or caste considerations. This way lies not only folly, but disaster. Let us help the backward groups by all means, but never at the cost of efficiency. How are we going to build our public sector or indeed any sector with second-rate people?*[4]

This salutary recommendation was ignored by all the States as it was clearly politically more rewarding to all parties to promise reservation to the largest possible number of castes. Not a single State adopted the economic test; it was the Supreme Court that had to create the concept of the 'creamy layer' – i.e. the more affluent amongst the backward classes – and stipulate that it be excluded.

4. Jawaharlal Nehru, *Letters to Chief Ministers 1947-1964*, vol. 5, Oxford University Press, 1959, pp. 456-7.

The Mandal Commission – A seriously flawed report

It was only in the year 1979 that the Union of India got around to appointing a second commission, popularly known as the Mandal Commission, for determining the criteria for defining 'socially and educationally backward classes' and to examine the desirability of providing for reservation in public services and posts in favour of such backward classes of citizens. It is interesting to note that even the terms of reference of the Mandal Commission never used the expression 'any backward classes' and referred only to 'socially and educationally backward classes'. The report of this Commission was submitted on December 31, 1980, and it relied almost exclusively on caste as the predominant criterion for reservation in Government jobs.[5]

Significantly, Indira Gandhi never implemented this report, although it was tabled in Parliament first in 1982. She fully knew of its serious defects and the disastrous long-term consequences of purely caste-based reservations. To her credit, it must be said that she was completely free from any caste-prejudice and never used the Mandal Commission Report or even the Kalelkar Commission report to garner votes for her party. After her tragic assassination, her son Rajiv Gandhi stormed to victory on a massive sympathy wave, winning almost four-fifths majority in the Lok Sabha. He too did not implement the Mandal Commission Report. For all practical purposes, the report had been given a quiet burial.

But the sympathy for Rajiv Gandhi soon evaporated and the Congress Party fared badly in the 1989 elections, and V. P. Singh became the Prime Minister for a short while. The rivalry between Singh and Devi Lal[6] was bitter. Alarmed at the huge success of Devi Lal's political rally at the Boat Club lawns in New Delhi, V.P. Singh, to save his personal political fortune, resurrected the Report and, by announcing a 27% reservation for OBCs, altered the political landscape of the country forever.

What was this Mandal Commission Report and why was it seriously flawed?

The Mandal Commission was appointed by the President under Article 340. Its main task was to recommend the criteria to be used

---

5. A detailed examination of the methodology adopted by the Mandal Commission can be found in the minority judgment of Kuldip Singh, J. at pp. 742-43, 747-49 of the decision reported in All India Reporter (AIR).
6. A Haryana politician and leader of the Jat community. He was the Deputy Prime Minisiter in this short-lived Government.

to determine socially and educationally backward classes which were not adequately represented in public services and posts either in the Union or in any States. The Commission had sent out a questionnaire consisting of eleven questions which were almost completely based on caste. The questionnaire specified eleven indicators which were broadly divided into three groups:

A. Social

(i) Castes/classes considered as socially backward by others.

(ii) Castes/classes which mainly depend on manual labour for their livelihood.

(iii) Castes/classes where at least 25% females and 10% males above the State average get married at an age below 17 years in rural areas and at least 10% females and 5% males do so in urban areas.

(iv) Castes/classes where participation of females in work is at least 25% above the State average.

B. Educational

(v) Castes/classes where the number of children in the age group of 5-15 years who never attended school is at least 25% above the State average.

(vi) Castes/classes where the rate of student drop-out in the age group of 5-15 years is at least 25% above the State average.

(vii) Castes/classes amongst whom the proportion of matriculates is at least 25% below the State average.

C. Economic

(viii) Castes/classes where the average value of family assets is at least 25% below the State average,

(ix) Castes/classes where the number of families living in *Kuccha* house is at least 25% above the State average.

(x) Castes/classes where the source of drinking water is beyond half a kilometer for more than 50% of the households.

(xi) Castes/classes where the number of households having taken consumption loan is at least 25% above the State average.

The social indicators were given weightage of three points; educational and economic indicators, two and one point respectively. On the basis of these indicators, the Mandal Commission identified 3743 castes that were 'backward classes' and were eligible for 27% reservation in public employment. With 22.5% reservation for Scheduled castes and Scheduled Tribes (SC/ST) and 27% for other backward classes (being persons belonging to the 3743 castes), 49.5% of all public jobs would now be reserved under the quota system. Was there any scientific method or detailed survey that was carried out to determine the above list? The Mandal Commission candidly admitted that it had to rely on highly inadequate data.

It was admitted that surveys were carried out only in 0.06% of the villages. Many castes were simply included because they were mentioned in the first Backward Classes Commission report headed by Kaka Kalelkar! Barring Gujarat, no other State had given any worthwhile information or data. There was also a vast disparity between the number of castes that had been recognized as backward by the Kalelkar Commission and by the State Government. For example, while the Kalelkar Commission recognized 366 backward classes in Maharashtra, the State Government recognised only 196. On the other hand, the number of castes recognised by the Commission was 156 in Tamil Nadu while the State Government had recognized 1245 castes. Highly discriminatory figures were prevalent in almost all the States.[7]

It is a great national tragedy that 27% of public employment is now reserved for members of 3743 castes that have been determined on a highly arbitrary basis. Palkhivala and K.K. Venugopal pointed out serious flaws in the preparation of this list and it is indeed shocking that six out of nine judges accepted the report by completely glossing over these fatal defects. Even an elementary student of statistics would have unhesitatingly rejected the report. The defects as pointed out by Palkhivala and, more particularly, by K.K. Venugopal, can be summarized as follows:

(i) The Mandal Commission identified 3743 castes as 'backward classes' based on caste which is precisely what the Constitution prohibits.

7. For a brilliant and detailed study of the Mandal Commission see, *Falling over backwards* by Arun Shourie, Rupa & Co.

(ii) The Mandal Commission had to determine the desirability of making reservation in public services which was not done.

(iii) Under Article 16(4), it was necessary to decide whether a particular backward class was inadequately represented in the State services. No survey whatsoever was done to determine whether any of the 3743 castes were represented inadequately.

(iv) The socio-educational field survey was, in the words of Justice Kuldip Singh, an 'eye-wash'. In every district, only two villages and one urban block were taken into consideration! Thus, only 0.06% of the total villages were surveyed.

(v) Out of the 3743 castes, only 406 were subjected to socio-educational field survey i.e. only 10.85% of the castes were subjected to survey to determine backwardness.

(vi) A large number of castes in the list were simply added from the State lists. Thus, out of the 260 castes identified from the Union Territory of Pondicherry, the majority were merely picked up from the State list without any independent verification.

(vii) The Mandal Commission pointed out that Haryana, Himachal Pradesh, Assam, Pondicherry, Rajasthan, Orissa, Meghalaya and Delhi had notified lists of Other Backward Classes without there being any enquiry into their conditions. Andaman and Nicobar, Arunachal Pradesh, Chandigarh, Dadra and Nagar Haveli, Goa, Daman and Diu, Lakshadweep, Madhya Pradesh, Manipur, Mizoram, Nagaland, Sikkim, Tripura and West Bengal had never prepared a list of OBCs. If the Mandal Commission was to merely adopt the State lists without any investigation, there was no reason to have the Commission at all.

(viii) There was no explanation as to why the 1961 census was adopted when the 1971 census was available.

(ix) The Mandal Commission had criticized the earlier Kalelkar Report but still adopted several castes from that report.

(x) Remarkably, the Mandal Commission identified backward classes amongst non-Hindus by inventing castes for them and despite the fact that the concept of caste was anathema to Christianity, Islam and Sikhism.

(xi) The Mandal Commission also relied on the 1931 census. It totalled the population of Scheduled Castes, Scheduled Tribes, forward Hindu castes and all other non-Hindus. This totalled to 56.3% of the population. It then assumed that 43.7% of the balance must be backward and proceeded to state that a similar percentage of non-Hindus must also be backward and thus arrived at the figure of 52%!

(xii) The Mandal Commission relied on the 1931 census for computing the percentage of backward classes, completely ignoring the demographic changes of the last 50 years and the fact that India of 1931 included Pakistan, Bangladesh and Burma.

In the light of the above revelations, it is incredible that the majority proceeded on the basis that the Mandal Commission Report was valid and upheld the reservation based on such a flawed report. Having been approved by six out of nine judges, the Mandal Commission Report now gets the Supreme Court's approval even though it is statistically flawed, historically inaccurate and logically absurd.

Despite all these flaws, the V.P. Singh Government issued an Office Memorandum (O.M.) dated 13th August, 1990, that provided, for the first time, 27% of reservation for OBCs in public service. Even this O.M. used the term 'socially and educationally backward classes', but the idea was clearly to provide for caste-based reservations. This O.M. led to a widespread public agitation, particularly in North India, and clashes between pro and anti reservationists. The attempt at self-immolation by Rajeev Goswami truly portrayed the 'fiery' nature of this controversy which threatened, probably for the first time since the Emergency, the very foundation of our Constitution.[8] But the opportunistic Office Memorandum did not help V. P. Singh, and his coalition lost the election to a Congress-led coalition in 1991. In a conciliatory measure, the newly elected coalition Government with

---

8. Ramchandra Guha discusses this in a detailed manner in his excellent book, *India after Gandhi*, pp. 605-612.

Narasimha Rao as the Prime Minister came out with another O.M. dated 25th September, 1991, which modified the earlier O.M. and provided for an additional 10% reservation for other economically backward sections of society who were not covered by the existing schemes of reservation.

Adjudication on top of a volcano

It was in this charged atmosphere that a Bench of nine Judges was specially constituted to adjudicate on complex constitutional questions involving the interpretation of Article 16:

- (i) Can backward classes be identified on the basis of caste alone?
- (ii) Whether Article 16(4) is an exception to Article 16(1)?
- (iii) Whether reservations can cross the ceiling limit of 50%?
- (iv) Whether the 'creamy layer' is to be excluded?
- (v) Whether reservation in the matter of promotion is permitted under Article 16?

Before proceeding further, reference must be made to Art. 16(1), 16(2) and 16(4) which will help in a better understanding of the controversy.

> *16(1) There shall be equality of opportunity for all citizens in matters relating to employment or appointment to any office under the State.*
>
> *16(2) No citizen shall, on grounds only of religion, race, caste, sex, descent, place of birth, residence or any of them, be ineligible for, or discriminated against in respect of, any employment or office under the State.*
>
> *16(3) ...*
>
> *16(4) Nothing in this Article shall prevent the State from making any provision for the reservation of appointments or posts in favour of any backward class of citizens which, in the opinion of the State, is not adequately represented in the services under the State.*

'Merit and Merit alone'

Nani Palkhivala and several other senior advocates appeared on behalf of the petitioners, challenging the two controversial O.M.s. For Palkhivala, this litigation was also an opportunity to express his views on qualities such as merit and industry that formed the bedrock of his own personal and professional life. Palkhivala painted the picture of a divisive India, ridden by factionalism and caste feuds, and strenuously contended that caste based reservations would be a step in the wrong direction and wreck the secular character of our Constitution. The Mandal Commission, he submitted, had ignored its basic mandate which was to examine the desirability or otherwise of making provision for the reservation of appointments or posts in favour of OBCs in public services. The report would revitalize casteism and cleave the nation into two – forward and backward. He also strongly felt that the effect of such reservation would be the death knell of meritocracy.

In a way, life came full circle for the man who gave us the 'basic structure' doctrine, when he placed reliance on this doctrine in *Indra Sawhney*. He contended that a secular, unified and caste-less society was a basic feature of the Constitution, and this formed the rationale for caste being a prohibited marker under various provisions of the Constitution including Articles 15(1) and 16(1). When this was the case, caste could never be the basis for determining 'backward classes' referred to in Article 16(4). Criticizing the Mandal Commission Report, which formed the basis for the impugned memoranda, he contended that this Report treated the expression 'backward classes' as being synonymous with backward castes and identified backward classes solely and exclusively on the basis of caste, ignoring all other considerations including poverty. Further, the Report even invented castes for non-Hindus where none existed. Thus, the Report had successfully divided the nation into two sections, backward and forward, placing 52% of the population in the former section. Acceptance of this Report, he submitted, would spell disaster for the unity and integrity of India.

Apart from the inherent divisiveness in using caste as a criterion, Palkhivala also stressed the ill effects that such a reservation policy would have on efficient administration. He submitted that if the recommendations of the Commission were implemented, it would result in the sub-standard replacing the standard and the reins of power passing from meritocracy to mediocrity. Reservation necessarily entailed the appointment of less meritorious persons, resulting in the lowering of efficiency in the administration. The mandate of Article 335, he argued, was that reservations should be so operated as not to affect the efficiency of administration. All other constitutional provisions such as Articles 16 and 46 were subject to this mandate. Therefore, in any event, reservations could not exceed 30%, the figure referred to in Dr. Ambedkar's speech in the Constituent Assembly.

Quite akin to his approach in the *Bank Nationalization* case,[9] Palkhivala scrutinised the Mandal Commission Report in a forensic manner and pointed out several inaccuracies, some of them glaring in nature, in the reservation policy as put in place by the impugned O.M.s. He submitted that Article 340 of the Constitution authorised the President to appoint a Commission for investigating the conditions of 'socially and educationally backward classes' within the territory of India. The terms of reference of the Mandal Commission also used the expression 'socially and educationally backward classes'. This being the case, the Mandal Commission could not have prepared a list of 'other backward classes' for the purpose of reservations under Article 16(4).

Palkhivala pointed out several defects in the method adopted by the Mandal Commission for ascertaining backwardness, including:

(i) issuing questionnaires to hardly one percent of the population;

(ii) relying on obsolete material such as the caste census of 1931;

(iii) rewriting the Hindu *varna* system by adding intermediate or middle castes;

(iv) identifying 3743 castes to be backward classes when the First Commission had managed to identify only 2399 backward classes and the Anthropological Survey of India had published a project report identifying only 1057 backward classes.

Palkhivala contended that the Central Government had, for extraneous reasons, accepted the Mandal Commission Report and issued the impugned O.M.s despite these inaccuracies. He sought to buttress this by relying on vitiating facts such as acceptance of this report without any discussion or debate in Parliament notwithstanding its far-reaching consequences, implementation of this report through an executive order and not through an Act of Parliament, and providing reservations for 'other backward classes' in Union services for the first time based on a 10 year old report.

---

9. *R.C. Cooper v. Union of India*, AIR 1970 SC 564 : (1970) 1 SCC 248.

Palkhivala also prepared supplemental written submissions and pointed out that the *Mandal* case had an unprecedented constitutional sweep and the difference between the earlier cases and the *Mandal* case was the difference between a hillock in Delhi and the Himalayas. He pointed out that the Mandal Report had no constitutional sanctity as its findings were completely beyond the scope of Article 340 which enabled the appointment of a Commission only to investigate the conditions of socially and educationally backward classes of citizens and to suggest steps to remove their difficulties and improve their conditions. With a sense of deep anguish, Palkhivala argued that the Mandal Report, if implemented, would 'bury the ideal of equality 50 fathoms deep'. The net result would be that 3743 so called 'backward classes', representing more than half the population, would be entitled to preferential treatment in admission to colleges and universities, employment and promotion. The so called 'forward castes' would be reduced to the status of second class citizens. The Constitution had emphatically rejected casteism but this was revived by the Mandal Report.

The Union of India as well as several States supported the policy of reservation as introduced by the impugned Memoranda and contended that the words 'backward classes' as used in Article 16(4) could only have meant the *shudras* or the 'middle castes'. Given the widespread caste-based politics, no political party – ruling or opposition – could afford to oppose any reservation policy that created an additional 27% quota. The bar contained in Article 16(2) against discrimination on the basis of caste, it was argued, would not apply to the identification of 'backward classes' based on caste. The relevant consideration for a caste to qualify as a 'backward class' was only paucity or inadequacy of representation in the apparatus of the Government, and not poverty. Reservations were neither an economic reform measure nor a poverty alleviation programme, but a programme of historical compensation. On this premise, it was argued that the Mandal Commission was correct in its identification of 'backward classes'. The Union also adopted the justification given by the Mandal Commission for relying on the 1931 census, which was that figures of caste-wise population were not available beyond 1931 since systematic caste-wise enumeration of population was discontinued in 1931. The Mandal Commission simply assumed that the *inter se* rate of population growth among various castes over the period from 1931 to 1981 would remain more or less the same, and concluded that these castes formed 52% of the total population of India based on such assumption. This conclusion was endorsed by the Union, which also contended that the scope of judicial review over the methodology adopted by the Mandal Commission was extremely limited in nature and confined to whether the exercise of power was a fraud on the Constitution.

The Union opposed Palkhivala's call for 'merit and merit alone' as the standard for appointment by submitting that the marks obtained at the examination/test/interview at the stage of entry into service was not an indicia of the inherent merit of a candidate. Though members of the 'other backward classes', due to their backwardness, may not be able to perform as well as the general category candidates in the selection examination, they would do so in course of time. The Union thus defended its stand on the ground that the starting point being different for 'other backward classes' and open category candidates, a gentle push in the form of reservations was permissible.

A divided verdict

The arguments put forth by Palkhivala found favour with only three of the nine judges. Six judges, in three separate opinions, upheld the controversial O.M. dated 13th August 1990. The majority opinion of Jeevan Reddy J. speaking on behalf of himself and Kania C.J., M.N. Venkatachaliah and A.M. Ahmadi JJ, declared that 'a caste is nothing but a social class – a socially homogenous class,' and that 'it was mainly these classes the Constituent Assembly had in mind though not exclusively – while enacting Article 16(4)'. The majority reasoned that caste, occupation, poverty and social backwardness were closely intertwined and justified caste-based reservations. The Union could start with any caste, apply the criteria of backwardness evolved by it to that caste, and determine whether it qualified as a backward class or not. Accepting the contention of the Union, the majority held that reservation under Article 16(4) was not in favour of a 'caste' but a 'backward class', and in such a situation, the bar of Article 16(2) would not apply at all. The majority also held that the expression 'other backward classes' was different, and broader, in its meaning and scope when compared with the expression 'socially and educationally backward classes' contained in Article 15(4). The thrust in Article 16(4), according to the majority, was mainly on social backwardness, resulting from years of historical discrimination. However, the majority also clarified that 'other backward classes' need not be similar in their backwardness to Scheduled Castes and Scheduled Tribes, in order to avail the benefits of reservation.

Certain portions of the second O.M. dated September 15, 1991, were read down and the expression 'poorer sections' was interpreted to mean those who are socially and economically more backward and not on economic criteria alone. Similarly, the word 'preference' was also read down to mean an equitable apportionment of the benefits of reservations between the backward, and more backward and it was for the States to notify the castes/classes which came within these categories.[10]

Merit and efficiency of administration

The majority did not agree entirely with Palkhivala's submissions on the impact of reservations on merit and efficiency of administration. Steering clear of the controversial question of whether reservations were *per se* anti-meritorian, the majority confined itself to observing that efficiency, competence and merit were not synonymous concepts and hence, it was wrong to treat merit as being synonymous with efficiency in administration. Merit, according to the majority, was only one component of the efficiency of an administrator. Despite acknowledging the fact that reservations implied the selection of a less meritorious person, the majority justified this compromise as being the cost paid for deliverance of the constitutional promise. The majority also expressed the hope that this small difference in merit that may be allowed at the stage of initial recruitment would disappear in course of time, when beneficiaries of the reservation would compete with others and improve their own efficiency. Apart from this response, the majority also placed certain limitations on reservations relying on the principles of merit and efficiency of administration.

No reservation for promotions

The first of such limitations was the unequivocal pronouncement that reservations would be confined to the initial appointment alone, and not extended to the promotion stage. The observations by the majority in this regard are important.

> *While it is certainly just to say that a handicap should be given to backward class of citizens at the stage of initial appointment, it would be a serious and unacceptable inroad into the rule of equality of opportunity to say that*

10. This was the view of Kania C.J., Venkatachaliah, Ahmadi and Jeevan Reddy JJ. It would be too lengthy to discuss the views of other five judges on this office memorandum.

> *such a handicap should be provided at every stage of promotion throughout their career. That would mean creation of a permanent separate category apart from the mainstream – a vertical division of the administrative apparatus. The members of reserved categories need not have to compete with others but only among themselves. There would be no will to work, compete and excel among them. Whether they work or not, they tend to think, their promotion is assured. This in turn is bound to generate a feeling of despondence and 'heart-burning' among open competition members. All this is bound to affect the efficiency of administration...At the initial stage of recruitment reservation can be made in favour of backward class of citizens but once they enter the service, efficiency of administration demands that these members too compete with others and earn promotion like all others... They are expected to operate on equal footing with others. Crutches cannot be provided throughout one's career. That would not be in the interest of efficiency of administration nor in the larger interest of the nation.*

The second limitation placed by the majority was the declaration that it would be advisable to keep certain posts outside the ken of reservations even at the stage of initial appointment, either on account of the nature of duties attached to such posts or their level in the official hierarchy. The majority gave an illustrative list of such posts and concluded that since these posts formed a category of their own, reservations therein may not be consistent with the 'efficiency of administration' as contemplated by Article 335. To this extent and no more, Palkhivala's submissions on merit and efficiency of administration were accepted.

Ceiling limit of 50% on total reservations

Palkhivala's contention that the percentage of reservations should be confined to 30% since reservations were the exception and not the norm, was also rejected. Relying on the decision in *State of Kerala v. N.M. Thomas*,[11] the majority held that Article 16(4) was a facet of, and not an exception to, Article 16(1). However, the majority placed a cap of 50% on total reservations for appointments made every year. This was inconsistent with the view that Article 16(4) was not in the nature of an exception and has

11. AIR 1976 SC 490 : (1976) 2 SCC 310.

been bitterly criticized by Seervai.[12] If Article 16(4) was not an exception, theoretically there could be 100% reservation. The majority did not attempt to address this inconsistency at all.

Exclusion of creamy layer

The majority also put in a caveat in so far as reservations for 'other backward classes' was concerned, in the form of a constitutional requirement to exclude the 'creamy layer' in these castes from the benefits of reservation. 'Creamy layer' in this context meant those individual members found in any caste who had already made such significant strides in social, educational and economic progress as to render them undeserving of the benefits of reservation. Unfortunately, in several States, repeated attempts have been made to so define the creamy layer that only a microscopic percentage of the OBCs are excluded. For instance, the State of Bihar promulgated an Ordinance making the creamy layer applicable to professionals whose income was above Rs. 10 lakhs per annum and to businessmen whose turnover was more than Rs. 10 crores! For civil servants, the provisions were even more shocking. The creamy layer would apply only to officers whose spouse was also a graduate *and* the spouse also owned a house in an urban area. It was also necessary that either of the parents of the Class-I civil servant should also have been directly recruited to a Class-I service. There was absolutely no logic to this Ordinance and it effectively made a mockery of the direction of the Supreme Court to exclude the creamy layer. The result is that the benefits of reservation seldom reaches the intended beneficiaries and the Supreme Court's insistence on excluding the creamy layer remains a voice in the wilderness.

Article 16(4) referred to reservations for backward classes and the Central Government had uniformly emphasized the importance of the 'economic test' as the basis for reservation. Therefore, a person could belong to a forward class and yet be backward on account of impoverishment. On the other hand, a person may belong to a backward class but be very wealthy and would not require any kind of protection or reservation. Palkhivala pointed out that Dhanik Lal Mandal himself was a rich *zamindar*[13]

12. Seervai, *Constitutional Law of India*, 4th edition, Vol. 2, pp. lvii-xcv.
13. A landholder or landlord in British India responsible for collecting and paying to the Government the taxes on the land under his jurisdiction. *Zamindars* were holders of large extents of land.

but yet would be entitled to the benefits of reservation merely because he belonged to a 'backward class'.

The Supreme Court's majority decision has permanently enshrined casteism and the economic test, in reality, has been virtually abandoned. The 'creamy layer' test often remains a theoretical safeguard. The benefits of reservation are often taken away by those who do not deserve it. The really deserving tragically never get the benefit of reservation or any affirmative policy. Dr. Ambedkar wanted reservations only for a limited period but the Supreme Court's decision has now ensured that caste-based reservations will continue as long as the Constitution exists.

Skirting the fatal flaws

The majority rejected Palkhivala's objections to the methodology adopted by the Mandal Commission. The majority refrained from scrutinizing the inaccuracies in the Mandal Commission Report on the ground that this was merely a recommendatory Report and only the constitutional validity of the O.M.s that relied on this Report were in issue before the Constitution Bench. Despite the O.M.s having endorsed this report in large measure, the majority concluded that the Government of India had not accepted the list of OBCs contained in the Mandal Commission Report in its entirety. The fact that the O.M. dated 13th August, 1990, directed that only those classes common to both the Mandal List and the respective State Lists would qualify as 'backward classes' for the purposes of Article 16(4), prompted the majority to conclude that the lists prepared by the Mandal Commission would have no real significance. It is clear that the Mandal Commission's findings were wholly unsustainable and the majority conveniently skirted the unanswerable submissions of Palkhivala and K.K. Venugopal on this issue.

Justices Ratnavel Pandian and P.B. Sawant wrote concurring opinions. Justice Pandian took an extreme position in this matter as he even disagreed with the cap of 50% imposed by the majority. His views on the exclusion of creamy layer were also in divergence with the position taken by the majority. The learned judge branded the petitioners as 'anti-reservationists' and even committed the error of observing that Article 16(4) was a fundamental right, when it was a settled position of law that no one could claim a right to reservation and that the decision to provide for reservations was purely within the domain of governmental policy.

Inadequate representation in the services

An essential requirement of Article 16(4) is that reservations are intended for those backward classes of citizens that are not adequately represented in the services of the State. If a particular backward class was more than adequately represented, it should not get the benefit of reservation. This makes it clear that a blanket reservation quota, applicable to all backward classes, is not permitted. But the Mandal Commission did not make any attempt to determine the backward classes that were adequately represented.

Sadly, the six judges, who constituted the majority, did not address this critical issue.

The dissenting views

Justices Kuldip Singh and R.M. Sahai struck clear notes of dissent. The former accepted the argument raised by Palkhivala and other counsel that caste-based reservations would be antithetical to the secular structure of the Indian Constitution. He reasoned that Hinduism, from which the caste system flowed, was not the only religion in India. Caste being an anathema to various religious groups such as Muslims, Christians, Sikhs, Buddhists and Jains, as well as religious denominations such as Arya Samajis and Brahmo Samajis, reliance on caste as the basis for determination of 'other backward classes' would disrupt the peaceful co-existence of all these communities. Focusing on the inaccuracies and inadequacies in the methodology adopted by the Mandal Commission, Justice Kuldip Singh held that any identification of 'backward classes' had to commence with a determination of their existing representation in the Government services. Inadequacy of representation was the pre-condition for reservations under Article 16(4). Hence, the State had to first make a determination of those communities that were under-represented in the Government services and then examine whether it was their backwardness that caused such under-representation. If the answer to both these questions was in the affirmative, only then could that community be treated as a 'backward class' eligible for the benefit under Article 16(4). The Mandal Commission, apart from failing to appreciate this, had proceeded on the legal fallacy that the expression 'backward class of citizens' meant the same thing as 'socially and educationally backward classes of citizens' in Article 15(4). According to Justice Singh, the former expression was much wider in its scope. By identifying 'backward classes' using the criteria for 'social and educational backwardness' the Mandal Commission had removed from the zone of consideration other classes that could have been identified on the basis of occupation, economic standards, environment, backward area, residence, etc.

He also observed that the 'terms of reference' of the Mandal Commission required it to assess the desirability of providing reservations. This exercise was not conducted at all. Though 3743 castes were identified as 'backward classes', the Commission had overlooked the extent of representation these castes already had in public services. The socio-educational field survey conducted by the Commission was a mere eye-wash because only two villages and one urban block in each district of the country were taken into consideration for the purpose of such study. Thus, only a meagre .06% of the total number of villages in the country was surveyed. Moreover, only 406 out of 3743 castes were subjected to this field survey. Many of the castes found their place in the Mandal Commission Report due to their prior inclusion in the lists of backward classes prepared by different States. The blind adoption of these State lists by the Mandal Commission without conducting any independent inspection was not correct.

Apart from these infirmities, the Mandal Commission even invented castes for non-Hindus, and imagined the population of 'other backward classes' in the country to be 52%. Justice Singh made his contempt for the report quite clear by remarking: 'A collection of so-called backward castes by a clerical act based on drawing-room investigation cannot be the backward classes envisaged under Article 16(4).'

Justice Sahai's opinion was also along the same lines and he too felt that caste could never have been employed as a criteria for determination of 'backward classes'.

Dr. Justice T.K. Thommen wrote another well-reasoned dissenting opinion and he summed up his stand thus:

> *It is generally a combination of factors such as low birth and demeaning occupation, or lack of any occupation, that has historically subjected classes of people to invidious discrimination and humiliating isolation and consequential poverty and social and educational backwardness. These are questions of fact which must be ascertained before the qualifying backwardness is identified. To disregard any one of these factors, particularly the most compelling reality of Indian life originating in low castes and demeaning occupations generally associated with them, such as that of*

scavenger, sweeper, fisherman, dhobi, barber and the like, and resulting in abject poverty, is to ignore the relevant criteria in identifying backwardness warranting reservation. What is sought to be identified for the purpose of reservation is not caste or religion, but poverty and backwardness caused by historical discrimination and its continuing evil effects. Caste may be a guide in this search, just as occupation or residence may be a guide, but what is sought to be identified is none but backwardness stemming from historical discrimination. If caste is more often than not a guide in the search for backwardness and if the lowest of the low castes has for historical reasons become the indicium of backwardness of the kind attracting reservation, caste in the absence of any better guide is a factor to be taken into account along with other factors such as poverty, illiteracy, physical and mental disabilities and other diseases caused by malnutrition, unhygienic conditions and the like. What the Constitution prohibits is not caste or non-discriminatory and inoffensive customs and practices based on castes; or ameliorative measures to uplift the downtrodden poverty stricken members of low castes; what it prohibits is exclusionary discrimination based solely on caste or any other criterion enumerated in Article 15(1) or Article 16(2). Any one or all of such criteria along with any other relevant criterion, such as poverty, illiteracy, disease, etc. may be legitimately used to identify backwardness for the purpose of reservation.

Bitter criticism of the decision by Seervai

The decision of the Supreme Court in the *Mandal* case has been bitterly criticized by the great jurist H.M. Seervai. Lamenting the steep fall in the quality of judgments involving constitutional law, he observed:

> *It is submitted that the judgments of six majority judges on Article 16(4) have reached the rock bottom. For the same reasons it is further submitted that never have six Supreme Court judges served the Bench, the Bar and the general pubic so ill as Reddy J., Kania C.J. Venkatachaliah, Ahmadi, Pandian and Sawant JJ. had served them.*[14]

---

14. Seervai, *Constitutional Law of India*, 4th edition, Vol. 2, p. xcv.

It is submitted that perhaps the criticism is too harsh but the fact remains that the decision of the Supreme Court has enshrined caste as the primary basis for reservation. However, to be fair, the Supreme Court imposed salutary safeguards by insisting that reservation cannot cross 50%, that there should be no reservations in promotion, and that seats/posts which could not be filled up cannot be carried forward. Indeed, Seervai also compliments the Supreme Court for its decision on two important points. By majority of 8:1, the Supreme Court held that the words 'socially and educationally backward classes' cannot be read into Article 16(4). It showed that the Constitution did not intend to restore the benefit only to those who are socially and educationally backward. Secondly, it was held that reservation cannot extend to promotion as this would seriously impair the administrative efficiency that is mandated by Article 335.

The Aftermath

Palkhivala was deeply disappointed by the judgment. In a two-part article in the *Times of India*,[15] he wrote: 'I am sure V.P. Singh was sincere when he said that after the Supreme Court judgment in the *Mandal* case he could die in peace. But his policy has ensured that the nation will not live in peace...' He pointed out that though 20 separate questions were framed by the majority, only one was vital: whether reservations are permissible on the basis of caste? The majority decision had pointed out that reservations must exclude the creamy layer and that the inclusion or exclusion on castes must be periodically reviewed. These conditions, according to Palkhivala, were incapable of being complied with. The majority decision would fracture and cleave the nation and would revive casteism.

In more ways than one, the decision in *Indra Sawhney* was a classic case of tight-rope walking by the judiciary. To be fair to the majority, they did strive to balance it all the way. Though caste-based reservations were permitted, the creamy layer was directed to be excluded from the benefits of such reservations. Limits were placed on reservations insofar as super-specialities and posts requiring superior skills were concerned. The nine-judge Bench also unequivocally held that reservations should not be extended to the stage of promotions. The carry-forward rule whereby unfilled

---

15. November 24 and 25, 1992. The judgment was delivered on November 16, 1992.

reserved posts were carried on and added to the reservation quota for the next year was held to be unconstitutional. Even at the stage of initial appointment, reservations could not, under ordinary circumstances, exceed 50%.

Unfortunately, Parliament has, in blatant disregard of the principles laid down in *Indra Sawhney*, amended the Constitution and introduced Articles 16(4A) and 16(4B). These provisions have now been held to be constitutionally valid by the Supreme Court in *M. Nagaraj v. Union of India*,[16] subject to a few safeguards.

The Constitution as it stands today permits reservations for Scheduled Castes and Tribes at the stage of promotion with consequential seniority and also allows for 'carry forward' of unfilled reserved quota seats. Castes that were placed in the reservation quota long ago and have benefited from the same for more than one generation today staunchly protect their 'backward' status. This is truly the only country in the world where one fights to be recognised as backward. It is also a paradox that, as the years go by, there is no reduction in the list of backward classes. The Constitution contemplated reservation for a limited period so that those who were disadvantageously placed could get the benefit of easier admission to educational institutions or easier entry into public jobs. Undoubtedly, this was necessary to create a level playing field because persons belonging to the Scheduled Castes and Scheduled Tribes did not have the equal opportunity to compete with forward communities. Reservation, undoubtedly, was necessary but it should have been a temporary feature. The Supreme Court has repeatedly called upon the States to periodically review the extent of backward classes but again this has not been done. Politically, it is clearly impossible to remove a particular caste once it has been classified as 'backward class'. It is also a matter of deep regret that there is increasing demand to be notified as a SC, ST or backward class. These are political decisions made without any kind of statistical data to identify the backwardness or inadequate representation in the services under the Central or State Governments.

In large measure, the seeds for these fissiparous tendencies were sown by the Mandal Commission Report and Palkhivala's attacks on the anti-secular character of this report have been proved to be right.

---

16. (2006) 8 SCC 212 : AIR 2006 SC 71.

Justice Krishna Iyer, a former Supreme Court judge who has delivered landmark judgments for the underprivileged, cautioned that the general doctrine of backward classes would bring in 'back-door casteism' and subvert the scheme for a casteless society by creating vested interest in the 'plums of backwardism'. Justice Iyer had also pointed out the dangers of communal manipulation of Article 16(4) under political pressure. The grim forebodings of Justice Iyer have come true and are firmly entrenched today.

And even greater danger looms ahead. The fallout of the Mandal decision has increased the clamour for reservation in private sector employment. Some States have already passed legislation in this behalf but these have not been brought into force. Even more dangerous is the move to extend reservation to religious minorities. After dividing the country on caste lines, the next step is to divide it on a religious basis – all with the hope of winning a few more votes at the next elections. Sixty years after we became a republic, our politicians have a single-minded determination to systematically destroy the glorious dreams of our founding fathers.

No one is opposed to reservation or affirmative action; but the least that could have been done was to properly determine the backward classes and then restrict the benefit to those classes that were not adequately represented in public employment. Finally, reservations, based on the Mandal Commission Report, are now cast in concrete.

The Election Commission Case

Defending the Integrity and Role of the CEC

Almost fifty years after he had argued his first case in the Bombay High Court, Palkhivala appeared for T.N. Seshan, the then Chief Election Commissioner, before the Supreme Court.[1] Unfortunately, this was not a case which Palkhivala would have liked to be remembered for and could hardly be called his swansong.

An important feature of Indian democracy is the sheer size and complexity of a general election. The Constitution of India created an Election Commission to supervise the conduct of free and fair elections. In 1951, the Representation of the People Act was passed and various rules governing elections were framed from time to time. Article 324 created the Election Commission, headed by the Chief Election Commissioner (CEC), that was in charge of the entire election process. The Election Commission would also have 'such number of other Election Commissioners as may be prescribed by the President from time to time.' The office of the CEC was thus very important and he could not be removed except by a process of impeachment as in the case of a Supreme Court judge.

After the first decade, elections were often marred by violence and booth capturing. Several political parties indulged in employing *goondas* and other anti-social elements to capture booths, took away ballot boxes and stuffed them with ballot papers. Various voters were threatened or intimidated during the election process. In some cases, the incidence of violence and booth capturing reached serious proportions and, in some constituencies, elections became a farce. Several criminals, who were accused of serious crimes like murder, extortion, dacoity and other serious offences, became MLAs and MPs. The criminalization of politics

1. *T.N. Seshan, Chief Election Commissioner v. Union of India,* (1995) 4 SCC 611 : (1995) 5 JT 337.

was, and continues to be, the biggest blot on Indian democracy. The election of a successful candidate could be challenged only by instituting an election petition before the High Court and often this took two to three years to decide. In some cases, by the time the petition was heard, the five year term of the elected candidate would be virtually over. In several cases, the Chief Election Commissioner was a silent spectator to the serious violations of election laws.

In this gloomy scenario, came the appointment of T. N. Seshan, who was a very senior civil servant, as Chief Election Commissioner on December 12, 1990. He quickly began to clean up the political system and this was accompanied by widespread media publicity. Strictly enforcing the election laws, Seshan was a one-man-army against politicians who were used to flouting the rules and getting away with it. As Seshan could not be removed except by the impeachment process, he was able to do several daring things and brought political parties to their knees. After a long time, he was the one man who taught corrupt politicians a lesson and the common citizen simply loved him. Seshan became a national hero and, to his credit, was single-handedly able to implement election laws and regulations that had hitherto been observed in the breach. Until Seshan's arrival, there was widespread use of money and liquor to illegally garner votes, and the greater the money power and muscle power of a political party, the greater was its chance of success. Indeed, a situation was reached whereby it was virtually impossible for an honest citizen to contest elections. In this background, Seshan's determined efforts to clean up the system were widely welcomed.

Seshan took on all political parties. He ruthlessly postponed elections and took strong legal action even against senior leaders. But there was one fatal flaw in his method of working and that was his enormous love for publicity. Seshan frequently appeared in the media and was much sought after as a speaker. He even began to portray himself as the saviour of Indian democracy. Indeed, in one interview, he also hinted that after his retirement, he would enter politics which he later did. Finally, he perhaps made the big mistake of trying to place himself on par with Supreme Court judges in matters of protocol.

Seshan was thus effective but also abrasive. As a civil servant, his contemporaries often called him rude and arrogant. One senior civil servant remarked that Seshan had the classic Indian trait of being subservient to his superiors and tyrannical to his subordinates. Therefore, he was not very popular with either the political class or other members of the executive. In short, Seshan the individual became much bigger than the constitutional post of Chief Election Commissioner. Excessive publicity, which helped him in the beginning, eventually proved his undoing.

It was, therefore, decided to clip his wings and an Ordinance[2] was passed to convert the Election Commission into a three-member body. Seshan would now have to exercise powers with two more Election Commissioners. This trio was entrusted with the task of supervising elections. Where there was a conflict between the three Commissioners, the decision would be by majority! In other words, if the Central Government (read – ruling party) could appoint two partisan civil servants of their choice as Election Commissioners, then they could easily overrule Seshan on important decisions.

The Ordinance substituted the following sections for the original:

> *Section 9: The business of the Election Commission shall be transacted in accordance with the provisions of the Act.*
>
> *Section 10(1): The Election Commission may, by unanimous decision, regulate the procedure for transaction of its business as also allocation of its business, amongst the Chief Election Commissioner and the other Election Commissioners.*
>
> *(2) Save as provided in sub-section (1), the business of the Election Commission shall, as far as possible, be transacted unanimously.*
>
> *(3) Subject to the provision of sub-section (2), if the Chief Election Commissioner and the other Election Commissioners differ in opinion on any matter, such matter shall be decided according to the opinion of the majority.*

This was an effective way to cut Seshan to size. To add salt to Seshan's wounds, the Ordinance also equalized the salary payable to the Chief Election Commissioner and the other Election Commissioners, and equated the age of retirement of the Chief Election Commissioner and the other Election Commissioners.

2. The Chief Election Commissioner and Other Election Commissioners (Conditions of Service) Amendment Ordinance, 1993.

This ordinance was challenged before the Supreme Court in four writ petitions and the first was filed by Cho Ramaswamy,[3] the second by the incumbent Chief Election Commissioner, T.N. Seshan himself and by two other writ petitioners.[4]

In his later years, Palkhivala had developed a seething dislike for most politicians and justifiably so. He was simply appalled at the extent of corruption and the narrow parochial policies pursued by most political parties. With coalition politics firmly in place, it was increasingly clear that each party did not hesitate to sacrifice the national interest for their individual votebanks. A party with just a few seats in Parliament could wield an enormous clout and most of them did not hesitate to use it to get a few cabinet berths in order to unashamedly make money. In recent years, there have been widespread reports of the accumulation of fortunes by politicians which are quite unbelievable.

Therefore, despite his failing health, Palkhivala appeared for T.N. Seshan, as he considered the case to be of great public importance. The general public impression was that the Ordinance would seriously undermine the functioning of the Election Commission which had, by all accounts, done remarkably well in curbing election malpractices during Seshan's tenure.

Palkhivala came to Delhi and conferences with other lawyers appearing for Seshan were held over two days at Tata House which stretched late into the night. Even in 1995, at the age of 76, his capacity for hard work had not diminished and he was mentally very alert. He also prepared written submissions to be handed over to the court, as he had done in some of the important cases in the past. By the time the case reached hearing, the Ordinance had been replaced by the Chief Election Commissioner and Other Election Commissioners (Conditions of Service) Amendment Act, 1994, in which the above two sections were incorporated.

In the course of his address, Palkhivala bestowed high praise on Seshan and pointed out the various steps he had taken to make elections free and fair. But his words of praise created no impression on the judges who were obviously aware of Seshan's various acts of self-glorification and his attempts to project his own image before the public. Rather, the effect on the judges was opposite of that intended.

---

3. A leading Tamil writer and journalist.
4. B.K. Rai and Common Cause, a registered society.

The written submissions submitted by Palkhivala indicate five main grounds urged by him;

(i) Sections 9 and 10 were be beyond the legislative competence of Parliament which had no power to direct as to how 'the business of the Election Commission shall be transacted'. Similarly, Parliament could not pass any law making either the Election Commissioners equal to the CEC or providing that in case of any difference of opinion between them the matter would be decided by the majority.

(ii) Article 324 prohibited the removal of the CEC except by a process of impeachment. Sections 9 and 10 removed the CEC from power which is tantamount to removing him from office.

(iii) The first proviso to Article 324(5) prohibited any variation in the conditions of service of the CEC. When Seshan was appointed on December 12, 1990, he was the sole repository of all powers under Article 324 but by the amendment, he had to suffer humiliation of being overridden by the other two civil servants.

(iv) Sections 9 and 10 made a mockery of Article 324 in two ways: first, they placed the CEC and the Election Commissioners on a footing of equality; and, secondly, the two Election Commissioners could be removed from office on the recommendations of the CEC; but, while in office, they could reduce the CEC to a mere figurehead. This was an arbitrary and whimsical scheme.

(v) Sections 9 and 10 were a fraud on the Constitution as they were designed and calculated to defeat the whole purpose of having an Election Commission free from control of the executive and the legislature. The undisputed facts showed that CEC was acting in a truly independent manner and whenever he went wrong or overstepped his limits he was be rightly controlled by the judiciary.

The written submissions finally referred to the period of 45 days after the two Election Commissioners were appointed on 1st October, 1993. During this time, the two Election Commissioners frequently overruled Seshan and the functioning of the Election Commission was paralysed.

The Supreme Court had to give an interim order on November 15, 1993, giving Seshan complete overall control of the Commissioner's work and making it clear that he alone would be entitled to issue instructions to the staff and to outside agencies and that no other Election Commissioner could do so.

In Palkhivala's favour were certain observations made in an earlier judgment, *S.S. Dhanoa v Union of India.*[5] In this case, it was made clear that the Chief Election Commissioner was not the first among equals; his was a superior office that had special privileges. The CEC could not be removed except by impeachment and his tenure, conditions of service and salary could not be varied adversely. Even in the Constituent Assembly, Dr. Ambedkar stated that the other members of the Election Commission were not to have the same status as the Chief Election Commissioner.[6]

G. Ramaswamy and Ram Jethmalani continued the arguments and they too made elaborate and detailed submissions challenging the validity of the two sections but their arguments too were in vain.

Justice Ahmadi wrote the judgment of the Constitution Bench in *Seshan's* case. All four petitions were dismissed and the Act was upheld on the ground that the scheme of Article 324 envisaged a multi-member body headed by a Chief Election Commissioner. The observations in *Dhanoa's* case were partly overruled. Some of the observations in the judgment of Ahmadi J. are a reaction to the high praise bestowed on Seshan by Palkhivala. The Court reminded the petitioner and the counsel that:

> *Nobody can be above the institution which he is supposed to serve. He is merely the creature of the institution, he can exist only if the institution exists. To project the individual as mightier than the institution would be a grave mistake. Therefore, even if the Election Commission is a single-member body, the CEC is merely a functionary of that body; to put it differently, the alter ego of the Commission and no more.*

The most damaging remarks to Seshan himself were made in para 30 of the judgment:

> *We may incidentally mention that the decisions taken by the CEC from time to time postponing elections at the last*

5. AIR 1991 SC 1745 : (1991) 3 SCC 567.
6. *Constituent Assembly Debates* (CAD), Vol VIII, p. 905.

moment, of which he has made mention in his petition, have evoked mixed reactions. This we say because the CEC uses them to lay the foundation for his contention that the entire exercise was mala fide. Some of his other decisions were so unsustainable that he could not support them when tested in court. His public utterances at times were so abrasive that this Court had to caution him to exercise restraint on more occasions than one. This gave the impression that he was keen to project his own image. That he has very often been in the newspapers and magazines and on television cannot be denied. In this backdrop, if the Government thought that a multi-member body was desirable, the Government certainly was not wrong and its action cannot be described as mala fide. Subsequent events would suggest that the Government was wholly justified in creating a multi-member Commission. The CEC has been seen in a commercial on television and in newspaper advertisements. The CEC has addressed the Press and is reported to have said that he would utilise the balance of his tenure to form a political party to fight corruption and the like [Sunday Times (Bombay) dated 25-6-1995]. Serious doubts may arise regarding his decisions if it is suspected that he has political ambitions, in the absence of any provision, such as, Article 319 of the Constitution. The CEC is, it would appear, totally oblivious to the sense of decorum and discretion that his high office requires even if the cause is laudable.

The allegation of *mala fides* on the part of the Government in pushing through the ordinance was also brushed aside with the following observations:

Assuming the present CEC had taken certain decisions not palatable to the ruling party at the Centre as alleged by him, it is not permissible to jump to the conclusion that that was the cause for the Ordinance and the appointments of the ECs. If such a nexus is to weigh, the CEC would continue to act against the ruling party to keep the move for a multi-member Commission at bay. We find it difficult to hold that the decision to constitute a multi-member Commission was actuated by malice. Therefore, even though it is not permissible to plead malice, we have examined the contention and see no merit in it. It is wrong

> *to think that the two ECs were pliable persons who were being appointed with the sole object of eroding the independence of the CEC.*

Another factor that seems to have weighed with the court while passing strictures against Seshan was the various letters written by him to the Home Secretary and the Prime Minister to equate himself with judges of the Supreme Court – especially his attempt to amend the Warrant of Precedence to reflect his exalted status.

The entire case was a total fiasco for the petitioners. The judgment clearly showed that the proceedings in court were overshadowed by the personality of Seshan and his ego. As can be seen from the above excerpts, these clearly made a difference to the case and the Supreme Court was determined to put Seshan in his place.

The judgment does not even mention the names of Palkhivala, G. Ramaswamy or Ram Jethmalani and other eminent counsel who appeared. In the judgment, except the plea that the amendment was a fraud on the Constitution, the detailed submissions of Palkhivala have not even been discussed.[7] There are no reasons given as to why they partly overruled the earlier decision in *Dhanoa* case. It was indeed sad that Palkhivala's last important case had to end in this manner.

In the end, Seshan was cut to size but serious damage was done to the office of the CEC. For all his faults, Seshan did a remarkable job of cleaning up the system and made us all aware of the critical role that the EC plays in ensuring free and fair elections.

❋

---

7. This point is discussed perfunctorily in para 23 of the judgment.

Chapter 6

Income Tax Matters

While Palkhivala's contribution to constitutional law was immense, he shot to national fame at a young age only as a tax lawyer. Without question, he had perhaps the largest income tax practice till the mid-60s. His increased involvement with the House of Tatas resulted in a reduction in his court appearances.

In this chapter, an attempt has been made to highlight important cases that he argued under Income Tax Acts of 1922 and 1961. Undoubtedly, there is bound to be a dispute on the cases that have been left out. As far as possible, cases have been chosen only where a new principle was laid down or where the judgment of the court has been recognised as a landmark verdict. It was not possible to cover decisions from all the High Courts where Palkhivala appeared. Several important cases which he argued before the Tribunal have also been left out.

In many cases, the points involved were not confined merely to the Income Tax Act or other tax laws like Wealth Tax or Super Profits Tax. One finds that several cases involved myriad branches of law including the Transfer of Property Act, 1882, Stamp Act, 1899, Hindu law, sales tax statutes and other commercial laws like the Indian Contract Act, 1872, the Sale of Goods Act, 1930 and the Negotiable Instruments Act, 1881. Equally wide was the range of assessees whom Palkhivala represented. They included not only limited companies but spiritual leaders, individuals, Princes, Nawabs, the Nizam, Baronets, trustees, executors, wards, testators, assignees, firms and managing agents, association of persons (AOP) and professionals like Chartered Accountants. In view of the numerous cases and topics involved, this chapter has been divided into thirteen main headings.

1. Palkhivala's early appearances for the Department

The old Income Tax Reports show that Palkhivala and G.N. Joshi, a lawyer who appeared for the Department with great distinction for many years, had appeared together for the Commissioner of Income Tax in two cases. Interestingly,

Sir Jamshedji Kanga appeared for the assessee. In the first case,[1] the question was whether amounts received from the insurance company under a 'Consequential Loss Policy' was liable to tax as income. A major fire destroyed the factory building of the assessee and its manufacturing activity came to a grinding halt. In 1944, the company received Rs. 14 lakhs from the insurance company and Kanga argued that this was not 'income' but was received as an indemnity under the insurance policy; it should be looked as a windfall and not an amount earned in the course of the business of the company. The stand of the Department was that under the policy these amounts were paid to the company as an indemnity for the 'loss of profits' because of cessation of its manufacturing activity. Unfortunately, for Kanga, the issue was settled by an earlier Privy Council[2] decision and the Bombay High Court had no hesitation in answering the question in favour of the revenue. The arguments of Palkhivala are not mentioned in the judgment.

On the same day,[3] Kanga appeared for another assessee and Palkhivala appeared for the Commissioner. This case[4] was more complex and the court had to deal with the liability of a partnership firm to pay super tax. The judgment is worth reading for the excellent arguments of Kanga who tried to interpret the seemingly contradictory sections and submitted that the assessee was not liable to pay super tax. The expression 'no tax' in the relevant statutory provisions, according to Kanga, would include not only income tax but also super tax. Equally interesting is the manner in which Chagla has dealt with all his submissions and rejected them. The judgment contains important observations on the interpretation of statutes. Once again, Palkhivala's arguments are not mentioned in the judgment but the questions were answered in favour of the revenue. For the record, Palkhivala succeeded in both the cases in which he appeared for the Revenue.

2. Basic concepts

2.1 *Heads of income*

United Commercial Bank, during the assessment year 1945-46, earned interest of Rs. 23,62,815 on its investment in securities but made a loss of Rs. 8,86,972 in its banking operations. It had also a

1. *Raghuvanhi Mills Ltd. v. CIT,* (1949) 17 ITR 520 : AIR 1949 Bom 377.
2. *Rex v. B.C. Fir and Cedar Lumber Co.,* (1932) A.C. 441.
3. March 18, 1949. Chagla never reserved his judgments and dictated them in open court as soon as the arguments concluded.
4. *Kikabhoy Chandabhoy v. CIT,* (1949) 17 ITR 523 (Bom).

carried forward loss of Rs. 3,21,929 which was computed after setting off its business loss against its business income.

Palkhivala argued that if the securities are held as a trading asset, as in the case of a banking company, the interest income must be taxed as business income. Examining the scheme of the Income Tax Act, the Supreme Court held that tax is to be charged on the total income at the rates prescribed in the Finance Act. Each head of income – salary, interest on securities, property, business, capital gains etc. is separate, exclusive and specific. The court referred to English cases which dealt with 'schedules', akin to our heads of income, and held that any income falling under one head cannot be put under any other head. Palkhivala's argument was rejected and it was held that income from securities, even for a bank, cannot be treated as business income.[5]

But Palkhivala raised another interesting argument and partly succeeded on this point. Under Section 24(2) of the 1922 Act, a loss could be carried forward and set-off against profits from the 'same business'. He argued that the word 'same business' signifies the identity of business in which the loss has occurred and does not refer to the head of income under which profits are chargeable. Dealing in money and credit and dealing in securities are acts done in the course of banking business. Interest from securities does not cease to be profits and gains of the banking business merely because it falls under a separate heading for the purpose of chargeability. Section 24 permitted set-off of loss in computing the aggregate income. The Supreme Court accepted this plea and remanded the case to the High Court to decide whether UCO Bank had held the securities as part of its banking business. This decision was subsequently followed in several cases and it established the mutual exclusivity of the heads of income.

A similar question arose in the case of *Bihar State Co-operative Society v. CIT,*[6] where the bank had made deposits with another bank and had earned interest from the same. The question before the Supreme Court was whether this interest formed a part of the business income of the assessee or whether it was income from 'other sources'. Palkhivala argued that the business of the bank was dealing in money and credit and that laying out monies in deposit with other banks was only a mode of conducting its business. He claimed that there were two reasons why the money was kept in

---

5. *United Commercial Bank v. CIT,* (1957) 32 ITR 688 : AIR 1957 SC 918.
6. (1960) 39 ITR 114 : AIR 1960 SC 789 : [1960] 3 SCR 58.

another bank. First, it ensured that monies that were not immediately required still earned interest. Secondly, if and when money was required to meet a demand, it was easily available for disbursement. C.K. Daphtary, one of the finest legal minds and a very persuasive counsel, was the Solicitor-General who appeared for the Income Tax Department. He argued that the monies so invested did not form a part of the 'carrying out of the business' of a bank, since the bank's business was only to deal in money and credit.

The Court, however, ruled against the Revenue and held that for a bank, money is its stock-in-trade or circulating capital, and its normal business is to deal in money and credit. It reasoned that it was not correct to hold that the business of banks consisted only in receiving deposits and lending money to its members or such other societies as are mentioned in the objects. When a bank keeps its money in another bank, it is readily available to meet the demand of its depositors if and when the need arises, and this is a legitimate mode of carrying on its banking business. Banks always have to keep sufficient cash or easily realisable securities. In the court's opinion, that is an act done in what is truly the carrying on or carrying out of a business. On this ground, the Court upheld Palkhivala's contention that income from deposits formed a part of business income.

Dilip Kumar Roy,[7] a disciple of late Sri Aurobindo, was a well known singer and a writer of books on religion and philosophy. He received cash gifts from his devotees which were sought to be taxed. Palkhivala raised three main arguments. He contended, firstly, that singing *bhajans* and writing books on philosophy was not a vocation at all. However, this contention was rejected by the court by citing another judgment where the Supreme Court had held that teaching *Vedanta* amounted to a vocation. The second contention raised was that the amounts in question were not amounts received as payment for conducting the vocation or business. He argued that these were amounts paid as gifts for personal esteem and veneration. This ingenious argument was accepted by the Bombay High Court, after it discussed several case law cited by him on the point. The test was that if the amount was given in appreciation of a person's expertise in a field, then it was not an amount received from the business or profession, but in the nature of a gift. On the other hand, if it was paid to reward a

---

7. *Dilip Kumar Roy v. CIT*, (1974) 94 ITR 1 (Bom).

person for services rendered to the payer in that field, then they would be treated as income. The third contention was that, in any event, the amounts received by the assessee are impressed with the character of a trust. The Court did not consider this plea since it had already ruled that there was no taxability on these amounts.

2.2 *Accrual of income*

One of the most oft-cited decisions of the Supreme Court is *E.D. Sassoon & Co. Ltd. v. CIT.*[8] A galaxy of eminent counsel appeared in this case. M.C. Setalvad, the Attorney-General, C.K. Daphtary, the Solicitor-General, B.J.M. Mackenna (a British barrister practicing in the U.K.) and Palkhivala. The Supreme Court laid down important principles on when income can accrue or arise and these are followed till this day.

E.D. Sassoon and Co. Ltd.[9] sold the managing agencies of three textile mills for Rs. 76 lakhs and this was credited to its Capital Reserve Account. The transfer/sale of the three mills took place in June, July and December of 1943 i.e. during the financial year ending March 31, 1944. The managing agency commission for the assessment year 1944-45 was paid to three companies which had purchased the managing agencies.[10]

As the transfer took place at different times during the financial year ending on March 31, 1944, the Department and the Tribunal held that the commission should be taxed in the hands of the managing agency till the date of transfer; in effect, the managing agency commission should be apportioned between Sasoon and the three companies that had purchased the managing agency on a *pro rata* basis.

On a careful examination of the managing agency agreement, the Supreme Court held that the right to receive remuneration or commission was payable to the managing agents only at the end of each such period of service. The contract of employment was an entire and indivisible contract. The Supreme Court rightly noted

8. AIR 1954 SC 470 : (1954) 26 ITR 27.
9. The Sassoons (1792-1864) set up business in Bombay in 1833 and in Hong Kong in 1844. With extensive business interests in India and China, Sassoons were the wealthiest family in India and China. Victor Sassoon, the last male heir in the Sassoon Baronetcy was crippled while in service with the British Air Force in the Second World War and died in 1961. The title 'died out' with him as he had no children.
10. Palkhivala appeared for one of these companies *viz.* Chidambaram Mulraj & Co. Ltd.

the difficulty in the case: the transferors had worked for a portion of the year but were not entitled to any amount and the transferees, who worked only for part of the year were entitled to the whole income for the year. But what was relevant was the income that had accrued to the person on a strict interpretation of Section 4(1)(a) of the 1922 Act, and no question of the work done for the broken period or any equitable consideration would make any difference to the question of chargeability.

Justice N.H. Bhagwati's judgment deserves to be read and his observations on the concepts of accrual, income, receipt and other fundamentals of accounting and income tax law remain valid even today.

In *CIT v. Shoorji Vallabhdas and Co.*,[11] the commission payable to a managing agency was reduced in a later year in respect of commission payable in a previous year. Since the assessee followed the mercantile system of accounting, the Revenue claimed that the higher commission had accrued and tax was payable on that sum. Palkhivala's contention, accepted by the Bombay High Court, was that the question whether the income accrued or not was not a mere matter of cogency of the entries made in the account books of the assessee, but was essentially one of substance and of the real nature of what happened. He argued that a mere book entry was not conclusive of whether the assessee had become entitled to the sums or not and that the agreement between the assessee and its principal to receive a lower commission was a matter of business expediency. What was crucial was the real commission which the agent was entitled to in consequence of the agreement between the parties. This decision was later affirmed by the Supreme Court.[12]

In 1977, Palkhivala argued an important case on accrual of income.[13] It all began with signing of an agreement on June 22, 1955 in the United States. Under this agreement, Carborandum Co. Inc. entered into an agreement for rendering of technical knowhow services to manufacture bonded abrasives and coated abrasive products. The agreement also required the American company to provide factory design and layouts, manufacturing specifications, furnishing comprehensive technical information and providing the Indian company with a Resident Factory Manager and other technical personnel. During the initial training period,

11. (1959) 36 ITR 25 (Bom).
12. *CIT v. Shoorji Vallabhdas & Co.*, (1962) 46 ITR 144 (SC).
13. *Carborandum Company v. CIT*, (1977) 108 ITR 335 : AIR 1977 SC 1259.

the employees of the Indian company were also trained so that they could replace the foreign employees as quickly as possible. The American company was to receive 3% of the net sales as technical fees under the agreement.

The ITO took the view that 5% of the technical fee was earned in India and this amount was liable to Indian income tax. Usually, the ITOs pass orders which are completely in favour of the Revenue but this was a rather unusual case where the ITO granted substantial relief. The Commissioner, perhaps taken aback by this unusual fairness, revised the order and directed 75% of the technical fee to be treated as accruing or arising in India.

The American company naturally went up in appeal and the Tribunal set aside the Commissioner's orders. In fact, the Tribunal took the view that even 5% of the fees did not accrue or arise in India but as the American company had not appealed against the findings of 5%, the Tribunal confirmed the order of the Income Tax Officer and allowed the appeal. The Tribunal noted that services were rendered by the American company outside India and the agreement had also been signed outside India. The American employees who worked in India were, under the agreement, treated as employees of the Indian company and paid accordingly. Thus, no income accrued or arose to the American company in India.

In the Madras High Court, the case took a strange turn. The entire fees earned by the American company were held to accrue or arise in India because, according to the High Court, the agreement clearly established a 'business connection between the two companies'. Therefore, the fees could be taxable as accruing or arising from such business connection and were liable to tax under Section 41(1)(c) and Section 42 of 1922 Act.

Palkhivala appeared for the American company in the Supreme Court and assailed the High Court order which confirmed the tax liability on the ground of 'business connection' when this ground had never been raised at any time. He further went on to argue that even if there was a 'business connection', the High Court failed to examine the question of apportionment under Section 42(3) of the Act. Even on the principle of apportionment, the tax liability could not be more than 5% as held by the Income Tax Officer.

Agreeing with Palkhivala's submissions, the Supreme Court found that the High Court had wrongly confirmed the demand based upon 'business connection' when this ground was never raised before the Tribunal or lower authorities. However, it examined the case on merits and discussed the meaning of the expression 'business connection' and the theory of apportionment. If only part of the operations were carried on in the taxable territories, then the profits and gains of the business that are taxable in India will be those that are attributable to the operations carried on in India.

The Supreme Court, after examining the agreement, held that no part of activity had been carried on by the American company in India as no income accrued or arose within the Indian territory. Once again, since the American company had not filed the appeal against the addition of 5% by the ITO, this portion was confirmed.

2.3 *Tax should be on real income*

Assessees are often subjected to absurd and arbitrary treatment by the laws of income tax. For instance, Section 23A of the 1922 Act required companies to distribute a minimum percentage of their income and if they did not do so, the shortfall was *deemed* to have been distributed and the deemed divided was added to the total income to individual shareholders and taxed in their hands! Thus, individual shareholders had to pay tax on dividend they never received.

On the contrary, if a company declared 'excess dividend', it was liable to pay additional income tax. If a company made profits and declared dividend in excess of a stipulated percentage, that company had to pay additional income tax. Thus, companies that declared less dividend created an additional tax liability in the hands of the shareholders, while companies which declared higher dividends had to pay additional income tax.

The levy of this additional income tax was questioned before the Bombay High Court in *CIT v. Khatau Makanji Spinning and Weaving Company Ltd.,*[14] The company had paid dividend from the profits of the earlier years as the profits of the relevant assessment year were not adequate. Palkhivala argued that the additional income tax could be levied only with reference to the total income of that previous year. While the Finance Act, 1953 provided for levy of additional income tax, the charging section in the Income Tax Act, 1922 had not been amended. This argument was accepted by Chief Justice Chagla who ruled that the Finance Act, 1953 had 'misfired' by not providing that the accumulated

---

14. (1956) 30 ITR 841 : AIR 1956 Bom 733.

profits would also be treated as part of the total income of the previous year. This judgment was affirmed by the Supreme Court which also held that Parliament had failed to suitably draft the provisions of the Finance Act, 1953. Section 3, the charging section made it clear that tax could be levied only on income and nothing else.

Chief Justice Chagla rightly pointed out that for a charge to be legal under Section 3 of the 1922 Act (or) Section 4 under the 1961 Act, it must be a tax on the income of the assessee and on nothing else.

If the charge is a tax on something else, then it is not a proper or valid charge. He gave an excellent example: Parliament may levy tax at the rate of 50% of the wealth of the assessee or it may say that if the assessee's wealth is Rs. 5 lakhs or Rs. 10 lakhs, he will be liable to pay tax at a particular rate in relation to his total income. Clearly, levying tax at a percentage of the wealth would have no relationship to the total income while fixing the rate on the basis of the wealth would be valid as, in the latter case, the assessee would pay tax on his total income.

The excess dividend fastened a liability on a company to pay additional tax irrespective of a company's total income. For example, a company may pay dividend out of accumulated profits of the earlier years and, hypothetically, this may even be more than the total income of the assessee. Justice Chagla observed that as long as the charge is on the total income of the previous year, there is no limitation upon the power or authority of Parliament to fix any rate it pleases. But there is a limit upon the power of Parliament that is inherent in the nature of the tax which can be imposed under the charging section that prescribes the subject matter of the tax and it is necessary that the rate must be relatable to the subject matter of the tax. If it does not relate to the subject matter, then the conclusion must be that Parliament is not taxing income but is taxing something else. Justice Chagla also pointed out that the object of Parliament could be achieved in different ways but if it 'misfires' in achieving its objective in a proper manner, the court will be obliged to strike it down. Parliament could have treated the excess dividend declared as a notional income and may add a part of the total income of the previous year or it could have provided certain alternatives to levy tax. The ambit of the charging section is clear and it must be a tax on income. The Finance Act which levies tax on the excess dividend paid had traveled beyond the ambit of Section 3 and was not valid.

Another important case that dealt with additional income tax was *CIT v. Elphinstone Spinning and Weaving Mills Company Ltd.*[15] In this case, the assessee had made profits but the depreciation allowance was substantially higher, converting the profit into a loss for income tax purpose. Nevertheless, the company declared dividend and this was treated as 'excess dividend' and the company made liable to additional income tax. The Department argued that total income would also include a loss and this interpretation was accepted by the Tribunal. In a very well written judgment, Justice Hidayatullah analyzed the provisions of the Income Tax Act, 1961 and the relevant Finance Act in the background of legal principles laid down in leading English cases. He held that the word 'additional income tax' must refer to a state of affairs in which there was already tax liability. The words 'charge on the total income' were not appropriate to cover a case where there was a loss. Finally, the expression 'dividends payable out of such profits' would not apply when there were no profits. Unless the words 'on the total income' were modified by Parliament, the courts could not help the draftsman by a favourable construction. On a plain reading of the statutory provisions, no additional tax could be levied unless there was total income in the previous year. The court ruled: 'There is no doubt that if the words of a taxing statute fail, then so must the tax.'

Justice Hidayatullah cited with approval an excellent observation of Chief Justice Chagla:

> *There seems to be no logic, there seems to be no reason nor principle why a distinction should be made between the case of two such companies. But if life is not logic, income-tax is much less so, and it is clear that we cannot impose tax upon a subject by implication or because we think that the object of the Legislature was a particular object.*

In both these cases, the judgments of the Bombay High Court deserved to be read in full.

Very, very few judges today would have the boldness and courage to decide a case in the manner that Chief Justice Chagla did.

2.4 *Sticky loans*

All banks have the problem of defaulting borrowers. When even the recovery of the principal amount becomes extremely difficult, these advances are treated as 'sticky loans'. Naturally, the defaulter

15. (1960) 40 ITR 142 : AIR 1960 SC 1022.

does not pay the instalments and no interest is received by the bank. At the same time, according to the mercantile system of accounting, the interest technically accrues to the bank at the end of each accounting year. Therefore, banks have a piquant situation where the interest on 'sticky advances' is unlikely to be received but accrues as income. Banks, therefore, do not credit this amount to the Profit and Loss Account but show it as a part of 'Interest Suspense Account'. This system had been followed for several years and interest credited to suspense account was not treated as its income. The Income Tax Department had approved this practice by issuing circulars in 1924, 1952 and 1973 which was uniformly followed by several banks. In 1975, for the first time, the Kerala High Court took a discontent view in *Catholic Bank of India v. CIT*[16] and this view was followed in a later case concerning the State Bank of Travancore.[17] The bank took up the matter in appeal and unfortunately, by a majority of 2:1 the Supreme Court[18] upheld the view of the Kerala High Court. Palkhivala argued that what can be taxed are real profits and gains and not hypothetical profits or gains. One could not adopt the doctrinaire theory of accrual and treat the accrual of such interest as income when it was highly unlikely that this amount would ever be received. An irrevocable loan was a bad debt which is deductible under Section 36(1)(vi) while sticky loan is a loan to which a high degree of improbability of recovery attaches in a particular year or years depending on the financial position of the concerned borrower. Palkhivala pointed out that over 50 years, this distinction was recognized by the Central Board of Revenue (later Central Board of Direct Taxes) and by the Reserve Bank of India. All banks, although following the mercantile system of accounting had credited interest on sticky loans to 'interest suspense account' and was not treated as its taxable income. Reference was made to the standard accounting textbooks and the International Accounting Standards (IAS 18). The decision of the Kerala High Court was clearly wrong, he submitted.

Justice V.D. Tulzapurkar accepted the arguments of Palkhivala but Justices Sabyasachi Mukharji and Ranganath Mishra held against all the banks.[19] When the Central Board of Direct Taxes

16. 1964 Ker LT 653.
17. (1975) 110 ITR 336.
18. *State Bank of Travancore v. CIT*, AIR 1986 SC 757 : (1986) 158 ITR 102 : (1986) 2 SCC 11.
19. The dissenting view of Justice Tulzapurkar was subsequently restored in *UCO Bank v. CIT*, 1999 AIR SC 2082 : (1999) 237 ITR 889 : (1999) 4 SCC 599.

had accepted this view, there was no need for the Kerala High Court and the Supreme Court to take a different view. The net result was that banks had to pay income tax on interest which was highly unlikely to be recovered. Now, a bank had to pay Rs. 40 as income tax on interest of Rs.100/- which was not received. Strangely, the majority observed that the real income theory would apply in limited fields where the reality of the situation prevents accrual of income. The Supreme Court failed to note that the reality of the situation in the case of sticky loans did not result in accrual of income. The stark reality was that there could be no real accrual when the income was unlikely to be received. Although there was no real income, the Supreme Court went on to hold that banks could not treat interest as accrued and then treat it as part of interest suspense account.

The majority observed that they wanted to adhere to the basic fundamentals of the law with clarity and consistency rather than be carried away by common clichés. Ironically, it was the Supreme Court's decision that ignored the basic fundamentals of tax law and wrongly treated interest income on sticky loans as taxable despite a contrary practice followed consistently for several decades and approved by the highest executive authority in the hierarchy of direct taxes – the Central Board of Revenue (before 1963) and by the Central Board of Direct Taxes.

Thirteen years later, the correctness of the *State Bank of Travancore* case once again came up for consideration before the Supreme Court in *UCO Bank v. CIT.*[20] Two Constitution Bench decisions of the Supreme Court on the scope of circular had not been considered in the *State Bank of Travancore* case. More importantly, on October 9, 1984, the Board issued another circular stating that if no interest had been received for three-consecutive years, interest credited to the suspense account by banking companies will not be subject to tax. This circular was also not brought to the attention in the earlier Supreme Court decision which was rendered in 1986. Consequently, the majority decision in the *State Bank of Travancore* case[21] (decided by a Bench of three judges) was contrary to the law laid down by the two Benches of five judges.

The Supreme Court also overruled the decision of a Bench of two judges of the Supreme Court in *Kerala Financial Corporation v.*

20. (1999) 4 SCC 599 : (1997) 237 ITR 889 : AIR 1999 SC 2082.
21. AIR 1986 SC 757 : (1986) 158 ITR 102 : (1986) 2 SCC 11.

CIT.[22] In the end, Palkhivala's arguments prevailed. It is sad that banks had to face unnecessary hardship for 13 years because the High Courts and the Supreme Court wrongly insisted on taxing interest on sticky loans when the Central Board of Direct Taxes itself had no objection to granting banks much needed relief and not taxing this amount.

2.5 *The law applicable to any assessment year*

Section 3 of the Territorial Waters, Continental Shelf, Exclusive Economic Zone And Other Maritime Zones Act, 1976, extends the sovereignty of India to the 'territorial waters' which is 12 nautical miles from the shore. Section 6 of this Act defines the continental shelf to extend to a distance of 200 nautical miles from the shore and the Central Government can extend any enactment for the time being in force in India to any part of the continental shelf. Accordingly, the Income Tax Act, 1961 was extended to the continental shelf from April 1, 1983. Palkhivala successfully argued that the Income Tax Act, 1961 would not apply for the period April 1, 1982 to March 31, 1983. The Income tax Department had unjustifiably recovered income tax on salaries paid to employees of a foreign drilling company engaged by the Oil and Natural Gas Commission (ONGC) even for the period prior to the notification. In the end, the Bombay High Court directed refund of tax recovered with 15% interest because the employees had rendered service beyond the 12 nautical mile limit and were not liable to pay income tax on their salaries till the notification come into force on April 1, 1983.[23]

3. Business income and expenditure

3.1 *Income – Revenue or capital*

An interesting case that dealt with the consequences of devaluation was *CIT v. Tata Engineering and Locomotive Company Ltd.*[24] Telco had remitted USD 33,850 to purchase capital goods and to incur expenditure connected therewith and a sum of USD 30,382.96 was spent on capital account. Telco had also earned commission of USD 36,123 in foreign exchange and also received about USD 9,000 as reimbursement of expenses that was incurred

22. (1994) 4 SCC 375 : (1994) 210 ITR 129 : AIR 1994 SC 416.
23. *McDermott International Inc v. Union of India*, (1988) 173 ITR 155 : (1988) 70 CTR 481 (Bom).
24. AIR 1966 SC 1506 : (1966) 60 ITR 405 : [1966] 3 SCR 235.

in India for an American company. These amounts were permitted to be retained in the US for purchase of capital goods.

The rupee was devalued in 1949.[25] As the Government of India imposed certain additional restrictions and the goods became more expensive, the assessee repatriated USD 49,500. A surplus of Rs. 70,147 resulted on account of devaluation and the question was whether the surplus was a trading profit or an accretion to the capital account. The Department was represented by a brilliant lawyer, A.V. Viswanatha Sastri. He argued that if the commission had been allowed to be retained, any surplus on account of devaluation was liable to tax. Palkhivala argued that Telco was not a dealer in foreign exchange and the amount had not been retained for revenue purposes. The amount had been retained on capital account and to acquire a capital asset. Therefore, any profit made on realisation is capital appreciation, even though the foreign currency may have been originally acquired as a revenue receipt. In a brief but interesting judgment, Justice Sikri observed that the act of retaining money in dollars was only on capital account. There was no doubt that the commission earned was a revenue receipt and was liable to tax. Once this amount was retained abroad for purchase of capital equipment, it was an independent transaction and a first step to acquiring capital goods and any surplus arising as a result of devaluation would be only on capital account and not liable to tax.

In *CIT v. Asiatic Textile and Co.*,[26] the question before Justice Chagla of the Bombay High Court was whether a compensation paid for the surrendering of managing agency was a revenue or a capital receipt. The facts, he held, were an illustration of high finance at its highest and the 'manipulations left one completely bewildered'. But if these transactions were valid, then the assessee could not be taxed even if the court morally disapproved the transaction. Again, Palkhivala's opponent was G.N. Joshi who cited a large number of judgments from India and the United Kingdom. Palkhivala divided these cases into four categories, and Justice Chagla noted that since this was the most apt classification, he would follow the same and reach a conclusion on the issue.

---

25. The rate of exchange between the rupee and the dollar was USD1 : Rs. 3.340. After devaluation, the rate exchange became USD1 : Rs. 4.775. Over the years, the rupee has gone down in value and, in 2011, USD 1 is approximately equal to Rs. 45.00.
26. (1955) 27 ITR 315 (Bom) : AIR 1955 Bom 198.

The first category of cases was where the managing agent, instead of a year-on-year commission, accepts a lump sum for a particular time period irrespective of the amount of profits generated in that period. In this category, since the payment was for agency services to be rendered, and was being paid upfront, it was held to be a revenue receipt. The second category involved a variation or modification of an agency agreement which was incidental to the business carried on by the assessee. Here, the amount received for either modification or termination of the agency agreement was also a revenue receipt since the assessee had not lost an enduring source of business. In the third category, the agent accepted a lower rate of commission from the date of modification and accepted a lump sum as compensation. Since the contract was continuing, the lump sum was a revenue receipt. The fourth category of cases were those where the contract was in the ordinary course of the asssessee's business, but damages or compensation was paid for a breach of the agreement. The Court held that in these cases, the principle was that if an assessee is doing business in a commodity and in respect of that business various contracts have been entered into and some contracts are not carried out and compensation is paid to the assessee company, those contracts are incidental to the business and are entered into in the ordinary course of business. Therefore, even there it was a revenue receipt. By analysing these cases in this manner and classifying them, Palkhivala lucidly and effectively distinguished every judgment that was cited against him on a tricky issue of law. He then referred to several cases which had held that receipts on surrender of a capital asset were capital in nature. The Bombay High Court finally ruled that the payment made for the surrendering or termination of a managing agency agreement was a capital receipt.

3.2 *Expenditure – Revenue on Capital*

The expression 'enduring benefit' is extremely important in deciding whether an expenditure is revenue or capital in nature. If the assessee acquires an 'enduring benefit', the expenditure is capital in nature. The meaning of 'enduring benefit' was considered in detail in *CIT v. Coal Shipments Private Ltd.*[27] Although this decision was rendered in 1971, it concerned expenditure incurred from 1951-52 to 1955-56. After the World War II ended, it was decided

27. (1971) 82 ITR 902 : AIR 1972 SC 1634 : (1971) 3 SCC 736.

to resume the export of coal to Burma through an association called the Coal Exporters and Charterers Association. H. V. Low and Company Ltd., an important member of this Association, agreed not to export coal to Burma if others paid it Rs. 1 and 5 annas per tonne of coal exported. Coal was exported by the assessee until June, 1956 when this arrangement came to an end. Interestingly, the amount paid to Low and Company Ltd. was taxed in its hands but the expenditure was denied in the hands of the assessee on the ground that it was to secure a monopoly and should not be allowed as revenue expenditure.

The Supreme Court discussed various judgments on the aspect of 'enduring benefit'. It referred to an earlier judgment of Justice Hidayathullah who had held that none of the decisions were exhaustive or universal and each case had to depend on its own facts. He further observed that one should avoid the temptation of deciding cases by matching the colour of one case against the colour of another.[28] Coming back to the case pertaining to Low and Company Ltd., the court held that 'enduring benefit' need not be of a lasting character. At the same time, it should not be so transitory and ephemeral that it could be terminated at any time by the volition of any of the parties. It pointed out that the agreement with Low and Company Ltd. could be terminated at any time. It rejected the plea that the amount paid was to secure a monopoly. The Supreme Court apparently took note of the fact that there was no certainty of the duration of the arrangement and the same could be revoked at any time. The advantage was not of an enduring character. The payment related to the quantum of coal shipped to Burma in the course of trading activities and was not connected with the capital value of the asset. The agreement also required H.V. Low not to export coal to Burma during the relevant period. In this context also, the Supreme Court ruled that payment made to eliminate competition over some length of time may constitute capital expenditure but if the duration is uncertain and the agreement could be put to an end at any time, it could not be treated as capital expenditure. Ultimately, it was the uncertainty of the duration of the agreement that led the court to hold in favour of Palkhivala's client.

Another important case involving the question of revenue and capital expenditure was *Bhor Industries Ltd. v. CIT.*[29] The curious

---

28. *Abdul Kayoom v. CIT*, (1962) 44 ITR 689, 703 : AIR 1962 SC 680.
29. (1963) 48 ITR 376 (Bom).

facts were that a company had agreed to pay a percentage of its annual profits to the local ruler each year as consideration for not allowing any competing entity to run a similar business in the ruler's territory. There were also payments made to the ruler to ensure that additional property tax and factory taxes were not collected from the assessee for that business.

Palkhivala argued that although the assessee acquired monopoly rights, it should be allowed as a revenue expenditure because the payment was conditional only if the assessee made profits. The Bombay High Court rejected Palkhivala's contention and ruled that the protection acquired by the company went to appreciate the whole of the capital asset. Consequently, the amount paid for acquiring monopoly rights to the erstwhile ruler was not a revenue expenditure because the assessee had acquired an advantage for the enduring benefit of the business.

An unusual case arose under the Administration of Evacuee Property Act, 1959.[30] Aboobaker Abdul Rahman owned the Imperial Cinema Theatre and several other immovable properties in Bombay. Subsequently, Aboobaker and his three sons formed a partnership to run the cinema business. After partition, two sons migrated to Pakistan and Aboobaker expelled them from the partnership firm. The business was thus continued by Aboobaker and his third son as the remaining partner. The shares of the two sons who had migrated to Pakistan and were expelled were declared to be evacuee property. In 1950, Aboobaker died and his third son took over the business as sole proprietor. Without going into slightly complex facts, it may be stated that the Custodian-General initiated proceedings and the dispute was whether the properties could be treated as evacuee property under the above Act. The son who remained in India incurred substantial legal expenses to defend the proceedings and claimed them as business expenditure. The Income Tax Appellate Tribunal disallowed the claim on the ground that the legal expenses were incurred for the protection of his person and not for the protection of the properties of the business. Palkhivala went through several provisions of the 1959 Act and the rules made thereunder. Referring to Schedule VII, List-III, Entry 41 of the Constitution of India, he pointed out that the Act was concerned only with 'evacuee property' and not the person who was an evacuee. The legal expenditure incurred was to preserve

30. *Ebrahim Aboobaker v. CIT*, (1971) 81 ITR 664 (Bom).

his business and its properties. G.N. Joshi,[31] for the Department, submitted that the dominant purpose of the Act was to declare a person as an evacuee and the dispute relating to property of such an evacuee was a subsidiary question. The Bombay High Court accepted Palkhivala's argument that the legal expenditure had been incurred for preventing a declaration that the business of the Imperial Cinema Theatre was an evacuee property. Accordingly, the legal expenditure incurred was allowable as revenue expenditure under Section 10(2)(xv) which is analogous to Section 37 of the Income Tax Act, 1961.

In *CIT v. Bombay Samachar Ltd.*,[32] the assessee published newspapers and had borrowed money on which interest was claimed as revenue expenditure. It was alleged that it had advanced monies to a sister concern on which no interest had been charged. The Tribunal and the High Court noticed that the amounts due from the sister concern were not really loans but were debit balances and the assessee had been allocated shares towards this amount. On facts, there was no diversion of any amount to the sister concerns. There was no dispute that the amounts borrowed had been used for the purpose of the assessee's business. It was not open to the Department to take the plea that if the assessee had been diligent in collecting the outstandings from others, it would have reduced its indebtedness and saved interest. Once an amount had been borrowed and used for the purpose of business, the interest had to be allowed. The Department could not reject a claim of interest on the ground that the assessee had ample resources and need not have borrowed the money. This decision once again establishes that in commercial matters, the Department cannot substitute its wisdom as to what the assessee ought to have done.

3.3 *Writing-off amounts due – An allowable expenditure*

CIT v. Chandulal Keshavlal,[33] dealt with the important principle of allowing as expenditure amounts that were *given up* on grounds of commercial expediency. The assessee had to receive a certain amount as managing agency commission during the relevant assessment year. At the request of its principal, the agency agreed to

---

31. He was also a junior of M.C. Setalvad and a profound lawyer. Setalvad has acknowledged his contribution in appearing for several important constitutional cases.
32. (1969) 74 ITR 723 (Bom).
33. (1960) 38 ITR 601 : AIR 1960 SC 738.

accept a lesser sum as its commission. The Department claimed that the sum which was foregone was not an allowable expenditure in the hands of the managing agency. There was no evidence that this sum was wholly and exclusively written-off for the purposes of the managing agency business. No benefit had accrued to the managing agent and only his principal had benefited. In the absence of any benefit to the business of the managing agency, the deduction could not be permitted. The arguments of Palkhivala have unfortunately not been mentioned.

The Supreme Court referred to an excellent decision of Justice Vivian Bose in *Eastern Investments Ltd. v. CIT*,[34] where the judge ruled that if a transaction is entered into for commercial expediency and there is no allegation of fraud or oblique motive, the expenditure incurred must be allowed. He rightly observed that most commercial transactions are entered into for mutual benefit of both sides and each side hopes to gain something for itself. But for income tax purposes, the test is not whether every party benefited or whether it was a prudent transaction that had resulted in ultimate gain to the assessee. Bose J. also held that it did not matter if a third party had benefited as long as the transaction was properly entered into as part of the assessee's legitimate commercial undertaking in order to facilitate the carrying on of its business. The test was whether it was properly entered into as part of the assessee's legitimate commercial undertaking and in order to facilitate the carrying on of its business.

In an English case,[35] the holding company had written-off an amount due from its subsidiary and claimed it as a deduction. The court had observed that the writing-off of this small amount was part of a business transaction and would better enable the subsidiary to continue to carry on its business. In the same way, by giving up a part of its managing agency commission, the obvious intention was to strengthen the principal company which would then benefit the managing agent.

Additionally, the Supreme Court then observed that the Tribunal had come to a conclusion that the expenditure was indeed written-off wholly and exclusively for the purpose of business. This finding of fact could not be disturbed by the High Court or the Supreme Court if there was evidence upon which the Tribunal had arrived at such a conclusion.

---

34. (1951) 20 ITR 1 : AIR 1951 SC 278.
35. *Odhams Press Ltd. v. Cook*, (1941) 9 ITR (Suppl) 92.

3.4 *Fines and penalties cannot be deducted*

Can a fine imposed on an assessee be claimed as business expenditure? This interesting question came up for consideration before the Bombay High Court in *CIT v. Haji Aziz and Abdul Shakoor Bros.*[36] This firm imported dates from Iraq in violation of the then Sea Customs Act, 1867. The firm paid Rs. 82,250/- as redemption fine in lieu of confiscation and claimed this as a deduction under Section 10(2)(xv) of the Indian Income Tax Act, 1922 [corresponding to Section 37 of the present Act]. The Bombay High Court disallowed the expenditure and this was confirmed by the Supreme Court. Penalty cannot be claimed as a deductible expense as it is not a commercial loss or expenditure incurred in the course of carrying on its business. The court ruled that infraction or violation of the law is not a normal incidence of business; and a penalty imposed for contravention of a specific statutory provision cannot be treated as an expenditure incurred to enable a person to carry on trade.

Palkhivala ingeniously argued that there could be three consequences of a breach of law:

(i) confiscation or a redemption a fine in lieu of confiscation;

(ii) personal penalty;

(iii) prosecution in a criminal court.

An expenditure incurred to save or salvage a business was an allowable expenditure. The redemption fine was with regard to the assessee's stock-in-trade and not against the firm. It was intended for the release of the stock-in-trade of the assessee and would be an allowable expenditure. Thus, an ingenious distinction was sought to be drawn between an amount spent to release seized or confiscated goods and that spent for the release of a person who may be arrested.

The Supreme Court rejected Palkhivala's arguments and observed that any amount paid as penalty was for the infraction or breach of the law and, as held by the High Court, could not be a normal incidence of a company's business. Section 37 of the Income Tax Act, 1961 was later retrospectively amended in 1988

---

36. (1955) 28 ITR 266 : AIR 1955 Bom 350 : (1955) 57 Bom LR 485 (Bom) – affirmed by the Supreme Court in (1961) 41 ITR 350 : AIR 1961 SC 663.

with effect from 1962 by which any payment incurred for any purpose which is 'an offence or which is prohibited by law' is not allowable as a business expenditure.

3.5 *Distinction between provision and reserve*

The important distinction between a 'provision' and a 'reserve' was considered by the Supreme Court in the case of *Metal Box Ltd. v. Its Workmen,*[37] where the question was whether a sum set aside for the payment of gratuity would be a provision or a reserve for the computation of net profits of the company. The Court held, at the outset, that the principles governing what was a provision or a reserve were well known in commercial circles. Provisions are made for anticipated losses and contingencies and are charges against profits and therefore, taken into account against gross receipts in the profit and loss account and the balance sheet. On the other hand, reserves are appropriations of profits, the assets by which they are represented being retained to form part of the capital employed in the business. Provisions are usually shown in the balance-sheet by way of deductions from the assets in respect of which they are made whereas general reserves and reserve funds are shown as part of the proprietor's interest.

The workmen of Metal Box argued that the sum set aside was a 'reserve', because the exact sum that was payable in the coming year was not known precisely. Since the amount could not be computed accurately, it was argued that this was merely a 'reserve' that had to be added back to the gross profits for the distribution of bonus. The management of Metal Box, represented by Palkhivala, relied on a judgment of the House of Lords in *Southern Railway of Peru Ltd. v. Owen,*[38] where the company set aside an amount that was payable as retirement benefit to the employees retiring in the coming year. Even though it was not a certain event that all employees due to retire in the coming year would actually retire, the House of Lords held that this amount was a 'provision' because it was a liability that was certain, and that it could be quantified to a degree of accuracy. In an important observation, the Court held that if under the Income Tax Act, an estimated liability, ascertainable with substantial accuracy, can be taken into account for calculating the true profits and gains, there was no reason why the position under the Payment of Bonus Act should be any

---

37. (1969) 73 ITR 53 : AIR 1969 SC 612.
38. [1957] AC 334 (HL).

different. On this ground, the Court held that the amounts set aside for payment of gratuity were a 'provision' and not a 'reserve'.

This judgment continues to be a leading judgment on the distinction between a 'provision' and a 'reserve'. Even though this judgment was delivered in the context of the Payment of Bonus Act, 1965, it has had far-reaching consequences in cases arising under the Companies Act and the Income tax Act.

3.6 *Deductions for bad debts and current repairs*

(a) Bad debts

In *CIT v. Abdullabhai Abdulkader,*[39] the assessee was an agent of a non-resident. While executing a transaction of behalf of his principal, the assessee paid taxes on the transaction, but failed to collect them from his principal. He sought to write this off as a bad debt. The Revenue, represented by the Advocate-General, argued that since this was not a debt incurred during the course of the business, there could be no deduction claimed on it as a bad debt 'in respect of' a business. Justice Chagla, yet again, rejected these contentions. Accepting the arguments made by Palkhivala for the assessee, Chagla J., held an obligation to discharge a liability may arise out of business custom or out of a legal obligation and both stood on the same footing. A businessman may have to stand surety for someone in order that he should get monies for his own business. The custom of the business may require that that was the only method whereby he could get monies in order to finance his own business, and the question might arise, if he has to discharge the surety debt, whether that debt is a business debt or not. If the custom is established and the requirement of the business is proved, then it would be a business debt. Similarly, the law may cast an obligation upon the assessee to discharge a liability. In this case, since the Income tax Act imposed a liability upon the assessee by reason of his business connection with the non-resident to discharge the tax liability of his principal, the discharging of the liability was incidental to the business.

A very incisive passage in this judgment reads:

> *The Advocate-General rather naively suggested that the assessee need not have done this business with the non-resident, in which case there would have been no liability*

39. (1957) 31 ITR 72 (Bom).

> *imposed upon him and no debt would have arisen. Even though all powerful, the Taxing Department cannot dictate to an assessee what type of business he should carry on and with whom he should deal; the Taxing Department must accept the business such as it is which the assessee carries on, because it is the profits of that business that the Taxing Department seeks to tax.*

But this decision was reversed in appeal by the Supreme Court[40] which held that the loss incurred was not in its own business but the liability arose because of the business of another person and that was not a permissible deduction. This is clearly incorrect. The liability to pay tax as an 'agent' of the non-resident arose because the business that the assessee carried on was for his foreign principal. If this tax could not be recovered, then it should be allowable as a deduction.

(b) Current Repairs

A textile mill replaced parts in more than 75% of its looms to increase the efficiency of its business. The old parts that were replaced had become completely worn out, they were heavy in weight and were also of a construction which made them not easily workable. Further, these old parts were not available in the market and if an attempt had been made to prepare parts similar in kind or to acquire them, the cost would have been disproportionately high. The assessee company therefore replaced these parts with the parts of a new type which were lighter in weight, easy to operate, conformed to international labour standards and were superior to the old parts. The looms had been worked with the old parts for a period of 60 years and no need had arisen during all these years to replace them. The question before Justice Chagla was whether this expense was deductible as 'current repairs'?[41]

While Palkhivala's submissions are not mentioned in the case, Justice Chagla succinctly explained the meaning of the two terms 'current' and 'repairs'. He held that the expression 'repairs' must be understood in contradistinction to 'renewal' or 'restoration'. A building, machinery, plant or furniture may be renewed or restored either wholly or in part, in which case the amount expended would not be in respect of repairs, but when renewing or restoring a

---

40. *CIT v. Abdullabhai Abdulkadar*, AIR 1961 SC 701 : (1961) 41 ITR 545.
41. *New Shorrock Spinning & Mfg. Co. v. CIT*, (1956) 30 ITR 338. This decision was later approved by the Supreme Court in *Ballimal Naval Kishore v. CIT*, (1997) 2 SCC 449 : (1997) 224 ITR 414 : AIR 1997 SC 851.

building, machinery, plant or furniture a need may arise to set right certain defects or flaws and an amount may be spent for this purpose. The result may be that although the original asset was preserved and maintained, no new asset had come into existence and no additional advantage accrued to the assessee. The simple test he laid was: whether the expenditure for repairs had been incurred to preserve and maintain an already existing asset?

The object of the expenditure, he held, is not to bring a new asset into existence, nor is its object the obtaining of a new or fresh advantage. Regarding the word 'current', he held that they are such repairs which are attended to when the need for them arose and are not allowed to fall into arrears or be accumulated. If a building, machinery, plant or furniture needs some repairs and those repairs are attended to as and when the need arose, then the repairs are current repairs. He held that the Tribunal's reasoning that the repairs were done 60 years after the start of the factory was erroneous. The question to be asked was whether the repairs were allowed to accumulate or whether the assessee did them at the time when they were supposed to be done? On this ground, Justice Chagla held in favour of Palkhivala's client that these were, indeed, 'current repairs'.

The deduction for current repairs has continued to be a vexed question and, unfortunately, the pragmatic and liberal approach adopted by Chief Justice Chagla has not been followed. In *CIT v. Saravana Spinning Mills Pvt. Ltd.,*[42] the question was whether replacement of ring frames was allowable as a deduction on account of 'current repairs'. The South India Research Association had given a report that the process of converting fibre into yarn was a continuous, interlinked process. The report qualified that the output emerging on various intermediate stages of production could not be sold or marketed or used for any purpose and the entire textile mill should be considered as a plant commencing from the blow room to the winding section. All the items of a machinery were part of an integrated textile mill and the expenditure incurred on replacing any one of the items of a machinery would be allowable as a revenue expenditure.

Despite this report, the Supreme Court went on to hold that the manufacturing process in the textile mill was not continuous and integrated. It is not known on what basis the Supreme Court came to such a conclusion when there was a report from a specialized association. The question whether the process is

42. (2007) 293 ITR 201 : (2007) 7 SCC 298.

continuous and interlinked is a question of fact. This question of fact was never in question before the High Court and the Supreme Court should not have taken a contrary view on facts and disallowed the claim for deduction. Indeed, the Supreme Court took a narrow and restricted view that is in stark contrast to the broad and liberal approach adopted by Chief Justice Chagla.

3.7 *Fictitious payment is income*

Ramadas Dossa[43] was a cotton broker and he made payments to six individuals, the amounts ranging from Rs. 9,00,000/- to one C.M. Ghanekar and Rs. 4,707/- to one Dharsey Chapsey. On enquiry, it was found that three of them were *benamis* for Ramnarain Sons Ltd., a well known company and the remaining three were fictitious. The monies were paid to these individuals but were actually meant for this company. The magnitude of fraud is indicated by the fact that Ghanekar was just 28 years old and earned a salary of Rs. 100 per month. The Tribunal held that huge payments were made to men of straw and as Dossa was a party to the concealment of income of Ramnarain Sons Ltd., he was made liable to tax on all these payments.

Chief Justice Chagla endorsed the moral indignation felt by the Tribunal and condemned the conduct of Dossa. He then added:

> *But the Income Tax Act, as we have often observed, unfortunately does not concern itself with moral considerations. The Income Tax Act is concerned with a very limited question as to whether the amount brought to tax constitutes the income of the assessee. At worst, the finding of the Tribunal concerns to this that the assessee helped Ramnarain Sons Ltd. to conceal its income and by permitting Ramnarain Sons to put forward benamidars with whom the assessee dealt, the profits earned and not be brought to tax.*

Dossa had actually made payments to three known individuals who were *benamidars* of Ramnarain Sons Ltd. but these payments could not be treated as his income. But on the payments made to three fictitious persons, Dossa would be liable to pay income tax.

3.8 *Deductions under Section 80J and Rule 19A*

The enormous hard work involved in the preparation of a case is evident from the judgment in *Indian Oil Corporation v.*

---

43. *Ramadas Dossa and Co. v. CIT,* (1956) 29 ITR 1001 (Bom).

S. Rajagopalan.[44] Dinesh Vyas briefed Palkhivala and thereafter the case did not come for hearing for some time. When it was finally listed for hearing, Palkhivala reached Bombay the previous night and Vyas was worried whether he would recollect all the facts. There was no time for a further briefing and Palkhivala came straight to court. Vyas recollects that he remembered all the facts and the legal issues and made a brilliant presentation. This case is an illustrative example of his phenomenal memory: once briefed, he would remember all the essential points and did not require further meetings or conferences.

Two interesting questions arose for consideration in this case. First, whether the assessee had to create a development rebate reserve in respect of new plant and machinery which was installed or put to use in a particular year even though there were no profits made during that year? The Department argued that unless a reserve was created, IOC would not be eligible for development rebate. The second question was the method of computing 'capital employed' under Rule 19A for granting deduction under Section 80J of the Income Tax Act, 1961.

As regards the first question, Palkhivala argued that a reserve could be created only out of profits and the statute did not contemplate the creation of an illusory debit entry in the profit and loss account and a corresponding illusory credit entry in the development rebate reserve account. If the total income of the assessee is nil, there cannot be an obligation on the part of the assessee to create a reserve as a condition for carrying forward development rebate when it is being actually allowed. The assessee had to create a reserve only out of assessed profits and if there were no such profits in the year of installation or use, no reserve need be created. If the Department's contention was accepted, the assessee would have to borrow money to create the reserve. The Bombay High Court referred to various High Court decisions extensively and held that IOC was not obliged to create a reserve if there was no taxable income in the relevant years for enabling it to carry forward the development rebate to the following years.

---

44. (1973) 92 ITR 241 (Bom)—The decision was wrongly overruled on the development rebate issue in *Shri Shubhlaxmi Mills Ltd. v. Addl. CIT*, (1989) 2 SCC 465 : (1989) 177 ITR 193 : AIR 1989 SC 1406. The Supreme Court based its decision on an Explanation inserted in the section by Finance Act, 1966 with retrospective amendment from 1961.

The second question related to the benefit of Section 80J[45] and the Department took a strange stand on the interpretation of Rules 19A(2) and 19A(3) that prescribed the manner of computing the capital employed. Rule 19A(2) required that the aggregate value of the assets of the undertaking rule to be computed in a particular manner. But Rule 19A(3) stated that the aggregate of the assets as ascertained under Rule 19A(2) must be subject to a deduction 'of the aggregate amounts of the borrowed monies and debts due by the assessee'. IOC owned four industrial undertakings and claimed the benefit of Section 80J for each of them. The Department took the assets in each of the four industrial undertakings separately and deducted the *entire borrowings* of IOC from each of these undertakings! As the total borrowings of IOC obviously exceeded the aggregate of the assets of each individual undertaking, IOC was completely denied the benefit of Section 80J.

The Bombay High Court, noting the absurdity of this interpretation, gave a reasonable interpretation to rule 19A(3) to make it workable. It held that after the words 'borrowed monies and debts due by the assessee' in this sub-rule, the words 'in respect of the industrial undertaking in which the capital employed is to be computed' should be added. This is an excellent example of purposive construction by adding words into a statute to make it workable. It rejected the objection of the Department which relied on the famous statement of Rowlatt J:

> *...in a taxing Act one has to look merely at what is clearly said. There is no room for any intendment. There is no equity about a tax. There is no presumption as to a tax. Nothing is to be read in, nothing is to be implied. One can only look fairly at the language used'.*[46]

The Bombay High Court accepted that the court cannot put a beneficial interpretation on the provisions of a taxing statute on the basis of a presumed interpretation of the legislature. But Rowlatt J., it remarked, had not said that common-sense had no place in the interpretation of a taxing statute. The court must interpret a statute so as to avoid an absurd construction. This High Court judgment by Justice J.L. Nain is very well written and deserves to be read.

---

45. Section 80J granted a deduction of 6% on the 'capital employed' from the gross total income of the assessee.
46. *Cape Brandy Syndicate v. Inland Revenue Commissioners*, [1921] 1 K.B. 64, 71.

3.9 *What is 'actual cost'?*

Another classic decision on first principles was *Challapalli Sugars Ltd. v. CIT.*[47] In the 1922 Act, the expression 'actual cost' had not been defined unlike the present definition contained in Section 43(6) of the 1961 Act. The assessee company had borrowed a large amount from a financial institution in setting up its sugar factory. The interest paid during the relevant year and for the period prior to the commencement of the business was Rs. 2,38,614/- a large amount in 1958. The assessee claimed that interest paid should be added to the cost of plant and machinery and it was entitled to depreciation and development rebate on the aggregate of the amount paid for the plant and machinery *plus* the interest paid prior to the commencement of the business. The dispute, in effect, was whether interest paid prior to commencement of operation of the plant could be capitalised. This is most obvious to any person today but was an unusual concept fifty years ago. The ITO rejected the claim on the ground that interest was paid on a year to year basis as an admissible item of revenue expenditure and no depreciation could be allowed on the capitalised amount to the extent that has been incurred on account of interest. However, both at the first appellate stage and before the Tribunal, the assessee succeeded; it was held that not only interest but all expenditure which had been incurred for acquiring and installing the asset should be capitalized and form part of actual cost. Surprisingly, the Andhra Pradesh High Court reversed this view.

Justice Khanna, in a well reasoned judgment, observed that as the expression 'actual cost' had not been defined, it should be construed in a sense which no commercial man would misunderstand. He then proceeded to examine the meaning of the words 'cost' and 'price', in accordance with normal rules of accountancy and as understood in commercial and industrial circles. He referred to various accounting and auditing textbooks and an interesting decision of the Chancery Division delivered in 1960, where it was held that interest on debentures could be charged to capital during the period of construction.[48] Khanna J. also referred to Section 208 of the Companies Act, 1956 which specifically provided for payment of interest on the share capital of a company with a large gestation period. This section enabled interest paid to be included in the capital as part of cost of the

---

47. (1975) 98 ITR 167 : AIR 1975 SC 97.
48. *Hinds v. Buenos Ayres Grand National Tramways Company Ltd.*, (1906) 2 Ch. 654

construction of work or building. This decision merits careful reading. The Supreme Court held that the interest paid on borrowed funds for acquisition and installation of plant and machinery before the commencement of production could be added to the actual cost. Major projects with a large gestation period could now capitalise the interest and claim depreciation, development rebate, and later, investment allowance on the aggregate of the actual purchase price plus interest and other expenditure that had been incurred.

3.10 *Public are substantially interested*

The requirement of a minimum dividend under Section 23A of the 1922 Act did not apply to companies in which 'the public are substantially interested'. Naturally, this expression became the subject matter of a great deal of litigation. Broadly speaking, companies having not less than 25% of shareholding by the public would be deemed to be companies in which 'the public are substantially interested'. Ironically, if too much dividend was paid, the company had to pay additional income tax.[49]

The Bombay High Court ruled that shares owned by directors had to be excluded in calculating the limit of 25%. Before the Supreme Court, Palkhivala successfully argued that merely because shares were held by directors, they could not be treated as belonging to a group or not belonging to the public. It could be demonstrated that directors were not being controlled by one individual or if it could be shown that these directors had purchased the shares out of their own funds and there was no element of control. The mere relationship of being a director did not mean that these shares should be excluded in computing the 25% limit.[50] While the issue was apparently simple, this case had a chequered history and the chaotic uncertainty is best described by Palkhivala himself in his preface to the Seventh Edition of his commentary on the Income Tax Act, 1956 wherein he observed:

> *The legal quibbles which arise out of the definition of 'company in which the public are substantially interested' sometimes entail a litigation co-extensive with the best part of a businessman's life. For instance, in the case of*

49. *CIT v. Khatau Makanji Spinning and Weaving Company Ltd.*, (1956) 30 ITR 841 : AIR 1956 Bom 733; *CIT v. Elphinstone Spinning and Weaving Mills Company Ltd.*, (1960) 40 ITR 142 : AIR 1960 SC 1016.
50. *Raghuvanshi Mills Ltd. v. CIT*, AIR 1961 SC 743 : (1961) 41 ITR 613.

Raghuvanshi Mills Ltd. the only question involved was whether the company was one in which the public were substantially interested and the dispute related to the assessment year 1943-44. The case had to go to the Income-Tax Tribunal four times, to the Bombay High Court five times and to the Supreme Court twice. In 1969, the final conclusion was reached as to whether for the year 1943-44 the company should be treated as one in which the public were substantially interested! (74 ITR 823). It is the gravest mistake to make the company's basic rate of tax depend on a test so arbitrary and so elusive. The mistake should be rectified – at least as a concession to the shortness of human life.

3.11 *Reconstruction – Benefit permissible for expansion*

Another case where Palkhivala was able to get a judgment of the Calcutta High Court reversed was *Textile Machinery Corporation Ltd. v. CIT.*[51] This judgment continues to be a leading authority on the meaning of the word 're-construction'. The assessee manufactured boilers, machinery parts and railway wagons. In 1957, it set up a steel foundry and a year later, a jute mill was set up. The steel foundry manufactured castings which had earlier been purchased from other suppliers. In the jute mill, the bulk of the output was used by the assessee. The steel foundry and the jute mills were divisions and not separate companies. The assessee claimed the benefit of Section 15C of the Income Tax Act, 1922 which was the predecessor of Section 80J of the Income Tax Act, 1961. Briefly, it granted a deduction of 6% per annum of the capital employed in a newly established undertaking provided it:

> *(2)(i) is not formed by the splitting up, or the reconstruction of, business already in existence or by the transfer to a new business of building, machinery or plant, previously used in any other business;*

The Income Tax Officer disallowed the claim on the ground that almost 60% of the output of the steel foundry and 90% of the output of the jute mill was consumed by the assessee itself. The deduction was not available because these new divisions were merely an expansion of the existing business. The assessee was successful before the Tribunal which held that the two

51. AIR 1977 SC 1134 : (1977) 107 ITR 195 : (1977) 2 SCC 368.

undertakings had been newly established and were housed individually in separate buildings and required separate industrial licences. The fact that a major part of their output was captively consumed in the assessee's business did not make any difference. The High Court held otherwise and disallowed the claim. In the Supreme Court, Palkhivala argued that if the Department's submission was accepted, it would amount to adding a new category in Section 15C(2) and if a newly established undertaking manufacture articles to supplement the principal industrial activity, the benefit under Section 15C would be disallowed. This would be adding words to Section 15C and re-writing it. On facts, there was no dispute that the two divisions were newly constructed. The court ruled that the true test was not whether the expression 'new industrial undertaking' connoted expansion of the existing business of the assessee but whether the new industrial undertaking was separate and distinct from the existing business. The fact that the output of the new industrial undertaking is only partly sold in the open market and the balance captively consumed was not a ground to deny the benefit under Section 15C.

The Supreme Court then discussed the word 're-construction' which had not been defined in the Act. Once the new undertakings are independent production units which have not been formed by transferring the assets of the old business to the new undertakings or if the identity of the new undertaking is absorbed and lost in the old business, no 're-construction' takes place.

This judgment was immensely beneficial to several other assessees who got the benefit of Section 15C. This thwarted the attempt of the Department to deny the benefit of this Section on grounds not contemplated in the Act. It also enabled several units to expand their businesses by starting new divisions. Even if the output of a new division was captively consumed in the parent factory, the benefit could not be denied.

4. Income from salaries

4.1 *Is compensatory allowance a perquisite?*

The ambit and scope of the word 'perquisite' was called into question in the case of *CIT v. D.R. Pathak.*[52] The Bombay High Court had to consider whether 'city compensatory allowance' (CCA)

52. (1975) 99 ITR 14 (Bom). D.R. Phatak, ironically, was an Income-tax Officer working in Bombay and received CCA of Rs. 741/-. The decision was beneficial to all employees throughout India who received a similar allowance.

could be taxed as a perquisite or not. The Court also had to rule on whether, then, it would fall under Section 10(14) of the Income Tax Act, 1961 and be exempt from income-tax. The Revenue tried to make a distinction between expenditure incurred *for* the performance of duties and expenditure incurred *in* the performance of duties, and argued that expenditures that were incurred *for* the performance of duties were not exempt under this provision. Palkhivala argued, on the other hand, that this was an unjustified distinction to make. His submission was that even personal expenses incurred at a time outside office hours would be exempt, because but for his employment, he would not incur such an expenditure. The Court agreed with Palkhivala's arguments, that the very definition of the expression 'compensatory allowance' showed that it was an allowance granted to meet personal expenses necessitated by special circumstances. Thus, the argument that there was no nexus with the actual performance of the duty itself was rejected.

4.2 *Compensation – Whether profits in lieu of salary:*

In *CIT v. ED Sheppard,*[53] the Bombay High Court had to decide whether the compensation paid to an employee on his leaving service could be liable to income tax under the head of 'profits in lieu of salary'. Sheppard was an employee of a firm that converted itself into a company. His employment with the firm had to be terminated and he received shares in the company as compensation. He was then employed again by the company. The Department argued that Sheppard had not suffered any loss of employment and therefore, the shares received by him should be treated as consideration for past services. Palkhivala argued that the shares received were for loss of employment and loss of future prospects. The Court agreed with Palkhivala and held that the payment, was, in fact, a payment of compensation and not a distribution of profits in lieu of salary. The Court said that in the ultimate analysis, it had to decide whether this receipt was one of capital or revenue in nature and since it was not a revenue receipt, it could not be taxable under the head 'salaries'.

4.3 *Concessional rates of interest – Whether a perquisite?*

A loan granted by the employer at a lower rate of interest for acquisition of a house was not a perquisite. Palkhivala pointed out

---

53. (1960) 39 ITR 14 (Bom) – affirmed in AIR 1963 SC 1343 : (1963) 48 ITR (SC) 237 by a majority of 3:1.

that this was not part of the service contract and therefore could not be taxed as a perquisite in the employee's hand. This was a case that Palkhivala argued with Dinesh Vyas before the Tribunal.[54]

5. Capital gains

Henry Gannon, a British resident, left India in 1944 and died soon after in England. He owned a large number of shares and appointed James Anderson as the executor of his will. Anderson sold certain shares and distributed the proceeds according to Gannon's will. The Income Tax Department was quick to levy capital gains tax on the sale of shares. Anderson protested and the question arose whether a sale by an administrator of a deceased shareholder would be liable to capital gains tax. The law provided that distribution of capital assets in accordance with a will are not liable for capital gains tax. Palkhivala lost the case before the Bombay High Court and the Supreme Court.[55] Both the courts held that *'distribution of capital assets'* was different from *'distribution of sale proceeds of a capital asset'*. Palkhivala argued, and perhaps rightly, that this made no difference and that the expression 'distribution of capital assets' would also cover the sale of these assets and the subsequent distribution of the sale proceeds. But this argument was rejected and the court held that the exemption would only apply when the assets were distributed as such and not when the assets were sold and the sale proceeds given away. The court observed that what the law had done was to state that the distribution of assets would not be treated as a transfer which was quite different from the executor selling the assets and then distributing the sale proceeds. The Supreme Court's judgment is indeed confusing and illogical. If a person making a will has three houses and directs that these properties should be divided equally amongst his three children, there would be no capital gains tax. But if he directed that the property should be sold and the money distributed equally amongst his three children, it would attract capital gains tax! But the view of the Supreme Court is the law and must prevail.

One of the most important judgments of the Supreme Court on capital gains is *K.P. Varghese v. ITO.*[56] Varghese had bought a property for Rs. 16,500 and after a few years, he sold it to his

---

54. *Pednekar K.P. v. ITO*, (1983) 6 ITD 483.
55. *CIT v. James Anderson*, AIR 1964 SC 1761 : (1964) 51 ITR 345
56. AIR 1981 SC 1922 : (1981) 131 ITR 597 : (1981) 4 SCC 173.

children for the same price. Under Section 52(2) of the Income Tax Act, 1961 if the Income Tax Officer felt that the fair market value of the capital asset exceeded the sale price declared by the assessee by more than 15%, the fair market value is to be taken as the value for the purposes of income tax. From a writ petition before the Kerala High Court, the case eventually reached the Supreme Court where Palkhivala appeared for an intervener – Mafatlal Gagalbhai & Co. Private Ltd. He argued that Section 52(2) would not apply when the income received by the assessee is actually the income disclosed by the assessee in its return. It would be unfair to impose income tax on income that was never received by an assessee and simply because the fair market value of the property was higher than the consideration received by the assessee. Palkhivala argued that this could never have been the intention of Parliament.

Justice Bhagwati, in a superb judgment, held that even though tax statutes had to be construed literally, in cases where the literal interpretation produced an absurd result, there was scope for the Court to even 'do violence' to the statute. In this case, he applied the mischief rule that was immortalised by the *Heydon's case*[56a] in England and held that this provision was enacted to make sure that assessees did not sell their properties for a higher consideration but disclosed a much lower amount. But there was no allegation made that Varghese had actually received a higher sale price for the property from his children.

Justice Bhagwati pointed out that a literal interpretation of Section 52(2) would lead to absurd and unintended consequences. A person may enter into agreement to sell his property to Mr. X for a certain price but the actual sale may take place after a few years by which time, the market price may have increased by more than 15%. Could it be said that there was understatement of consideration? The following observations of Justice Bhagwati are important:

> *It would indeed be most harsh and inequitable to tax the assessee on income which has neither arisen to him nor is received by him, merely because he has carried out the contractual obligation undertaken by him...It would indeed be strange if obedience to the law should attract the levy of tax on income which has neither arisen to the assessee nor has been received by him... We must, therefore, eschew literalness in the interpretation of Section 52(2), and try to arrive at an interpretation which avoids this*

56a. [1584] EWHC Exch J 36 (1 January 1584).

> *absurdity and mischief and makes the provision rational and sensible, unless of course, our hands are tied and we cannot find any escape from the tyranny of the literal interpretation.*

Another important case under Section 52 was *ICI (India) Pvt. Ltd. v. CIT.*[57] Imperial Chemical Industries Ltd. (ICI) was a multinational incorporated in the United Kingdom and the assessee was its 100% Indian subsidiary. ICI planned a scheme to invest funds in three Indian companies which required the parent English company advancing large loans to its 100% Indian subsidiary and the loan amounts were then used to subscribe shares of three Indian companies. This was done with the approval of the Reserve Bank of India and the concerned Department of the Government of India at the 'highest level'. The Indian subsidiary would continue to hold shares and did not have to pay any interest on the loan if the three companies in which the funds were invested did not declare any dividend. If dividend was declared, by the three companies, 5½% was to be remitted to the English company and the balance retained by the Indian subsidiary. There was a provision in the scheme enabling the English company to require the Indian subsidiary to transfer its shares to its parent subsidiary as and when required by the parent English company.

This scheme was operated from 1956 to 1959 when drastic changes were made by the Finance Act, 1959 and inter-corporate dividends became liable to be taxed. This drastically affected the scheme because dividends paid by the three companies to the 100% subsidiary were taxed and when the Indian subsidiary paid dividends to the English company, it was taxed once again! The structure of the scheme was no longer viable and the Indian subsidiary was asked to transfer all its shareholdings in the three companies to the parent English company at par or face value.

While all these transactions were approved by the Reserve Bank of India and the Government of India, the Income Tax Department sought to invoke Section 52 alleging that the transfer of shares by the Indian subsidiaries to the parent company was effected with the object of evading or reducing the liability to pay capital gains tax. The Tribunal held that there was no intention to avoid capital gains tax because there was no liability to capital gains in 1953 and the shares were transferred only in February 1961, during the assessment year 1962-63. There was nothing surprising

---

57. AIR 1972 SC 1524 : (1972) 83 ITR 710 : (1972) 3 SCC 370.

about the arrangement not being very formal. In a neat observation, the Tribunal held:

> *We have to find out the object of the transaction. It is removed in point of time from the result. In such a case one cannot try to infer the object from the results. We really have to put ourselves at a point of time when the transaction was conceived. Taking the materials before us, we consider that there is nothing to suggest that the parties had the capital gains tax in their mind in 1953 and later when they put through the aforesaid transactions. We have, therefore, to hold that the factual requisites of Section 52 have not been established here.*

The High Court took a contrary view and held that the assessee was indeed liable under Section 52. Palkhivala then appeared for the assessee in the Supreme Court and argued that the intention or object to avoid or reduce liabilities to capital gains were questions of fact and did not depend on inference of facts from the evidence or material before the Tribunal. When the transaction was entered into in 1953 and approved by the statutory authorities, the intention was to make investments in India and it was felt that the investment could best be made through a 100% subsidiary. When the subsequent changes in the law made the scheme unviable, the English company invoked its power to have all the shares transferred to itself. This finding of the Tribunal was supported by the evidence and was quite reasonable. The Supreme Court took a practical view and accepted the arguments of Palkhivala. Interestingly, it observed that merely because the amount involved was large that would not justify a reference on a question of law. There was nothing to suggest that the parties had avoidance of capital gains in mind when they prepared the scheme; there was no justification for invoking Section 52. The view of the Calcutta High Court was rightly reversed.

6. Other sources of income – Dividend

Justice S.R. Tendolkar of the Bombay High Court had to decide whether an unusual arrangement amounted to a 'dividend' under Section 2(6A) of the Income Tax Act.[58] The assessees were shareholders of the Navjivan Mills Ltd. which had invested its profits in the purchase of shares of the Bank of India (before

58. *Kantilal Manilal v. CIT*, (1956) 30 ITR 569 (Bom) – affirmed in *Kantilal Manilal v. CIT*, AIR 1961 SC 1038 : (1961) 41 ITR 275.

nationalization). This bank offered rights' shares to their shareholders at Rs. 100 per share, and Navjivan Mills Ltd. instead of purchasing the shares, decided to offer the rights' issue of the bank to their shareholders. Palkhivala argued that from the point of view of company law, the resolution of the directors to offer these rights cannot possibly be looked upon as a declaration of 'dividend'. A dividend, can only be declared by the shareholders of the company. The only right that the directors have is to recommend a dividend to the meeting of the shareholders.

But the High Court rejected Palkhivala's argument and observed that the definition of dividend was inclusive and even if distribution of the right to acquire shares in Bank of India could not be regarded as a dividend within the *extended meaning* of definition in the former Section 2(6A), it was still dividend within the *ordinary meaning* of that expression. The distribution was taxable in the hands of the shareholders who received the right to purchase shares. Palkhivala appeared before the Supreme Court but once again without success.

7. Taxation of trusts – Five interesting cases

(i) The case of the late Nizam of Hyderabad is one of the most fascinating trust cases. In 1950, the Nizam created several trusts and one of them was the 'Family Trust' which had a corpus of Rs. 9 crores in Government securities. This staggering amount would be equivalent to not less than Rs. 500 crores today. The complex trust deed had 175 equal units and these were broken up as follows: five units constituted a fund called a 'Reserve Fund', 3½ units constituted a 'Family Trust Expenses Fund' and the remaining 166½ units were divided amongst his relatives mentioned in a schedule to the trust deed. Part I of this schedule mentioned two wives and their children, and Part II mentioned the names of other wives, sons, daughters, daughters-in-law, sons-in-law, would-be-sons-in-law and certain 'other ladies of the palace'. It maintained a ratio of 2:1 between male and female children which meant that the sons got twice as much as the daughters.

The trust deed made detailed provisions as to what should be done on the death of any of the beneficiaries. For example, the Nizam had 15 daughters and each was allotted three units. Two thirds of this share or 2 units was to be given to the daughter as income and the remaining 1/3rd was to be set apart as a reserve fund to be utilized towards unforeseen or emergency expenses. There were separate provisions for sons-in-laws and future husbands of unmarried daughters. The trust also specified a complex but clear method of these shares devolving on the heirs of deceased beneficiaries. The Income Tax Department sought to levy wealth tax at the maximum marginal rate on the ground that the beneficiaries were indeterminate and their individual shares could not be determined.

Justice P. N. Bhagwati brilliantly marshalled the complex facts involved in the case. Palkhivala appeared for the trustees and argued that since Section 3 of the Wealth Tax Act, unlike the Income Tax Act, did not mention 'association of persons', no wealth tax could be imposed on the trustees. The Court, however rejected this argument and held that since Section 3 started with the words 'Subject to the other provisions of this Act', it would be subject to Section 21 which specifically mentioned trustees. Palkhivala argued that a trust would be subject to wealth tax on the basis of the beneficiaries on the relevant valuation date which is usually March 31 of each year. During the year, some beneficiaries may die and their shares will devolve in accordance with the trust deed. Palkhivala's argument was that if it was possible to say with certainty and definiteness as to who were the beneficiaries on the valuation date, the trust could not be taxed at the maximum marginal rate. Examining the various provisions of the trust deed carefully, Justice Bhagwati observed that on the valuation date of each year it was indeed possible to identify the beneficiaries and their specific shares. The trust deed had provided for every possible contingency and even if a beneficiary died during the year, the beneficiaries who were to succeed him could be easily ascertained and identified. The trust was therefore not liable to tax at the maximum marginal rate. Consequently, the court held that the remainderman's interest could not be brought to tax under the Wealth Tax Act, 1957. However, after this judgment, Section 21(1A) was inserted in the Wealth Tax Act to plug this loophole.

(ii) In *J.K. Trust v. CIT*,[59] the Supreme Court dealt with an interesting question: can a business itself be treated as 'property' under the Income Tax Act, 1961? A trust was the managing agent of certain textile mills and received remuneration which was then used for the objects of the trust. The Bombay High Court held that a managing agency could not be regarded as trust property and the income from that business would not be entitled for exemption

59. AIR 1957 SC 846 : (1957) 32 ITR 535.

under Section 4(3) of the Income Tax Act, 1961. But the Supreme Court reversed the view of Chief Justice Chagla and held that the word 'property' was a term of the widest import and, subject to any express limitation or qualification would signify every possible interest which a person can acquire, own and enjoy. Business, by this test, would undoubtedly be property.

(iii) In *Sole Trustee, Loka Shikshana Trust v. CIT*,[60] the Court had to decide whether the running of a newspaper and journals were for the purposes of education and fell within the scope of the definition of 'charitable purpose' under Section 2(15) of the Income Tax Act, 1961. The trust was carrying out various activities such as founding and running reading rooms and libraries, promoting *Kannada* and helping organisations that were engaged in similar areas of work. The income from the business of publishing a newspaper was sought to be taxed as income from business since there were 'profits' and the definition of 'charitable trust' excluded 'the carrying on activity for profit'.

Palkhivala raised two points: first, that the profit was only an incidental consequence of the charitable activities, and secondly, the expression in Section 2(15) covered only 'private profit' and not profits made for public purposes. He argued that the primary purpose of the trust was that of education and that the newspaper was published only to further that purpose. The Revenue relied on a speech made by the Prime Minister in Parliament regarding the amendments to this provision. Palkhivala however argued that speeches made on the floor of the house could not be used to interpret taxing statutes, since tax legislation had to be interpreted strictly.

The court rejected both the arguments of Palkhivala and held that the income from the running of the newspapers was taxable. It held that the activity of running a newspaper did not fall within the scope of 'education' but under general public utility. In any case, the court held that the exemption would not apply to the assessee. However, in a separate opinion, Justice Beg held that if there was a restriction in the trust deed that stipulated that the profits of the trust were also to be used for the purposes of the trust, then the assessee could be exempted from tax. However, since there was no restriction on how the profits were to be utilised, the profits were held to be taxable. The Supreme Court has, twenty-five years later,

---

60. (1975) 101 ITR 234 : AIR 1976 SC 10 : (1976) 1 SCC 254.

affirmed this latter view of Justice Beg in the decision of *Addl. CIT v. Surat Art Silk Cloth Manufacturers' Association.*[61]

(iv) In the case of *Manilal Dhanji v. CIT,*[62] the assessee had put away a certain sum in trust where the beneficiary was his daughter. She would be entitled to an income from the trust property only after she attained majority. In the relevant year, the amount had earned an interest that was sought to be taxed in the hands of the father as trustee. Palkhivala made an interesting argument regarding the nature of accrual. He argued that the daughter had no right to receive the money until her majority. Since there was no income in the hands of the beneficiary, he argued that there could be no tax on the trustee. The Court accepted this contention and held that there could be taxability only once the income was paid to the assessee on her attainment of majority.

(v) In *Hakim Abdul Hamid v. CIT,*[63] Hakim Abdul Hamid, his brother and mother were partners of a pharmaceutical concern called 'Hamdard Dawakhana'. The movable properties of this firm were given to a wakf and the same business was carried on in the name of the wakf. Under the wakf deed, the business income was to be divided into three portions namely:

- (i) One-eighth of the total business profit of the wakf business was to be transferred to a reserve fund;
- (ii) Out of the *balance,* seven-eighths was to be spent on charities; and
- (iii) One-eighth to be paid to the *mutawalli* (Manager), namely, Hakim Abdul Hamid.

Hamid's mother died in 1949 and his brother migrated to Pakistan. He purchased the share of his evacuee brother which also was earmarked for charitable purposes. The wakf deed contained complex provisions as to how the reserve fund was to be utilized. While there was no dispute about the exemption to amounts spent on charities and the taxability of the amount paid to the sole *mutawalli,* the Department denied exemption to the business profit that was transferred to the reserve fund and sought to tax it at the maximum rate. Palkhivala argued that the reserve fund, under the wakf deed, was also for the benefit and development of the business

61. (1980) 121 ITR 1 : AIR 1980 SC 387 : (1980) 2 SCC 31.
62. (1959) 35 ITR 467 (Bom) : AIR 1959 Bom 506 – affirmed in (1962) 44 ITR 876 : AIR 1963 SC 433.
63. *Hakim Abdul Hamid v. CIT,* (1973) 90 ITR 203 (Del-FB).

held under trust which was carried on for charitable purposes. The reserve fund was meant to meet future contingencies and also for being spent for charity. The reserve fund had the same character as the wakf business. Some part of it was to be ploughed back into the business.

A Full Bench of the Delhi High Court accepted Palkhivala's arguments and held that the creation of the reserve fund was necessary in the interest of the trust or wakf. If the trust business was to yield profits which were to be utilized for the purpose for which the trust was created, then it was necessary that a portion of the profit should be transferred to the reserve fund. The trust and the reserve fund had a two-fold purpose *viz.* for being used for the benefit of the community at large and, particularly, for the maintenance of the *mutawalli*. The court held that there would be an exemption under the Income Tax Act, 1922 to the extent the reserve fund was used for charitable purposes. As mentioned earlier, 1/8th of the amount was transferred to the reserve fund and the balance 7/8th was applied for religious or charitable purpose and was eligible for exemption.

8. Hindu law

Balkrishna Purushottam Purani owned immovable properties that earned him rental and dividend income. He died leaving behind three widows[64] and two daughters. The Department sought to assess the three widows as an 'association of persons' and wanted to tax the aggregate income received by them. In the Income Tax Act, the definition of 'person' is very wide and includes not only individual companies, partnership firms but also 'association of persons' and 'body of individuals'. The Bombay High Court held that widows could not be treated as an 'association of persons' and the income they earned could only be taxed in their individual hands.

Before the Supreme Court, Palkhivala argued that co-widows under the *Mitakshara* succession law were co-heirs to the estate of the deceased husband, and they took as joint-tenants with rights of survivorship and equal beneficial enjoyment. An 'association of persons' will mean two or more individuals who come together to start a business or a joint venture. The Supreme Court agreed with

64. Before the Hindu Marriage Act, 1955, there was no bar against a Hindu male from having more than one wife. Balakrishna died in November, 1947 and, therefore, all the three were legally wedded wives.

Palkhivala and accepted the point that widows had only received dividends and rental income. There was no finding or evidence that the three widows, after the death of their husband, had combined in a joint enterprise to produce income.[65]

The term 'association of persons' (AOP) is not defined under the Income Tax Act and, to this day, the principles laid down in this case are used to determine whether there is a valid AOP or not.

Another important case involving Hindu law was *Goli Eswariah v. CGT,*[66] where the *karta* of a Hindu undivided family (HUF) blended his self-acquired property with that of the family. The question was whether this was a gift to the HUF. This was a highly contentious issue as the High Courts of Andhra, Madras, Allahabad, Kerala and Mysore had given conflicting judgments on this point. When a coparcener threw his property into the common stock, it was a unilateral act by which he gave up his separate interest in his property. There was no physical mixing of this property with the property of the family; it was an act of his own volition and intention by waiving his separate rights either the family rejecting or accepting it. A peculiar feature of the *Mitakshara* school of Hindu Law was that the family could neither reject nor accept it. By this reasoning, the Court held that there was no gift under the Transfer of Property Act, since there was no donor and donee. This judgment led to an amendment in Section 64(2) of the Income Tax Act, 1961 whereby, even if the individual owner of a property impressed it with the character of common property, any income was taxed in the hands of the transferor (the individual) and similar amendments were also made to the Gift Tax and Wealth Tax Acts.

9. Other taxes

9.1 *Estate duty*

In *Khorshed Shapoor Chenai v. Asst. CED,*[67] the assessee's lands had been acquired for building a pharmaceutical plant, but the compensation was assessed and paid to his successors after his death. Estate duty was charged on these lands and calculated on the basis of the compensation paid. The successors challenged this compensation in a civil court under Section 18 of the Land

---

65. *CIT v. Indira Balkrishna,* AIR 1960 SC 1172 : (1960) 39 ITR 546.
66. (1970) 76 ITR 675 : AIR 1970 SC 1722 : (1970) 2 SCC 390.
67. (1980) 122 ITR 21 : AIR 1980 SC 775 : (1980) 2 SCC 1.

Acquisition Act, 1894. Pursuant to this, the Civil Court paid enhanced compensation and the revenue sought to levy (additional) estate duty by re-opening the assessment through a notice. The assessee challenged the notice before the High Court of Andhra Pradesh in a writ petition, but it was dismissed. Palkhivala appeared for the assessee in the Supreme Court, and made two basic submissions. He first argued that the enhanced compensation could not form a part of the estate duty since the right to receive compensation had already been enjoyed by the assessee. The Court rejected this argument holding that a distinction cannot be drawn between compensation and enhanced compensation, and that they were both facets of the same transaction. However, the Court accepted Palkhivala's argument that an assessment for the purposes of estate duty could not be opened on the ground that additional compensation had later been granted by a civil court. The Supreme Court held that the estate duty officers had to ascertain the value of the properties in the estate and levy duty thereon. When the assessee had revealed all information to the Revenue and the Revenue chose to impose estate duty based on the compensation amount initially paid, it was not open to the Revenue to later contend that duty had escaped assessment. On this ground, the notice for re-opening of the assessment and demand of additional estate duty was quashed by the Supreme Court.

This judgment is very important in the context of levy of capital gains on enhanced compensation that is received later and on the determination of wealth on the valuation date when the enhanced compensation is received much later by the assessee.

Palkhivala, assisted by late K.R. Ramamani,[68] successfully argued one of the most important cases on estate duty before the Tribunal. S. Anantharamakrishnan was the founder of the Amalgamations Group – a leading industrial house of Southern India – who died in 1964, when the estate duty was at a savage rate of 85%. The group consisted of approximately 30 companies and the estate duty liability was discharged by these companies and subsequently allowed as a revenue expenditure in their hands.

9.2 *Wealth Tax*

A judgment that will remain the leading authority for the meaning of the word 'debt' is *Kesoram Industries and Cotton Mills*

68. An eminent tax lawyer of the Madras High Court and was the partner of Subbaraya Aiyar, Padmanabhan and Ramamani

Ltd. v. CWT.[69] The Supreme Court had to decide whether the *provision* made for the payment of super tax, income tax and wealth tax would be a 'debt owed' under Section 2(m) of the Wealth Tax Act, 1957.[70]

Palkhivala argued unsuccessfully before the Calcutta High Court. On appeal before the Supreme Court, he once again urged that the liability to pay tax arose because of the charging section and it was only the quantification which was postponed till the Finance Act of each year was passed. Therefore, a provision for tax payable was a 'debt owed'. Viswanatha Sastri, on the other hand, argued that what could be deducted was only an ascertainable amount and the obligation to pay income tax arose only on the passing of the Finance Act. Therefore, on March 30 of each year, there was no 'debt owed' within the meaning of the Section 2(m) of the Wealth Tax, 1957.

In a brilliant judgment, Justice Subba Rao analysed the meaning of the expression 'debt owed'. The verb 'owe' meant 'to be under an obligation to pay' and did not really add anything to the meaning of the word 'debt'. Therefore, what did the word 'debt' mean? After analyzing various decisions, the Supreme Court adopted a simple and clear definition given by Lord Lindley:[71]

> *a debt is a sum of money which is now payable or will become payable in the future by reason of a present obligation, debitum in prasenti, solvendum in futuro.*

The liability to pay income tax was a present liability although it may become payable after it is quantified in accordance with the rates prescribed by the Finance Act. The court explained the relationship between the Income Tax Act which was a permanent act and the Finance Act, which is passed every year. The latter only prescribes the rate of tax. If for some reason the Finance Act is not passed, the rates of the preceding year would continue (unless the Finance Bill proposes a lower rate). Therefore, on the valuation date of March 31 of each accounting year, the tax liability is known and the provisions made for super tax, income tax, wealth tax was eligible for deduction while calculating the net wealth. The court also pointed out the distinction between a 'debt' and 'liability'. A sum of money which is definitely payable, although in future, is a

69. (1966) 59 ITR 767 : AIR 1966 SC 1370.
70. There were two other issues in this judgment, but this is the most contentious.
71. *Webb v. Stenton,* (1883) 11 Q.B.D. 518, 527.

'debt' but a sum payable upon a contingency is not a debt until the contingency has happened. Similarly, a claim for damages will not become a debt till the court delivers its judgment.

Palkhivala argued an interesting case before the Special Bench of the Tribunal. Chartered Accountants and other professionals usually maintain accounts on cash basis and paid income tax only on the fees that are actually received. The Department contended that outstanding fees for services rendered constituted a debt due and was liable to be included as an asset in computing the net wealth. The Special Bench, in a well reasoned decision, held[72] that the outstanding fees could not be treated as an asset. This was a welcome relief to several professional assessees and, mercifully, the Wealth Tax Act was not amended to nullify this decision.

9.3 *Expenditure Tax*

The Revenue sought to impose expenditure tax on the legal heirs of the Maharaja of Morvi even though the Expenditure Tax Act was enacted after his death.[73] Palkhivala filed a writ petition on behalf of his wife in the Bombay High Court challenging the show cause notice demanding the tax. He argued that while the Expenditure Tax Act might have effect for the relevant assessment year, since it was enacted after the assessee's death, it cannot be imposed on him. A person could not be made liable to taxes that did not even exist during his lifetime. In other words, a taxing statute cannot be applied to persons who are not in existence at the time of its enactment. G. N. Joshi, Palkhivala's regular opponent before the Tax Bench, argued that since there were provisions in Section 18 of the Expenditure Tax Act by which an assessment could be made against a person's estate or on his legal heirs even after his death, tax could be imposed. Palkhivala countered this argument by stating that a tax could be imposed under Section 18 only when the person was liable to the tax but had died before he paid the same. Consequently, Sections 18 and 24B of the Income Tax Act, 1922, could not be made applicable to cases where a liability to tax did not arise during the lifetime of the person.

---

72. *Shah N.M. v. Second WTO*, (1982) 1 ITD 244 (SB).
73. *H.H. Vijayakunverba Maharani of Morvi. v. S. Narayanan*, (1962) 45 ITR 223 (Bom) : AIR 1962 Bom 254. Earlier, Palkhivala had appeared for this assessee's mother-in-law or the Queen Mother.

This case introduced the 'aspect' theory in Indian constitutional law.[74]

10. Miscellaneous

10.1 *Board circulars*

The judgment in *K. P. Varghese*[75] is equally important for reiterating the binding nature of circulars on the Department. Section 52(2), on a literal interpretation, would apply to all transfers but two circulars of the Central Board of Direct Taxes clarified that this sub-section had limited operation and did not apply to honest and *bona fide* transactions or where the consideration was correctly disclosed or declared by the assessee. The amendment was intended to deal with only cases where there was understatement of consideration. K.P. Varghese's case was precisely what Parliament did not want to tax; all he had done was to sell his property to his children at the cost price. Justice Bhagwati, in an oft-quoted judgment, observed that these Board circulars are binding even if they were not in accordance with the strict interpretation of statutory provisions. He relied on two earlier decisions,[76] one of which was argued by Palkhivala.

Finally, the Supreme Court reversed the decision of the Division Bench of the Kerala High Court and allowed the appeals. The principles laid down in this decision on the interpretation of statutes are noteworthy. The application of Section 52(2) was tempered because of this judgment, but the fact that it remains on the statute books even today perhaps suggests that the interpretation put by Palkhivala on this Section was incontrovertible.

Ellerman Lines Ltd. was a British company whose ships carried cargo all over the world and some ships came to India as well. Rule 33 of the Income Tax Rules, 1922 prescribed certain methods of arriving at a proportionate part of income liable to income tax and the only question was whether the British company was entitled to claim a deduction for investment allowance under the UK tax laws, which corresponded to development rebate under the Indian Income Tax Act, 1922. Palkhivala referred to a letter of the Central Board of Revenue (the predecessor of the Central Board of Direct

---

74. *Federation of Hotel & Restaurant Assn. of India v. Union of India,* AIR 1990 SC 1637 : (1989) 3 SCC 634.
75. *K.P. Varghese v. ITO*, AIR 1981 SC 1922 : (1981) 131 ITR 597. This case has also been discussed under 'Capital Gains', *supra.*
76. *Navnit Lal C. Jhaveri v. K. K. Sen*, (1965) 56 ITR 198 : AIR 1965 SC 1375 and *Ellerman Lines Ltd. v. CIT*, (1971) 82 ITR 913 : AIR 1972 SC 524.

Taxes and the Central Board Excise and Customs) stipulating that investment allowance granted in U.K. was to be allowed while calculating the taxable income of the British shipping company. The circular imposed a condition that the quantum of investment allowance should not exceed the development rebate which was allowable under the Indian Income Tax Act, 1922.

The Solicitor-General of India argued that these circulars could not abrogate or modify the provisions of the Act but the Supreme Court held that the instructions issued by the Board of Revenue were binding on the assessing authorities *even if they deviated from the provisions of the Act.*

10.2 *Valuation of shares*

In early 1962, Palkhivala argued an important case before a seven-judge Bench.[77] Shirinbai Kooka, a wealthy Parsi lady, had invested in a large number of shares before and after 1939-40. Initially, she was only an investor and paid tax on her dividend income. In the financial year 1945-46, she decided to carry on the business of trading in shares and converted her shares into her stock-in-trade on April 1, 1945 and adopted the market price of these shares as the cost to the business. During that year, she received Rs. 5.50 lakhs[78] from the sale of shares. Palkhivala argued that Kooka's profit was the difference between the selling price received and the market value of these shares on April 1, 1945, while the Department argued that the profit was the difference between the selling price and the original cost of the shares when they were purchased before or after 1939-40.

In Palkhivala's way was a five-judge verdict rendered in 1952.[79] Sir Kikabhai Premchand was a dealer in silver and shares and, following the mercantile system of accounting, he valued these assets at cost price prevailing at the beginning and at the end of the year. In the calendar year 1942, he withdrew some of the silver and shares from his business and transferred them to certain trusts where he was also the managing trustee. The Department sought to tax him on the difference between the cost price of the silver and shares and their market price on the date of their transfer to the trusts. The great Justice Vivian Bose, speaking for the majority,

77. *CIT v. Bai Shirinbai Kooka*, AIR 1963 SC 477: (1962) 46 ITR 86.
78. At current prices, this should be equivalent to about Rs.10 crores today. This is based on the vaue of gold in 1945 and its value today.
79. *Sir Kikabhai Premchand v. CIT*, AIR 1953 SC 509 : (1953) 24 ITR 506.

rejected the Department's contention and observed that the act of withdrawal of silver and shares was not a business transaction and Kikabhai neither made a profit nor a loss from the it. Justice Bose observed that what can be taxed is the income, profits and gains made in the relevant accounting year and not any potential gain that an assessee could have made. An assessee, he said, could not trade with himself nor could he make profit or loss out of transactions with himself. Thus, the Supreme Court, held that the withdrawal had to be at cost price. Interestingly, in *Sharkey v. Wernher*,[80] a judgment rendered later, the House of Lords held that the valuation at the time of withdrawal should be at the market price.

When *Kooka's* case first came for hearing, it was posted for hearing before a seven-judge Bench to consider whether *Kikabhai's* case required reconsideration. After a careful examination of that case and a few English decisions, the Supreme Court held that the issue in *Kikabhai's* case was the converse of *Kooka's* case. In the earlier case, there was no sale of shares or silver while in the latter shares were actually sold. Applying ordinary commercial principles, the profits on the sale of shares would be the difference between what the shares cost the business and what they fetched the business. The 'cost' to business would be their market price on the date of their conversion from investments to stock-in-trade i.e., April 1, 1945. Palkhivala's argument was thus accepted by the majority.

10.3 *Method of accounting*

McMillan & Co. Ltd., was an English company that published and sold books and magazines in various parts of the world. While it maintained proper accounts at its head office, it adopted an unusual method in India: a fixed percentage of the marked price was adopted as the 'cost or production' and the Indian profits were determined accordingly. The Income Tax Officer accepted this method but disallowed some items of expenditure and an alleged bad debt. McMillan appealed and the Appellate Assistant Commissioner (AAC) enhanced the income after rejecting the books of account.

The AAC found that the percentage adopted as 'cost of production' resulted in a profit margin of 25% of the Indian

80. (1955) 36 TC 275 (HL).

operations whereas the international percentage of profit was more than 37%. This gap was too wide and called for some explanation particularly because the Indian unit did not maintain an Indian trading and profit and loss account. The method of accounting adopted in India was not proper and the AAC enhanced the income by adopting the international profit margin of 37%. McMillan appealed and was successful before the Bombay High Court. The Income Tax Department took up the matter in further appeal to the Supreme Court.

Palkhivala argued that in an appeal preferred by the assessee, the AAC could not reject the books of account or the method of accounting which had been accepted by the ITO. Analysing various sections of the Income Tax Act, 1922, he argued that there were two classes of cases: in one class, there was an 'objective determination' based on objective facts and, in another class, a 'subjective determination' by the ITO. In the first class, the entire hierarchy of officers are included but in the second class, the decision could be taken by the named officer only. The proviso to Section 13 of the old Act enabled the ITO to reject the computation of profits by the assessee if there was no regular method of accounting employed by the assessee or the method employed was such that 'the income, profits and gains cannot properly be deducted therefrom'. According to Palkhivala, the power to accept or reject the books was vested only with the ITO. Once he accepted the method of accounting, his determination became final and the AAC cannot reject them in an appeal filed by the assessee. However, if the method of accounting is rejected, then the assessee can appeal and the AAC has to then decide whether the rejection is valid or not.

The argument for the Revenue was that the AAC had very wide powers under Section 31(3) which enabled him to 'confirm, reduce, enhance or annual the assessment'. Such wide powers would include the power to examine and determine whether the method of accounting adopted by the assessee was proper or not.

Palkhivala's arguments must have been very persuasive as Justice S.K. Das, who delivered the majority judgment,[81] complimented him, but rejected his reasoning:

---

81. *CIT v. McMillan & Co.*, AIR 1958 SC 207 : (1958) 33 ITR 182. Justice N. H. Bhagwati dissented and the verdict was 2:1. Justices S. K. Das and J. L. Kapur were in the majority.

> *By what we must admit is a very adroit and plausible piecing together of some of these sections, learned counsel has built up his argument that in the present case the opinion of the Income-tax Officer that the income, profits and gains can be properly deduced from the method of accounting regularly employed by the assessee is a subjective determination of the Income-tax Officer alone, and the opinion of no other officer or authority can be substituted therefore.*

The majority held that while the argument was persuasive, Palkhivala was reading too much into the words 'in the opinion of Income Tax Officer' occurring in the proviso to Section 13 of the Income Tax Act, 1922. The powers of the AAC were very wide and he could reject the method of accounting even if the ITO had accepted it. Carefully analysing the sections, the majority rightly pointed out the fallacy in Palkhivala's arguments. The AAC has to determine the income liable to tax, and to do so, he is entitled to correct any error made by the ITO, including the acceptance of the method of accounting.

10.4 *A Maharani's maintenance allowance*

The Queen Mother of the erstwhile princely State of Morvi received a maintenance allowance from 1922 which was paid from the treasury. This was paid when she was the queen and when her son became the ruler, he discontinued the allowance but granted her a village to maintain her status and dignity. After independence, Morvi became a part of Saurashtra and the grant of the village stood cancelled. As attempts to get it back proved futile, the Queen Mother was paid Rs. 60,000/- per annum in lieu of the loss of this village. Under a special tax concession order, widows or mothers of former rulers were not liable to pay tax on the 'maintenance allowance' received by them. The Department denied exemption on the ground that this was not a maintenance allowance but amounts paid to maintain the Queen's status and dignity. This plea was accepted by the High Court but on further appeal before the Supreme Court, Palkhivala was able to persuade the Supreme Court to reverse this finding.[82] The Supreme Court observed that if the entire facts and circumstances were taken into consideration, the inescapable conclusion was that the sum of Rs. 60,000/- was paid only as a maintenance allowance even though the resolution passed had used the words 'status and dignity'.

---

82. *H.H. Maharani Kesarkunverba v. CIT,* AIR 1960 SC 1343 : (1960) 39 ITR 283.

10.5 *Powers of the Tribunal*

Another case which is remarkable for the arguments of Palkhivala and C.K. Daphtary is the *Keshav Mills* Case.[83] This decision is of general importance because the Supreme Court examined the ambit and scope of its own power to review and revise its earlier decisions. With regard to tax references, the Supreme Court laid down the extent of the powers of the High Court to direct the Income Tax Appellate Tribunal to call for additional evidence. Chief Justice P.B. Gajendragadkar, speaking for a seven-judge Bench, meticulously analysed the facts and rendered a judgment that is remarkable for its precision. Keshav Mills, which had its office in the princely State of Baroda, sold textile goods and payments were received through banks in British India or by hundies drawn on British Indian shroffs and merchants. The Department contended that the payments had accrued in British India and liable to tax under the Indian Income Tax Act, 1922. When the matter reached the High Court, the judges felt that further facts were required to determine taxability and they directed the Tribunal to submit a supplementary statement of case.

There was an interesting twist to this case. While the matter was remanded for getting the supplementary statement of the case, the Supreme Court gave a judgment (in another case) which dealt with the role of the post office in sending and receiving cheques.[84] The court held that if the sender merely delivered the cheque to the post office for transmission to the addressee, it acts only as the agent of the sender. On the other hand, if the sender sends the cheque at the request or direction of the addressee to send it through post, then the post office is the agent of the addressee. This had serious consequences because if the post office was treated as the agent of the addressee and the letter was posted in British India, then the payment would give rise to assessable income in British India. Thus, posting of the cheques in Delhi amounted to payment in Delhi and the income would accrue in British India.

When the matter came up before the Bombay High Court, it was once again sent back to the Tribunal to decide whether the cheques and *hundies* were sent by post at the request of the addressee. In view of the Supreme Court decision, the matter had been considerably simplified and would require the facts to the

83. *Keshav Mills Co. v. CIT,* AIR 1965 SC 1636 : (1965) 56 ITR 365.
84. *CIT v. Ogale Glass Works Ltd.*, AIR 1954 SC 429 : (1954) 25 ITR 529.

considered again. The Tribunal gave its second supplementary statement and the High Court eventually held against the assessee.

Palkhivala successfully argued that the High Court, while deciding the income tax reference, could call upon the Tribunal to make a supplementary statement of the case but it could not direct the collection of additional material and evidence while calling for supplementary statement. The High Court could only direct the inclusion of material which was on record but which had not been earlier included in the statement of case.

The court accepted Palkhivala's argument and set aside the decision of the Bombay High Court. The net result was that the High Court had to exclude the additional evidence that had been collected and decide the case only on the earlier material on record.

Chief Justice Gajendragadkar held that the High Court did not have the power to direct the Tribunal to collect additional material or evidence that was not on record. The scheme of the Income Tax Act indicated that the evidence had to be led in primarily before the Income Tax Officer, though additional evidence could be adduced before the appellate authority or the Tribunal, subject to the prescribed procedure. When the Tribunal had fully heard the matter and the case was referred to the High Court for determination of the question of law, there was no scope for any further or additional evidence.

Apart from this, the Supreme Court dealt with an important question on the scope of Article 141 and the power of the Supreme Court in reviewing its earlier decisions. On this constitutional question, the Supreme Court laid down parameters as to when the earlier decision could be departed from.

With the subsequent amendments to the Income Tax Act, 1961, the Tribunal does not have to make a statement of case and appeals now lie to the High Court only on 'substantial questions of law.' To that extent, the observations in *Keshav Mills* may be academic. The Supreme Court brilliantly analysed the submissions of Palkhivala and Daphthary, and the judgment continues to be a memorable one.

From 1998, appeals lie to the High Courts from orders passed by the ITAT only if the case involves 'a substantial question of law'. By a strange twist of fate, the meaning of this phrase was authoritatively laid down in a civil case argued by Palkhivala before a Bench of five judges.[85] A suit for damages was filed before the

85. *Chunnilal V. Mehta & Sons v. Century Spinning Mills Co. Ltd.*, AIR 1962 SC 1314 : [1962] Supp (3) SCR 549.

Bombay High Court and the plaintiff was unsuccessful both before the single judge and the Division Bench. An application was filed for a certificate under Article 133(1)(a)[86] of the Constitution which enabled the High Court to certify that a case involved a substantial question of law, thus enabling a party to appeal to the Supreme Court.

The Bombay High Court rejected this application as well and Palkhivala, requested the Supreme Court to decide the meaning of the phrase 'substantial question of law'. There were conflicting decisions of various High Courts. The Supreme Court held that a substantial question of law does not mean a question that is of general importance. A substantial question of law was that which arose between the parties involved in a particular case.

After noticing the conflict of views of what constituted a substantial question of law, Justice Mudholkar, in a passage that has become a classic, held:

> *The proper test for determining whether a question of law raised in the case is substantial would, in our opinion, be whether it is of general public importance or whether it directly and substantially affects the rights of the parties and if so whether it is either an open question in the sense that it is not finally settled by this Court or by the Privy Council or by the Federal Court or is not free from difficulty or calls for discussion of alternative views. If the question is settled by the highest Court or the general principles to be applied in determining the question are well settled and there is a mere question of applying those principles or that the plea raised is palpably absurd, the question would not be a substantial of law.*

The Supreme Court considered the views of various High Courts and agreed with the view of the Madras High Court. It observed that the view taken by the Bombay High Court was 'rather narrow' and that taken by the former Nagpur was 'too wide'.

However, on the merits, the Supreme Court did not accept Palkhivala's interpretation of a particular clause of the managing agency agreement and dismissed the appeal. But the judgment was

86. This Article was subsequently amended by the Constitution (Thirtieth Amendment) Act, 1972 and the Constitution (Forty-fourth Amendment) Act, 1978.

immensely useful for several other litigants and effectively determined the scope of Section 100 of the Code of Civil Procedure which, from 1976, confined second appeals only on 'substantial questions of law.'

Apart from second appeals under the Civil Procedure Code, appeals lie only on substantial questions of law against the orders passed by several *quasi* judicial Tribunals. Thus, the civil case argued by Palkhivala continues to be the leading decision on the point even after 50 years.

10.6 *Purposive interpretation*

Another excellent example of the Supreme Court's purposive interpretation is the *Central Board of Direct Taxes v. Aditya V. Birla.*[87] Aditya Birla was a qualified engineer from the prestigious Massachusetts Institute of Technology and had several years of experience in manufacturing and selling staple fibre. He was engaged as a consultant by the Thai Rayon Co. Ltd., based in Bangkok, Thailand. He claimed 50% deduction on the remuneration received by him from that company under Section 80RRA of the Income Tax Act, 1961. This Section granted deduction to the remuneration received by an Indian citizen from 'an employer' and for 'services rendered outside India.'

The Department took the view that the money earned by Aditya Birla was as a consultant and not as an employee, and the deduction under Section 80RRA was not permissible. Palkhivala argued that the object of Section 80RRA was to encourage foreign exchange earnings being remitted to India by Indian technicians and the word 'employer' used in Section 80RRA should not be narrowly construed.

Justice Sabyasachi Mukherji, who delivered a number of judgments on tax laws, both at the Calcutta High Court and the Supreme Court, accepted Palkhivala's submissions. If the object of the Section was kept in mind, there was no warrant, he held, to restrict the meaning of the word 'employer' and 'remuneration'. Section 80RRA should not be confined only to salaries received by employees and even consultants would be eligible for deduction on the remuneration or fees that they may receive. This is an excellent example of a broad liberal interpretation given to an income tax provision in contrast to the hyper-technical approach that is sometimes adopted on the ground that exemption provisions should be construed strictly.

---

87. AIR 1988 SC 420 : (1988) 170 ITR 137 : 1988 Supp SCC 120.

11. International taxation

A very interesting case on double taxation was argued by Sir Nusserwanji Engineer and Palkhivala way back in 1953.[88] A company had its registered office in Bombay and a branch in Karachi that, by the assessment year 1949-50, became a part of Pakistan. When British India was split into the two Dominions of India and Pakistan, a double-taxation avoidance agreement was entered into between the two countries and incorporated in Section 49AA of the Income Tax Act,1922. It was the first double-taxation agreement that India had entered into with any country, and was necessitated by the sudden partition. The company, being resident and ordinarily resident in India, was chargeable to income tax on its total world income which would include the profits obtained in Karachi, Pakistan. This company had appointed Parekh Cotton Company Ltd. as its managing agent which had to be paid 20% of the net annual profits. The Department argued that as the assessee had itself split the commission between that payable to the branches at Bombay and Karachi, it could not claim the commission attributable to the Karachi profits as a deduction in calculating the Indian profits.

The Bombay High Court pointed out that the assessee carried on only one business and the net profit had to be ascertained by pooling together profits earned in all the branches and deducting therefrom all the expenses and the fact that part of the profits was in foreign territories would make no difference. This view of the Bombay High Court was later confirmed by the Supreme Court where R.J. Kolah appeared for the assessee. The Supreme Court decision is also important because it was held that the eligibility to a particular deduction will depend on the provision of law relating thereto and *not the view taken by the assessee of its rights.* If he is entitled to a deduction of the whole commission, then the assessee cannot be estopped merely because it had erroneously allocated a part of it towards the profits earned in Karachi.

Electronics Corporation of India Ltd. v. CIT,[89] raised the important question of the extra-territorial operation of the Income Tax Act, 1961. Section 9(1)(vii) was introduced by the Finance Act, 1976. In this clause, fees for technical service is deemed to

---

88. *C. Parekh and Co. (India) Ltd. v. CIT*, (1953) 24 ITR 24 (Bom) : AIR 1954 Bom 75 – affirmed in *CIT v. C. Parekh & Co. (India) Ltd.*, (1956) 29 ITR 661 : AIR 1958 SC 775.
89. (1990) 183 ITR 43 : AIR 1989 SC 1707 : 1989 Supp SCC 642.

accrue or arise in India if they are payable by the Government or an assessee who is a resident unless the fees are payable for services outside India. If the fees were payable by a non-resident, it is deemed to accrue or arise in India if it is payable for services utilized in India or able to make or earn from any source in India. Under Article 245(2), no law made by Parliament 'shall be deemed to be invalid on the ground that it would have extra territorial operation'.

Would this Article enable Parliament to tax income which neither arose in India nor was earned abroad by an Indian residing in India? As a general rule, tax is levied either when a person is a resident in a particular country or where the source of that income arises in that country. If there is neither residence nor source, the general international practice is not to impose tax on such individual or income. However, recent experience shows that the Income Tax Department has aggressively sought to tax income which has neither arisen from a source in India nor earned by a person resident in this country. Unfortunately, there was no clear pronouncement on the limits of Parliament's competence to levy tax that has an extra-territorial operation. Palkhivala was able to raise sufficient doubts on the ambit and scope of Article 245(2). Realising the importance of the issue involved, Justice Pathak decided to refer this issue to a Bench of five judges with these words:

> *But the question is whether a nexus with something in India is necessary. It seems to us that unless such nexus exists Parliament will have no competence to make the law. It will be noted that Article 245(1) empowers Parliament to enact law for the whole or any part of the territory of India. The provocation for the law must be found within India itself. Such a law must have extra territorial operation in order to subserve the object, and that object must be related to something in India. It is conceivable that a law should be made by Parliament in India which has no relationship with anything in India. The only question is then whether the ingredients in terms of the impugned provision indicate a nexus. The question is one of substantial importance specially as it concerns collaboration agreements with foreign companies and other such arrangements for the better development of industry and commerce in India. In view of the great public importance of the question, we think it desirable refer to these cases to a Constitution Bench, and we do so order.*

By a strange quirk of fate, Electronics Corporation withdrew this case and the issue remained undecided for two decades. Recently, a five judge Bench has dealt with this issue and laid down the scope of Parliament's power to legislate on extra-territorial aspects or causes and its power to legislate for any territory other than the territory of India or any part of it.[90] Despite this latest decision, the law on this subject still remains unclear.

In an earlier case, Jusice Venkatarama Iyer had pointed out the difference between *extra-territorial legislation* and laws that had *extra-territorial operation.*[91] The distinction between these two categories is critical but outside the scope of this book.

In *CIT v. H.E.H. Mir Osman Ali Bahadur,*[92] was an interesting case that involved international law, municipal law and a covenant between the Government of India and the Nizam of Hyderabad. The Nizam claimed that he was immune from Indian taxation upto January 25, 1950 as he was a sovereign till then and this plea was accepted by the High Court which also held that as he ceased to be a sovereign from the next day when India became a republic, the income that accrued to the Nizam thereafter was liable to tax. Palkhivala argued that, under international law, a foreign sovereign was exempt from taxation under English common law which was also the law of India before the Constitution came into force. Reference was made to leading text-books on international law and also certain articles in American journals that dealt with immunity from taxation of foreign State-owned property. The Supreme Court rejected Palkhivala's argument and held that the Nizam had never acquired an international personality under international law and there was a serious doubt whether the Nizam could be treated as a foreign sovereign. Tracing the history of various developments that took place in Hyderabad till January, 1950 the Supreme Court held that the Hyderabad State never acquired an international personality under international law and its ruler was not entitled to claim immunity from taxation of his income or his properties.

12. The swan song

One of the last cases that Palkhivala argued before the Supreme Court was perhaps the *Builders Association of India v. Union of*

---

90. *G.V.K. Industries Ltd. v. ITO*, (2011) 4 SCC 36 : (2011) 332 ITR 130 : (2011) 3 SCALE 111.
91. *Bengal Immunity Co. Ltd. v. State of Bihar*, AIR 1955 SC 661 : [1955] 2 SCR 603.
92. AIR 1966 SC 1260 : (1966) 59 ITR 666.

India.[93] By this time, a heart surgery and a few cerebral strokes had taken their toll. This case was a writ petition filed under Article 32. The judgment does not indicate against which order the writ petition was filed. The case was concerned with the interpretation of the words '*construction*, manufacture or production of any *article or thing*, not being an article or thing specified in the list in the Eleventh Schedule'. In *CIT v. N.C. Budharaja and Company,*[94] the Supreme Court had held that the word 'construction' was relatable to 'article or thing' and would not apply to immovable structures like dams, bridges, buildings or roads. The word 'construction' was referable to the construction of ships. The writ petition filed under Article 32 was to reconsider this judgment rendered by Justice Jeevan Reddy. In the latter judgment, Justice Jeevan Reddy again presided over the Bench. The submissions of Palkhivala are neatly summarised on three grounds. He argued that the word 'construction' was to be read independent of and not in association with the word 'manufacture or production of any article or thing'. So read, the word 'construction' would take within its sweep all types of construction like dams, building and bridges. Palkhivala also referred to an opinion of the Law Ministry and a reply of the Ministry of Finance on this issue. Secondly, he referred to a circular issued in the context of Section 32AB which contained similar words and clearly pointed out that 'it may be clarified that the business of construction is an eligible business for the purpose of this provision'. A third contention was not seriously pressed. Justice Jeevan Reddy dismissed the writ petition on the ground that there was no reason to reconsider their earlier judgment. It is submitted that the Supreme Court was wrong in adopting a narrow approach to the meaning of the word 'construction'. When the Finance Ministry itself issued a circular that the construction business was eligible under Section 32AB, Justice Reddy distinguished it by stating that this circular did not clearly state that construction of all types was included! Obviously, it is not necessary for the Government to state that all types of construction are eligible. Indeed, the circular should have been enough for the Supreme Court to reconsider its earlier decision. Further, if the intention of this provision was to encourage capital formation, there was no reason why the word 'construction' should have been given a restricted meaning. It is submitted that Palkhivala was right and the Supreme Court was wrong in rejecting this submission.

---

93. (1994) 209 ITR 877 : AIR 1994 SC 2740 : 1995 Supp (1) SCC 41.
94. (1993) 204 ITR 412 : AIR 1993 SC 2529 : 1994 Supp (1) SCC 280.

13. Will we ever learn?

Palkhivala's involvement in tax cases spanned five decades from 1945 to 1995. He gave his first budget speech in 1957 and continued to be a bitter critic of the avalanche of amendments and chronic tinkering with tax laws. Only a few budgets like the one presented by C. Subramaniam in 1976 and by V.P. Singh in 1986 received praise from Palkhivala. In the preface to various editions of his commentary on income tax, Palkhivala lamented the inherent unfairness and total lack of concern for the economic consequences of the changes in our tax laws.

During his life time, Palkhivala saw the Income Tax Act, 1922 consisting of less than a hundred sections replaced by the 1961 Act consisting of about 300 sections. Within a few years, the 1961 Act was mutilated by an average of more than fifty amendments per year! No other country comes even close to this legislative hyperactivity. What is equally sad is that amendments are seldom debated in Parliament and complex changes are made in the Act without any discussion.

In 2012, the Direct Taxes Code is likely to replace the Income Tax Act, 1961. It is almost certain that the new Code will suffer the same fate because the evil practice of repeated amendments, several of them retrospective, will continue.

The tragedy is that repeated amendments have failed to check rampant tax evasion. Weak administration and pervasive corruption make it simple and profitable for taxes to be evaded. Statistically, the chances of a rich tax payer being prosecuted and sent to jail for tax evasion are less than his being killed in a road accident. Successive voluntary disclosure schemes have made a mockery of the penal provision. Looking back, nothing has really changed in the last 50 years and it is unlikely that any meaningful reforms will be made in the coming decade. Palkhivala's criticism and suggestions made over the years were substantially in vain. The only redeeming feature is that tax rates are now far more reasonable than the earlier days when the maximum income tax rate was 97.75% of the total income of the assessee!

However, as a lawyer, Palkhivala had the enormous satisfaction of appearing before outstanding judges who did not hesitate to strike down a bad law or answer the tax reference in favour of the assessee regardless of the amount of tax involved. The maxim that tax laws, in cases of ambiguity, should be interpreted in favour of tax prayer has been virtually abandoned by most of the High

Courts and the Supreme Court. While the courts have been highly pro-active in public interest litigation, there is a perceptible tendency to decide cases in favour of the Revenue when cases are evenly balanced or even where the scales are slightly tilted towards the assessee. It is sincerely hoped that this trend is reversed and we can once again expect landmark decisions like *Bai Shirinbai Kooka, E.D. Sasoon, Keshav Mills,* or *Poona Electric Supply,*[95] in the years ahead.

❋

95. *Poona Electric Supply v. CIT,* AIR 1966 SC 30 : (1965) 57 ITR 521. This was another outstanding judgment by Justice Subba Rao but Palkhivala did not argue this case. The great A.V. Viswanatha Sastri had appeared for the assessee.

Chapter 7

Indirect Taxes

Central excisc – Significant contribution

The general impression is that Nani Palkhivala mainly appeared in cases involving income tax and constitutional law. Surprisingly, his contribution to the development of the law of central excise is significant but not generally recognised. Central excise duty is levied on the manufacture of 'goods' and Entry 84 of List I of Schedule VII to the Constitution of India reads as follows:

> *84. Duties of excise on tobacco and other goods manufactured or produced in India except:*
>
> *(a) alcoholic liquors for human consumption,*
>
> *(b) opium, Indian hemp and other narcotic drugs and narcotics*
>
> *but including medicinal and toilet preparations containing alcohol or any substance included in sub-paragraph (b) of this entry.*

An examination of this Entry shows that duty can be levied on goods (movable property) which are *manufactured* or *produced* in India. But the definition of the word 'manufacture' in the Central Excise Act, 1944, is not helpful. It does not define the word 'manufacture' at all. Before 1985, it merely stated that the word 'manufacture' would 'include all incidental and ancillary processes'. This problem is not uncommon in the field of taxation. Neither the Income Tax Act, 1922 nor the 1961 Act has precisely defined the word 'income'. Section 2(24) of the Income Tax Act, 1961, gives an inclusive definition: it reads '"income" includes…' and proceeds to enumerate several categories which would not be income in the ordinary sense of the word. Similarly, there was (and is) no proper definition of the word 'manufacture'. The Central Excise Act, 1944, was initially called 'Central Excises and Salt Act, 1944'. The levy of duty on salt was abolished after independence –

undoubtedly, in recognition of the historical importance of Gandhiji's salt satyagraha. After the Dandi march, no Government in independent India could ever think of levying duty on salt. The provisions relating to salt were finally deleted in 1996.

Although the Act came into force in 1944, very few items were subjected to central excise duty. Till the mid 1970s, the tax collection through direct taxes was far in excess of the duties of excise and customs. There was hardly any litigation in indirect taxes but the absence of a clear definition of the word 'manufacture' resulted in a vacuum which could not continue for long. After manufacture, the second most important issue in central excise law is the 'valuation' of goods.[1] Thus, 'manufacture' and 'valuation' are the twin pillars on which the entire edifice of central excise law is built. By a remarkable coincidence, Palkhivala appeared in six cases which laid down the basic principles defining the scope of 'manufacture' and 'valuation'.

Meaning of the word 'manufacture'

Till this day, the 1963 decision of the Supreme Court in what is popularly called the *DCM case,*[2] laying down the ambit and scope of the word 'manufacture', continues to hold good. The judicial meaning given to this word has not been improved upon and this decision will remain the most important decision on 'manufacture' as long as central excise duty continues to be levied. The Union of India was in appeal before the Supreme Court. Three companies viz. (i) Delhi Cloth and General Mills Ltd. (ii) Modi Sugar Mills Ltd., and (iii) Ganesh Flour Mills Ltd., challenged the demand of duty on refined oil. All three manufactured *vanaspati* (hydrogenated refined oil) from groundnut oil and *til* oil (sesame oil) purchased from the open market or from the manufacturers of such oil. These two oils were refined and major impurities removed from them. This involved the process of refining which removed coloured, suspended and 'mucilaginous'[3] matters. The refined oil was then subjected to hydrogenation resulting in *vanaspati*. The Central Excise Department sought to levy duty on the process of

---

1. Excise duty is mainly levied on *ad valorem* basis. In a few cases, it is levied at a specific rate of Rs. x per tonne or per kilolitre. Section 4 of the Act lays down the manner in which the assessable value has to be computed. Rules have also been framed to determine the assessable value in certain cases.
2. *Union of India v. Delhi Cloth & General Mills Ltd.*, AIR 1963 SC 791 : [1963] 1 SCR 586.
3. From the noun 'mucilage' which means a viscous secretion or bodily fluid; an adhesive solution or glue (Oxford Dictionary).

refining on the ground that it amounted to manufacture and attracted levy of central excise duty. Before the High Court, the assessee had filed affidavits of experts contending that *vanaspati,* made after refining oil, would not be liable to excise duty as the process did not amount to manufacture. The Punjab High Court accepted these contentions and allowed the writ petitions. At the relevant time, writ petitions by parties in Delhi were filed before the Punjab High Court as Delhi did not have a High Court to entertain these writ petitions. (Haryana State had not yet come into being.)

Aggrieved by the decision of the Punjab High Court, the Union of India filed three appeals before the Supreme Court. G. S. Pathak, an eminent counsel, who subsequently became the Vice President of India, was engaged on behalf of the Union of India. The three manufacturers briefed N. C. Chatterji and A. V. Viswanatha Sastri, both equally eminent counsel. Indeed, Viswanatha Sastri was a towering colossus. He was a retired judge of the Madras and Andhra Pradesh High Courts and commenced practice in the Supreme Court after retirement. In the early 1960s, he had perhaps the largest practice in the Supreme Court. He had few equals in his knowledge and grasp of civil and tax law.

Hindustan Lever Ltd. intervened in the matter and engaged the services of Palkhivala through Dadachanji & Co.

The stand of the Government was that the process of purification or refining of oil results in a new manufactured product called 'refined oil'. The Supreme Court has discussed the arguments of Pathak in detail but there is no reference to the arguments of Palkhivala or the other counsel who appeared for the assessees. The Department raised an alternate plea: manufacture would take place if the raw material undergoes some change by application of one or more processes. This was a dangerous proposition and would have been disastrous to the industry. In effect, the word 'manufacture' would be equated with a mere process and excise duty would be payable even if no new product came into existence. The mere activity of painting or electroplating would amount to manufacture even though it continued to be the same piece of steel or other metal. The Supreme Court referred to a passage from an American judgment which was quoted in Vol. 26 of 'Words and Phrases'. The passage is important and reads:

'"Manufacture" implies a change but every change is not manufacture, yet every change of an article is the result of treatment, labour and manipulation. But something more is necessary and there must be transformation; a new and different article must emerge having a distinctive name, character or use'.

Thus, the Supreme Court laid down a threefold test to determine what is manufacture. The inputs must be transformed to such a degree that there is a new and different article having a distinctive *name, character and use.*

This threefold test continues to be applied till this day to determine whether an activity amounts to manufacture. A decision on this question will decide the fate of a particular industry's liability to pay excise duty. If an activity amounts to manufacture, excise duty is payable and that particular assessee comes within the scope and ambit of the Central Excise Act and all the myriad rules and regulations that have been framed thereunder. He has to take out a licence/registration, submit returns and comply with all the procedural formalities. On the other hand, if the activity is not manufacture, he escapes not only the liability to pay duty but also the onerous task of complying with complex rules and regulations that are subject to frequent changes.

Apart from manufacture, the Supreme Court also considered the meaning of the word 'goods'. It pointed out that the Act did not define 'goods' but defined 'excisable goods' to mean goods specified in the First Schedule to the Central Excise Act. After referring to Vol. 18 of 'Words and Phrases' and a decision of a New York Court, the court noted the definition of the word 'goods' in Webster's Dictionary which, *inter alia,* mentions that goods are commodities that are bought and sold by merchants and traders. The court went on to hold that before duty could be levied, the article must be something which ordinarily comes to the market to be bought and sold.

The Supreme Court then rejected the alternate plea of the Union of India that processing should be equated to manufacture. The Department contended that 'manufacture' would include any process which was incidental or ancillary to the completion of the manufactured product. Therefore, the word 'manufacture' should be equated with any process. The Supreme Court, in a far reaching decision, observed that the definition only makes it clear that the word 'manufacture' has been used to include processes incidental to the manufacture of an article. The definition was not made with a view to make mere processing of goods liable to excise duty. The net result of this landmark decision is that while every manufacturing activity involves one or more processes, a process will not amount to manufacture unless the activity of processing satisfies the three-fold test, viz. a new article having a distinctive *name, character and use* emerges.

Interestingly, the Supreme Court laid down that excisable goods must be those which can ordinarily come to the market to be bought and sold. In other words, if the article is something which cannot be marketed, duty cannot be levied. This position was made clear several years later in *CCE v. Bhor Industries.*[4] Most practitioners of central excise believe that the marketability test was laid down by the Supreme court in the *Bhor Industries Ltd.* case, often forgetting that the principle had already been laid down in the *DCM* case.

The *DCM* case, in laying down the three-fold test, has been immensely useful in determining the meaning of 'manufacture'. The principles are laid down with remarkable clarity by Das Gupta J. and they enable determination of whether a particular activity amounts to manufacture. It also clearly demarcates the difference between processing and manufacture. The case is equally important for laying down the test of marketability and to determine what constitutes 'goods'. Thus, in one case, three landmark principles were laid down by the Supreme Court which have stood the test of time.

The next important case in the field of manufacture in which Palkhivala had an important role to play was *South Bihar Sugar Mills Ltd. v. Union of India.*[5] Palkhivala appeared for Tata Chemicals Ltd. as intervener.[6] In addition, this company had also filed a separate writ petition raising the same question of law. The South Bihar Sugar Mills manufactured sugar by the carbonation process and paid excise duty on the sugar so manufactured. The Central Excise Department took the plea that during the process of manufacture of sugar, carbon dioxide was generated and this gas was compressed. According to the department, such carbon dioxide was dutiable at 50% *ad valorem.* Initially, the demand of duty was challenged before the Punjab High Court which dismissed the writ petition and an appeal was filed before the Supreme Court.

4. 1989 (40) ELT 280 : AIR 1989 SC 1153 : (1989) 1 SCC 602.
5. AIR 1968 SC 922 : [1968] 3 SCR 21.
6. Ravinder Narain, formerly a partner of Dadachanji & Co., and now a Senior Advocate practising in the Supreme Court, had to inform Palkhivala of any important taxation case pending in the Supreme Court. If the case could adversely affect Tatas, Palkhivala would appear as an intervener for the concerned Tata company.

S.V. Gupte, who subsequently became the Attorney-General of India, appeared for the sugar company. Palkhivala was for the intervener and the Attorney-General, C.K. Daphtary, appeared for the Union of India. Ravinder Narain assisted Palkhivala in that case and he recollects that Gupte argued first and contended that carbon dioxide gas was not liable to excise duty. The Supreme Court was initially not inclined to accept this argument.

When Palkhivala's turn came, he took an interesting and different plea. He contended that the gas generated was not carbon dioxide at all but was only 'kiln gas'. Such kiln gas that was generated in the course of manufacture of sugar was not carbon dioxide as known to the market. Palkhivala submitted that merely burning limestone with coke generated a mixture of gases and one of the constituents therein was carbon dioxide. He further submitted that the manufacturing process was an integrated and continuous one which generated not only carbon dioxide but also nitrogen, whose content was 53% as against the carbon dioxide content of 32-35%. The mixture of gases generated was popularly known as 'kiln gas' in the sugar industry and by manufacturers of soda ash. Kiln gas was not marketable since it could not be brought to the market for being bought and sold as such. It would require an elaborate plant to extract carbon dioxide from kiln gas before it could be marketable.

As per specifications laid down by the Indian Standards Institution (ISI) – (now known as Bureau of Indian Standards or BIS) - carbon dioxide sold commercially had to be 99% pure and supplied in steel cylinders under a minimum pressure of 1000 lbs per sq. inch. On the other hand, kiln gas had a carbon dioxide content of only 50-60% and was compressed to a pressure of 40-45 lbs per sq. inch. Therefore, carbon dioxide, as contemplated by item 14-H of the old Central Excise Tariff, would not include kiln gas.

The arguments, as dealt with by the Supreme Court, indicate extensive references to technical literature and books on chemical technology. The Supreme Court accepted the arguments of Palkhivala and allowed the appeals. The Supreme Court observed that commercial carbon dioxide must have a content of at least 99% and was usually sold in steel cylinders – either in liquefied or in solidified form. In the present case, it was neither.

The Supreme Court then made some observations which are important and can be usefully applied to other cases as well. The

Revenue submitted that kiln gas could be sold in the same condition to other companies through a pipeline. The Supreme Court observed that such a method would be uneconomical and could hardly be expected to be employed by the trade even though it was theoretically possible to do so. The judgment of the Punjab High Court was set aside and the appeal allowed.

It is thus remarkable that the two main cases that defined 'manufacture' were argued by Palkhivala. It is also a tribute to the eminent judges of the Supreme Court that their judgments have stood the test of time and are still critical to determine whether an activity amounts to manufacture or not.

'Valuation' – The Voltas case

Once an activity amounts to manufacture, it becomes liable to excise duty and that leads us to the important question of valuation. On what value does excise duty have to be paid? Is it on wholesale price or retail price or on some other formula prescribed by law? Before 1975, Section 4 of the Central Excise Act, 1944 stipulated that the assessable value shall be deemed to be the wholesale cash price at which an article of '*like kind and quantity is sold or is capable of being sold*' at the time of removal from the factory. In simple terms, duty was levied on the wholesale price at which the goods were sold or capable of being sold at the factory gate. The important feature to be noted in central excise is that the assessee could have both wholesale and retail transactions but the assessable value would be based only on the wholesale price. The assessee could have different selling prices but there would be only one assessable value – the value at which the goods were ordinarily sold in wholesale or capable of being sold in the course of wholesale trade.[7]

The first major case on valuation before the Supreme Court was *A.K. Roy v. Voltas Ltd.*[8] The facts are interesting and important. Voltas manufactured air-conditioners and water coolers and 90-95% of them were directly sold to the customers at list prices. These were retail transactions. The remaining 5-10% were sold to wholesale dealers in different parts of the country at the list price less 22% discount. The Assistant Collector demanded duty on the

---

7. The text of the old Section 4 is set out in the Appendix. The present Section 4 which came into force on 1.7.2000, treats the transaction value as the assessable value.
8. AIR 1973 SC 225 : 1977 ELT J177 (SC) : (1973) 3 SCC 503.

retail price, whereas Voltas contended that excise duty was payable only on the list price after deducting discount of 22% i.e the wholesale price. This would constitute the assessable value for levy of excise duty. Thus, the wholesale cash price at which 5-10% of air-conditioners were sold was to be the basis for levy of duty on air-conditioners. In fact, this had been accepted by the Central Excise Department right until 1962. But the Assistant Collector of Central Excise confirmed the demand and levied duty on the retail price from 1962 onwards. This order was challenged before the Appellate Collector who confirmed the order of the Assistant Collector. Against this order, Voltas filed a writ petition before the Bombay High Court which allowed the writ petition.[9]

A.K. Roy was the Collector of Central Excise and he filed an appeal before the Supreme Court. Palkhivala appeared for Voltas before the Supreme Court. Referring to Section 4 and earlier decisions on the subject, the Supreme Court pointed out that even if 90-95% of the goods had been sold directly to the consumers, it would not affect the wholesale price of the remaining 5-10%. The price charged for 5-10% of the total sales would still constitute wholesale cash price for the purpose of Section 4(a). Accordingly, 100% of the turnover would be assessed on the wholesale price at which 5-10% of the goods had been sold. Secondly, the Supreme Court pointed out that for wholesale prices to exist, it would not be necessary that there should be a wholesale market actually at the factory gate. The law contemplates notional wholesale buyers' market wherein similar articles could be bought and sold. It was not necessary for a market to exist in a physical sense. And then came one sentence in para 21 of the Supreme Court's judgment which created unprecedented turmoil and triggered the filing of literally hundreds of cases in various High Courts:

> *Excise is a tax on the production and manufacture of goods.*[10] *Section 4 of the Act therefore provides that the real value should be found after deducting the selling cost and selling profits and that the real value can include only the manufacturing cost and the manufacturing profit. The Section makes it clear that excise is levied only on the amount representing the manufacturing cost plus the*

9. At the relevant time, there was no Tribunal. The Customs, Excise and Gold (Control) Appellate Tribunal (CEGAT) started functioning in 1982. It is now called CESTAT - gold control is out and service tax is in.
10. See *Union of India v. Delhi Cloth & General Mills,* [1963] Supp 1 SCR 586 : AIR 1963 SC 791.

manufacturing profit and excludes post-manufacturing cost and the profit arising from post-manufacturing operation, namely selling profit.[11] *(emphasis supplied).*

These observations on post-manufacturing expenses (PME) had a far reaching effect on central excise revenue. In hundreds of cases, almost all High Courts issued interim orders preventing the Department from collecting duty on any item that constituted post-manufacturing expenses. Certain High Courts went to the extent of stating that levy of duty on the wholesale price would amount to a sales tax which Parliament was not competent to levy. The net result was that excise duty was levied only on manufacturing cost and all post-manufacturing expenditure had to be excluded.

Meanwhile, Parliament substituted a new Section 4 with effect from October 1, 1975.[12] The new Section was far more elaborate than its predecessor. The new Section expressly provided that central excise would be a levy on the wholesale price at the factory gate and provided deduction of the following items: durable and returnable packing charges, trade discount, freight charges and indirect taxes (sales tax, octroi, excise duty). Despite the clear provisions of the new Section and the fact that *Voltas* case was decided under the old Section, the High Courts continued to hold that no excise duty could be levied on post-manufacturing expenses.

In the *Voltas* case, Palkhivala was briefed by Dadi Engineer, Senior Partner of Crawford Bayley & Co. and Ravinder Narain of J.B. Dadachanji & Co. When he realised that several High Courts had taken the observations of Justice Mathew out of context and had passed interim and final orders preventing levy of excise duty on post-manufacturing expenses, he informed Dadi Engineer that this was not the real ratio of *Voltas* at all. *Voltas* was concerned with the question of levying excise duty on wholesale price even when most of the goods were sold in retail. It was wrong, according to Palkhivala, to take one sentence out of context and not pay duty on the wholesale price.

---

11. Judgment by Justice K.K. Mathew. The other judges on the Bench were Justices A.N. Grover and A.K. Mukherjea.
12. This Section was in force till 1.7.2004 when the new pattern of levying excise duty on transaction value was introduced.

The Bombay Tyres case

Nevertheless, Palkhivala did press this argument before the Supreme Court in what is perhaps the most important case on valuation. The issue as to whether the assessable value excluded post-manufacturing expenses came up before the Supreme Court in the case of *Union of India v. Bombay Tyres International Ltd.*[13] A batch of cases was posted for hearing before the Supreme Court. Palkhivala led the batch for the assessees and K. Parasaran, the Solicitor-General at that time, appeared for the Union of India. After hearing detailed arguments for several days, the Supreme Court made a brief order on May 9, 1983. It pointed out the rules regarding valuation under the old Section 4 and then set out the principles that would apply under the new Section 4. It clearly rejected the theory of excluding post-manufacturing expenses. A detailed and unanimous judgment was given on October 7, 1983 by Justice R.S. Pathak, who later became the Chief Justice of India.[14] The decision is remarkable for its brevity and the manner in which it dealt with the first principles of central excise and tax laws.

The main argument that was made in this case was that excise duty could not be levied on post-manufacturing expenses. The Union of India could levy duty only on the manufacturing cost and 'manufacturing process'. Therefore, to the extent the levy was on the wholesale price, it would be bad in law as the levy included post-manufacturing expenses. The Supreme Court rejected this contention. It pointed out that the levy of excise duty was on manufacture or production of goods. But it was not necessary that the stage of collection should synchronise with the completion of the manufacturing process. Therefore, even though central excise was levied on manufacture or production, the point at which the excise duty could be collected depended entirely on administrative convenience. Generally, it was collected when the article left the factory for the first time. Merely because the goods became the subject matter of assessment only when they are sold did not mean that excise duty was not on manufacture. They referred to an important passage from Seervai's classic commentary on the Constitution[15] wherein the great jurist pointed out that every tax had two elements: the person, thing or activity on which tax is imposed and the amount of tax. To put it differently, the two

13. AIR 1984 SC 420 : (1984) 1 SCC 467.
14. Justice R.S. Phatak was also a judge of the International Court of Justice at the Hague from 1989 to 1992.
15. *Constitutional Law of India,* H.M. Seervai, 2nd edition, Vol. 2, p. 1258.

elements are the subject matter of a tax and the measure of a tax. Thus, the Supreme Court rejected the plea that excise duty could be levied only on manufacturing cost plus manufacturing profits and overruled the view taken by almost all the High Courts that excise duty could not be levied on post-manufacturing expenses. Indeed, the Gujarat High Court had gone to the extent of holding that the levy of excise duty on the wholesale price would really mean a sales tax, and, therefore, Parliament did not have the legislative competence to levy tax on the wholesale price. Sales tax being a State subject, Parliament would have no power to levy central excise duty on the sale pricc of the goods.

The case for the Union of India was argued brilliantly by K. Parasaran, the former Attorney-General. Other advocates who were present at the hearing of this batch of cases, recollect that the submissions made by Parasaran were remarkable. He argued that Parliament had the right to adopt any basis for determining the assessable value of excisable goods and that the measure for assessing the levy need not correspond completely to the nature of the levy. As long as the measure of the tax had a nexus with the charge, it was sufficient. The judgment of the Supreme Court discussed important decisions of the Privy Council which dealt with the fundamental nature of excise duty. Unlike later judgments on excise duty, the *Bombay Tyres'* decision was admirably brief and yet comprehensive; it put at rest the controversy that had plagued the High Courts for almost a decade. One sentence in the *Voltas* case on post-manufacturing profits had triggered a tidal wave of litigation which benefited no one except the lawyers. The 1984 judgment of the Supreme Court put an end to the controversy on the inclusion of post-manufacturing expenses. Excise duty was to be levied on the wholesale price at the factory gate which would include all expenses that were incurred even after the manufacturing stage. In effect, indirect expenses and overheads that were incurred were also includible in the assessable value.[16]

Thus, Palkhivala played an important role in helping formulate the fundamental propositions on manufacture and valuation. But

---

16. Unfortunately, the Department and the assessees did not live happily ever after on the subject of valuation. Soon afterwards, a new controversy on post-removal expenses came up for consideration in the Supreme Court. Section 4 was amended to levy duty not only on the factory gate price but also on the price at which the goods were sold at the depot. Further amendments were made and, today, the assessable value is on the transaction value on which the goods are sold to the wholesale buyer. Litigation on valuation, although at a reduced level, has unfortunately continued.

his role in central excise is not limited to these two issues alone. He played an important role in three other areas of central excise and these relate to promissory estoppel, the concept of 'related person' and the levy of duty on a job-worker.

In *Godfrey Philips Ltd. v. Union of India*,[17] the Department had issued a circular stating that the cardboard boxes or the outers in which the cartons of cigarettes were packed need not be included in computing the assessable value. Therefore, the cost of the cardboard carton was not to be added to the assessable value. Despite this circular, the Department began to include the same after the decision in the *Bombay Tyres* case. The assessees questioned the action of the Department and the matter ultimately reached the Supreme Court. The court held that when the Board had issued a circular permitting the deduction of these items, it was not open to the Department to act contrary to the same. The assessees had acted on the basis of the circular and the Department would be prohibited from acting against the circular by the principle of promissory estoppel. The *Godfrey Philips* case became a landmark decision on this subject and was an authority for the doctrine of promissory estoppel. Palkhivala appeared in this matter but there is little reference to his arguments in the judgment.

Apart from promissory estoppel, the Supreme Court, by a majority of 2:1,[18] laid down a further proposition that if the packing was done to ensure smooth transportation and was not necessary to sell the goods in wholesale, such cost of packing or the cost of such packing could not be included in the assessable value. It is submitted that this ruling on packing clearly amounted to judicial legislation and created a new deduction not contemplated by the Act. This observation also led to a further bout of litigation on packing costs. Justice Bhagwati, in the minority, rightly held that there was no basis for the deduction of packing for smooth transportation.

Related person

The concept of 'related person' has also given rise to a considerable amount of litigation. This is partly due to the unhappy drafting of Section 4(4)(c) which defines a related person as follows:

---

17. AIR 1986 SC 806 : 1985 (22) ELT 306 : (1985) 4 SCC 369.
18. The court was unanimous on the issue of promissory estoppel.

> *'related person' means a person who is so associated with the assessee that they have interest, directly or indirectly, in the business of each other and includes a holding company, a subsidiary company, a relative and a distributor of the assessee and any sub-distributor of such distributor.*
>
> *Explanation.—In this clause 'holding company', 'subsidiary company' and 'relative' have the same meanings as in the Companies Act, 1956 (1 of 1956.)*

This definition indicates that persons who are interested in the business of each other would be treated as 'related persons'. The definition also expressly includes within its ambit even distributors of manufactured products. There is no difficulty in understanding the concept of holding company and subsidiary company, and relative, since these are all defined in the Companies Act, 1956. What was controversial was the meaning of the expression *'have interest, directly or indirectly in the business of each other'*. This was the concept of mutuality of interest. But what is 'mutual interest' and what is meant by 'interest in the business of each other'? These complicated issues were argued by Palkhivala in another important case.[19]

The facts of the *Atic Industries* case are interesting and complicated and reveal the genius of Palkhivala in persuading the Supreme Court to accept a purposive interpretation of a badly drafted provision. Atic Industries Ltd. manufactured different kinds of dyes. Its shares were held equally by an Indian company Atul Industries Ltd. ('A' Ltd.) and a foreign company Imperial Chemical Industries Ltd., London ('I' Ltd.). Initially, this foreign company had a 100% subsidiary called Imperial Chemical Industries (India) Ltd. After 1974, the non-resident shareholding in any Indian company could not exceed 40% of its share capital. Therefore, 60% of the shareholding of the Indian subsidiary was offered to the public and only 40% was held by the parent company – Imperial Chemical Industries Ltd., London. The name of the Indian company was changed to Crescent Dyes and Chemicals Ltd. ('C' Ltd.).

'A' Ltd. and 'C' Ltd. purchased substantial quantities of the dyes manufactured by Atic Industries at a commercial price and resold these dyes at a higher price to other buyers. Note that 40% of the

---

19. *Union of India v. Atic Industries Ltd.*, 1984 (17) ELT 323 : (1984) 3 SCC 575 : AIR 1984 SC 1495.

share capital of 'C' Ltd. was held by 'I' Ltd., which, in turn, held 50% of the shares of the manufacturer – Atic Industries. It was common ground that the transaction between the assessee and the two wholesale purchasers ('A' Ltd. and 'C' Ltd.) was on principal to principal basis and no extra-commercial consideration entered into the determination of the wholesale price charged by the assessee.

The above complex shareholding pattern was the basis for the Department treating Atic Industries and their wholesale distributors, namely 'A' Ltd. & 'C' Ltd., as 'related persons' and demanding duty on the selling price charged by the latter two companies from their customers. The Department submitted that the manufacturer and the distributors were related because they had interest, directly or indirectly, in the business of each other.

In a short and lucid judgment, Justice Bhagwati held that it was not enough for the manufacturer to have an interest in the business of the distributor or *vice versa*. It was essential that both the assessee and the person alleged to be related, ought to have interest, direct or indirect, in the business of each other. The interest must be mutual although the quality or degree may vary. Applying this test, it held that although 'A' Ltd. had interest in the business of Atic Industries due to its 50% shareholding, it could not be said that Atic Industries had any interest, direct or indirect, in the business carried on by 'A' Ltd. The position regarding 'C' Ltd. was stronger. Although 'C' Ltd. was a wholesale buyer on principal to principal basis, Atic Industries could not be said, by virtue of this circumstance, to have any interest, direct or indirect, in the business of 'C' Ltd.

Deciding this case was no easy task. The judgment of Justice Bhagwati demonstrates his remarkable grasp of the commercial realities of a particular case.

Excise duty on job-work

Another landmark case argued by Palkhivala related to valuation and had a far-reaching impact on the manufacture of goods by small-scale units with the brand names of multinationals and large Indian companies.

Food Specialties Ltd. (FSL), an Indian company, entered into an agreement with Nestle Products India Ltd., (Nestle), a subsidiary of a Swiss based foreign company, to manufacture condensed milk, baby food and infant cereals. Under the agreement, FSL was to manufacture goods and supply them to

Nestle as per the quantities ordered. The goods were manufactured as per the detailed specification of Nestle. FSL had no interest in the trade mark and undertook not to sell the product to any person other than Nestle. Thus, FSL would sell the goods to Nestle at a certain wholesale price and Nestle would then sell it at a higher price. (The higher price of Nestle was mostly on account of the heavy cost of advertisements and other overheads.) The Department submitted that the value of the goods should include the value of the trade mark and such value could be added to the wholesale price at which the goods were sold by FSL to Nestle. The Supreme Court rejected this contention and held that the value of the trade mark could not be added. The goods were made by FSL and it is irrelevant as to who owned the trade mark. Duty could be levied only on the wholesale price at which the goods were sold.

This decision had a far-reaching effect on outsourcing and job-work. It paved the way for large multinationals to get their goods manufactured by smaller manufacturers. There was no need to add the value of a trade mark to the wholesale price. Thus, large multinationals would get their products manufactured through smaller manufacturers at a substantially lesser cost. The smaller manufacturers would sell the goods to Hindustan Lever, Colgate-Palmolive, or Procter and Gamble at a wholesale price without the need for adding the value of the trade mark. Until the late 1980s, several cosmetics were subject to savage rates of excise duty reaching upto 105%. These absurd rates of taxation led almost all multinationals and large Indian companies to get cosmetics and toiletries manufactured by hundreds of small-scale units. The reason was that if the goods were manufactured by a small-scale unit, there was no excise duty upto a turnover of Rs. 5,00,000/- and concessional rate of about 50% was applicable upto a turnover of Rs. 15 lakhs. This led to a series of amendments to discourage such outsourcing. Mercifully, the rates of tax also came down. Ultimately, the cat and mouse game ended with the levy of excise duty on the maximum retail price (MRP) on several household products, including cosmetics and toiletries.

Palkhivala had an equally important role to play in determining the principles of valuation, although he was not successful in the *Bombay Tyres* case. In fairness, it must be stated that the Supreme Court's interpretation was correct and the argument of Palkhivala was rightly rejected.

Customs – Novel arguments

Surprisingly, Palkhivala has argued only one reported customs case in the Supreme Court. *Collector of Customs v. Nathella Sampathu Chetty.*[20] Section 178A of the Sea Customs Act, 1878, shifted the burden of proof on the person from whom gold, gold articles, diamonds, precious stones and certain other notified goods were seized. About 1,000 *tolas* of gold[21] were seized from an employee of Nathella Sampathu Chetty when he alighted from the Bombay Express at the Madras Central station. The Collector of Customs was not satisfied with the explanation of the source from which the gold had been obtained. Finding that the gold was *prima facie* smuggled, he directed confiscation. A writ petition before the Madras High Court was successful and an appeal was preferred to the Supreme Court by the Collector of Customs. Palkhivala submitted that Section 178A of the Customs Act was constitutionally invalid as it violated Articles 14, and 19(1)(f) – the right to equality and the right to acquire property respectively. Palkhivala also explained the special features of gold and how difficult, if not impossible, it was to identify its source. He submitted that Section 178A imposed an impossible burden on the importer and based his argument on six grounds.[22] The arguments were indeed novel but were rejected in a detailed judgment rendered by Justice Rajagopala Ayyangar.

Sales tax – Only tenable propositions

Nani Palkhivala's appearances in sales tax cases were far fewer than those in direct taxes. The reported sales tax cases where Palkhivala had appeared in the Supreme Court are less than a dozen. This list may not be exhaustive as in several cases his name may not be mentioned either in the judgment or as one of the counsel who appeared. Bansi Mehta, an eminent Chartered Accountant, recollects that Palkhivala was asked to appear for the Sales Tax Department by the late Shri Wankhede who was then the Finance Minister of Maharashtra.[23] Palkhivala did so for almost 18 months, and, barring a few cases, the Department succeeded in almost all the matters. Possibly, there was a clash of interest as the clients for whom he appeared in income tax cases would be the

---

20. AIR 1962 SC 316 : [1962] 3 SCR 786.
21. Approximately 12 kgs. 1 *tola* equals approximately 12 grams.
22. *Collector of Customs v. Nathella Sampathu Chetty*, AIR 1962 SC 316, 326-327 (para 21): [1962] 3 SCR 786.
23. The famous Wankhede Stadium in Mumbai is named after him.

clients against whom the sales tax references had to be argued. Later, he stopped appearing for the Sales Tax Department.

What was the reason for this extraordinary success? Palkhivala, in a speech, remarked that he would never argue a hopeless case. If he felt that the Sales Tax Department had no case, he would inform the High Court at the beginning of the hearing. In this way, the High Court knew that Palkhivala would not argue an untenable proposition of law; cases that were contested had important issues that required the attention of the court.

N.C. Mehta, a leading specialist in sales tax cases, was the advisor to all the Tata companies on sales tax matters. He remembers discussing several sales tax cases with Palkhivala. On important amendments, N.C. Mehta would discuss the sales tax implications with Palkhivala and they would then decide the course of action to be adopted by the Tata companies.

A number of important constitutional cases have arisen in sales tax disputes. Strangely, barring two cases, Palkhivala never argued any important case that involved constitutional principles in this area. The two main exceptions are the *Builders' Association* case[24] where the Supreme Court dealt with Articles 286 and 366(29A) and certain constitutional entries and the *Telco*[25] case where the court dealt with Article 19(1)(g). Almost all the cases dealt with levy of tax on inter-State sales. It is necessary to give a very brief background on sales tax before the cases are discussed.

The erstwhile Madras Presidency was the first province to levy sales tax in 1939. Interestingly, the then elected Government was headed by C. Rajagopalachari whom Palkhivala admired immensely. It is fair to state that sales tax laws of most of the then Provinces followed the Madras pattern. For most Provinces, sales tax soon became the most important source of revenue. Under the Government of India Act, 1935, the power of taxation was distributed between the Federal Government at Delhi and the Provincial Governments in various parts of British India. (This excluded the then princely States). Thus, while income tax was to be levied by the Centre, the levy of sales tax was allocated to the Provincial Governments. The earlier case law indicates a veritable frenzy by the Provinces to levy sales tax on any contract that had

---

24. *Builders' Association v. Union of India,* AIR 1989 SC 1371, 1375-1380 : (1989) 2 SCC 645.
25. *Tata Enginering and Locomotive Company Ltd. v. State of Bihar,* AIR 1965 SC 40 : [1964] 6 SCR 885.

even a remote connection with a particular Province. This was done on the principle of 'territorial nexus'. In most cases, a Province sought to levy sales tax even if only one or some of the ingredients that resulted in a sale occurred in that particular Province. For example, in Assam and Bengal, sales tax was levied if the goods were in existence in that particular Province at the time of the contract for sale. Therefore, if goods situated in Calcutta were sold on the basis of a contract made in Madras, sales tax was levied by the Bengal Government on the ground that the goods were in that Province. At the same time, the Province of Madras would also levy sales tax on the ground that the contract was entered into in Madras! In Bihar, if the goods were manufactured in that province, it was treated as a sufficient nexus to levy sales tax. The widest net was cast in the Central Provinces and Berar where sales tax could be levied if the goods were found in that Province *at any time* after the contract for sale or purchase was made! This led to multiple levies of sales tax by different provinces on the same contract for sale leading to a heavy burden on the ultimate consumer.

The chaotic situation that prevailed was noticed by Dr. Ambedkar and he introduced draft articles to reduce the adverse effects of multiple taxation in the Constituent Assembly. Dr. Ambedkar informed the Assembly that sales tax had caused a great deal of difficulty in the matter of freedom of trade and commerce. He further stated that 'this kind of chaos ought not to be allowed' and proposed to limit sales tax. These articles restrained States from levying sales tax on sales that had taken place outside the State or those which were in the course of import or export. For an interesting legislative history of sales tax in the pre-independence years, see the judgment of Venkataramaiah J in the *Builders' Association* case.[26]

The law reports show that Palkhivala appeared in a few important sales tax cases in the Supreme Court and reference can be made to a few of them. In 1960, Palkhivala appeared for the Bombay Chamber of Commerce and Industry which intervened in an important case that involved the interpretation of the expression 'in the course of import' in Article 286(1)(b). A cargo of sugar was sold when the ship was on the high seas to the Government of India which cleared the sugar on payment of the appropriate

26. *Builders' Association v. Union of India,* AIR 1989 SC 1371, 1375-1380 : (1989) 2 SCC 645.

customs duty. Strangely, a writ petition under Article 32 was filed directly in the Supreme Court against the order of the Assistant Collector of Sales Tax! Palkhivala succeeded and it was held that the sugar was sold 'in the course of import' and the order of the Assistant Collector was set aside.[27] Today, no such writ petition would be entertained, particularly under Article 32 by the Supreme Court or even under Article 226 by any High Court. The importer's petition would be dismissed straight away and he would be asked to file an appeal. Surprisingly, there is no discussion in this judgment as to how a writ petition would lie directly under Article 32. What was the fundamental right of the private limited company that was violated?

In another case filed directly before the Supreme Court under Article 32, the Tata Iron & Steel Company Ltd. had challenged the order passed by the Commercial Tax Officer, West Bengal, that sought to levy sales tax on transactions that had already suffered central sales tax. An objection was raised that the petition was not maintainable since no fundamental right of the company was infringed. The Supreme Court held that a threat to recover tax without authority of law would infringe the fundamental right of a citizen under Article 19(1)(g) and the petition was held to be maintainable. This is clearly incorrect as a company is not a citizen. This writ petition should have been dismissed on this ground alone.[28] On merits, the court observed that the sales were inter-State sales and the West Bengal Government had no jurisdiction to tax this transaction. Palkhivala succeeded in this case by a slender margin of 3:2.

Palkhivala had left standing instructions with Ravinder Narain to intervene on behalf of the Tata group of companies if any legal question that affected their interest arose for consideration in the Supreme Court.[29] One such case was filed by Ashok Leyland Ltd., challenging the levy of sales tax on inter-State transactions. The Central Sales Tax Act came into force in 1956, and, before this enactment there were several cases where the State Governments had collected tax on transactions which amounted to inter-State

---

27. *J.V. Gokul & Company Pvt. Ltd. v. Assistant Collector of Sales Tax,* AIR 1960 SC 593: [1960] 2 SCR 852.
28. *Tata Iron and Steel Company Ltd. v. S.R. Sarkar,* AIR 1961 SC 65 : [1961] 1 SCR 379 (Indeed, another petition filed by Tata Engineering and Locomotive Co. Ltd. was rightly dismissed by the Supreme Court in 1965 and this decision is discussed later in this chapter).
29. Today, interveners are not allowed to make oral submissions but have to file only written submissions.

sales and the High Courts had set aside the demand for tax in these cases. To avoid drastic financial consequences of having to refund these taxes, Parliament passed the Sales Tax Validation Act, 1956. This Act declared that no law of any State that levied sales tax on inter-State sales or purchases between April 1, 1951 and September 6, 1955 would be deemed to be invalid. All taxes that were collected by various State Governments were deemed to be validly collected. Thus, all the High Court judgments were set at naught. In the *Ashok Leyland* case, Setalvad appeared for this company and Palkhivala intervened on behalf of Telco. In view of the Validation Act, both the appeals were dismissed.[30]

Another important case argued by Palkhivala was *Singareni Collieries Company Ltd. v. CCT.*[31] The Andhra Pradesh Government sought to levy sales tax on coal that had been allotted to buyers outside that State. At the relevant time, coal was a controlled commodity and could be purchased only on the directions of the Coal Commissioner issued under the Colliery Control Order, 1945. In an interesting judgment, the Supreme Court upheld Palkhivala's argument that coal was transported from the collieries to consumers outside Andhra Pradesh and the transactions must be regarded as 'inter-State sales' and they were not liable to tax under the Hyderabad General Sales Tax Act, 1950. The facts of this case are interesting and show enormous attention to detail. The appeals related to three years 1954-1955, 1955-56 and 1956-1957. These three years were, in turn, divided into four sub-periods and Palkhivala successfully argued that sales tax could not be levied for any sub-period:

(i) Between April 1, 1954 to September 6, 1955, the transactions were not taxable because of the Explanation to Article 286(1). Under this Explanation, only the State in which the goods were *actually delivered* would have the right to levy sales tax. In the present case, coal was actually delivered only in States other than Andhra Pradesh on the basis of orders of the Coal Commissioner.

(ii) Between September 7, 1955 to September 10, 1956, the transactions were not taxable because they were covered by the Explanation to Article 286(1) and also because they were inter-State sales. On September 6, 1955, the

30. *Ashok Leyland Ltd. v. State of Madras*, AIR 1961 SC 1433 : [1962] 1 SCR 607.
31. AIR 1966 SC 563 : [1966] 2 SCR 190.

Supreme Court had held[32] that the State Legislatures could not tax inter-State sales unless Parliament empowered them to do so by a law passed under Article 286(2). Parliament passed the Constitution (Sixth Amendment) Act, 1956 on September 10, 1956, reserving to itself the power to levy tax on inter-State sales, and also omitting the Explanation to Article 286(1). Thus, till September 10, 1956, the Hyderabad State could not levy sales tax unless the delivery took place inside that State.

(iii) During the next period, September 11, 1956 to January 4, 1957, the transactions were not taxable for a very interesting reason. Although Constitution (Sixth Amendment) Act, 1956 was effective from September 10, 1956, the Central Sales Tax Act, 1956 came into force only on January 4, 1957. Therefore, during this period, the State Government could not levy tax because the sales of coal were inter-State sales and the Central Government could not levy tax because there was no Central Act in force!

(iv) For the last period – January 4, 1957 to March 31, 1957 – Palkhivala submitted that only Central Sales Tax was leviable; no sales tax was payable to the State of Andhra Pradesh.[33]

All these contentions were accepted and Singareni Collieries did not have to pay sales tax in Andhra Pradesh for any of the four sub-periods in the three financial years. Equally impressive in this case is the careful marshalling of facts by Justice J.C. Shah.

In 1967, Palkhivala argued one more case for Telco.[34] The State of Bihar once again sought to levy tax on sales that were cleared from stockyards located in States other than Bihar. The Assistant Commissioner of Sales Tax held that sales made from stockyards located in other States were also subject to Bihar sales tax and an assessment order was passed. Instead of filing an appeal, the company filed a writ petition before the Patna High Court on the ground that the Sales Tax Department had wrongly assumed

---

32. *Bengal Immunity Co. Ltd. v. State of Bihar,* AIR 1955 SC 561 : [1955] 2 SCR 603.
33. The State of Andhra Pradesh was formed in 1953.
34. *Tata Engineering and Locomotive Co. Ltd. v. Asst. Commissioner of Commercial Taxes,* AIR 1967 SC 1401 : [1967] 2 SCR 751.

jurisdiction to tax outside sales. The assessment was contrary to the overwhelming evidence on record. The High Court dismissed the writ petition on the ground that Telco should have filed an appeal to the statutory authorities and not come to the High Court directly. On appeal to the Supreme Court, in a strong judgment, Justice Hidayatullah pointed out that there were exceptional cases when the High Court ought to interfere under Article 226. If the assessing authorities act under an invalid law or act arbitrarily without the sanction of law, the High Court can interfere to avoid hardship to an assessee. The Supreme Court remanded the case to the Patna High Court so that the Assistant Commissioner could at least file a counter to the stand taken by Telco. The High Court was asked to ascertain whether there was any basis to levy Bihar sales tax on sales made from stockyards outside Bihar. This case, decided in 1967, demonstrates the arbitrariness of revenue authorities to make absurd demands to meet revenue targets.

Such absurd demands continue to plague assessees, particularly the honest ones, till this date. There is an unfortunate tendency of several High Courts to summarily dismiss writ petitions on grounds of 'alternate remedy' even where the demand made in a show cause notice is absurd. The refusal to entertain writ petitions also increases corruption at the lower levels. The observations of Justice Hidayatullah are very important and emphasise the need for High Courts to prevent the miscarriage of justice by not denying access to justice in genuine cases of hardship.

Three years later, Palkhivala appeared in another case for Telco where the Supreme Court laid down an important principle that no assessment could be made by sampling. It appears that the Assistant Commissioner of Sales Tax treated vehicles sent to stockyards in different States as subject matters of inter-State sales and sought to levy Central Sales Tax. In fact, Telco had paid local sales tax in Bihar when the trucks were sent to different stockyards in various States. Telco's stand was that the movement of trucks to various stockyards was not pursuant to any firm contract and was not in the course of inter-State sales. The Department took one sample transaction and presumed that all vehicles sent to various stockyards were as inter-State sales and liable to sales tax. The Supreme Court allowed the appeal and observed that the Assistant Commissioner ought to have examined individual transactions to determine whether an inter-State sale or a local sale had taken place at different stockyards. It was wrong to assume that all transactions were of a similar nature and levy tax on the basis of a sample transaction.[35]

In 1971, there was another litigation between the State of Bihar and Telco. Once again, it was a case involving inter-State sales and A.K. Sen, the former Law Minister and an eminent Senior Counsel, appeared for the State of Bihar. On merits, the State's appeal was dismissed.[36] In 1973, Palkhivala appeared in another sales tax case but not for the Tatas. Once again, the dispute related to inter-State sales and Palkhivala appeared for Kelvinator, a leading manufacturer of refrigerators.[37] The assessee had its factory at Faridabad in Haryana and manufactured refrigerators under three different brand names. These were sent to the company's godown in Delhi and the distributors placed purchase orders after the goods reached Delhi. The court held that the movement of goods from Faridabad to Delhi was not under any contract of sale and the transactions could not be treated as inter-State sales under the Central Sales Tax Act, 1956.

The last, and perhaps the most important, sales tax case argued by Palkhivala was in 1989 and is popularly referred to as the *Builders' Association of India v. Union of India*.[38] Before discussing this case, one has to go back to 1948 when the Madras Government amended the definition of sale to include 'works contract'. This was successfully challenged before the Madras High Court in 1954[39] and eventually before the Supreme Court in 1958.[40] It held that when a person engages a contractor to construct a building, the contract cannot be split into two different parts. The State Governments have the power to levy sales tax only on 'sale'. This would mean the sale of goods which involves transfer of property from the seller to the buyer. There is no concept of a seller and buyer in a works contract. In a significant observation, the Supreme Court pointed out that the State Governments could not artificially expand their taxing power by treating a works contract as a sale when it did not have the essential ingredients of a sale.

---

35. *Tata Engineering & Locomotive Co. Ltd. v. Asst. Commissioner of Commercial Taxes,* AIR 1970 SC 1281 : (1970) 1 SCC 622.
36. *State of Bihar v. Tata Engineering & Locomotive Co. Ltd.,* AIR 1971 SC 477 : (1970) 3 SCC 697.
37. *Kelvinator India Ltd. v. State of Haryana,* AIR 1973 SC 2526: (1973) 2 SCC 551.
38. *Builders Association of India v. Union of India,* AIR 1989 SC 1371: (1989) 2 SCC 64.
39. *Gannon Dunkerley Ltd. v. State of Madras,* AIR 1954 Mad 1130: (1954) 5 STC 216.
40. *State of Madras v. Gannon Dunkerley Ltd.,* AIR 1958 SC 560: [1959] SCR 349.

The Forty-sixth Amendment, amongst other things, amended the Constitution to permit levy of sales tax on the transfer of property in goods involved in a works contract. Article 366(29A)(b), inserted by this Amendment, reads as follows:

> *(29A) 'tax on the sale or purchase of goods' includes:*
>
> *(a) ...*
>
> *(b) a tax on the transfer of property in goods (whether as goods or in some other form) involved in the execution of a works contract.*

Thus, the State Governments were empowered to levy sales tax on the bricks and cement that would be transferred in a construction contract. After the Forty-sixth Amendment, a number of States made laws to levy sales tax on works contract. The State Governments were under the impression that they could levy tax on works contract without any restriction. Some States went to the extent of levying sales tax on the entire building that was constructed.

Harish Salve remembers Palkhivala's brilliant performance in the *Builders' Association of India v. Union of India*,[41] which is a landmark decision settling the essential principles applicable to the levy of sales tax in respect of a 'works contract' after the Forty-sixth Amendment. Palkhivala was engaged to appear for one of the parties but did not turn up when the batch of cases was called out. Another senior counsel commenced arguments and Salve recollects that this counsel had great difficulty in explaining the concepts of a sale, a 'works contract' and the impact of the Forty-sixth Amendment. For about 30 minutes, he was repeatedly questioned by the Bench and, in particular, by Justice Venkataramaiah. Salve thought that the case was lost. Palkhivala trooped in 35 minutes after the case started. In a brilliant turnaround, Palkhivala was able to lucidly explain the legislative history of the levy of tax in respect of a 'works contract' and the scope of Articles 286, 366(29A) and Entry 54 of List II in the Seventh Schedule to the Constitution. Palkhivala pointed out the dangerous consequences of accepting the view put forth by the Union of India. Palkhivala, according to Salve, single handedly saved this case. A contrary view would have been disastrous.

In a very good judgment, the Supreme Court pointed out that the Forty-sixth Amendment did not confer a greater freedom on

41. AIR 1989 SC 1371 : (1989) 2 SC 645.

the State Governments to levy sales tax on the sale of goods. All that it did was to make it possible for the State Governments to levy sales tax on the price of goods and materials that were used in a works contract. Thus, in the construction of a house, the State Governments could now levy tax on the goods that were involved in the execution of the works contract. This would be treated as a deemed sale, but there was no power with the State Governments to levy sales tax on the entire building that was constructed. The Supreme Court pointed out that even though the State Governments had the power to levy sales tax in respect of a works contract, this power was subject to the restrictions contained in Article 286 and other provisions of the Constitution. The Forty-sixth Amendment only enabled them to levy sales tax on the goods and materials that were used in a composite works contract. This was a major relief for the construction industry and also served as a useful check on the power of the State Governments to levy tax in respect of a works contract. Going by the past experience and the insatiable need for more revenue, the State Governments would certainly have run riot and proceeded to levy tax on the works contract itself i.e. on the entire building.

Justice Venkataramaiah expressed a sense of anguish at the States trying to tax building activities as it could affect housing schemes for the poor and the under-privileged. He wanted the States to consider making suitable classification for lessening the tax burden on housing for the poor. He observed:

> *In exerting this power particularly in relation to transfer of property in goods involved in the execution of 'works-contracts' in building activity, in so far as it affects the housing-projects of the under-privileged and weaker sections of society, the State might perhaps be pushing its taxation-power to the peripheries of the social limits of that power and, perhaps, even of the constitutional limits of that power in dealing with unequals.*

The words of the late Justice Venkataramaiah have obviously fallen on deaf ears. Far from lessening the tax burden, the Central Government has now levied service tax on the labour portion of works contract. Now sales tax or VAT (Value Added Tax) is levied on the materials that are used in construction activity and service tax is levied on the labour portion. No part of a building thus goes untaxed. In addition, all the materials like cement and steel have also suffered excise duty and education cess. To add to the cost, several State Governments have levied horrendous rates of stamp duty. There is virtually no concern for the hapless citizens who have to perhaps spend the greater part of their working life in procuring and repaying a housing loan. It is estimated that taxes and duties approximately constitute almost 30% of the cost of an apartment.

After 1989, Palkhivala does not seem to have appeared in any major sales tax case.

❋

Chapter 8

Labour Cases

Not many know that Palkhivala appeared in a number of labour cases. D.M. Popat[1] recalls that Chief Justice Chagla and Justice Tendolkar constituted a very quick Bench and would finish pending tax references within two months! Therefore, tax work before the Bombay High Court did not occupy him throughout the year. By a convenient coincidence, the Income Tax Appellate Tribunal functioned (and continues to function) mainly in the forenoon. (The afternoons are reserved for dictating orders). On the other hand, in Bombay, the Labour Tribunals worked in the afternoon. Palkhivala would thus finish income tax appeals in the forenoon and rush to the Labour Tribunals and courts in the afternoon. He mainly appeared for the management and was particularly effective in cases that involved accounting issues. At that time, the calculation of bonus and other labour dues was still in the nascent stage and legal principles were yet to be crystallised. Palkhivala's accounting expertise was very useful in arguing these cases.

The law reports indicate that he had argued quite a few important labour cases in the Supreme Court. Palkhivala, at age 39, appeared for the Imperial Bank of India (which became the State Bank of India) and the Central Bank of India before a five-judge Bench that had to decide questions relating to the payment of bonus to the bank employees. M.C. Setalvad appeared for a few other banks. The Banking Companies Act, 1949, was amended in 1956 to permit payment of industrial bonus in pursuance of a settlement or award. The Supreme Court held that the amendment in 1956 did not have any retrospective effect. It, in effect, prohibited the payment of industrial bonus to bank employees before this year.[2] The verdict may be harsh but this was the effect of the law.

---

1. Senior Partner, Mulla and Mulla & Craigie Blunt & Caroe, Advocates & Solicitors, Mumbai.
2. *Central Bank of India v. Their Workmen*, AIR 1960 SC 12 : (1960) 1 SCR 200.

In the same year (1959), he appeared before another Bench for Dunlop Rubber Co. (India) Ltd. Once again, this was an appeal from the Industrial Tribunal and a question arose whether changes in service conditions could be made by the Bombay Tribunal without taking into account the conditions of service in different parts of the country. Palkhivala's argument was that in a company having all India operations, the conditions of service must be uniform. However, this plea was rejected and the Supreme Court held that service conditions could be different if there were unusual features in a particular region.[3]

In 1960, Palkhivala appeared before the Supreme Court for a number of textile mills from Ahmedabad and succeeded on a technical plea.[4] In appeals against the orders of the Industrial Tribunal, the Federal Court and the Supreme Court had earlier held that industrial adjudication could involve the creation of a new obligation which may not be permissible in an ordinary civil suit.[5] Industrial adjudication was intended to further social justice and secure peace and harmony between employers and workmen. But the Industrial Tribunal, the court held, could not determine the quantum of bonus in a general manner. It was necessary to arrive at the quantum of bonus to be awarded in the case of each concern. Further, the Tribunal could not apply what was popularly called the 'Full Bench formula' as set out in the *Associated Cement Companies* case.[6] When the employers and the workmen had signed the 1953 agreement for bonus for five years, it was not open to the industrial court to extend it for one more year. The Supreme Court, by majority, allowed the appeal 'with regret'.[7]

In another case later that year, Palkhivala again succeeded on a technical plea. A reference made by the Government covered all demands of the workmen except the demand for inspection of accounts in connection with certain service charges. The Tribunal, however, directed access to the account books, and this was set aside as being outside its jurisdiction. The Tribunal had also granted the demand for a wage increase without any definite

---

3. *Dunlop Rubber Co. (India) Ltd. v. Workmen*, AIR 1960 SC 207 : (1960) 2 SCR 51.
4. *New Maneck Chowk Spg. & Wvg. Co. Ltd. v. Textile Labour Assn.*, AIR 1961 SC 867: [1961] 3 SCR 1.
5. *Western India Automobile Association v. Industrial Tribunal*, AIR 1949 FC 111; *Rohtas Industries Ltd. v. Brijnandan Pandey*, AIR 1957 SC 1: [1956] SCR 800.
6. *Associated Cement Companies Ltd. v. Workmen*, AIR 1959 SC 967 : [1959] SCR 925.
7. *New Maneck Chowk, ibid.*

finding about the financial capacity of the company to meet such increase in liability; this was also set aside.[8]

In 1966, Palkhivala appeared for the Reserve Bank of India where the court discussed the scope of Article 43 of the Constitution that made payment of living wages part of the Directive Principles of State Policy.[9] The employees were represented by A.S.R. Chari, a very capable counsel with Marxist leanings. Justice Hidayatullah complimented Chari in the judgment by observing: '*we have been addressed by able and very moving arguments on behalf of the employees by Mr. Chari*'. At another place, he noted that Chari had made his submissions with '*customary earnestness and ability and with commendable restraint*'. Palkhivala was also complimented to a lesser degree for showing concern for the employees' point of view and agreeing to consider their demands favourably on some of the less important issues. It is some indication of Palkhivala's stature at the Bar that he was called upon to appear for the Reserve Bank of India even in an industrial dispute.

The penultimate major labour case in which Palkhivala appeared was the famous *Jalan Trading* case,[10] where certain provisions of the Payment of Bonus Act, 1965, were challenged. This Act made payment of minimum bonus mandatory. A writ petition was filed by Punalur Paper Mills Ltd. and M.C. Setalvad appeared for the company. Palkhivala appeared not only for the Jalan Trading Company which had preferred an appeal from the Industrial Court of Bombay but also for several other textile mills and the Tata Oil Mills Ltd. The Supreme Court in the *Associated Cement Companies* case[11] had laid down a formula for payment of bonus and this was popularly called the 'Full Bench Formula'. In 1965, the Payment of Bonus Act made it mandatory to provide bonus to all employees then drawing a salary of Rs. 1,600/- or less per month. Bonus, which originally contemplated a payment to workmen out of profit, soon became a statutory obligation and had to be paid even if profits were not earned. The Act also provided for payment of minimum and maximum bonus. The Supreme Court struck down Section 33 which imposed *retrospective* liability to pay bonus from 1963 only on those companies that had a dispute pending on the

8. *Airlines Hotel Private Ltd. v. Workmen,* AIR 1962 SC 676.
9. *All India Reserve Bank Employees' Assn. v. Reserve Bank of India,* AIR 1966 SC 305 : [1966] 1 SCR 25.
10. *Jalan Trading Company v. Mill Mazdoor Sabha,* AIR 1967 SC 691 : [1967] 1 SCR 15.
11. *Associated Cement Companies Ltd. v. Workmen,* AIR 1959 SC 967 : [1959] SCR 925.

issue of bonus immediately before May 29, 1965 – the date on which Payment of Bonus Ordinance had come into force. Such companies had to pay bonus even if they did not have adequate profit. If there was no pending dispute on May 29, 1965, then an employer was liable to pay bonus only if there were adequate profits from 1960 to 1965. This was held to be completely arbitrary. A classification merely based on the existence of a dispute on a pending date was unreasonable and liable to be struck down. Similarly, Section 34 was also struck down as it sought to impose an arbitrary ratio to cover the distribution of surplus profits. Further, the Supreme Court struck down Section 39 which conferred extensive powers on the Central Government.

After the *Jalan Trading* case, Palkhivala argued his last important labour case,[12] that has ironically been subsequently cited and followed in several income tax cases. Every company had to pay bonus on the basis of allocable surpluses calculated under the Payment of Bonus Ordinance which subsequently became the Payment of Bonus Act, 1965. Metal Box Co. of India Ltd., while calculating the allocable surplus, claimed deduction for the gratuity payable to its employees. It had introduced a gratuity scheme for its employees, other than officers, and claimed deduction for the estimated liability towards payment of gratuity. Now, the amount of gratuity depended on the number of years of service, wages and the last wages drawn was determined on the basis of actuarial valuation. The company made provision on the basis of such estimated liability and debited the estimated amounts to the profit and loss account. When an employee actually retired, the amount of gratuity payable to him was debited against the provision that had been made earlier. Consequently, the actual payment was not debited to the profit and loss account. The employees argued that the company could get deduction only on the amount that was actually paid each year. An estimated liability towards gratuity based on actuarial valuation was not deductible. Even if such estimated liability was deductible, such appropriation towards a future liability would be a reserve and would have to be added back to the Second Schedule. In a landmark decision, the Supreme Court held that the assessees maintaining their accounts on the mercantile system could claim deduction for accrued gratuity even if gratuity was paid at a future date. It is not necessary deductions should be claimed only on the amounts actually expended or paid.

---

12. *Metal Box Co. of India Ltd. v. Workmen*, AIR 1969 SC 612 : (1969) 73 ITR 53.

When working out the net profit, a businessman can claim a deduction for the liability which is properly ascertainable; even if the liability is to be discharged at a future date, a deduction can be claimed for the discounted present value of such liability. If such deductions were permissible under the Income Tax Act, 1961, to arrive at the true profits and gains, there was no reason why the same could not be done under the Payment of Bonus Act, 1965. The Supreme Court also held that the amounts debited to the Profit and Loss account on actuarial basis could not be treated as a 'reserve'; as the amounts were set aside to discharge the known liability to pay gratuity, it was a provision. In a classic passage, the court held:

> *'An amount set aside out of profits and other surpluses, not designed to meet a liability, contingency, commitment or diminution in value of assets known to exist at the date of the balance sheet is a reserve but an amount set aside out of profits and other surpluses to provide for any known liability of which the amount cannot be determined with substantial accuracy is a provision'.*

This case continues to be one of the leading authorities on the distinction between the meaning of a 'provision' and a 'reserve' in commercial accounting.

After the *Metal Box* case, Palkhivala does not seem to have argued any important labour case.

❄

Chapter 9

Representing India

International Cases

The Kutch – Sind dispute

Soon after his 46th birthday, Palkhivala was asked to represent the Government of India before an International Tribunal constituted to decide a long pending boundary dispute between India and Pakistan.[1]

Unlike income tax appeals which were confined to determination of questions of law, the case before the International Tribunal involved extensive examination of documentary evidence starting from 1819 until 1947, when both India and Pakistan became independent. As this was a boundary dispute, Palkhivala also had to examine numerous maps. Ably assisted by an excellent team of officials, Palkhivala's arguments were instrumental in India getting 90% of the Great Rann of Kutch. Apart from his back-breaking schedule in dealing with cases and opinions in India, Palkhivala now had to constantly travel to Geneva and London for this case which was to last almost three years.

K.V. Kamath, in his excellent biography,[2] has set out Palkhivla's arguments in detail. Palkhivala went into the historical records and began with the treaty between the Ruler of Kutch and the East India Company that assured British protection to the State of Kutch. He then went into the historic origin of Sind and how it eventually became a part of British India. It took fifteen years, between 1855-1870, to demarcate the boundary between the princely State of Kutch and the province of Sind. But disputes continued and were eventually resolved by the then Government of

---

1. Five years later, he was to represent India once again before the International Civil Aviation Organization and the International Court of Justice.
2. M.V. Kamath, *Nani Palkhivala: A life*, pp. 124-134.

India which came out with a map in 1914 that delineated the boundary limits of Sind and Kutch.

After independence, India and Pakistan were partitioned and a new boundary was drawn on the basis of the Radcliffe Award,[3] and boundary disputes between the two countries surfaced again.

Kamath has set out Palkhivala's scatching criticism of the arguments put forth by Pakistan.[4] He argued that Pakistan case was based on three theories:-

(a) *The General Theory of Confusion*: Pakistan's case was that the map-makers and the administrators were all generally confused as to where the boundary really lay.

(b) *The Special Theory of Confusion*: Pakistan's contention was that certain people were especially confused on particular occasions when they treated the whole of the Rann as belonging to Kutch.

(c) *The Theory of a Century of Error*: This theory virtually suggested that, for a hundred years, everybody made an error as to what precisely were the boundaries of the territory conquered by the British in 1843 when they took control of Sind.

The Arbitral Tribunal painstakingly considered these submissions and passed an award running into 579 pages.

Kutch was a princely State under the suzerainty of the British Crown but the province of Sind formed part of British India. British India was partitioned under the Indian Independence Act, 1947 and eventually became the Republic of India and the Islamic Republic of Pakistan. After independence, the province of Sind merged with Pakistan while Kutch and other native states on the western border merged with India. There was a running dispute between the two countries on the exact demarcation of the boundary between Sind and Kutch (which later became part of the State of Gujarat) in the Great Rann of Kutch. While India claimed that there was no territorial dispute as the boundary was well established along the northern-edge of the Rann of Kutch as shown in the pre-partition maps, Pakistan claimed that there was a dispute involving 3500 sq. miles of territory. The borders between India

3. Viscount Cyril Radcliffe was a leading barrister and became a Law Lord. In 1962, he was made hereditary peer.
4. Kamath M.V., *Nani Palkhiivala: A life*, pp. 126-127.

and Pakistan was always tense and the first major war between India and Pakistan broke out in 1965.

On June 30, 1965, an agreement was reached between India and Pakistan which *inter alia*, provided: (i) there would be cease-fire commencing at 3 a.m. on July 1, 1965; (ii) restoration of *status quo* as on January 1, 1965 in the area of Gujarat and West Pakistan border; with a view to reduce tension along the entire India-Pakistan border. (iii) a Tribunal would be constituted consisting of three persons, none of whom was to be a national of either India or Pakistan. However, each country could nominate one member and the Chairman was to be jointly selected by both countries. If they failed to agree, the Secretary General of the United Nations would nominate the Chairman.

While India nominated Alex Bebler, a judge of the Constitution Court of Yugoslavia, Pakistan nominated Nasrollah Entezam, an Iranian diplomat who had earlier served as President of the General Assembly of the United Nations. As both countries could not agree upon a Chairman, the Secretary General of the United Nations nominated Gunnar Lagergen, then the President of the Court of Appeals for Western Sweden as the Chairman of the Tribunal.

The hearings began from February 1966 at the Hotel De Ville, Geneva and later, the venue shifted to the Palace of Nations in the same city. Eventually, the hearings lasted for two years. By drawing of lots, India was to make the opening statement. The Tribunal had to consider extensive documents, maps and photographs. The Tribunal was also shown documentary films produced by Pakistan. The award indicates that the total documents ran to 10,000 pages in addition to 350 maps produced as evidence.[5] The award, by majority, awarded was 90% of the disputed to India and Pakistan got the balance including much of the high ground where the heaviest fighting took place. The Indian nominated judge, Alex Bebler ruled the entire disputed territory in favour of India. The strength of India's presentation can be seen in the fact that, Nasrollah Entezam, the judge nominated by Pakistan made the following observations in his short concurring judgment:

> *In an early stage, I considered that Pakistan had made out a clear title to the northern half of the area shown in the Survey Maps as the Rann. I have now had the advantage of*

5. The interested reader can access the award at http://untreaty.un.org/cod/riaa/cases/VolXVII/1-576.pdf.

reading the Opinion of the learned Chairman, and in the light of it I concur in and endorse the judgment of the learned Chairman.

The implementation of the award was not free from controversy. Palkhivala declared the award as a victory for India since 90 per cent of the land claimed had been awarded in its favour. However, the award of Kanjarkot, Chhadbet, Dharabanni, Priol Valo Kun and the two inlets on either side of Tharparkar to Pakistan was resented by the Indian public and politicians. While Prime Minister Indira Gandhi said that the award was not entirely judicial and had taken 'certain political considerations' into account, she did not advocate its repudiation. Strangely, M.C. Chagla, a former Chief Justice of the Bombay High Court and Minister for External Affairs, bitterly criticised the award and termed it a political rather than a judicial verdict and argued against its implementation.[6] Taking a contrary position, Jayaprakash Narayan and C. Rajagopalachari advocated acceptance of the award. In Pakistan, surprisingly, the award was free from public controversy barring a few grumblings of disappointment in some quarters.[7]

The award was also challenged before a Constitution Bench of the Supreme Court of India in *Maganbhai Ishwarbhai Patel v. Union of India,*[8] where the petitioners challenged the authority of the Indian Government to cede Indian territory without the approval of Parliament. The Court held that the territory was genuinely disputed and cannot be considered to be a cession of territory requiring a constitutional amendment.

The demarcation work on the ground began in March, 1968 and was completed in June, 1969 with the erection of 906 concrete boundary pillars along 408 kilometeres of the disputed territory. The field teams were given a discretion to settle differences upto 100 yards without referring back to their parent Governments. The boundary became effective from the midnight of July 5, 1969 and the Tribunal was dissolved in Stockhom, Sweden.[9]

It is also of contemporary relevance that the Tribunal's Award excluded the short agreed border from the head of Sir Creek

6. Chagla was then a member of the Rajya Sabha.
7. See Mukund G. Untawale, 'The Kutch Sind dispute: A Case Study in International Arbitration', 23 I.C.L.Q. 818. For another interesting article, see J. Gillis Wetter, 'The Rann of Kutch Arbitration', 65 Am.J. Int'l L.346 (1971).
8. (1970) 3 SCC 400 : AIR 1969 SC 783.
9. See Mukund G. Untawale, 'The Kutch Sind dispute: A Case Study in International Arbitration', 23 I.C.L.Q. 818.

eastward. Both India and Pakistan had agreed to exclude the boundary from the head of Sir Creek downward to the west. After many rounds of talks at various levels, both countries have still not been able to resolve the dispute and this has been a thorn in Indo-Pakistan relations to the present day. The regular arrest and alleged ill-treatment of fisherman on both sides for violation of claimed sovereign territory remains a constant irritant.

Banning Pakistani aircraft in Indian airspace

On January 30, 1971, an Indian Airlines aircraft took off from Srinagar airport and was to land at Jammu. On board were 32 persons including the Captain, co-pilot and two inflight attendants. Two hijackers on board soon forced the pilot at gunpoint to take the aircraft to Lahore. After landing, they asked the passengers and crew to disembark and blew up the aircraft. All this while, Pakistani authorities remained mute spectators.

India swiftly reacted to this outrageous act and banned, with immediate effect, all Pakistani aircraft from flying over the territory of India. This had drastic consequences since Pakistan at that time consisted of East Pakistan which required their aircraft to fly over India. Pakistani aircraft would now have to reach Dacca via Colombo which obviously resulted in a huge increase in the cost of travel apart from longer travel duration. When India demanded the handover of all the hijackers, Pakistan refused on the ground that they were not Indians but Kashmiris![10]

In response to the ban, Pakistan filed a complaint before the International Civil Aviation Organisation. The ICAO Tribunal had its seat in Montreal, Canada. India, represented by Palkhivala, raised a preliminary objection to the maintainability of the complaint itself as this was not a question relating to the interpretation or the application of the provisions of the convention or the transit agreement. On July 29, 1971, the Council rejected India's preliminary objections on the jurisdiction of the ICAO.

International Court of Justice

On August 30, 1971, the case was taken to the International Court of Justice (ICJ) by India under Article 84 of the Chicago Convention, Article II of the Transit Agreement, read with Articles

---

10. Over the last 60 years, nothing has really changed and Kashmir continues to be a simmering problem.

36 and 37 of the Statute of the International Court of Justice. Palkhivala was Chief Counsel for India and opened arguments. Here, Pakistan raised objections to the ICJ's jurisdiction. Pakistan was represented by Yahya Bakhtiar, later Attorney-General for Pakistan. Bakhtiar subsequently became famous for defending former President Zulfiqar Ali Bhutto.[11]

The oral arguments reveal an intense intellectual duel marked by unfailing courtesy – both on the part of counsel and judges. Another striking feature of the record is how organized the oral presentation of Palkhivala was. He addressed every point, then responded to questions from the judges and finally summarised the arguments for the convenience of the court. Every argument is referenced to the relevant document along with page number of the record. His arguments were based on many grounds: historical, logical, and legal. His application of logic to international law and illustrated by examples was particularly incisive.

The net result was that India succeeded on the point of the ICJ's jurisdiction by a majority of 13:3, but failed to convince the Court that the ICAO was incompetent to entertain Pakistan's complaint. Hence, the matter was 'remanded' to the ICAO whose competence to entertain the complaint was recognized. However, the court refused to define the exact extent of the competence and left it for future adjudication.

Matters on the ground overtook the pace of international judicial processes. While this matter was being heard in the ICAO Council and the ICJ, India and Pakistan went to war again and the newly independent State of Bangaldesh came into being.

Palkhivala's appearances for India before the International Court of Justice and two Tribunals are the finest testimony to his reputation and versatility. In the Kutch-Sind dispute, he was just 46 years old! The combination of brilliance and eloquence made him one of the most persuasive counsel to have argued not only in Indian Courts but in international fora as well.

❃

11. Bhutto was sentenced to death and later executed.

Appendices

Appendix I

The Copyright Case

Sampath Iyengar v. Sir Jamshedji B. Kanga

In the High Court of Judicature at Madras
Ordinary Original Civil Jurisdiction
C. S. No. 350 of 1951

A.C. Sampath Iyengar, Plaintiff v. (1) Sir Jamshedji B. Kanga,
(2) N.A. Palkhivala, (3) N.M. Tripathi Ltd., Defendants

(a) **Plaint under Order 4, Rule 1 Original Side Rules and Section 6 and 7 of the Copyright Act, 1911**

The aforesaid plaintiff begs to state as follows:

(1) The plaintiff is an Advocate of this Honourable Court. The permanent address of the plaintiff is 'Kesava Prasad', 29, Luz Church Road, Mylapore, Madras. The address for service of the plaintiff is that of his Advocate Sri S. Krishnamachariar, 27, Law Chambers, High Court Buildings, Madras.

(2) The first defendant is an advocate of the Bombay High Court and his address for service is – Advocates' Chambers, High Court Buildings, Bombay.

The second defendant also is an advocate of the Bombay High Court and his address for service is Advocates' Chambers, High Court Buildings, Bombay.

The third defendant is a law publishing company having office at Princess Street, Bombay 2, and the same is the address for its service.

(3) The plaintiff is the author of a literary work entitled 'The Indian Income-tax Act'. The first edition of the same was published in 1941, the second edition in 1945 and the third in the year 1947. Volume I of the fourth edition was published in November 1951 and Volume II is expected to be released in the new year 1952.

(4) The plaintiff's book is a highly popular book consulted by all Income-tax practitioners and courts and lawyers and particularly by the Income-tax Department. The Central Board of Revenue, Government of India, has awarded priority of recognition to the plaintiff's book. The plaintiff is the owner of the copyright in the said book including the 1947 edition of the same.

(5) During the close of the year 1950, the defendants 1 and 2 as joint authors and defendant 3 as publisher brought out a book entitled 'The Law and Practice of Income Tax'. In that book, the defendants

have infringed the plaintiff's copyright in his 'Indian Income-tax Act' and especially the 1947 edition. The defendants have reproduced substantial portions of the plaintiff's book in a material form and they have largely utilised the labours of the plaintiff. The defendants have converted the plaintiff's property in his book, in several contexts and in several places.

(6) The plaintiff thereupon, through his solicitors, caused notice to be sent to all the defendants on 1st August 1951 charging them with infringement of copyright and demanding of the defendants compensation and adequate amends. The defendants by their solicitors prayed for time and after some correspondence finally intimated by their notice dated 12th September, 1951, refuting the plaintiff's charge and declining to make any amends, much less any compensation.

(7) The plaintiff learns that defendants have sold all the copies published by them. The defendants have in consequence made unlawful gain and caused damage to the plaintiff.

(8) The plaintiff files herewith marked as document 'C', a list of some instances in parallel columns of the acts of piracy committed by the defendants. The books themselves are herewith filed – the plaintiff's work being marked as Document (A) and defendants' as Document (B). The plaintiff craves leave to refer to the said documents in greater detail and also to submit further instances of infringement and piracy.

(9) The plaintiff submits that he is entitled to a decree for injunction restraining the defendants in future from reproducing a similar work, and for compensation by way of damages for the defendant's infringement of plaintiff's copyright and his conversion of the plaintiff's property in his (plaintiff's) work.

(10) The plaintiff's book was published in Madras City and was also sold in the State of Madras amongst other places. The defendants have published and sold many copies of their book in the Madras State and in the Madras City directly and through agents. Hence a part of the cause of action has arisen within the jurisdiction of this Hon'ble Court. The said cause of action arose in 1947 and subsequently when the plaintiff's book was published and being sold and in 1950 and 1951 when the defendants printed, published and sold their infringing copies in Madras City and Madras State and elsewhere.

(11) The plaintiff values the suit for the purpose of Court fees and jurisdiction at Rs.10,500/- and pays a court fee of Rs. 768.10.0

Details of the valuation

(1)	Valuation for making account of the damages awardable to the plaintiff.	.. Rs.10,000
	Plaintiff is prepared to pay extra court fee on such further sum as may be awarded by the Court	
(2)	Valuation for Injunction Relief	.. Rs. 500
	Total	.. Rs.10,500

(12) The plaintiff therefore prays for a decree:

(a) directing an account to be taken of the number of copies printed and published by the defendants of their book entitled 'The Law and Practice of Income Tax' and sold by them, or any of them, or by their agents or servants and of the profits made by them thereby.

(b) for payment to the plaintiff as and by way of damages for the profits so made by the defendants or such portion thereof as may be determined by this Honourable Court.

(c) for an injunction restraining the defendants, their servants and agents from reproducing or authorising reproduction of any further edition or reprint of the defendants' book entitled 'The Law and Practice of Income Tax' and from their committing any act of infringement or conversion of the plaintiff's copyright in his work entitled 'The Indian Income-tax Act'.

(d) for costs of this suit and

(e) for such further and other reliefs as this Honourable Court may deem fit and proper in the circumstances of this case.

Counset for Plaintiff **Plaintiff**

Verification

I, A.C. Sampath Iyengar, the plaintiff abovenamed do hereby declare that what is stated in paragraphs 1 to 6 and 8 to 12 are true to my knowledge and what is stated in paragraph 7 is stated on information and belief and I believe the same to be true.

Dated at Madras this day 22nd November, 1951.

Plaintiff

Documents filed with the plaint

A. 'The Indian Income-tax Act' by Plaintiff 1947.

B. 'The Law and Practice of Income-tax' by defendants 1950.

C. 'List of some instances of the acts of piracy by the defendants'

Plaintiff

In the High Court of Judicature at Madras
Ordinary Original Civil Jurisdiction
C.S. No. 350 of 1951

A.C. Sampath Iyengar, Plaintiff v. (1) Sir Jamshedji B. Kanga, (2) N.A. Palkhivala, (3) N.M. Tripathi Ltd., Defendants

Under Order 4 Rule 1 Original Side Rules and Sections 6 and 7 of the Copyright Act, 1911.

(b) The Written Statement of Kanga & Palkhivala

1. These defendants say that no part of the cause of action has arisen in Madras and no part of the alleged conversion or alleged infringement of the Plaintiff's copyright has taken place in Madras. The defendants submit that this Hon'ble Court has no jurisdiction to entertain or try this suit.

2. Without prejudice to the above, these defendants say that the 3rd defendants who are the publishers of these defendants' book had the sole right to sell and they alone have sold the first edition of this defendants' book. These defendants have not published or sold any copy or copies of their book anywhere. These defendants, therefore, submit that in any event so far as these defendants are concerned, this Honourable Court has no jurisdiction to entertain or try this suit.

3. Without prejudice to the aforesaid submissions and contentions, these defendants submit that the plaintiff is not entitled to an injunction as prayed for, since he has come to Court after great delay. These defendants' book was published in or about October 1950 and the entire edition was sold out by February 1951. The book became widely known on its publication and these defendants believe that the plaintiff was aware of the book and its contents before the edition was sold out by February 1951. The plaintiff sent to these defendants his Solicitors' notice dated 1st August 1951, which was received in Bombay on or about the 4th August 1951. The plaintiff's 93-page compilation in book form, which contained particulars of the alleged infringement, was received by the 2nd and 3rd defendants on or about the 6th or 7th August 1951. The 2nd and the 3rd defendants by their Attorneys' letter dated the 14th of August 1951 totally denied the false charge of infringement and stated that a detailed reply would be sent upon the return to India of the 1st defendant who was at that time in Europe. Upon the return of the 1st defendant from Europe, a detailed reply was sent to the plaintiff by the defendants' Attorneys' letter dated the 12th of September 1951, again totally denying the false charges levelled by the plaintiff against the defendants. These defendants will rely on and crave leave to refer to the correspondence referred to hereinabove when produced. The present prayer for injunction in the suit filed at the end of November 1951 is a belated one, and these defendants submit that the same should be refused on the ground of laches and delay.

4. With reference to paragraph 3 of the Plaint these defendants say that the portions of the plaintiff's book in respect of which infringement is alleged do not constitute original literary work.

5. With reference to para 4 of the Plaint, these defendants are not aware of and do not admit the statements made therein save and except that the plaintiff is the owner of the copyright in his book.

6. With reference to para 5 of the Plaint, these defendants deny that they have infringed the plaintiff's copyright in his 'Indian Income-tax Act', and/or specially the 1947 edition thereof, or that they have reproduced substantial or any portion or portions of the plaintiff's book in a material form or at all, or have at all utilized the labours of the plaintiff, or have converted the plaintiff's property in his book in any context or in any place or in any manner whatever. These defendants say that the plaintiff has no cause of action against the defendants.

7. With reference to para 6 of the Plaint, these defendants deny that by their Solicitors' letter they prayed for time. These defendants will rely on and crave leave to refer to the correspondence between the Attorneys of the parties when produced.

8. With reference to para 7 of the Plaint, these defendants deny that they have made any unlawful gain or caused any injury to the plaintiff.

9. With reference to para 8 of the Plaint, Document 'C' has been dealt with hereinafter. These defendants deny that they have committed any act of

infringement or piracy whatsoever. These defendants say that the plaintiff is bound to give particulars of the alleged infringement or piracy, and is not entitled to submit any further instances or particulars of alleged infringement or piracy at any time he chooses.

10. With reference to para 9 of the plaint, these defendants deny all the allegations and submissions contained therein.

11. With reference to para 10 of the plaint, these defendants deny that they have published or sold any copy or copies of their book in the Madras State or in the Madras City directly or through agents. These defendants say that the 3rd defendant alone (and not these defendants) published and sold copies of these defendants' book, but even the said publication and sales by the 3rd defendant were effected wholly in Bombay and nowhere else. These defendants say that all offers or orders for the book from Madras City and elsewhere were accepted by the 3rd defendant in Bombay; all the contracts were effected and made in Bombay; and all such contracts were executed and performed by the 3rd defendant wholly in Bombay in each and every case. These defendants repeat that no part of the alleged cause of action against the defendants or in any event against these defendants, has arisen within the jurisdiction of this Honourable Court. These defendants deny that the alleged cause of action arose in 1947 or subsequently. These defendants deny that they or the 3rd defendants have printed, published or sold a single copy of these defendants' book in the Madras State or the Madras City.

12. With reference to para 12 of the Plaint, these defendants deny that the plaintiff is entitled to any of the reliefs claimed.

13. These defendants say that their commentary on the Indian Income Tax Act is the result, first, of a careful and independent study of each and every case cited therein and the various provisions of the Act as amended from time to time, and secondly, of their practical experience as Income Tax practitioners.

14. The 1st defendant has commanded a very large Income Tax practice for some decades and has seen in active practice the evolution and growth of case law on the subject from the very commencement of the Indian Income Tax Act, 1922. The 1st defendant has figured as Counsel in innumerable cases in which the principles enunciated in these defendants' book have been dealt with and applied and in which the cases cited in these defendants' book have been referred to and considered. The 2nd defendant also commands a considerable practice in the field of Income Tax and other fields. The 2nd defendant himself read for the purpose of writing these defendants' book, not only the head-note but the judgment in each of the cases cited in these defendants' book, without exception.

15. With particular reference to Document 'C', these defendants say as follows:

> 'These defendants say that they followed the usual and well-established plan and arrangement of a legal commentary in writing their book. These defendants say that the sources of their commentary, apart from their practical experience as practitioners, are case law and the provisions of the Statute, both of which are, naturally, also the source of the plaintiff's commentary. These common sources explain the few so-called 'similarities', if at all there be any, to which the plaintiff refers in his document 'C'. These defendants say that the phrases and sentences in respect of which the plaintiff charges these defendants with piracy in the said Document 'C' can be easily traced to well known decided cases accurately cited at the

appropriate places in these defendants' book, or to the language of the very section or Rule to which the commentary relates. These defendants will substantiate at the hearing of the suit their case on this point by pointing out the particular decided cases and the particular sections or Rules in which the various phrases have become the current coin of Income-Tax law, and these defendants say and submit that the plaintiff's claim to copyright in respect of them is untenable.'

16. These defendants say that they have copied, borrowed or adopted nothing whatsoever from any part of the plaintiff's book in point of matter, style, arrangement or plan or in any other particular; nor have they committed any act of piracy or any infringement at all of the plaintiff's copyright in any place or in any manner. These defendants say that they have incorporated in their commentary what in their opinion were the correct propositions of law and the most appropriate decided cases and the best passages or phrases from Law Reports, and that they were not deterred or debarred from doing so by reason of the possibility that any of such propositions, cases, passages or phrases might have been adopted or dealt with by previous commentators. These Defendants say that save in cases where they have been tied down to the language of the Statutes or a decided case, these defendants' style and mode of expression are patently different from the plaintiff's. These defendants say that even a cursory comparative glance at the two commentaries would clearly indicate these defendants' originality of thought, substance, expression and presentation on every topic. These defendants say that if any casual 'similarities' of phrase or expression at all appear on the surface here and there, they are inevitable in any lengthy commentaries on the same Statutes of which the principles are well settled by a large body of case law. But the treatment and development by these defendants of all topics including the topics referred to in Document 'C' are entirely different from the plaintiff's; while the matter and substance of these defendants' commentary, no less than the style and order of treatment, owe nothing whatever to the plaintiff's publication.

17. With further particular reference to Document 'C', these defendants say that in Document 'C' the plaintiff has vainly tried to set up cases of similarity where none in fact exist. These defendants say that the Document 'C' has been prepared in a very misleading manner. In several places in Document 'C', in quoting passages from these defendant's book, the plaintiff has omitted references to decided cases given accurately in these defendants' book, or has presented passages from these defendants' book in a truncated form or in an inverted order, so as to give to the plaintiff's commentary a false colour of originality and to give the corresponding portions of these defendants' commentary a false air of plagiarism; whereas a reference to and examination of the decided cases or the commentary on the topic as a whole in these Defendants' book would immediately negative any idea of these defendants' having copied from the plaintiff's book. These defendants say that many of the topics dealt with in the passages cited in Document 'C' are topics which occur very frequently in Income Tax practice and the principles' and cases applicable are extremely well known and are repeatedly cited. Document 'C' shows that the plaintiff apparently claims copyright in the language and phraseology of classic judgments, in well known legal expressions, in elementary propositions of law and, on occasions, even in ordinary words of English language which are the only appropriate words in a particular context. These defendants say that the plaintiff's claim is fantastic. These defendants crave leave to refer in detail to every passage given in Document 'C' at the time of hearing of the suit.

18. These defendants repeat that if their book is read as a whole or at least the commentary on any given topic is read as a whole and compared with the plaintiff's commentary, it would be immediately apparent, as the truth is, that these defendants' commentary is the result of entirely independent study and is strikingly different from and owes nothing whatever to the plaintiff's book.

19. These defendants say that the suit is false and vexatious and submit that it should be dismissed with costs.

Written Statement drawn by:)	Sd/- J.B. Kanga
Messrs. Gagrat and Co., and)	**Defendant No.1**
Settled by R.J. Kolah Esqr.,)	Sd/- N.A. Palkhivala
Advocate, High Court, Bombay.)	**Defendant No.2**

We, Sir Jamshed Behramji Kanga of Bombay, Indian Inhabitant, residing at Walkeshwar Road, Bombay, the 1st defendant abovenamed and Nani A. Palkhivala, also of Bombay, Indian Inhabitant, residing at Slater Road, Grant Road, Bombay, do respectively solemnly declare that what is stated in paragraphs 2, 3 (part), 4, 5, 6, 7, 8, 9, 10, 11 (part), 12 (part), 13, 14, 15, 16, 17 and 18 of the foregoing Written Statement is true to my[1] own knowledge and what is stated in the remaining paragraphs 1, 3 (part), 11 (part) and 12 (part) is stated on information and belief and [2]I believe the same to be true.

Dated this 25th day of January 1952.
Sd/-
Defendants 1 & 2
King & Patridge
Attorneys for the Defendants

In the High Court of Judicature at Madras
Ordinary Original Civil Jurisdiction
The Hon'ble Mr. Justice Panchapakesa Ayyar

C.S. No. 350 of 1951

A.C. Sampath Ayengar, Plaintiff vs. Sir Jamshedji B. Kanga and two others, Defendants

(c) Judgment

This is a suit filed by the A.C.Sampath Ayyangar,[3] an advocate of this Court, against Sir Jamshedji Kanga, an advocate of the Bombay High Court, and Mr. N.A. Palkhivala, another advocate of the Bombay High Court, and N.M. Tripathi Ltd., Bombay, Booksellers and Publishers, for alleged infringement of his copyright in his book, 'The Indian Income-tax Act', Ex. P-1, by the first and second defendants pirating passages from the book and doing various other acts of infringement like adopting similar treatment, analysis, commentaries on sections, compilation and knitting, and quoting the very passages from his commentary and from extracts quoted from the decisions by the plaintiff, and using his characteristic phraseology and coined expressions, and headings, and adopting his

1. The word 'my' instead of 'our' is typed in the original written statement.
2. 'I' has been wrongly mentioned in the written statement, it should have been 'me'.
3. Although the plaintiff's name is 'A.C. Sampath Iyengar' is the plaint, the judgment has used 'A.C. Sampath Ayyangar'.

criticisms of sections and decisions, and even his italics, through cunningly changing a word here and a word there and transposing passages in footnotes to the body of the book and passages in the body of the book to the footnotes in a dishonest attempt to camouflage the piracy in the book titled 'The Law and Practice of Income-tax', Ex P-2, written by defendants 1 and 2 and published by the third defendant, in 1950, in Bombay. The suit was filed in this Court as copies of Ex. P-2 were said to have been sold in Madras City in 1950 and 1951. The plaintiff prayed for an account to be taken of the number of copies printed and published by the defendants of their book, Ex. P-2, and for payment to the plaintiff, by way of damages, the profits made by the defendants, or such portion thereof, as determined by this Court, for infringing his copyright and converting his book, Ex. P-1, dishonestly, in the book Ex. P-2, and for an injunction restraining the defendants, their servants and agents, from reproducing or authorising the reproduction of any further edition or re-print of Ex. P-2 or any further infringement or conversion of the plaintiff's copyright in Ex. P-1, and for costs. The plaintiff valued the relief for damages regarding conversion at Rs.10,000/-, and expressed his readiness to pay any further court-fee on any larger sum of damages found due to him on taking accounts. He also valued the relief for injunction at Rs. 500/-. According to him, he had published the first edition of his book, 'The Indian Income-tax Act' in 1941, the second edition in 1945, and the third edition, Ex. P-1, in 1947. Volumes I and II of the fourth edition, Exhibits D-5 and D-5(a), were published in 1952. The defendants were said to have sold out their first edition of the book, Ex. P-2, and to be intending to publish a second edition. The plaintiff filed along with the plaint, documents A, B and C, they being now marked as Ex. P-1, Ex. P-2 and Ex. P-3. Ex. P-3 contains a list of the alleged passages, headings, phraseology, etc., said to have been pirated from Ex. P-1 by the defendants in Ex. P-2. The plaintiff alleged that he had given a notice through his solicitors to the defendants about the alleged infringement of his copyright in Ex. P-1, on 1st August 1951, charging them with infringement of copyright and demanding compensation and adequate amends, and alleged that the defendants, by their solicitors, prayed for time, and, after some correspondence, intimated by their notice, dated 12th September 1951, refuting the plaintiff's charge and declining to pay compensation or make amends. There was a slight error in this allegation as the defendants had denied any infringement of copyright even in their very first reply to the notice and had only asked for time for a more detailed reply after defendant 1, who was then in England, returned to India. The plaintiff had also not filed along with their plaint, the detailed reply given by the defendants regarding the passages alleged to have been pirated by him. He had filed his plaint on 22nd November 1951.

Along with the plaint, he had also filed an application (Appln. No.4436 of 1951) for restraining the defendants by an exparte interim injunction from publishing the second edition of their book pending the disposal of the suit, and for costs. To this application also, he had not annexed a copy of the defendants' detailed reply denying the infringement of his copyright in any manner or fashion and meeting in detail the allegations of piracy regarding the several passages, etc. named by him in his notice. Krishnaswami Nayudu J. passed an *ex parte* interim order of injunction on 30th November 1951. The defendants, however, filed a written statement vigorously contending the suit as frivolous, and prayed for setting aside the *ex parte* order of injunction, alleging that there was no infringement of copyright whatsoever and that the *ex parte* order had been obtained on wrong allegations and without disclosing their reply to the passages etc., relied on by the plaintiff for proving piracy. In their written statements, they had denied that there was any act of copying or piracy on their part from Ex. P-1, and had alleged that their book, Ex. P-2, was an independent compilation of defendant 2 (guided and supervised by defendant 1) by going to the original Act, decisions, Income-tax Manual, etc., which were all 'common sources' available for any man inclined to write a commentary on the Income-tax Act, provided he utilised his own labour, skill and brains, as defendants 1 & 2 did. They also contended that this court had no jurisdiction to try the suit, as no part of cause of action had arisen in Madras and no part of the alleged conversion or infringement of copyright had taken place in Madras. Krishnaswami Nayudu J., by his order dated 22nd January 1952, dissolved the interim injunction granted by him *ex parte* on 30th November 1951, after recording an undertaking by the defendants to maintain a correct and true account of the sales of the new edition when it was brought out, and to file accounts in Court once a quarter and give the plaintiff copies of such statements. He directed the suit itself to be posted to 18th March 1952 for trial and disposal subject to part-heard, evidently because the very same matters involved in the suit would have to be considered and decided in the injunction application, if he proceeded with it separately. I may add that the second defendant has filed an affidavit in this Court on 22nd April 1952 stating that the second edition of Ex. P-2 has not yet been released for sale and so no copies of it have been sold, and no accounts of sale could be filed, and filing a nil account.

When the suit came on for hearing before me, the learned Attorney-General for India,[4] who appeared for the defendants, withdrew the contention regarding jurisdiction, and stated that the defendants submitted to the jurisdiction of this Court, and that no issue need be framed regarding it. Therefore, the following issue was framed.

> 'Whether the defendants or any of them have infringed the plaintiff's copyright? Whether the similarities, if any, referred to in Ex. C. to the plaint are due to common sources to which the plaintiff and the defendants have had access and to phraseology and ideas familiar to Income-tax law? Whether the similarities, if any, resulting from the use and employment of common sources and of expressions and ideas familiar in Income-tax law, can constitute 'infringement of the plaintiff's copyright?"'

Then the plaintiff was examined as P.W.1. Because of certain contentions raised by the parties about the passages, etc., which could be relied on by the plaintiff for proving his case, I passed the following order, dated 7th April 1952, after hearing the arguments on both sides:

> 'In view of the divergent contentions of the learned advocates on both sides, it has become necessary for me to pass an order now defining the passages etc., on which the plaintiff can be allowed to rely for proving the alleged infringement of copyright of his book, Ex. P-1, by the defendants in their book, Ex. P-2, now that the issues have been framed and the evidence of the plaintiff, as P.W.1, has begun, and his cross-examination is in progress. When T.M. Krishnaswami Ayyar, the learned counsel for the plaintiff, had opened his case and proceeded with it in part, he agreed to stop midway so that the learned Attorney-General for India, (who was appearing for the defendants and had to go away urgently the next day to attend to his engagements already fixed up in Bombay, Nagpur, Delhi,

4. M.C. Setalvad who appeared because of the enormous amount of respect he had for Sir J.B. Kanga.

etc.,) might address the Court shortly on the main points of law arising in this copyright case, which was, according to him, the first case relating to a commentary on an Act. I too agreed so that the Court and the defendants might have the benefit of the arguments of the learned Attorney-General, in addition to the arguments of their other counsel. But the fact remains that Mr. T.M. Krishnaswami Ayyar has not finalised his 'opening' and his referring to the passages etc., alleged to be pirated, and that he is entitled to finish his 'opening' now or at the end of the evidence of the plaintiff, as he likes. It was urged by the learned counsel for the defendants that the plaintiff should not be allowed to enlarge the examples of infringement of copyright beyond the examples in the suit notice given to the defendants, and the examples given in the plaint, viz., those given in Ex. C. which is now marked as Ex. P-3., and the further examples given in Ex. P-4. They relied on a passage in Copinger and James in their 'Law of Copyright' (8th edition) at page 174. The learned authors say there, after observing that a general allegation that the defendants' work contains pirated passages, and a verification by affidavit of those passages are sufficient:

'But if a plaintiff brings an action to protect a work, *being only entitled to copyright in a small part of such work,* he ought to tell the defendant in his claim what that part is; otherwise costs unnecessarily incurred must be borne by the plaintiff.'

According to the learned counsel for the defendants, this will apply to every case where the *Court finds* that the plaintiff is entitled to copyright only in a small part of such work. But, I have no doubt whatever that the passage applies only where the *plaintiff claims* to be entitled to copyright in a small part of such work, and not where *the court* holds like that. The Court can hold like that only after hearing the evidence and the arguments, and not before hearing, or in the course of hearing, the evidence. No Court in Indian Republic (whose Constitution puts 'Justice' in the forefront) will come to a *decision* about the title of the plaintiff, before hearing his case and arguments. The very fact that Copinger and James go on to say that in such a case the plaintiff ought to tell the defendant in his claim what part of the work he claims to have copyright in, shows that it is *the plaintiff' assertion of* title that is contemplated in the passage and not *the Court's finding of title*, as no plaintiff can tell the defendant what the Court holds him to be entitled, till the Court itself gives its decisions to that effect. In my opinion, the case put by Copinger and James is perfectly understandable and simple, as it refers to a case like an anthology of poems or essays (for instance, 'Palgrave's Golden Treasury', or a volume of 'Collected Essays') where the plaintiff claims copyright only in one of the poems or essays included in the book, and is therefore claiming title to copyright only in that small part of such work, and is asked to tell the defendant what part of the work he claims copyright in. But this suit is not a case like that. This is a case where the plaintiff has written a huge commentary on the Indian Income-tax Act, the book itself coming to more than 900 pages, excluding the various appendices and additions coming to a few hundred pages more, and has claimed copyright in *the whole work*, Ex. P-1, though, doubtless, he does not claim copyright in the portion of the book containing the sections of the Indian Income-tax Act, or in the extracts from 'The Income-tax Manual' given for the information of the Income-tax Officers, and where the defendants, in their

* Note: The certified copy of the judgment contains several portions which are underlined. These are shown in italics in this book.

written-statements, have conceded that the *plaintiff has copyright in his book.* It is not a case like an anthology of poems or essays; nor is it a case where the plaintiff claims copyright only *in a small portion* of the work. It is a case where the plaintiff claims copyright in his entire commentary, forming more than half the book, and asserts that the defendants in their book of comparable dimensions, Ex. P-2, have copied *substantial passages* from his book and commentary, which he claims to be his *original* artistic work in the sense of the word 'original' in the Copyright Act. The defendants were well aware of this, and cannot be said to have been taken by *surprise.* In paragraph 5 of the plaint, the plaintiff claimed copyright in his book, Ex. P-1, and said that the defendants had reproduced *substantial portions* of his book in material form and had largely appropriated and utilized the labours of the plaintiff. Of course, copyright is given in order to prevent the breaking of the maxim, 'Thou shalt not steal'. In paragraph 8 of the plaint, the plaintiff went to say that he was filing document 'C', which is now Ex. P-3, showing the list of *some instances,* in parallel columns, of the acts of piracy committed by the defendants. He adds that both the books, his and the defendants', are filed as documents 'A' and 'B', now Ex. P-1 and P-2, and that he *craves leave to refer to the said documents in greater detail and also to submit further instances of infringement and piracy.* The defendants, in their written-statements, not only attacked Ex. C., now Ex. P-3, as not containing anything *original* by the plaintiff, but also denied 'specifically that they had pirated, in their book, any portion or passage from the plaintiff's book. That being so, the well-known rule of law referred to by Copinger and James before the passage quoted, and also mentioned by Halsbury in his Laws of England, Vol VII, at pages 568 and 586-587, will govern the situation. The passage in Halsbury, at page 568, runs as follows:

> 'It is an infringement of the copyright in a copyright work to produce a work, or any substantial part thereof, in any material form whatsoever, without the consent of the owner of the copyright.'

The passage at pages 586-587 runs:

> 'By reason of these presumptions, a plaintiff cannot be compelled to give particulars of his title *before it is put in issue.* It is not necessary for a plaintiff who complains of infringement to specify the parts of the defendant's work which he thinks have been pirated from his work; it is sufficient for him to allege generally that the defendant's work contains passages which have been pirated from the plaintiff's work and the Court will compare the two works.'

But, of course, no Court can be expected, or required, to embark on the wholly inconceivable task of comparing two huge books, like these, running to two thousand pages, by itself, in solitude. The Judge will go mad if he embarks on such a gargantuan venture. He will rely on the plaintiff's advocate to help him, and the opposing counsel also incidentally, by mentioning the passages, sentences, phrases, turns of thought, idiosyncrasies, conclusions, analysis, discussions, mistakes etc., on which he relies mainly in the case, *as soon as the issues are framed* (as Halsbury and Copinger both 'contemplate, and the heading rulings in such cases require) so that every one, including the Judge and the opposing counsel, may know the face and forefront of his grievance; and the learned counsel for the defendants will, naturally, concentrate on those passages etc., with, of course, reasonable latitude and liberty to both sides to gravitate from those passages etc., to the extent necessary to make their meaning, import and implication clear. That is the rationale of asking the plaintiff's counsel to point out to the Court the passages etc., on which he relies as showing the piracy.

Mr. T.M. Krishnaswami Ayyar, for the plaintiff, relies upon the passages etc., to be marked by him by tomorrow morning[5] in Ex. P-3, the passages and points mentioned somewhat briefly in Ex. P-4, which he treats as 'Heads of Points', the examples in three pages in the suit notice, which have been marked as Ex. P-5(a), and those in two sheets which he put in today, and now marked as Ex. P-6.

This is not a case where the defendants are alleged to have unauthorisedly *reprinted the entire book of the plaintiff,* in the fashion of the persons who pirated Shakespeare's First Folio editions. Nor is it a case where whole pages have been severely copied, as in *Macmillan v. Cooper.*[6] It is a case where only short passages, phrases, turns of expressions, idiosyncrasies, rulings cited, italics, structure, sequence, context, plan, arrangement, analysis, 'conclusions etc., are alleged to have been pirated, and even they are alleged to have been cunningly camouflaged in order to hide the piracy. So, it is important that the passages etc., relied on by the plaintiff, should be set out, now that the issues have been framed, and before the evidence of the plaintiff is closed, so that the Court may not be asked to read and compare for itself an unending series of pages and passages and examples, and so that the defendants may not be called on to undertake to prove that none of the pages or passages in their book are in any way a colourable limitation, or camouflaged duplication, of the plaintiff's pages and passages. It is with that intention, and in order to bring about that much-needed clarity, which will save the Court's time, that I am passing this order limiting the scope of the claim made by the plaintiff regarding the pirated passages etc., By this means alone can the evidence proceed in sensible and intelligible way, instead of getting nebulous and sailing in an unchartered sky. By this way alone can the *Court judge* finally whether the defendants have stolen the labour, skill and brain capital of the plaintiff.

Mr. T.M. Krishnaswami Ayyar, for the plaintiff will be allowed, therefore, to rely on the passages marked in Ex. P-3 and on the examples shown in Ex. P-4, P-5(a) and P-6 are *aides-memoir* and it follows, therefore, that reasonable latitude will be given to the plaintiff's advocate regarding what he intended to bring out by the points mentioned briefly, and already dealt with, or to be dealt with hereafter by him, more specifically in his 'opening'.

In my opinion, most of the numerous passages etc. quoted in Ex. P-3, P-4, P-5(a) and P-6, can be effectively argued on by the learned counsel themselves, and decided on by the Court, without putting the plaintiff or the defendants to the necessity of affirming or denying, often meaninglessly, things which are in black and white in the books themselves. But, of course, I leave that to the discretion and good sense of the learned counsel on both sides.

The learned counsel for the defendants stated that as Ex. P-3, P-4, P-5(a) and P-6 have been marked, it may be their duty to go over *every instance mentioned therein* and put it to P.W.1 or other witness for the plaintiff. I cannot quite agree. There are exhibits and exhibits, like books and books; some are intended to be proved in every detail; some are merely marked as *aides-memoir* to be glanced at and referred to and to apprise the Court and the other side about what is relied on, without the need to take every instance and put it to the witnesses.

It was also urged by the learned counsel for the defendants that in every phrase, passage, term etc., alleged to have been pirated, the *originality* of the plaintiff must be proved by questioning him about it. Now, the *originality* required in a commentary

---

5. The words 'tomorrow morning' find a place in the judgment!
6. I.L.R. 48 Bom 308 (P.C.)

on an Act, or in a dictionary, or a multiplication table, or a Book of Proverbs, will be of a low order, and not, like a Shakespeare's play, or a Botticelli painting, or a Michael angelo statue, or a Beethoven song, or a poem of Sheley, or a discovery by Marconi, novel or ingenious. It need not have original or inventive thought or imagination. It is enough if there is originality in the sense that the author has made it his own by his labour, skill and use of brains. In such cases of Originality *in this sense,* little purpose will be served by asking persons claiming such originality whether they are original, because they will only say that they are original 'in the copyright sense', as P.W.1 went on saying regarding many phrases, passages etc., put to him. But, it is obvious also that even originality in this sense, which alone can be claimed in the usual run of even good commentaries on Acts, must be protected by the Court, to the extent of the protection given by law, just as even the poor man's trifling coppers, earned by slaving all day long, must be protected as much as the rich man's millions in gold, easily earned by an inborn gift for clever speculation or contract. I do hope that the advocates on both sides, while examining or cross-examining the witnesses on this point of *originality* or *substantial copying,* will rely more on their arguments to Court and reference to the books (Ex. P-1 and P-2 already mentioned) than in putting questions to the witnesses in each case. But, even here, I leave it to their discretion and good sense.'

In view of this order, the plaintiff finally relied on Exhibits P.3, P.4, P.5(a) and P.6 as the passages etc., constituting the infringement of copying subject to the very limited latitude given by me to go, by way of explanation and clarification, beyond what was stated as heads of points etc., In view of this, issue (1) was amended by me, on 8th April 1952, after hearing both sides, by substituting the phrase 'Exhibits P-3, P-4, P-5(a) and P-6' for the original phrases 'Ex. C. to the plaint'. Thereafter, the plaintiff's examination, as P.W.1, was completed, and the second defendant was examined as D.W. 1. The plaintiff filed exhibits P-1 to P-17, and the defendants filed exhibits D-1 to D-13.

This is a case, it will be noticed from the order dated 7-4-1952, involving considerations of complicated questions of fact and law. There is no wholesale re-print of Ex. P-1 by the defendants; not even whole pages reproduced as they are. I have to give a finding on issue (1) after carefully considering the various contentions regarding the passages said to be copied, expressions borrowed, style, treatment, sequence, knitting together topics, analysis, opinions, criticisms, italics, etc., said to have been copied by the defendants from the plaintiff's book, Ex. P-1, in their book, Ex. P-2, before I can decide whether the defendants, or any of them, have infringed the plaintiff's copyright, and whether the similarities, if any, referred to in exhibits P-3, P-4, P-5(a) and P-6 are important enough to be noticed or are trivial and common place, or are due to common sources, to which the defendants have had access, and to phraseology and ideas familiar to Income-tax law and known to any lawyer conversant therewith. These questions of fact are, of course, to be determined in the light of the facts elucidated in the oral and documentary evidence, and cannot be decided by referring to any ruling, as each case must depend on its own facts. The further questions whether the similarities, if any, resulting from the use and employment of common sources and of expressions and ideas familiar to Income-tax law, do constitute an infringement of the plaintiff's copyright, and, if so, whether the plaintiff is entitled to an injunction, or merely to damages, and whether the plaintiff is entitled to any relief at all, in the light of the evidence, are mixed questions of fact and law. I have been helped very greatly in the elucidation of the law and the clarification of the facts by the lucid and learned arguments of Mr. T.M. Krishnaswamy Ayyar for the plaintiff, both in his opening and closing, and of the learned Attorney-General for India and Mr. Kolah for the defendants regarding the law and of Mr. H.M. Seervai regarding the facts.[7]

I shall first deal with the law necessary for deciding this case. There is no serious dispute regarding the law, between the learned counsel on both sides. The Indian law of copyright is stated in the Copyright Act of 1914 which is only based on the British Copyright Act of 1911, except for some differences regarding certain matters which are not relevant to this case, as they do not affect the points raise herein. So, for the purpose of this case, the law in India is the same as the law in England. It has been stated tersely and lucidly in Halsbury's Laws of England (IInd edition, 1932) Vol VII, paragraphs 822 to 826 and 882 and 883, which paragraphs are reproduced below, omitting the references to the footnotes, and with some portions italicised by me.

'822: No person is entitled to copyright in any work, whether published or unpublished, except under and in accordance with the provisions of the Copyright Act, 1911, (in India of course, the Copyright Act, 1914) under which provisions copyright, as therein defined, is conferred in respect of published, and unpublished, *original* literary, dramatic, musical, and artistic works. Ideas or opinions are not the subject-matter of copyright, but only the form in which ideas or opinions are expressed, and then only to the extent that a substantial part of the form must not be plagiarised.

823: Only original works are protected, but it is not requisite that the work should be the expression of original or inventive thought, for Copyright Acts are not concerned with the originality of ideas, but with the expression of thought, and, in the case of a literary work, with the expression of thought in print or writing. The originality which is required relates to the expression of the thought. It is not required that the expression should be in an original or novel form or that the work should not be copied from another work; it should originate from the author. Thus a report of a speech, a photograph of a picture, and a translation of a foreign work, are protected; and so too is a book of mathematical calculations, if independently worked out, even though in form identical with an existing book. The owner of copyright has, in short, no monopoly in the subject matter. Others are at liberty to produce the same result, provided they do so independently, and, though they are not the first in the field, their work is none the less 'original' in the sense in which that would be used in the Copyright Act, 1911. But if no skill or labour is employed in producing the particular form in which the work is expressed there will be no copyright in it, although it may embody an original idea or opinion; there is therefore no copyright in news as such, but only in the form in which it is expressed, and there is no

7. In an interview, T.R. Andhyarujina, who was H.M. Seervai's junior, said that Seervai was briefed not only because he had been Kanga's junior but also because he would take one case at a time and not leave the court when the case was being conducted. On the other hand, M.C. Setalvad and Kolah made their submissions and left. N.A. Palkhivala was also not present in court throughout the hearing. Only H.M. Seervai and Mr. N.A. Palkhivala stayed in Chennai (Madras) throughout the hearing.

copyright in an advertisement slogan, or in the name of a horse selected as a probable winner.

824: The skill and labour necessary in order to fulfill the test of originality in the sense above indicated may consist in the compilation of dictionaries, directories, maps or road-books, or in the mere preparation of lists, though there will be no copyright if the list conveys no useful information whatever. It may only consist in the improvement of an existing work as in bringing up to date a directory, or a read-book, 'or in bringing out a new edition of an existing work, provided that the work is so enlarged and improved as to constitute in reality a new work. The new edition, if it fulfils that condition, becomes a separate subject of copyright. A list of tours for travellers has been protected on the ground that there was not only a selection, but also a condensation and an arrangement which would be of value to the traveling public; on the other hand, the labour of arranging time-tables obtained from a common source in such a way that they should be more convenient for travellers starting from a particular town was not thought sufficient to entitle the resultant work to protection. But the labour of compiling a programme where time, skill and money were expended upon the form and arrangement is sufficient to enable the compiler to restrain the copying of his work.

There may be copyright in the notes to a non-copyright text if knowledge, skill, and taste is employed in their preparation, notwithstanding that the matter contained in the notes is to be found in standard works on the subject, or that the notes largely consist of apt quotations from non-copyright sources. The head-note of a law report is entitled to protection, for it is a thing upon which much skill and exercise of thought is required to express in clear and concise language the principle of law to be deduced from the decision to which it is pre-fixed.

A selection of non-copyright poems which can only be made as the result of careful reading, study, and comparison, and the exercise of taste and judgment, is entitled to copyright; for the same reason there is copyright in an arrangement of old music, in a pianoforte score of an opera, in law reports, and in a list of words selected as being suitable for a telegraph code.

825: Copyright cannot exist in a work of grossly immoral tendency, nor in a work which is blasphemous or seditious. A work which contains false statements to the knowledge of the plaintiff which are calculated to deceive the public is not entitled to the protection of the Court, and a work which, though it embodied new matter, itself infringed copyright, was refused protection on that ground. Probably no work which is contrary to public policy will be protected.

826: Whereas the Copyright Act, 1842, gave protection to 'books', an expression which was defined as including a volume, pamphlet, sheet of letterpress, sheet of music, map, chart or plans, separately published, copyright under the Copyright Act, 1911, extends to all literary works, and the words 'literary work' cover work which is expressed in print and writing, irrespective of the question whether the quality or style is high, and are used in sense of written or printed matter. The expression 'literary work' also includes maps, charts, plans, tables, and compilations. The change of description of the work to be protected brought about by the Act, 1911, from 'books' to 'literary works' has not cut down, or altered to his detriment, the right of a person claiming copyright.

But there is no copyright in a mere collection of words, which is not a compilation, and the collection of which has not involved any literary skill.

The name or title of a book or other work is not the subject-matter of copyright unless it is of such length as to constitute a literary composition of the author; it is, however, actionable to misrepresent to the public the authorship of a work by using the title similar to one identified with another work.

882: Copyright is the sole right to produce or reproduce a work which is capable of being the subject of copyright protection or any substantial part thereof in any material form whatsoever, and to perform, on in the case of a lecturer to deliver, the work of any substantial part hereof in public. It being necessary, however in view of the many methods employed in the reproduction of copyright works, and of certain older decisions in respect thereof, to explain this definition, the Copyright Act, 1911, contains further definitions of what the right includes. Copyright includes, if a work is unpublished, the sole right to publish the book or any substantial part thereof. It also includes the sole right to produce, reproduce, perform, or publish any translation of a work; it includes, as in the case of a dramatic work, the sole right to convert it into a novel or other non-dramatic work in the case of a novel or other non-dramatic work, or of an artistic work, to convert it into a dramatic work, by way of performance in public or otherwise; and in the case of literary, dramatic or musical work, to make any record, perforated roll, cinematograph film, or other contrivance by means of which the work may be mechanically performed or delivered. It also includes the sole right to authorise any of the acts aforesaid.

883: Copyright is infringed by any person who, without the consent of the owner of the copyright, does anything the sole right to do which is conferred on the owner of the copyright. But no absolute monopoly is given to authors analogous to that conferred upon inventors by the grant of letters patent, and if it can be shown, as a matter of fact that two precisely similar works, were produced entirely independently of one another, the author of the work published first cannot restrain the publication by the other author of that author's independent and original work. The right is merely a negative right to prevent the appropriation of the labours of an author by another. Thus a similarity or even identity, if it were conceivable between two plays or two places of music due to coincidence does not constitute an infringement by the second of the first, and a person may take a photograph of an object which has already been photographed, or make an independent engraving of a picture from which an engraving has already been made, without

> committing an infringement of the first photograph or engraving. Nor is it an infringement of copyright to reissue copies of a work which have already been lawfully made, nor to reproduce only the idea conveyed by or embodied in a copyright work without copying the form in which the idea is expressed.
>
> But, on the other hand, it is an infringement of copyright to produce a work similar to a copyright work, although the defendant has never seen the plaintiff's work, but has copied an intermediate copy, which he was entitled to copy, for in that case the defendant has used, though indirectly, the material form in which the plaintiff has expressed himself. The fact that the defendant acted innocently is no defence, for copyright is a proprietary right, and, if it is invaded the element of motive or intention on the part of the defendant is wholly irrelevant.'

In view of the exhaustive statement of the law, accepted as sound law by both sides even in the India of today, I need only refer very briefly to the other rulings relied upon by the one side or the other. In *Jarrold v. Houlston,*[8] it has been held that if any person, by his pain and labour, collects and reduces into the form of a systematic course of instructions those questions which he may find an ordinary person asking in reference to the common phenomena of life, with answers to those questions and explanations of those phenomena, whether such explanations and answers are furnished by his own recollection of his former general reading or out of works consulted by him for the express purpose, the reduction of questions so collected, with such answers, under certain heads and in scientific form, is sufficient to constitute an original work of which a copyright will be protected. But another person, may originate another work in the same general form, provided he does so from his own resources and makes the work he so originates the work of his own, by his own labour and industry bestowed upon it. It was held also that in determining whether an injunction should be ordered, the question in a matter where the plaintiff's work is not 'original' in the sense of novel, is, how far an unfair or undue use has been made of the work. It was further held that if, instead of searching into the common sources and obtaining his subject-matter from there, a man avails himself of the labour of his predecessor, adopts his arrangement and questions, or adopts it with a colourable variation, it will be an illegitimate use. It was held further that where a man copied or took any idea or language from any work and falsely denied it, it will be a strong indication of *animus furandi.* The learned Vice-Chancellor, who decided the case, added that if the Court is led to the conclusion that there has been piracy, it will not grudge the labour that may be required in order to ascertain how far the injunction should extend, and it was also stated that the injunction could be confined to the portion pirated, where it was separable. That was a case of an illegal piracy of Dr. Brewer's book 'Guide to Science', which did not lay claim to any originality with reference to the scientific doctrine contained in it, by the defendant in his book 'The Reason Why'. The injunction granted was confined to lectures 2 and 3 and 5 to 25 in 'The Reason Why'. The Vice-Chancellor referred to three legitimate uses of a compilation like 'The Guide to Science' by a later compiler. These three uses will also apply to a compilation of a labour

8. Revised Reports, Vol. 112, p. 357. This has been wrongly mentioned as footnote 1 in the judgment. Footnotes in this book will not tally with the original footnotes because certain additional footnotes have also been added.

commentary like the plaintiff's book, Ex. P-1, in addition to two other uses I shall mention. The first was an independent right to look into the 'common sources' which were unprotected by copyright, and to make such use of them, as the second author deemed fit. In this case, that will apply to the right of the defendants 1 and 2 to look into the Income-Tax Act, the Income Tax Manual decided cases, Select Committee Reports, etc. and make such use of those non-copyright matters as they deemed fit subject not copying wholesale the extracts prepared by another. The second was that if a subsequent author found a work like Dr.Brewer's and, on perusing it, was struck by seeing that the author had been led up to particular questions and answers by the perusal of some other work, to have recourse himself to the same work, although possibly he would not have thought of doing so, but for the perusal of the plaintiff's book. The third legitimate use was held to be this. The author of a subsequent work, after getting his own work with great pains and labour into a shape approximating to what he considered a perfect shape, can look through the earlier work, to see whether it contains any heads which he has forgotten.

As early as 1809, it was held by Lord Chancellor – Eldon, in *Longman v. Winchester,*[9] that there can be copyright in a compilation like a Court Calendar or a road-book, and that there can be piracy regarding such compilations with no pretence to originality in the sense of discovery or invention. It was held that though regarding maps, road-books, calendars, etc., if the later publisher applied the same skill, intelligence and diligence, the result would be much the same as the original publisher's work, the Court would interpose to prevent a re-publication of a work which the labour and skill of another person had supplied to the world, and that no man had a right to steal another's labour and take advantage of the selections already made by another, though he could not be prevented from dealing again with the same subject and giving the public the fruit of his original labour on the subject, the subject being open to all the world. A copy from the previous work verbatim and literatim would be a fit subject for an injunction regarding the portions so copied.

In *Kelly v. Morris,*[10] it was held by the Vice-Chancellor that the compiler of a directory or guide book, containing information derived from sources common to all, which must of necessity be identical in all cases if correctly given, is not entitled to spare himself the labour and expense of original inquiry by adopting and re-publishing the information contained in previous works on the same subject, and that he must obtain and work out the information independently for himself, and that the only legitimate use which he can make of previous work is for the purpose of verifying the correctness of his results. Certain portions of the Imperial Directory of London containing a copy of the Post Office London Directory were covered by an injunction in that case.

In *Pike v. Nicholas,*[11] it was held that an author who had been led by a former author to refer to older writers might, without committing piracy, use the same passage in the older writers which were used by the former author.

In *Cox v. Land and Water Journal Company,*[12] it was held that there can be copyright even regarding a list of hounds[13] prepared, and piracy possible therein,

9. English Reports Vol. 33, 987.
10. Law Reports Equity Cases Vol. I page 697.
11. Law Reports and Chancery Appeals Vol. 5 page 25.
12. Law Reports Vol. 9 page 324.
13. The word 'hounds' appears in the judgment.

though, where the list was liable to frequent changes and a correct list was not easily obtained, it would be only a case for damages and not for injunction.

In *Trade Auxiliary Company v. Middlesborough and District Tradesmen's Protection Association,*[14] it was held by Cotton L.J., Lindley, L.J. and Lopes L.J. that there can be copyright regarding business forms and bills of sale and deeds of arrangement, and that piracy was possible therein.

In *Lamb v. Evans*[15] copyright and piracy were held to be possible in trades directory consisting of a series of advertisements though, it was held to be not possible in a single advertisement.

In *Walter v. Lane,*[16] the House of Lords held that a person, who makes notes of a speech delivered in public (here Lord Roseberry's speech), transcribes them, and publishes in a newspaper a verbatim report of the speech, is the 'author' of the report, within the meaning of the Copyright Act, and is entitled to the copyright in the report and can assign the copyright and maintain an action regarding infringement of copyright. Lord Halsbury was one of the learned judges who gave the decision.

In *Muffatt and Paige Limited v. George Gill and Sons Ltd. and Francis Marshall,*[17] an annotated edition of Shakespeare's play 'As you Like It' with some novel features was held to be covered by copyright and to be capable of piracy, and even copying whole passages from it from memory (Mr. Marshall was held to have an extraordinary memory and to have seen and read the book alleged to have been pirated) would be piracy, and an injunction was granted regarding the portions of the compilation pirated.

In *University of London Press Limited v. University Tutorial Press Ltd.,*[18] examination papers were held to fall under the term 'original literary work', under the Copyright Act, and to be capable of copyright and piracy.

In the *Educational Company of Ireland v. Fallon and Getz,*[19] it was held that an author writing a book for another firm containing practically the same kind of lessons, and intended practically for the same class of pupils, as the one the copyright of which was given by him to a previous publisher, would be committing breach of copyright, and an injunction was granted regarding the publication of the second book.

In *G.A.Cramp & Sons Limited v. Frank Smythson Limited,*[20] the House of Lords held that copying common place tables from pocket diaries would not amount to an infringement of copyright where no special labour, or skill or knowledge or judgment or literary taste had been used in the preparation of the original tables.

In *Deeks v. H.G.Wells,*[21] a case from Canada, the Privy Council held that an infringement of copyright in a literary work may be proved by intrinsic evidence consisting of a large number of similarities, of like omission, of plan, of phrase and of common mistakes; but that such evidence must be of the most cogent force sufficient to give rise to an irresistible inference that the one work was copied from

---

14. LR Vol. 40, p.425.
15. 1893 I Chancery 280.
16. 1900 AC 539.
17. Law Times Reports, Vol. 86, 465.
18. 1916 II LR 601.
19. 1919 Irish Reports Vol.I, page 62.
20. LR 1944 House of Lords 329.
21. 64 MLJ 193.

the other, before it can be accepted as against the oath of respectable and responsible people that there was no copying in fact. It was a case where the suggested similarities could be explained by the nature of the work and the authorities to which the authors had recourse, which were common to both. The Privy Council held that where experts were called to point out the coincidence, similarities and omission to be found in the two works, they could not be permitted to offer their opinion that the one should have been copied from the other. That case had been brought by Florence A. Deeks against the famous author H.G.Wells, complaining that he had seen and read her manuscript and converted it and used it in his book 'The Outline of History'. Respectable and responsible people, who would otherwise be believed by the Court, swore that H.G.Wells never saw the manuscript in question. The plaintiff, relied on several similarities, between her manuscript and Well's book as evidence of H-G.Wells's having seen and used her manuscript. The Privy Council held that H.G.Wells was not proved to have seen and read the manuscript and dismissed the plaintiff's prayer for injunction, negativing the alleged infringement of copyright.

Now, I came to the Indian cases cited before me. In *Jogesh Chandra Chaudhuri v. Mohini Chanda Ray*,[22] Imam J., of the Calcutta High Court held that though it is generally true that in the reports of judgments, the reporter has no copyright, it cannot be said that in the selections of cases and in the arrangement of the reporting, the reporter has not the protection of the law, and that though any man is entitled to report such judgments as he obtains by expenditure of his own time, labour and money, he cannot be allowed to avail himself of other people's industry, where he fails to exert his own energies. In that case, the defendant had reproduced not only the judgments which had been reported by the plaintiff in his 'Calcutta Weekly Notes', in the defendant's 'Calcutta Case Law', but had also reproduced parts of the plaintiff's reports which formed no part of the judgments and had taken from the plaintiff's reports, extracts and facts which had been collected by the plaintiff from recourse to the cases at considerable expense of skill, labour and brains.

In *Macmillan Company Limited v. Cooper*,[23] a case relating to the publication by the defendant of 'Plutarch's Life of Alexander, North's Translation abridged', copying almost verbatim several pages of the notes appended to a similar book of the plaintiff, on which considerable skill, labour and brains had been utilized, the Privy Council held that the text of North's translation was not covered by copyright, as the plaintiff had not spent sufficient knowledge, labour , judgment or literary skill on it, but that the plaintiff was entitled to the copyright in the notes and that copyright had been infringed by the defendant by copying from the whole notes servilely, with all the mistakes therein. There was absolute verbatim identity of some of the notes in both the books. So the injunction was granted regarding the passages in the notes so servilely copied.

In *Mohini Mohan Singh v. Sita Nath Basak*,[24] it was held by a bench of the Calcutta High Court that whether a work is a colourable imitation of another must necessarily be a question of fact; but mere similarity will not be enough, as it might be due (1) to mere chance, (2) to both works being taken from a common source, (3) to the plaintiff's work being taken from the defendant's and (4) the defendant's work being taken from the plaintiff's, and that each case must depend

22. 26 Indian Cases 30.
23. ILR 48 Bom 308. This was a decision of the Privy Council.
24. AIR 1931 Cal 233.

upon its own circumstances. It was held further that in the case of works not original in the proper sense of the term, but prepared from materials which are open to all, the principle is that a person is not at liberty to use or avail himself of the labour which another has bestowed for the purpose of producing his works – that will be taking away the result of another man's labour, or, in other words, his property, and that colourable imitation of another's work could also be covered by an injunction. That case related to a school book of the plaintiff being copied by the defendant.

In *Kartar Singh Giani v. Ladha Singh*,[25] a Bench of the Lahore High Court held that copyright means the sole right to produce or reproduce the whole or any substantial part of a book in any material form whatsoever, and that the copyright in a work shall be deemed to be infringed by another person, who, without the consent of the owner of the copyright, reproduces the whole or a portion thereof, but that any person can go to a common source and produce a book on the same subject as a result of his own independent research and labour and that there would be no infringement of copyright in such cases. It dismissed the plaintiff's prayer for injunction in that case on that ground.

In *Gopaldas v. Jagannadha Prasad*,[26] a case of two works on Koka Shastra, a Bench of the Allahabad High Court held that copying was proved, as the defendant had reproduced substantial portions of the plaintiff's book, and held that the mere fact that the defendant had added some additional matter in his book to what he had pirated from the plaintiff's book, did not make his book any the less an infringement of the plaintiff's copyright, as he had reproduced a substantial part of the plaintiff's book.

Though the learned Attorney-General for India stated that he was not able to find a case where copyright was held to be possible in a commentary on an Act, with very little scope for even second-rate originality in it, Mr. T.M. Krishnaswamy Ayyar, for the plaintiff, was able to cite *Stevens v. Wildy,*[27] where the Vice-Chancellor held that there was copyright in a book entitled 'The Joint Stock Companies' Winding Up Act, 1848, with an introduction, notes and forms', and that it could be infringed where whole passages, or the actual words, had been taken in many instances, and that an injunction could be granted. His actual words are:

> 'I do not wish to speak harshly of the nature of the defendant's work; but, I cannot help saying that his book appears in a great degree to have been completed by taking in many instances the actual words as they stand in the plaintiff's work'.

That ruling will apply to the case of a commentary on the Indian Income-tax Act also, as in this case, and will protect even the fifth-rate originality required in such commentaries where, of course, no responsible commentator can traverse beyond the meaning of the sections or the decided cases, and will be generally bound down, as in a vice, regarding the topics to be dealt with, headings to be considered, section analysis, conclusions, omissions etc. Indeed, the very fact that defendant 1 and 2, in paragraph 5 of their written statement stated that they were not disputing that the plaintiff was the owner of the copyright in his book,

---

25. AIR 1934 Lahore 777.
26. ILR 1938 All. 370.
27. The learned judge has not given the citation in the judgment. This case is also not cited in the latest (fourth) edition of *Halsbury's Laws of England.*

Ex. P-1, will itself show their consciousness that there could be copyright in such commentaries on Acts. The law in all modern countries is growing from day to day, like democracy and democratic conceptions. So such commentaries on Acts, with the fifth-rate originality required therein, will be more and more common, as time goes on, and will have to be protected, wherever justified, under the Copyright Act, in the interests of the authors and the publishers of such commentaries which though common, like paddy-growing, will have to be protected like the paddy growing in each man's field. The essence of the copyright law is the maxim, 'Thou shalt not steal' as already stated, and the infringer of the copyright can be imagined as, in effect, saying, 'I cannot grow paddy, as it takes too long, but I can easily steal the paddy grown laboriously by others'. It will be obvious that the similarity of the paddy grown in one field with that in another will not be a conclusive, or even important, test to prove stealing or piracy, and that independent use of skill, labour and brains in growing the paddy will be the test in commentaries on Acts, as in this case.

Of course, the admission of the defendants regarding the copyright of the plaintiff in his own book, Ex. P-1, will not affect their rights to attack the contention that portions of Ex. P-1 have been plagiarised in Ex. P-2, by pointing out that the plaintiff has no copyright in those portions, by reason of their being extracts from common sources not covered by copyright, and open to all the world, like the Income-tax Manual, Select Committee Reports, decisions of Courts, quotations from well-known commentaries, usage of expressions, phrases and words well known in law or idiom, or by showing that the so-called original contributions of the plaintiff in those words, phrases, passages etc., are not covered by the Copyright Act under the rulings of the Privy Council in *Macmillan & Co. v. Cooper,*[28] regarding the text of North's translation of Plutarch's Life of Alexander (as a part from the notes) and in *G.A.Cramp & Co. v. Frank Smith,*[29] on the ground that sufficient knowledge, labour, judgment or literary skill had not been expended on such alleged contribution to make them 'original literary work'.

It is also obvious, on the rulings cited above, and even from mere considerations of sense and commonsense, that the relief to be given in a copyright case depends on the facts of the case. Sometimes, an injunction will be granted in whole, sometimes in part, sometimes not at all, but only damages given in lieu of injunction, and sometimes no relief at all will be given where there has been no infringement of copyright on the ground that there is either no original literary work involved in the passage etc., complained of, or a substantial portion, as understood in the copyright cases, by the consideration of the quality or quantity, was copied. A judge has to pass a decree to suit the case. Thorns are food for a camel but not for a man, and toys are required only for a man with children and not for one without any and law applies to all men but decrees generally only to the parties and ought to be passed with reference to each case as the old Hindu law-givers declared in *Mimansas* and *Nyayasastras* two thousand years ago. Of course, when considering the question of a substantial portion being copied, mere quantity will not be the test. Even if only a small quantity is taken, it will do if the quality of it is vital and useful. That will be like taking the cornea from a healthy eye of a neighbour and having it engrafted to one's own defective eye to improve the vision and efficiency of one's eye. In the case of competing works, a small quality pirated from a previous work will also be enough to prove infringement of

28. 48 Bom. 308.
29. 1944 AC 329.

copyright as the sales of the prior work will be affected and the sales of the latter work will be advanced by such piracy. Of course, the primary object should be competition and it cannot be held to be the primary object in some cases. Thus, every woman bringing forth a child makes that child, incidentally, compete, in this world of competition, with 2,400 million other human beings. But here, the primary object in bringing forth a child is not to make it compete with the other 2,400 million human beings but to fulfill herself and get satisfaction for herself by having her own child. So too, able lawyers, like defendants 1 and 2, having vast Income-tax practice in the Bombay High Court and Supreme Court, when writing a commentary on Income-tax, will not be held to have done it primarily to compete with the plaintiff but only to fulfill themselves and to have the satisfaction of writing a good commentary. The plaintiff himself, by writing his book, competed with at least three other good commentaries existing before him, like those of Pal, Sundaram and A.N. Aiyar, and it cannot be said that his primary object was to compete with them. Whether he read some of those commentaries, like those of A.N. Aiyar, which he did not read and yet added that he did not consider to be of much use, and that it contained no useful information, though he had never read it is immaterial in this connection.

The examination of P.W. 1 and D.W. 1 was elaborate and detailed, and D.W. 1 fared better in cross-examination than P.W. 1. He stood a detailed and skilful cross-examination exceedingly well, and was not materially unshaken on any point, and struck me as a competent and alert lawyer, who was thoroughly conversant with the Income-Tax Act and law and was very well-informed with every part of his book, and could give a cogent account of any part of it, regarding the scheme, arrangement, analysis, conclusion, criticism etc. He struck me also as giving his evidence in a straight forward fashion. P.W. 1 was not able to stand the cross-examination so well because of his emotion, and often gave answers, which cannot be said to be satisfactory, was not able in some cases to refer to other portions of his book, or to the Act, or the Income-tax Manual, or the decided cases, so quickly as D.W. 1 possibly due to his greater age. Memory is notoriously stronger in a younger man. The Hindu psychologists have said that facts stick in the memory of people below 16 like inscriptions on rocks, in the memories of people between 16 and 80 like writing on paper or slate, fading with time, and, after 80, is like writing on water! Thus in the course of P.W. 1's cross-examination when asked:

Q. You agree that the phraseology in the defendant's book is taken from the sections and the rules themselves as far as this commentary is concerned?

A. If they are taken, they are taken.

Q. Income must accrue abroad before it can be remitted to this country...the transaction cannot be held to result in any accrual of profits abroad on behalf of the branch office?

A. If it is there, it is there. You can argue that.

Q. Is the presentation in any sense similar?

A. Why not? The defendant has copied from my commentary.

Q. Have you any doubt when I say that these words which are taken from the decision itself?

A. I do not know.

There are some more such examples. Again, he sometimes gave his answers in a huff, in sheer narration and chagrin. Thus, being put out on being told that he had not cited cases in support of some of his propositions, and having had to admit it, and being also put out on seeing that the cases referred to in a previous commentary could be legitimately used, under the rulings, by the author of a subsequent commentary, if he went into the original sources thus indicated and spent some skill, labour and brains on them himself, he answered that he would not give any authorities for any of his propositions in any future edition of his book, evidently in order that subsequent commentators might not go to the original sources, aided by such citations, and extract the same passages and propositions like himself therefrom, forgetting that a commentary which cites no cases would not to be worth the paper on which it is written, especially when it is not an original work in the primary sense, like a work on 'Jurisprudence' by a well-known authority like Salmond, or on the 'Rule of Law' by a well-known authority like Dicey, or on 'Ancient Law' by a well-known authority like Maine, or on 'Hindu Law' by a well-known authority like Mayne, and is only a pedestrian commentary with a fifth rate originality. No lawyers will invest their monies on such a commentary citing no decisions, and even laymen will not waste their money on it, as the opinions of an author like that will be of no use to them, without the decision of courts, which, whether right or wrong, are binding till they are upset or modified. So too, the plaintiff was making many assertions without adequate proof. This is illustrated by the following extract from his evidence:

Q. You claim damages in this case?

A. Yes.

Q. What for?

A. For conversion of my property, the outcome of my brains, which is the author's capital, as the learned Law Lords put it. My capital is gone away, thanks to the defendants.

Q. You complain that your copyright has been infringed by the defendant?

A. Yes, The sale of the copies of the defendants' book is due to a very great extent to the book being a reproduction of the major portion of my ideas, my own experience, my method of expression, my method of analysis, my treatment of the subject etc.

This last is too tall a claim to make regarding a book by two very eminent lawyers, like defendants 1 and 2, the first of whom was the Advocate-General of Bombay Province for years, and was in charge of Income-Tax practice from almost the inception of the Income Tax Act and argued 90% of the Income-Tax Cases in that province, which is well-known as the leading province for Income-Tax assessment, and whose income ran to several thousands a month, and the second of whom, though young and hardly 32, has very high academic distinctions and a brilliant career at the Bar and in courts, and is a Professor of Law in the Bombay Law College and had intensive Income-tax practice, first along with defendant 1 and then independently, in which capacity he got no less than Rs. 60,000/- as income in 1950. The plaintiff did not pretend, much less prove, that he had higher intelligence or practice or income than the defendants. A perusal of the book, Ex. P-2, has convinced me that it will sell by its own merits, – it has systematic arrangement, clear analysis, sound opinions, citation of cases for every point, etc., and then it will not have to depend one jot on the alleged similar phrases, expressions etc., said to have been copied from the plaintiff's book, Ex. P-1, though I cannot at all agree with Mr. Seervai, the learned counsel for defendants 1 and 3, that the plaintiff's book Ex. P-1, is like a godown and that the defendants' book is like a well-arranged store. It cannot be however denied by comparing the two books, that Ex. P-2 is slightly more systematic in arrangement, and that the treatment therein is slightly more lucid, clear, idiomatic, systematic, logical and up-to-date because of its later date.

It is an unfortunate feature in this case that both sides, having legal antagonism, made allegations against each other, which cannot be said to be either wise or valid. Thus, Mr. Seervai, for the defendants, reading the passage from P.W. 1's evidence that he had not carefully perused detailed reply of the defendants, to the passages sent to them in his notice dated 1-8-1951, as proofs of piracy, and on the fact that the plaintiff had not attached this detailed reply to his application for *ex parte* interim injunction before Krishnaswami Nayudu urged that the plaintiff had falsely and maliciously suppressed the detailed reply from the Court, when applying for the *ex parte* injunction, so that the Court might not, on perusing the reply, refuse it summarily, and in order to pursue his false, frivolous and vexatious suit and drag the defendants from Bombay to Madras, leaving their own work, and get damages from them, if he could, by hook or by crook. While I agree that the plaintiff, as an advocate, suing two other advocates in such a matter, should have attached the detailed reply to his application for *ex parte* interim injunction, I am not satisfied that he had any of the evil motives attributed to him. The plaintiff's reply in the passage relied on was. ' I did not look into the notice carefully. I was mainly concerned to find out whether they were amenable to acknowledge and make some amends. When I found out that they were not prepared, I thought it was idle for me to go through the material…As I told you, I was not concerned with examining meticulously the contents of the annexures. We wanted to know what their reaction would be, and it was not favourable. So I did not attach much importance to it…I was satisfied that there was a good case for me in a court of law. I did not care to know what the defence would be. Your defence is a matter that has to be established in a court of law.' Now, it is too much to take the statements in the above passage as proving any of the evil motives attributed to the plaintiff. His reference to the defendants making some amends need not necessarily show a great and getting money from them by way of blackmail. Nor need his not reading the reply notice carefully, though it is expected of any plaintiff to read the reply notice carefully in such cases before rushing to court, prove that he was intent on filing a suit which he knew to be false, frivolous and vexatious. Nor will his stating that he was satisfied that there was a good case for him in a Court of law, and that he did not care to know what the defence would be, and that the defence was a matter that had to be established in a court of law, prove satisfactorily any of the evil motives attributed. A man fanatically convinced of the truth of his case (the plaintiff strikes me as one such man) rarely cares to know the opponent's point of view. This is notoriously so with religious fanatics and fierce litigants. Thus, fanatical Hindus, Muslims and Christians will not care to read and understand the case of their opponents, being firmly convinced in the truth of their own convictions. That appears to me to be the real fact with the plaintiff, like a jealous mother of a puny child, or like a jealous husband or wife, suspecting all the world of having intentions of robbing or injuring the child, the wife or husband, as the case may be, there are jealous authors suspecting the whole world to be conspiring to steal from their books. When that is the case, there is no need for assuming that the plaintiff knew his case to be false, frivolous and vexatious, and persisted in the suit in order to drag the defendants to Madras and wring out of them damages, if he could, by hook or by crook. As Mr. T.M. Krishnaswamy Ayyar, for the plaintiff, rightly urged, a litigant, even though an advocate, is not bound to hear the other side, like a judge. The maxim of natural justice, *audi alteram partem* (hear the other side) applies to judges, and arbitrators etc., analogous to them, and not to litigants, and political and religious leaders of opposite factions. The attribution of these evil motives is, in my opinion, not at all proved any more than the attribution by the plaintiff of the sales of the defendants' book to alleged copying of passages etc. from his book. So too, the plaintiff attributed dishonest camouflage to the defendants in order to hide their copyings from his book, by omitting or altering a word, splitting up one sentence in his book into two, one paragraph into two, and transferring comments under one section to another section, from one part of the commentary to another part of the commentary, from the body of the commentary to the foot-note, from the foot-note to the body to the commentary, and converting headings into the body of the commentary and the body of the commentary into headings. As we shall see later on, this is entirely unsustainable on a cross-examination, however plausible it may seem on first impression. So too, the defendants asserted that the plaintiff, with a view to claiming a false originality, did not cite the relevant cases for several important propositions he enunciated in his commentary and passed off these propositions as his own the real fact appears to be that the plaintiff was not really so systematic and methodical as the defendants, and did not cite cases for every proposition separately. P.W. 1 admitted, in the course of his evidence, that all the propositions cited by him in Ex. P-1 were only culled from the Income-Tax Act or the decided cases etc., and were not his original propositions in the primary sense or the term. There are some more instances of such charges and counter-charges of a vitriolic nature made by one side against the other and not satisfactorily proved by the evidence or the facts relied on.

Now, I shall state briefly a few necessary facts before going on to discuss the issues in detail. The plaintiff was a practising advocate in this State till about 1948 (when he gave up practice) and had decent practice. In 1941, he took to Income-Tax practice and appeared in some cases including one before Leach, C.J., and one before Patanjali Sastri, J. He then conceived the idea of writing his book, the first edition of which he brought out in 1941 itself. This first edition took him 2 ½ years to prepare. He knew that there were the commentaries of Sundaram and A.N. Aiyar on the Income-Tax Act, before he himself began writing his commentary; but, according to him, he did not look into any commentary or even into the Income-Tax Manual for the purpose of writing his book, and bought only an unofficial publication containing the bare Act, by one Krishnamurthi Ayyar, as, in his opinion, Government Acts and Manuals contained innumerable mistakes! He went to the cases himself and extracted from them the passages he deemed fit and took the help of his assistants, including Mr. Krishnamachari, one of his counsels now, for preparing the cases, extracts from the Income-Tax Manual etc., for incorporating in his book. He incorporated them only after his own verification and using his own discretion. He also discussed with Income-Tax practitioners and others many questions of Income-Tax Law including fanciful and hypothetical questions, in order to make an original contribution to the law on the subject. He had looked into Sundaram's commentary 12 or 15 or 24 times in the course of his Income-tax practice, but not for the purpose of writing his book. The first edition of his book was priced at Rs.12/- a copy, and 2,000 copies were printed and sold out. The second edition was brought out in 1945. It took him one year to prepare and was priced at Rs.20/- a copy, and 2,000 copies were printed and sold out. The third edition of his book, the edition represented by

Ex. P-1 was brought out in 1947. It took him one year to prepare. It was priced at Rs.25/- per copy, and, 2,500 copies were printed and sold out. The 4th edition of his book, in two volumes, was brought out in 1952 after the filing of this suit. It took him two years to prepare this edition and it was priced at Rs.37.80 pre-publication, and Rs.42.80 post-publication, and 5,000 copies were printed as the Income-Tax Department had given top priority to his book and were expected to order 1,500 copies themselves. His book received well-deserved excellent opinions regarding its thorough and exhaustive exposition of a complex branch of the law from Sir George Rankin and Lord Macmillan and others, and was referred to in a case in the Orissa High Court and was said to have been referred to by the first defendant himself in an Income-Tax Full Bench case in 1945 in the Bombay High Court. The first defendant himself was said to have expressed a very favourable opinion on that book, though that opinion was only conveyed to P.W.-1 through an intermediary (who was not called by the plaintiff). The opinion could not be given in the evidence of P.W.-1, as amounting to hearsay, and as that fact was intended indirectly to show that the first defendant had a good opinion of the plaintiff's book and had therefore a motive in order to pirate to make his own book a goodseller.

When the plaintiff, who holds the copyright in his book was thus expecting very good sales of his fourth edition, which he had taken in hand, he saw in a Calcutta book-stall, a copy of Ex. P-2, and suspected piracy therein from his book. He consulted some of his friends in Madras, but, as he had left off practice in 1948, and was an advisor to the Chambers of Commerce, there were no assistants in Madras to help him, and the lawyers he wrote to said that they had not looked into the books and could not say whether there was any piracy. Anyway, as he looked into P.2, deeper, he became convinced of his suspicion that portions of his book, Ex. P-1, had been pirated by the defendants in their book, Ex. P-2, and that Ex. P-2 was being sold out rapidly because of such pirated portions, and resolved to file this suit against the defendants. But when he asked his solicitors, Sanderson and Morgan, to issue the suit notice to the defendants, they wanted him to satisfy them that there was a plausible case for issuing a suit notice to two advocates like the defendants. So, he prepared hastily a list of passages etc. pirated (those are contained in Ex. P-5) and gave them to the solicitors. These passages ran to 93 pages and are now comprised in Ex. P-5 and contain alleged instances of similar language and expression of thought, instances of mistakes committed by the plaintiff which, strange to say, occurred in the defendants' book also, sameness of system of treatment, similarity in the analysis of the problems and in summing up, selections of the plaintiff's passage and compilations so as to give continuity of thought and incisiveness, which selections were reproduced in the defendant's book, piracy of the marginal notes in Ex. P-1 by the defendants in Ex. P-2 (which portion is the one marked as Ex. P-5a here) and instances of paraphrasing. The plaintiff stated that he prepared Ex. P-5 in haste, and after a superficial perusal of Exs. P-1 and P-2. Later on, as already stated, he filed this suit and applied for interim injunction, and has eventually added Exs. P-3, P-4 and P-6, to Ex. P-5a, the portion in Ex. P-5 now relied on, in addition to Exs. P-3, P-4 and P-6.

The second defendant conceived the idea of writing Ex. P-2 in March 1947. He consulted the first defendant, in whose chambers he had worked for long, and the 1st defendant agreed by the end of April 1947 to guide and supervise the work. The second defendant began systematically examining every relevant case in the Tax Cases, Income-Tax Reports etc; and took notes and extracts. He also relied on the notes and extracts of rulings he had prepared for conducting his own cases, along with the first defendant or independently, and took advantage of that vast experience also for writing this book. He also referred to Income-Tax Manual and recognised authorities like Konstam, Halsbury, Simon etc., for Income-Tax law, and, as a result of his independent thinking and application of labour, skill and brains, wrote the book, Ex. P-2, discussing complicated problems with the first defendant, Mr. Kolah and others in his chambers and talking also to Mr. Dalal, an expert in Insurance Law, regarding the reference to Insurance Law in Ex. P-2. He got also some extracts of the Select Committee incorporated in Ex. P-2 from a Bombay attorney, Nadir Mulla, in connection with certain cases of his or of the first defendant in the High Court. He had been referring from 1947 to 1950 the commentaries on the Income-Tax Act of Pal, Sundaram and A.N. Aiyar and the plaintiff, whenever occasion required, and on the points required, but swore that he had not those commentaries before him for the purpose of writing his book. These books were with Mr. Mistry, Mr. Kolah etc. in the same chambers. D.W. 1 admitted that he remembered the opinions of the plaintiff on some 20 points (by virtue of his seeing Ex. P-1 for practice) when he was writing his book, Ex. P-2 and that his pointed attention was drawn by Mr. Dalal to a point on which the plaintiff had expressed a contrary opinion from his, but swore that he did not have the plaintiff's book before him for the purpose of writing his book and that he did not copy anything from Ex. P-1 either word, or phrase, passage or italics, case or foot-note, conclusion or criticism, arrangement or sequence, topic or subject, all of which he took only from the Act, Income-Tax Manual, decided cases etc., common sources with no copyright in them. He took three years to complete his work which was also deservingly praised by leading journals and lawyers, and was, he said, surprised and pained at this charge of plagiarism and infringement of copyright.

In this connection, I may add that I have perused the commentaries of Mr. Sundaram, Mr. A.N. Aiyar, the plaintiff and the defendants on the Income-Tax Act, thought not the commentary of Mr. Pal (who has faded out since), and I am satisfied that all of them are good commentaries and that the plaintiff's and defendants' commentaries are particularly good, though Ex. P-2 is, of these two, slightly more full, up-to-date, methodical, lucid and systematic than Ex. P-1. The attacks on Ex. P-2 by the plaintiff, as a book which sold primarily because of the passages etc. copied from his book, and the attack of the defendants on Ex. P-1 as a book, with false claim of originality and resembling more a godown than a well-arranged store are, in my opinion, untenable and uncalled for; equally with the opinion of the plaintiff, as P.W.1, without reading A.N. Aiyar's commentary, that it was of not of much use and was not worthwhile.

Before proceeding further, I say as well deal with some other important matters of revised law and fact requisite for disposing of this case. Firstly, it is well-settled that an author or a co-author of a subsequent work will be liable for infringement of copyright, if that is found by the Court, even if he has never seen the plaintiff's work and has only copied from it through an intermediary copy which he was entitled to copy, as already seen from the extract from Halsbury's Laws of England Vol. VII (para 863) and is supported by numerous cases. He will also be liable, even though he has not directly used the previous work when writing his book but has only copied the portion held to be an infringement *from memory,* as held in *Muffatt and Paige Limited v. George Gill and Sons Ltd. and Francis Marshal,*[30] where Francis Marshall had copied whole passages and sentences from the

30. Law Times Reports Vol. 86, 465.

plaintiff's edition of 'As you Like It' from memory. He had been proved to have an extraordinary memory. So too, in this case, even if the 2nd defendant had not plaintiff's book, Ex. P-1, before him when he wrote his book, Ex. P-2, it would be enough if the plaintiff succeeds in proving that a substantial portion of his book had been copied from his book, Ex. P-1, in Ex. P-2, by the second defendant's having remembered and copied from memory such portions, the second defendant admittedly referred to Ex. P-1 numerous times during the course of his practice, before and when writing the book, Ex. P-2. If he is proved to have had passages from P.W.-1's book in any notes prepared by him for the purpose of his original practice in the High Court, or for helping the first defendant in his Income-tax cases in High Court and had referred to them for the purpose of writing Ex. P-2, that too will be enough. All that depends on an appreciation of the evidence in the case.

It is also equally well-settled that a co-author of a book, held by a Court to be an infringement of the copyright in a previous book, in whole or in part, will be equally liable with another co-author, even if he did not take the same part, or indeed any part at all, in bringing out the book alleged to contain the piracy, and even though he is innocent of actual knowledge of the piracy. So, the first defendant, Sir Jamshedji Kanga, a co-author of Ex. P-2 with the 2nd defendant, will be equally liable with the second defendant, Mr. Palkhivala, his co-author and the third defendant, the publishers, in case it is held that there has been an infringement of the copyright in the plaintiff's book, Ex. P-1, in the defendants' book, Ex. P-2, even though his part in the work was mainly of a supervisory and advisory character, and the actual writing of Ex. P-2 had been done by the co-author, the second defendant, as mentioned by the first defendant in the Foreword to Ex. P-2. The learned Attorney-General for India, who appeared for the defendants, in the course of his address to me, while mentioning (as did D.W. 1 in his evidence) that the first defendant's part in the book, Ex. P-2, was confined to guiding and supervising and advising the second defendant, his junior for a long time, and in scrutinizing and approving of the entire typed manuscript of Ex. P-2, submitted to him by the second defendant, and of all the propositions of law contained therein, relying on his phenomenal memory of all the leading cases in Income-tax law from his vast experience of such cases as Advocate-General of Bombay, etc., as in advising the second defendant to alter or modify some of the propositions stated in the typed manuscript, said that the first defendant took the fullest responsibility for every single thing found in Ex. P-2 and in styling this case as false, frivolous and vexatious equally with the second defendant, and was perfectly willing to be held liable for infringement of copyright, if found by the Court, equally with the second and third defendants. That, of course, is the law. The argument of Mr. T.M. Krishnaswamy Ayyar for the plaintiff, that the second defendant might have committed the alleged acts of piracy without the aid, knowledge or approval of the first defendant, and that therefore, the first defendant's status as Advocate-General of Bombay from 1922-35, and a leading Income-tax advocate with a vast income taking part in moulding the evolution of Income-tax law almost since its inception in the leading Income-tax province of India should be ignored, will, of course, be only relevant for considering the truth and the possibility of the piracy, and not for considering the liability for it, if found to be true, as Mr. T.M. Krishnaswamy Ayyar himself frankly admitted. Indeed, the first defendant had, in the detailed reply to the plaintiff's notice, as emphatically repudiated the alleged acts of piracy as the 2nd defendant, and had characterized the grievance of the plaintiff and the proposed action by the plaintiff as false, frivolous and vexatious, just as the 2nd defendant had done.

That there is no proprietorship in ideas or opinions, under the Copyright Act, but only in the form in which those ideas or opinions are expressed, and that even such copyright in the *form* will only be established when a substantial portion of that form is plagiarised, as is clear from paragraph 822 of Vol VII of Halsbury's Laws of England, already extracted above, and is supported by numerous decisions given in the foot-notes in Vol. VII. It is enough if I cite one more case, *Hollinrake v. Truswell.*[31] In that case, the plaintiff claimed copyright in a cardboard pattern sleeve containing upon it scales, figures, and descriptive words for adapting it to sleeves of any dimensions. Lord Herschell L.C., and Lindley and Davey L.J., reversing the decision of Wright J., held that this could not be the subject of copyright, though it could be the subject of a patent of an instrument or tool.

It is well settled now that taking even a small but significant quantity for a competing purpose may amount to infringement of copyright (See *Trade Auxiliary Co., v. Middleborough and District Tradesmen's Protection Association,*[32] at page 429 of the decision already quoted). In *Mawman v. Tegg,*[33] quoted with approval in *Jarrold v. Houlston,*[34] where 2,160 lines out of 2,17,000 lines, or about one percent, of a previous work were admitted to be copied, it was held that infringement of copyright had been committed and that it was a proper case for an injunction. Of course, in our case, there is no admission of copying even of a single line or word from the plaintiff's book, Ex. P-1, in the defendants' book, Ex. P-2. Mr. T.M. Krishnaswamy Ayyar, for the plaintiff, now admits that the major portion of the book, Ex. P-2, is an independent work of the second defendant, and may not amount to breach of copyright, and confines himself to the instances in Exhibits P-3, P-4, P-5(a) and P-6 not withdrawn. Those instances may amount to one to two percent of the plaintiff's book, or the defendants' book, each being roughly equal to the other in size. Of course, if the plaintiff establishes copying of the plaintiff's original literary work by the defendants even regarding that one to two percent, he would have made out a case of infringement, though whether an injunction should be granted, or only mere damages, would still be a matter for the Court to decide.

Mr. T.M. Krishnaswami Ayyar relied on another proposition from *Jarrold v. Houlston,*[35] viz., that when the defendants denied positively that any ideas or language had been copied or taken, and the Court is yet compelled to come to the conviction that however the second defendant might satisfy his own conscience, no other person can reconcile that denial with the facts developed by a comparison of the works in question, the Court, in such a case, might take the denial itself against the defendants as proof of *animus furandi*. That is so, and is not disputed by the learned counsel for the defendants. But, of course, as urged by the learned counsel for the defendants, the converse also will apply, and, however much the plaintiff might satisfy his own conscience that there is copying of his ideas or language by the defendants, he cannot possibly succeed, or get any relief (except perhaps being relieved from paying the defendants' cost) when the Court, after a careful comparison of the works in question, has come to the conclusion that there has been, in fact, no copying from his book.

Mr. T.M. Krishnaswami Ayyar, for the plaintiff, next relied on another proposition from *Jarrold v. Houlston,*[36] viz., that the collocation and phraseology

---

31. 1894 (3) Ch. Page 420.
32. Reports. Vol. 40. P. 425 at 429.
33. 26. R. R. 112.
34. R.R. 112 page 357.
35. *Ibid.*
36. *Ibid.*

of the previous work, if copied substantially, will not only be an infringement but will be none the less an infringement if some words etc., are altered in order to bring about a colourable variation ingeniously and purposely in the collocation and phraseology in order to camouflage and hide the copying and plagiarism. That proposition too, is correct, and is not disputed by the learned counsel for the defendants.

Another proposition was relied on by Mr. T.M. Krishnaswami Ayyar, namely, that when infringement of the copyright in a previous book by the author of a subsequent work is proved it will be of no answer to the action for injunction, or damages, for breach of copyright, to say that much additional and original matter, the result of the subsequent author's own independent research and thought, has been added. That proposition also is correct, and is laid down in many cases and is not disputed by the learned counsel for the defendants. The added matter may only be relevant in such a case for the purpose of considering whether an injunction should issue in respect of such matter also, as going inseparably with the pirated matter, or no injunction need be given regarding such matter.

The learned counsel for the defendants relied upon a proposition of law called from *Jarrold v. Haywood*,[37] and quoted with approval in *Kartar Singh v. Ladha Singh*,[38] to the effect:

> 'If any part of a work complained of is a transcript of another work, or with colourable additions and variations prepared without any real independent literary labour, such portion of the work is piratical. It is impossible to establish a charge of piracy when it is necessary to track some passages and lines through hundreds of pages or when the authors of a work challenged as piratical honestly applied their labour to various sources of information'

That proposition, which was accepted by a Bench of Lahore High Court and with which I entirely agree, is undoubtedly correct, and was not disputed by Mr. T.M. Krishnaswami Ayyar for the plaintiff, his contention being merely that the plaintiff's case is not one like that.

The learned counsel for the defendants relied on another proposition taken from *Kartar Singh v. Ladha Singh*[39] to the following effect:

> 'All laws which put a restraint upon human activity and the enterprise must be construed in a reasonable and generous spirit. Under the guise of the copyright, a plaintiff can ask the Court to close all the avenues of research and scholarship and all frontiers of human knowledge.'

and that the law of Copyright must be interpreted in a just and liberal spirit in the light of the above observations of the Bench, supported by numerous other decisions, English and Indian. That proposition also is undoubtedly correct and is not disputed by Mr. T.M. Krishnaswami Ayyar for the plaintiff, his contention being that even the most liberal interpretation of the Copyright Act would still leave the plaintiff's case for infringement unaffected.

The next proposition of Mr. T.M. Krishnaswami Ayyar was that even an attempted sale of work infringing the copyright in a previous work would confer jurisdiction on Court, and that an injunction could be asked for. He relied on the

37. 18 WR 279.
38. AIR 1934 Lahore 777.
39. *Ibid.*

ruling of the Allahabad High Court in *Om Prakash v. Radhey Shyam*,[40] in support of this contention. This is correct, but is not material for our purpose now in this case as the learned Attorney-General for India, for the defendants, has, even at the very outset, given up the defendants' contention that this Court had no jurisdiction to try this suit, and had stated that the defendants had acquiesced in the jurisdiction of this Court.

Mr. T.M. Krishnaswami Ayyar, for the plaintiff, next relied on the proposition that a subsequent author of a similar work, admitting that he had seen the previous work, from which he is charged with pirating a substantial portion for the purpose of his practice, but not for writing the subsequent work, must be held to have used the previous work for writing the subsequent work, if he is proved to have been writing the subsequent work even during the period he was consulting the previous work for practice, as it is impossible to put the two uses of the book in water-tight compartments. That proposition is one of *fact*, and must depend on the evidence. No cut and dry decision can be given, except in the light of the facts proved in each case. The matter becomes of importance because the second defendant, as D.W. 1 admitted having consulted the plaintiff's book, Ex. P-1, for his practice from 1944 onwards not only before the idea of writing this book occurred to him in 1947, but continued to refer to the plaintiff's book for his practice even during 1947 to 1950, when he was gathering materials and writing his book and passing the proofs thereof.

The next proposition of Mr. T.M. Krishnaswami Ayyar, for the plaintiff, was that, as the 2nd defendant admitted that when writing his book, Ex. P-2, the plaintiff's book, Ex. P-1, was all the time in his very chambers with Mr. Kolah, a friend and colleague of his, it must be presumed that he had access to the book, Ex. P-1, and must have used it even for writing Ex. P-2. He relied on the observations of Wittenberg in his book 'The Protection and Marketing of Literacy and Property', p. 89 about 'access'. Here the argument is obviously based on the analogy of a presumption of adultery drawn in a divorce case, when a young man and a young woman are alone with each other in the same bedroom at night, and could have had access, and should be presumed to have had access, or to the presumption in Mohammadan Law, in its theory of valid interval, when a man and his wife, of co-habitable age, are alone are presumed to be likely to have had sexual intercourse. I cannot agree that a man's being alone with a book belonging to a colleague in the same chambers, is in an exactly similar position to the young man and young woman being alone in a bed-room at night or a man and wife being alone under the Mohammadan Law. Each case must depend on the evidence in that case. Here it depends on whether I accept the testimony of D.W. 1, denying such use of the book while writing his book, or reject it, for any reason, including this. Of course, as already stated, infringement of copyright can be established even if the book from which a substantial passage is pirated is not actually before the subsequent author pirating it, and even if he does so from mere memory, as Marshall did in the case already referred to. Here again, it is a question of a fact and apprehension of evidence.

The next proposition of Mr. T.M. Krishnaswami Ayyar was that even in the case of the extracts from judgments and select committee reports not covered by copyright, there will be infringement of copyright, if there has been expenditure of skill, taste, labour and brains in such selections by the previous author, and the very same selections are copied servilely by the subsequent author, with all the tell-

40. ILR 1948 All 20.

tale mistakes, which serve to show piracy. That is so, as would be clear from the decisions already cited including that in *Jogesh Chandra Chowdary v. Mohini Chandra Ray.*[41] In that case, not only selections of the cases in the Calcutta Weekly Notes, but also the arrangement was copied by the defendant in his 'Calcutta Case Law'. He also reproduced facts, notes etc., attached to the plaintiff's report and forming his own independent contribution. I am prepared to hold that even if a man proceeds to copy the entire judgments or extracts therefrom made by another in his book, without copying the notes independently appended thereto, he will be committing breach of copyright, if he does not, by his own labour, skill and brains, get those judgments (which are not subject to copyright) himself. Thus, if a man starting a journal called 'My Law Journal' copies the cases reported in any issue of the Madras Law Journal, in their very order, without using his own labour, skill and brains, he would be undoubtedly committing breach of copyright. It was held in *Gopaldas v. Jagannath Prasad,*[42] that the fact that the defendant produced something like the plaintiff's work, does not necessarily create an infringement, for it is always possible to arrive at the same result from independent sources, or by coincidence, and it must be shown that the defendant had derived the work from the plaintiff's book; but, where the number and details of the similarity are too many to be due to mere chance, and they have been evidently copied from the plaintiff's work, even including the tell-tale inadvertent slips and errors, and with slight colourable variations, and the defendant had adopted the plaintiff's arrangement and has put the plaintiff's matter in his book in the same order and sequence, and the defendant gives a wrong explanation for these similarities, and is unable to name the correct books from which he took his material, there is no room for doubt that the defendant got this matter from the plaintiff's. Similarity should not be due to coincidence or culling from common sources by independent use of labour, skill and brains, and must be substantial.

Lastly, Mr. T.M. Krishnaswami Ayyar further urged that similarity in the scheme of the book, arrangement on topics, headings, phrases, conclusions, criticisms, common passages, common mistakes, idioms etc., would be proof of copying and infringement of copyright. This is a matter for determination in the light of evidence in each case. If similarity between two works was not due to coincidence or copying from common un-copyright matters, and was substantial, and not inane, common and inevitable, and so cogent that no one would believe any denial, the argument of Mr. T.M. Krishnaswami Ayyar would be correct, but not otherwise, as held in *Robl and another v. Palace Theatre Limited and another.*[43] It is also clear that where the copying is trivial or inane, common or inane, common or inevitable, it would not be held to be infringement of copyright, though the question of triviality of the copying or its inane, common or inevitable nature, too, is a matter of fact and has to be decided on the evidence in the case. Thus, inane similarities, as the comparison mentioned in Shakespeare's 'Henry IV' between two countries, or a continuation that one man has copied his features from another, because he has got two eyes, two ears, a nose, a mouth, two arms and two legs, like the other, will be too inane for this purpose. So too, it is inevitable for any geographer of a country to name the principal mountains, rivers, towns etc., of that country. So too, it will be very common for people to describe certain things in the same way, like the five Pandavas as 'Yudhishtara, Bhima,

41. 26 Indian Cases 30.
42. ILR 1938 All 370.
43. Times Law Reports, 28, page 69.

Arjuna, Nakula and Sahadeva' etc. That will also not be anything worth taking notice of by Courts. So too, the adoption, from the common stock of mankind, of legal expressions etc., leaving no room for taste or judgment or skill or labour or brains, will not carry copyright in them and that copying them will be no infringement, as held by the Privy Council in *G.A.Cramp & Sons Limited v. Frank Smith & Son Ltd.,*[44] and other cases.

The learned counsel on both sides agree that the question regarding the infringement of copyright in this case by the defendants, or otherwise, must be treated as one single question, by surveying and comparing the two books as a whole. That view is undoubtedly correct, and has been laid down in many decisions. Mr. T.M. Krishnaswami Ayyar, for the plaintiff, specially urged that all the various heads under which he tried to prove copying and infringement of copyright, and the various items under each head, in Exs.P-3, P-4, P-5(a) and P-6 were only intended to be taken as a whole, for the purpose of arriving at a decision whether infringement of copyright in the plaintiff's book in Ex. P-1 by the defendants in Ex. P-2 has been proved, and that he was relying on all the instances cumulatively, and not singly and separately. Now, as the Hindu-Law givers have held even in the days of the Mauryas, in considering the cumulative effect of separate facts, there are three things to be kept in mind, Firstly, the *utility* of such cumulative facts in some cases. Thus, while one rope will not be able to hold an elephant, ten ropes, twisted together, will easily hold it. Secondly, the *futility* of such cumulative facts in some cases. Thus, it has been remarked, by them, that one thousand blind men cannot muster one eye between them. Thirdly, the *danger* in looking at such cumulative facts without proper care, like the man who is said to have spent his time contemplating the various coils of a cobra, ignoring the head, and got bitten to death by it! In other words, one should not lose the wood for the trees, to use the English phrase corresponding to this idea.

I have very carefully and anxiously considered the various points urged in Exs. P-3, P-4, P-5(a) and P-6 and the various headings, so skillfully and lucidly put before me by Mr. T.M. Krishnaswami Ayyar and answered by the learned counsel for the defendant. After the most careful consideration, I have arrived at the conclusion that though, on first impression, a few of the passages, phrases, words and quotations, etc. relied on by the plaintiff might seem to have been copied by the second defendant from Ex. P-1 in Ex. P-2 – those coming at the most to 2 ½ pages out of 1000 pages – still, even those, on careful scrutiny, cannot be said to have been satisfactorily proved to have been copied by him from Ex. P-1, and could have been got by him out of his own independent thinking or by referring to the common non-copyright sources. The burden of proving copying lies heavily on the person alleging such copying, as, under our law, any man, asserting a thing, must prove it, if he is to get the relief asked for. Thus, a man alleging that a murder has been committed by A, must prove that A committed the murder; but, if A alleges, in his defence, that he did not commit the murder, but saw B committing it and wants that statement about B's being the murderer to be believed, he must prove that B committed the murder. So, in this case, the burden of proving copying by the second defendant from Ex. P-1 lies heavily on the plaintiff, and I am clearly of opinion, after carefully considering the entire evidence and argument that he has utterly failed to prove it, and has only left a kind of vague suspicion that those 2 ½ pages might not have been copied from his book by defendant 2 from memory of the passages etc. I believe D.W. 1's

44. Law Reports 1944 House of Lords 329.

evidence on oath that he did not refer to Ex. P-1 when he was writing Ex. P-2. He struck me as a straightforward witness giving out the truth to the best of his belief. In such a case, where the witness is believed by Court on his evidence on oath, similarities and other things, which would otherwise count, will have little value, as held in *Deeks v. Wells*.[45] Of course, it is just possible (it is a mere possibility, with no proof) that the second defendant, who had been using Ex. P-1 for his practice from 1944 to 1950, and right through the period when he was writing his book, and admitted having remembered twenty views of the plaintiff expressed in Ex. P-1, and to have controverted one view of the plaintiff specifically, might have sub-consciously remembered some more views and put them in Ex. P-2, and that may account for the 2½ pages referred to by me above. But that is *a mere surmise*, and not either a matter of evidence or of inference, or even of a justifiable presumption. Therefore, I must give the benefit of the doubt to the second defendant even regarding these 2 ½ pages. It is also obvious that the above 2½ pages of dispersed matter extracted from many judgments (non-copyright matter) in a book of one thousand pages, even if found to be copied, may not amount to a substantial portion of the plaintiff's book, and may not justify an injunction or even damages, though it might be technically petty piracy of a kind. But, as stated already, there is no need to discuss the matter further, as there is no proper proof that he took even those 2½ pages or any portion thereof from Ex. P-1, and he could have got those portions independently by his own labour and put them in his book, from his own independent selection from those common sources not covered by copyright. These also amount only to a very small fraction of the entire extracts from judgments incorporated in Ex. P-1 or Ex. P-2, and both authors went to the original sources.

Now, I shall deal, briefly and rapidly, with the various heads under which Mr. T.M. Krishnaswami Ayyar sought to prove copying and infringement of copyright. The first was the alleged inspiration for the book Ex. P-2 on the book, Ex. P-1. Now, the inspiration given by one book, for writing another book on the same subject or a different subject, may not amount at all to breach of copyright. Many a great author has been inspired to write a better book on a subject by seeing a good book by another on that subject. It is not also one of the things complained of in Exs. P-3, P-4, P-5(a) and P-6. Further, there is the famous story of a celebrated decision of Maryadarama, the Chief Justice of the Chola Empire in the 11th century A.D., on this very matter. A country rustic sat under a tree. A food-seller was also there selling iddlis and sambhar. The rustic ate his meal of homely rice, bundled up by his wife in his dhoti, exhilarated by the smell of the nice sambhar of the food-seller. Seeing him sniff his nose with enjoyment, and consume his food with relish, the food-seller demanded from the rustic at least a small sum for the service he had taken from the smell of sambhar for his inspiration and rapid consumption of rice. On his refusal, he went to court, and Chief Justice Maryadarama held that for the smell of his sambhar, the food-seller must get the smell of the rustic's rupees, and had a bag of rupees thrust against the food-seller's nose as damages! Of course, that only damaged his nose, and did no more good! The matter of modelling one's book after another is also not of very great importance for breach of copyright purposes. Many a great author has modelled his book on the work of some author before him. That is why there is the Shakespearean School, the Wordsworthean School, the Shelley School, etc., and that is the natural way of human progress, and no sensible man will complain about it. Of course, in the present case, there is no proof that the second

45. 64 M.L.J. 193.

defendant was inspired to write his book, Ex. P-2, by seeing Ex. P-1, or that he modelled Ex. P-2 on Ex. P-1. According to him, he modelled it on the standard commentaries, like Mulla's C.P.C., Transfer of Property Act, etc., and it will be noticed that Mulla had his commentary out long before the plaintiff did. So, it is no argument to say that the plaintiff's commentary also resembles Mulla's commentary. It may be that the plaintiff also modelled his commentary on standard commentaries like Mulla's. Two persons taking a photograph of the same object will get much the same picture; but the first taker cannot accuse the second taker of copying his picture.

The second head under which Mr. T.M. Krishnaswami Ayyar tried to prove copying and infringement was that 50 to 80 percent of the topics, subjects and headings dealt with in both the books, Ex. P-1 and Ex. P-2, were common, and that, therefore, the headings in Ex. P-2 must have been copied from Ex. P-1. The argument is unconvincing and totally unproved. In the case of commentaries on Acts, as in histories, geographies etc., at least 50 to 80 per cent of the subjects, topics and headings must be common. No man, who has written about the mountains of India, can ask a succeeding author to leave out the Himalayas, already dealt with by him; or, at least, the Western Ghats, in his book! Especially when dealing with an act like the Income-tax Act, full of bristles piercing into the rich man's flesh, no intelligent commentator can afford to ignore a single topic, subject or heading, arising from the Act, if he is not to lose all prospects of a good sale for his book. The complained of headings in both the books, like the extracts complained of from judgments are all taken from common sources.

The third argument of Mr. T. Krishnaswami Ayyar related to the similarity of the beginning, ending sequence, etc. in many commentaries between the two books, and, therefore, the probability of the similar things in Ex. P-2 being a copy of Ex. P-1. This is also quite untenable. Just as any man writing about human life will have to refer to birth, growth, marriage and death, and any man writing about wealth must write about its acquisition, development, alienation and elimination. So too, commentators must proceed like this in such commentaries 'money' and 'money's worth' must follow as naturally as a mountain and a river, and can only follow in that sequence. The cases of similarity are few and of no importance. Besides, two intelligent commentators on the Income-tax Act – I hold that both the plaintiff and the second defendant are equally intelligent and alert- must agree on at least 80 percent in their arrangement, sequence, development and analysis. The analysis similarity is also confined to a ____ from _____.[46] Besides, the analysis of matter by two qualified people must be more or less the same. So too the analysis of subjects by two qualified commentators.

The next head under which Mr. T.M. Krishnaswami Ayyar wanted to prove copying and infringement of copyright was the common conclusions to which the plaintiff and the defendants came on most of the vital matters involved. That is also, in my opinion, inevitable, as it cannot be expected that the Income-Tax Act is so absurd, or the decisions so futile, that two intelligent men can come to opposite conclusions on more than a very few topics. They must necessarily agree in their conclusions regarding most of the topics. But, here, it is curious, and it shows the absence of pirating, that these two learned and clever authors differed on two or three topics, one being right in one or two, and the other in the rest. Thus, the plaintiff

---

46. Several portions in the judgment have been added by the learned judge and the handwriting in this particular portion is incomprehensible and has, therefore, been left blank.

was of the opinion in the third edition of his book Ex. P-1 that profits earned by a man selling stolen property, habitually received by him, would not be taxable, whereas the second defendant held that they could be taxed, not only as trade profits, but also as income derived from other sources, and the plaintiff has adopted, in his fourth edition, the view that they are taxable as income from other sources, but, of course, independently, by following the reasoning in a case in 1948. So too, the plaintiff adopted one opinion, and the defendant the contrary opinion, regarding a certain matter, and the Supreme Court recently decided, in two different decisions on the same point, in favour of the plaintiff's view. These are only examples to show that each author seems to have considered the matter himself, independently, and arrived at his own conclusion.

The next point urged by Mr. T.M. Krishnaswami Ayyar was the citing of common decisions and quoting of common extracts. Now, this is also inevitable in every modern country governed by rulings and precedents. Judge-made law, far from becoming unimportant, is assuming greater importance in every civilized country, and, in our country, due to writs, where the judges are given greater powers of indirect law-making than they ever had before. In such a state of law, it is obvious that the rulings would be eagerly sought after by every intelligent commentator and put into his book, whatever his view might be about the judge's wisdom, which view also he will rarely disclose, lest the sale of his book should be affected prejudicially. So, all the rulings must inevitably find their place in any intelligent commentary. Here, we find also several cases where the rulings cited by each of these able commentators are different and several where the common rulings are few and the additional rulings are many more, showing independent application of labour, skill and brains by the second defendant, and his not relying on the plaintiff's application of his labour, skill and brains.

The next head on which Mr. T.M. Krishnaswami Ayyar relied was common criticisms of sections, omissions and lapses on the part of the legislators, etc. Thus, both these commentators pointed out that the proviso to one section was utterly useless, because a proviso could not override the substantial provision in that section, and that the Act in one place had overlooked the provision in another section for taxing a certain income, when naming various incomes liable to be taxed there. But, even there, the two commentators showed their characteristic differences; the plaintiff characterised the provision in the proviso as *brutum fulmen*, (it ought to be, correctly, *brutum fulmen*), or an empty threat, whereas the second defendant characterized it as a pointless provision arising from the over-anxiety of the draftsman.

The next head on which Mr. T.M. Krishnaswami Ayyar relied was common marginal headings. This is covered by Ex. P-5(a). I have looked into this matter and I find that almost all the marginal headings are taken either from sections, or from the Income-tax Manual, or from well-known rulings or commentaries. So, this head is useless for proving piracy.

The next head was common grouping of sections in both the books; but, such groupings are indicated even in the Income-tax Manual, and must occur to any intelligent commentator, even if it is not so indicated. A man who is to comment on the Income-tax Act is not expected to be a fool unable to find out which section goes with which other section. There is, as already stated, the Income-tax Manual, which has been laboriously compiled, like the Land Acquisition Manual, by able and experienced administrators for the use, primarily, of the Government servants carrying out the duties under the Act.

The next thing relied on by Mr. T.M. Krishnaswami Ayyar was the mistakes committed by the plaintiff in his book, Ex. P-1, being copied servilely by the second defendant in Ex. P.-2. Now, common mistakes, though they can arise even by accident, by two men committing the same mistakes independently, like two men falling into the same well at night, are generally good evidence of copying, if they are numerous and convincing, as held in numerous decisions. But, unfortunately for the plaintiff, the four common mistakes relied on by him in Ex. P-5, at pages 62 to 66, had to be given up as wholly untenable and were given up, I have no doubt, very wisely. Therefore, an attempt was made to prove three more alleged mistakes of the plaintiff said to have been copied by the second defendant. The first was the alleged copying of the wrong sentence of the plaintiff at page 29. The plaintiff has written, at page 29 of his book, Ex. P-1 the sentence 'In short, Income-tax Acts are not necessarily restricted in their application to lawful business only', and has cited, in the foot-note, *The Canadian Minister of Finance v. Smith,*[47] as the authority for the proprietor. The defendant has, at page 66 of his book, the sentence 'In the leading case of *Minister of Finance v. Smith* (24), Lord Haldane said 'The Income Tax Acts are not necessarily restricted in their application to lawful businesses only'. This, according to Mr. T.M. Krishnaswami Ayyar, is servile copying by the second defendant from the plaintiff's book, Ex. P-1, which contained the alleged mistake, by adding the word 'not' to what Lord Haldane had actually said. Lord Haldane's exact words in that case, which appear at page 198, are: 'Their Lordships have no reason to differ from the conclusion reached in that case; but they must not be taken to assent to any suggestion sought to be based on the words used by the learned Lord Justice that Income-tax Acts are necessarily restricted in their application to lawful businesses only.' It will be noted at once that the second defendant must have gone to the original decision, for three reasons. Firstly, the plaintiff has not, in his book, given the name of Lord Haldane, and the second defendant could not have known it except by going to the decision; secondly, the plaintiff has not given the exact page, 198, from which the quotation is taken, and the second defendant has used the correct word 'businesses', used by Lord Haldane in the judgment, instead of the wrong word 'business' used by the plaintiff. Nor am I satisfied that it is a case of mistake at all on the part of the plaintiff and the second defendant in their books to be as correct as any other view, especially as Simon, one of the greatest authorities on Income-tax, has taken the same view. We need not now bother ourselves with considering whether receipts from habitually selling stolen property is taxable as profits of trade or as income from other sources. It will be a profitable discussion. The point is that the plaintiff has not committed any mistake, and the defendant is not proved to have committed the same mistake, much less to have copied from the plaintiff's mistake. The second defendant alone has used the quotation mark. One further thing that supports the second defendant's contention, namely, that he read the case himself and took the sentence as is given in his book in his notes in that form with the word 'not' added, and got confirmed that the word 'not' was there by looking at the decision of Yahya Ali, J. in *Mohammed Abdul Karim & Co. v. Commissioner of Income Tax,*[48] and by looking at Simon later on, is the fact that Yahya Ali, J., an experienced judge of this Court, has given the dictum of Lord Haldane in the very same form as the 2nd defendant with the word 'not' added. Now, a commentator cannot be generally expected to be wiser than judges of High Courts, who are statutorily learned men. They can

47. 1927 AC 193.
48. 16 I.T.R. 412 at 416.

very well rely on passages and quotations and summarises in judgment of High Courts without again going to the original authority, which may be hard to get at, as it was for the second defendant, at that time.

Mr. T.M. Krishnaswami Ayyar urged, with great plausibility, that Yahya Ali J. must have taken the sentence in question from the plaintiff. That may or may not be so. I myself think that it may possibly be so. But there is no proof that the second defendant, when getting confirmed from Yahya Ali J.'s judgment , knew or suspected that Yahya Ali, J. had taken it from the plaintiff. Indeed, as the plaintiff's name is not mentioned at all by Yahya Ali, J., I cannot infer that Yahya Ali, J., must have been seen the plaintiff's book and got the sentence from it. It is only a mere surmise. Of course, it will be a good thing if judges who rely on sentences from commentaries quote the commentator's name also, as that will be only doing them justice and will also be of some service to the commentators. So this instance also fails.

The next instance of common mistake relied on was the second defendant's referring to 'receiving and reselling' of stolen property and to the plaintiff's having by an error mentioned 'receive and resell' in his third edition, and even the fourth edition, after having put 'receive and reset' in his first two editions. It was urged by Mr. T.M. Krishnaswami Ayyar that the word in the English Tax Cases was 'resetting', and not 'reselling', and that 'resetting' means 'receiving' in that context. But that meaning was not known even to me when I first read it, and I took the word 'resetting' to be a mistake for 'reselling' till Mr. T.M. Krishnaswami Ayyar discovered the true meaning of 'resetting'. There is also, as the second defendant pointed out, the possibility of a man's receiving stolen property from a thief, by paying him a pittance, and reselling it to another person at a profit. Therefore, the word 'receive and resell' will not be nonsensical or meaningless or incorrect even in that context. So, I see no mistake committed by the plaintiff in putting 'receiving and reselling', for 'receiving and resetting', and no mistake also in the second defendant's using the words 'receiving and reselling'. The very fact that the second defendant could give an intelligible explanation for his phrase 'receiving and reselling' would show that he has applied his brains to the matter. So, this instance also fails.

The last, and 11th hour, instance of alleged common mistake copied in Ex. P-2 from Ex. P-1 is contained in item 12 of Ex. D-1. Mr. T.M. Krishnaswami Ayyar stated that the plaintiff wrongly relied on *I.R.C. v. Morton,*[49] as an authority for the proposition stated therein, and that the second defendant also relied on the same overruled case as an authority. But the curious thing is that the so-called ruling which is said to have overruled *I.R.C. v. Morton,*[50] does not say or show that the said ruling was overruled regarding the proposition for which it was quoted by both these learned commentators. So it is not even proved to be a common mistake. But, even assuming it was overruled, I can very well see two commentators in India independently being ignorant of the latest English Case overruling a slightly earlier English case, after the independence of India and the non-concern of Indians with the English Courts and their decisions. So, by mere chance, these two authors could have exhibited the same ignorance regarding the alleged overruling, which itself is, in my opinion, not at all proved. So, one of the pillars relied on by Mr. T.M. Krishnaswami Ayyar for proving copying and infringement of copyright has collapsed.

---

49. Citation not available in the judgment.
50. Citation not available in the judgment.

Another important pillar relied on by Mr. T.M. Krishnaswami Ayyar for proving copying and infringement of copyright is the similarity of several passages in Ex. P-1 and Ex. P-2 containing the effect of certain important decisions. His argument was that the words in the decisions were adapted by the plaintiff when digesting the decisions and utilizing them for his purpose, and that the second defendant servilely copied those adaptations of the plaintiff. There is no substance at all in this. Ex. D-1 shows the untenability of this claim. No passage is proved to have been copied. Now, I shall consider some of the passages. None of the adaptations of passages from the judgments, claimed by the plaintiff, are of any significance excepting three. The remaining ones consist merely of removing a word here and a word there, a comma here and a comma there, adaptations not at all requiring the use of labour, skill or brains, and, therefore falling within the rulings of the Privy Council and House of Lords stated above; such mechanical and prosy[51] adaptations involve no use of labour, skill or brains, and will not have copyright in them, and will not involve breach of copyright by copying them. I shall first give the best of the three exceptions as it deserves to be discussed at some length, and the other two instances also briefly; the other things do not really deserve to be discussed at all. The one matter which deserves some detailed discussion is at page 29 of Ex. P-1, the plaintiff's book, and at page 66 of the defendant's book, Ex. P-2. The passage in question runs in the plaintiff's book as follows:

> 'The Revenue merely looks at an accomplished fact, viz., of profits having been earned, and assess the same. The assessee might be prosecuted for the crime and yet be charged on the profits.'

The passage in the defendants' book, at page 66, runs as follows:

> 'The revenue merely looks at an accomplished fact; by bringing the profits to tax, it does not condone or take part in the illegal enterprise. The assessee may be prosecuted for the offence and at the same time taxed upon the profits arising out of its commission'.

The source for both these commentaries is admittedly the observation of Rowlatt J. in his judgment in *Mann v. Nash*.[52] The passage from the judgment relevant for our purpose runs as follows:

> 'Does the State keep its revenue eye open and its eye of justice closed? I must say I do not feel the force of that observation at all. Would it have made any difference, I ventured to ask in the argument, 'if the State had kept both its eyes open and prosecuted the man for the lottery and taxed him for the profits at the same time?...The Revenue representing the State, is merely looking at an accomplished fact.'

It is obvious that the passage 'The Revenue representing the State, is merely looking at an accomplished fact' is not altered to any appreciable extent by the plaintiff, as the alteration by him is purely verbal and does not involve any use of the brains, as a rhetorical question by the learned Judge has been converted into a simple proposition understandable by one and all. It is just possible, in my opinion, that the second defendant might have remembered this adaptation by the plaintiff, in Ex. P-1, when he read the book for his practice and put it in his book. But there is no proof of...[53] The second defendant must have gone to the original

51. The word 'prosy' is used rarely and the Oxford Dictionary defines it as 'showing no imagination; commonplace or dull.'
52. 16 T.C. 524
53. This sentence is not complete in the certified copy.

judgment, as he has used the words 'at the same time' found in the judgment and not found in Ex. P-1. Ex. P-1 does not give the page, 530, at which the passage is found, but only page 523, the beginning of the judgment. Anyway, copying is not proved; and, even proved, it would be so small a piracy that I would not have seriously taken notice of it excepting for disallowing the defendants their costs. The second defendant was not able to say whether he found the passage summarised like that into a straight proposition in any other book, and finally said that he himself summarised it like that. Perhaps, he did, I am not, however, fully satisfied that he did not remember from his reading of Ex. P-1, for his practice, this particular adaptation by the plaintiff and take it, honestly and unconsciously, and put it into his book. Anyway, I leave it at that.

As regards the other instances of adaptation given by Mr. T.M. Krishnaswami Ayyar, they involve so very little skill, labour and brains that any independent commentator can easily adapt the passages himself like that. As I have already held, there are two other legitimate uses of a previous commentary or a book, besides the three uses mentioned in *Jarrold v. Houlston*.[54] The fourth use is to be inspired, by reading a good book, to write a similar or better book on the same or different subject. The fifth use is to build your book on that good book by adopting the good features in it. The world is not so full of good books that a good book should not be initiated in such an innocent way. The arrangement of Mulla in his Civil Procedure Code and Transfer of Property Act and other standard commentaries had better be adopted by every commentator on any Act including the Panchayat Courts Act, so that he may get a methodical and systematic, independent and intelligible, treatment. I do not think Mulla will or can complain of breach of copyright by such modelling of commentaries on his standard commentaries. I consider that, here, the second defendant might have modelled his adaptations from judgments or summaries of judgments in a very few cases. I put them at *three cases* out of a *thousand* on the plaintiff's adaptations and there is nothing wrong, or anything in the nature of a breach of copyright, there.

An example of this is found on page 340 of the plaintiff's book and on page 328 of the defendant's book. At page 340 of the plaintiff's book, he has extracted or summarised the passage in these terms:

> 'Fixed capital is what the owner turns to profit by keeping it in his own possession. Circulating or floating capital is what he makes profit of, by parting with it and letting it change masters'.

In Ex. P-2 there is the following corresponding passage:

> 'Fixed capital is what the owner turns to profit by keeping it in his own profession (mistake for possession); circulating capital is what he makes profits of by parting with it and letting it change masters.'

The original passage in the judgment of Viscount Haldane in *John Smith & Son v. Moore,*[55] runs as follows:

> 'Adam Smith described fixed capital as what the owner turns to profit by keeping it in his own possession, circulating capital as what he makes profit of by parting with it and letting it change masters.'

Commentators, especially of an intelligent variety, do not quote more than what is actually necessary and to the point. When quoting Lord Haldane, they

---

54. R.R. Vol. 112 p. 357.
55. 12 T.C. 266 at page 282.

will, naturally, fight shy of mentioning Adam Smith whose saying he had adopted as his own. Therefore, it would be natural for any intelligent commentator to leave out the beginning phrase 'Adam Smith described', and the inevitable necessity of changing the word 'as' into 'is' will arise, to make the sentence grammatical and English. It may be, that even here, the second defendant remembered the plaintiff's adaptation and that made him adapt likewise. It may not be also, as already stated, as any intelligent commentator could have easily done the same thing. Indeed, Mahajan J. has the very same adaptation in a reported case and he is not proved to have got it from the plaintiff. This is a border line instance, like the third instance I am going to refer to now. That instance is found at page 111 of the plaintiff's book and at page 88 of the defendant's book runs as follows:

> 'The turning of investment to account was not merely incidental, but was the essential feature of the business, speculation being among the appointed means of the company's gains.'

The passage in the defendant's book at page 88, runs thus:

> 'The turning of investment to account was not merely incidental but was the essential feature of the business, speculation being among the appointed means of the company's gains.'

The passage in the judgment of Lord Justice Clerk from which both the commentators have drawn the above passage is found in *Californian Copper Syndicate (Limited and Reduced) v. Harris,*[56] and is as follows:

> 'This was that the turning of investment to account was not to be merely incidental, but was, as the Lord President put it in the case of the Scottish Investment Company, the essential feature of the business, speculation being among the appointed means of the Company's gains.'

The plaintiff, like an intelligent commentator, has dropped out the unwanted clauses about what the Lord President put it in the case of the Scottish Investment Company, for the same reason that Adam Smith was dropped out in the previous passage cited. Any intelligent commentator must do that in the interest of economy of space and pointedness of comment. It is quite possible that the second defendant also independently did likewise. It is also just possible that memory of the plaintiff's adaptation lingered in his mind unconsciously, and that he put the same adaptation in his book, Ex. P-2. The matter is not free from doubt, and the burden of proof is on the plaintiff, I must hold that, in all these three cases, also where I entertained some little doubt, it is not at all proved that the second defendant copied the passages from the plaintiff's book. It is also immaterial, as the passages copied are not sufficient to constitute a substantial copying justifying injunction or damages. There is no need to discuss any more passages etc., as to copying of adaptations by the second defendant, as the similarity is less and less and the adaptations involve less skill than the three instances referred to by me and can be more easily adapted in the same way independently by any other intelligent commentator. A look at Ex. D-1 will show how untenable the plaintiff's claims are in most of the cases relied on by him. I may say here that I am perfectly satisfied that the second defendant did go to the original sources and cases in all the instances, as his description of the cases, citation of other cases, correction of errors, if any in Ex. P-1,[57] all show. Whether

56. 5 Tax Cases 159 at 167.
57. The reference should be to Ex. P-2. The plaintiff's book is Ex. P-1.

he adopted the adaptations of the plaintiff in the three cases referred to above, from unconscious memory of Ex. P-1 and his appreciation of such adaptations, I cannot say conclusively. But I am satisfied that in none of the three instances also is there proof that he did copy from the plaintiff's book, and the burden is heavily on the plaintiff. Of course, it must have chagrined the plaintiff to see that where he had adapted or summarised passages, similar summaries and adaptations were in some cases found in the defendant's book without acknowledging their debt to him for these adaptations. To receive censure or ridicule (one of his views in Ex. P-1 was admittedly referred to as absurd in Ex. P-2) and not be given praise, is one of the things which chagrin, irritate and anger authors. That is, in my opinion, one of the underlying causes for the plaintiff's filing this thin and unconvincing suit and for his irritability and emotion in giving his answers in the witness-box.

Coming to the summaries of the law and the statements of the law, etc., and the words, phrases etc. said to have been copied by the second defendant and set out in Exs. P-3, P-4, P-5(a) and P-6, I am not at all satisfied that they have been so copied. No doubt, there are numerous words and phrases common between Ex. P-1 and P-2. But most of these words are current words, of precise and definite significance in law, and must be used by any intelligent commentator. Thus, phrases like 'ambit of taxation', 'the taint of illegality', are found in exactly the same phrasing in leading authorities of undisputed ability like Halsbury and Simon, Dicey and Salmond. For the plaintiff to expect later commentators on the Indian Income-Tax Act to coin new phrases for themselves is to ask for the impossible, and, even though, at one stage, I think by error, it was claimed by the plaintiff that some of the words and phrases were coined by himself (see Ex. P-4), it was very properly given up by him the moment its untenability was pointed out to him, and he said that he had only used them in a particular collocation. Now, the word 'collocation' is a trap and snare, as it is capable of more mis-use than use. Such polysyllabic words have given more hopes to plaintiffs than judges have been able to fulfil! I am not satisfied that the plaintiff has proved at all that any of his passages or phrases, or words in Ex. P-1 have been copied by the defendants in Ex. P-2. Even words like 'bond-washing' and 'Earning year' which look at first sight to be somewhat simple and therefore likelier to be copied than the commoner coins will, on careful examination, be found to be only rarer coins (of law) available for richer people. 'Bond washing' is a well-known word in the Stock-exchange, and, of course, all stock-jobbers are rich or ought to be. The words 'Earning year' are found in reported decisions. I need not bother with words like 'in due course', 'all the more so', 'the effect of the section' etc. relied on by the plaintiff as his last straw. I want to point out here that the plaintiff's claim that the second defendant borrowed even his faulty idioms is not proved. Both these authors might have indulged in faulty idioms, but I do not see any faulty idiom of the plaintiff being pirated by the other. And why should he do so ? Nobody steals rubbish!

The next thing urged by Mr. T.M. Krishnaswami Ayyar is that the very camouflaging similar expressions found in Exhibits P-1 and P-2 in eight different ways, as by putting words, expressions, phrases, comments, etc., occurring in the earlier part of his book and in the latter part of defendant's book, and *vice versa*; transferring them from one section to another; transferring them from one topic to another; transferring them from the top of the page to the bottom of the page and *vice versa*; transferring them from headnote to the body and *vice versa*; splitting one sentence into two and one paragraph into two, and combining two sentences into one and two paragraphs into one, would show the defendants' copying from Ex. P-1, and their desperate attempt to hide such copying by this eight-fold device, reminiscent of the spider and the web! I cannot agree. It is only when copying is proved that camouflage becomes important. To say that a man has a motive to commit a murder will not be evidence that he committed the murder. If the murder is proved, the motive may be of some use as evidence, but not otherwise. So, here, when copying is not proved, the alleged camouflage, which itself is not proved, will be of no use whatever.

The last item, regarding common italics, need not detain us a moment. Indians, as a race, are very fond of italicizing things. One well-known Indian statesman, for instance, read a book three times, underlining one-third of the book each time, and, at the end of the process, found the whole book underlined! It is not as if that all the words italicized by the plaintiff are italicized by the second defendant. Of this number, a good number will have to be italicized by anybody, as constituting foreign words, like *bona fide*, and some words will be italicized by any Indian, like the word 'nil'. Indians have a great fascination for 'zeros', and 'nils' and even call God 'Pujya', (the 'Supreme Zero). The remaining italics might have been done by the second defendant by accident, or might have been done by an unconscious impulse generated by his unconscious memory, by having read Ex. P-1 or any other commentary, containing the same italicised words, during his practice. But we will be simply involving ourselves in the realm of conjecture if we go further into this subject. So, I will leave the subject at that.

In the end, therefore, I am of the opinion that, though the plaintiff really believed that portions of his book had been copied and pirated by the defendants, and that too, just at a time when his book was given top priority, and the fourth edition costing Rs. 37-80 unlike the lesser price of the older set and coming out editions and 5,000 copies of which were being printed, there is really no proof that any portion of the plaintiff's book has been really copied or pirated by the defendants in Ex. P-2. Only a vague suspicion remains that at the most, about 2 ½ pages, covered by the instances given above and some more examples too laborious to be stated in this long judgment, might have been imitated or copied by the second defendant, relying on his maximum memory, generated in having referred to the plaintiff's book, Ex. P-1, on numerous occasions between 1944 and 1950, and, be it remembered, during the entire period of his preparing and writing his book, Ex. P-2. I am not satisfied that the plaintiff was moved by any desire for pelf in issuing the notice, and, of course, he has lost some money by launching this ill-advised litigation in which he has not succeeded. Authors act on impulses which will not be appreciated[58] by hard businessmen who only take the money factor into account. I have no doubt whatever that the plaintiff was sincere in believing that a portion of his book had been pirated, though, of course, he was quite wrong in his thinking so and has indulged in some untenable and extreme statements, in his emotion, as P.W.1.

In the end, therefore, this suit deserves to be dismissed without costs. The learned counsel for defendants 1 and 3 and the second defendant on his own behalf, say that they do not press for costs. There is no need for me, therefore, to discuss the matter as regards costs any further. I direct all the parties of this suit to bear their own costs.

Sd/- ASP.
26th April 1952.

❄

---

58. It is not clear whether the word is 'appreciated' or 'approved' in the handwritten correction of the learned judge.

Appendix II

The Fundamental Rights Case[1]

Propositions submitted
before the Supreme Court
by
N.A. Palkhivala, *Senior Advocate*

Writ Petition No. 135 of 1970

In The Matter of:

His Holiness Kesavananda Bharati, Petitioner vs. The State of Kerala and another, Respondents.

Propositions regarding the true construction of Article 368 as it stood before the Twenty-fourth Amendment in 1971, in support of the submissions that:

(*a*) Parliament had no power to destroy or impair the essential features, the basic elements or the fundamental principles of the Constitution; and

(*b*) Article 368 did not prevail over or override Article 13.

1. The whole ratio of the majority judgments as well as the minority judgments in *Golak Nath case*,[2] turns entirely on the meaning to be attached to two words – the word 'law' in Article 13(2) and the word 'amendment' in Article 368. Therefore the crucial question is – what is the precise meaning to be attached to these two words. To start with any assumption that the word 'amendment' should be construed in its widest sense is to start with the answer instead of starting with the question.

2. The minority judgments in *Golak Nath case*, as also the earlier cases, proceeded on the assumption that the power of amendment dealt with by Article 368 was plenary. This assumption is wholly without foundation.

3. Article 368 referred only to the topic of constitutional amendment but was silent as to the subject-matter in respect of which the amending power could be exercised, and was equally silent as to the extent or width of the amending power.

4. It was only the proviso which enumerated the Articles the amendment of which required the concurrence of at least half the States. But even the proviso did not make it clear whether the institutions dealt with by it, e.g., the State Legislatures and the High Courts, could be destroyed by Parliament in the exercise of its amending power with the concurrence of half the States.

1. The written submissions or propositions were published in (1973) 4 SCC (Jour). 1. We thank Shri Surendra Malik of Eastern Book Company for permitting us to reproduce them here.
2. [1967] 2 SCR 762 : AIR 1967 SC 1643.

5. Article 368 used the word 'amendment' which is of the most elastic ambit; and the primary question is really of ascertaining the fair and reasonable meaning to be attached to that word in the context of Article 368, having regard to the genesis and general scheme of the Constitution, the basic constitutional structure behind the text of the constitutional document, and all other relevant circumstances which will be adverted to later.

6. It is clear beyond doubt that one of the well-settled meanings of the word 'amend' is that which would preclude the power to alter or destroy the essential features, the basic elements, the fundamental principles of the Constitution; and it is submitted that the word 'amendment' bore that meaning in Article 368. There is inherent evidence within the Article itself to support this view:

(*a*) Whereas the Constitution is given by the people unto themselves, the power to decide upon amendments (with or without the concurrence of half the States) is given to the five-year Parliament which is merely a creature of the Constitution. This point is of such profound significance that it will be elaborated later as a separate topic.

(*b*) Article 368 did not start with the *non-obstante* clause 'notwithstanding anything in this Constitution'.

(*c*) Article 368 was drafted in a very low key. It used the word 'amendment' simplicitor whereas even less significant amending powers in the other parts of the Constitution use the words 'add' 'alter' 'repeal' or 'vary', in addition to the word 'amend'. *See* Articles 31-B; 35(*b*); 252(2); 372; 372-A(2); V Schedule Para 7 and VI Schedule Para 21. Further, Article 368 merely talked of 'an amendment of this Constitution' and did not extend the amending power to 'all or any of the provisions of this Constitution'.

(*d*) On the construction of the word 'amendment' suggested by the Respondents, all fundamental rights could be taken away by Parliament by the requisite majority, whereas much less significant matters required the concurrence of at least half the States under the proviso to the Article. The basic human freedoms are of the most fundamental importance to all the States and to all their citizens. For instance, every State is interested in ensuring that Articles 14, 15 and 16 are respected and its citizens are not discriminated against, and that its religious and linguistic minorities are protected under Articles 29 and 30. Likewise, Article 32 is of no less importance to the citizens of the States than Article 226. Is it conceivable that while the Constitution required the States' concurrence for matters of much less moment, it intended the essential features of the Constitution (which included the basic human freedoms) to be entirely at the mercy of a two-thirds majority at the Centre?

(*e*) Under Article 368, the assent of the President to the Bill was necessary before the Constitution could stand amended. Under Article 60 the President has to take an oath that he will 'preserve, protect and defend the Constitution'. Any proposed amendment which struck at the core of the Constitution would require the President, if he was true to his oath, to refuse his assent. It is reasonable to assume that the Constitution did not intend to create a constitutional crisis by permitting Parliament to destroy all or any of the basic features of the Constitution and by enjoining the President at the same time to be true to his oath and preserve, protect and defend the Constitution by refusing assent. On the other hand, on the construction put by the Petitioners on the word 'amendment', such glaring inconsistency between the President's oath and the Parliament's power is avoided.

(*f*) Article 368 deals only with 'amendment of this Constitution'. The preamble is not a part or provision of the Constitution. (1960) 3 SCR 250, 282. (*See* also Annexure 'I' in which the same view is expressed about the preamble to the United States Constitution). Therefore, the preamble cannot be amended under Article 368. Secondly, the very nature and contents of the preamble are such that it is incapable of being amended. It refers to the most momentous event in India's history and sets out what the people of India resolved to do for their unfolding future. No Parliament can amend or alter past history.

If the preamble is unalterable, it necessarily follows that those features of the Constitution which are necessary to give effect to the preamble, are unalterable. Fundamental Rights are intended to give effect to the preamble, (1959 SCR 995, 1018-9). They cannot be abridged or taken away.

(*g*) It is most important to note that the provisions of Article 368 itself can be amended under that very Article. If the word 'amendment' is to be read in the widest sense contended for by the Respondents, Parliament would have the power to get rid of the requisite majority required by Article 368 and make any constitutional amendment possible by a bare majority. Further, Parliament would have the power to reduce India to a status which is neither sovereign nor democratic nor republican, and where the basic human rights are conspicuous by their absence. After doing that Parliament may:

(*i*) repeal Article 368 and expressly provide that the Constitution should hereafter be unamendable, or

(*ii*) amend Article 368 and provide for, say, 99 per cent majority for future amendments of the Constitution including any future amendment of Article 368 itself.

7. For the foregoing reasons, which are based upon the provisions of Article 368 itself, apart from other significant reasons which will be adverted to later, it is submitted that Article 368 should not be read as expressing the death-wish of the Constitution or as a provision for its legal suicide. It is fairly clear that Parliament cannot arrogate to itself under Article 368 the role of the Official Liquidator of the Constitution.

Propositions on behalf of the Petitioners regarding the true construction of Article 13 as it stood before the 24th Amendment in 1971; in support of the submissions that

(*a*) constitutional amendment, whether under Article 368 or otherwise, was 'law' within Article 13(2) and was void to the extent to which it contravened Fundamental Rights; and

(*b*) Article 368 did not prevail over or override Article 13.

I. Article 13(1) and (2) is not redundant

It is a misconceived argument that Article 13(1) and (2) is redundant and, therefore, the question whether Parliament can abridge Fundamental Rights by constitutional amendment should be decided without reference to Article 13(2). The observations of Kania, C.J., in the *Gopalan case*,[3] which are passing observations made in discussing the provisions of the Constitution generally, have been explained by Hidayatullah, J., in the *Sajjan Singh case*.[4] So far from being redundant, Article 13 serves the most useful purpose of dealing clearly and comprehensively with the four dimensions of the bar which it imposes:

(*a*) the authorities against whom the bar is imposed;

(*b*) the categories of law to which it applies;

(*c*) the laws in point of time which it covers; and

(*d*) the effect of the bar.

These four aspects are dealt by Article 13 as follows:

(*a*) The bar is imposed against the State, i.e. the totality of all the forces of the State, even including statutory corporations and autonomous authorities.[5]

(*b*) All categories of law are covered by the bar – from the highest (constitutional amendments) to the humblest (bye-laws); and all executive Orders and Notifications are equally covered under Article 13(2).

(*c*) All laws in force under Article 372 and all laws to be brought into force at any future date are brought within the scope of the bar.

(*d*) The effect of the bar is to render the law absolutely void, so as to leave no room for the U.S. theory of a law being 'relatively void'.[6]

To say that Article 13(2) is superfluous in the context of the alleged power to take away Fundamental Rights by constitutional amendments, is to beg the question. The primary purpose of Article 13(2) is to prohibit the making of any law, including constitutional law, which takes away or abridges Fundamental Rights. The Preamble makes it clear that the object of the Constitution is to secure the basic human freedoms, and this security or guarantee would be meaningless if the legislatures against whom the guarantees operate is itself at liberty to abrogate the guarantees.

II. 'Constitution as by law established'

It is clear beyond doubt, and is admitted in the minority judgments in the *Golak Nath case*,[7] and in the earlier judgments in the *Sankari Prasad case*,[8] and the

---

3. [1950] SCR 88 at 100.
4. [1965] 1 SCR 933 at 961.
5. See *Rajasthan State Electricity Board v. Mohanlal*, [1967] 3 SCR 377, 385.
6. *Behram Khurshed Pesikaka v. State of Bombay*, [1955] 1 SCR 613, 651-4.
7. [1967] 2 SCR 762, at 907 and 930.
8. [1952] SCR 89 at 106.

Sajjan Singh case,[9] that the word 'law' is comprehensive enough to include both ordinary law and constitutional law. But it is sought to be argued that:

(*a*) the result of an exercise under Article 368 is not a 'law', and

(*b*) that the word 'law' in Article 13(2) does not include constitutional law or constitutional amendment.

As regards argument (*a*) referred to above, it is submitted that the proposition that upon the procedure laid down in Article 368 being followed, the end-product is not a 'law', is erroneous.

The forms of oath in the Third Schedule refer to 'Constitution as by law established'. These words postulate:

(*a*) that the Constitution itself was originally established by law; and

(*b*) that every amendment thereto has likewise to be established by law in order that it may take effect. This necessarily involves and implies that every Amending Act under Article 368 is a 'law'.

The decisions of the Privy Council in *McCawley v. King*,[10] and *The Bribery Commissioner v. Ranasinghe*,[11] establish that constitutional amendment is a 'law', whether it is a controlled Constitution or whether there is a sovereign legislature under an uncontrolled Constitution.

As regards argument (*b*) noted above, it is submitted that there is no basis for the suggestion that the word 'law' in Article 13(2) has to be read in a restricted sense so as to exclude constitutional amendments. On the contrary, there are overriding considerations, set out below, which warrant the conclusion that the 'law' contemplated by Article 13(1) and (2) is every category of law, including constitutional law.

III. Article 13(1) covers constitutional law

Article 13(1) enacts that all laws in force immediately before the commencement of the Constitution are void to the extent of their inconsistency with the Fundamental Rights. Article 395 repealed the Indian Independence Act, 1947, and the Government of India Act, 1935, but not the constitutional laws of the Indian States or some other constitutional laws of British India. The Privy Purse case *Madhav Rao Scindia v. Union of India*,[12] establishes that the Covenants and the Merger Agreements entered into by the rulers with the Dominion of India were constitutional law; in fact, they have been called in the aforesaid case 'Constitutions in little'. These Covenants and Merger Agreements were in force at the commencement of the Constitution and they continued to remain in force. Further, in some of the States, the line between constitutional law and non-constitutional law was blurred, since the Ruler has absolute powers to take any legislative or executive action. Several laws of Indian States, constitutional as well as ordinary, continued after the commencement of the Constitution under Article 372.[13]

It is fairly clear that such constitutional laws, which stood unrepealed, would be void under Article 13(1) to the extent of their inconsistency with Fundamental

9. [1965] 1 SCR 933 at 950-1.
10. 1920 AC 691.
11. 1965 AC 172.
12. [1971] 3 SCR 9, 37-8 : (1971) 1 SCC 85.
13. *See* AIR 1960 SC 1312, Paras 3 and 15: [1961] 1 SCR 957, 962-3 : AIR 1954 SC 680 : [1953] SCR 404, 412.

Rights. This means that the expression 'all laws in force' in Article 13(1) would include constitutional law. The word 'law' in Article 13(2) could not have a different meaning. Therefore, the word 'law' in Article 13(2) included constitutional amendments.

It is further submitted that even assuming there had been no constitutional laws in force at the commencement of the Constitution which would be void under Article 13(1), that would be merely a fortuitous circumstance and would not derogate from the validity of the proposition that the word 'law' in 'Article 13(1) and the word 'law' in Article 13(2) included constitutional law. Since quite obviously all former constitutional laws throughout India were not repealed by Article 395, it must be held that when drafting Article 13(1) it was intended that the former constitutional laws should be hit by that Article.

IV. No limitation on the word 'law' in Article 13(2)

The Preamble, the scheme of the Constitution, the historical background, the intrinsic evidence of the solemn guarantees in Part III as well as the intrinsic evidence in other provisions dealing with constitutional amendments, all lead to the inference that the word 'law' in Article 13(2) was used in its ordinary sense as embracing constitutional law and there is no reason for reading the word in a restricted sense so as to confine it to ordinary laws. The Petitioner's argument merely requires the word 'law' to be used in its ordinary sense without the addition of any limiting words.

The real question is not whether there are any words of limitation in Article 368, but whether there are any words of limitation in Article 13(2). The minority decisions in the *Golak Nath case*, which refuse to read a limitation upon the words of Article 368 overlook that their own view reads a limitation upon the wide word 'law' in Article 13(2). If a limitation has to be read in either of these two Articles, there is no reason why it should be read in such a way as to enable Parliament to destroy Part III which is the foundation on which the fabric of the Constitution is reared.

V. Constitutional amendments under Articles 4 and 169 and Schedules V and VI

The argument that the word 'law' in Article 13(2) excludes constitutional law or constitutional amendment, is inconsistent with the scheme of the Constitution. The Parliament has power under Articles 4 and 169, and Para 7 of Schedule V and Para 21 of Schedule VI, to make amendments to the Constitution by a bare majority and without following the procedure laid down in Article 368. If the word 'law' in Article 13(2) does not cover constitutional amendments *ex hypothesi* it would not cover constitutional amendments made under the aforesaid provisions of the Constitution by a bare majority. The consequences of this view are so startling as to be patently unacceptable:

(*a*) If Article 13(2) does not operate as a bar, then under Article 4 read with Article 2 or 3 Parliament would have the power to create a new State and amend the Fourth Schedule so as to give the new State no representation in the Council of States or a representation which is indisputably unfair and which denies to the inhabitants of that State equality before the law as compared to the inhabitants of other States.

(*b*) If Article 13(2) does not apply, amendments could be made in the Fifth Schedule which deals with the administration of Scheduled Areas, to provide that none of the Fundamental Rights shall apply to the Scheduled Areas. Or, a provision could be made in Para 5 of the Fifth Schedule that the Governor shall have the power to make regulations denying to Scheduled Tribes the right to move freely throughout the territory of India and confining them to certain ghettos as Negroes are confined in South Africa, or denying the Scheduled Tribes all religious freedom and prohibiting them from worshipping their Tribal Gods.

(*c*) The Sixth Schedule which deals with the administration of Tribal Areas in Assam could likewise be amended to enable laws to be made or executive action to be taken in those areas, which may be patently inconsistent with Fundamental Rights.

Thus on the Respondent's construction of the word 'law' in Article 13(2) as excluding constitutional amendments, Parliament would have the power to reduce the Scheduled Tribes under the Fifth Schedule and the Assam Tribes under the Sixth Schedule to the level of second-class citizens and deny them the most elementary civil liberties – and that too by legislation passed by a bare majority like any ordinary law. The Constitution is reduced to an absurdity when an ordinary law of Parliament passed by a bare majority injuriously affecting the aforesaid Tribes would be void as violating Fundamental Rights; but the same law passed by the same bare majority and by exactly the same procedure would be valid if it seeks to incorporate those violations in Schedule V or VI. Correctly speaking, there is no difference between ordinary legislative power and constituent power in such a case. The Indian Constitution is undoubtedly a controlled Constitution. To say that under a controlled constitution a law prohibited by constitutional limitations can yet be passed as a constitutional amendment by a bare majority, is a contradiction in terms.

It is submitted that this is a conclusive argument which clinches the issue. Article 13(2) has necessarily to be read as including constitutional amendments made, for example, in exercise of the power conferred by Para 7 of Schedule V and Para 21 of Schedule VI. If such constitutional amendments were covered by the word 'law' in Article 13(2), it must obviously follow that constitutional amendments under Article 368 were also included and that the word 'law' in Article 13(2) embraced all constitutional amendments as much as ordinary law.

It is significant to note that even the 24th Amendment has merely added the following clause to Article 13:

> '(4) Nothing in this Article shall apply to any amendment of this Constitution made under Article 368.'

This means that constitutional amendments under Articles 4 and 169, Para 7 of the Fifth Schedule and Para 21 of the Sixth Schedule are still within the ambit of Article 13; and consequently the word 'law' in Article 13(2) did include and continues to include constitutional amendments.

VI. Consequences of the contrary view

If constitutional law is not covered by the word 'law' in Article 13(2), the integrity of India and the 'unity of the nation' referred to in the Preamble would be directly at stake. The Fundamental Rights could be amended so as to make them applicable to certain parts of India and not to others, to certain communities of India and not to others. Overtly favourable treatment could be given to the members of a political party, as is done in several other countries, and not to the rest of the citizenry. The South would be at the mercy of the North; minorities at the mercy of the majority; secularism at the mercy of religious fanaticism; and the process of disintegration of the Republic could well begin. The Petitioner's submission, giving a fair and natural meaning to the word 'law' in the context of Article 13(2), denies to Parliament the power of reducing the Constitution to a caricature of its present self.

If Parliament has an unfettered power of amendment, as claimed by the Respondent, even the two-thirds majority in Article 368 could be reduced to a bare majority, and the Fundamental Rights would thereafter be without any safeguard whatsoever. Alternatively, an amendment could be made in Part III to provide that if a Parliamentary Act or a State law starts with a declaration that the Fundamental Rights shall not apply to that law, such a law cannot be challenged on the ground of violation of any of the Fundamental Rights. In fact, the 25th Amendment is one category of such a law.

VII. Evidence of proceedings before the Constituent Assembly

The proceedings before the Constituent Assembly support the Petitioner's viewpoint:

(*a*) On April 29, 1947, an interim report on Fundamental Rights was placed before the Constituent Assembly and there was a debate on that interim report (see *Constituent Assembly Debates*, Vol III, pp. 399 to 436). On April 29, 1947, Shri K. Santhanam moved an amendment in Clause 2 which corresponded to the present Article 13 as follows:

> 'Shri K. Santhanam: Sir, I gave notice of an amendment but I will move it in a somewhat modified form in terms of a suggestion made by Sardar Patel. I move that in Clause 2 for the words 'nor shall the Union or any unit make any law taking away or abridging any such right', the following be substituted:
>
> 'Nor shall any such right be taken away or abridged except by an amendment of the Constitution.'
>
> The only reason is that if the clause stands as it is then even by an amendment of the Constitution we shall not be able to change any of these rights if found unsatisfactory or inconvenient. In some Constitutions they have provided that some parts of the Constitution may be changed by future constitutional amendments and other parts may not be changed. In order to avoid any such doubts I have moved this amendment and I hope it will be accepted.
>
> The Hon'ble Sardar Vallabhbhai Patel: 'Sir, I accept the amendment' (*Constituent Assembly Debates*, Vol. III, pp. 415-6).

In the draft prepared by the Constitutional Advisor in October 1947, Clause 9(2) corresponding to the present Article 13(2) was so worded as to exclude constitutional amendments from being rendered void under that article:

> '(2) Nothing in this Constitution shall be taken to empower the State to make any law which curtails or takes away or which has the effect of curtailing or taking away any of the rights conferred by Chapter II of this Part except by way of amendment of this Constitution under Section 232 and any law made in contravention of this sub-section shall, to the extent of the contravention, be void.'

But the Drafting Committee omitted the words excluding constitutional amendments, and in the draft Constitution as settled by the Drafting Committee, constitutional amendments were not excluded from the bar of Clause 8(2) corresponding to the present Article 13(2):

'(2) The State shall not make any law which takes away or abridges the rights conferred by this Part and any law made in contravention of this clause shall, to the extent of the contravention, be void;'

(*b*) Pt. Jawaharlal Nehru referred to Fundamental Rights as 'something that you want to make permanent in the Constitution' and Dr. Ambedkar referred to them as being excluded from the ambit of Articlc 368 (1967 Vol. 2 SCR 762 at 791-2) (See *Constituent Assembly Debates*, Vol. III, pp. 465-6 and *Constituent Assembly Debates*, Vol. IX, p. 1661).

(*c*) All the living members of the Committee of the Constituent Assembly, which was entrusted with the task of drafting the Chapter on 'Fundamental Rights', are unanimously of the view that they intended the Fundamental Rights to be beyond the reach of parliamentary majorities. (Writ Petition No. 135 of 1970, Vol. II, pp. 99-100).

VIII. Inalienable natural rights

The Fundamental Rights, with very few exceptions, are inalienable natural rights. Since the rights embodied in Part III are inalienable, it must necessarily follow that they cannot be taken away by Parliament by law, whether the law is entitled 'Constitution Amendment' or is labelled as ordinary law.

> 'The very purpose of a Bill of Rights was to withdraw certain subjects from the vicissitudes of political controversy, to place them beyond the reach of majorities and officials and to establish them as legal principles to be applied by the courts. One's rights to life, liberty and property, to free speech, a free press, freedom of worship and assembly, and other Fundamental Rights may not be submitted to vote; they depend on the outcome of no elections.'[14]

'The great purposes of the Constitution do not depend on the approval or convenience of those they restrain.'[15]

'Man being what he is, cannot safely be trusted with complete immunity from outward responsibility in depriving others of their rights. At least such is the conviction underlying our Bill of Rights.'[16]

> 'Our protection against all kinds of fanatics and extremists, none of whom can be trusted with unlimited power over others, lies not in their forbearance but in the limitations of our Constitution.'[17]

When we are dealing with the Fundamental Rights, 'we are dealing with principles of liberty and justice 'so rooted in the traditions and conscience of our

14. Per Jackson in *West-Viginia State Board of Education v. Barnette*, (1943) 87 L Ed 1628 at 1638 : 319 U.S. 624 at 638.
15. *Jackson, Erreson v. Board of Education*, 330 US 1, 28.
16. Frankfurter: *Joint Antifascist Ref. Comm. v. McGrath*, 341 US 123, 171.
17. Jackson: *American Comm. Assn. v. Douds*, 339 US 382, 439.

people as to be ranked as fundamental' – something without which 'a fair and enlightened system of justice would be impossible'.'[18]

If the basic human rights are to be fundamental and not fragile, it is impossible to hold that they can be abolished by an Act of Parliament merely by being called a Constitutional Amendment Act. A constitutional limitation would be no limitation at all if Parliament can do away with the limitation at its will. Constitutional guarantees which are away from extinction only by a bare majority or a two-thirds majority of a five-year Parliament are no guarantees at all.

Further, the opposite view involves the inexplicable anomaly that a five-year Parliament which even by a unanimous vote cannot abridge a single Fundamental Right by ordinary law, can repeal by a requisite majority the entire Chapter on Fundamental Rights merely by calling the law a Constitutional Amendment.

IX. Freedoms reserved by the people for themselves

Our Constitution is given by the people, in the exercise of their sovereignty unto themselves:

1954 SCR 541 at 555;
(1960) 3 SCR 250 at 281-2.

The Fundamental Rights are merely the expression of the basic freedoms reserved by the people for themselves:

(1967) 2 SCR 762 at 792;
1950 SCR 88 at 198.

If the freedoms are reserved by the people for themselves, all the functionaries and agencies under the Constitution have to respect those freedoms and, *ex hypothesi*, no functionary or agency can destroy those freedoms.

X. Reference to 'the State' in Article 13(2)

Article 13(2) imposes a limitation on the power of 'the State' which is a term of the largest possible import. The significance of the word 'State' is vital to the present case. Part III gives protection to the citizen and guarantees him the basic human rights against the totality of all the forces of the State. If the State in its most comprehensive sense cannot make a law to take away or abridge Fundamental Rights, Parliament which is only one of the functionaries or agencies of the State cannot pass such a law under Article 368. In other words, when the State, i.e. the totality of all the legislative and executive forces throughout India, is interdicted from passing a certain law, it is not possible to exclude or exempt constitutional amendments. The all-comprehensive concept of the State harmonises with the all-comprehensive concept of the 'law' in Article 13(2). The juxtaposition contemplated by Article 13(2) is not of 'Parliament' and 'ordinary law', but of all agencies comprised in the State and all branches of the law.

XI. Fundamental Rights exist even in times of Emergency

Even in times of crisis when a Proclamation of Emergency is issued, all Fundamental Rights continue to be in force except those dealt with by Article 19, and even the provisions of Article 19 are merely suspended and not abrogated during the period of Emergency (Article 358). Further, when the Proclamation of Emergency is in operation, the President has the power under Article 359 to suspend the enforcement of the Fundamental Rights in a court of law, but the

18. Frankfurter: *West Va. State Board of Education v. Barnette*, 319 US 624, 652.

Rights continue to exist and can be enforced after the Emergency ceases. It is inconceivable that the same Constitution which intended the Fundamental Rights to remain in existence even during the period of Emergency, at the same time intended to empower any five-year Parliament to take away those Rights altogether in normal times.

Propositions on behalf of the Petitioner on the point that in the exercise of its amending power under Article 368, Parliament cannot alter or destroy the essential features of the Constitution:

1. It has been already submitted that just as there are inherent and implied limitations on the legislative power to make ordinary laws, e.g. the unexpressed limitation which disentitles the legislature to encroach upon the judicial domain,:

(1971) 1 SCR 288, 294-7 : (1970) 2 SCC 280;
(1970) 3 SCR 745, 751 : (1970) 1 SCC 509;
(1970) 1 SCR 388, 392-3 : (1969) 2 SCC 283;
(1967) 1 AC 259, 287, 288, 290 (*PC*);
1940 IR 136.
1950 IR 67.

Lane's: *The Australian Federal System, 1972*, pp. 4, 94-5.

there are, likewise, inherent and implied limitations on the other species of legislative power, i.e. the power to make amendments to the Constitution.

2. These inherent and implied limitations disentitle Parliament to alter or destroy any of the essential features, basic elements or fundamental principles (hereinafter called 'the essential features' or 'essential elements') of the Constitution. However, Parliament may amend them without altering or destroying them.

3. The principle of inherent or implied limitations on Parliament's power to amend a controlled Constitution stems from three basic features which, by definition, must be present in every controlled Constitution of a Republic:

(*a*) The ultimate legal sovereignty resides in the people.

(*b*) Parliament is only a creature of the Constitution.

(*c*) The power to alter or destroy the essential elements of a Constitution is an attribute of ultimate legal sovereignty.

If Parliament has the power to destroy the essential elements, it would cease to be a creature of the Constitution, the Constitution would cease to be controlled, and all the other institutions and authorities under the Constitution would be entirely at the mercy of a single institution, *viz.* Parliament.

A power given by the Constitution cannot be construed as authorising a destruction of other powers given in the same instrument – and this rule applies *a fortiori* to the power of amendment.

4. It is true that the borderline cannot be precisely drawn between amendments which would be valid and those which would be invalid on the principle that the essential features are beyond Parliament's amending power; nor would it be possible to specify exhaustively the amendments which would be invalid on that principle. But that is no argument against accepting the aforesaid principle:

> '...In modern times opinions have sometimes been expressed to the effect that natural justice is so vague as to be practically meaningless. But I

would regard these as tainted by the perennial fallacy that because something cannot be cut and dried or nicely weighed or measured therefore it does not exist. The idea of negligence is equally insusceptible of exact definition, but what a reasonable man would regard as fair procedure in particular circumstances and what he would regard as negligence in particular circumstances are equally capable of serving as tests in law, and natural justice as it has been interpreted in the courts is much more definite than that....'

Per Lord Reid, *Ridge v. Baldwin*, 1964 AC 40 at 64-5.

'But such a lack of generality in criminal legislation need not, of itself, involve the judicial function, and Their Lordships are not prepared to hold that every enactment in this field which can be described as *ad hominem* and *ex post facto* must inevitably usurp or infringe the judicial power. Nor do they find it necessary to attempt the almost impossible task of tracing where the line is to be drawn between what will and what will not constitute such an interference. Each case must be decided in the light of its own facts and circumstances, ...'

Per Lord Pearce, *Liganage v. Queen*, (1967) 1 AC 259 at 289-90.

In re *Delhi Laws Act, 1912*, [1951] SCR 747, this Hon'ble Court held that the essentials of a legislative function could not be delegated, although it is not possible to enumerate precisely what those essential principles are nor is it possible to specify exhaustively those elements of legislation which cannot be delegated.

5. The following are some of the essential features of the Constitution:

(*i*) The supremacy of the Constitution. Ours is a controlled 'Constitution' *par excellence*. All institutions, including Parliament, are merely creatures of the Constitution and none of them is its master.

(*ii*) The Sovereignty of India. This country cannot be made a satellite, colony or dependency of any foreign country.

(*iii*) The integrity of the country. The unity of the nation, transcending all the regional, linguistic, religious and other diversities, is the bed-rock on which the constitutional fabric has been raised.

(*iv*) The democratic way of life, which connotes much more than merely the people's right to vote and elect representatives to power. In totalitarian, authoritarian and Fascist countries also, the people have such a right to vote and elect, but the equal freedom to choose between different parties and the freedom to oppose are denied.

(*v*) The Republican form of Government. India cannot be transformed into a monarchy.

(*vi*) The guarantee of basic human rights to all its citizens to ensure JUSTICE, social, economic and political; Liberty of thought expression, belief, faith and worship; Equality of status and of opportunity. These rights are categorised and elaborated as Fundamental Rights in Part III of the Constitution. Parliament cannot damage or abrogate the essence of any of these rights. (See, further, the Annexure).

(*vii*) A secular State, that is, a State in which there is no State religion.

(*viii*) A free and independent judiciary. Without it, all other rights would be writ in water.

(*ix*) The dual structure of the Union and the States. Entries in the Legislative Lists or other powers may be transferred from the Union to the State or *vice-versa,* but not so as to imperil the existence of either the Union or the States.

(*x*) The balance between the legislature, the Executive and the judiciary. None of the three organs can use any of its power to destroy the powers of the other institutions, nor can any of them abdicate its power in favour of another.

(*xi*) A Parliamentary form of Government as distinct from a Presidential form of Government.

(*xii*) The amendability of the Constitution as per the basic scheme of Article 368. That article itself can be amended but not so as to destroy its basic scheme. For instance, Article 368 cannot be amended so as to:

(*a*) empower Parliament to alter or destroy any of the essential features of the Constitution;

(*b*) make the Constitution literally or practically unamendable;

(*c*) make it generally amendable by a bare majority in Parliament;

(*d*) confer the power of amendment either expressly or in effect on the State legislatures;

(*e*) delete the proviso and deprive the States of the power of ratification which is today available to them in certain broad areas.

ANNEXURE

The Historical Background regarding Fundamental Rights

The historical background is of great importance. The difference in basic approach, which results in some Constitutions having guaranteed fundamental rights and others not having them, 'may be traced mainly to the spirit and genius of the nation in which a particular Constitution has its birth'.[19] The history of India prior to the promulgation of the Constitution, has perhaps not been paralleled in its essential features in any other country:

(*a*) For several decades the national leaders had been struggling to achieve independence and had envisaged a Constitution for free India which would provide basic human rights which could not be withdrawn under any circumstances. (See Granville Austin's: '*The Indian Constitution: Corner-stone of a Nation*', pp. 52-59, reproduced in the Compilation filed on 23rd November, 1972).

(*b*) India was to become a free democracy for the first time in its 5000 years old history. Since freedom had not become a way of life in this country, the basic human rights had to be carefully protected and preserved.

19. See *McCawley v. King,* 1920 AC 691 at 703.

(*c*) The country was welded together into one nation under one Central Legislature for the first time in its history. The fundamental rights represented the solemn balance of rights between citizens from various parts of India, 'the fundamental conditions on which *inter se* they accepted the Constitution'.[20]

(*d*) A sense of security and safety had to be created in the minds of the people when there were such tremendous diversities of religion, race, caste, creed, language, culture, etc., particularly in the minds of the religious and linguistic minorities.

(*e*) Economic and political thinking in the country ranged from antiquated feudalism to extreme leftism, and the necessity arose of putting the Fundamental Rights beyond the reach of the party in power and the State.

Since the question essentially is as to the intention of the founding fathers of the Constitution – did they intend that Parliament should have the power to destroy fundamental rights? – the above background is not only relevant but significant on the question as to the real intention.

The makers of the Constitution had a large number of foreign models before them in which there were provisions for amending the essential features of the Constitution by means of Referendum and other modes of ascertaining the wishes of the people in whom the ultimate legal sovereignty resides. The absence of any such provision in our Constitution clearly shows that the founding fathers of our Constitution did not want to provide in the original Constitution itself any channel for altering or destroying the basic constitutional structure. It is inconceivable that they intended to empower Parliament to destroy any of the essential features of the Constitution. In particular, it is inconceivable that after having provided the most complete and comprehensive guarantees of the basic human freedoms known to any Constitution of the world, the Constitution-makers still intended that any Parliament for the time being in session may take away or abridge all or any of those basic freedoms.

* * * * *

Propositions on behalf of the Petitioner on the necessity of taking into account the consequences of each of the rival contentions regarding the width of the power of amendment, the question of abuse of power being wholly irrelevant to the issue of the true scope of the power.

The word used in Article 368 is 'amendment', a word of ambiguous import and elastic ambit. The principle of inherent and implied limitations means deducing what is left unsaid from what is said, and perceiving what is implicit in the express provisions and scheme of the instrument. The entire attempt is to fathom the true intention of the Founding Fathers of the Constitution.

The submission of the Petitioner is that:

(*a*) according to one of the well-settled meanings of the word 'amend', the power of amendment in Article 368 does not comprise the power to alter or destroy any of the essential features, basic elements or fundamental principles of the Constitution (hereinafter called 'essential features');

20. Cf. *Bribery Commissioner v. Pedrick Ranasinghe*, 1965 AC 172 at 193-4.

(*b*) in any event there are inherent and implied limitations on the power.

The Respondents controvert both (*a*) and (*b*). They submit that the power of amendment comprehends the power to alter or destroy the essential features; that there are no inherent or implied limitations; and that the power is absolute and limitless.

Thus this Hon'ble Court has to decide upon; (*i*) the meaning of the word 'amendment' and (*ii*) the existence of inherent and implied limitations. The conclusion on these two distinct questions would resolve the most crucial issue arising in the case:

the scope and width of the power of amendment.

In ruling on this most crucial issue, it is not only desirable but imperative to consider the consequences of the plea of limited power and also of the plea of limitless power. To form a value judgment on this central point while ignoring the consequences of each rival view, is to form no value judgment at all. The Constitution is an organic whole and presents an integrated scheme; and it is judicially impossible to determine the width of one power without considering its effect on other powers and institutions.

The test of the true width of a power is not how probable it is that it may be exercised, but what can possibly be done under it.

The question of abuse or misuse of power is entirely irrelevant. To say that taking into account consequences involves consideration of abuse of power is to confuse the extent of power with its exercise, and its scope with the manner of its use. When the question is as to the width of the power, the hope and expectation that it will never be used is as wholly irrelevant as an imminent danger of its use.

* * * * *

Propositions on behalf of the Petitioner regarding the Constitution (Twenty-fourth Amendment) Act, 1971

The Twenty-fourth Amendment has sought to achieve five results:

(*i*) It has inserted an express provision in Article 368 to indicate that the source of the amending power will be found in that Article itself.

(*ii*) It has made it obligatory on the President to give his assent to any Bill duly passed under that Article.

(*iii*) It has substituted the words 'amend by way of addition, variation or repeal....' in place of the bare concept of 'amendment' in the original Article 368.

(*iv*) It makes explicit that when Parliament makes a constitutional amendment under Article 368 it acts 'in exercise of its constituent power.'

(*v*) It has expressly, provided, by amendments in Articles 13 and 368, that the bar in Article 13 against abridging or taking away any of the Fundamental Rights should not apply to any amendment made under Article 368.

The petitioner does not dispute that the amendments covered by (*i*) and (*ii*) above are within the amending power of Parliament.

If the amendments covered by (*iii*) and (*iv*) above are to be construed as empowering Parliament to exercise the full constituent power of the people themselves, and as vesting in Parliament the ultimate legal sovereignty of the people, and as authorising Parliament to alter or destroy all or any of the essential features, basic elements and fundamental principles of the Constitution (hereinafter called 'essential features'), the amendments must be held to be illegal void.

Likewise if the amendment covered by (*v*) above is construed as authorising Parliament to damage or destroy the essence of all or any of the Fundamental Rights, the amendment must be held to be illegal and void.

If the aforesaid construction is correct, it is submitted that the Twenty-fourth Amendment would be void and illegal for the following reasons:

(1) A creature of the Constitution cannot increase its own constituent power

The limited power of Parliament to amend the Constitution conferred by Article 368 prior to the Twenty-fourth Amendment is hereinafter referred to as 'the constituent power'.

A creature of the Constitution, as the Parliament is, can have only such constituent power as is conferred by the Constitution which is given by the people unto themselves. While purporting to exercise that constituent power, Parliament cannot increase that very power. No doubt, Parliament had the power to amend Article 368 itself, but that does not mean that Parliament could so amend Article 368 as to change its own constituent power beyond recognition. A creature of the Constitution cannot enlarge its own power over the Constitution, while purporting to act under it, any more than the creature of an ordinary law can enlarge its own power while purporting to act under that law. The power of amendment cannot possibly embrace the power to enlarge that very power of amendment, or to abrogate the limitation, inherent or implied, in the terms on which the power was conferred. The contrary view would reduce the whole principle of inherent and implied limitations to an absurdity.

(2) A creature of the Constitution cannot arrogate to itself the power to alter or destroy the essential features of the Constitution

In any view of the matter, Parliament as a functionary created under the Constitution had no competence so to amend the Constitution as to empower itself to alter or destroy the essential features of the Constitution. If the Twenty-fourth Amendment does confer such a power on Parliament, it would mean that, instead of the Constitution continuing to be supreme, it is now Parliament which is supreme and the Constitution is made subservient. In other words Parliament which is constituted under the Constitution has purported to make itself the master of the Constitution instead of being the functionary or creature of the Constitution as it was before the amendment, and has converted the controlled Constitution into an uncontrolled Constitution.

On the aforesaid construction, what Parliament has actually purported to do in the Twenty-fourth Amendment is to effect a silent revolution, since it has sought to overthrow the supremacy of the Constitution and make itself supreme. The fact that the revolution has been silent, peaceful and unperceived, does not make it any the less a revolution. Revolution is the only word to denote the substitution of one supremacy for another and to indicate the transfer of the ultimate legal sovereignty from the people to Parliament which is sought to be done by the Twenty-fourth Amendment. 'An attempt by the majority to change the fundamental law in violation of self-imposed restrictions is unconstitutional and revolutionary' (*American Jurisprudence*, Vol. II, Section 25, pp. 629-30).

(3) Parliament cannot abridge or destroy basic human rights and fundamental freedoms which were reserved by the people for themselves when they gave to themselves the Constitution

The Twenty-fourth Amendment purports to empower Parliament to take away or abridge all or any of the fundamental rights. This means that Parliament is made competent to destroy the basic human rights and the fundamental freedoms which were reserved by the people unto themselves when they gave themselves the Constitution and provided for the functioning of a Parliament. What is reserved by the people for themselves cannot possibly be destroyed by a functionary of the Constitution.

(4) Parliament cannot do indirectly what it was enjoined by the Constitution not to do directly

On a proper reading of the word 'amendment' in Article 368 as it stood originally and also on the principle of inherent and implied limitations, Parliament had no power to alter or destroy any of the essential features of the Constitution. If this is the correct position under the Constitution as given by the people unto themselves, it must necessarily follow that Parliament cannot abrogate the limits of its own constituent power. It cannot do in two stages what it could not do in one stage. It cannot first repeal the limitations on its own constituent power and then purport to do what was forbidden by those limitations.

Alternative Submission Regarding the Twenty-Fourth Amendment

Without prejudice to the above and in the alternative, it is submitted that if the Twenty-fourth Amendment is at all to be held valid, it can only be on a 'reading down' of the amended provisions of Articles 13 and 368, which reading would preserve the original inherent and implied limitations on the constituent power. The restricted reading would be that even after the Twenty-fourth Amendment:

(*a*) Parliament would have no power to alter or destroy the essential features of the Constitution;

(*b*) fundamental rights are among the essential features of the Constitution and, therefore, the essence of any of the fundamental rights cannot be altered or destroyed even when they are sought to be abridged.

It is submitted that if this Hon'ble Court is at all pleased to hold the Twenty-fourth Amendment to be valid, it should only be on the aforesaid restricted interpretation which would permit amendments only within the basic framework of the Constitution in which all the essential features are preserved.

There are clear authorities for the proposition that the Court may 'read down' a statute in order to bring it within the competence of the authority enacting it, when on a wider construction the Statute would have to be held void as being beyond the law-making authority's competence.[21]

Such restricted construction is possible in the present case for the following reasons:

---

21. In re *The Hindu Women's Rights to Property Act*, 1941 FCR 12 at 26-32; *R.M.D. Chamarbaugwalla v. Union*, [1957] SCR 930 at 936-39; *Kedarnath Singh v. State of Bihar*, [1962] Supp 2 SCR 769 at 810-11; *Arora v. State of U.P.*, [1964] 6 SCR 784 at 797; *Shah & Co. v. State of Maharashtra*, [1967] 3 SCR 466 at 477; *Seshammal v. State of Tamil Nadu*, (1972) 2 SCC 11 at 22-25.

(*a*) In a broad sense the expression 'constituent power' may include the power to amend the Constitution, whether the amending power is limited or unlimited.

(*b*) While the words 'amend by way of addition, variation or repeal' are, generally speaking, words of wide import, in a given context they are capable of being read as not authorising the alteration or destruction of essential features. In other words, these newly inserted words are not necessarily inconsistent with the limitation which enjoins the preservation of essential features, although in other contexts they may well comprehend changes in or abrogation of the essential features. In short, these newly inserted words may involve, but do not necessarily involve, the power to abrogate or destroy the essential features.

(*c*) The lifting of the bar of Article 13(2) against amendments under Article 368 is again not necessarily inconsistent with the essential features being beyond the amending power. If the bar in Article 13(2) is validly lifted, it can mean that Parliament can abridge any of the fundamental rights but not so as to damage or destroy the essence or core of any of those rights.

(*d*) The whole point about implied and inherent limitation is that they apply where the empowering words are seemingly wide enough to cover what the limitations prohibit. On the original Article 368, two submissions have been made on behalf of the Petitioner:

(*i*) the bare word 'amendment' is not to be read in the wide sense of 'amendment by way of addition, variation or repeal', and

(*ii*) even if it is to be read in the aforesaid wide sense, the inherent and implied limitations would still apply.

In other words, if the bare word 'amendment' in the original Article 368 were to be read in the wide sense of 'amendment by way of addition, variation or repeal', even then the implied and inherent limitations would have cut down the scope of the amending power prior to the Twenty-fourth Amendment. It is clear that since the inherent and implied limitations would have applied even if what is now enacted explicitly was implicit in the bare word 'amendment', they apply with equal vigour after the change in the language of Article 368.

The inherent and implied limitations can be ruled out only by express words to the contrary. They would cease to apply only if there were compelling words, e.g., an express power conferred on Parliament to alter or abrogate any of the essential features of the Constitution. In that event the Court would have no option but to strike down the conferment of such a power.

Additional Propositions on Behalf of the Petitioner on the Constitution (Twenty-Fourth Amendment) Act, 1971, Regarding the Lifting of the Bar Imposed by Article 13(2)

I. First submission

Article 13(2), as it stood before the Twenty-fourth Amendment, had two elements:

(*i*) the bar against the State making any ordinary law which abridges or takes away any of the fundamental rights; and (*ii*) the bar against any constitutional amendment which abridges or takes away any of the fundamental rights.

The first bar is an essential feature of the Constitution and it has been left untouched by the Twenty-fourth Amendment.

The second bar is also an essential feature of the Constitution. The effect of the bar is that while Parliament may add to or amend the fundamental rights, the amendment cannot take the form of abridgment or taking away of any of the fundamental rights. Since the bar against such constitutional amendments is an essential feature of the Constitution, the purported lifting of the bar by the Twenty-fourth Amendment is illegal and void.

II. Second submission in the alternative

An argument may be urged as follows: To distinguish the second bar from the first and to hold that while the first is an essential feature of the Constitution, the second is not. The first is an essential feature, since it is clearly basic to the constitutional scheme that the State should be restrained from abridging or taking away any of the fundamental rights, But the second bar stands on a different footing, since in the working of the Constitution, Parliament may find it necessary to abridge a fundamental right without damaging or destroying its core or essence and in that event it may propose to lift the second bar of Article 13(2) in the exercise of its amending power. Since each fundamental right is itself an essential feature and its core or essence cannot be destroyed or damaged in the exercise of the amending power, no damage could be done to the core and essence of any of the Fundamental Rights by the lifting of the second bar. In other words, it may be urged that the Fundamental principles underlying the original Constitution are the following:

(*a*) Subject to (*b*) dealt with below, the 'State' as defined in Article 12 should be powerless to abridge or take away any of the Fundamental Rights;

(*b*) Parliament in the exercise of its amending power should be powerless to damage or destroy the core or essence of any of the Fundamental Rights, and even if it assumes the power to amend any of them, the amendment should not reach the point of such damage or destruction.

In this view of the matter, it would be possible to decide the present case entirely on the principle of inherent and implied limitations and the true construction of the words of Article 368 conferring the amending power, without any reference to Article 13(2) at all.

Without prejudice to the first submission and in the alternative, the Petitioner submits that if the aforesaid second bar against constitutional amendments imposed by Article 13(2) is held not to be an essential feature of the Constitution, then the position after the Twenty-fourth Amendment is as follows:

(*a*) The provision of the Twenty-fourth Amendment, lifting the bar in Article 13(2) against constitutional amendments under Article 368, should be held to be valid.

(*b*) However, the bar would continue to apply against constitutional amendments made under other provisions of the Constitution namely Articles 4, 169, 244-A, Para 7 of the Fifth Schedule, and Para 21 of the Sixth Schedule. Any constitutional amendments made under any of these provisions would have to observe the bar of

Article 13(2), and such amendments cannot abridge or take away any of the Fundamental Rights. The reason is that it is only amendments made under Article 368 which are exempted from the application of Article 13(2) by the Twenty-fourth Amendment. This difference may be justified on the ground that whereas under Article 368 a special majority is necessary, under the other amending provisions only a bare majority of Parliament is sufficient.

(*c*) The power to amend the Constitution under Article 368 continues to be subject to the inherent and implied limitations which prevent Parliament from altering, damaging or destroying any of the essential features of the Constitution. Every Fundamental Right is an essential feature of the Constitution. The net result is that a constitutional amendment under Article 368 may abridge a fundamental right but if after the lifting of the bar in Article 13(2), the degree of abridgment is such as to damage or destroy the essence or core of that right, the constitutional amendment would be illegal and void.

Propositions on behalf of the Petitioner regarding the Constitution (Twenty-fifth Amendment) Act, 1971

The ground for holding the 25th Amendment illegal and void is that, as already submitted, even if the 24th Amendment is held to be valid, it can only be on a restricted interpretation of the power of amendment conferred on Parliament by Article 368 as altered by the 24th Amendment. The restricted the interpretation would be that even after 24th Amendment and even if the bar of Article 13(2) was validly lifted, the inherent and implied limitations continue to attach to Parliament's amending power under Article 368 with the result that:

(*a*) Parliament would have no power to alter, damage or destroy the essential features of the Constitution; and

(*b*) each fundamental right being an essential feature of the Constitution, no constitutional amendment can damage or destroy the essence or core of any of the Fundamental Rights.

It is in the light of this legal position that the validity of the 25th Amendment has to be considered.

The 25th Amendment has made three material changes:

(*i*) It has amended Article 31(2) in two respects:

(*a*) it substitutes the word 'amount' for the concept of 'compensation' for property acquired or requisitioned; and

(*b*) it has provided that the acquisition or requisition law shall not be called in question on the ground that the whole or any part of the 'amount' is to be given otherwise than in cash.

(*ii*) It has provided that the fundamental right to acquire hold and dispose of property under Article 19(1)(f) cannot be invoked in respect of any such law as is referred to in Article 31(2).

(*iii*) It has inserted Article 31-C as an overriding Article which makes the various fundamental rights conferred by Articles 14, 19 and 31 inapplicable to certain categories of laws passed by Parliament or by any State Legislature.

It is submitted that all the amendments covered by (*i*), (*ii*) and (*iii*) above, damage or destroy the essence or core of the fundamental rights which they deal with; and consequently the whole of the 25th Amendment Act is illegal and void.

The aforesaid three features of the 25th Amendment are dealt with below seriatim:

I. Amendment of Article 31(2)

It is submitted that the right to property is one of the essential features of the Constitution, like all the other fundamental rights. Further, it is the handmaid to various other fundamental rights. A very few examples may suffice to illustrate this point. The right to freedom of the Press under Article 19(1)(*a*) would be meaningless if a publisher could be deprived of his printing plant and the building in which it is housed without compensation. The fundamental right under Article 19(1)(*c*) to form trade unions would be denuded of its true content if the property of a trade union could be acquired by the State without compensation. The right to practise any profession or to carry on any occupation, trade or business under Article 19(1)(*g*) would be merely a right to do forced labour for the State if the net savings from the fruits of a citizen's personal exertion are liable to be acquired by the State without compensation. The freedom of religion in Article 26 would lose a great deal of its efficacy if the institutions maintained by a community for its religious and charitable purposes could be acquired without compensation. The common man who may have put his life-savings in shares or in other forms of property is directly affected by the denial of the right to compensation. Under the amended Article 31 and amount may be fixed by the State on a basis which need not be disclosed even to members of the legislature which passes the law and which may have no relation to the value of the property sought to be acquired. In other words, the amended Article 31 in substance and effect authorizes confiscation of any citizen's property, however small that property may be in value. Such a law which has nothing to do with concentration of wealth and permits any common citizen's property to be virtually confiscated involves destruction of the essence or core of the right to property.

The other amendment of Article 31(2) is that even the 'amount' which does not satisfy any of the principles of compensation need not be paid in cash but may be given in the form, say, of a promise to pay at a future date, and that cannot be made a ground of challenge to the validity of the law. This amendment amounts in effect to compounding the injustice. In these days of mounting inflation and the State tendency to repudiate even solemn constitutional guarantees, a Government's promise to pay at a future date may be almost worthless. This part of the amendment serves to emphasise the point that the change in Article 31(2) effected by the 25th Amendment is really intended to authorise confiscation of the bulk of any property which a State may choose to acquire or requisition. It may be noted that Article 31(2) has nothing to do with estates, zamindaris, land reforms or agrarian reforms which are specifically dealt with by Article 31-A and to which Article 31(2) is wholly inapplicable.

II. Amendment to make Article 19(1)(f) inapplicable to acquisition and requisition laws

The right to acquire, hold and dispose of property under Article 19(1)(*f*) is subject under Article 19(5) to reasonable restrictions in the interests of the general public. Since all reasonable restrictions in the public interest are already permitted under Article 19(5), the only object of making Article 19(1)(*f*) inapplicable can be to enable acquisition and requisition laws under Article 31 to contain restrictions and provisions which are unreasonable or not in the public interest.

If Article 19(1)(*f*) applies, an acquisition or requisition law which permits a property to be taken without the owner being heard where the rules of natural justice would require the owner to be heard, would be void as offending that

Article. See *R.C. Cooper v. Union*, (1970) 3 SCR 530 at 577 : (1970) 1 SCC 248. But after the 25th Amendment, such rules of natural justice can be flagrantly violated and a man's property can be acquired or requisitioned and the 'amount' fixed, without giving him a hearing in cases where natural justice would require such hearing to be given; and the Land Acquisition Act can be amended to provide that any man's land or house can be acquired without any notice to the owner to show cause against the acquisition or to prove what 'amount' should be fairly paid to him for the property acquired. This clearly damages the essence or the core of the fundamental right under Article 19(1)(*f*) to acquire, hold and dispose of property.

III. Article 31-C which validates Constitution-breaking laws

Article 31-C damages or destroys the core or essence of at least seven essential features of the Constitution.

1. There is a fine but vital distinction between two cases:

(*a*) where the fundamental rights are amended to permit laws to be validity passed which would have been void before the amendment; and

(*b*) the fundamental rights remain unamended but the laws which are void as offending those rights are validated by a legal fiction that they shall not be deemed to be void.

The question is not one merely of legislative device. In the first case the law is constitutional in reality. In the second case the law is unconstitutional in reality but is deemed by a fiction of law not to be void; with the result that Constitution-breaking laws are validated and there is a repudiation or abrogation of the Constitution *pro tanto*.

If the second case is permissible as a proper exercise of the amending power, the Constitution would be reduced to a scrap of paper. If Article 31-C is valid, it would be equally permissible to Parliament so to amend the Constitution as to declare all laws to be valid which are passed by Parliament or State Legislatures in excess of their legislative competence, or which violate any of the basic human rights enshrined in Part III or the freedom of inter-State trade in Article 301. It would be equally permissible to have an omnibus Article that 'notwithstanding anything contained in the Constitution, no law passed by Parliament or any State Legislature shall be deemed to be void on any ground whatsoever'. The insertion of only one such Article would toll the death-knell of the Constitution.

The true legal effect of Article 31-C is that it gives a blank charter to Parliament and all the State Legislatures to defy and ignore the Constitution.

Article 31-C clearly damages or destroys the supremacy of the Constitution which is one of the essential features of the Constitution.

2. Article 31-C not only subordinates the fundamental rights to the Directive Principles of State policy but virtually abrogates the fundamental rights in respect of laws which the legislature declares to be for giving effect to the Directive Principles. One of the essential features of the Constitution is that the right to enforce the fundamental rights in the Court is guaranteed (Article 32), whereas the Directive Principles are not so enforceable (Article 37). The fundamental rights are clear-cut and precise, in contrast to the vague contours of the Directive Principles. To abrogate the fundamental rights when giving effect to the Directive Principles is to destroy one of the essential features of the Constitution. Ignorance and arbitrariness, injustice and unfairness, would hereafter not be open to challenge on the touchstone of the invaluable basic rights, if Article 31-C is valid.

3. It is one of the essential features of the Constitution that it can be amended only in the 'form and manner' laid down in Article 368 and according to that Article's basic scheme.[22] This essential feature is sought to be abrogated by Article 31-C. That Article has the effect of virtually authorizing abrogation of the fundamental rights while they still remain ostensibly on the Statute Book. The public criticism and debate which would be invoked by a proposal to abridge a particular fundamental right is avoided, although various fundamental rights are effectively silenced. The absurd situation is that, whereas an amendment of a single fundamental right would require a majority of at least 2/3rds of the members of Parliament present and voting (Article 368), a law falling within Article 31-C which overrides and violates several fundamental rights can be passed by a simple majority.

4. Every fundamental right is an essential feature of the Constitution. Article 31-C purports to take away a large number of these fundamental rights altogether in the field covered by that Article. It provides for the wholesale smothering of various rights which are independent of the right to property and are totally irrelevant to the Directive Principles laid down in Article 39(*b*) or (*c*). Even the rights to:

equality before the law;

freedom of speech and expression;

to assemble peaceably and without arms;

to form associations or unions;

to move freely throughout the territory of India;

to reside and settle in any part of the territory of India;

to practise any profession or to carry on any occupation, trade or business;

to retain property except when deprived by authority of law;

which are so vital for the survival of democracy, the rule of law, and the integrity and unity of the Republic, can be violated under Article 31-C under the cloak of avoiding concentration of economic power.

5. A citizen is not even permitted to raise the question whether the proposed law will result, or is reasonably calculated to result, in securing the Directive Principles laid down in Article 39(*b*) or (*c*). The wrong done to the people who are deprived of their basic freedoms is aggravated by protection to laws, which, in reality, may not be at all calculated to give effect to the Directive Principles. This would be so even on the basis that on a proper construction of Article 31-C, Article 39(*b*) or (*c*) must have direct relevance to the law and its subject-matter, because even in such a case a question may still arise whether the law is so framed or conceived that it will secure the Directive Principles in question.

One of the essential features of the Constitution is the right to move the Supreme Court for the enforcement of the other fundamental rights (Article 32). The essence of core of this right is gone when the fundamental rights are made unenforceable for the purpose of giving effect to the Directive Principles and at the same time the Court is precluded from considering whether the law is such that it can possibly secure the Directive Principles in question.

---

22. Cf. *Trethowan case*, 1932 AC 526.

6. One of the essential features of the Constitution is that no State Legislature can amend the fundamental rights or any other part of the Constitution. This essential feature is repudiated by Article 31-C which empowers even State Legislatures to pass laws which virtually involve a repeal of the fundamental rights. The wholly irrational consequence is, whereas State Legislatures cannot abridge a single fundamental right, it is now open to them to supersede a whole series of such rights. In substance, the power of amending the Constitution is delegated to all the State Legislatures – which is not permissible under Article 368.[23]

7. One of the essential features of the Constitution is the provision for the protection to minorities and their cultural and educational rights. The fundamental rights under Articles 14, 19 and 31 which are sought to be superseded by Article 31-C are necessary to make meaningful the specific rights of the minorities which are guaranteed by Articles 25 to 30. Under the guise of giving effect to Directive Principles, a number of steps can be taken which can seriously affect the position of regional, linguistic, cultural and other minorities.

The proviso inserted by the Twenty-fifth Amendment to Article 31(2) is very telltale. It expressly provides that where the property of an educational institution established and administered by a minority is acquired, the amount fixed for the acquisition should be such as not to restrict or abrogate the right guaranteed under Article 30(1). The clear implication is that when property is acquired in other cases, an amount can be fixed which restricts or abrogates any of the other fundamental rights – for instance, the rights to freedom of speech and expression Article 19(1)(*a*), to form associations or unions Article 19(1)(*c*), or to practise any profession or carry on any occupation, trade or business Article 19(1)(*g*), or the right of religious community to establish and maintain institutions for religious or charitable purposes (Article 26). Further, if a law violates the rights of the minorities under Articles 25 to 30, such a law would be no law at all and therefore deprivation of property under such a law would violate Article 31(1). But since Article 31(1) is one of the Articles abrogated by Article 31-C, minorities can be deprived of their properties, held privately or upon pubic charitable or religious trust, by a law which clearly violates their rights under Articles 25 to 30.

In conclusion, it would be no exaggeration to say that Article 31-C is a monstrous outrage on the Constitution. It has a built-in mechanism for the dissolution of the true democracy that India has been so far, cessation of the rule of law, disintegration of the nation, and the birth of a totalitarian regime.

* * * * *

Propositions on behalf of the Petitioner regarding the true Construction of Article 31(2) substituted by the Constitution (Twenty-fifth Amendment) Act, 1971

I. True construction of Article 31(2)

It is significant to note that before the 25th Amendment, Article 31(2) provided for the payment of compensation when any property was acquired or requisitioned for a public purpose and contained the provision inserted by the Fourth Amendment that the adequacy of such compensation should not be called in question in any court. The 25th Amendment substituted the word 'amount' for 'compensation'.

---

23. *See* 1919 AC 935, 945 (*PC*); [1967] 2 SCR 650, 653-4, 659-60; 1951 Canada Law Reports Supreme Court, 31 at 37-38.

The Petitioner submits that the true construction of Article 31(2) as substituted by the 25th Amendment involves the following:

(*a*) 'Amount' is not a legal concept at all, unlike 'compensation'. Therefore the will of the State is the only yardstick for fixing the amount. Thus the amount fixed may be such as may amount to virtual confiscation of the property or the bulk of it.

(*b*) The Supreme Court held in the *Bank Nationalisation case*,[24] that if the principles which were irrelevant to the concept of compensation were adopted, the law would be struck down. But that decision was with reference to the word 'compensation' which appeared in Article 31(2) before the 25th Amendment. Since the word 'amount' is not a legal concept at all, there is no basic norm by reference to which the relevance or irrelevance of principles can be judged.

(*c*) Since the amount fixed or the principles adopted may be arbitrary and may have no relation or relevance to the value of the property acquired, the essence or core of the right to property is damaged, if not destroyed, by Article 31(2).

(*d*) Not only does Article 31(2) virtually abrogate the right to property, but it can have a similar effect on the other fundamental rights, e.g. the rights enumerated in Article 19 and the rights of the minorities and of religious freedom (see the examples on page 3 of the Propositions on the 25th Amendment tendered on 8th December, 1972). This is made clear by the proviso to Article 31(2) which has also been inserted by the 25th Amendment. The implication of that proviso is that the State may fix such an amount for acquisition of property as may restrict or abrogate any of the other fundamental rights the exercise of which would be affected by the deprivation of the property without just compensation – and the only exception to this power of the State is the case dealt with in the proviso of educational institutions established and administered by a minority referred to in Article 30(1).

It is submitted that what is stated above is the correct interpretation of Article 31(2) substituted by the 25th Amendment and that it must therefore be held to be void on the ground that it damages or destroys the core or essence of the right to property and of several other fundamental rights; and that 'reading down' of the Article would not be proper.

II. Alternative submission regarding Article 31(2)

Without prejudice to the above and only in the event of this Hon'ble Court coming to the conclusion that Article 31(2) as substituted by the 25th Amendment should be held valid on a restricted interpretation, it is submitted that the restricted interpretation would have to proceed on the following basis:

(*a*) Article 31(2) still appears as a fundamental right by reference to which the validity of ordinary laws is to be judged. Therefore it must be read as providing a standard or measure. If the 'amount' and the 'principles' are entirely at the will or whim of the State, there would be no meaning in keeping Article 31(2) as a fundamental right and in making payment an essential feature of that fundamental right.

24. [1970] 3 SCR 530.

(*b*) The word 'amount' is used in the context of a Constitution which specifically continues to provide in Article 19(1)(f) the right to acquire, hold and dispose of property. Further, the word 'amount' occurs in Article 31(2) which provides not for expropriation or confiscation but for compulsory acquisition or requisition for a public purpose. Article 31(2) makes it a condition of the validity of the acquisition or requisition law that it must fix an amount or specify the principles for determining the amount. Article 31(2) embodies the principle of eminent domain which necessarily involves the obligation of the State to pay for what is taken. Therefore the amount must be such as would not abrogate the right to property, since such abrogation would be inconsistent with:

(*i*) the inherent and implied limitations on Parliament's power under Article 368 to abrogate any fundamental right;

(*ii*) Article 19(1)(f) which preserves the right to property; and

(*iii*) the Statement of Objects and Reasons which does not indicate that the right to property was intended to be abrogated by the 25th Amendment.

Consequently, the true standard or measure is that the amount or the principles must have a reasonable relation to the property and its value. In short, the word 'amount' which is literally amorphous crystallises into shape and form in the context of Article 31(2).

On the above interpretation, the right to property may be said to have evolved in the Indian Constitution through the following stages of dilution:

(*i*) Property could be taken by the State only on payment of full compensation, the adequacy of the compensation being justiciable. (This was the Constitution in its original form).

(*ii*) The State could take property on payment of 'compensation' in the legal sense, although that compensation may be inadequate; the adequacy of the compensation being non-justiciable. (This stage was reached by the Fourth Amendment in 1955).

(*iii*) The State may take property for an amount which may not represent 'compensation' in the legal sense, but which must have a reasonable relation to the value of the property taken and which would prevent the acquisition from amounting to confiscation or expropriation. (This is the effect of the 25th Amendment).

(*c*) The 'principles' referred to in Article 31(2) would be such principles as are relevant and appropriate to the determination of such an 'amount' as is referred to in (*a*) above. Just as principles which were irrelevant to the legal concept of 'compensation' made the acquisition law invalid prior to the 25th Amendment, if any principles are adopted which are irrelevant to the concept of amount as explained in (*a*) above, the law would be invalid.

(*d*) Where the law itself fixes the amount, it may indicate the principles on which it has been arrived at, or the Court may enquire on what broad principles it has been fixed. The contrary view would involve the unacceptable position that Article 31(2) gives the option to the State either to specify principles which cannot be arbitrary or to specify an amount which can be arbitrary. The only correct view can be that whether the law fixes the amount or specifies the principles, the amount or the principles must converge on the same result.

(*e*) Since Parliament has no power to damage or destroy the core or essence of any of the fundamental rights, the very limits on its amending power would involve the conclusion that the power under Article 31(2) cannot be so exercised, and the amount fixed or determined cannot be so low, as to damage or destroy the core or essence of the other fundamental rights, e.g. the freedom of the Press, the right to form trade unions and the religious freedom and the rights of the minorities in Articles 25, 26 and 29.

On the above construction, the effect of the proviso to Article 31(2) would be as follows:

The proviso would give a wider protection in respect of educational institutions of a minority than would be available under (*e*) above. The reason is that the proviso requires such an amount to be fixed or determined as would not restrict the right under Article 30(1), which is a higher safeguard than the rule prohibiting damage to the essence or core of the other fundamental rights. If the amount to be paid on acquisition has to be such that it would not restrict the right under Article 30 (1), it would have to be an amount higher than the amount which would be sufficient not to damage the essence of that right. Whereas on the principle of inherent and implied limitations it is only the core or essence of the fundamental rights which is protected, the proviso to Article 31(2) protects the right under Article 30(1) in its full amplitude and not merely its core or essence.

* * * * *

Additional argument in support of the plea that the 'amount' or 'principles' under Article 31(2) cannot be arbitrary but have to be reasonable.

Assuming Article 31(2) as substituted by the 25th Amendment is to be regarded as legal and valid, there is an additional reason for holding that the 'amount' and 'principles' referred to therein have to be reasonable in relation to the property and its value.

Article 31(2) may be regarded as vesting the State with a discretion to fix the amount. It is well-settled that where a discretion is granted by any law, it is implicit in the grant of such discretion that it must be exercised reasonably. If the discretion is exercised arbitrarily or unreasonably, it would mean that the discretion has not been exercised at all. These principles which are well-settled in respect of discretion conferred by ordinary statutes apply a *fortiori* to Article 31(2) which safeguards the citizen's fundamental right to property against the State. The condition on which the State is permitted by Article 31(2) to exercise the power of acquiring or requisitioning property is that discretion must be exercised in fixing the amount or specifying principles. If a law fixes an amount unreasonably or if the Court finds that in arriving at the amount the State has adopted principles which are unreasonable or irrelevant to the property and its value, the exercise of the State's discretion would be arbitrary. In such a case the Court would strike down the law on the ground that the constitutional requirement of the exercise of discretion has not been satisfied.

In *Roberts v. Hopwood*,[25] the House of Lords held that where a statute permitted a Borough Council to employ such servants as may be necessary on such 'wages as (the Council) may think fit', the discretion conferred upon the Council by the Statute must be exercised reasonably, and that the fixing by the Council of an arbitrary sum for wages without regard to existing labour conditions was not an exercise of that discretion.

Lord Buckmaster's observations in that case at pp. 587 and 590 are very pertinent. At page 590 Lord Buckmaster says:

> '.... they did not base their decision upon the ground that the reward for work is the value of the work reasonably and even generously measured, but that they took an arbitrary principle and fixed an arbitrary sum, which was not a real exercise of the discretion imposed upon them by the statute.'

Lord Atkinson's observations at pp. 597 and 599 are again pertinent. On page 599 Lord Atkinson says that on a fair construction of the statute it means that 'in each and every case the payment of all salaries and wages must be 'reasonable'.' This means that the test of reasonableness is treated as implicit in the conferment of discretion by the law.

Lord Wrenbury's classic words are at page 613:

> 'I rest my opinion upon higher grounds. A person in whom is vested a discretion must exercise his discretion upon reasonable grounds. A discretion does not empower a man to do what he likes merely because he is minded to do so – he must in the exercise of his discretion do not what he likes but what he ought. In other words, he must, by use of his reason, ascertain and follow the course which reason directs. He must act reasonably.'
>
> By this test, the legal position is that so long as the discretion is exercised reasonably under Article 31(2), the Court will not interfere even though the return may not amount to compensation in the eye of the law or the principles may not cover all the essential elements of the legal concept of 'compensation'.

Inadequacy of the amount is non-justiciable, but only where the State action is within the constitutionally permissible limits. Arguments regarding the reasonable exercise of discretion (i.e. the reasonable relation of the amount or principles to the property and its value) and the bar against damaging any of the fundamental rights go to the constitutional limitations upon State action under Article 31(2), and are therefore justiciable. They deal with the constitutional condition which is required to be satisfied before the power of acquisition or requisition can be validly exercised. There is a world of difference between the proposition that adequacy of the amount shall not be called in question and the proposition that arbitrary exercise of discretion or power shall not be called in question.

* * * * *

25. (1925) AC 578.

Proposition on behalf of the Petitioner in support of the point that the right to property is one of the essential features of the Constitution

I. Every fundamental right is an essential feature of the Constitution

Every fundamental right is an essential feature of the Constitution. If the Constitution-makers had thought that a particular right was not an essential feature, they would not have included it in the category of fundamental rights. In respect of the rest of the Constitution it is for the Court to decide whether a particular provision or institution constitutes an essential feature or not. But when it comes to the fundamental rights, all controversy is eliminated and what the Constitution-makers specified as fundamental must necessarily be treated as a fundamental feature of our Constitution.

II. The importance of the right to property

Without prejudice to the above and assuming any inquiry is at all possible as to whether the right to property should be treated as one of the basic elements of our Constitution, it is submitted that:

(*a*) the intrinsic value of the right,

(*b*) its necessity for the meaningful exercise of various other fundamental rights, and

(*c*) its importance to the proper functioning of the Constitution as a whole;

leave no doubt that the right to property is one of the basic elements of our Constitution.

Property is necessary for the subsistence and well-being of men. No man would become a member of a community in which he could not enjoy the fruits of his honest labour and industry. The preservation and security of property is one of the primary objects of the social compact that induce men to unite in society. There can be no dispute or debate about this proposition, though there may be different opinions as to the quantum of property that a person should be allowed to hold.

III. Legislative history

(*a*) Section 299 of the Government of India Act, 1935 recognised the right to property and contained a safeguard against expropriation without compensation or acquisition of property for a non-public purpose.

(*b*) Article 17 of the Universal Declaration of Human Rights also recognises the right to private property. India is a signatory to that Declaration.

(*c*) The Constituent Assembly examined the Constitutions of several countries, which guarantee basic rights. In '*Constituent Assembly of India, Constitutional Precedents* (*Third Series*) *1947*)', it is stated as follows:

'Broadly speaking, the rights declared in these Constitutions relate to equality before the law, freedom of speech, freedom of religion, freedom of assembly, freedom of association, security of person and security of property. Within limits these are all well-recognised rights and it may be useful to draw attention to them by embodying them in the Constitutional Charter.'

(*d*) The debates in the Constituent Assembly when the draft articles corresponding to Article 19(1)(f) and Article 31 came up for discussion clearly indicate that the framers of our Constitution attached sufficient importance to property to incorporate it in the chapter on fundamental rights and rejected suggestions and contentions to the contrary. The provision regarding freedom of trade and intercourse which was originally in the chapter on fundamental rights was later on removed from that chapter and put into a separate part, in view of the suggestions by some members in the Constituent Assembly. It is significant to note that similar suggestions in respect of Article 31 (corresponding to Article 24 of the draft Constitution) were not accepted. Pandit Jawaharlal Nehru categorically stated that in the Indian Constitution there was no room for expropriation or acquisition without compensation. That basic feature of the Constitution was departed from only in the case of legislation regarding abolition of zamindari and land tenure reforms and such legislation was accordingly expressly saved by clauses (4) and (6) of Article 31. Whilst there may be difference of opinion as to the quantum and extent of compensation that should be paid for acquisition of property, it was an essential feature of the Indian Constitution as framed and enacted that there could not be any expropriation of private property or acquisition without compensation.

IV. Right to property necessary for the meaningful exercise of other fundamental rights

The right to property is essential for the effective and meaningful exercise of various other fundamental rights. A very few examples would suffice to illustrate this point. The right to freedom of the Press under Article 19(1)(*a*) would be meaningless if a publisher could be deprived of his printing plant and the building in which it is housed without compensation. The fundamental right under Article 19(1)(*c*) to form trade unions would be denuded of its true content if the property of a trade union could be acquired by the State without compensation. The right to reside and settle in any part of the territory of India, which is guaranteed by Article 19(1)(*e*), would be meaningless if the State could expropriate the citizen's hut or house or household effects. The right to practise any profession or to carry on any occupation, trade or business under Article 19(1)(g) would be merely a right to do forced labour for the State if the net savings from the fruits of a citizen's personal exertion are liable to be acquired by the State without compensation. The freedom of religion in Article 26 would lose a great deal of its efficacy if the institutions maintained by a community for its religious and charitable purposes could be acquired without compensation.

V. Necessity of the right to property for the normal working of the Constitution

It would be no exaggeration to say that without the right to property it would be impossible to work the Constitution. For example, many of the legislative Entries, including Entries which set out the subject-matters in respect of which taxes can be levied, necessarily pre-suppose the right to private property. The existence of the separate States would be in direct jeopardy if the right to private property did not exist. The democratic way of life, the very institution of Parliament with its necessary incidents like free elections, freedom to oppose and the right to dissent would all be paralysed if the right to private property did not exist.

Propositions on behalf of the Petitioner regarding the ambit of the amending power in different Constitutions

And

Parliament providing a channel like referendum for ascertaining the people's will.

I. The amending power in our Constitution must be construed on its own terms

The scope and width of Parliament's amending power under Article 368 must be determined on its own terms and the other world Constitutions are of no assistance in solving this question. Some of the material features which have a bearing on this issue are:

(*a*) Our historical background. National leaders struggled for several decades to achieve independence and envisaged a Constitution for free India which would provide inalienable basic human rights; the country became a free democracy for the first time, and was welded together into one State also for the first time, in its five thousand years old history; the necessity of creating a sense of security and safety in the minds of numerous religious, linguistic and regional minorities made it imperative that fundamental rights should be beyond the reach of the party in power.

(*b*) Amending powers are conferred by different Articles in our Constitution – Articles 4, 169, Para 7 of the Fifth Schedule and Para 21 of the Sixth Schedule – in significantly different terms which have a direct bearing on the scope and width of the amending power.

(*c*) In the original draft of the Constitution prepared by B.N. Rau, there was a significant contrast between the word 'amendment' in the clause corresponding to the present Article 368 and the conferment of amending power in wider term in Clause 238 which was later omitted. Further, Mr Kamath's amendment which would have widened the scope of the amending power in Article 368 was rejected. Thus the proceedings before the Constituent Assembly clearly support the view that Parliament's amending power under Article 368 was intended to be restricted as contended by the Petitioner.

(*d*) Our Constitution has an extraordinarily forceful and meaningful Preamble which contains guarantees reflecting the pledge contained in the Objectives Resolution of 1946.

(*e*) The people are in no way associated with the amending power in Article 368, but the decision is purely that of a creature of the Constitution, viz. Parliament; and even the States are wholly dissociated from the amending process except in the cases falling within the proviso to Article 368.

There is no other Constitution in the world which affords a parallel to the Indian Constitution as regards the abovementioned cumulative features and other relevant circumstances. Therefore it would be futile to consider the scope of the amending power in other Constitutions.

II. Constitutions of other countries

The amending power has widely varying scope and width in the Constitutions of different countries. Relevant extracts from the Constitutions of 61 countries are given in a separate compilation.

It is most significant to note that where the amending power rests with the people of a Republic, in whom the ultimate legal sovereignty resides, the position is quite different as compared to cases where the amending power resides in a creature of the Constitution, e.g., the Indian Parliament. Inherent and implied limitations which apply to a Parliament constituted under a controlled Constitution do not apply to the people. People may, in the exercise of their ultimate legal sovereignty alter, damage or destroy an essential feature of their Constitution by way of amendment (apart from questions of limitations on the people's power arising from the Preamble or the principle of inalienable and natural human rights).

III. The U.S.A. Constitution

Article V of the U.S.A. Constitution affords no analogy to Article 368, as is clear from the following:

(*a*) The features and the historical background peculiar to India, do not exist in the case of the U.S. Constitution.

(*b*) Article V in the U.S.A. Constitution has been read as associating the people with the amending process, since that article expressly provides for the calling of Conventions for amending the Constitution. The fact that Conventions have been rarely called is not relevant. The necessity of calling Conventions (instead of letting the legislature make the decision) would really arise when the basic human freedoms are sought to be abridged or taken away or any other essential feature of the Constitution is sought to be altered, damaged or destroyed. Such amendments have not been made in the U.S.A. But the very fact that the people are capable of being associated with the exercise of the amending power distinguishes Article V from our Article 368.

(*c*) The decision to have an amendment is not made by the Congress (corresponding to our Lok Sabha) but is made by 3/4ths of the State legislatures or Conventions. The Congress can only initiate a Proposal.

(*d*) Two-thirds of the State Legislatures may ask for amendments, and in such a case Congress does not even initiate a Proposal.

(*e*) The decisions of the Supreme Courts of the States in U.S.A. are not relevant, since they turn upon the terms and background of the State Constitutions. For instance, the case reported in *Southern Reporter*, Second Series, Vol. 81, page 881 is irrelevant, since that case deals with the Constitution under which an amendment would become valid only 'when approved by the qualified electors' (see the first para of that Vol. at page 882).

IV. Can Parliament amend our Constitution so as to provide a channel for a decision by the people regarding amendments?

One possible view of the matter is that having regard to the historical background which is referred to above and which is set out in detail in the

Annexure to the Propositions No. P-5/12-B, the Constitution-makers did not intend that any essential feature of our Constitution should be permitted to be altered, damaged or destroyed, even by the people, although all amendments may be made by Parliament which do not have such an effect. It may be urged that it was precisely for this reason that the Constitution-makers, having the various constitutional precedents before them, deliberately chose to make no provision for amendment by the people by a referendum or convention. (Ascertainment of the will of the people as regards constitutional amendments may be done in one of the well-settled constitutional modes, of which referendum is a well-favoured example. For the sake of brevity, the word 'referendum' is used hereinafter *to denote any of the available channels* for enabling the people's will to be expressed as regards constitutional amendments).

The other view of the matter is that a referendum was not provided for originally in the Constitution because it might have made it very difficult to have the Constitution accepted on those terms by the diverse sections of the public who would have viewed a referendum with grave misgivings; but that does not rule out the constitutional possibility of Parliament at any future stage amending the Constitution so as to provide a channel for the decision of the people on a referendum regarding amendments which are beyond the constitutional limits of the Parliament's amending power.

If the latter view is correct, Parliament can amend the Constitution to provide such a channel for ascertaining the will of the people regarding constitutional amendments. The most important point is that the provision must be such that:

(*a*) the decision can be made directly by the people on the precise proposal being submitted to them, and

(*b*) the *issue of amendment* must be presented to the people in absolute isolation, so that it does not get mixed up with other political questions and with political party affiliations or preferences.

Thus it must satisfy the criteria of directness and speciality of the people's decision (*See* Dr. Conrad's Article, pp. 405, 408 and 412).

If the latter view is right and Parliament can amend the Constitution to provide for a referendum, two views would again be possible as regards the scope of the people's amending power:

(*a*) It may be urged that the people would have on a referendum complete and absolute power to deal with any of the essential features of the Constitution.

(*b*) The other view would be that even the people on a referendum would have their amending power limited in two respects. Firstly, they cannot so amend the Constitution as to make it inconsistent with any part of the Preamble; and, secondly, they cannot take away the natural and inalienable rights or the basic human freedoms.

In this case it is not necessary to decide the questions regarding Parliament's competence to amend the Constitution so as to provide for a referendum and the extent and scope of the people's amending power on a referendum.

Note: A summary of submissions of all the other counsel who appeared in *Kesavananda Bharati* and Palkhivala's reply are given at (1973) 4 SCC Journal 35-52.

❄

Appendix III

Letters to Mrs. Gandhi in June, 1975 & November, 1975

Friday, 27th June 1975

My dear Prime Minister,

I spoke to Mr. Gokhale, the Law Minister, yesterday at 1 o' clock, requesting him to convey to you that, with great regret, I had decided to withdraw from the Appeal in view of the developments in the morning. I would have normally called upon you personally and explained the position, but in the circumstances of yesterday, it did not seem feasible. Then I again spoke to Mr. Gokhale twice in the afternoon and I do hope you got the message before it was released to the Press at about 6 p.m. yesterday. I was very anxious that you should know about it from me first.

The statement I released to the Press was the following:

> 'While I adhere to my views regarding the legal merits of the Prime Minister's Appeal against the Allahabad High Court's Judgment in the Election Petition against her, the measures taken by the Government this morning are such that, consistently with my lifelong convictions and the values I cherish, I have requested the Law Minister to convey to the Prime Minister my decision to withdraw as Counsel from the Appeal.'

Unfortunately, pre-censorship did not permit even this perfectly innocuous statement to be printed!

A letter does not seem a satisfactory mode of communication on a matter like this. I do hope I shall have the opportunity of meeting you at an early date.[1]

With warm regards,

Yours sincerely,
Sd./- N.A. Palkhivala

Mrs. Indira Gandhi,
Prime Minister of India,
New Delhi.

An Attempt to Review the Kesavananda Bharati Case

This is what Palkhivala wrote to Prime Minister Indira Gandhi. The letter is dated 9 November, 1975:

My dear Indiraji,

I am personally very happy that the litigation regarding your election is at long last over. There has never been any doubt in my mind that the judgment of the

1. There is no record of Palkhivala having met Mrs. Gandhi after writing this letter.

Allahabad High Court was erroneous on facts and in law and you deserved to succeed on every count – regardless of the subsequent amendments to the Constitution and to the Representation of the Peoples Act. Please accept my sincerest felicitations.

There is one matter about which I have been thinking for some time of writing to you but I did not want to do so till the Supreme Court's verdict in your case was pronounced. It is about the application made by the government to the Supreme court to reconsider the *Bank Nationalisation* case, and the *Kesavananda Bharati* case, in which the Supreme Court held that Parliament in exercise of its amending power cannot alter or destroy the basic structure of the Constitution.

I have nothing to say about the *Bank Nationalisation* case, because the question is purely academic. Subsequent amendments of the Constitution have superseded that judgment and most of the laws passed before the amendments have been put in the Ninth Schedule to prevent the ratio of the *Bank Nationalisation* case being applied to them.

However, I am most distressed and perturbed by the government's attempt to get the judgment in *Kesavananda's case* overruled. May I earnestly request you to consider the following points:

(1) The Supreme Court has already upheld the amendments which have virtually abrogated the right to property. Further, the court has also upheld the validity of Article 31C under which if any central or state law is intended to give effect to the economic policies of the state, not only would the right to property be altogether non-existent but even the basic human freedoms including equality before the law, freedom of speech and expression, the rights to form associations and to move throughout the territory of India, also stand abrogated. The optimum latitude of action is thus already assured to the government.

(2) If Parliament is given an unlimited power of amending the Constitution, the high degree of probability is that the basic structure of the Constitution which postulates a free democracy and the unity and integrity of the country will vanish within a few years. After you, who will be able to hold the entire country together? The States will fight for greater autonomy than is desirable. It is, to my mind, inconceivable that freedom and the unity of the country can survive for long after Parliament's supremacy over the Constitution is established.

(3) The basic structure of the Constitution is the real safeguard of the minorities. They are bound to feel grave apprehension at the prospect of the structure being held alterable. How many of your successors will share your own exemplary non-communal outlook?

(4) The happenings in Bangladesh show how thin is the veneer of civilized political behavior. With limitless amending power, the rule of law will itself disappear in the foreseeable future.

(5) What the country needs today more than anything else is stability and the healing of wounds. Both would suffer a severe setback if the most important ruling under our Constitution is attempted to be unsettled.

(6) Jammu and Kashmir, Tamil Nadu and Gujarat are, according to my information, going to oppose the attempt to arm Parliament with absolute power. But for Congress rule, the leaders of almost all states would adopt the same attitude, because the very existence of the states and their powers would be in jeopardy.

(7) India, Pakistan, Burma and Ceylon got their independence at about the same time, and of these countries. India is the only one with political stability. The

greatest credit for this achievement is due, apart from the outstanding personality of your father and yourself, to the basic structure of our Constitution.

(8) Your own case has been argued in the Supreme Court on the basis that *Kesavananda's* case represents the law of the land. It would look strange that within three days of the historic judgment in your favour, the court should consider whether that very case should be overruled.

(9) *Kesavananda's* case occupied the court for five months and the judgment was delivered only two and a half years ago. There are, and can be, no new arguments. Nothing has happened in between except the resignation of the old and the appointment of new judges. What would be the future of jurisprudence after we start the sorry precedent of seeking to unsettle the most momentous of rulings at brief intervals?

I beseech you, dear Indiraji, to consider the consequences of seeking to have the judgment in *Kesavananda's* case overruled. We have reached a historic moment when two roads diverge in the woods and your own decision at this juncture can have an imponderable impact for the good of the country.

Please forgive me for inflicting this long letter on you. I would not have done so but for my conviction that you always have an open mind and that your decision can save the Constitution, ensure the onward march of the nation on our chosen path, prevent several months of waste of the court's time and avoid the state of uncertainty and misgivings which is such an unfailing solvent of progress.

The hearing in the Supreme Court on the correctness of *Kesavananda's* case begins tomorrow. It need not continue unless the government wants it to. Believe me, my respectful appeal to you is not made out of any lack of confidence in the case for holding Parliament's amending power to be limited, but it is based upon my belief that it would be a great gesture on your part to withdraw the state's plea for unsettling the law. I shall be very happy to call upon you if you so desire.

With warm regards,

Yours sincerely,
Sd./- N.A. Palkhivala

Appendix IV

Important Written Submissions, Articles and the Bhopal Affidavit

IN THE SUPREME COURT OF INDIA CIVIL
ORIGINAL JURISDICTION

WRIT PETITION (CIVIL) NO.805 OF 1993

T.N. Seshan, Chief Election Commissioner of India, Petitioner –Versus Union of India and others, Respondents

PROPOSITIONS FILED ON BEHALF OF THE

PETITIONER

by

MR. NANI A. PALKHIVALA

On 1st October 1993, two Notifications were issued – the first by which the composition of the Election Commission was increased to three (including the Chief Election Commissioner), and the second by which Mr. G.V.G. Krishnamurthy and Mr.M.S.Gill were appointed the new members of the Election Commission.

The argument that these two Notifications were malafide and were void for a number of reasons, has been already advanced ably and adequately by Mr.G.Ramaswamy, Senior Advocate. These propositions are not concerned with that point. They only deal with the second point also raised in the petition.

The second point assumes that the enlargement of the Election Commission and the appointment of the two individuals as Election Commissioners were valid. The second point is that even assuming that the enlargement of the Election Commissioners were valid, the two sections quoted below which were introduced by the Chief Election Commissioner and other Election Commissioners (Conditions of Service) Amendment Act, 1994, are invalid and void.

The two Sections (hereinafter referred to as 'the impugned Sections') run as follows:

> '*Sec. 9* : The business of the Election Commission shall be transacted in accordance with the provisions of the Act.
>
> *Sec. 10(1):* Election Commission may, by unanimous decision, regulate the procedure for transaction of its business as also allocation of its business, amongst the Chief Election Commissioner and the other Election Commissioners.

Save as provided in Sub-sec. (1), the business of The Election Commission shall, as far as possible, be Transacted unanimously.

Subject to the provision of Sub-sec. (2), if the Chief Election Commissioner and the other Election Commissioners differ in opinion on any matter, such matter shall be decided according to the opinion of the majority.'

The following are the principal grounds for holding the impugned sections invalid and void.

First, the impugned sections are beyond the competence of Parliament.

(i) Parliament has no power to pass any law as to how 'the business of the Election Commission shall be transacted'.

(ii) Parliament has no power to pass any law putting the Chief Election Commissioner and the Election Commissioners on a footing of equality, and to provide in effect that on any matter where there is difference of opinion, 'such matter shall be decided according to the opinion of the majority'.

Secondly, Article 324 of the Constitution says that the Chief Election Commissioner 'shall not be removed from his office except in like manner and on the like grounds as a Judge of the Supreme Court'. The impugned sections virtually remove the Chief Election Commissioner, and in this way Parliament did indirectly that it could not do directly. The Chief Election Commissioner is removed from power which is tantamount to removing him from office. In other words, Parliament acted in a manner which would leave no self-respecting Chief Election Commissioner with any option but to resign.

Thirdly, in the first proviso to Article 321(5) of the Constitution, 'the conditions of service of the Chief Election Commissioner shall not be varied to his disadvantage after his appointment'. The impugned sections vary the most vital condition of service to the Chief Election Commissioner's disadvantage. When the Chief Election Commissioner's appointment was made on 12th December 1990, he was the sole repository of all powers under Article 324 regarding 'the superintendence, direction and control of the preparation of the electoral rolls for, and the conduct of, all elections to Parliament and to the Legislature of every State and elections to the offices of President and Vice-President'. Today, he has to suffer the humiliation of being overridden by two civil servants.

Fourthly, the impugned sections constitute a mockery of Article 324 of the Constitution in two ways:

(i) No doubt the Chief Election Commissioner and the Election Commissioner together constitute the Election Commission. But they are not placed on a footing of equality by the Constitution. (*See Annexure 1*). Incidents of the Prime Minister and a Chief Minister making decisions contrary to the majority view in the Cabinet is a well established feature of the Constitution. (See *Annexure 2*). The same features are implicit in Article 324 which deals with the Election Commission.

(ii) There is another way in which the Constitution is mocked. The two Election Commissioners become liable to be removed from office on the recommendation of the Chief Election Commissioner, but while they continue in office the arbitrary and whimsical scheme approved by Parliament makes it possible for them to reduce the Chief Election Commissioner to a mere figurehead.

Fifthly, the impugned sections constitute a fraud upon the Constitution inasmuch as they have been designed and calculated to defeat the whole purpose of having an Election Commission which would be free from control of the executive. The whole purpose of Article 324 is to make a provision for ensuring that elections are free and fair and are not manipulated by the executive or the legislature. India has reached the nadir of corruption and electoral malpractices. Undisputed facts leave no doubt that the Chief Election Commissioner was truly independent and refused to kowtow to any individual, however highly placed, in the legislature or the executive. Whenever the Chief Election Commissioner went wrong or overstepped the limits of his power and jurisdiction, he was rightly controlled by the judiciary. The whole purpose of introducing the impugned sections is to make it impossible for him to act in a spirit of independence.

It is well established that the court will not uphold any act, legislative or executive, which constitutes a fraud upon the power or misuse of power in bad faith. (See *Annexure 3*). The undisputed events of the past five years speak far more eloquently than any words can, as to the object of the appointment of the two Election Commissioners.

The first period extended from 12th December 1990 to 1st October 1993 when the two Election Commissioners were appointed. During this period, the Chief Election Commissioner acted independently exactly as the Constitution intended the Chief Election Commissioner to act.

The second period was from 1st October 1993 to 15th November 1993 when the Chief Election Commissioner was paralyzed or destabilized and was unable to perform his statutory duties and functions. During those 45 dark days, the Election Commission, as contemplated by the Constitution, could not and did not function.

The third period is from 15th November 1993 up-to-date. On 15th November 1993, this Hon'ble Court issued rule in this petition and passed an interim injunction as follows:

> 'In W.P. No. 805/93 notice on the application for interim Stay as well as on the application for production of the documents. Until further orders, to ensure smooth and effective working of the Commission and also to avoid confusion both in the administration as well as in the electoral process, we direct that the Chief Election Commissioner shall remain in complete overall control of the Commission's work. He may ascertain the views of other Commissioners or such of them as he chooses, on the issues that may come up before the Commission from time to time. However, he will not be bound by their views. It is also made clear that the Chief Election Commissioner alone will be entitled to issue instructions to the Commission's staff as well as to the outside agencies and that no other Commissioner will issue such instructions.'

During the last 15 months, the Election Commission has functioned effectively and independently, as contemplated by the Constitution. The petitioner can pray for no better final order than an order ensuring the continuation of the constitutional mandate.

MANDAL COMMISSION'S REPORT

(ii) Propositions submitted by N.A. PALKHIVALA
Unconstitutional and unacceptable features of the Mandal Report

1. The Terms of Reference require the Commission 'to examine the desirability or otherwise of making provision for the reservation of appointments or posts . . .

in public services'. This most vital part of the Terms of Reference was wholly ignored by the Commission. Before making its recommendations for reservation under Art. 16(4), the Commission was bound, by the Terms of Reference, to determine the desirability or otherwise of such reservations. The Commission did not at all investigate whether reservations in different States had resulted in the sub-standard replacing the standard and the reins of power passing from meritocracy to mediocrity; and whether they had resulted in demoralization and discontent, for instance, in the police force.

2. The basic structure of the Constitution envisages a cohesive, unified, casteless society – in which casteism, petrified and ossified for centuries should become merely the dust on the shelf of Indian history. By emphatically ensuring a fresh lease of life to the canker of casteism for a long, indefinite future, the Report fractures the nation and violates the basic structure of the Constitution. It would revitalize casteism, cleave the nation into two – forward and backward and open up new vistas for internecine conflict and fissiparous forces, and make backwardness a vested interest. It will undo whatever has been achieved in the last forty-three years towards creating a unified, cohesive society.

3. The progress of India has been from casteism to egalitarianism. It has been from feudalism to freedom: and equality is the very heart of a free republic. The bedrock of the Report is discrimination in reverse; it is discrimination against merit and calibre. By denying equality, it violates the basic structure of the Constitution.

4. The perpetually recurring theme of the Report is the inequality bred in Indian society by casteism. With this background in mind, the Commission doubts whether the ideal of equality (Arts. 14, 15 and 16) can be applied in practice in India (pp. 21-23, chap. VI).

5. The Report virtually rewrites Art. 16(4) by substituting *caste* for class. Caste is made the sole test – *not just the paramount test but the sole and exclusive test* – for quota eligibility (pp. 54-56, chap. XII).

6. Every other test – economic or non-economic – is wholly rejected: 'The substitution of caste by economic tests will amount to ignoring the genesis of social backwardness in the Indian society' (p. 4, para 1.21). The Commission ignored the basic point that it was not concerned with the genesis of social backwardness in Indian society but with the determination of 'backward class' for the purposes of Art. 16(4). The suggestion made by a large section of the public that multiple criteria, including economic tests, should be adopted (p. 43, para 10.4) was brushed aside.

7. Every single piece of evidence or material adverted to by the Commission was only for the purpose of determining whether a caste was backward, and not whether a member or family in the caste was backward. The indicators (criteria) invoked to determine backwardness are invariably applied to the caste and not to the individual; and even in dealing with castes, economic indicators have the lowest weightage (p. 52, paras 11.23 and 11.24).

8. By adopting caste as the exclusive test of a backward class, the Commission deliberately shuts its eyes to the fact that there are crores of backward individuals in forward castes and crores of forward individuals in backward castes. Forty-three years of independence have changed the social, educational and economic landscape beyond recognition (e.g change in 'Varna' of Chief Ministers (p. 38, para 9.15). By making caste the sole consideration, the Commission has

(a) included for preferential treatment all members of backward castes, however wealthy; and

(b) excluded all members of forward castes, however poor and deserving.

It is well settled that a classification would be upheld, only if it bears a reasonable relation to the subject-matter of the legislation or executive action. The Report makes such an unreasonable and irrational classification that the children of some of the wealthiest families, and of Mandal himself, who was a rich zamindar, would be entitled to preferential treatment because they spring from the so-called backward castes (pp. 50-56, chaps. XI and XII). Some aberrations are corrected in deciding whether a caste is backward or forward (p. 55, para 12.9); but no aberration, however startling, is sought to be corrected when dealing with families or individuals within the same caste, though such correction could easily be done by economic tests. The gross injustice which would be perpetrated by implementing the Report can be conclusively demonstrated by taking the very example of Mohan and Lallu (p. 23, paras 6.17 to 6.21), and by merely exchanging the castes given in the Report (i.e. by assuming that Mohan comes from a wealthy backward caste family and Lallu comes from an impoverished forward caste family).

9. Castes are the building blocks of the Report. The Commission deplores the facts that (a) casteism is still the paramount reality of Indian life, and (b) caste is the football in the political game which political parties play (pp. 18-20, chap. V). Going beyond the Terms of Reference, the Commission has devoted whole chapters to tracing the sordid history of castes and casteism which are a blot on Indian society (pp. 5-36, chaps. II toVIII).

10. The basic inherent contradiction in the Report is that while *deploring the indisputable evils of casteism,* the Commission itself wants caste *to be made the sole test of reservations in employment, admissions, and promotions.*

11. The Report invents castes for non-Hindus. The obsession with casteism and the desire to apply the same yardstick to all Indians impelled the Commission to identify backward classes among non-Hindus also by the exclusive test of caste, regardless of any economic or other tests (pp. 55-6, paras 12.11 to 12.18) and regardless of the fact that caste is anathema to Christianity, Islam and Sikhism.

12. Under constitutional law, a decision cannot be regarded as valid which is vitiated by non-application of mind. The recommendations for reservations are so sweeping and so widespread as to leave no doubt that there has been no application of mind. They apply to all posts and all services in toto under the Central Government – all civil and administrative services, the armed forces, public sector undertakings, nationalized banks, all universities and affiliated colleges, all private sector undertakings which receive financial assistance from the government in any form; and the recommended quotas are not only for employment or admission but even for promotions at all levels (p. 58, paras 13.13 to 13.16 and the Summary on p. 64). Further, in every field of Government service, the recommendation is for carrying forward for three years the unfilled reserved quota (p. 58, para 13.13). The most momentous of all issues – *the security of the State* – if appointments and promotions in the armed forces are made on caste basis, never entered the mind of the Commission.

13. Efficiency of administration which is the paramount consideration in dealing with reservations for weaker sections under Art. 335, is not considered or adverted to at all in any part of the substantive Report. It is merely referred to in passing in the final Chapter on Recommendations (p. 57, para 13.2).

14. Even regarding backward castes, the materials before the Commission were woefully inadequate. Worse, the evidence was partisan and biased (p. 47, paras 10.46 and 10.47). The dividing line between the forward and the backward castes is too vague and varies from State to State (p. 39, paras 9.24 and 9.25). Many advanced castes were included in the lists of backward castes maintained by the States and several truly backward castes were left out (p. 43, para 10.6). Essential data was non-existent. 'Hardly any State was able to give the desired information' (p. 37, para 9.4). As regards the representation of OBCs in Government services, the information received by the Commission was 'too sketchy and scrappy for any meaningful inference which may be valid for the country as a whole' (p. 38, para 9.14). 'No State Government could furnish figures regarding the level of literacy and education amongst Other Backward Classes (p. 39, para 9.30). 'No list of OBCs is maintained by the Central Government, nor their particulars are separately compiled in Government offices' (p. 41, para 9.47). The practice of mentioning the caste in service records was discontinued by the Government by 1951.

15. The census records in 1931 were hopelessly obsolete. They were not only patently out-of-date but referred in British India as it then was, i.e. including Pakistan, Bangladesh and Burma, and excluding the Indian States. Still they were taken into account because they constituted the last census records to proceed on the caste basis (p. 56, paras 12.19 and 12.20).

16. The sample survey was totally inadequate. The survey covered only two villages and one urban block in any district (p. 51, para 11.15). The original recommendation of the Experts Panel for a larger sample survey was rejected for lack of time (p. 50, para 11.10). That means the survey covered less than one out of 500 villages. Such a survey is scientifically untenable, as admitted by the Commission itself (p. 53, para 11.27).

17. The whimsicality and irrationality which characterize the Report are almost beyond belief. In ascertaining whether a caste was backward, the Commission even applied the test of the stigma of 'criminality', though one would have thought that criminal castes hardly qualify for reservations in public service (p. 54, para 12.6). While Article 16(4) contemplates reservation for a backward class which is not adequately represented in State service, the Commission reversed the constitutional mandate and took inadequate representation in public services as an 'important test' of the caste being backward (p. 54, para 12.6).

18. The minute of dissent by Shri L. R. Naik makes it clear that the recommendations of the majority of the Commission would not achieve the objective of the Constitution and the only result would be that the intermediate backward castes would benefit at the expense of the depressed backward castes. He draws pointed attention to the tendency 'fast developing among Intermediate Backward Classes to repeat the treatments or rather ill-treatments they themselves have received from times immemorial at the hands of the upper castes, against . . . . the Depressed Backward Classes' (Second Part of the Report, p. 230).

19. The Commission failed to give any weight whatever to the reasons why for all the past decades the Union Government had not made reservations on caste basis in the areas of employment, admissions and promotions. In particular, the Commission gave short shrift to the reasons why no effect was given to Kalelkar's Report based on caste (1955):

(a) Kalekar's Report had listed 2399 castes as backward. Dealing with this list the Union Government said, 'if the entire community, barring a few exceptions, has thus to be regarded as backward, the really needy would be swamped by the multitude and hardly receive any special attention or adequate assistance, nor would such dispensation fulfil the conditions laid down in Article 340 of the Constitution' (p. 2, para 1.8). This objection would apply *a fortiori* to the Mandal Report which lists 3743 backward castes. Like the expanding universe, the list of backward castes is ever expanding. Many more are already waiting in the wings to receive recognition.

(b) The Union Government had always held the consistent view that 'it would be better to apply economic tests than to go by caste' (p.4, para 1.20);

The Mandal Commission had no use for the words of wisdom contained in Kalekar's own letter forwarding his Report to the President, 'I am definitely against reservation in Government Services for any community for the simple reason that the services are not meant for the servants but they are meant for the service of society as a whole ...' (p. 3, para 1.17).

The Commission wholly ignored the unanswerable view point of Pandit Nehru in his letter to Chief Ministers sent on June, 27, 1961:

> '. . . help should be given on economic considerations and not on caste . . . . I dislike any kind of reservation, more particularly in service. I react strongly against anything which leads to inefficiency and second-rate standards . . . . . The only real way to help a backward group is to give opportunities of good education . . . . But if we go in for reservations on communal and caste basis, we swamp the bright and able people and remain second-rate or third-rate. I am grieved to learn of how far this business of reservation has gone based on communal consideration. It has amazed me to learn that even promotions are based sometimes on communal or caste considerations. This way lies not only folly, but disaster. Let us help the backward groups by all means, but never at the cost of efficiency. How are we going to build our public sector or indeed any sector with second-rate people?' (Jawaharlal Nehru, Letters to Chief Ministers 1947 – 1964, Vol.5, Oxford University Press, 1989, pp. 456 – 7).

Proposed implementation in phases:

The facts that the Government Notification dated 13th August, 1990 does not adopt the Mandal recommendations in the first stage for the armed forces, for promotions in civil service, and for educational institutions, is wholly irrelevant to the question arising in these petitions. If the Report is constitutionally valid, it can be implemented in phases; and it has been expressly announced by the Government in Parliament that they *propose to implement it in phases* and it has also been announced outside Parliament by members of the Central Cabinet that the Mandal Report would be implemented 'in toto' and 'without any dilution'.

The position under the Constitution

I. The basic structure of the Constitution envisages the creation of a free society:

(i) which is cohesive and unified and has obliterated casteism, and

(ii) where all persons are assured of equality before the law.

II. In order to take care of the weaker sections of the people (Art. 46), there are three distinct and separate exceptions to the incandescent ideal of equality:

First, Articles 330 and 332 provide for mandatory reservations of seats in the Central and State Legislatures for those whom the Constitution regards as the weakest of the weak – the Scheduled Castes and Scheduled Tribes, – and not for any other backward class.

Secondly, the State has the discretionary power under Article 15(4) to make 'any special provision for the advancement of any socially and educationally backward classes of citizens'. For instance, special financial or educational institutions may be established under Article 15(4) for certain castes provided they can be designated as 'socially and educationally backward classes'. But Article 15(4) has nothing whatsoever to do with reservations in services under the State.

Thirdly, Article 16(4) deals with reservations in services under the State.

The following points emerge from the provisions regarding reservations in services under the State:

(a) Only the weakest of the weak sections – the Scheduled Castes and Scheduled Tribes – have a right under Article 335 to be considered for preference in public services and even they have only the right to have their claims considered 'consistently with the maintenance of efficiency of administration'.

(b) The less weak sections – other Backward Classes – may have reservations in pubic services made for them purely in the discretion of the Government under Article 16(4).

(c) The Government's discretion under Article 16(4) has to be fairly and judicially exercised in the context of the scheme of the Constitution. Reading Article 16(4) and Article 335 together, it is evident that if efficiency of administration cannot be sacrificed even in favour of Scheduled Castes and Schedule Tribes, much less can it be sacrificed in favour less weak sections, the other Backward Classes.

(d) Article 15(4) refers to socially and educationally backward classes because in the context of Article 15(4) which deals with discrimination in their favour in point expenditure out of public revenues, caste symbolizing social and educational backwardness may be relevant. By contrast, Article 16(4) does not refer to social backwardness at all. In Article 16(4), the expression used is 'backward class' simpliciter, which can embrace economic backwardness but can never justify caste (social backwardness) as a paramount criterion. The nuances of 'backwardness' in the context of Art. 16(4) are only those which are germane to selection for service under the State, where caste is irrelevant.

(e) The fact that caste or social backwardness can never be the paramount criterion or consideration under Art. 16(4) is proved by another feature of the constitutional scheme. Even the lowest castes - the Scheduled Castes and Scheduled Tribes - have reservations in the Central and State Legislatures under Article 334 only for a period of 50 years (after the latest amendment) from the commencement of the Constitution. If reservations could be made under Art. 16(4) on the paramount ground of caste or social backwardness, casteism would be perpetuated in Government service indefinitely.

To recapitulate what Krishna Iyer J. said in *State of Kerala v. N.M. Thomas* [1976 (1) SCR 906] – (a) To travel beyond the special treatment permissible under Art. 16(4) and evolve a general doctrine of backward classification is to over-power the basic concept of equality and bring in a back-door casteism, subverting the scheme of a casteless society (p. 969). (b) The solution to the problem lies elsewhere and not with the higher 'backward' groups who have a vested interest in the plums of backwardism; otherwise, the solemn undertakings in Arts, 14 to 16 may be reduced to a 'teasing illusion or promise of unreality' (p. 973). (c) The securing of benefits under Art. 16(4) by political pressure or communal manipulation for all manner of castes would run the high risk of unconstitutional discrimination (p. 981).

III. No doubt under Art. 340, the Commission has 'to investigate the conditions of socially and educationally backward classes' but such investigation is for various purposes of the Constitution. The Commission can make recommendations under Art. 340 for action under Art. 15(4) for socially and educationally backward classes. But it cannot make recommendations for reservations under Art. 16(4) on the paramount ground of caste or social backwardness. The basic fallacy underlying the Mandal Report is its unstateable assumption that it is entitled to make recommendations for reservations under Art. 16(4) in services under the State, on the exclusive ground – not even paramount but the sole ground - of caste or social backwardness.

MANDAL CASE – I

(iii) SC Verdict will 'Cleave Nation'[1]—Article on the Mandal judgment by N.A. Palkhivala

Last week, the Supreme Court pronounced its decision in the Mandal case. The six judgments cover 910 pages. Understandably, brevity is not the forte of a people who were the first to evolve eternity and infinity.

Discrimination against any citizen on the ground only of caste is prohibited by Article 15(1) and likewise, such discrimination against any citizen in respect of any employment or office under the state is prohibited by article 16(2). Article 15(4) permits the state to make 'any special provision for the advancement of any socially and educationally backward classes of citizens or for the scheduled castes and the scheduled tribes.'

The crucial provision is continued in Article 16(4) which permits, the state to make 'any provision for the reservation of appointments or posts in favour of any backward class of citizens which, in the opinion of the state, is not adequately represented in the services under the state'. Whereas 'caste' is referred to in Articles 15(1) and 16(2) as a prohibited ground of discrimination, the word used in Articles 15(4) and 16(4) is 'class' to denote the group which may qualify for permissible preference or reservation.

The Mandal report identifies 52 percent of the total population of India as Other Backward Classes (OBCs) – over and above the 22.5 percent who are the scheduled castes and scheduled tribes and are already entitled to reservation in Union government service. Never before in history, and no where else in the world today, have reservations been prescribed for the overwhelming majority of the population of any country.

The Mandal report applies (a) to all employment, civil and military under the government; (b) to employment in all public sector enterprises; (c) to private sector enterprises which in any manner receive any financial assistance from the state or any public sector undertaking; (d) to admission and engagement in all

1. This two part article appeared in the Times of India (November 24 and 25, 1992) just eight days after the judgment was delivered on November 16, 1992.

universities and affiliated colleges; and (e) to promotions at all levels in the areas covered by (a) to (d) above.

The V.P. Singh government which issued the memorandum dated August 13, 1990, proposed to implement the Mandal report in phases and announced that the report would be implemented 'in toto' and 'without any dilution'. However, it proceeded on the basis that in the first stage the Mandal recommendations would not be adopted for the armed forces, for promotions in civil service and for educational institutions. For OBCs, 27 percent reservations were made, over and above the existing 22.5 percent for the scheduled castes and the scheduled tribes.

The memorandum dated September 25, 1991 issued by the present government adopted the 1990 memorandum with the amendments that (i) within the 27 percent reservations, preference should be given to candidates belonging to poorer sections of the backward castes, and (ii) an additional ten percent of the vacancies should be reserved for other economically backward classes of the people. No criteria were issued for determining the poorer sections or the other economically backward classes.

In the majority judgments of the Supreme Court, no fewer than 20 separate questions were framed and answered. The vital question was only one: are reservations on the basis of caste permissible under article 16(4)?

The majority judgments answered this question in the affirmative and upheld the two memoranda with the important qualifications that (a) the 'creamy layer' of backward classes should be excluded, because otherwise they would tap up all the benefits of reservations meant for that class; (b) within four months the government should 'specify the basis of exclusion – whether on the basis of income, extent of holding or otherwise – of the creamy layer'; (c) the inclusion or exclusion of a caste or a section of a caste would have to be periodically reviewed to take care of changing circumstances; (d) permanent commissions should be appointed within four months by the Central Government and by the state governments to decide regularly the cases which would arise involving questions whether a particular caste or a section of a caste was rightly included or excluded; and all further proceedings in such matters can be taken only in the Supreme Court; (e) 'a backward caste cannot be determined only and exclusively with reference to economic criterion' and, therefore, the ten percent additional reservation made by the second memorandum of September 25, 1991 was illegal and void; (f) armed forces and some higher civilian posts to be selected by the Government, should be outside the purview of caste reservations; (g) reservations cannot be applied to promotions: 'crutches cannot be provided throughout one's career'.

The six judgments of the Supreme Court fall into two categories – the majority judgments which partially uphold the memoranda but subject to qualifications and conditions which are incapable of being complied with, without an unforgivable waste of public time and energy; and the minority judgments which state the law plainly and bluntly, *viz.*, that the memorandums providing for reservations on caste basis are unconstitutional and void.

I am sure Mr. V.P. Singh was sincere when he said that after the Supreme Court judgment in the Mandal case he could die in peace. But his policy has ensured that the nation will not live in peace. The poisonous weed of casteism has been replanted 'where it will trouble us a thousand years, each age will have to reconsider it'.

It is submitted that the majority judgments in the Mandal case are erroneous in law and need to be overruled in the national interest and in the long-term interests of the backward castes themselves. The basic structure of the Constitution envisages a cohesive, unified, casteless society – in which casteism, petrified and ossified for centuries, should become merely the dust on the shelf of Indian history. By ensuring a fresh lease of life to the canker of casteism for a long and indefinite future, the judgment fractures the nation and disregards the basic structure of the Constitution.

The decision would revitalize casteism, cleave the nation into two – forward and backward – and open up new vistas for internecine conflicts and fissiparous forces, and make backwardness a vested interest. It will undo whatever has been achieved since independence towards crafting a unified, integrated nation.

The progress of India has been from casteism to egalitarianism. It has been from feudalism to freedom; and equality is the very heart of a free republic.

The majority judgments will revive casteism which the Constitution emphatically intended to end; and the pre-independence tragedy would be re-enacted with the roles reversed – the erstwhile underprivileged would now become the privileged. The desperate tale of the forward caste woman in Kerala who, merely with a view to gaining admission for her son in a medical college, deposed before a magistrate in the presence of her husband that the son was her illegitimate offspring by a Harijan, does not seem to have attracted the attention of our 'low arousal' people. The majority view will result in the sub-standard replacing the standard and the reins of power passing from meritocracy to mediocrity. Caste will be given precedence over merit and caliber. Article 16(4) has been virtually rewritten by substituting 'caste' for 'class'.

(To be continued)

(The author appeared in the Supreme Court in the Mandal case)

Part II

The crucial point is that under the majority judgments of the Supreme Court, it is the members belonging to certain castes only who are eligible to be considered for reservations. When you have removed the creamy layer, what you are left with are still the members of certain castes only. The sections of society which fall outside those designated castes do not qualify for reservations, however socially and educationally backward they may be.

It is undisputed that 45 years of independence have changed the social, educational, and economic landscape beyond recognition. There are crores of backward individuals in forward castes and crores of forward individuals in backward castes. By making caste the essential condition, the majority judgments have (A) included for reservations all members of backward castes who do not belong to the creamy layer, and (B) excluded all members of forward castes, however backward and deserving. Such a classification can never be upheld, because it does not bear a reasonable relation to the subject matter of the action.

A backward class may be given the benefit of Article 15(4) or Article 16(4), but the class must consist of a homogeneous group – the element of homogeneity should be the backwardness characterizing the class. In other words, the link or the thread holding the class together should be the backwardness of the members. Such a link or thread can never be supplied by caste. Excluding the creamy layer of the caste would not get rid of the vice that the only link or thread binding the benefited class together is caste. In other words, a classification may be justified on the ground that it is a backward 'class', but never on the ground that it is a backward 'caste' or a 'section of a backward caste'.

This principle was precisely enunciated by the Constitution Bench in *Triloki Nath* (1969), *Pradip Tandon* (1975), *Jayashree* (1977), *Akil Bhartiya Soshit* (1981). These judgments were cited before the Supreme Court and are referred to in the majority judgment without disapproval, but they are inexplicably overlooked.

The majority judgments gave no weight to the reasons why for all the past decades the Union government had not made reservations on caste basis in areas of employment, admission and promotions, and why the practice of mentioning the caste in service records was discontinued by the Government in 1951. The last census records to proceed on caste basis are those of 1931 which, though hopelessly obsolete, were relied upon by the Mandal Commission because they were the latest census records to proceed on the caste basis.

Kaka Kalelkar's own letter forwarding his report (1955) to the President said, 'I am definitely against reservations in government services for any community, for the simple reason that the services are not meant for the servants but they are meant for the service of society as a whole'. Kalelkar's report, which was not accepted by the then Government had listed 2,399 castes as backward. Dealing with this list, the Union Government said, 'if the entire community, barring a few exceptions, has thus to be regarded as a backward, the really needy would be swamped by the multitude and hardly receive any special attention or adequate assistance'. This objection would apply a *fortiori* to the Mandal report which lists (not exhaustively) 3,747 backward castes. Like the expanding universe, the list of backward castes is ever-expanding. Many more are already waiting in the wings to receive attention.

The last word on the subject may be left with Pandit Jawaharlal Nehru who, in his letter to the chief ministers in June 1961 said, 'I dislike any kind of reservation, more particularly in service. I react strongly against anything which leads to inefficiency and second-rate standards .... The only real way to help a backward group is to give opportunities for a good education ... but if we go in for reservations on communal and caste basis, we swamp the bright and able people and remain second-rate or third-rate .... It has amazed me to learn that even promotions are based sometimes on communal or caste considerations. This way lies not only folly, but disaster. Let us help the backward groups by all means, but never at the cost of efficiency.'

Reading Article 16(4) and Article 333 together, it is evident that when efficiency of administration cannot be sacrificed even in favour of the scheduled castes and the scheduled tribes, much less can it be sacrificed to favour less weak sections, *viz.*, the other backward classes. The majority judgments accept this proposition. How will the Government ensure the fulfillment of the condition of 'efficiency of administration' or lay down satisfactory criteria to exclude the creamy layer of backward castes in a country where less than one percent of the population are income-tax payers.

The unacceptable consequences of the majority view are well illustrated by the fact that the majority struck down the part of the memorandum dated September 25, 1992 which provides for additional reservation of 10 percent for other economically backward classes, on the ground that while caste backwardness is relevant under Article 16(4), economic backwardness is not.

The minority judgments of Justices Thommen, Kuldip Singh and R.M. Sahai lay down the correct law. They proceed on the footing that casteism is anathema to the Constitution and that it can never be the basis of reservation.

A momentous responsibility lies on the present Government. No doubt, it is bound by the law as laid down by the majority judgments of the Supreme Court, but it is not bound to continue the policy of reservations, in view of the qualifications and conditions indicated in those judgments. In other words, the Governments' decision under Article 16(4) to continue to make or not to make reservations has to be fairly and judiciously exercised in the light of the conditions and qualifications which would now have to be complied with. The Government has to decide whether it is in the national interest to open up a pandora's box in a country which is already plagued by unmanageable problems.

It has to decide whether it will opt for populism, persist in the policy of reservations and convert this country into a paradise for lawyers, or whether it will take a u-turn and give the moral leadership which is the hallmark of statesmen who bravely take on the role of 'movers of people, mobilisers of opinion'.

By practicing in reservations, the Government will get deplorably enmeshed in unending litigation and waste the nation's resources, time and energy on an unimaginable scale. In law, the Government is entitled to say that having regard to the conditions and qualifications imposed by the Supreme Court, it is not in the national interest to persist in the system of reservations. Such a stance would require courage and statesmanship of the highest order, and would mark a turning point in the history of a country which has been too long content to run a third-class democracy under a first-class Constitution.

(concluded)

(iv) Affidavit of N.A. Palkhivala in Support of Defendant's Motion for Dismissal on Forum Non Conveniens Grounds

STATE OF MAHARASHTRA

UNION OF INDIA

N.A. Palkhivala, being duly sworn, deposes and says:

I took the M.A. Degree (1942) from St. Xavier's College, Bombay, and the LL.B. Degree (1944) from Government Law College, Bombay. I am a Senior Advocate of the Supreme Court of India (corresponding to English QC) and have wide practice before the Supreme Court of India, the Bombay High Court and other High Courts of India.

I was a Professor of Law at Government Law College, Bombay, for several years, and was appointed the Tagore Professor of Law at the Calcutta University. I was a Member of the First Law Commission of India (1955) and also of the Second Law Commission (1958).

In 1975, I was elected an Honorary Member of The Academy of Political Science, New York. The Honorary Degree of LL.D. was conferred upon me by the Princeton university, New Jersey, in 1978, and by the Lawrence university, Wisconsin, in 1979.

From 1977 to 1979 I served as Ambassador of India to the United States of America.

'I have done the State some service'. Thrice India had to present its case before international forums and I was engaged as the Counsel for the Indian Government on all the three occasions – the Rann of Kutch case before the Special Tribunal appointed by the United Nations in Geneva (1962 – 65); the case regarding Pakistan's alleged right to overfly India before the International Civil Aviation Organization (ICAO) Tribunal in Montreal (1971), and the appeal therefrom to the International Court of Justice at the Hague (1971 – 72).

I have been and am the Counsel for some of the largest corporations, Indian and foreign, which had or have business operations in India. I was the Chief Counsel for the citizen in cases which has substantially shaped the growth of our constitutional law, particularly the first five cases mentioned on pp. 6 and 7 below.

I am the author of numerous articles, and several books including :

'We, the People', 1984

'India's Priceless Heritage', 1980

'Our Constitution Defaced and Defiled', 1974

'The Law and Practice of Income Tax', 7th edition updated, 1982 and

'Taxation in India' (co-author of the book published by the Harvard University), 1960.

At present I hold a number of positions on the Board of Directors of some of the major companies in India, including:

Chairman	: The Association Cement Cos. Ltd. Tata Exports Ltd.
Deputy Chairman	: Tata Engineering and Locomotive Co. Ltd.
Vice Chairman	: Associated Bearing Co. Ltd.
Director	: Tata Sons Ltd. The Tata Iron & Steel Co. Ltd. National Organic Chemical Industries Ltd. The Press Trust of India Ltd.

I am the Chairman of the Income-Tax Appellate Tribunal Bar Association and President of the Forum of Free Enterprise.

I have reviewed the Affidavit dated July 31, 1985 affirmed by Mr. Bud G. Holman, and that dated December 14, 1985 affirmed by Mr. J.B. Dadachanji. I say that Mr. Holman's statements regarding the adequacy of the Indian legal system and Indian courts are correct, and Mr. Dadachanji has presented a true picture of the state of the law and administration of justice in India.

I have seen the Memoranda and Affidavits filed in opposition to Union Carbide's Motion regarding Forum Non Conveniens. In those papers it has been stated that Indian legal system is 'deficient' and 'inadequate'. I am constrained to say that it is gratuitous denigration to call the Indian system deficient or inadequate.

The Indian legal system is essentially based upon the common law of the United Kingdom. The Code of Civil Procedure, 1908, which continues in force, is based upon the procedure in the courts of the United Kingdom. The Indian Evidence Act is also based upon the law of evidence in the United Kingdom, while the Indian Penal Code, again, codifies the criminal law of the United Kingdom. There is a basic similarity in essentials between the American legal system and the Indian legal system, since they both have had their origin in the jurisprudence of the United Kingdom.

A legal system is not a structure of fossils but is a living organism which grows through the judicial process and statutory enactments. Thus in course of time systems which were once similar become different in some respects. We do not have the jury system in India in civil or criminal matters, nor do we have the type of 'discovery' which is a specialty of the American procedure. While it is true to say that the Indian system today is different in some respects from the American system, it is wholly untrue to say that it is deficient or inadequate. Different is not to be equated with deficiency.

The Indian legal system does not provide an identical forum – identical to the American forum; but it does provide an adequate alternative forum. The differences between the two systems spring from the differences in the history, culture and economic development of the two countries. There are some questions of substantive and procedural law which Indian and US systems have answered differently – for instance, the practice of contingency fees, the way to handle class actions, and how broad and costly 'discovery' should be. Different countries have different answers to these problems. Contingency fees which are permitted in the United States are prohibited in the United Kingdom, Canada and India as serious public evils and as being against public policy. To brand the Indian system as being inadequate because its method of dealing with class actions or meeting the need of discovery is different from the American method, is to betray good chauvinism but poor international perspective.

It would be a work of supererogation to repeat the authorities and detailed documentation which have been sufficiently deployed in Mr. J.B. Dadachanji's Affidavit. On the basis of those very authorities and documentation, I respectfully submit the following broad considerations on the strident points urged in support of the plea that the Indian courts are not an adequate alternative forum.

The Indian judiciary

The Indian judiciary is wholly competent to deal with any dispute in any field of law, and has, in the 35 years of the history of our Republic, ably dealt with far more complex issues than those arising from the gas plant disaster at Bhopal.

The Supreme Court of India, in the range of its power and the sweep of its jurisdiction, is without a rival in human history. Its writ runs over more than one-seventh of the human race. It has jurisdiction in every domain of the law – constitutional and ordinary, civil and criminal, social and industrial.

It has not only the power to strike down executive action as being illegal but also the power to declare any law made by Parliament or by any State Legislature to be void – as being in violation of fundamental rights or otherwise *ultra vires* the Constitution. There is no injustice which the Supreme Court is powerless to redress. Articles 32 and 136 (1) of the Constitution are reproduced in Appendix 'A'.

The charge that the Indian judiciary is not 'innovative' is baseless. To say that our Supreme Court is super-innovative would be closer to truth. The Constituent Assembly which framed our constitution deliberately rejected the due process clause and provided in Article 21 of our Constitution that 'no person shall be deprived of his life or personal liberty except according to procedure established by law'. But the Supreme Court, by enviable innovative techniques, has evolved the principle that 'procedure established by law' is no different from procedural 'due process of law'. Further, by construing the words ' personal liberty' in the widest sense, the Supreme Court has made the Indian Constitution approximate in this respect to the U.S. Constitution. The categories of personal liberty are never closed; and 'due process' – created entirely by the judicial process – reigns supreme.

Our Supreme Court has dealt with cases where the legal issues presented a far greater challenge to judicial capacity to evolve the law than is presented by the Bhopal case. A few examples would suffice.

In *R. C. Cooper v. Union of India,* AIR 1970 SC 564, the Supreme Court held that the nationalization of the 14 biggest banks in India could be successfully challenged by a single shareholder of a single bank, when the Board of Directors of none of the 14 banks were courageous enough to question governmental action.

In *Madhavrao Scindia v. Union of India,* AIR 1971 SC 530, the Supreme Court struck down the executive ruse of abolishing the privy purses and privileges of the Maharajas and Princess of India by resorting to governmental derecognition of the Maharajas and Princes.

In *Kesavananda Bharati v. Union of India,* AIR 1973 SC 1461 the Supreme Court handed down a decision which is India's finest contribution to world jurisprudence. The Supreme Court held that the power to 'amend' the Constitution did not involve the power to make the Constitution lose its identity or to change its basic structure; that the Constitution was not a jellyfish but had basic features which could not be abrogated; and that Parliament, invested with the power to amend any part of the Constitution, could not act as the Official Liquidator of the Constitution. In 1975 when Emergency brooded over the country, and when the voice of opposition was totally silenced and Parliament enacted a vicious law to the effect that no citizen could claim freedom under the Constitution or on any principle of common law, natural law or rules of natural justice, a specially constituted Full Bench of the Supreme Court stoutly refused to review its two-year old decision in Kesavananda Bharti's case.

Part IV of our Constitution contains Directive Principles of State Policy which are 'fundamental in the governance of the country and it shall be the duty of the State to apply these principles in making laws.' (Article 37 of the Constitution). In *Minerva Mills v. Union of India* (AIR 1980 SC 1789), the Supreme Court, while giving due weight to the Directive Principles of State Policy, refused to hold that the Fundamental Rights could be sacrificed at the alter of Directive Principles.

In *Motilal Padampat Sugar Mills v. Uttar Pradesh* (AIR 1979 SC 621), the Supreme Court took the doctrine of Promissory Estoppel (which estops the Government from pleading executive necessity and going back on its earlier promise) an important step further, and held that it was not merely available as a defence but could supply a cause of action for instituting legal proceedings.

There is no doubt that the Indian judicial system can fairly and satisfactorily handle the Bhopal litigation. The only thing special about these cases is the number of claimants; but that can hardly be treated as a factor which puts the cases beyond the competence of Indian judges. After all, mass tort is merely a species of mass litigation, and Indian courts have admirably handled even those cases of mass litigation which have affected the lives and destinies of millions.

The gas plant disaster at Bhopal was an unmitigated tragedy. The plant itself was the product of highly complex technology, but complexity of the technology cannot be equated with complexity of legal issues. The principles of liability and damages involved in the Bhopal cases are all well established in India. The complexity is not in the nature of determination of legal issues but in the application of the law to the events which took place in Bhopal. Well settled law is to be applied to an unusual occurrence.

The Indian Bar

To say that the Bar in India is ill-equipped to deal with the Bhopal cases is a slanderous reflection on the legal profession in India, unredeemable by the plea of truth.

There are 250,000 lawyers in India. They constitute an All India Bar – in other words, any of them is entitled to appear in the Bhopal case.

A galaxy of talent is available to the claimant in India. India is a poor country, but it is rich in talent and culture. Several lawyers have expressed their willingness to assist the claimants in India without charging a fee. I am proud to say that the tradition of public service still animates the Indian Bar, – the first five constitutional cases mentioned on pp. 6 and 7 above, each of which lasted over some months, were argued in the Supreme Court for the citizen by the Bar without charging any fees, even when the clients were so wealthy as the 14 major banks and the Maharajas. There are nobler spurs to professional excellence than contingency fees.

One of the 'short comings' alleged against the Indian Bar is that there are no tort 'specialists' among Indian lawyers. It is true that the Indian Bar does not display that degree of specialization which often spells commercialization, – the degree of specialization which made a famous American remark (of physicians) that a specialist in diseases of the left leg will not treat diseases of the right. But are we sure that a generalist is less useful to society than a specialist in ambulance-chasing? Again, can a legal firm be said to be ill-equipped to deal with mass litigation because the number of partners in any partnership is limited by Indian law to twenty?

Further, since the Government of India has taken over the conduct of the Bhopal cases on behalf of the claimants, the highest law officers in the State – the Attorney General and the Solicitor General of India, and the Advocate General of the Madhya Pradesh State – would be available to the claimants.

The substantive law of torts in India

The law of torts is well established in India and has been enforced for more than a century. India is an excellent example of how a country can have a fairly developed and stable tort law without having an avalanche of tort litigation. Concepts of negligence, contributory negligence, absolute liability, different types of damages which can be awarded, etc., are all well recognized. Some tort law has been codified in the form of special statutes, as pointed out on pp. 16 – 18 of Mr. Dadachanji's affidavit.

The law of torts in India is the same as that which prevails in the United Kingdom, subject to modifications by our statutes which are not relevant here. That law of torts was in force in India prior to the promulgation of the Constitution in 1950; and Article 372(1) of the Constitution provides that subject to its other provisions, 'all the law in force in the territory of India immediately before the commencement of this Constitution shall continue in force therein until altered or repealed or amended by a competent legislature or other competent authority.' Therefore, to say that the Indian law of torts is inadequate or inadequately evolved, is tantamount to saying that the U.K. law of torts is inadequate or inadequately evolved.

It is untrue to allege that India is industrially backward or that an adequate legal system which is normally attendant upon industrial development does not exist. According to some economists, India is the tenth most industrialized country in the world, and has the third largest number of engineers and scientists of any country. Apart from having its own satellites in space, it has atomic power stations. Only this week, Mr. Rajiv Gandhi, the Prime Minister of India, was at a function to dedicate one of our atomic power plants and research centres to the nation.

KALPAKKAM. (Tamil Nadu), December 16.

The Prime Minister, Mr. Rajiv Gandhi, here today urged Indian nuclear scientists to 'take a leap ahead, so that we catch up with the most advanced technology in the world'.

'We must look to the third millennium,' Mr. Gandhi observed as he dedicated to the nation the Madras Atomic Power Station (MAPS). He also renamed the Reactor Research Centre as the 'Indira Gandhi Centre for Atomic Research'.

The large and distinguished international gathering at the dedication included the Chairman of Atomic Energy Commission and top nuclear scientists from many countries including Pakistan.

The Times of India, December 17, 1985

India has codified laws regarding anti-pollution, environment control, industrial safety, hazardous waste, etc.

The Indian system is undoubtedly capable of evolving the law to cope with advances in technology in the unfolding future. If the Bhopal litigation represents an opportunity for the further development of tort law in India, that chance should not be denied to India merely because some might say that the American legal system is ahead in development.

Procedure and procedural delays

The charge of inordinate delays in the administration of justice in India would be perfectly valid in a treatise dealing with the Indian legal system. But it is wholly inapt and untenable as regards the Bhopal case.

The special law passed by the Parliament of India, The Bhopal Gas Leak Disaster (Processing of Claims) Act, 1985, ('the Bhopal Act') and the scheme framed thereunder, enact specific and well-conceived measures to deal with the cases 'speedily, effectively, equitably and to the best advantage of the claimants.' The Bhopal Act by itself is wholly sufficient to insulate Bhopal claimants from the law's proverbial delays. There is no 'inadequacy' or 'deficiency' in the Indian legal system which cannot be set right by the Government of India within a matter of days. The Bhopal Act is a good example of how innovative the Government itself can be when it comes to dealing with an unparalled situation. Under our well settled law, the Government itself can set up, and has on several occasions set up, a special tribunal; and cases can be assigned to a special judge to ensure their speedy handling.

The year that has rolled by since the tragedy occurred leaves no doubt that the unprecedented Bhopal case will receive unprecedented treatment in India. The Government has already taken the unusual step of substituting itself in place of all claimants and of organizing legal redress in a manner which would be difficult to improve upon. The claimants have no less a champion than the sovereign Union Government. It would be ludicrous to suggest that when these very cases have been chosen by the Government for exceptional protection under its wing, the Government would be unable or unwilling to ensure their hearing without delay.

There have been countless cases in India where a single judge has been directed by a higher court to deal with a particular matter on a day to day basis, or special tribunals have been constituted, or the Supreme Court itself has issued orders for the speedy and expeditious disposal of important cases. The case of *M.C. Mehta v. Union of India* (Writ Petition No. 12739 of 1985) referred to on page 7 of Mr. Dadachanji's Affidavit, shows how in a similar case of oleum gas leak from a chemical plant in Delhi, the Court swung into action within two days of the disaster in the current month. Is there any reason to assume that the courts would not act expeditiously for thousands of victims of the Bhopal tragedy, when they did so for far fewer sufferers of the gas leak in Delhi?

The reason for the choice of the attractive American forum

Equality before the law is guaranteed by the Constitution of India to all persons – citizens and non-citizens alike. Article 14 of the Constitution provide that 'The State shall not deny to any person equality before the law or the equal protection of the laws within the territory of India.' Hence, if the Bhopal cases are tried in India, the quantum of damages to be awarded to the claimants would be under the same law which is applicable to all other cases of similar tort, irrespective of the nationality or residence of the corporation sued. Today, the Government itself is the biggest litigant in India, and deaths and injuries are caused in innumerable cases where the State acts through its multitudinous agencies. If the Bhopal cases are tried in India, the same principles of law and measure of damages applied therein would also have to be applied in countless cases in the future. It is not difficult to see in Article 14 the genesis of the condemnation of the Indian forum as 'inadequate' and the choice of the American forum as 'adequate'.

The ends of justice often require the truth to be faced squarely and stated bluntly. Indian courts are inadequate only in the sense that they are an inadequate instrument for procuring the fabulous damages which American juries are prone to award. Since the Affidavit is confined to the Indian legal system, I shall make no submission on the question whether 'forum shopping' should be permitted as a means of virtually getting American aid thinly disguised as 'damages'. It is a fortuitous circumstance – but not without significance – that $9.5 billion which I believe represents the total aid given by the USA to the Indian Republic over the last 35 years is exceeded by the aggregate claims made on behalf of the Bhopal victims.

Sd/- Nani Ardeshir Palkhivala
DEPONENT

VERIFICATION

I, the Deponent above named, do hereby verify that the contents of the foregoing affidavit are based on my experience as a practicing lawyer and on legal research done by me and under my direction and believed to be true.

Verified at Bombay on this 18th day of December, 1985.

Sd/- Nani Ardeshir Palkhivala

DEPONENT

/ true copy /

APPENDIX 'A'

Articles 32 and 136(1) of the

Constitution of India

PART III

FUNDAMENTAL RIGHTS

32. Remedies for enforcement of rights conferred by this Part.

(1) The right to move the Supreme Court by appropriate proceedings for the enforcement of the rights conferred by this Part is guaranteed.

(2) The Supreme Court shall have power to issue directions or orders or writs, including writs in the nature of habeas corpus, mandamus, prohibition, quo warranto and certiorari, whichever may be appropriate, for the enforcement of any of the rights conferred by this Part.

(3) Without prejudice to the powers conferred on the Supreme Court by Cl. (1) and (2), Parliament may by law empower any other court to exercise within the local limits of its jurisdiction all or any of the powers exercisable by the Supreme Court under Cl. (2).

(4) The right guaranteed by this article shall not be suspended except as otherwise provided for by this Constitution.

136. Special leave to appeal by the Supreme Court

(1) Notwithstanding anything in this Chapter, the Supreme Court may, in its discretion, grant special leave to appeal from any judgment, decree, determination, sentence or order in any cause or matter passed or made by any court or tribunal in the territory of India.

❄

Appendix V

Text of Articles 32 and 136 of the Constitution of India

Part III

Fundamental Rights

Right to Constitutional Remedies

Article 32: Remedies for enforcement of rights conferred by this Part

(1) The right to move the Supreme Court by appropriate proceedings for the enforcement of the rights conferred by this Part is guaranteed.

(2) The Supreme Court shall have power to issue directions or orders or writs, including writs in the nature of *habeas corpus, mandamus, prohibition, quo warranto* and *certiorari*, whichever may be appropriate, for the enforcement of any of the rights conferred by this Part.

(3) Without prejudice to the powers conferred on the Supreme Court by clause (1) and (2), Parliament may by law empower any other court to exercise within the local limits of its jurisdiction all or any of the powers exercisable by the Supreme Court under clause (2).

(4) The right guaranteed by this article shall not be suspended except as otherwise provided for by this Constitution.

Part IV

The Union Judiciary

Article 136: Special leave to appeal by the Supreme Court

(1) Notwithstanding anything in this Chapter, the Supreme Court may, in its discretion, grant special leave to appeal from any judgment, decree, determination, sentence or order in any cause or matter passed or made by any court or tribunal in the territory of India.

(2) Nothing in clause (1) shall apply to any judgment, determination, sentence or order passed or made by any court or tribunal constituted by or under any law relating to the Armed Forces.

Appendix VI

Selected Opinions

This appendix is a compendium of 11 opinions given by N.A. Palkhivala. Apart from his court work, he had a large volume of opinion work. Several business entities sought his opinions on taxation, corporate laws and other allied subjects. Lawyers specializing in tax or company law often have an extensive opinion practice. Several companies are faced with complicated statutes which are difficult to understand. These opinions help a company in choosing the right course of action. In many cases, opinions are also taken to ensure that a company or its executives are not faced with penal consequences.

We have chosen just 11 out of the numerous opinions that he gave in his career. Palkhivala's opinions were always brief and not burdened with the citation of too many cases. We often find that opinions run to several pages with copious extracts from reported judgments. Palkhivala rarely extracted passages from judgments. His answers were always to the point and written in simple, concise and lucid English. Except in a few opinions, the names of the clients have been changed to maintain confidentiality.

(1)

This opinion concerns the Monopolies Restrictive Trade Practices Act, 1969 (MRTP Act) which was enacted at the zenith of Indian socialism. Between 1967- 73, the ruling party nationalised coal mines, oil refineries and 14 major banks. The growth of any large undertaking was frustrated by numerous legislative speed-breakers and road blocks. Amongst the worst was the MRTP Act. If a company whose total assets by itself or with any interconnected undertaking was more than Rs. 20 crores, it had to be registered under Section 26 of that Act and subjected to numerous restrictions. In this opinion, Palkhivala advised the former Tata Oil Mills Co. and three other undertakings that they did not have to get registered under this Act. An indication of the enormous erosion in the value of rupee is the reference in the opening para of the opinion that the total value of the assets of TOMCO, Lakme and the third company was less than Rs. 20 crores! Today, it would be impossible for even mid-size companies to get an office accommodation at this price in Bombay.

OPINION

The Tata Oil Mills Company Limited ... Querist

The Tata Oil Mills Co. Ltd., ('TOMCO') holds more than 50% of the share capital in each of the following companies:-

Lakme Ltd.

International Fisheries Ltd.

The above two companies being subsidiaries of TOMCO are inter-connected with TOMCO under Section 2(g) of the Monopolies and Restrictive Trade Practices Act, 1969 ('the Monopolies Act'). The total value of the assets of TOMCO and of the aforesaid two subsidiaries taken together is less than Rs. 20 crores.

The question is, whether TOMCO should get registered under Section 26 of the Monopolies Act. Having regard to the facts stated in the Note dated the 6th August, 1970, I do not think TOMCO is required to be registered under Section 26 of the Monopolies Act. Section 26 of the Monopolies Act does not apply to TOMCO or to any of the aforesaid two companies which are inter-connected with TOMCO.

In deciding whether TOMCO or any of the above two companies is 'dominant', two principles are material for the purpose of the present case. First, the statistics published by the Central Government alone can be taken into account in determining whether or not a company is 'dominant' in relation to the total production of goods of any description. If figures are not published by the Central Government as regards the total production of a particular category of goods, the question of an undertaking being 'dominant' cannot be decided. (See Explanation IV to Section 2(d) of the Monopolies Act). Secondly, the figures of the three calendar years preceding the calendar year which itself precedes the year in which the question of dominance arises, i.e. 1966, 1967 and 1968 in the present context, must be available before the question of dominance can be determined (see Explanation VI to Section 2(d) of the Monopolies Act). In the present case, the figures published by the Central Government do not show that TOMCO is 'dominant' within Section 2(d) of the Monopolies Act. As far as Protein Isolate is concerned, TOMCO has not yet commenced commercial production of it and will only do so some time during the course of the current calendar year. The licence for commercial production of Protein Isolate was obtained by TOMCO only in April 1970.

One of the questions is as to how the value of assets is to be determined under Section 2(w) of the Monopolies Act. There are various interpretations possible. In this case, it is not necessary to decide which is the correct interpretation. One view is that the assets referred to in the definition are only those assets which can depreciate or diminish in value, i.e. fixed assets. However, the better view seems to be that the expression 'value of assets' should be construed as comprising all assets, whether fixed or current, after making provision for depreciation, renewal or diminution in value and after deducting at least current liabilities from the current assets; and the resultant net figure may be treated as the value of assets. Even ignoring the loans from banks and debentures, and taking into account only the current liabilities and provisions, the value of the assets of TOMCO and the two subsidiaries comes to an aggregate figure of much less than Rs. 20 crores.

Industrial Perfumes Ltd. is under the same management, within Section 2(g)(iii)(c) of the Monopolies Act, as Lakme Ltd., and International Fisheries Ltd., and therefore, the three companies may be treated as inter-connected undertakings, i.e. as inter-connected with one another. But a separate and distinct question is whether this fact is enough to make Industrial Perfumes Ltd. inter-connected with TOMCO under Section 2(g)(vii) of the Monopolies Act. In my opinion, the word 'through' in that section is crucial. It suggests that the statutory test of inter-connection must be satisfied through the intermediate company which is alleged to result in inter-connection. 'Through' connotes a lineal connection and not a collateral relationship. In the present case, Industrial Perfumes Ltd., and the two subsidiaries of TOMCO are inter-connected, but it cannot be said that Industrial Perfumes Ltd. is inter-connected with TOMCO through either of the subsidiaries. In any view of the matter, the value of the assets of TOMCO, the subsidiaries and Industrial Perfumes Ltd. all taken together, is less than Rs.20 crores if the current liabilities are deducted as they should be.

The last question is whether Industrial Perfumes Ltd. would have to be registered under Section 26 of the Monopolies Act. At least in one category of goods, namely, Citronellol, Industrial Perfumes Ltd. has more than one-third of the Indian market today. However, the figures published by the Government for the calendar years 1966, 1967 and 1968 would have to be looked at in order to see whether Industrial Perfumes Ltd. is dominant within Section 2(d) [Explanation IV and Explanation VI to Section 2(d)]. In any event, this question is not material at present, because even assuming Industrial Perfumes Ltd. is a dominant undertaking, the value of its assets (after deducting the current liabilities and provisions) is less than Rs. 1 crore, and consequently it would not fall within Section 20(b) of the Monopolies Act.

In the above circumstances, I advise TOMCO and the three companies not to apply for registration under Section 26 of the Monopolies Act.

Sd/- N. A. Palkhivala
11th September, 1970

Chamber No. 3,
High Court Annexe,
Bombay – 1

(2)

An opinion concerning taxability of salary. Palkhivala does not set out the facts but deals with seven questions. Interestingly in question No. 5, Palkhivala advises discontinuance of the practice of recovering small amounts from senior executives because this would result in a higher tax burden on them.[1]

OPINION

A & Company ... Querist

Question 1: Section 16(1) of the Income-tax Act, 1961 runs as follows:

'16. The income chargeable under the head 'Salaries' shall be computed after making the following deductions, namely:

(i) In respect of expenditure incidental to the employment of the assessee, a sum calculated on the basis provided hereunder, namely:-

(a)	Where the salary derived from such employment does not exceed Rs. 10,000	20 percent of such salary;
(b)	Where the salary derived from such employment exceeds Rs. 10,000	Rs. 2,000 plus 10 percent of the amount by which such salary exceeds Rs. 10,000 or Rs. 3,500, Whichever is less;

Provided that

(i) where the assessee is in receipt of a conveyance allowance from his employer; or

(ii) where any motor car, motor cycle, scooter or other moped is provided to the assessee by his employer for use by the assessee, otherwise than wholly and exclusively in the performance of his duties; or

(iii) where one or more motor cars are owned or hired by the employer of the assessee and the assessee is allowed the use of such motor car or all or any of such motor cars otherwise than wholly and exclusively in the performance of his duties,

the deduction under this clause shall not exceed one thousand rupees.'

The deduction under the aforesaid clause is expressed as a percentage of the salary. Therefore, if the employee serves for less than twelve months, the deduction will be a percentage of the salary received for the broken period of the year for which he serves. However, the maximum amount of deduction, viz. Rs. 3,500/- is not stated to be for the whole year. Therefore, in a case where Rs. 2,000/- plus 10

1. This opinion, surprisingly, does not contain the name of the querist or the facts. The questions have simply been set out and answered.

percent of the total salary is excess of Rs. 10,000/- is more than Rs. 3,500/-, an employee would be entitled to the maximum deduction of Rs. 3,500/- even if he serves for only a part of the year. In short, the maximum ceiling of Rs. 3,500/- is not related to the period of employment and is not to be reduced by the fraction-of-twelve-months for which the employee serves.

Question 2: The reasoning which applies to answer to Question 1 would also apply here. Therefore, if the employee is in receipt of a conveyance allowance for even a part of the accounting year, say, only one month of the accounting year, the maximum ceiling of deduction would be Rs. 1,000/- under the proviso to Section 16(i).

Question 3: Some employees of the querist who own a car are reimbursed by the Querist at a fixed rate per kilometer for the mileage done on the Company's business. At present the querist reimburses the employees at the rate of 61 paise per kilometer. (The rate could be higher when the cost of running a car increases). Such reimbursement cannot be treated as conveyance allowance. Therefore, in such cases clause (i) of the proviso would not apply, and the employees would be entitled to deduction in terms of the substantive part of Section 16(i).

Question 4: In the case of some employees, the Querist provides a motor car for the employee for business and personal use; but for the personal use of the car, the querist recovers from the employee the full perquisite value in terms of Rule 3 of the Income Tax Rules, 1962. In such cases, since the Querist recovers the full value of the perquisite (i.e. use of the car for the employee's personal use), it cannot be said that the Querist provides a car for the employee's personal use. Therefore, in such cases, neither clause (ii) nor clause (iii) of the proviso would apply; and the employee would be entitled to the maximum deduction in terms of the substantive part of Section 16(1).

Question 5: In case of a few senior executives, cars owned by the Querist are permitted to be used by the executive both for the purpose of Company's business as well for the executives' personal use; but the Querist recovers Rs. 60/- per month on account of the personal use and the employee shows in his Return of Income the prescribed perquisite value for personal use of the car, less Rs. 60/-. In such case, clause (ii) or clause (iii) of the proviso would still apply and the deduction under Section 16(i) would stand reduced to Rs. 1,000/-. Therefore, I strongly advise the Querist to discontinue immediately this practice which results in an unnecessarily larger fiscal burden on the executives.

Question 6: The Querist provides free transport to certain categories of employees. The free transport takes the form of a motor car, station-wagon or mini-bus. These vehicles are used for taking the employees from their homes to the office and taking them back from the office to their homes. The important fact is that the employees who are given this facility are not at all entitled to use the motor car, station-wagon or mini-bus for their personal use; and, secondly, no employee is individually given this transport facility. The employees are always transported in a group.

In my opinion, such group transport facility merely for transport to and from the office would not be covered by clause (ii) or (iii) of the proviso to Section 16(i); and the employees would be entitled to the full deduction permissible under the substantive part of Section 16(i). In the context of present day conditions and the wholly inadequate public transport system, I am of the view that group transport cannot personally be regarded as a perquisite. It would not be necessary for the Querist to make any recovery from the employees in respect of such group transport facility.

Question 7: The Querist provides motor cars to senior executives to be used for the company business as also for the private or personal purposes of the executives. In the past, when a car provided by the Querist was sent for servicing/repairs, the Company provided the executive with a stand-by car. The Querist recovers from the executive the full perquisite value of the car in terms of Rule 3(c)(ii) of the Income Tax Rules, 1962. In the interest of economy it is proposed that the practice of having stand-by or relief cars will be discontinued and, during the period that the car is under servicing/repairs, the executive will be reimbursed the actual expense incurred by him on transport, whether on the Company's business or for personal use. Such reimbursement will be subject to a reasonable limit per day as fixed by the Querist.

Although the Querist would continue to recover from the employees the full perquisite value of the car in terms of Rule 3(c)(ii) then for the period that the car is under servicing/repairs, the proposal to reimburse the employee an amount on account of transport for personal use during the period that the car is under servicing/repairs would necessarily raise two questions – (a) whether the employee should be assessed on the basis that he has a received a perquisite in respect of the reimbursement for personal use, which would presumably exceed the standard perquisite value in terms of Rule 3(c)(ii) and (b) whether the employee is in receipt of a conveyance allowance within clause (i) of the proviso to Section 16(1).

In the circumstances, I am clearly of the opinion that the best and safest line of action for the Querist is to reimburse the executive only the expense incurred by him on transport on Company's business during the period that the car is under servicing/repairs; and the Querist should not reimburse anything at all on account of transport for personal use by the executive.

The amount of the aforesaid reimbursement should be debited to the account, 'General Administration-Traveling'.

If there is no reimbursement on account of expenses on transport for the personal use of the employee, no question would arise of any perquisite or of any tax liability on that account in the hands of the employees; and, further they would get the full deduction under the substantive part of Section 16(i).

Sd/-
N.A. Palkhvala.
June 8, 1974.

Chamber No. 3,
High Court Annexe,
Bombay – 1.

(3)

A short and simple opinion on the calculation of depreciation under section 205 of the Companies Act, 1956. Palkhivala agrees with the earlier opinion of former Chief Justice J. C. Shah that a company need not take into account extra shift depreciation despite a circular to the contrary. He took the view that the circular proceeded on a clear misreading of section 205(2) and should be ignored.

OPINION

ABC Steel Products Ltd. ... Querist

The question is as regards the correct interpretation of Section 205 of the Companies Act, 1956 ('the Act'). I am in broad agreement with the reasoning and conclusion of Mr. J.C. Shah in his Opinion dated 11th May, 1982. Section 205 permits depreciation to be debited to the profit and loss account either according to the written down method or the straight line method. If a company adopts the straight line method, there is no provision in the Act which would require the company to take into account extra shift depreciation or multiple shift depreciation. It is a characteristic feature of the straight line method that a uniform amount year after year over the entire duration of the estimated life of the plant should be provided by way of depreciation. The Circular No.8/19(205)/64-PR dated 15th September, 1964 seems to suggest that the Company, even while adopting the straight line method, should take into account extra and multiple shift allowances. The Circular proceeds upon a clear misreading of Section 205(2) and should be ignored. Such a Circular which is contrary to the statute has no legal effect.

A company may work extra shift in one year and not in the next. It is wholly illogical to suggest that a variable allowance like extra shift allowance should be taken into account when following the straight line method of depreciation which, as stated above, aims at providing the same amount of depreciation year after year.

Sd/-
N.A. Palkhivala,
December 1, 1982

Bombay.

(4)

This opinion, given in 1985, concerns the scope of sections 309, 310 and 314 of the Companies Act, 1956 and the question that was considered was whether the remuneration paid to a solicitor, who was also a director, would require Central Government approval.

OPINION

ABC Ltd. ... Querist

The Querist is a public limited company. One Mr. S.V. Divecha, a solicitor and advocate, was in the employment of the Querist from 1st April 1960 till he retired on 9th April 1985. Since he was also a whole-time director of the Querist, he also ceased to hold the office of director. Subsequently, Mr. Divecha was appointed as additional director on 17th April 1985.

Mr. Divecha has resumed his professional practice. It is contemplated that the Querist may from time to time, as and when the occasion arises, obtain Mr. Divecha's advice on specific matters, and for such professional services he will submit his bill of costs to the Querist. The Querist has not engaged the services of Mr. Divecha by giving him any retainer nor is there any obligation, express or implied, on the Querist's part to consult him. The Querist's solicitors are the instructing attorneys, M/s Crawford Bayley & Co., but the Querist may consult Mr. Divecha in view of his intimate knowledge and experience in regard to the wide range of questions facing the pharmaceutical industry in general and the Querist in particular.

The question is whether the provisions of Sections 309, 310 and 314 of the Companies Act, 1956 ('the Act') would be attracted as regards the remuneration paid by the Querist to Mr. Divecha for his professional services.

The proviso to Section 309(1) runs as follows:

'Provided that any remuneration for services rendered by any such director in any other capacity shall not be so included if—

(a) the services rendered are of a professional nature, and

(b) in the opinion of the Central Government, the director possesses the requisite qualifications for the practice of the profession.'

Section 309(4) provides for a ceiling on the remuneration payable monthly, quarterly or annually or by way of commission to directors who are neither in the whole-time employment of the company nor are managing directors.

Section 310 provides in effect that a director's remuneration shall not be increased unless such increase is approved by the Central Government.

Section 314(1) enacts that no director of a company 'shall hold any office or place of profit' except in accordance with the provisions of that section.

The relevant sections of the Act – Sections 198, 309 and 310 – have been interpreted by the Kerala High Court in *R. Gac Electrodes Ltd. v. Union of India*, [1982] 52 Comp. Cas 288 at 291. The material portion of the judgement reads as under:[2]

> 'Section 198 of the Act fixes a ceiling for managerial remuneration. Section 309 provides for the determination of the remuneration of directors. Section 309(1), as amended, ropes in the remuneration paid to a director for services rendered by him in any other capacity also. The combined effect of ss. 198 and 309 is that by the payment of remuneration for services rendered by a director in any capacity other than that of a director, his total remuneration cannot go above the ceiling fixed by s. 198. In other words, no remuneration can be paid to a director for services rendered by him in any other capacity, if he is getting the maximum managerial remuneration he is entitled to under s. 198. But, it is to be noted that there is an exception to the above rule. The exception is that if the services rendered are of a professional nature, the remuneration payable to a director for that, will not come within the restriction imposed by s. 309(1). Provision for this is there in the proviso to s. 309(1), which was also inserted by the 1965 amendment. But the exception is subject to a condition. The condition is that the Central Government should certify that the director concerned possesses the requisite qualifications to practice that profession. So, if a director renders a professional service not in his capacity as director and the Central Government certifies that he is having the requisite qualifications to practice that profession, the remuneration paid to him for that service will not form part of the managerial remuneration to which he is entitled, and the payment of which is to be limited to the ceiling fixed by s.198. The net result is that the remuneration for professional service rendered by a director will not be a remuneration to be determined under s. 309 in accordance with s. 198. Then the further question is whether s. 310 which provides for increase of remuneration has anything to do with the payment of remuneration for professional services. The increase can only be an increase in remuneration. As per s. 309, the remuneration payable to a director takes in only managerial remuneration and remuneration for services of a non-professional nature rendered by him

2. This is a rare case where Palkhivala has reproduced a lengthy passage from a Kerala High Court judgment in his opinion.

in any other capacity and remuneration the increase for which permission is required under s. 310 will take in only the above remuneration. As remuneration for services of a professional nature will not be a remuneration determined under s. 309(1) the payment of the same to a director will not increase the remuneration he is entitled to under s. 309(1). So, it goes without saying that for the payment of remuneration for services of a professional nature no previous sanction of the Central Government under s. 310 is necessary. So, no Form No.26 application also need be filed. What is required is a certificate from the Central Government as insisted by the proviso to s. 309(1).'

In *Ruby Mills Ltd. v. Union of India,* [1985] 57 Comp Cas 193 at 197 the Bombay High Court took the same view as the Kerala High Court and observed, *inter alia,* that Section 310 would have no application to remuneration for professional services. The government would be in no position to determine the value of professional services rendered by a solicitor or advocate.

In my opinion, the judgments of the Kerala High Court and the Bombay High Court are correct except on one point. In both the cases, it was held that it is necessary to make an application under proviso (b) to Section 309(1) to the Central Government for its opinion whether the director possess the requisite qualifications for the practice of a profession. In my view, on a fair reading of the proviso to Section 309(1), the Central Government is not required to exercise any judgment in the matter as to whether a gentleman duly qualified as a solicitor and with decades of experience as a solicitor possesses 'the requisite qualifications for the practice of the profession'. The Central Government's opinion is called for only when, for argument's sake, fees are paid to a person about whose professional qualifications there is a doubt. In such cases of doubt, the Central Government's opinion would prevail provided a reasonable man would come to the conclusion entertained by the Government. But in a case where there is no manner of doubt as to the professional qualifications of a person, the question of seeking the Central Government's opinion under the proviso to Section 309(1) cannot arise. It is not conceivable that recognized degrees and long years of practice as members of professional bodies, duly recognized by law, would possibly be ignored by the Government which has to act reasonably. I am conscious that the Government takes a contrary view and requires the Government's approval to be obtained even for qualified and experienced solicitors. In my opinion, such a view is incorrect; but the Querist may act upon the Government's view if it wants to avoid a dispute.

In the very exhaustive and well-thought out Case for Opinion, a number of cases have been cited and points of view presented, which converge upon the same conclusions as are indicated above. I am broadly in agreement with the reasoning and conclusions reached in the Case for Opinion.

I now proceed to answer briefly the questions raised in the Case for Opinion.

Question (1): If the Querist chooses to avail itself of the professional services of Mr. Divecha, who is a qualified solicitor and advocate, is the Querist obliged to make an application to the Central Government under the proviso to sub-section (1) of section 309 of the Companies Act, 1956?

Answer: No. In my opinion, it is not necessary to make any application to the Central Government for its view on the question whether Mr. Divecha possesses the requisite qualifications for the practice of his profession. The answer to this question is self-evident. A law cannot be so read as to necessitate wholly useless paper work. By way of analogy, one may refer to Section 256 of the Income Tax

Act which provides that a question of law arising from the Tribunal's order has to be referred to the High Court; and yet, it is well-settled that where the answer to the question is self-evident:

CIT v. Chander Bhan Hariharan Lal, 60 ITR 188 (SC); *CIT v. Indian Mica Supply Co. Ltd.*, 77 ITR 20 (SC); *Mathuraprasad Motilal v. CIT*, 30 ITR 695; *Mangaldas Verma v. CIT*, 25 ITR 175; *Kirpaldas Motandas v. CIT*, 10 ITR 505; *CGT v. Kusumben Mahadevia*, 122 ITR 38 (SC); *Tirath Ram Ahuja Ltd. v. CIT*, 103 ITR 15; *CIT v. National Newsprint & Paper Mills Ltd.*, 114 ITR 398, 401; *CIT v. Hanumanbux Inderchand*, 125 ITR 248;

or when the question is of an academic nature:

CIT v. Himangshu Sekhar Chakravarty, 94 ITR 318, 319 (SC),

no reference need be made to the High Court–although there are no words in Section 256 to that effect. Likewise, Section 309(1) of the Act must be so construed as to enact that opinion of the Central Government is not required to be sought where the answer regarding 'the requisite qualifications for the practice of the profession' is self-evident.

Question (2): If remuneration is paid to a director for professional services is it remuneration for the limited purpose of including it in the computation of 11% of the managerial remuneration as stipulated in Section 198 of the Act or does it constitute remuneration under any other provision of Section 309 of the Act?

Answer: The remuneration paid to a director for professional services is not remuneration for the purpose of determining managerial remuneration under Section 198, nor is it remuneration which falls within the restrictions imposed by Section 309.

Question (3): If the Querist pays to Mr. Divecha fees for his professional services are the provisions contained in sub-section (4) of Section 309 attracted.

Answer: No. Any fees paid to Mr. Divecha for professional services would fall outside Section 309(4).

Question (4): In the event of the Querist paying fees to Mr. Divecha for professional services rendered by him would the provisions of Section 310 be attracted keeping in view of the fact that Mr. Divecha will be paid fees for attending meetings of the Board of Directors of the Querist.

Answer: No. Section 310 has no application to fees paid for professional services rendered by a professional consultant who happens to be a director. It is impossible to take the view that the Government can sit in judgment under Section 310 on the value of professional services rendered to a company.

Question (5): If the Querist consults Mr. Divecha in his professional capacity from time to time and pays his fees but without paying him any salary and/or retainer fee could it be said that Mr. Divecha is holding an office or place of profit as contemplated by Section 314 of the Act?

Answer: No. Merely because Mr. Divecha would render professional services to the querist from time to time without being paid a fixed salary or a retainer fee, it cannot be said that he holds any office or place of profit within Section 314 of the Act.

Bombay.

Sd/-
N.A.Palkhivala,
November 1, 1985

(5)

In this opinion, Palkhivala considered the vexed question of whether the provisions of Section 115J dealing with Minimum Alternate Tax (MAT) should be considered while making advance payment of tax under Section 207. His opinion that it should not was short-lived as subsequently all the provisions of the Income Tax Act were made applicable in the context of MAT as well.

OPINION

XYZ Ltd. ... Querist

The Querist is a public limited company. It has sought my opinion on two questions arising under the Income Tax Act, 1961 ('the Act').

The first question is whether the Querist should consider the provisions of Section 115J when making advance payment of tax under Section 207 of the Act.

In my opinion, the Querist is not bound to take Section 115J into account for the purpose of filing an estimate, and of payment of advance tax.

Section 207 of the Act which imposes the basic substantive liability to pay advance tax, runs as follows:

> '207. *Liability for payment of advance tax.*—Tax shall be repayable in advance during the financial year, in accordance with the provisions of Sections 209 to 219 (both inclusive), in respect of the total income of the assessee which would be chargeable to tax for the assessment year immediately following that financial year, such income being hereafter in this Chapter referred to as 'current income'.

Section 2(24) of the Act defines 'income' as including twelve specified categories of receipts. In Section 2(24) there is no reference whatever to Section 115J or to any part of the book profits which is taxable as income under that Section (Section 115J).

Section 2(45) of the Act runs as follows:—

> '2. *Definitions.*—In this Act, unless the context otherwise requires,—
>
> (45) "total income" means the total amount of income referred to in Section 5, computed in the manner laid down in this Act.'

I am clearly of the opinion that the provisions of Section 115J are to be ignored for the purpose of filing an estimate and for making payment of advance tax. My reasons for coming to this conclusion are the following:

(a) Advance tax is payable only on 'income' under Section 207 to 212 of the Act. 'Income' is defined in Section 2(24) of the Act, and no part of that definition covers any amount assessable under Section 115J. In fact, Section 115J is an intruder in the Act and its provisions are totally alien to the scheme of the Act. Any reference to an amount assessable under Section 115 unless the context expressly or by necessary implication compels such inclusion.

(b) The expressions 'total income' and 'current income' are used in various places in Sections 208 to 212. These expressions refer to 'income' as defined in Section 2(24) and 'total income' as defined in Section 2(45). Neither the expression 'total income' nor the expression 'current income' is used in the Act anywhere else as including the amount assessable under Section 115J. On the other hand, the definition of 'total income' necessarily postulates computation 'in the manner laid down in this Act', and 'current income' under Section 207 means the total income of a particular period. Thus, 'total income' and 'current income' are concepts which indicate the total of income computed under different heads specified in the Act. By contrast, Section 115J purports to tax an amount which has never been computed in the manner laid down in the Act at all.

(c) The operative part of Section 115J enacts that 'the total income ... chargeable to tax for the relevant previous year shall be deemed to be an amount equal to thirty percent of such book profit'. This provision embodies a pure legal fiction by which the total income for a particular amount. This legal fiction applies only for the purpose of Section 115J and cannot be extended to other provisions of the Act. It is well-settled that a legal fiction can operate only within the field of the definite purpose for which the fiction is created.[3]

This fiction in Section 115J has been created only for the purpose of that section and not for the purpose of advance tax.

The second question on which my opinion is sought is the following:

> 'The Querist at present closes its accounts on 31st December, if the Querist continues to have the calendar year as its financial year for the purposes of the Companies Act, will the Querist be liable to pay tax under Section 115J?'

My answer to the above question is in the negative. In the case of a company like the Querist of which the accounting year ends on 31st December, Section 115J of the Act would have no application at all.

Under sub-section (1) of Section 115J, the total income is 'deemed to be an amount equal to thirty percent of such book profit.' 'Book profit' means, under the Explanation to Section 115J(1), 'the net profit as shown in the profit and loss account for the relevant previous year prepared in accordance with the provisions of Parts II and III of the Sixth Schedule to the Companies Act, 1956' as increased by certain specified amounts and as reduced by other specified amounts. Sub-section (1) and the Explanation can apply only to those companies which have prepared their accounts for the previous year relevant to the assessment year. The statute does not contemplate preparation of accounts for the previous year relevant to the assessment year. The statute does not contemplate that preparation of accounts for the purpose of Section 115J is to tax a company on the basis of the accounts which it presents to its shareholders, the whimsical idea being that even if a company has no taxable profits, it must still pay tax on the basis of the profits which it has shown to its shareholders. That is why the Explanation refers to 'Book Profit', i.e. the profit which the company shows in its accounts. Any doubt on this

---

3. *CIT v. Amarchand Shroff,* 48 ITR (SC) 59; *CIT v. Ajax Products Ltd.*, 55 ITR (74), 750-1(SC); *ITO v. Ponnose,* 75 ITR 174, 178 (SC); *CIT v. Vaoial Lallubhai,* 86 IT 2, 8 (SC); *CIT v. Vina,* 58 ITR 100; *Motilal Harilal & Co. Ltd. v. CIT,* 45 ITR 557; *Arvind Bhogilal v. CIT,* 105 ITR 764, 780, 784-8; *Amritlal Somebhai v. CIT,* 116 ITR 833, 837; *Radhadevi Mohatta v. CIT,* 129 ITR 229, 242-3.

point is dispelled by the expression 'book profit' means the net profit *as shown* in the profit and loss account...'. The words 'as shown' postulate a pre-existing document which is available to the Assessing Officer at the time when he makes the assessment. The words which follow – 'prepared in accordance with the provision of ... the Companies Act, 1956' merely go to indicate that the book profit is that which emerges from the profit and loss account prepared in compliance with the Companies Act, as distinct from the taxable profit determined as per the Act. The concept of a profit and loss account prepared in accordance with the provisions of the Companies Act specially for a previous year as defined in the Act is, to my mind, wholly foreign to Section 115J. The correctness of this view is borne out by the following further considerations:-

(a) The rule of strict construction applies *a fortiori* to provisions which create an artificial or vicarious liability to tax or which are penal in character:[4]

Strict construction of Section 115J would altogether rule the view that Section 115J contemplates special preparation of the profit and loss account for a previous year other than the regular accounting year of the company.

(b) The whole scheme of sub-section (1) and the Explanation to Section 115J leaves no doubt that the Section applies to a profit and loss account which has been prepared by a company for its own purpose as per the Companies Act and which is pre-existing before the assessment is taken up.

(c) The various adjustments (increases and reductions) to be moved to the book profit as disclosed by the profit and loss account also indicate that the profit and loss account is one to which the directors had applied their minds at the time when they signed the accounts for the company's own accounting year.

(d) The whole scheme of Section 115J proceeds on the footing of a change in the figure of taxable profit by the book profit. There is no mandate for changing the accounting year of the book profit for the previous year of the taxable profit. In other words, it is in respect of the same previous year that the taxable profits are ignored and the section directs attention to the book profit. If for the relevant previous year, of which the profits fall to be assessed under the Act, there is no profit and loss account and no book profit, there is nothing on which Section 115J can operate.

In the circumstances of the case, my advice to the Querist is that it should let its accounting year end on 31st December as heretoforth. It should present its accounts to its shareholders for the period ended 31st December, 1988. In assessment proceedings for the year 1989-90, the Querist should maintain that

---

4. *CIT v. Manilal Dharji,* 44 ITR 876, 881 (SC); *CIT v. Kashevlal Patel,* 55 ITR 637, 640 (SC); *CIT v. Chuancas & Co.,* 55 ITR 17 28 (SC); *Philip Thomas v. CIT,* 49 ITR (SC) 97, 101; *CIT v. Prem Bhai Parekh,* 77 ITR 27, 30 (SC); *CIT v. Sarathy Mudaliar,* 83 ITR 170, 173 (SC); *Bhogilal Leherchand v. CIT,* 25 ITR 523; *Desai v. Ramamurthy,* 34 ITR 409; *Rahi Laxmi Pal Factory v. ITO,* 103 ITR 517, 524 (PP); *Bhagawati Trading Co. Ltd. v. CIT,* 109 ITR 353, 359-60; *CIT v. Hindustan Export & Import Corporation Pvt. Ltd.,* 139 ITR 691, 699; *CIT v. Bhupender Singh Atwal,* 140 ITR 928, 936.

Section 115J has no application to the case of the Querist since the Querist has no profit and loss account prepared in accordance with the provisions of the Companies Act for the previous year ended 31st March, 1989, and that it is not required by Section 115J to prepare any profit and loss account for such a previous year. If and when the Assessing Officer takes the view that the Querist should prepare a profit and loss account as per the Companies Act specially for the purpose of Section 115J for the period ending 31st March 1989, the Querist should file a writ petition in the High Court for appropriate relief.

Bombay
September 29, 1988.

N.A. Palkhivala

(6)

This opinion deals with the conversion of partnership into a private limited company and the tax implications arising thereunder. The answers are very brief and precise and the opinion does not refer to a single reported case.

OPINION

M/s PQR (a firm) ... Querist

The querist is a registered partnership firm having its main office in Bombay and two manufacturing units at Madras. The firm has four individual partners and a private limited company. Two minor sons have been admitted to the benefits of the partnership firm.

The proposal is to convert the Querist partnership into a private limited company. The business of the Querist will be taken over along with all its assets and liabilities at book value by the private limited company. The shareholders of the private limited company will be the same as the seven members of the Querist partnership–the five partners and the two minors admitted to the benefits of the partnership. The ratio of their shareholding in the private limited company will be the same as their profit-sharing ratio in the Querist firm.

I now proceed to answer briefly the questions raised in the Case for Opinion.

Question (1): Whether on such conversion capital gains tax (either short-term or long-term) is chargeable or not?

Answer: No. There will be no capital gains tax leviable. All the assets will be transferred at book value. There will be no transfer of goodwill as a separate asset. Wherever depreciation has been allowed in the past on any of the assets of the querist, the book value represents the written down value of those assets and they would be transferred at such book value to the limited company. In these circumstances, no capital gains tax can at all arise to the Querist firm.

Question (2): Whether the provisions of new sub-Section (4) to Section 45, which has been enacted from A.Y. 1988-89, are attracted or not?

Answer: No. Section 45(4) of the Income-tax Act, 1961 ('the Act') would have no application. The firm will be kept alive after the proposed transfer and the firm will do some small new business. Thus, there will be no distribution of any capital assets among the partners.

There should be a slump sale of the business as a going concern by the querist to the limited company. In other words, there should not be the sale of any separate asset but there should be a slump sale of the business as a going concern and as a single asset. The whole business should be transferred as one asset for shares of a face value equal to the net worth of the partnership.

Question (3): Whether the benefit of investment allowance granted to the partnership will be withdrawn on such conversion or whether the case will be covered under sub-Section (7) of Section 32A of the Act and benefit will not be withdrawn on such conversion?

Answer: No. The benefit of investment allowance granted to the Querist firm in the past will not be withdrawn. (See Section 32A(7) of the Act).

It would be best to form a limited company with initial token capital contributed by the partners and the minors as the sole shareholders in the same proportion in which they share the profits of the firm.

Question (4): Whether the provisions of Chapter XX-C of the Act would apply?

Answer: No. The provisions of Chapter XX-C of the Act would have no application to the present case. The entire business as a single asset would be transferred as a going concern and to such a case Chapter XX-C has no application.

Question (5): What is the position of goodwill when the firm has not valued goodwill in the past or at the time of such conversion?

Answer: Goodwill nowhere appears in the books of the Querist firm and it will nowhere appear in the balance sheet of the limited company.

Question (6): What is liability under gift-tax?

Answer: There would be no liability under the Gift-tax Act. In a case like this which is purely a case of business reorganization, no question of gift-tax can possibly arise.

Question (7): What should be the share capital of a private limited company, viz. partner capital in the firm?

Answer: The sole shareholders of the limited company should be the partners (and the minors admitted to the benefits of partnership) of the Querist firm and the share capital of the limited company should be divided among them in the same proportion in which they share the profits of the Querist firm. I take it that the capital account of each partner and each minor is roughly in the same proportion as the profit-sharing ratio. To avoid any needless dispute, I suggest that the capital account of each partner and each minor in the Querist firm should first be made to correspond approximately to their profit-sharing ratio and then the transfer of the whole undertaking may be effected to the limited company. But this need *not* be done if the limited company is to take over the partners' credit balances as liabilities due to the company's creditors.

Question (8): What are the implications of stamp duty?

Answer: The stamp duty would be payable according to the State law.

Question (9): If conversion/takeover is not possible, please suggest the other method for converting our firm into a private limited company with least damage.

Question (10): If conversion or takeover by succession is possible, what are the formalities to be completed for takeover?

Answer: The proposal contained in the case for opinion represents the best method of achieving certain objectives which the partners of the querist have in mind. The limited company would be the successor to the partnership. The stamped document should be sufficient for the purpose, except that immovable properties would have to be transferred according to the formalities regarding stamp duty etc. in force in the relevant State

Question (11): Partnership firm has many rented premises in its name in Bombay. Whether there will be any adverse effects on the tenancy rights of these premises by such conversion of the firm into a private limited company. If so, what should be the way out?

Answer: The premises leased to the Querist firm do not appear in the books of account at all and those rented premises should not be transferred.

In respect of the premises taken by the Querist firm as tenants, a notice has already been received from the landlord terminating the tenancy. Thus, the Querist firm is merely a statutory tenant. Therefore, it is not even possible in law for the Querist to transfer the rented premises.

For the reasons which I have discussed in conference, there should be no sub-letting of such rented premises by the Querist firm to the limited company. The premises should be allowed by the Querist firm to be used by the limited company on a purely gratuitous licence.

Question (12): What should be the modus operandi to execute this scheme of conversion keeping in view all the applicable provisions of various relevant Acts so as to minimize the damages, if any?

Answer: I have nothing to add.

Sd/-
N. A. Palkhivala
Bombay November 30,1989

(7)

Palkhivala had to consider whether a discount on 'commercial paper' would amount to 'interest' under section 2(28A) of the Income Tax Act, 1961 and, consequently, whether person responsible for paying subscribers investment in the commercial paper, in the form of discount would require to deduct tax at source under section 194A.

OPINION

ABC Capital Markets Ltd. ... Querist

The Querist is a wholly owned subsidiary of a nationalised bank and functions as a merchant bank. It provides various financial services to the corporate sector.

The Reserve Bank of India recently issued the 'Non-Banking Companies (Acceptance of Deposits through Commercial Paper) Directions, 1989' ('the said Directions'). The object of the said Directions is to empower companies other than banking companies to issue short term money market instruments such as Commercial Paper, subject to their fulfilling certain norms.

The Commercial Paper ('CP') can be issued by companies only in the form of Usance Promissory Notes and are negotiable by endorsement and delivery. The CP may be issued for a period of not less than three months and not more than six months and at such discount as may be determined by the company issuing the CP. On maturity of the CP, the holder of the CP presents the instrument for payment to the issuing company.

No interest is payable to the holder of the CP and the rate of discount is negotiated and settled between the issuer and the subscriber. The original subscriber can sell the CP to any party in the secondary market at discounted rates.

The CP is thus a short-term unsecured promissory note issued by a company to fund its business activities at cheaper rates than normal borrowings.

There is no fixed rate of discount. The discount at which the CP is to be issued will be determined freely by market forces. Obviously, the amount of discount would get reduced as the CP approaches the date of maturity. The CP may change hands several times before the date of maturity. The subscriber to the CP will get no interest on his investment but the financial benefit to him would be in the form of discount on the face value of the CP.

The Income Tax Act, contains the definition of interest:

'(28A) interest means interest payable in any manner in respect of any moneys borrowed or debt incurred (including a deposit, claim or other similar right or obligation) and includes any service fee or other charge in respect of the moneys borrowed or debt incurred or in respect of any credit facility which has not been utilized.'

Section 194A of the Act provides for deduction of tax at source at the time when the interest is paid to, or credited to the account of the payee.

I now proceed to answer briefly the questions raised in the Case for Opinion:

Question (a): Whether *prima facie* the discount to such face value can be termed as 'interest' within the meaning of Section 2(28A) of the Act?

Answer: No. The discount is not interest either under the general law or within the definition of 'interest' in Section 2(28A) of the Act.

Question (b): Whether the return on the subscriber's investment in the CP, in the form of discount, can be termed as 'interest other than interest on securities' within the meaning of Section 194A of the Act whereby a deduction at source is required to be made by the person responsible for paying such income by way of interest other than interest on securities?

Answer: No. As stated above, the discount is not interest at all and, therefore, the question of deducting any tax at source under Section 194A does not arise. The discount is really a financial benefit, not amounting to, or in the form of interest – to the person who lays out his capital on the purchase of the CP.

Question (c): If either Section 193 or 194A is applicable and, consequently, tax is to be deducted at source, at what stage will it have to be deducted at source.

Answer: Does not arise.

Question (d): Will the obligation to deduct tax at source lie with the intermediary holders of the CP also or would it be the sole responsibility of the issuer to do so by instructing the paying agent who would be one of the bankers to the issuer?

Answers: Does not arise. The absurdity of regarding the discount as a form of interest is shown by the impossibility of deducting tax at source as per Section 194A of the Act. There would normally be a number of intermediary holders of the CP as the CP changes hands in the money market. The machinery of Section 194A is not at all designed to provide for deduction of tax at source when the CP changes hands before the date of maturity.

Question (e): Whether there is any responsibility on the part of the paying agent to deduct tax at maturity. Further, the issuer will know the discount price at the time of issue and the question therefore arises as to whether the issuer has to recover tax at source on the difference between originally discounted price of CP and its face value?

Answer: Does not arise. There can be no question of deducting tax at source from the amount of the discount.

Sd/
N.A. Palkhivala,
September 24, 1990

Bombay

(8)

This opinion, on Section 370 of the Companies Act, 1956, dealt with the difference between a loan and a 'deposit'. Briefly, the question was whether a sum of Rs. 12 lakhs given as deposit to Associated Cement Companies Ltd., would amount to a loan? If it was a loan, then the monies could not be advanced without the prior permission of the Central Government. Palkhivala pointed out the distinction between the two words and the absurd consequences that would result if deposits were treated as a 'loan'.

Ex parte:

Cement Agencies Limited ... Querist

OPINION

The directors of the querist were served with a notice by the Registrar of Companies, dated 26th November 1973, asking them to show cause why legal action should not be taken against them for the alleged contravention by the Querist of the provisions of Section 370 of the Companies Act, 1956 ('the Act').

In this notice, it has been stated as follows:

'It is noticed from the audited accounts of the above mentioned company for the year ending 31st December 1971 that as against its paid up capital and Reserve of Rs. 10.47 lacs, the company advanced Rs. 12 lacs as deposits to M/s Associated Cement Companies Limited without the prior approval of the Central Government. It is, therefore, apparent that the above mentioned company has contravened the provisions of Section 370 of the Companies Act, 1956, since these amounts were advanced without obtaining prior approval of the Central Government'.

The above-mentioned paragraph seems to indicate that a deposit of moneys is the same as, and is to be equated with, a loan of moneys within Section 370 of the Act.

In my opinion, there is a definite distinction between a deposit of money and a loan of money. This has been made clear by the Courts both in India and in England and is emphasised by the Limitation Act, 1963. Articles 21 and 22 in the Schedule to that Act prescribe different periods for the limitation of actions for moneys lent and moneys deposited. The Limitation period in the case of a loan begins from the time when the loan is made, and the limitation period in the case of a deposit begins from the day the demand for the money is made.

If deposits of moneys with bodies corporate were to be treated as loans within Section 370 of the Act, then the consequences would be, logically speaking, that deposits with Scheduled Banks would also come within the scope of Section 370 of the Act. The Company Law Department has consistently held in all cases that deposits with Scheduled Banks would not come within the scope of Section 370 of the Act. To treat certain deposits of moneys, and not others, as being within Section 370 of the Act, would be to give an inconsistent construction to the section, unjustified by any canon of interpretation.

Even if, for argument's sake, it is held that a deposit of money and a loan of money are not mutually exclusive terms and that a deposit may involve a loan of money, the correct position is that Section 370 of the Act deals with loans not amounting to deposits. In other words, if the transaction is one which involves a loan but the loan is given in such circumstances that in law it is of the nature of a deposit, then Section 370 of the Act would have no application at all. Even though a loan and a deposit are not mutually exclusive terms, in the context of a statutory provision, the word 'loan' may be used in the sense of a loan not amounting to a deposit. (see the Privy Council's judgment in *Nawab Major Sir Mohammed Akbar Khan v. Attar Singh and others* (63 Indian Appeals, page 279) and *Ram Janki Devi & Anr. v. M/s Juggilal Kamalapat,* [1971] 3 SCR 573 at 577). In the present case, Section 370 must be construed as dealing with loans not amounting to deposits, because otherwise, as stated above, the absurd position would be that not only fixed deposits with banks but even cash deposits in the current account of a limited company with a bank would be subject to the ceiling laid down in Section 370.

I am, therefore, of the opinion that the deposit of Rs. 12,00,000/- by the Querist with M/s Associated Cement Companies Limited could not be said to be a loan to M/s Associated Cement Companies Limited within Section 370 of the Act. There has, therefore, been no violation or contravention of that section by the querist.

Sd/-
N.A. Palkhivala
3rd December 1973

Chamber No. 3,
High Court Annexe,
Bombay – 400001.

(9)

A short but interesting question was whether non-banking financial companies could pay a higher interest on deposits. This opinion, given in 1992, justified the higher rate of interest ignoring the new proviso inserted in Rule 8 of the Companies (Acceptance of Deposits) Rules, 1975.

OPINION

XYZ Ltd. .. Querist

The Querist is a public limited company which accepts deposits from its shareholders and from the public. Such acceptance of deposits is regulated by Section 58A of the Companies Act, 1956, and the Companies (Acceptance of Deposits) Rules, 1975, as amended from time to time. These rules apply to non-banking and non-financial companies.

The Querist has been accepting deposits from its shareholders and from the public at a rate of interest not exceeding the rate prescribed from time to time.

By a Notification dated 10th January, 1992, the Government increased the rate of interest from 14% to 15% per annum 'with effect from 10th January,

1992'. On that date, the Querist had a large number of deposits which had not matured and which will mature at some date in the future. The crucial question is whether the Querist is at liberty in law to give interest at the higher rate as from 10th January, 1992 on such pre-existing deposits.

By the said Notification dated 10th January, 1992, in Rule 8 of the Companies (Acceptance of Deposits) Rules, 1975, the following additional proviso was inserted before the Explanation:

'Provided further that where a company permits a depositor to renew his deposit, before the expiry of the period for which such deposit was accepted by the company, for availing of the higher rate of interest, the company shall pay interest to such depositor at higher rate if -

(i) such deposit is renewed in accordance with the other provisions of these rules and for a period longer than the unexpired period of the deposit, and

(ii) the rate of interest as stipulated at the time of the acceptance or renewal of deposit is reduced by one percent for the expired period of the deposit and is paid or adjusted or recovered accordingly.'

I am clear in my mind that the Querist would be fully justified in law in paying the increased rate of interest from 10th January, 1992 on all pre-existing deposits, without complying with the above-quoted proviso. My reasons in support of this opinion are as follows:

First, the Querist is *not* offering an option to the depositor either to continue the deposit at the old rate or to withdraw the old deposit and make a fresh deposit earning interest at the increased rate. The increase in the rate is automatic and the depositor has no option in the matter.

Secondly, in law it amounts merely to a case of variation in the terms of the contract. The variation is made by the company unilaterally and the variation is accepted by the depositor because it is obviously for his own benefit. Such a variation in terms of the deposit cannot possibly amount to surrender of the old deposit or renewal of the deposit. There is nothing under the Companies Act or under the Rules made thereunder to prevent such a variation for the remaining period of the deposit after 10th January, 1992.

Thirdly, the aforesaid proviso can apply only to those cases where a deposit is surrendered before it matures and a fresh deposit is made in order to earn the higher rate of interest. In other words, the above-quoted proviso does not create any legal fiction but it only deals with those cases where *in reality* a deposit is prematurely withdrawn and a fresh deposit made with a view to earning the higher rate of interest. The whole of the said Rule 8 deals with premature repayment of a deposit. In the present case, there is no premature repayment of the deposit at all; the same deposit continues but at an increased rate of interest. The new proviso to Rule 8 specifically deals with cases 'where a company permits a depositor to renew the deposit, before the expiry of the period for which such deposit was accepted by the company'. Therefore, by its very terms the said proviso has no application at all where no deposit is prematurely withdrawn but the deposit in fact and in reality continues to run its course at an increased rate of interest.

Fourthly, if the above-quoted proviso is construed as being applicable to cases like the present, it would be unconstitutional as not being either reasonable or in the public interest:

(a) If the Proviso proceeds on the erroneous belief or assumption of the rule- making authority that the case will be one of premature withdrawal of a deposit, the said proviso would be on that ground alone illegal and invalid. 'The beliefs or assumptions of those who frame Acts of Parliament cannot make the law':

Per Lord Radcliffe, *IR v. Dowdall*, 33 TC 259, 287 (HL); *Davies v. Davies*, 44 TC 273, 294 (HL), 72 ITR 444, 465; *ITO v. Maniram* 72 ITR 203, 211 (SC); *Ayrshire v. IR*, 27 TC 331 (HL), 16 ITR Suppl 80. See also *CIT v. Saroop*, 153 ITR 1, 9.

Much less can an erroneous belief or assumption of the rule-making authority make the law.

(b) Millions of manhours would be literally wasted arranging for refunds of a portion of the interest already paid by the different companies and making and accepting fresh deposits. The only beneficiaries of such an irrational rule would be the paper industry and the printing press.

In the light of what I have stated above, the Querist would be perfectly entitled to pay interest at the higher rate on pre-existing deposits which have been accepted in the past, and wholly ignore the above-quoted Proviso added to Rule 8.

Sd/-
N.A. Palkhivala
February 04, 1992.

Bombay

(10)

In 1994, Palkhivala dealt with an important question of whether construction and other related activities would be eligible for investment allowance. In CIT v. Budharaja, 204 ITR 412, the Supreme Court had answered this question in the negative and held that construction of dams, bridges, buildings, roads and canals would not be entitled for the benefit of investment allowance. Palkhivala rightly took the view that the Supreme Court's opinion was erroneous and that the matter required reconsideration. Eventually, the matter was reconsidered in Builders Association of India v. Union of India [1994] 209 ITR 877 (SC) but Palkhivala was unsuccessful. It is submitted that the view of the Supreme Court in both the cases was incorrect.

OPINION

ABC Industrial Co. Ltd. ... Querist

The Querist is an industrial undertaking and has many manufacturing and other business groups. One of the groups is in construction related activities. This group undertakes civil, mechanical and electrical contracts. It constructs buildings, sport stadia, airport terminus buildings, office buildings etc. and also undertakes contracts on turn-key basis involving all the three related activities, namely, civil, mechanical, and electrical. The mechanical jobs involve work like installing heavy equipment; and electrical jobs involve work like laying overhead cables on the railway tracks, construction of transmission towers, etc.

The Querist was granted investment allowance under Section 32A of the Income-tax Act, 1961 ('the Act') for a number of years in the past. In the earlier assessment years the Querist had claimed investment allowance with reference to the plant and machinery acquired and put to use for the purpose of its construction and other related activities and was granted the same at the assessment stage only.

The problem has now been created by the decision of the Supreme Court in the case of *CIT v. Budharaja,* (204 ITR 412, 429-34). In that case the Supreme Court held that the assessee is not entitled to investment allowance under Section 32A of the Act because that Section 'does not comprehend within its ambit - construction of a dam, a bridge, a building, a road, a canal and other similar constructions'.

Consequent upon the aforesaid decision of the Supreme Court, the Income-tax Department has issued a notice under Section 148 of the Act for the Assessment Year 1983-84 with the object of withdrawing the investment allowance granted to the Querist and similar others companies in the past. The Querist expects to get similar notices for the subsequent years and if the reassessments for all the years are made by withdrawing the investment allowance already granted, there will be a tax demand of a few crores of rupees on the Querist. Besides, interest that may become payable under various sections of the Act may also be demanded.

In the past, construction companies were allowed the benefit of development rebate under Section 33 of the Act and later the benefit of investment allowance under Section 32A of the Act.

In my opinion, the aforesaid decision of the Supreme Court is, with respect, erroneous. My basic reasons for coming to this conclusion are the following:

(i) Section 32A applies in respect of a ship, aircraft, machinery or plant which is owned by the assessee and 'is wholly used for the purposes of the business carried on by him'. These words are wide enough to include the business of constructing dams, bridges, buildings, etc.

(ii) Section 32A(b)(iii) refers to 'any other industrial undertaking for the purposes of business of construction, manufacture or production of any article or thing'. First, the phrase 'industrial undertaking' is wide enough to cover the business of undertaking the construction of major project. Secondly, the word 'construction' should be construed as standing by itself, and it cannot possibly go with any article or thing. The concept of 'construction of any article or thing' makes no sense at all, clearly indicating that the word 'construction' stands by itself, and the words 'manufacture or production' go with article or thing.

(iii) The Supreme Court did not consider the point at all that the word 'construction' should be construed by itself and that the Court was not called upon to consider whether a dam or a bridge was covered by the word 'article' or 'thing'. This is the crucial and decisive point in the case, and any decision given without considering this point is bound to be patently erroneous. Nowhere in the judgment is this point considered, and this raises the presumption that the Counsel for the assessee did not raise this point.

(iv) The words of Section 32A being plain and unambiguous, no question arose of looking at the legislative history. But the Court tried to take into account legislative history and erroneously inferred that the legislative history was against major construction projects being regarded as coming within the ambit of Section 32A. In any event, the Court should have considered that the Income Tax Act is today in a total mess. It has been changed and developed in such an illogical, capricious and erratic manner that it would be positively unsafe to look at the legislative history when the words of a section are clear beyond doubt.

(v) Unfortunately, the Court heard together cases under Section 80HH and Section 84, along with cases under Section 32A. The net result was that considerations which may have been relevant under those other Sections were erroneously imported into cases which were under Section 32A.

(vi) The Income-tax Department itself had for years taken the view that development rebate under Section 33 and its successor investment allowances under Section 32A were both allowable in the field of construction business. On the material point these two sections remain unaltered and yet the Department whimsically decided to urge the view that construction business fell outside the ambit of those sections. This is the curse of tax administration in India. The element of uncertainty is introduced not merely by arbitrary legislative changes in the law at the whim and fancy of individuals, but also by erratic administration of the law even when the law continues to remain unaltered by the legislature.

(vii) It is impossible to find a rationale for the view that construction of ships was intended to be covered by Section 32A, whereas all other types of construction work were intended to be denied the benefit of that section.

(viii) Section 32A(2)(c) refers to the 'business of repairs of ocean-going vessels or other powered craft'. These words cannot possibly refer to the 'manufacture or production of any article or thing' and clearly point to the fact that the Section is intended to apply to businesses other than the business of manufacturing or producing any article or thing.

I now proceed to answer briefly the question raised in the Case for Opinion:-

Question (A): The action that the Querist should take to get the Supreme Court to reconsider its decision and also, in the meantime, to stall the reassessment proceedings as have been, and will be, initiated by the assessing authorities.

Answer: I have no doubt in my mind that the question should be once again taken to the Supreme Court, and the Court should be requested to constitute a larger Bench to reconsider and overrule the aforesaid decision of the Division Bench in 204 ITR 412. The matter concerns not only the Querist but affects every single person involved in 'construction' business in the broad sense. Besides, past assessments would be robbed of their finality by the reopening of assessments which were correctly made in the first instance. The Builders Association should take up the matter and fight out the issue. In my opinion, there is a strong case for over-ruling the decision in 204 ITR 412 on the grounds indicated above.

The House of Lords and the Supreme Court have ruled in a number of cases that if the interpretation of a fiscal enactment is open to doubt, the construction most beneficial to the subject should be adopted:

Atkinson v. Goodlass, 31 TC 447, 462 (HL); *CIT v. Shahzada Nand,* 60 ITR 392, 400 (SC); *CIT v. Kulu Valley Trans,* 77 ITR 518, 530 (SC); *CIT v. Vegetable Products,* 88 ITR 192 (SC); *CIT v. Naga Hills Tea,* 89 ITR 236, 240 (SC); *CED v. Kanakasabai,* 89 ITR 251, 257 (SC); *CIT v. Madho Jatia,* 105 ITR 179, 184 (SC).

They have further ruled that a provision for deduction, exemption or relief should be construed liberally and in favour of the assessee;

CIT v. South Arcot Soc. 176 ITR 117, 199 (SC); *CIT v. UP Co-op Fed,* 176 ITR 435, 441 (SC); *Broach Soc v. CIT,* 177 ITR 418, 422 (SC); *CIT v. Strawboard,* 177 ITR 431, 434 (SC).

In *Bajaj Tempo v. CIT,* 196 ITR 188, the Supreme Court observe that a provision to a taxing statute granting incentive for promoting growth and development should be construed liberally. Even assuming the interpretation I have suggested above amounts to a liberal interpretation, it would still be justified having regard to the fact that Section 32A grants an incentive for promoting growth and development.

If any reassessment proceedings are started for any of the past years, the Department should be requested not to proceed further in the matter till the question is reconsidered by the Supreme Court. If this request remains unheeded, the Querist should take appropriate proceedings in the appropriate court to obtain a stay order restraining the Department from proceeding further with the proposed reassessments.

Sd/-
N. A. Palkhivala

Bombay — May 16, 1994.

(11)

By 1994, Palkhivala had a series of strokes and did not keep good health. Nevertheless, this opinion elaborately dealt with complicated legal issues arising out of 'asset securitization'. Palkhivala has discussed the impact of the Indian Trusts Act, the Motor Vehicles Act, the Benami Transactions (Prohibition) Act, 1988 as well as principles relating to trust law.

OPINION

XYZ Bank N.A. ... Querist

The Querist is a body corporate, incorporated in the U.S.A. It is also carrying on the business of banking in India.

One of the recent developments in the financial markets of the world is the concept of 'asset securitization'. Briefly, asset securitization involves the packaging of loans or similar financial assets and selling them in the form of securities. In other words, the concept of asset securitization is one which transfers illiquid assets such as loans on the balance sheet of a lender into a marketable security and if properly structured, the result can be that the loans are taken off the balance sheet of the lender. Globally, the Querist is one of the largest issuers of the asset backed securities.

The Querist proposes to acquire some receivables from the lenders/banks in whose hands the receivables would be in the form of loan repayment, and from leasing/hire purchase companies in whose books the receivables would be in the form of lease rentals or hire purchase instalments.

The Querist, as the 'Purchaser' of the receivables would enter into an agreement with a leasing/hire purchase company (hereinafter called 'the Seller') to purchase loan instalments/lease rentals/hire purchase instalments (hereinafter called 'the Receivables').

Under the terms of the proposal 'the Seller would offer' to sell the Receivables; but the agreement to purchase any specific Receivables would come into existence only after the Purchaser would have advised the Seller about the Receivables, the Purchaser is willing to purchase. After the selection is made by the Purchaser and the price is determined, the Purchaser will convey to the Seller his acceptance of the Seller's offer.

There are two distinct ways in which the proposed scheme of securitization can be achieved. The first is where the Querist may purchase the debt, i.e. take an assignment of the debt. When the Querist purchases the debt, he requires the legal title to the debt, and if the debt is not paid on the due date, the Querist as the purchaser or assignee of the debt would have the right to file a suit for recovery. The other is where the Querist may not take an assignment of the debt but let the debt continue to vest in the intending Seller who would hold the debt in trust for the Querist.

Neither of the two ways set out above of achieving asset securitization is hit by The Benami Transactions (Prohibition of the Right to Recover Property) Act, 1988. In other words, both the ways of achieving asset securitization are open under the Indian law.

It is well settled under Indian law that when funds are held in trust or in a fiduciary capacity by 'x' and 'x' goes into liquidation, the funds held in trust are not available to the official liquidator or receiver.

On the above facts, my opinion is sought on the following questions:

Question (a): Whether in the event of the Seller having received the purchase consideration of a receivable from the Beneficiary will he be entitled to claim any interest in that receivable or that the Beneficiary can claim that the entire beneficial interest in that receivable has been acquired by him on account of his having made full payment of the consideration for that receivable?

Answer: Where the full payment has been made by the Beneficiary, the Seller would have no interest in the Receivable and the Beneficiary can claim that the entire beneficial interest in that Receivable was acquired by him when he made the full payment of the consideration.

It is a well settled position under Indian law that even when a debt has not been assigned but the beneficial interest in the debt has been transferred, the lender has no subsisting beneficial interest in the debt. Upon the lender going into liquidation or becoming insolvent, the liquidator/Official Assignee would not be entitled to keep the proceeds of the debt when they are realized:

Shanti Prasad Jain v. The Director of Enforcement, AIR 1962 SC 1764; *New Bank of India v. Pearey Lal*, AIR 1962 SC 1003; *Seth Jessa Ram Fatehchand v. Om Narain*, [1967] 2 SCR 429.

The law laid down in the above quoted cases has been reiterated by the Bombay High Court in:

Reserve Bank v. BCCI (Overseas) Ltd., (1998) 78 Company Cases 207; *Reserve Bank v. BCCI (Overseas) Ltd.*, (1998) 78 Com Cases 230.

Question (b): If the answer to query (a) is in the negative, whether in the event of the liquidation of the seller, the liquidator of the seller can claim any right to receive those receivables from the debtors in respect of which the seller has received full consideration for sale of the same from the beneficiary pending execution of the deed of assignment in favour of the beneficiary?

Answer: No.

Question (c): Whether the agreement for sale of the receivables will attract stamp duty as a deed of assignment particularly having regard to the contents of the agreement and the fact that the Querist thereunder still has to decide as to which receivables out of the receivables therein mentioned are to be purchased by him and at what price?

Answer: At the preliminary stage when the selection of the Receivables has not yet been made and the price for a receivable is not yet fixed, there is no agreement at all. It is only the stage of a proposal. Even afterwards when the proposal matures into an agreement, if there is an assignment of the debt, stamp duty would be payable. But if the agreement between the parties takes the form of no assignment of the debt but merely transfer of the beneficial interest in the debt, no stamp duty would be payable as on sale of the debt, since the legal title in the debt would not be transferred.

Question (d): Whether the seller is entitled to repossess the motor vehicle and to apply for a duplicate registration certificate under sub-section (5) of Section 61 of the Motor Vehicles Act, 1988 even though he has assigned his right to receive hire purchase instalments arising on account of the hire purchase of that vehicle.

Answer: If only the equitable interest is transferred, the seller would continue to be entitled to exercise his right under Section 51(5) of the Motor Vehicles Act. It is desirable that the querist should purchase only the equitable interest in the debt and not take an assignment of the debt. This would preserve the privity of contract between the original borrower and the original lender.

Litigation in India normally continues for a length of time which makes eternity intelligible. In those circumstances, it would be eminently in the interest of the Querist that it does not take on the risk of having to sue a debtor from whom a receivable is due but lets that risk fall on the original party who is entitled to recover the receivable.

Question (e): Generally, if any.

Answer: Economic considerations are paramount and the guiding principles is that of the economic substance of a transaction, so far as accounts of a company are concerned. For example, if shares are held by a bank, in its own name according to the Reserve Bank of India guidelines, when the beneficial ownership of the shares belongs to the customer, the shares are not entered in the accounts of the bank.

Likewise, if a company has not assigned a debt but has only sold the beneficial interest in the debt to a third party, the accounts would be certified by auditors as correct even where the debt has ceased to appear in the books of the seller; the sale proceeds received on the sale of the beneficial interest would be reflected in the bank balance or other assets of the company.

In answer to question (d) above, I have said that it seems desirable that the Querist should purchase only the equitable interest in the debt (the receivable) and not take on assignment of the debt. In that connection I should like to deal here specifically with the repeal of Section 94 of the Indian Trusts Act, 1882 by Section 7 of the Benami Transaction Act, 1988. Section 94 of the Indian Trusts Act dealt with 'constructive trusts'. In my opinion, it would clearly be a mistake to read the repeal of the said Section 94 by the Benami Transactions Act, 1988 as abolishing the law of equity which evolved the doctrine of constructive trusts, resulting trusts and implied trusts. In the present case, the provisions of Article IX of the Agreement between the parties, which is annexed as Annexure 8 to the case for opinion expressly contemplates that the seller would hold the receivable in trust for the other party.

The law in force today in India on this point may be summarized as follows:-

(a) The rule of equity which obliges the legal owner to hold a particular property in trust for the beneficial owner has been in force in India since the last century and it continues to be in force. It would definitely apply to the scheme adumbrated in the case for opinion. The purchaser of the beneficial interest in the receivables would be entitled to enforce the rule of equity and compel the legal owner of the receivable to hold the receivable for his (the purchaser's benefit).

(b) The whole purpose of the Benami Transactions Act, 1988 is to prohibit benami transactions. If legal drafting had not been devalued, like everything else in India, and if the drafting of our laws had been today of the old standard, what the draftsman would have said is that notwithstanding anything contained in Sections 91, 92 and 94 of the Indian Trusts Act, 1882 the provisions of the Benami Transaction Act, 1988 would prevail and they would supersede the provisions of those three Sections of the Indian Trust Act, 1882.

(c) Even taking the aforesaid three Sections of the Indian Trust Act, 1882 to have been repealed, the principles of equity underlying those Sections still continue to be in force in India.

(d) Even after the enactment of the Benami Transactions Act, 1988, the Bombay High Court has upheld the aforesaid equitable principles in the two cases referred to earlier:

Reserve Bank v. BCCI (Overseas) Ltd., (1993) 78 Company Cases 207; *Reserve Bank v. BCCI (Overseas) Ltd.*, (1993) 78 Company Cases 230.

(e) In any event, where there is an express contract between parties, which is not prohibited by the Benami Transactions Act, 1988 or any other statute, that 'A' will hold a certain asset in trust for 'B', the court would enforce the contract which is perfectly legal.

Sd/-
N. A. Palkhivala
October 3, 1994.

Bombay

Subject Index

A

B

J

K

M

N

O

P

R

S